NEW BOOKS FROM IA

SOUTHERN REGION DEMUs
Kevin Robertson and Hugh Abbinnett

A pictorial tribute to the various classes of Southern Region diesel-electric multiple-units that replaced steam over much of the SR's non-electrified network. A companion to the earlier volumes on DMUs and EMUs, the authors have produced a highly informative and exciting volume on a little published topic.

Paperback | 282 x 213 mm | 80 pages | 978 0 7110 3511 9 | £16.99

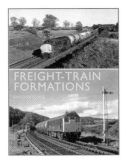

FREIGHT–TRAIN FORMATIONS
Kevin Robertson and Hugh Abbinnett

Featuring freight trains on BR from the end of steam, *Freight-Train Formations* is a largely pictorial examination of the train formations operated to handle the variety of freight traffic that the railways have carried over the past 40 years. Alongside the photographic content, the book also includes information derived from the TOPS system to provide an accurate record for modellers of individual trains.

Hardback | 282 x 213 mm | 96 pages | 978 0 7110 3447 1 | £20.00

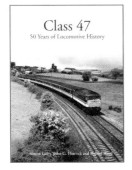

CLASS 47: 50 YEARS OF LOCOMOTIVE HISTORY
Simon Lilley, John G. Hiscock and Robert Ward

Introduced in 1962, the Brush Type 4s – or Class 47s – were the most numerous design of diesel electric locomotive to see service on British Rail. Produced to mark the 50th anniversary of the class's introduction to service, this is a comprehensive reference to the type and its operational record.

Hardback | 292 x 216 mm | 192 pages | 978 0 86093 648 0 | £29.99

Rail Guide

2013

Colin J. Marsden

First published 2010
Reprinted 2010, 2011, 2012
This Fourth Edition first published 2013

ISBN 978 0 7110 3739 7

Published by Ian Allan Publishing.

An imprint of Ian Allan Publishing Ltd, Hersham, Surrey KT12 4RG.
Printed in Malta.

Visit the Ian Allan Publishing website at www.ianallanpublishing.com

Distributed in the United States of America and Canada by BookMasters Distribution Services.

Front Cover Top: *During 2012 Colas started to introduce Class 56s as their core heavyweight long distance freight motive power. On 25 May 2012, No. 56094 is seen piloting Class 47 No. 47739* Robin of Templecombe *past Barrow-on-Trent powering the 11.51 Washwood Heath to Boston steel train.* **John Tuffs**

Front Cover Bottom: *Following the introduction of Class 172s on London Midland, a number of Class 150/1s were transferred to First Great Western. Set No. 150129 is seen passing Langstone Rock, Dawlish Warren on 23 May 2012 forming an Exmouth to Paignton local service.* **CJM**

Back Cover Top: *New to service in 2012 are a small fleet of overhauled Mk3s fitted with sliding plug passenger doors, for use on Chiltern Railways main line services between London Marylebone and Birmingham. Car No. 12602 is illustrated at Marylebone.* **Antony Christie**

Back Cover Bottom: *The former West Coast Mk3 Driving Van Trailers (DVTs) now work for a number of main line operators, including Arriva Trains Wales, who use a vehicle at the remote ends of Class 67 powered Holyhead to Cardiff express services. Car No. 82306 is illustrated at Newport attached to Class 67 No. 67002 during a driver training run on 17 July 2012.* **CJM**

Acknowledgement – The Author would like to record his thanks to the many railway staff who have provided invaluable information for the production of this book. Also to the many photographers, especially Nathan Williamson, Antony Christie, Stacey Thew, John Binch and Brian Morrison, for providing many of the images. I would also like to express my thanks to Keith Ewins for reading the updated manuscript. **CJM**

Welcome to the 2013 edition of the Ian Allan *ABC Rail Guide*, the only comprehensive listing of all locomotives, multiple-units, coaches and track machines provided by operator.

It is amazing quite how many changes to the UK fleet are reported each year, with over 5,000 changes from our 2012 listings incorporated in this new edition. This clearly reflects the ever-changing scene of our railways.

While no major new classes were introduced during the review period, significant changes were recorded. For example, the Class 57/3s were replaced on Arriva Trains Wales services by Class 67s, a high proportion of Virgin Class 390 *Pendolino* sets were increased from nine to 11 vehicles and reclassified as 390/1, the Virgin Trains Class 57/3 fleet was heavily reduced with examples transferred to Direct Rail Services and Network Rail, while confirmation was received that new Vossloh Class 68 mixed traffic diesel locos had been ordered for Direct Rail Services. Also the go-ahead had been given for construction of the new InterCity replacement stock.

New and extra Class 350 *Desiro* and Class 377 *Electrostar* sets were ordered from Siemens and Bombardier, ensuring a continued cascade of middle-aged stock to other routes.

A major hitch in the UK franchise policy emerged in mid-2012, when initially First Group were awarded the West Coast franchise; after massive lobbying by the present operator Virgin Rail Group and public outcry, the franchise award was stopped by the Government and major new guidelines on franchise appointments were to be announced by early 2013. This franchise hold-up also saw the next tranche of franchise changes deferred, including East Coast and Great Western.

Only one new loco was delivered in the UK during 2012, No. 70099, a General Electric trials loco built in Turkey to the same design as the Freightliner Class 70s.

In *Rail Guide 2013* we continue to provide listings of Network Rail certified track machines. This year we have included the Rail Head Treatment Train (RHTT) vehicles for the first time.

The smaller operators in the freight sector and the private operators have seen the most significant changes, with several previously withdrawn Class 56s being returned to main line use by Colas Rail Freight, and operators such as Harry Needle Railroad and British American Railroad expanding their fleets and operations.

In autumn 2012 GBRf announced it had obtained the use of three more Class 66s previously stored in Europe to cover expanding business needs.

On the export front, Porterbrook and Europhoenix continued their export of ex-BR electric locos to Hungary and Bulgaria, with Europhoenix also exporting Class 56s to Hungary.

The Editor of the *ABC Rail Guide* welcomes correspondence about omissions or corrections or suggestions for further items to be included.

We hope you enjoy following the UK rail scene in 2013, but please always remember to keep safe, do not trespass on the railway and keep an eye open around you and if you see anything suspicious please notify the British Transport Police or a railway official.

Colin J. Marsden
Dawlish, January 2013

Information in Rail Guide 2013 is correct to 15 January 2013

An expanding UK freight operator is Colas Rail Freight, which now operates a fleet of Class 47, 56, 66 and 86 main line locomotives. All are painted in the operator's distinctive black, orange and lime livery. On 7 November 2012, Class 56 No. 56087 passes Dawlish Warren and is about to traverse the South Devon coast with an empty log train bound for Teigngrace on the Newton Abbot to Heathfield line. **CJM**

Train Operators, The Association of Train Operating Companies, and Network Rail welcome rail enthusiasts and photographers, but in today's safety led railway and with the continued concerns about possible transport terrorism, guidelines are very important and we encourage all to follow these published guidelines as much as possible. They are available to view and download from the National Rail and ATOC websites, but are reproduced in full below to assist you with this information. ■

The Official Railway Enthusiasts Guidelines

■ Network Rail welcomes rail enthusiasts to our stations.

■ The following guidelines are designed to help you to have a safe and enjoyable experience. Please keep them with you when you are at Network Rail managed stations.

■ You may also wish to take a copy of the Railway by-laws which are available from the Office of Public Sector Information website.

Before you enter the platform

■ When you arrive at a station, please let the staff at the Network Rail Reception Desk know that you are on the station. This will help keep station staff informed so that they can go about their duties without concern as to your reasons for being there.

■ You may require a platform ticket to allow access to platforms.

While you are on the platform

■ You need to act safely & sensibly at all times.
  ● Stay clear of the platform edge and stay behind the yellow lines where they are provided.
  ● Be aware of your surroundings.

Please DO NOT:
  ● Trespass on to the tracks or any other part of the railway that is not available to passengers.
  ● Use flash photography because it can distract train drivers and train despatch staff and so is potentially very dangerous.
  ● Climb on any structure or interfere with platform equipment.
  ● Obstruct any signalling equipment or signs which are vital to the safe running of the railway.
  ● Wear anything which is similar in colour to safety clothing, such as high-visibility jackets, as this could cause confusion to drivers and other railway employees.
  ● Gather together in groups at busy areas of the platform (e.g. customer information points, departure screens, waiting areas, seating etc.) or where this may interfere with the duties of station staff.

■ If possible, please try to avoid peak hours which are Monday – Friday 6:00am (06.00) – 10:30am (10.30) and 3:30pm (15.30) – 7:30pm (19.30).

Extra Eyes and Ears

■ If you see anything suspicious or notice any unusual behaviour or activities, please tell a member of staff immediately.

■ For emergencies and serious incidents, either call:
  The British Transport Police on 0800 40 50 40.
  The Police on 999, or 101

■ Your presence at a station can be very helpful to us as extra "eyes and ears" and can have a positive security benefit.

Photography

■ You can take photographs at stations provided you do not sell them. However, you are not allowed to take photographs of security related equipment, such as CCTV cameras.

■ Flash photography on platforms is not allowed at any time. It can distract train drivers and train despatch staff and so is potentially very dangerous.

■ Tripod legs must be kept away from platform edges and behind the yellow lines. On busy stations, you may not be allowed to use a tripod because it could be a dangerous obstruction to passengers.

Railway By-laws

For safety & ease of travel on the railway system (which includes passengers, staff, property and equipment), the by-laws must be observed by everyone. A copy of the by-laws can be obtained at stations or downloaded from the Office of Public Sector Information website.

General

Train operators must put the safety of their passengers and staff first. You may very occasionally be asked by station staff to move to another part of the station or to leave the station altogether. Station staff should be happy to explain why this is necessary. If you are travelling by train, they may ask you to remain in the normal waiting areas with other passengers. If this occurs, please follow their instructions with goodwill as staff have many things to consider, including the safety & security of all passengers, and are authorised to use judgement in this regard.

Below: *The use of full length trains as mobile advertising displays has continued over the past year with several new 'total wrap' contracts being agreed. The operation to totally wrap a train in high quality graphics has been possible due to high definition plastic laminate now being available which is produced away from a railway environment and then applied using pre-cut shapes by contractors in just a few hours. The strength of advertising in this way is debatable. When a train arrives at a station passengers are more interested in boarding than reading the outside; also being so close to the vehicles, the full impact of the advert is lost. While travelling through the countryside few people can stop and have time to take in the full advertising message, especially when phone numbers and web addresses have to be absorbed. This Lycamobile full train advertising is applied to one Class 378 and one Class 319. No. 319218 is seen at King's Cross Thameslink.* **Antony Christie**

Contents

Arriva Trains Wales
Trenau Arriva Cymru

Address: ✉ St Mary's House, 47 Penarth Road, Cardiff, CF10 5DJ

📠 customer.relations@arrivatrainswales.co.uk

✆ 0845 6061 660

ⓘ www.arrivatrainswales.co.uk

Managing Director: Tim Bell

Franchise Dates: 7 December 2003 - 6 December 2018

Principal Routes: Cardiff to Swansea and West Wales
Cardiff Valleys
Cardiff - Hereford - Shrewsbury - Crewe - Manchester Piccadilly
Cardiff - Hereford - Shrewsbury - Chester - Bangor - Holyhead
Manchester - Crewe - Bangor - Holyhead
Shrewsbury - Pwllheli / Aberystwyth
Swansea - Shrewsbury

Depots: Cardiff Canton (CF), Chester (CH), Holyhead* (HD)
Machynlleth (MN), Shrewsbury* (SX) * Stabling point

Parent Company: Deutsche Bahn AG (DB Regio)

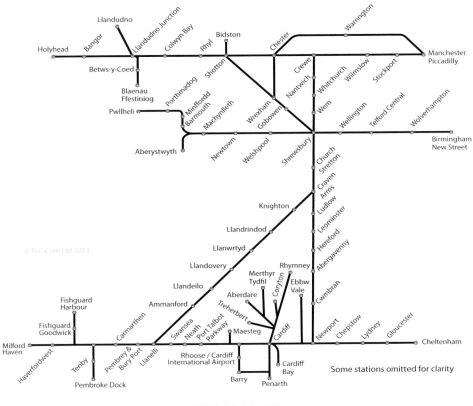

Class 67

Vehicle Length: 64ft 7in (19.68m)
Height: 12ft 9in (3.88m)
Width: 8ft 9in (2.66m)

Engine: EMD 12N-710G3B-EC
Horsepower: 2,980hp (2,223kW)
Electrical Equipment: EMD

Number	Depot	Pool	Livery	Owner	Operator
67001	CE	WATN	ATW	ANG	DBS/ATW
67002	CE	WATN	ATW	ANG	DBS/ATW
67003	CE	WATN	ATW	ANG	DBS/ATW

Right: *DB-S Class 67s, repainted into Arriva Trains Wales colours, took over the Welsh Assembly Government-sponsored Cardiff to Holyhead express service from mid-2012, when modified Mk3 DVTs using the TDM method of push-pull control were also introduced. The first three locos of the '67' fleet are dedicated to the service. On 29 March 2012, No. 67002 is seen passing Ponthir with the afternoon Holyhead-bound service.*
Antony Christie

Class 121

Length: 64ft 6in (19.66m)
Height: 12ft 8½in (3.87m)
Width: 9ft 3in (2.81m)

Engine: 2 x Leyland 150hp
Horsepower: 300hp (224kW)
Seats (total/car): 65S

Number	Formation DMBS	Depot	Livery	Owner	Operator	Note
121032	55032	CF	ATW	ATW	ATW	Previously Departmental No. 977842

■ Operated exclusively on Cardiff Queen Street to Cardiff Bay shuttle service.

Right: *Arriva Trains Wales operates one 'heritage' DMMU vehicle on its Cardiff Queen Street to Cardiff Bay, 'shuttle' service. The Class 121, No. 55032, built by Pressed Steel in 1960, passed to Departmental stock and after withdrawal was fully refurbished and taken over for Cardiff area use. Painted in full Arriva Trains Wales livery and allocated to Cardiff Canton, the vehicle departs from Cardiff Queen Street for Cardiff Bay.* **CJM**

Class 142

Vehicle Length: 51ft 0½in (15.55m)
Height: 12ft 8in (3.86m)
Width: 9ft 2¼in (2.80m)

Engine: 1 x Cummins LTA10-R per vehicle
Horsepower: 460hp (343kW)
Seats (total/car): 90S, 46S/44S

Number	Formation DMS+DMSL	Depot	Livery	Owner	Operator
142002	55543+55593	CF	ATW	ANG	ATW
142006	55547+55597	CF	ATW	ANG	ATW
142010	55551+55601	CF	ATW	ANG	ATW
142069	55719+55765	CF	ATW	ANG	ATW
142072	55722+55760	CF	ATW	ANG	ATW
142073	55723+55769	CF	ATW	ANG	ATW
142074	55724+55770	CF	ATW	ANG	ATW
142075	55725+55771	CF	ATW	ANG	ATW
142076	55726+55772	CF	ATW	ANG	ATW
142077	55727+55773	CF	ATW	ANG	ATW
142080	55730+55776	CF	ATW	ANG	ATW
142081	55731+55777	CF	ATW	ANG	ATW
142082	55732+55778	CF	ATW	ANG	ATW
142083	55733+55779	CF	ATW	ANG	ATW
142005	55705+55701	CF	ATW	ANG	ATW

Name applied
142072 *Myfanwy*

Arriva Trains Wales

Left: *Arriva Trains Wales Cardiff Canton depot has an allocation of 15 Class 142s, deployed in conjunction with Class 143s, on the Cardiff 'Valley' line services. On 27 July 2012, set No. 142085 departs from Cardiff with a Bargoed-bound service.* **CJM**

Class 143

Vehicle Length: 51ft 0½in (15.55m)
Height: 12ft 2¼in (3.73m)
Width: 8ft 10½in (2.70m)

Engine: 1 x Cummins LTA10-R per vehicle
Horsepower: 460hp (343kW)
Seats (total/car): 92S, 48S/44S

Number	Formation DMS+DMSL	Depot	Livery	Owner	Operator
143601	55642+55667	CF	ATW	BCC	ATW
143602	55651+55668	CF	ATW	PTR	ATW
143604	55645+55670	CF	ATW	PTR	ATW
143605	55646+55671	CF	ATW	PTR	ATW
143606	55647+55672	CF	ATW	PTR	ATW
143607	55648+55673	CF	ATW	PTR	ATW
143608	55649+55674	CF	ATW	PTR	ATW
143609	55650+55675	CF	ATW	CCC	ATW
143610	55643+55676	CF	ATW	BCC	ATW
143614	55655+55680	CF	ATW	BCC	ATW
143616	55657+55682	CF	ATW	PTR	ATW
143622	55663+55688	CF	ATW	PTR	ATW
143623	55664+55689	CF	ATW	PTR	ATW
143624	55665+55690	CF	ATW	PTR	ATW
143625	55666+55691	CF	ATW	PTR	ATW

Name applied
143609 ***Sir Tom Jones***

Below: *Operating alongside the Cardiff-allocated Class 142 fleet are 15 refurbished Class 143s, all sport 2+2 high-back seating and operating as a common pool of 'Pacer' Class 14x sets. Set No. 143607 is seen arriving at Cardiff in July 2012 with its DMS vehicle leading coupled to a Class 142 set.* **CJM**

Class 150/2

Vehicle Length: 64ft 9¾in (19.74m)
Height: 12ft 4½in (3.77m)
Width: 9ft 3⅛in (2.82m)

Engine: 1 x NT855R5 of 285hp per vehicle
Horsepower: 570hp (425kW)
Seats (total/car): 128S, 60S/68S

Number	Formation DMSL+DMS	Depot	Livery	Owner	Operator
150208	52208+57208	CF	ATW	PTR	ATW
150213	52213+57213	CF	ATT	PTR	ATW
150217	52217+57217	CF	ATW	PTR	ATW
150227	52227+57227	CF	ATW	PTR	ATW
150229	52227+57227	CF	ATW	PTR	ATW
150230	52230+57230	CF	ATW	PTR	ATW
150231	52231+57231	CF	ATW	PTR	ATW
150235	52235+57235	CF	ATW	PTR	ATW
150237	52237+57237	CF	ATW	PTR	ATW
150236	52236+57236	CF	ATW	PTR	ATW
150240	52240+57240	CF	ATW	PTR	ATW
150241	52241+57241	CF	ATW	PTR	ATW
150242	52242+57242	CF	ATW	PTR	ATW
150245	52245+57245	CF	ATW	PTR	ATW
150250	52250+57250	CF	ATW	PTR	ATW
150251	52251+57251	CF	ATW	PTR	ATW
150252	52252+57252	CF	ATW	PTR	ATW
150253	52253+57253	CF	ATW	PTR	ATW
150254	52254+57254	CF	ATW	PTR	ATW
150255	52213+57255	CF	ATW	PTR	ATW
150256	52256+57256	CF	ATW	PTR	ATW
150257	52257+57257	CF	ATW	PTR	ATW

150258	52258+57258	CF	ATW	PTR	ATW		150279	52270+57279	CF	ATW	PTR	ATW
150259	52259+57259	CF	ATW	PTR	ATW		150280	52280+57280	CF	ATW	PTR	ATW
150260	52260+57260	CF	ATW	PTR	ATW		150281	52281+57281	CF	ATW	PTR	ATW
150262	52262+57262	CF	ATW	PTR	ATW		150282	52282+57282	CF	ATW	PTR	ATW
150264	52264+57264	CF	ATW	PTR	ATW		150283	52283+57283	CF	ATW	PTR	ATW
150267	52267+57267	CF	ATW	PTR	ATW		150284	52284+57284	CF	ATW	PTR	ATW
150278	52278+57278	CF	ATW	PTR	ATW		150285	52285+57280	CF	ATW	PTR	ATW

Right: *36 Class 150/2s operate for Arriva Trains Wales. These sets have all been facelifted in recent years and sport standard ATW livery. A plan is on the cards for a major refurbishment of these vehicles which is likely to see the newer ATW Class 158 livery applied. Set No. 150280 is seen arriving at Cardiff Cathays.* **CJM**

Class 153

Vehicle Length: 76ft 5in (23.29m)	Engine: 1 x NT855R5 of 285hp
Height: 12ft 3⅛in (3.75m)	Horsepower: 285hp (213kW)
Width: 8ft 10in (2.70m)	Seats (total/car): 72S

Number	Formation DMSL	Depot	Livery	Owner	Operator							
						153323	52323	CF	ATW	PTR	ATW
						153327	52327	CF	ATW	ANG	ATW
153303	52303	CF	ATW	ANG	ATW	153353	57353	CF	ATW	ANG	ATW
153312	52312	CF	ATW	ANG	ATW	153362	57362	CF	ATW	ANG	ATW
153320	52320	CF	ATW	PTR	ATW	153367	57367	CF	ATW	PTR	ATW

Right: *ATW operate a fleet of eight single-car Class 153s for longer distance lighter used routes, mainly in west Wales. The fleet, based at Cardiff Canton, sport Arriva Trains livery. The Class 153s were formerly marshalled as two-car Class 155 sets and rebuilt to give operators greater flexibility. Car No. 153367 is seen at Blaenau Ffestiniog from its 'new' smaller driving cab end.* **Murdoch Currie**

Class 158

Vehicle Length: 76ft 1¾in (23.21m)	Engine: 1 x Perkins 2006-TWH of 350hp per vehicle
Height: 12ft 6in (3.81m)	Horsepower: 700hp (522kW)
Width: 9ft 3¼in (2.82m)	Seats (total/car): 134S, 66S/68S

Number	Formation DMSL+DMSL	Depot	Livery	Owner	Operator							
						158829	52829+57829	MN	ATT	ANG	ATW
						158830	52830+57830	MN	ATT	ANG	ATW
158818	52818+57818	MN	ATT	ANG	ATW	158831	52831+57831	MN	ATT	ANG	ATW
158819	52819+57819	MN	ATT	ANG	ATW	158832	52832+57832	MN	ATT	ANG	ATW
158820	52820+57820	MN	ATT	ANG	ATW	158833	52833+57833	MN	ATT	ANG	ATW
158821	52821+57821	MN	ATT	ANG	ATW	158834	52834+57834	MN	ATT	ANG	ATW
158822	52822+57822	MN	ATT	ANG	ATW	158835	52835+57835	MN	ATT	ANG	ATW
158823	52823+57823	MN	ATT	ANG	ATW	158836	52836+57836	MN	ATT	ANG	ATW
158824	52824+57824	MN	ATT	ANG	ATW	158837	52837+57837	CF	ATT	ANG	ATW
158825	52825+57825	MN	ATT	ANG	ATW	158838	52838+57838	CF	ATT	ANG	ATW
158826	52826+57826	MN	ATT	ANG	ATW	158839	52839+57839	CF	ATT	ANG	ATW
158827	52827+57827	MN	ATT	ANG	ATW	158840	52840+57840	CF	ATT	ANG	ATW
158828	52828+57828	MN	ATT	ANG	ATW	158841	52841+57841	CF	ATT	ANG	ATW

Arriva Trains Wales

■ All sets are fitted with operational European Rail Traffic Management System (ERTMS) equipment for operation on the Cambrian Line.

Left: *The revised ATW livery applied to the refurbished Class 158s looks impressive. On 26 March 2012, set No. 158825 is seen departing from Severn Tunnel Junction station.* **Antony Christie**

Class 175/0
Coradia 1000

Vehicle Length: 75ft 7in (23.06m)
Height: 12ft 4in (3.75m)
Width: 9ft 2in (2.80m)

Engine: 1 x Cummins N14 of 450hp per vehicle
Horsepower: 900hp (671kW)
Seats (total/car): 118S, 54S/64S

Number	Formation DMSL+DMSL	Depot	Livery	Owner	Operator
175001	50701+79701	CH	ATW	ANG	ATW
175002	50702+79702	CH	ATW	ANG	ATW
175003	50703+79703	CH	ATW	ANG	ATW
175004	50704+79704	CH	ATW	ANG	ATW
175005	50705+79705	CH	ATW	ANG	ATW
175006	50706+79706	CH	ATW	ANG	ATW
175007	50707+79707	CH	ATW	ANG	ATW
175008	50708+79708	CH	ATW	ANG	ATW
175009	50709+79709	CH	ATW	ANG	ATW
175010	50710+79710	CH	ATW	ANG	ATW
175011	50711+79711	CH	ATW	ANG	ATW

Left: *The Class 175 'Coradia 1000' units are allocated to the ATW depot at Chester and used mainly in the northern Wales area, as well as on longer distance North-South Wales services. The 'Coradia 1000' design comes in both two- and three-car formations. Two-car set No. 175001 is seen at Cardiff on 27 July 2011. All sets carry standard Arriva Trains Wales livery.* **CJM**

Class 175/1
Coradia 1000

Vehicle Length: 75ft 7in (23.06m)
Height: 12ft 4in (3.75m)
Width: 9ft 2in (2.80m)

Engine: 1 x Cummins N14 of 450hp per vehicle
Horsepower: 1,350hp (1,007kW)
Seats (total/car): 186S, 54S/68S/64S

Number	Formation DMSL+MSL+DMSL	Depot	Livery	Owner	Opt'r
175101	50751+56751+79751	CH	ATW	ANG	ATW
175102	50752+56752+79752	CH	ATW	ANG	ATW
175103	50753+56753+79753	CH	ATW	ANG	ATW
175104	50754+56754+79754	CH	ATW	ANG	ATW
175105	50755+56755+79755	CH	ATW	ANG	ATW
175106	50756+56756+79756	CH	ATW	ANG	ATW
175107	50757+56757+79757	CH	ATW	ANG	ATW
175108	50758+56758+79758	CH	ATW	ANG	ATW
175109	50759+56759+79759	CH	ATW	ANG	ATW
175110	50760+56760+79760	CH	ATW	ANG	ATW
175111	50761+56761+79761	CH	ATW	ANG	ATW
175112	50762+56762+79762	CH	ATW	ANG	ATW
175113	50763+56763+79763	CH	ATW	ANG	ATW
175114	50764+56764+79764	CH	ATW	ANG	ATW
175115	50765+56765+79765	CH	ATW	ANG	ATW
175116	50766+56766+79766	CH	ATW	ANG	ATW

Left: *Sixteen 'Coradia 1000' sets, classified as 175/1 and formed as three-car sets, share duties from Chester depot with the two-car Class 175/0 units. No. 175101 is viewed at Cardiff on 18 May 2012. The extra MSL vehicle increases the accommodation of the '175' by 68 standard class passengers.* **John Binch**

Class AC2E / TSO

Vehicle Length: 66ft 0in (20.11m)
Height: 12ft 9½in (3.89m)
Width: 9ft 3in (2.81m)
Seats (total/car): 62S

Number	Type	Depot	Livery	Owner	Operator					
5853	TSO	CF	ATW	ATW	ATW	5869(S)	TSO	LM	ATW	ATW -

Class AC2F / TSO

Vehicle Length: 66ft 0in (20.11m)
Height: 12ft 9½in (3.89m)
Width: 9ft 3in (2.81m)
Seats (total/car): 60S

Number	Type	Depot	Livery	Owner	Operator					
5965	TSO	CF	ATW	ATW	ATW	6119	TSO	CF	ATW	ATW ATW
5976	TSO	CF	ATW	ATW	ATW	6137	TSO	CF	ATW	ATW ATW
						6183	TSO	CF	ATW	ATW ATW

Vehicles 5913, 6013, 6035, 6162 and 6170 stored at Long Marston

Class AE2E / BSO

Vehicle Length: 66ft 0in (20.11m)
Height: 12ft 9½in (3.89m)
Width: 9ft 3in (2.81m)
Seats (total/car): 60S

Number	Type	Depot	Livery	Owner	Operator					
9503	BSO	CF	ATW	ATW	ATW	9509	BSO	CF	ATW	ATW ATW

Class AE2F / BSO

Vehicle Length: 66ft 0in (20.11m)
Height: 12ft 9½in (3.89m)
Width: 9ft 3in (2.81m)
Seats (total/car): 60S

Number	Type	Depot	Livery	Owner	Operator					
9521	BSO	CF	ATW	ATW	ATW	9524(S)	BSO	LM	ATW	ATW -
						9539	BSO	CF	ATW	ATW ATW

Right: A small fleet of Mk2 and Mk3 loco-hauled vehicles are operated by Arriva Trains Wales for use on the Cardiff-Holyhead express service funded by the Welsh Assembly Government. Mk2F TSO No. 5965 is illustrated. These vehicles are soon to be replaced by Mk3 stock under refurbishment. **CJM**

Class AJ1G / RFM

Vehicle Length: 75ft 0in (22.86m)
Height: 12ft 9in (3.88m)
Width: 8ft 11in (2.71m)
Bogie Type: BT10

Number	Type	Depot	Livery	Owner	Operator					
10249 (10012)	RFM	CF	ATW	DBR	ATW	10259 (10025)	RFM	CF	ATW	ATW ATW

Class AD1H / TSO

Vehicle Length: 75ft 0in (22.86m)
Height: 12ft 9in (3.88m)
Width: 8ft 11in (2.71m)
Bogie Type: BT10

Number	Type	Depot	Livery	Owner	Operator					
12176 (11064)	TSO	CF	BLG	DBR	ATW	12179 (11083)	TSO	CF	BLG	DBR	ATW
12177 (11065)	TSO	CF	BLG	DBR	ATW	12180 (11084)	TSO	CF	BLG	DBR	ATW
12178 (11071)	TSO	CF	BLG	DBR	ATW	12181 (11086)	TSO	CF	BLG	DBR	ATW

Mk3 Hauled Stock (NPCCS)

Length: 75ft 0in (22.86m)
Height: 12ft 9in (3.88m)
Width: 8ft 11in (2.71m)
Bogie Type: BT7

NZAG - DVT

Number	Depot	Livery	Owner	Operator					
82306 (82144)	CF	ATW	ATW	ATW	82307 (82131)	CF	ATW	ATW	ATW
					82308 (82108)	CF	ATW	ATW	ATW

Right: In 2011/12 three Mk3 Driving Van Trailers (DVTs) were converted at Brush Traction for Arriva Trains Wales use and renumbered in the 823xx series. Car No. 82306 is illustrated during a training run at Newport in July 2012, coupled directly to a Class 67. **Nathan Williamson**

c2c

Address: ✉ 10th Floor, 207 Old Street, London, EC1V 9NR
                ⌨ c2c.customerrelations@nationalexpress.com
                ✆ 0845 6014873
                ⓘ www.c2c-online.co.uk

Managing Director: Julian Drury
Franchise Dates: 26 May 1996 - 26 May 2013§
Principal Routes: London Fenchurch Street - Shoeburyness
                              Barking - Pitsea via Purfleet
                              Ockendon branch
                              London Liverpool Street - Barking (limited service)
Depots: East Ham (EM), Shoeburyness*
                              * Stabling point
Parent Company: National Express

§ Might be extended, re-franchising suspended

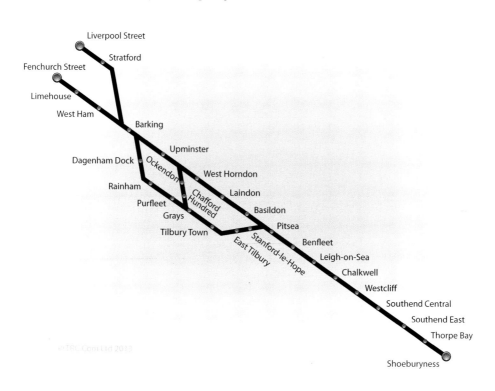

Class 357/0
Electrostar

Vehicle Length: (Driving) 68ft 1in (20.75m) Width: 9ft 2½in (2.80m)
(Inter) 65ft 11½in (20.10m) Horsepower: 2,011hp (1,500kW)
Height: 12ft 4½in (3.78m) Seats (total/car): 282S, 71S/78S/62S/71S

Number	Formation	Depot	Livery	Owner	Opt'r	Name
	DMSO(A)+MSO+PTSO+DMSO(B)					
357001	67651+74151+74051+67751	EM	NE2	PTR	C2C	Barry Flaxman
357002	67652+74152+74052+67752	EM	NE2	PTR	C2C	Arthur Lewis Stride 1841-1922
357003	67653+74153+74053+67753	EM	NE2	PTR	C2C	Southend City on Sea
357004	67654+74154+74054+67754	EM	NE2	PTR	C2C	Tony Amos
357005	67655+74155+74055+67755	EM	SPL‡	PTR	C2C	
357006	67656+74156+74056+67756	EM	SPL‡	PTR	C2C	Diamond Jubilee 1952 - 2012
357007	67657+74157+74057+67757	EM	NE2	PTR	C2C	
357008	67658+74158+74058+67758	EM	NE2	PTR	C2C	
357009	67659+74159+74059+67759	EM	NE2	PTR	C2C	
357010	67660+74160+74060+67760	EM	NE2	PTR	C2C	
357011	67661+74161+74061+67761	EM	NE2	PTR	C2C	John Lowing
357012	67662+74162+74062+67762	EM	NE2	PTR	C2C	
357013	67663+74163+74063+67763	EM	NE2	PTR	C2C	
357014	67664+74164+74064+67764	EM	NE2	PTR	C2C	
357015	67665+74165+74065+67765	EM	NE2	PTR	C2C	
357016	67666+74166+74066+67766	EM	NE2	PTR	C2C	
357017	67667+74167+74067+67767	EM	NE2	PTR	C2C	
357018	67668+74168+74068+67768	EM	NE2	PTR	C2C	
357019	67669+74169+74069+67769	EM	SPL‡	PTR	C2C	
357020	67670+74170+74070+67770	EM	NE2	PTR	C2C	
357021	67621+74171+74071+67771	EM	NE2	PTR	C2C	
357022	67672+74172+74072+67772	EM	NE2	PTR	C2C	
357023	67673+74173+74073+67773	EM	NE2	PTR	C2C	
357024	67674+74174+74074+67774	EM	NE2	PTR	C2C	
357025	67675+74175+74075+67775	EM	NE2	PTR	C2C	
357026	67676+74176+74076+67776	EM	NE2	PTR	C2C	
357027	67677+74177+74077+67777	EM	NE2	PTR	C2C	
357028	67678+74178+74078+67778	EM	NE2	PTR	C2C	London, Tilbury & Southend Railway 1854-2004
357029	67679+74179+74079+67779	EM	NE2	PTR	C2C	Thomas Whitelegg 1840-1922
357030	67680+74180+74080+67780	EM	NE2	PTR	C2C	Robert Harben Whitelegg 1871-1957
357031	67681+74181+74081+67781	EM	NE2	PTR	C2C	
357032	67682+74182+74082+67782	EM	NE2	PTR	C2C	
357033	67683+74183+74083+67783	EM	NE2	PTR	C2C	
357034	67684+74184+74084+67784	EM	NE2	PTR	C2C	
357035	67685+74185+74085+67785	EM	NE2	PTR	C2C	
357036	67686+74186+74086+67786	EM	NE2	PTR	C2C	
357037	67687+74187+74087+67787	EM	NE2	PTR	C2C	
357038	67688+74188+74088+67788	EM	NE2	PTR	C2C	
357039	67689+74189+74089+67789	EM	NE2	PTR	C2C	
357040	67690+74190+74090+67790	EM	NE2	PTR	C2C	
357041	67691+74191+74091+67791	EM	NE2	PTR	C2C	
357042	67692+74192+74092+67792	EM	NE2	PTR	C2C	
357043	67693+74193+74093+67793	EM	NE2	PTR	C2C	
357044	67694+74194+74094+67794	EM	NE2	PTR	C2C	
357045	67695+74195+74095+67795	EM	NE2	PTR	C2C	
357046	67696+74196+74096+67796	EM	NE2	PTR	C2C	

SPL‡ Queen's Diamond Jubilee
livery

Right: *In 2012 the c2c Class 357
'Electrostar' fleet was still considered
as the UK's most reliable train fleet.
With two sub-classes of Class 357,
maintained by East Ham depot, 46
Porterbrook-owned Class 357/0s are
in traffic. All are painted in National
Express white livery, with three sets
having Queen's Diamond Jubilee
branding added in 2012. Set No.
357006 is illustrated.* **John Binch**

c2c

Class 357/2
Electrostar

Vehicle Length: (Driving) 68ft 1in (20.75m) Width: 9ft 2½in (2.80m)
(Inter) 65ft 11½in (20.10m) Horsepower: 2,011hp (1,500kW)
Height: 12ft 4½in (3.78m) Seats (total/car): 282S, 71S/78S/62S/71S

Number	Formation DMSO(A)+MSO+PTSO+DMSO(B)	Depot	Livery	Owner	Operator	Name
357201	68601+74701+74601+68701	EM	NE2	ANG	C2C	*Ken Bird*
357202	68602+74702+74602+68702	EM	NE2	ANG	C2C	*Kenny Mitchell*
357203	68603+74703+74603+68703	EM	NE2	ANG	C2C	*Henry Pumfrett*
357204	68604+74704+74604+68704	EM	NE2	ANG	C2C	*Derek Flowers*
357205	68605+74705+74605+68705	EM	NE2	ANG	C2C	*John D'Silva*
357206	68606+74706+74606+68706	EM	NE2	ANG	C2C	*Martin Aungier*
357207	68607+74707+74607+68707	EM	NE2	ANG	C2C	*John Page*
357208	68608+74708+74608+68708	EM	NE2	ANG	C2C	*Dave Davis*
357209	68609+74709+74609+68709	EM	NE2	ANG	C2C	*James Snelling*
357210	68610+74710+74610+68710	EM	NE2	ANG	C2C	
357211	68611+74711+74611+68711	EM	NE2	ANG	C2C	
357212	68612+74712+74612+68712	EM	NE2	ANG	C2C	
357213	68613+74713+74613+68713	EM	NE2	ANG	C2C	*Upminster IECC*
357214	68614+74714+74614+68714	EM	NE2	ANG	C2C	
357215	68615+74715+74615+68715	EM	NE2	ANG	C2C	
357216	68616+74716+74616+68716	EM	NE2	ANG	C2C	
357217	68617+74717+74617+68717	EM	NE2	ANG	C2C	*Allan Burnell*
357218	68618+74218+74618+68718	EM	NE2	ANG	C2C	
357219	68619+74719+74619+68719	EM	NE2	ANG	C2C	
357220	68620+74720+74620+68720	EM	NE2	ANG	C2C	
357221	68621+74721+74621+68721	EM	NE2	ANG	C2C	
357222	68622+74722+74622+68722	EM	NE2	ANG	C2C	
357223	68623+74723+74623+68723	EM	NE2	ANG	C2C	
357224	68624+74724+74624+68724	EM	NE2	ANG	C2C	
357225	68625+74725+74625+68725	EM	SPL‡	ANG	C2C	
357226	68626+74726+74626+68726	EM	NE2	ANG	C2C	
357227	68627+74727+74627+68727	EM	SPL‡	ANG	C2C	
357228	68628+74728+74628+68728	EM	NE2	ANG	C2C	

SPL‡ Queens Diamond Jubilee livery

Below: *The 28 Class 357/2 sets are owned by Angel Trains and allocated to East Ham. They operate as one common pool with the Class 357/0 sets. All are painted in National Express white livery. Several sets from both sub-classes carry cast nameplates; these are fitted behind the driving cab at cant rail height. Set No. 357209 is illustrated.* **CJM**

Chiltern Railways

Address: ✉ 2nd floor, Western House, Rickfords Hill, Aylesbury, Buckinghamshire, HP20 2RX

🖱 Via website (www.chilternrailways.co.uk)

☎ 08456 005165

ⓘ www.chilternrailways.co.uk

Managing Director: Rob Brighthouse

Franchise Dates: 21 July 1996 - 21 December 2021

Principal Routes: London Marylebone - Birmingham Snow Hill
London Marylebone - Aylesbury
London Marylebone - Stratford-upon-Avon

Depots: Aylesbury (AL), Wembley*
* Stabling point

Parent Company: Deutsche Bahn AG (DB Regio)

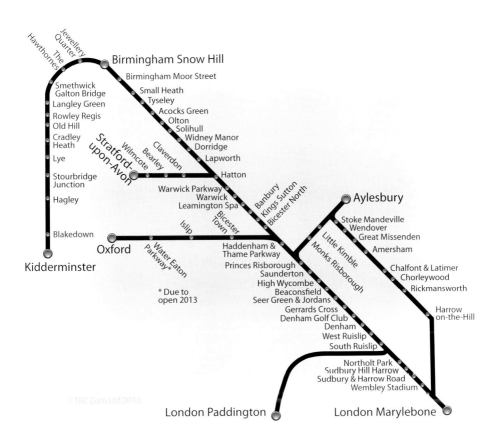

Chiltern Railways

Class 121

Length: 64ft 6in (19.66m)
Height: 12ft 8½in (3.87m)
Width: 9ft 3in (2.81m)

Engine: 2 x Leyland 150hp
Horsepower: 300hp (224kW)
Seats (total/car): 65S

Number	Formation DMBS	Depot	Livery	Owner	Operator
121020	55020	AY	BLU	CRW	CRW
121034	55034	AY	GRN	CRW	CRW

Left: *Heritage traction still survives working with Chiltern Railways. Two Class 121 'bubble' cars are based at Aylesbury for use on the Aylesbury to Princes Risborough line. Vehicle No. 55020 (illustrated) is painted in Chiltern blue, while No. 55034 has been restored to 1960s BR green. Both vehicles now have central door locking.* **John Wills**

Class 165/0 (2-car)
Networker Turbo

Vehicle Length: (Driving) 75ft 2½in (22.91m), (Inter) 74ft 6½in (22.72m)
Height: 12ft 5¼in (3.79m)   Engine: 1 x Perkins 2006 TWH of 350hp per vehicle
Width: 9ft 2½in (2.81m)   Horsepower: 700hp (522kW)
Seats (total/car): 183S, 89S/94S

Number	Formation DMSL+DMS	Depot	Livery	Owner	Operator
165001	58801+58834	AL	CRW	ANG	CRW
165002	58802+58835	AL	CRW	ANG	CRW
165003	58803+58836	AL	CRW	ANG	CRW
165004	58804+58837	AL	CRW	ANG	CRW
165005	58805+58838	AL	CRW	ANG	CRW
165006	58806+58839	AL	CRW	ANG	CRW
165007	58807+58840	AL	CRW	ANG	CRW
165008	58808+58841	AL	CRW	ANG	CRW
165009	58809+58842	AL	CRW	ANG	CRW
165010	58810+58843	AL	CRW	ANG	CRW
165011	58811+58844	AL	CRW	ANG	CRW
165012	58812+58845	AL	CRW	ANG	CRW
165013	58813+58846	AL	CRW	ANG	CRW
165014	58814+58847	AL	CRW	ANG	CRW
165015	58815+58848	AL	CRW	ANG	CRW
165016	58816+58849	AL	CRW	ANG	CRW
165017	58817+58850	AL	CRW	ANG	CRW
165018	58818+58851	AL	CRW	ANG	CRW
165019	58819+58852	AL	CRW	ANG	CRW
165020	58820+58853	AL	CRW	ANG	CRW
165021	58821+58854	AL	CRW	ANG	CRW
165022	58822+58855	AL	CRW	ANG	CRW
165023	58873+58867	AL	CRW	ANG	CRW
165024	58874+58868	AL	CRW	ANG	CRW
165025	58874+58869	AL	CRW	ANG	CRW
165026	58876+58870	AL	CRW	ANG	CRW
165027	58877+58871	AL	CRW	ANG	CRW
165028	58878+58872	AL	CRW	ANG	CRW

Left: *The main rolling stock used by Chiltern Railways is a fleet of 'Networker Turbo' Class 165s, introduced in the days of Network SouthEast. All are now refurbished, with revised interiors and front ends. The '165s' come in both two- and three-car formations. In this view, two-car set No. 165026 arrives at London Marylebone station.* **Antony Christie**

Class 165/0 (3-car)
Networker Turbo

Vehicle Length: (driving) 75ft 2½in (22.91m), (inter) 74ft 6½in (22.72m)
Height: 12ft 5¼in (3.79m)   Engine: 1 x Perkins 2006 TWH of 350hp per vehicle
Width: 9ft 2½in (2.81m)   Horsepower: 1,050hp (783kW)
Seats (total/car): 289S, 89S/106S/94S

Number	Formation DMSL+MS+DMS	Depot	Livery	Owner	Operator
165029	58823+55404+58856	AL	CRW	ANG	CRW
165030	58824+55405+58857	AL	CRW	ANG	CRW
165031	58825+55406+58858	AL	CRW	ANG	CRW
165032	58826+55407+58859	AL	CRW	ANG	CRW
165033	58827+55408+58860	AL	CRW	ANG	CRW
165034	58828+55409+58861	AL	CRW	ANG	CRW
165035	58829+55410+58862	AL	CRW	ANG	CRW
165036	58830+55411+58863	AL	CRW	ANG	CRW
165037	58831+55412+58864	AL	CRW	ANG	CRW
165038	58832+55413+58865	AL	CRW	ANG	CRW
165039	58833+55414+58866	AL	CRW	ANG	CRW

Class 168/0
Turbostar

Vehicle Length: 77ft 6in (23.62m)
Height: 12ft 4½in (3.77m)
Width: 8ft 10in (2.69m)
Engine: 1 x MTU 6R 183TD13H 422hp per vehicle
Horsepower: 1,688hp (1,259kW)
Seats (total/car): 278S, 60S/73S/77S/68S

Number	Formation DMSL(A)+MSL+MS+DMSL(B)	Depot	Livery	Owner	Operator
168001	58151+58651+58451+58251	AL	CRW	PTR	CRW
168002	58152+58652+58452+58252	AL	CRW	PTR	CRW
168003	58153+58653+58453+58253	AL	CRW	PTR	CRW
168004	58154+58654+58454+58254	AL	CRW	PTR	CRW
168005	58155+58655+58455+58255	AL	CRW	PTR	CRW

Right: *The original order for the 'Turbostar' DMU product range built by Adtranz (later Bombardier), were classified as '168' for Chiltern Railways. These sets sport an earlier less streamlined design of front end, than subsequent 'Turbostar' builds. The pioneer of the fleet, No. 168001, is seen at Birmingham Moor Street.* **Norman E. Preedy**

Class 168/1
Turbostar

Vehicle Length: 77ft 6in (23.62m)
Height: 12ft 4½in (3.77m)
Width: 8ft 10in (2.69m)
Engine: 1 x MTU 6R 183TD13H of 422hp per vehicle
Horsepower: 3/4-Car 1,266hp (944kW)/1,688hp (1,259kW)
Seats (total/car): 3-car - 208S, 59S/73S/76S, 4-car - 284S, 59S/73S/76S/76S

Number	Formation DMSL(A)+MS+MS+DMSL(B)	Depot	Livery	Owner	Operator	Notes
168106	58156+58756§+58456+58256	AL	CRW	PTR	CRW	§ is a MSL vehicle
168107	58157+58457+58757§+58257	AL	CRW	PTR	CRW	§ is a MSL vehicle
168108	58158+58458+58258	AL	CRW	PTR	CRW	
168109	58159+58459+58259	AL	CRW	PTR	CRW	
168110	58160+58460+58260	AL	CRW	PTR	CRW	
168111	58161+58461+58261	AL	CRW	EVL	CRW	58461 was originally 58661
168112	58162+58462+58262	AL	CRW	EVL	CRW	58462 was originally 58662
168113	58163+58463+58263	AL	CRW	EVL	CRW	58463 was originally 58663

Right: *With production orders for 'Turbostar' stock placed, a standard streamlined front was introduced, which has been used on all following orders as well as some EMU designs and the later Class 172s, but some sets incorporating a front gangway. Class 168/1 four-car set No. 168107 is illustrated at Birmingham Moor Street. This is one of only two Class 168/1s formed of four carriages; the remainder have just three.* **Norman E. Preedy**

Class 168/2
Turbostar

Vehicle Length: 77ft 6in (23.62m)
Height: 12ft 4½in (3.77m)
Width: 8ft 10in (2.69m)
Engine: 1 x MTU 6R 183TD13H of 422hp per vehicle
Horsepower: 3/4-Car 1,266hp (944kW)/1,688hp (1,259kW)
Seats (total/car): 3-car - 204S, 59S/76S/69S, 4-car - 277S, 59S/73S/76S/696S

Number	Formation DMSL(A)+MS+MS+DMSL(B)	Depot	Livery	Owner	Operator
168214	58164+58464+58264	AL	CRW	PTR	CRW
168215	58165+58465+58365+58265	AL	CRW	PTR	CRW
168216	58166+58466+58366+58266	AL	CRW	PTR	CRW
168217	58167+58467+58367+58267	AL	CRW	PTR	CRW
168218	58168+58468+58268	AL	CRW	PTR	CRW
168219	58169+58469+58269	AL	CRW	PTR	CRW

Chiltern Railways

Class 172/1

Vehicle Length: 73ft 4in (22.37m)
Height: 12ft 4½in (3.77m)
Width: 8ft 8in (2.69m)

Engine: MTU 6H1800 of 360kW
Horsepower: 965hp (720kW)
Seats (total/car): 121S, 53S/68S

Number	Formation DMS+DMS	Depot	Livery	Owner	Operator
172101	59111+59211	AL	CRW	ANG	CRW
172102	59112+59212	AL	CRW	ANG	CRW
172103	59113+59213	AL	CRW	ANG	CRW
172104	59114+59214	AL	CRW	ANG	CRW

Left: To augment their DMU suburban DMU fleet, Chiltern Railways introduced four two-car Class 172/1 sets in 2011. The stock were different from previous builds, using MTU power units and a diesel-mechanical rather than hydraulic transmission. Two sets, with No. 172102 nearest the camera, are seen stabled between duties at London Marylebone. **Antony Christie**

Class 67

Vehicle Length: 64ft 7in (19.68m)
Height: 12ft 9in (3.88m)
Width: 8ft 9in (2.66m)

Engine: EMD 12N-710G3B-EC
Horsepower: 2,980hp (2,223kW)
Electrical Equipment: EMD

Number	Depot	Pool	Livery	Owner	Operator	Name
67010	CE	WNTR	CRG	ANG	DBS/CRW	
67012	CE	WAWN	CRG	ANG	DBS/CRW	A Shropshire Lad
67013	CE	WNTR	CRG	ANG	DBS/CRW	Dyfrbont Pontcysyllte
67014	CE	WAAN	CRG	ANG	DBS/CRW	Thomas Telford
67015	CE	WAWN	CRG	ANG	DBS/CRW	David J. Lloyd

Left: The DB-S Class 67s used by Wrexham & Shropshire Railway until their demise in January 2011, together with the Mk3 rolling stock, passed to Chiltern Railways for use on their developing main line express services between London Marylebone and Birmingham. No. 67013 Dyfrbont Pontcysyllte is shown propelling a train for Marylebone out of Birmingham Moor Street on 22 August 2012. **Antony Christie**

Mk3 Hauled Stock (Passenger)

Vehicle Length: 75ft 0in (22.86m)
Height: 12ft 9in (3.88m) Width: 8ft 11in (2.71m)
Bogie Type: BT10

AJ1F - GFW *Seating 30F*

Number		Depot	Livery	Owner
10271	(10236/10018)	AL	CRG	DBR
10272	(10208/40517)	AL	CRG	DBR
10273	(10230/10021)	AL	CRG	DBR
10274	(10255/11010)	AL	CRG	DBR

AC2G - TSO/TSOL* *Seating 72S*

Number		Depot	Livery	Owner
12602	(12072)	AL	CRG	DBR
12603*	(12053)	AL	CRG	DBR
12604	(12131)	AL	CRG	DBR
12605*	(11040)	AL	CRG	DBR
12606	(12048)	AL	CRG	DBR
12607*	(12038)	AL	CRG	DBR
12608	(12069)	AL	CRG	DBR
12609*	(12014)	AL	CRG	DBR
12612	(12117)	AL	CRG	DBR
12613*	(12173/11042)	AL	CRG	DBR
12614	(12145)	AL	CRG	DBR
12615*	(12059)	AL	CRG	DBR
12616	(12127)	AL	CRG	DBR
12617*	(12174/11050)	AL	CRG	DBR
12618	(12169)	AL	CRG	DBR
12619*	(12175/11052)	AL	CRG	DBR

Above: *A major and impressive initiative was launched by Chiltern Railways in 2012: that of fitting sliding plug doors to its Mk3 passenger stock, a feature which would compliment Mk3s used by any operator. Painted in Chiltern Mainline livery, car No. 12603 is illustrated, clearly showing the revised plug door arrangement.* **Antony Christie**

Mk3 Hauled Stock (NPCCS)

Vehicle Length: 75ft 0in (22.86m)			
Height: 12ft 9in (3.88m)			
Width: 8ft 11in (2.71m)			
Bogie Type: BT7			

NZAG - DVT

Number	Depot	Livery	Owner	Number	Depot	Livery	Owner
82301 (82117)	AL	CRG	DBR	82303 (82135)	AL	CRG	DBR
82302 (82151)	AL	CRG	DBR	82304 (82130)	AL	CRG	DBR
				82305 (82134)	AL	CRG	DBR

Right: *To operate at the remote ends of Chiltern Railways Class 67 powered trains, a fleet of five Mk3 DVTs have been modified from the original West Coast vehicles and are now fitted with an auxiliary Penta TAD1352GE diesel engine and Meccalite alternator. This is located behind the driving cab, with one of the original sliding luggage doors now replaced by a ventilation grille. An underslung fuel tank is also fitted. Car No. 82301 is illustrated at Marylebone, with Arriva Trains Wales car No. 82307 on the right.*
Andrew Royle

Class 960 – Service Units

Class 121		Class 117	
Length: 64ft 6in (19.66m)	Engine: 2 x Leyland 150hp	Length: 64ft 0in (19.50m)	Engine: 2 x Leyland 150hp
Height: 12ft 8½in (3.87m)	Horsepower: 300hp (224kW)	Height: 12ft 8½in (3.87m)	Horsepower: 300hp (224kW)
Width: 9ft 3in (2.81m)	Seats (total/car): None	Width: 9ft 3in (2.81m)	Seats (total/car): None

Number	Formation	Depot	Livery	Owner	Operator	Notes
960014	977873	AL	BLG	CRW	CRW	Ex-Class 121 55022, Route Learning/Sandite
960301	977987+977992+977988	AL	GRN	CRW	CRW	Ex-Class 117, 51371/51375/51413 - used for water jetting

Class 01.5 (0-6-0)

Number		Depot	Pool	Livery	Owner	Operator	Name
01509 (433)	RH468043	AL	MBDL	BLU	CRW	CRW	*Lesley*

CrossCountry Trains

Address: ✉ Cannon House, 18 The Priory, Queensway, Birmingham, B4 6BS
🖱 info@crosscountrytrains.co.uk
☎ 0870 0100084
ⓘ www.crosscountrytrains.co.uk

Managing Director: Andy Cooper
Franchise Dates: 11 November 2007 - 31 March 2016
Principal Routes: Penzance/Paignton -
Manchester/Edinburgh/Aberdeen
Bournemouth - Manchester/
Edinburgh/Aberdeen
Birmingham - Stansted
Nottingham - Cardiff
Depots: Central Rivers (CZ),
Tyseley (TS),
Craigentinny (EC)
Parent Company: Deutsche Bahn AG
(DB Regio) / Arriva

Aberdeen
Stonehaven
Arbroath
Dundee
Leuchars
Cupar
Markinch
Kirkcaldy
Motherwell
Glasgow Central
Haymarket
Edinburgh
Dunbar
Berwick-upon-Tweed
Alnmouth
Morpeth
Newcastle
Chester-le-Street
Durham
Darlington
York
Manchester Piccadilly
Leeds
Doncaster
Stockport
Wakefield Westgate
Nottingham
Macclesfield
Congleton
Sheffield
Wilmslow
Crewe
Chesterfield
Stoke-on-Trent
Stafford
Wolverhampton
Birmingham New Street
Water Orton
Tamworth
Derby
Burton-on-Trent
Cheltenham Spa
Chepstow
Caldicot
Lydney
Gloucester
Bristol Parkway
Coleshill Parkway
Nuneaton
Narborough
Stamford
Bristol Temple Meads
Weston-super-Mare
Birmingham International
Leicester
Melton Mowbray
Oakham
Newport
Taunton
Tiverton Parkway
Coventry
Peterborough
Ely
Cambridge
Cardiff
Exeter St Davids
Dawlish
Teignmouth
Newton Abbot
Leamington Spa
Banbury
Oxford
Audley End
Totnes
Torquay
Reading
Stansted Airport
Paignton
Guildford
Plymouth
Liskeard
Bodmin Parkway
Par
Newquay
St Austell
Truro
Redruth
Camborne
St Erth
Basingstoke
Winchester
Southampton Airport Parkway
Southampton Central
Brockenhurst
Penzance
Bournemouth

© TRC.Com Ltd 2013

ABC Rail Guide 2013

Class 43 – HST

Vehicle Length: 58ft 5in (18.80m)
Height: 12ft 10in (3.90m)
Width: 8ft 11in (2.73m)
Engine: MTU 16V4000 R41R
Horsepower: 2,250hp (1,680kW)
Electrical Equipment: Brush

Number	Depot	Pool	Livery	Owner	Operator		Number	Depot	Pool	Livery	Owner	Operator
43207 (43007)	EC	EHPC	AXC	ANG	AXC		43321 (43121)	EC	EHPC	AXC	PTR	AXC
43285 (43085)	EC	EHPC	AXC	PTR	AXC		43357 (43157)	EC	EHPC	AXC	PTR	AXC
43301 (43101)	EC	EHPC	AXC	PTR	AXC		43366 (43166)	EC	EHPC	AXC	ANG	AXC
43303 (43103)	EC	EHPC	AXC	PTR	AXC		43378 (43178)	EC	EHPC	AXC	ANG	AXC
43304 (43104)	EC	EHPC	AXC	ANG	AXC		43384 (43184)	EC	EHPC	AXC	ANG	AXC

Above: *A fleet of five HST sets are at the disposal of CrossCountry Trains, allocated to Edinburgh Craigentinny depot, but usually only four are in traffic at one time. The sets are deployed on the core North East/Scotland to Devon and Cornwall routes, providing more seats than a Class 220 or 221 'Voyager' formation. Power car No. 43384 leads a northbound train past Cockwood, Devon.* **CJM**

HST passenger fleet

Vehicle Length: 75ft 0in (22.86m)
Height: 12ft 9in (3.88m)
Width: 8ft 11in (2.71m)
Bogie Type: BT10

GH1G - TF *Seating 40F*

Number	Depot	Livery	Owner
41026	EC	AXC	ANG
41035	EC	AXC	ANG
41193 (11060)	EC	AXC	PTR
41194 (11016)	EC	AXC	PTR
41195¤ (11020)	EC	AXC	PTR ¤ = TFD

GH2G - TS *Seating 82S*

Number	Depot	Livery	Owner
42036	EC	AXC	ANG
42037	EC	AXC	ANG
42038	EC	AXC	ANG
42051	EC	AXC	ANG
42052	EC	AXC	ANG
42053	EC	AXC	ANG
42097	EC	AXC	ANG
42234	EC	AXC	PTR
42290	EC	AXC	PTR
42342 (44082)	EC	AXC	ANG
42366 (12007)	EC	AXC	PTR
42367 (12025)	EC	AXC	PTR
42368 (12028)	EC	AXC	PTR
42369 (12050)	EC	AXC	PTR
42370 (12086)	EC	AXC	PTR
42371 (12052)	EC	AXC	PTR

Number	Depot	Livery	Owner	
42372 (12055)	EC	AXC	PTR	
42373 (12071)	EC	AXC	PTR	
42374 (12075)	EC	AXC	PTR	
42375 (12113)	EC	AXC	PTR	
42376 (12085)	EC	AXC	PTR	
42377 (12102)	EC	AXC	PTR	
42378 (12123)	EC	AXC	PTR	
42379* (41036)	EC	AXC	ANG	*=TSD
42380* (41025)	EC	AXC	ANG	*=TSD

GJ2G - TGS *Seating 67S*

Number	Depot	Livery	Owner
44012	EC	AXC	ANG
44017	EC	AXC	ANG
44021	EC	AXC	ANG
44052	EC	AXC	PTR
44072	EC	AXC	PTR

GH3G - TCC *Seating 30F/10S*

Number	Depot	Livery	Owner
45001 (12004)	EC	AXC	PTR
45002 (12106)	EC	AXC	PTR
45003 (12076)	EC	AXC	PTR
45004 (12077)	EC	AXC	PTR
45005 (12080)	EC	AXC	PTR

Train Operating Companies

CrossCountry Trains

Left: The entire CrossCountry Trains-operated HST fleet has been fully refurbished, with the high-quality work carried out by Wabtec of Doncaster. All vehicles sport a two-tone grey livery, offset by bright pink passenger doors and CrossCountry branding. In the upper illustration is Trailer Standard (TS) No. 42051, these vehicles seating 82 standard class passengers in the 2+2 style. In the lower illustration is Trailer First (TF) No. 41035, these vehicles seating 40 passengers in the 2+1 style. Both: **CJM**

Class 170/1
Turbostar

Vehicle Length: 77ft 6in (23.62m)
Height: 12ft 4½in (3.77m)
Width: 8ft 10in (2.69m)
Engine: 1 x MTU 6R 183TD13H 422hp per vehicle
Horsepower: 1,266hp (944kW)
Seats (total/car): 9F/191S 52S/80S/9F-59S

Number	Formation DMS+MS+DMCL	Depot	Livery	Owner	Operator
170101	50101+55101+79101	TS	AXC	PTR	AXC
170102	50102+55102+79102	TS	AXC	PTR	AXC
170103	50103+55103+79103	TS	AXC	PTR	AXC
170104	50104+55104+79104	TS	AXC	PTR	AXC
170105	50105+55105+79105	TS	AXC	PTR	AXC
170106	50106+55106+79106	TS	AXC	PTR	AXC
170107	50107+55107+79107	TS	AXC	PTR	AXC
170108*	50108+55108+79108	TS	AXC	PTR	AXC
170109*	50109+55109+79109	TS	AXC	PTR	AXC
170110	50110+55110+79110	TS	AXC	PTR	AXC

Vehicle Length: 77ft 6in (23.62m)
Height: 12ft 4½in (3.77m)
Width: 8ft 10in (2.69m)
Engine: 1 x MTU 6R 183TD13H 422hp per vehicle
Horsepower: 844hp (629kW)
Seats (total/car): 9F-111S 59S/9F-52S

Number	Formation DMS+DMCL	Depot	Livery	Owner	Operator		Number	Formation	Depot	Livery	Owner	Operator
170111*	50111+79111	TS	AXC	PTR	AXC		170114	50114+79114	TS	AXC	PTR	AXC
170112	50112+79112	TS	AXC	PTR	AXC		170115	50115+79115	TS	AXC	PTR	AXC
170113	50113+79113	TS	AXC	PTR	AXC		170116	50116+79116	TS	AXC	PTR	AXC
							170117	50117+79117	TS	AXC	PTR	AXC

* Fitted with passenger counters

Left: Built originally to operate on Midland Mainline services, the Class 170/1 sets in their two- and three-car formations are now operated by CrossCountry Trains, allocated to Tyseley depot near Birmingham. All sets have now been refurbished and sport standard CrossCountry livery, offset by website address details along the lower bodyside. Two-car set No. 170114 is seen at Cambridge forming a Stansted Airport service from the Midlands. **CJM**

Class 170/3
Turbostar

Vehicle Length: 77ft 6in (23.62m)
Height: 12ft 4½in (3.77m)
Width: 8ft 10in (2.69m)

Engine: 1 x MTU 6R 183TD13H 422hp per vehicle
Horsepower: 1,266hp (944kW)
Seats (total/car): 9F-191S 59S/80S/9F-52S

Number	Formation DMSL+MS+DMCL	Depot	Livery	Owner	Operator
170397	50397+56397+79397	TS	AXC	PTR	AXC
170398	50398+56398+79398	TS	AXC	PTR	AXC

Class 170/5
Turbostar

Vehicle Length: 77ft 6in (23.62m)
Height: 12ft 4½in (3.77m)
Width: 8ft 10in (2.69m)

Engine: 1 x MTU 6R 183TD13H 422hp per vehicle
Horsepower: 844hp (629kW)
Seats (total/car): 9F-111S 59S/9F-52S

Number	Formation DMSL+DMCL	Depot	Livery	Owner	Operator
170518	50518+79518	TS	AXC	PTR	AXC
170519	50519+79519	TS	AXC	PTR	AXC
170520	50520+79520	TS	AXC	PTR	AXC
170521	50521+79521	TS	AXC	PTR	AXC
170522	50522+79522	TS	AXC	PTR	AXC
170523	50523+79523	TS	AXC	PTR	AXC

Right: *Six two-car Class 170/5 sets are operated by CrossCountry. These share duties with all members of the Class 170 family used by the operator and can be seen on any CrossCountry '170' route. With bodyside advertising, set No. 170523 is seen traversing the Great Western main line between Cardiff and Newport near Coedkernew, while forming a Cardiff to Nottingham service.* **Antony Christie**

Class 170/6
Turbostar

Vehicle Length: 77ft 6in (23.62m)
Height: 12ft 4½in (3.77m)
Width: 8ft 10in (2.69m)

Engine: 1 x MTU 6R 183TD13H 422hp per vehicle
Horsepower: 1,266hp (944kW)
Seats (total/car): 9F-191S 59S/80S/9F-52S

Number	Formation DMSL+MS+DMCL	Depot	Livery	Owner	Operator
170636	50636+56636+79636	TS	AXC	PTR	AXC
170637	50637+56637+79637	TS	AXC	PTR	AXC
170638	50638+56638+79638	TS	AXC	PTR	AXC
170639	50639+56639+79639	TS	AXC	PTR	AXC

Below: *With its DMSL coach leading, three-car set No. 170638 is seen near Attenborough forming a Cardiff to Nottingham service. Again CrossCountry advertising is applied.* **Antony Christie**

CrossCountry Trains

Class 220
Voyager

Vehicle Length: 77ft 6in (23.62m)
Height: 12ft 4in (3.75m)
Width: 8ft 11in (2.73m)

Engine: 1 x Cummins 750hp per vehicle
Horsepower: 3,000hp (2,237kW)
Seats (total/car): 26F/174S 42S/66S/66S/26F

Number	Formation DMS+MS+MS+DMF	Depot	Livery	Owner	Operator
220001	60301+60701+60201+60401	CZ	AXC	HBS	AXC
220002	60302+60702+60202+60402	CZ	AXC	HBS	AXC
220003	60303+60703+60203+60403	CZ	AXC	HBS	AXC
220004	60304+60704+60204+60404	CZ	AXC	HBS	AXC
220005	60305+60705+60205+60405	CZ	AXC	HBS	AXC
220006	60306+60706+60206+60406	CZ	AXC	HBS	AXC
220007	60307+60707+60207+60407	CZ	AXC	HBS	AXC
220008	60308+60708+60208+60408	CZ	AXC	HBS	AXC
220009	60309+60709+60209+60409	CZ	AXC	HBS	AXC
220010	60310+60710+60210+60410	CZ	AXC	HBS	AXC
220011	60311+60711+60211+60411	CZ	AXC	HBS	AXC
220012	60312+60712+60212+60412	CZ	AXC	HBS	AXC
220013	60313+60713+60213+60413	CZ	AXC	HBS	AXC
220014	60314+60714+60214+60414	CZ	AXC	HBS	AXC
220015	60315+60715+60215+60415	CZ	AXC	HBS	AXC
220016	60316+60716+60216+60416	CZ	AXC	HBS	AXC
220017	60317+60717+60217+60417	CZ	AXC	HBS	AXC
220018	60318+60718+60218+60418	CZ	AXC	HBS	AXC
220019	60319+60719+60219+60419	CZ	AXC	HBS	AXC
220020	60320+60720+60220+60420	CZ	AXC	HBS	AXC
220021	60321+60721+60221+60421	CZ	AXC	HBS	AXC
220022	60322+60722+60222+60422	CZ	AXC	HBS	AXC
220023	60323+60723+60223+60423	CZ	AXC	HBS	AXC
220024	60324+60724+60224+60424	CZ	AXC	HBS	AXC
220025	60325+60725+60225+60425	CZ	AXC	HBS	AXC
220026	60326+60726+60226+60426	CZ	AXC	HBS	AXC
220027	60327+60727+60227+60427	CZ	AXC	HBS	AXC
220028	60328+60728+60228+60428	CZ	AXC	HBS	AXC
220029	60329+60729+60229+60429	CZ	AXC	HBS	AXC
220030	60330+60730+60230+60430	CZ	AXC	HBS	AXC
220031	60331+60731+60231+60431	CZ	AXC	HBS	AXC
220032	60332+60732+60232+60432	CZ	AXC	HBS	AXC
220033	60333+60733+60233+60433	CZ	AXC	HBS	AXC
220034	60334+60734+60234+60434	CZ	AXC	HBS	AXC

Below: *The mainstay of the CrossCountry main line operation is worked by a fleet of 'Voyager' and 'Super Voyager' stock formed in both four- and five-car formations. Class 220 No. 220028 is shown departing from Oxford with a Bournemouth to Manchester Piccadilly service. The set's DMF vehicle is leading.* **Antony Christie**

Class 221
Super Voyager

Vehicle Length: 77ft 6in (23.62m)	Engine: 1 x Cummins 750hp per vehicle
Height: 12ft 4in (3.75m)	Horsepower: 3,750hp (2,796kW)
Width: 8ft 11in (2.73m)	Seats (total/car): 26F/236S 42S/66S/66S/62S/26F

Originally fitted with tilt system to allow higher speeds over curves. Equipment now isolated

Number	Formation DMS+MS+MS+MS+DMF	Depot	Livery	Owner	Operator	
221119	60369+60769+60969+60869+60469	CZ	AXC	HBS	AXC	
221120	60370+60770+60970+60870+60470	CZ	AXC	HBS	AXC	
221121	60371+60771+60971+60871+60471	CZ	AXC	HBS	AXC	
221122	60372+60772+60972+60872+60472	CZ	AXC	HBS	AXC	
221123	60373+60773+60973+60873+60473	CZ	AXC	HBS	AXC	
221124	60374+60774+60974+60874+60474	CZ	AXC	HBS	AXC	
221125	60375+60775+60975+60875+60475	CZ	AXC	HBS	AXC	
221126	60376+60776+60976+60876+60476	CZ	AXC	HBS	AXC	
221127	60377+60777+60977+60877+60477	CZ	AXC	HBS	AXC	
221128	60378+60778+60978+60878+60478	CZ	AXC	HBS	AXC	
221129	60379+60779+60979+60879+60479	CZ	AXC	HBS	AXC	
221130	60380+60780+60980+60880+60480	CZ	AXC	HBS	AXC	
221131	60381+60781+60981+60881+60481	CZ	AXC	HBS	AXC	
221132	60382+60782+60982+60882+60482	CZ	AXC	HBS	AXC	
221133	60383+60783+60983+60883+60483	CZ	AXC	HBS	AXC	
221134	60384+60784+60984+60884+60484	CZ	AXC	HBS	AXC	
221135	60385+60785+60985+60885+60485	CZ	AXC	HBS	AXC	
221136	60386+60786+60986+60886+60486	CZ	AXC	HBS	AXC	
221137	60387+60787+60987+60887+60487	CZ	AXC	HBS	AXC	
221138	60388+60788+60988+60888+60488	CZ	AXC	HBS	AXC	
221139	60389+60789+60989+60889+60489	CZ	AXC	HBS	AXC	
221140	60390+60790+60990+60890+60490	CZ	AXC	HBS	AXC	
221141	60391+60791+-+60491	CZ	AXC	HBS	AXC	(Four-car set)

● A proposal has now been formulated for Class 220 and 221 sets to receive an additional intermediate pantograph vehicle, allowing dual diesel-electric operation. The project calls for the building of 57 new pantograph carriages and the rebuilding of other existing intermediate vehicles to pass 'train-line' power. No agreement for this project has yet been officially reached, but a contract is likely to be agreed soon. The vehicles would be built by Bombardier at Derby.

Below: *All but one of the 23 Class 221 'Super Voyager' sets are formed as five-car, the exception being the final set No. 221141. These sets were built with full tilting capability, but this has now been isolated. With its DMS coach nearest the camera, set No. 221124 is seen near Dawlish Warren with a Penzance to Aberdeen service in August 2012.* **CJM**

Passenger Train Operating Companies - CrossCountry Trains

East Coast

Address: ✉ East Coast House, 25 Skeldergate, York, YO1 6DH
✍ customers@eastcoast.co.uk
✆ 08457 225225
ⓘ www.eastcoast.co.uk

Managing Director: Karen Boswell
Operation Started: 13 November 2009*
Principal Routes: London King's Cross - Aberdeen/
Inverness, Edinburgh, Glasgow
Hull, Leeds, Bradford, Skipton
and Harrogate
Depots: Bounds Green (BN),
Craigentinny (EC)
Parent Company: InterCity East Coast (DfT)
(Directly Operated Railways Ltd)

* The Government took over operation
from 13 November 2009 and will
continue to operate the franchise as a
'stopgap' measure using the in-place
operational staff. A new franchise should
have taken over from 7 December 2013
but this has been further delayed by
changes to the franchise award process.

Class 43 – HST

Vehicle Length: 58ft 5in (18.80m)			Engine: MTU 16V4000 R41R			
Height: 12ft 10in (3.90m)			Horsepower: 2,250hp (1,680kW)			
Width: 8ft 11in (2.73m)			Electrical Equipment: Brush			

Number		Depot	Pool	Livery	Owner	Operator	Name
43206	(43006)	EC	IECP	ECG	ANG	ICE	Kingdom of Fife
43208	(43008)	EC	IECP	NXE	ANG	ICE	Lincolnshire Echo
43238	(43038)	EC	IECP	NXE	ANG	ICE	
43239	(43039)	EC	IECP	ECG	ANG	ICE	
43251	(43051)	EC	IECP	ECG	PTR	ICE	
43257	(43057)	EC	IECP	ECG	PTR	ICE	
43272	(43072)	EC	IECP	ECG	PTR	ICE	
43274	(43074)	EC	IECP	ECG	PTR	ICE	
43277	(43077)	EC	IECP	ECG	PTR	ICE	
43290	(43090)	EC	IECP	NXE	PTR	ICE	MTU Fascination of Power
43295	(43095)	EC	IECP	ECG	ANG	ICE	
43296	(43096)	EC	IECP	ECG	PTR	ICE	
43299	(43099)	EC	IECP	NXE	PTR	ICE	
43300	(43100)	EC	IECP	ECG	PTR	ICE	Craigentinny
43302	(43102)	EC	IECP	ECG	PTR	ICE	
43305	(43105)	EC	IECP	NXE	ANG	ICE	
43306	(43106)	EC	IECP	NXE	ANG	ICE	
43307	(43107)	EC	IECP	ECG	ANG	ICE	
43308	(43108)	EC	IECP	ECG	ANG	ICE	
43309	(43109)	EC	IECP	ECG	ANG	ICE	
43310	(43110)	EC	IECP	ECG	ANG	ICE	
43311	(43111)	EC	IECP	ECG	ANG	ICE	
43312	(43112)	EC	IECP	ECT	ANG	ICE	
43313	(43113)	EC	IECP	ECT	ANG	ICE	
43314	(43114)	EC	IECP	ECG	ANG	ICE	
43315	(43115)	EC	IECP	ECG	ANG	ICE	
43316	(43116)	EC	IECP	ECG	ANG	ICE	
43317	(43117)	EC	IECP	NXE	ANG	ICE	
43318	(43118)	EC	IECP	ECT	ANG	ICE	
43319	(43119)	EC	IECP	ECG	ANG	ICE	
43320	(43120)	EC	IECP	NXE	ANG	ICE	
43367	(43167)	EC	IECP	NXE	ANG	ICE	Deltic 50 1955 - 2005 v

A start was made in 2012 on replacing the National Express grey and white livery with an East Coast grey colour, shown on Class 43 No. 43308 arriving at London King's Cross. **Antony Christie**

Passenger Train Operating Companies - East Coast

East Coast

Class 91

						Vehicle Length: 63ft 8in (19.40m) Power Collection: 25kV ac overhead
						Height: 12ft 4in (3.75m) Horsepower: 6,300hp (4,700kW)
						Width: 9ft 0in (2.74m) Electrical Equipment: GEC

Number	Depot	Pool	Livery	Owner	Operator	Name
91101 (91001)	BN	IECA	ADV	EVL	ICE	Flying Scotsman (branding)
91102 (91002)	BN	IECA	ECG	EVL	ICE	City of York
91103 (91003)	BN	IECA	ECW	EVL	ICE	
91104 (91004)	BN	IECA	ECG	EVL	ICE	
91105 (91005)	BN	IECA	ECW	EVL	ICE	
91106 (91006)	BN	IECA	ECS	EVL	ICE	
91107 (91007)	BN	IECA	ECS	EVL	ICE	
91108 (91008)	BN	IECA	ECG	EVL	ICE	
91109 (91009)	BN	IECA	ECG	EVL	ICE	Sir Bobby Robson
91110 (91010)	BN	IECA	ADV	EVL	ICE	Battle of Britain Memorial Flight - Spitfire Hurricane Lancaster Dakota
91111 (91011)	BN	IECA	ECG	EVL	ICE	
91112 (91012)	BN	IECA	ECG	EVL	ICE	
91113 (91013)	BN	IECA	ECG	EVL	ICE	
91114 (91014)	BN	IECA	ECG	EVL	ICE	
91115 (91015)	BN	IECA	ECG	EVL	ICE	Blaydon Races
91116 (91016)	BN	IECA	ECG	EVL	ICE	
91117 (91017)	BN	IECA	ECG	EVL	ICE	West Riding Limited
91118 (91018)	BN	IECA	NXE	EVL	ICE	
91119 (91019)	BN	IECA	NXE	EVL	ICE	
91120 (91020)	BN	IECA	ECG	EVL	ICE	
91121 (91021)	BN	IECA	NXE	EVL	ICE	
91122 (91022)	BN	IECA	ECG	EVL	ICE	
91124 (91024)	BN	IECA	NXE	EVL	ICE	
91125 (91025)	BN	IECA	ECG	EVL	ICE	
91126 (91026)	BN	IECA	ECG	EVL	ICE	
91127 (91027)	BN	IECA	ECS	EVL	ICE	
91128 (91028)	BN	IECA	ECG	EVL	ICE	
91129 (91029)	BN	IECA	ECG	EVL	ICE	
91130 (91030)	BN	IECA	ECW	EVL	ICE	
91131 (91031)	BN	IECA	ECG	EVL	ICE	
91132 (91023)	BN	IECA	ECG	EVL	ICE	

A fleet of 31 Class 91s are allocated to Bounds Green in North London to operate the core East Coast services on the Leeds, Edinburgh and Glasgow routes. Some locos now sport full length promotional liveries, including No. 91110 which in mid-2012 was named and branded in recognition of the Battle of Britain Memorial Flight and unveiled at Railfest 2012 at York. The loco is seen at Newcastle with a conventional East Coast grey example.
Antony Christie

Mk3 HST Stock

Vehicle Length: 75ft 0in (22.86m)   Width: 8ft 11in (2.71m)
Height: 12ft 9in (3.88m)   Bogie Type: BT10

GK1G - TRFB *Seating 17F*

Number	Depot	Livery	Owner
40701	EC	NXE	PTR
40702	EC	NXE	PTR
40704	EC	NXE	ANG
40705	EC	NXE	ANG
40706	EC	NXE	ANG
40708	EC	ECT	PTR
40711	EC	NXE	ANG
40720	EC	NXE	ANG
40732	EC	ECG	PTR
40735	EC	NXE	ANG
40737	EC	NXE	ANG
40740	EC	NXE	ANG
40742	EC	NXE	ANG
40748	EC	NXE	ANG
40750	EC	NXE	ANG
40805	EC	NXG	ANG

GH1G - TF *Seating 48F*

Number	Depot	Livery	Owner
41039	EC	NXE	ANG
41040	EC	NXE	ANG
41043	EC	ECS	ANG
41044	EC	NXE	ANG
41058	EC	NXE	PTR
41062	EC	ECG	PTR
41066	EC	NXE	ANG
41083	EC	NXE	PTR
41087	EC	NXE	ANG
41088	EC	NXE	ANG
41090	EC	NXE	ANG
41091	EC	NXE	ANG
41092	EC	NXE	ANG
41095	EC	NXE	ANG
41097	EC	NXE	ANG
41098	EC	NXE	ANG
41099	EC	NXE	ANG
41100	EC	NXE	ANG
41115	EC	NXE	PTR
41118	EC	NXE	ANG
41120	EC	ECT	ANG
41150	EC	ECT	ANG
41151	EC	NXE	ANG
41152	EC	NXE	ANG
41154	EC	ECG	PTR
41159	EC	NXE	PTR
41164	EC	NXE	ANG
41165	EC	NXE	PTR
41170(41001)	EC	NXE	ANG
41185(42313)	EC	NXE	PTR
41190(42088)	EC	NXG	PTR

GH2G - TS (*TSD) *Seating 76/62*S*

Number	Depot	Livery	Owner
42057	EC	NXE	ANG
42058	EC	NXE	ANG
42059	EC	NXE	ANG
42063	EC	NXE	ANG
42064	EC	NXE	ANG
42065	EC	NXE	ANG

42091*	EC	ECT	ANG
42106	EC	NXE	ANG
42109	EC	NXE	PTR
42110	EC	NXE	PTR
42116*	EC	NXE	ANG
42117	EC	NXE	PTR
42123	EC	ECG	PTR
42125	EC	ECG	PTR
42127*	EC	NXE	ANG
42128*	EC	NXE	ANG
42130	EC	NXE	PTR
42134	EC	NXE	ANG
42146	EC	ECT	ANG
42147	EC	NXE	PTR
42150	EC	ECT	ANG
42154	EC	ECT	ANG
42158	EC	NXE	ANG
42159*	EC	NXE	PTR
42160	EC	NXE	PTR
42161*	EC	NXE	PTR
42163	EC	NXE	PTR
42171	EC	NXE	ANG
42172	EC	NXE	ANG
42179	EC	NXE	ANG
42180	EC	NXE	ANG
42181	EC	NXE	ANG
42182	EC	NXE	ANG
42186	EC	ECT	ANG
42188*	EC	NXE	ANG
42189*	EC	NXE	ANG
42190	EC	NXE	ANG
42191	EC	NXE	ANG
42192	EC	NXE	ANG
42193	EC	NXE	ANG
42198	EC	NXE	ANG
42199	EC	NXE	ANG
42205	EC	ECG	PTR
42210	EC	ECG	PTR
42215	EC	ECT	ANG
42219	EC	NXE	ANG
42226	EC	NXE	ANG
42228	EC	ECT	PTR

42235	EC	NXE	ANG
42237	EC	NXE	PTR
42238*	EC	NXE	ANG
42239*	EC	NXE	ANG
42240	EC	NXE	ANG
42241	EC	NXE	ANG
42242	EC	NXE	ANG
42243	EC	NXE	ANG
42244	EC	NXE	ANG
42286	EC	ECT	PTR
42306	EC	NXE	PTR
42307	EC	NXE	PTR
42322	EC	ECT	PTR
42323	EC	NXE	ANG
42326	EC	NXE	PTR
42330	EC	NXE	PTR
42335	EC	ECG	PTR
42340	EC	NXE	ANG
42352(41176)	EC	NXE	PTR
42354(41175)	EC	ECT	ANG
42355(41172)	EC	NXE	ANG
42357(41174)	EC	NXE	ANG
42363(41082)	EC	NXE	ANG

GJ2G - TGS *Seating 65S*

Number	Depot	Livery	Owner
44019	EC	NXE	ANG
44031	EC	NXE	ANG
44045	EC	NXE	ANG
44050	EC	ECT	PTR
44056	EC	NXE	ANG
44057	EC	NXE	PTR
44058	EC	NXE	ANG
44061	EC	NXE	ANG
44063	EC	NXE	ANG
44073	EC	ECG	PTR
44075	EC	NXE	PTR
44077	EC	NXE	ANG
44080	EC	NXE	ANG
44094	EC	ECT	ANG
44098	EC	NXE	ANG

Above: *Displaying National Express (the previous franchise operator's colours) with East Coast branding and dark blue passenger doors, Trailer First No. 41190 is illustrated. These vehicles seat 48 in the 2+1 style.* **Nathan Williamson**

Mk4 Stock

Vehicle Length: 75ft 5in (23m) Width: 8ft 11in (2.73m)
Height: 12ft 5in (3.79m) Bogie Type: BT41

AJ2J - RSB *Seating 30S*

Number	Depot	Livery	Owner
10300	BN	ECS	EVL
10301	BN	ECG	EVL
10302	BN	ECS	EVL
10303	BN	ECS	EVL
10304	BN	NXG	EVL
10305	BN	ECG	EVL
10306	BN	ECG	EVL
10307	BN	ECS	EVL
10308	BN	ECS	EVL
10309	BN	NXG	EVL
10310	BN	NXG	EVL
10311	BN	NXG	EVL
10312	BN	ECG	EVL
10313	BN	ECG	EVL
10315	BN	ECG	EVL
10317	BN	NXG	EVL
10318	BN	ECG	EVL
10319	BN	NXG	EVL
10320	BN	ECS	EVL
10321	BN	ECG	EVL
10323	BN	ECS	EVL
10324	BN	ECG	EVL
10325	BN	ECG	EVL
10326	BN	ECS	EVL
10328	BN	NXG	EVL
10329	BN	NXG	EVL
10330	BN	ECG	EVL
10331	BN	ECS	EVL
10332	BN	ECG	EVL
10333	BN	ECG	EVL

AD1J - FO *Seating 46F*

Number	Depot	Livery	Owner
11201	BN	ECG	EVL
11219	BN	ECS	EVL
11229	BN	NXG	EVL
11237	BN	NXG	EVL
11241	BN	ECG	EVL
11244	BN	ECG	EVL
11273	BN	NXG	EVL
11277(12408)	BN	ECS	EVL
11278(12479)	BN	ECS	EVL
11279(12521)	BN	NXG	EVL
11280(12523)	BN	ECS	EVL
11281(12418)	BN	NXG	EVL
11282(12524)	BN	ECS	EVL
11283(12435)	BN	ECS	EVL
11284(12487)	BN	ECG	EVL
11285(12537)	BN	ECG	EVL
11286(12482)	BN	ECG	EVL
11287(12527)	BN	ECG	EVL
11288(12517)	BN	ECG	EVL
11289(12528)	BN	ECG	EVL
11290(12530)	BN	ECG	EVL
11291(12535)	BN	ECG	EVL
11292(12451)	BN	ECG	EVL
11293(12536)	BN	NXG	EVL
11294(12529)	BN	ECG	EVL
11295(12475)	BN	NXG	EVL
11298(12416)	BN	ECS	EVL
11299(12532)	BN	ECS	EVL

AL1J - FOD *Seating 42F*

Number	Depot	Livery	Owner
11301(11215)	BN	ECS	EVL
11302(11203)	BN	ECS	EVL
11303(11211)	BN	ECS	EVL
11304(11257)	BN	ECS	EVL
11305(11261)	BN	ECS	EVL
11306(11276)	BN	NXG	EVL
11307(11217)	BN	ECS	EVL
11308(11263)	BN	NXG	EVL
11309(11262)	BN	NXG	EVL
11310(11272)	BN	ECS	EVL
11311(11221)	BN	ECS	EVL
11312(11225)	BN	ECG	EVL
11313(11210)	BN	ECG	EVL
11314(11207)	BN	ECG	EVL
11315(11238)	BN	ECG	EVL
11316(11227)	BN	ECG	EVL
11317(11223)	BN	ECG	EVL
11318(11251)	BN	ECG	EVL
11319(11247)	BN	ECG	EVL
11320(11255)	BN	ECG	EVL
11321(11245)	BN	ECG	EVL
11322(11228)	BN	ECG	EVL
11323(11235)	BN	ECG	EVL
11324(11253)	BN	NXG	EVL
11325(11231)	BN	ECG	EVL
11326(11206)	BN	NXG	EVL
11327(11236)	BN	NXG	EVL
11328(11274)	BN	NXG	EVL
11329(11243)	BN	NXG	EVL
11330(11249)	BN	NXG	EVL

AD1J - FO *Seating 46F*

Number	Depot	Livery	Owner
11401(11214)	BN	ECS	EVL
11402(11216)	BN	ECS	EVL
11403(11258)	BN	ECS	EVL
11404(11202)	BN	ECS	EVL
11405(11204)	BN	ECS	EVL
11406(11205)	BN	NXG	EVL
11407(11256)	BN	ECS	EVL
11408(11218)	BN	NXG	EVL
11409(11259)	BN	NXG	EVL
11410(11260)	BN	ECS	EVL
11411(11240)	BN	ECS	EVL
11412(11209)	BN	ECG	EVL
11413(11212)	BN	ECG	EVL
11414(11246)	BN	ECG	EVL
11415(11208)	BN	ECG	EVL
11416(11254)	BN	ECG	EVL
11417(11226)	BN	ECG	EVL
11418(11222)	BN	ECG	EVL
11419(11250)	BN	ECG	EVL
11420(11242)	BN	ECG	EVL
11421(11220)	BN	ECG	EVL
11422(11232)	BN	ECG	EVL
11423(11230)	BN	ECG	EVL
11424(11239)	BN	ECG	EVL
11425(11234)	BN	ECG	EVL
11426(11252)	BN	NXG	EVL
11427(11200)	BN	NXG	EVL
11428(11233)	BN	NXG	EVL
11429(11275)	BN	NXG	EVL
11430(11248)	BN	ECG	EVL
11998(10314)	BN	NXG	EVL
11999(10316)	BN	NXG	EVL

AI2J - TSOE *Seating 76S*

Number	Depot	Livery	Owner
12200	BN	NXG	EVL
12201	BN	ECS	EVL
12202	BN	ECS	EVL
12203	BN	ECS	EVL
12204	BN	NXG	EVL
12205	BN	NXG	EVL
12207	BN	ECS	EVL
12208	BN	NXG	EVL
12209	BN	ECS	EVL
12210	BN	ECG	EVL
12211	BN	ECG	EVL
12212	BN	ECG	EVL
12213	BN	ECG	EVL
12214	BN	ECS	EVL
12215	BN	ECG	EVL
12216	BN	NXG	EVL
12217	BN	ECG	EVL
12218	BN	NXG	EVL
12219	BN	NXG	EVL
12220	BN	NXG	EVL
12222	BN	ECG	EVL
12223	BN	ECG	EVL
12224	BN	ECG	EVL
12225	BN	ECG	EVL
12226	BN	ECG	EVL
12227	BN	NXG	EVL
12228	BN	ECG	EVL
12229	BN	ECG	EVL
12230	BN	NXG	EVL
12231	BN	ECS	EVL
12232	BN	ECS	EVL

AL2J - TSOD *Seating 68S*

Number	Depot	Livery	Owner
12300	BN	ECS	EVL
12301	BN	ECS	EVL
12302	BN	ECS	EVL
12303	BN	ECG	EVL
12304	BN	ECG	EVL
12305	BN	ECS	EVL
12307	BN	ECS	EVL
12308	BN	NXG	EVL
12309	BN	ECG	EVL
12310	BN	ECG	EVL
12311	BN	ECG	EVL
12312	BN	ECG	EVL
12313	BN	NXG	EVL
12315	BN	ECS	EVL
12316	BN	ECG	EVL
12317	BN	NXG	EVL
12318	BN	ECG	EVL
12319	BN	NXG	EVL
12320	BN	NXG	EVL
12321	BN	NXG	EVL
12322	BN	ECG	EVL
12323	BN	ECG	EVL

Passenger Train Operating Companies - East Coast

Number	Depot	Livery	Owner
12324	BN	ECG	EVL
12325	BN	NXG	EVL
12326	BN	ECG	EVL
12327	BN	ECS	EVL
12328	BN	NXG	EVL
12329	BN	ECS	EVL
12330	BN	ECG	EVL
12331(12531)	BN	NXG	EVL

AC2J - TSO *Seating 76S*

Number	Depot	Livery	Owner
12400	BN	ECG	EVL
12401	BN	ECS	EVL
12402	BN	ECS	EVL
12403	BN	NXG	EVL
12404	BN	ECG	EVL
12405	BN	ECS	EVL
12406	BN	NXG	EVL
12407	BN	NXG	EVL
12409	BN	ECG	EVL
12410	BN	ECG	EVL
12411	BN	ECS	EVL
12414	BN	ECS	EVL
12415	BN	ECS	EVL
12417	BN	ECS	EVL
12419	BN	ECS	EVL
12420	BN	NXG	EVL
12421	BN	ECS	EVL
12422	BN	NXG	EVL
12423	BN	ECG	EVL
12424	BN	NXG	EVL
12425	BN	NXG	EVL
12426	BN	ECG	EVL
12427	BN	ECG	EVL
12428	BN	ECG	EVL
12429	BN	NXG	EVL
12430	BN	NXG	EVL
12431	BN	ECG	EVL
12432	BN	ECG	EVL
12433	BN	ECG	EVL
12434	BN	ECG	EVL
12436	BN	ECS	EVL
12437	BN	ECS	EVL
12438	BN	ECS	EVL
12439	BN	ECG	EVL
12440	BN	ECG	EVL
12441	BN	ECG	EVL
12442	BN	ECG	EVL
12443	BN	ECG	EVL
12444	BN	ECG	EVL
12445	BN	ECG	EVL
12446	BN	ECG	EVL
12447	BN	NXG	EVL
12448	BN	ECS	EVL
12449	BN	NXG	EVL
12450	BN	ECS	EVL
12452	BN	ECG	EVL

Number	Depot	Livery	Owner
12453	BN	ECG	EVL
12454	BN	ECG	EVL
12455	BN	ECG	EVL
12456	BN	ECG	EVL
12457	BN	NXG	EVL
12458	BN	NXG	EVL
12459	BN	ECS	EVL
12460	BN	ECG	EVL
12461	BN	ECG	EVL
12462	BN	NXG	EVL
12463	BN	NXG	EVL
12464	BN	ECG	EVL
12465	BN	NXG	EVL
12466	BN	NXG	EVL
12467	BN	ECG	EVL
12468	BN	ECG	EVL
12469	BN	ECG	EVL
12470	BN	ECG	EVL
12471	BN	NXG	EVL
12472	BN	ECG	EVL
12473	BN	ECG	EVL
12474	BN	NXG	EVL
12476	BN	ECG	EVL
12477	BN	ECG	EVL
12478	BN	ECS	EVL
12480	BN	ECS	EVL
12481	BN	NXG	EVL
12483	BN	NXG	EVL
12484	BN	ECS	EVL
12485	BN	NXG	EVL
12486	BN	ECS	EVL
12488	BN	ECS	EVL
12489	BN	ECS	EVL
12513	BN	NXG	EVL
12514	BN	NXG	EVL
12515	BN	ECG	EVL
12518	BN	ECS	EVL
12519	BN	ECG	EVL
12520	BN	ECS	EVL
12522	BN	ECS	EVL
12526	BN	ECG	EVL
12533	BN	NXG	EVL
12534	BN	NXG	EVL

Number	Depot	Livery	Owner
12538	BN	NXG	EVL

NZAJ - DVT

Number	Depot	Livery	Owner
82200	BN	ECG	EVL
82201	BN	ECG	EVL
82202	BN	ECS	EVL
82203	BN	NXG	EVL
82204	BN	ECW	EVL
82205	BN	ADV	EVL
82206	BN	ECG	EVL
82207	BN	ECS	EVL
82208	BN	NXG	EVL
82209	BN	NXG	EVL
82210	BN	ECS	EVL
82211	BN	ECS	EVL
82212	BN	ECG	EVL
82213	BN	ECG	EVL
82214	BN	ECG	EVL
82215	BN	NXG	EVL
82216	BN	ECG	EVL
82217	BN	NXG	EVL
82218	BN	ECS	EVL
82219	BN	ECW	EVL
82220	BN	ECG	EVL
82222	BN	ECG	EVL
82223	BN	NXG	EVL
82224	BN	NXG	EVL
82225	BN	ECG	EVL
82226	BN	ECG	EVL
82227	BN	ECG	EVL
82228	BN	NXG	EVL
82229	BN	NXG	EVL
82230	BN	ECG	EVL
82231	BN	NXG	EVL

82205 carries Flying Scotsman advertising livery

Below: *Mk4 Trailer Standard Open End No. 12223 displays East Coast grey livery.* **Antony Christie**

Service Stock

HST and Mk4 Barrier Vehicles

Number	Depot	Livery	Owner	Former Identity					
6340	EC	NEG	ANG	BCK - 21251	6354	BN	NEG	ANG	BSO - 9459
6341	EC	NEC	ANG	BG - 92080	6355	BN	NEG	ANG	BSO - 9477
6346	EC	NEG	ANG	BSO - 9422	6358	BN	NEG	EVL	BSO - 9432
6352	BN	NEG	ANG	SK - 19465	6359	BN	NEG	EVL	BSO - 9429
6353	BN	NEG	ANG	SK - 19478	9393	EC	PTR	PTR	BG - 92196
					9394	EC	PTR	PTR	BG - 92906

East Midlands Trains

Address: ✉ 1 Prospect Place, Millennium Way, Pride Park, Derby, DE24 8HG
✒ getintouch@eastmidlandstrains.co.uk
✆ 08457 125678
ⓘ www.eastmidlandstrains.co.uk

Managing Director: David Horne
Franchise Dates: 11 November 2007 - 31 March 2015
Principal Routes: St Pancras - Sheffield/York/Leeds/Nottingham
Norwich/Skegness/Cleethorpes - Nottingham/Crewe/
Liverpool and Matlock
Depots: Derby (DY), Nottingham (NM), Neville Hill (NL)
Parent Company: Stagecoach Group

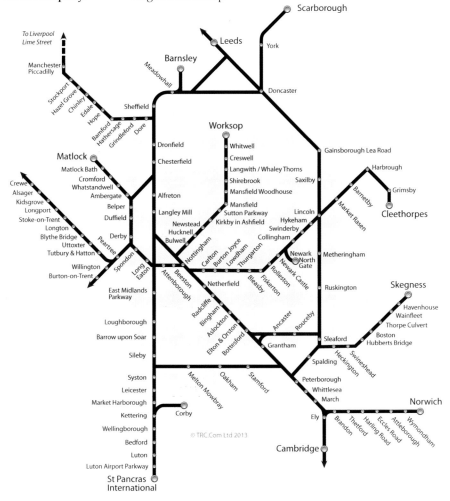

Class 08

Vehicle Length: 29ft 3in (8.91m)			Engine: English Electric 6K			
Height: 12ft 8⅝in (3.87m)			Horsepower: 400hp (298kW)			
Width: 8ft 6in (2.59m)			Electrical Equipment: English Electric			

Number	Depot	Pool	Livery	Owner	Operator	Name
08525	NL	EMSL	EMT	EMT	EMT	Duncan Bedford
08690	NL	EMSL	EMT	EMT	EMT	David Thirkill
08899	DY	EMSL	BLU	EMT	EMT	
08908	DY	EMSL	EMT	EMT	EMT	Ivan Stephenson
08950	NL	EMSL	EMT	EMT	EMT	David Lightfoot

Right: *To provide depot pilotage at East Midlands Trains depots the operator has several Class 08 0-6-0 diesel-electric shunting locos on its books. Four of the locos are painted in full East Midlands Trains livery with red cabs and fully overhauled. These locos are also named after rolling stock engineering staff. No. 08908* Ivan Stephenson *is seen inside the maintenance shed at Leeds Neville Hill.* **Ron Cover**

Class 43 – HST

Vehicle Length: 58ft 5in (18.80m)			Engine: Paxman VP185			
Height: 12ft 10in (3.90m)			Horsepower: 2,100hp (1,565kW)			
Width: 8ft 11in (2.73m)			Electrical Equipment: Brush			

Number	Depot	Pool	Livery	Owner	Operator
43043	NL	EMPC	SCE	PTR	EMT
43044	NL	EMPC	SCE	PTR	EMT
43045	NL	EMPC	SCE	PTR	EMT
43046	NL	EMPC	SCE	PTR	EMT
43047	NL	EMPC	SCE	PTR	EMT
43048	NL	EMPC	SCE	PTR	EMT
43049	NL	EMPC	SCE	PTR	EMT
43050	NL	EMPC	SCE	PTR	EMT
43052	NL	EMPC	SCE	PTR	EMT
43054	NL	EMPC	SCE	PTR	EMT
43055	NL	EMPC	SCE	PTR	EMT
43058	NL	EMPC	SCE	PTR	EMT
43059	NL	EMPC	SCE	PTR	EMT
43061	NL	EMPC	SCE	PTR	EMT
43064	NL	EMPC	SCE	PTR	EMT
43066	NL	EMPC	SCE	PTR	EMT
43073	NL	EMPC	SCE	PTR	EMT
43075	NL	EMPC	SCE	PTR	EMT
43076	NL	EMPC	SCE	PTR	EMT
43081	NL	EMPC	SCE	PTR	EMT
43082	NL	EMPC	SCE	PTR	EMT
43083	NL	EMPC	SCE	PTR	EMT
43089	NL	EMPC	SCE	PTR	EMT

Names applied

43048	T. C. B Miller MBE
43049	Neville Hill
43055	The Sheffield Star 125 Years
43076	In Support of Help for Heroes
43082	Railway Children The Voice for Street Children Worldwide

Right: *Main line services provided by East Midlands Trains are operated jointly by HST and Class 222 sets. The HST fleet of Class 43 power cars and Mk3 trailer vehicles are based at Leeds Neville Hill, but also receive maintenance at Derby Etches Park depot. All are painted in Stagecoach Rail-based livery scheme. An EMT HST led by power car No. 43044 is seen from the sharp end at Derby.* **Antony Christie**

Passenger Train Operating Companies - East Midlands Trains

East Midlands Trains

Class 153

Vehicle Length: 76ft 5in (23.29m)
Height: 12ft 3⅛in (3.75m)
Width: 8ft 10in (2.70m)

Engine: 1 x NT855R5 of 285hp
Horsepower: 285hp (213kW)
Seats (total/car): 66S

Number	Formation DMSL	Depot	Livery	Owner	Operator
153302	52302	NM	EMT	ANG	EMT
153308	52308	NM	EMT	ANG	EMT
153310	52310	NM	EMT	PTR	EMT
153311	52311	NM	EMT	PTR	EMT
153313	52313	NM	EMT	PTR	EMT
153319	52319	NM	EMT	ANG	EMT
153321	52321	NM	EMT	PTR	EMT
153326	52326	NM	EMT	PTR	EMT
153355	57355	NM	EMT	ANG	EMT
153357	57357	NM	EMT	ANG	EMT
153374	57374	NM	EMT	ANG	EMT
153376	57376	NM	EMT	PTR	EMT
153379	57379	NM	EMT	PTR	EMT
153381	57381	NM	EMT	PTR	EMT
153383	57383	NM	EMT	PTR	EMT
153384	57384	NM	EMT	PTR	EMT
153385	57385	NM	EMT	PTR	EMT

Left: East Midlands Trains has an allocation of 17 single-car Class 153 'bubble' cars for deployment on lesser used routes. All carry full East Midlands Trains blue livery and have been internally refurbished. No. 153355 (52355) is seen departing from Peterborough. **Antony Christie**

Class 156

Vehicle Length: 75ft 6in (23.03m)
Height: 12ft 6in (3.81m)
Width: 8ft 11in (2.73m)

Engine: 1 x Cummins NT855R5 of 285hp
Horsepower: 570hp (425kW)
Seats (total/car): 148S, 72S/76S

Number	Formation DMSL+DMS	Depot	Livery	Owner	Operator
156401	52401+57401	NM	EMT	PTR	EMT
156403	52403+57403	NM	EMT	PTR	EMT
156404	52404+57404	NM	EMT	PTR	EMT
156405	52405+57405	NM	EMT	PTR	EMT
156406	52406+57406	NM	EMT	PTR	EMT
156408	52408+57408	NM	EMT	PTR	EMT
156410	52410+57410	NM	EMT	PTR	EMT
156411	52411+57411	NM	EMT	PTR	EMT
156413	52413+57413	NM	EMT	PTR	EMT
156414	52414+57414	NM	EMT	PTR	EMT
156415	52415+57415	NM	EMT	PTR	EMT
156470	52470+57470	NM	EMT	PTR	EMT
156473	52473+57473	NM	EMT	PTR	EMT
156497	52497+57497	NM	EMT	PTR	EMT
156498	52498+57498	NM	EMT	PTR	EMT

Below: East Midlands Trains operates a fleet of 15 Class 156 units for longer distance domestic services, allocated to Nottingham Eastcroft depot. All sets are painted in standard Stagecoach blue livery with red/orange swirl ends and yellow passenger doors. All sets have recently been internally refurbished. Set No. 156408 is seen passing Loughborough. **Antony Christie**

Class 158

Vehicle Length: 76ft 1¾in (23.21m)
Height: 12ft 6in (3.81m)
Width: 9ft 3¼in (2.82m)

Engine: 158770-813 - 1 x Cummins NT855R5 of 350hp
Horsepower: 700hp (522kW)
Engine: 158846-862 - 1 x Perkins 2006TWH of 350hp
Horsepower: 700hp (522kW)
Engine: 158863-865 - 1 x Cummins NT855R5 of 400hp
Horsepower: 800hp (597kW)
Seats (total/car): 146S - 74S, 72S

Number	Formation DMSL+DMSL	Depot	Livery	Owner	Operator
158770	52770+57770	NM	SCE	PTR	EMT
158773	52773+57773	NM	SCE	PTR	EMT
158774	52774+57774	NM	SCE	PTR	EMT
158777	52777+57777	NM	SCE	PTR	EMT
158780	52780+57780	NM	SCE	ANG	EMT
158783	52783+57783	NM	SCE	ANG	EMT
158785	52785+57785	NM	SCE	ANG	EMT
158788	52788+57788	NM	SCE	ANG	EMT
158799	52799+57799	NM	SCE	PTR	EMT
158806	52806+57806	NM	SCE	PTR	EMT
158810	52810+57810	NM	SCE	PTR	EMT
158812	52812+57812	NM	SCE	PTR	EMT
158813	52813+57813	NM	SCE	PTR	EMT
158846	52846+57846	NM	SCE	ANG	EMT
158847	52847+57847	NM	SCE	ANG	EMT
158852	52852+57852	NM	SCE	ANG	EMT
158854	52854+57854	NM	SCE	ANG	EMT
158856	52856+57856	NM	SCE	ANG	EMT
158857	52857+57857	NM	SCE	ANG	EMT
158858	52858+57858	NM	SCE	ANG	EMT
158862	52862+57862	NM	SCE	ANG	EMT
158863	52863+57863	NM	SCE	ANG	EMT
158864	52864+57864	NM	SCE	ANG	EMT
158865	52865+57865	NM	SCE	ANG	EMT
158866	52866+57866	NM	SCE	ANG	EMT

Right: *Longer distance 'local' services on East Midlands Trains are operated by a fleet of 25 two-car Class 158s, including three sets (Nos. 158863-865) fitted with a more powerful 800hp Cummins engine on each carriage. The refurbished fleet carries Stagecoach main line white livery, but is slightly different from the similar South West Trains sets by having a ripple in the blue base colour band to the rear of the cab end doors. Set No. 158852 is illustrated at Ely. Note the '2' applied on the nose end, telling staff that it is the 52xxx vehicle of the set.*
Antony Christie

Class 222

Vehicle Length: 77ft 6in (23.62m)
Height: 12ft 4in (3.75m)
Width: 8ft 11in (2.73m)
Engine: 1 x Cummins OSK9R of 750hp per vehicle

Horsepower: 5,250hp (3,914kW)
Seats (total/car): 106F/236S
38S/68S/68S/62S/42F/42F/22F

Number	Formation DMS+MS+MS+MSRMB+MF+MF+DMRFO	Depot	Livery	Owner	Opt'r	Name
222001	60161+60551+60561+60621+60341+60445+60241	DY	SCE	EVL	EMT	The Entrepreneur Express
222002	60162+60544+60562+60622+60342+60346+60242	DY	SCE	EVL	EMT	The Cutlers' Company
222003	60163+60553+60563+60623+60343+60446+60243	DY	SCE	EVL	EMT	Tornado
222004	60164+60554+60564+60624+60344+60345+60244	DY	SCE	EVL	EMT	
222005	60165+60555+60565+60625+60443+60347+60245	DY	SCE	EVL	EMT	
222006	60166+60556+60566+60626+60441+60447+60246	DY	SCE	EVL	EMT	The Carbon Cutter

Vehicle Length: 77ft 6in (23.62m)
Height: 12ft 4in (3.75m)
Width: 8ft 11in (2.73m)
Engine: 1 x Cummins OSK9R of 750hp per vehicle

Horsepower: 3,750hp (2,796kW)
Seats (total/car): 50F/190S
38S/68S/62S/28F-22S/22F

Number	Formation DMS+MS+MSRMB+MC+DMRFO	Depot	Livery	Owner	Operator	Name
222007	60167+60567+60627+60442+60247	DY	SCE	EVL	EMT	
222008	60168+60545+60628+60918+60248	DY	SCE	EVL	EMT	
222009	60169+60557+60629+60919+60249	DY	SCE	EVL	EMT	
222010	60170+60546+60630+60920+60250	DY	SCE	EVL	EMT	
222011	60171+60531+60631+60921+60251	DY	SCE	EVL	EMT	

East Midlands Trains

222012	60172+60532+60632+60922+60252	DY	SCE	EVL	EMT	
222013	60173+60536+60633+60923+60253	DY	SCE	EVL	EMT	
222014	60174+60534+60634+60924+60254	DY	SCE	EVL	EMT	
222015	60175+60535+60635+60925+60255	DY	SCE	EVL	EMT	
222016	60176+60533+60636+60926+60256	DY	SCE	EVL	EMT	
222017	60177+60537+60637+60927+60257	DY	SCE	EVL	EMT	
222018	60178+60444+60638+60928+60258	DY	SCE	EVL	EMT	
222019	60179+60547+60639+60929+60259	DY	SCE	EVL	EMT	
222020	60180+60543+60640+60930+60260	DY	SCE	EVL	EMT	
222021	60181+60552+60641+60931+60261	DY	SCE	EVL	EMT	
222022	60182+60542+60642+60932+60262	DY	SCE	EVL	EMT	*Invest in Nottingham*
222023	60183+60541+60643+60933+60263	DY	SCE	EVL	EMT	

The backbone of the main line East Midlands Trains operation, sharing duties on the St Pancras to Derby, Sheffield and Nottingham corridor with HSTs are Bombardier-built Class 222s. The 222/0 fleet are a mix of seven- and five-car sets. All are refurbished and have a similar interior to the HST fleet. Set No. 222003 Tornado passes the closed wagon works at Toton with a southbound service. **Antony Christie**

Class 222/1

Vehicle Length: 77ft 6in (23.62m)
Height: 12ft 4in (3.75m)
Width: 8ft 11in (2.73m)
Engine: 1 x Cummins QSK9R of 750hp per vehicle

Horsepower: 3,000hp (2,237kW)
Seats (total/car): 33F/148S
22F/11F-46S/62S/40S

Number	Formation	Depot	Livery	Owner	Operator
	DMF+MC+MSRMB+DMS				
222101	60271+60571+60681+60191	DY	SCE	EVL	EMT
222102	60272+60572+60682+60192	DY	SCE	EVL	EMT
222103	60273+60573+60683+60193	DY	SCE	EVL	EMT
222104	60274+60574+60684+60194	DY	SCE	EVL	EMT

Left: *The Class 222/1 sub-class (four units) were originally built for First Hull Trains for use between Hull and London King's Cross. After Class 180s were deployed on this route, the '222s' were spare and transferred to East Midland Trains to join the rest of the fleet. As four-car sets, they are now used in a common pool with the Class 222/0 fleet following full refurbishment. Set No. 222103 is seen passing Cossington on the Midland Main Line with a southbound service.* **Nathan Williamson**

HST Passenger Fleet

Vehicle Length: 75ft 0in (22.86m)   Width: 8ft 11in (2.71m)
Height: 12ft 9in (3.88m)   Bogie Type: BT10

GK1G - TRFB *Seating 17F*

Number	Depot	Livery	Owner
40700	NL	SCE	PTR
40728	NL	SCE	PTR
40730	NL	SCE	PTR
40741	NL	SCE	PTR
40746	NL	SCE	PTR
40749	NL	SCE	PTR
40751	NL	SCE	PTR
40753	NL	SCE	PTR
40754	NL	SCE	PTR
40756	NL	SCE	PTR

GH1G - TF *Seating 46F*

Number	Depot	Livery	Owner
41041	NL	SCE	PTR
41046	NL	SCE	PTR
41057	NL	SCE	PTR
41061	NL	SCE	PTR
41063	NL	SCE	PTR
41064	NL	SCE	PTR
41067	NL	SCE	PTR
41068	NL	SCE	PTR
41069	NL	SCE	PTR
41070	NL	SCE	PTR
41071	NL	SCE	PTR
41072	NL	SCE	PTR
41075	NL	SCE	PTR
41076	NL	SCE	PTR
41077	NL	SCE	PTR
41079	NL	SCE	PTR
41084	NL	SCE	PTR

41111	NL	SCE	PTR
41112	NL	SCE	PTR
41113	NL	SCE	PTR
41117	NL	SCE	PTR
41156	NL	SCE	PTR

GH2G - TS *Seating 74S*

Number	Depot	Livery	Owner
42100	NL	SCE	PTR
42111	NL	SCE	PTR
42112	NL	SCE	PTR
42113	NL	SCE	PTR
42119	NL	SCE	PTR
42120	NL	SCE	PTR
42121	NL	SCE	PTR
42124	NL	SCE	PTR
42131	NL	SCE	PTR
42132	NL	SCE	PTR
42133	NL	SCE	PTR
42135	NL	SCE	PTR
42136	NL	SCE	PTR
42137	NL	SCE	PTR
42139	NL	SCE	PTR
42140	NL	SCE	PTR
42141	NL	SCE	PTR
42148	NL	SCE	PTR
42149	NL	SCE	PTR
42151	NL	SCE	PTR
42152	NL	SCE	PTR
42153	NL	SCE	PTR
42155	NL	SCE	PTR
42156	NL	SCE	PTR

42157	NL	SCE	PTR
42164	NL	SCE	PTR
42165	NL	SCE	PTR
42194	NL	SCE	PTR
42220	NL	SCE	PTR
42225	NL	SCE	PTR
42227	NL	SCE	PTR
42229	NL	SCE	PTR
42230	NL	SCE	PTR
42327	NL	SCE	PTR
42328	NL	SCE	PTR
42329	NL	SCE	PTR
42331	NL	SCE	PTR
42337	NL	SCE	PTR
42339	NL	SCE	PTR
42341	NL	SCE	PTR
42384¤	NL	SCE	PTR

¤ Modified from 41078

GJ2G - TGS *Seating 63S*

Number	Depot	Livery	Owner
44027	NL	SCE	PTR
44041	NL	SCE	PTR
44044	NL	SCE	PTR
44046	NL	SCE	PTR
44047	NL	SCE	PTR
44048	NL	SCE	PTR
44051	NL	SCE	PTR
44054	NL	SCE	PTR
44070	NL	SCE	PTR
44071	NL	SCE	PTR
44085	NL	SCE	PTR

Below: All of the East Midlands Trains HST passenger stock has now been refurbished, work carried out by Leeds Neville Hill depot. All cars sport a derivative of the Stagecoach main line white livery, complete with red passenger doors and a mid-blue window band. Car No. 44051, a TGS seating 63 standard class passengers is illustrated. **Nathan Williamson**

Service Stock

HST Barrier Vehicles

Number	Depot	Livery	Owner	Former Identity
6392	NL	PTR	PTR	BG - 81588/92183
6395	NL	PTR	EMT	BG - 81506/92148
6397	NL	PTR	PTR	BG - 81600/92190
6398	NL	MAI	EMT	BG - 81471/92126
6399	NL	MAI	EMT	BG - 81367/92994

Eurostar

Address: ✉ Eurostar, Times House, Bravingtons Walk, Regent Quarter,
London, N1 9AW
✎ new.comments@eurostar.com
✆ 08701 606 600
ⓘ www.eurostar.com

Managing Director: Nicolas Petrovic / Richard Brown
Principal Routes: St Pancras International - Brussels and Paris also serving
Disneyland Paris, Avignon and winter sport service
to Bourg St Maurice
Owned Stations: St Pancras International, Stratford International, Ebbsfleet
Depots: Temple Mills [UK] (TI), Forest [Belgium] (FF), Le Landy [France] (LY)

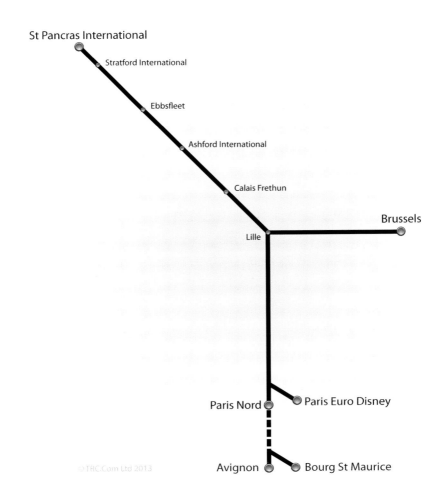

Passenger Train Operating Companies - Eurostar

Class 373

Vehicle Length: (DM) 72ft 8in (22.15m), (MS) 71ft 8in (21.84m)
(TS, TBK, TF, TBF) 61ft 4in (18.70m)
Height: 12ft 4½in (3.77m)
Width: 9ft 3in (2.81m)
Horsepower: 16,400hp (12,249kW)
Seats (total/car): 102F/272S, 0/48S/56S/56S/56S/56S/0/39F/39F/24F

Number	Formation DM+MSO+TSO+TSO+TSO+TSO+RB+TFO+TFO+TBFO	Depot	Livery	Owner	Operator	Name
UK sets (Class 373/0)						
373001	3730010+3730011+3730012+3730013+3730014+3730015+3730016+3730017+3730018+3730019	TI	EUS	EUS	EUS	Tread Lightly
373002	3730020+3730021+3730022+3730023+3730024+3730025+3730026+3730027+3730028+3730029	TI	EUS	EUS	EUS	Voyage Vert
373003	3730030+3730031+3730032+3730033+3730034+3730035+3730036+3730037+3730038+3730039	TI	EUS*	EUS	EUS	Tri City Athlon 2010
373004	3730040+3730041+3730042+3730043+3730044+3730045+3730046+3730047+3730048+3730049	TI	EUS*	EUS	EUS	Tri City Athlon 2010
373005	3730050+3730051+3730052+3730053+3730054+3730055+3730056+3730057+3730058+3730059	TI	EUS	EUS	EUS	
373006	3730060+3730061+3730062+3730063+3730064+3730065+3730066+3730067+3730068+3730069	TI	EUS	EUS	EUS	
373007	3730070+3730071+3730072+3730073+3730074+3730075+3730076+3730077+3730078+3730079	TI	EUS	EUS	EUS	Waterloo Sunset
373008	3730080+3730081+3730082+3730083+3730084+3730085+3730086+3730087+3730088+3730089	TI	EUS	EUS	EUS	Waterloo Sunset
373009	3730090+3730091+3730092+3730093+3730094+3730095+3730096+3730097+3730098+3730099	TI	EUS	EUS	EUS	Remembering Fromelles
373010	3730100+3730101+3730102+3730103+3730104+3730105+3730106+3730107+3730108+3730109	TI	EUS	EUS	EUS	Remembering Fromelles
373011	3730110+3730111+3730112+3730113+3730114+3730115+3730116+3730117+3730118+3730119	TI	EUS	EUS	EUS	
373012	3730120+3730121+3730122+3730123+3730124+3730125+3730126+3730127+3730128+3730129	TI	EUS	EUS	EUS	
373013	3730130+3730131+3730132+3730133+3730134+3730135+3730136+3730137+3730138+3730139	TI	EUS	EUS	EUS	
373014	3730140+3730141+3730142+3730143+3730144+3730145+3730146+3730147+3730148+3730149	TI	EUS	EUS	EUS	
373015	3730150+3730151+3730152+3730153+3730154+3730155+3730156+3730157+3730158+3730159	TI	EUS	EUS	EUS	London 2012
373016	3730160+3730161+3730162+3730163+3730164+3730165+3730166+3730167+3730168+3730169	TI	EUS	EUS	EUS	London 2012
373017	3730170+3730171+3730172+3730173+3730174+3730175+3730176+3730177+3730178+3730179	TI	EUS	EUS	EUS	
373018	3730180+3730181+3730182+3730183+3730184+3730185+3730186+3730187+3730188+3730189	TI	EUS	EUS	EUS	
373019	3730190+3730191+3730192+3730193+3730194+3730195+3730196+3730197+3730198+3730199	TI	EUS‡	EUS	EUS	
373020	3730200+3730201+3730202+3730203+3730204+3730205+3730206+3730207+3730208+3730209	TI	EUS	EUS	EUS	
373021	3730210+3730211+3730212+3730213+3730214+3730215+3730216+3730217+3730218+3730219	TI	EUS	EUS	EUS	
373022	3730220+3730221+3730222+3730223+3730224+3730225+3730226+3730227+3730228+3730229	TI	EUS	EUS	EUS	
Belgian sets (Class 373/1)						
373101	3751010+3731011+3731012+3731013+3731014+3731015+3731016+3731017+3731018+3731019	FF[S]	EUS	SNB	EUS	
373102	3751020+3731021+3731022+3731023+3731024+3731025+3731026+3731027+3731028+3731029	FF[S]	EUS	SNB	EUS	
373103	3751030+3731031+3731032+3731033+3731034+3731035+3731036+3731037+3731038+3731039	FF	EUS	SNB	EUS	
373104	3751040+3731041+3731042+3731043+3731044+3731045+3731046+3731047+3731048+3731049	FF	EUS	SNB	EUS	
373105	3751050+3731051+3731052+3731053+3731054+3731055+3731056+3731057+3731058+3731059	FF	EUS	SNB	EUS	
373106	3731060+3731061+3731062+3731063+3731064+3731065+3731066+3731067+3731068+3731069	FF	EUS	SNB	EUS	
373107	3731070+3731071+3731072+3731073+3731074+3731075+3731076+3731077+3731078+3731079	FF	EUS	SNB	EUS	
373108	3731080+3731081+3731082+3731083+3731084+3731085+3731086+3731087+3731088+3731089	FF	EUS	SNB	EUS	
French sets (Class 373/2)						
373201	3732010+3732011+3732012+3732013+3732014+3732015+3732016+3732017+3732018+3732019	LY	EUS	SNF	EUS	
373202	3732020+3732021+3732022+3732023+3732024+3732025+3732026+3732027+3732028+3732029	LY	EUS	SNF	EUS	
373203¤	3732030+3732031+3732032+3732033+3732034+3732035+3732036+3732037+3732038+3732039	LY	SNT	SNF	EUS	
373204¤	3732040+3732041+3732042+3732043+3732044+3732045+3732046+3732047+3732048+3732049	LY	SNT	SNF	EUS	
373205	3732050+3732051+3732052+3732053+3732054+3732055+3732056+3732057+3732058+3732059	LY	EUS	SNF	EUS	
373206	3732060+3732061+3732062+3732063+3732064+3732065+3732066+3732067+3732068+3732069	LY	EUS	SNF	EUS	

Train Operating Companies

Eurostar

Number	Formation (DM+MSO+TSO+TSO+RB+TFO+TBFO)	Depot	Livery	Owner	Operator	Name
373207	3732070+3732071+3732072+3732073+3732074+3732075+3732076+3732077+3732078+3732079	LY	EUS	SNF	EUS	*Michel Hollard*
373208	3732080+3732081+3732082+3732083+3732084+3732085+3732086+3732087+3732088+3732089	LY	EUS	SNF	EUS	*Michel Hollard*
373209	3732090+3732091+3732092+3732093+3732094+3732095+3732096+3732097+3732098+3732099	LY	EUS	SNF	EUS	*The Da Vinci Code*
373210	3732100+3732101+3732102+3732103+3732104+3732105+3732106+3732107+3732108+3732109	LY	EUS	SNF	EUS	*The Da Vinci Code*
373211	3732110+3732111+3732112+3732113+3732114+3732115+3732116+3732117+3732118+3732119	LY	EUS	SNF	EUS	
373212	3732120+3732121+3732122+3732123+3732124+3732125+3732126+3732127+3732128+3732129	LY	EUS	SNF	EUS	
373213	3732130+3732131+3732132+3732133+3732134+3732135+3732136+3732137+3732138+3732139	LY	EUS	SNF	EUS	
373214	3732140+3732141+3732142+3732143+3732144+3732145+3732146+3732147+3732148+3732149	LY	EUS	SNF	EUS	
373215	3732150+3732151+3732152+3732153+3732154+3732155+3732156+3732157+3732158+3732159	LY	EUS	SNF	EUS	
373216	3732160+3732161+3732162+3732163+3732164+3732165+3732166+3732167+3732168+3732169	LY	EUS	SNF	EUS	
373217	3732170+3732171+3732172+3732173+3732174+3732175+3732176+3732177+3732178+3732179	LY	EUS	SNF	EUS	
373218	3732180+3732181+3732182+3732183+3732184+3732185+3732186+3732187+3732188+3732189	LY	EUS	SNF	EUS	
373219	3732190+3732191+3732192+3732193+3732194+3732195+3732196+3732197+3732198+3732199	LY	EUS	SNF	EUS	
373220	3732200+3732201+3732202+3732203+3732204+3732205+3732206+3732207+3732208+3732209	LY	EUS	SNF	EUS	
373221	3732210+3732211+3732212+3732213+3732214+3732215+3732216+3732217+3732218+3732219	LY	EUS	SNF	EUS	
373222	3732220+3732221+3732222+3732223+3732224+3732225+3732226+3732227+3732228+3732229	LY	EUS	SNF	EUS	
373223	3732230+3732231+3732232+3732233+3732234+3732235+3732236+3732237+3732238+3732239	LY	EUS	SNF	EUS	
373224	3732240+3732241+3732242+3732243+3732244+3732245+3732246+3732247+3732248+3732249	LY	EUS	SNF	EUS	
373225¤	3732250+3732251+3732252+3732253+3732254+3732255+3732256+3732257+3732258+3732259	LY	EUS	SNF	SNT	
373226¤	3732260+3732261+3732262+3732263+3732264+3732265+3732266+3732267+3732268+3732269	LY	EUS	SNF	SNT	
373227¤	3732270+3732271+3732272+3732273+3732274+3732275+3732276+3732277+3732278+3732279	LY	EUS	SNF	SNT	
373228¤	3732280+3732281+3732282+3732283+3732284+3732285+3732286+3732287+3732288+3732289	LY	EUS	SNF	EUS	
373229	3732290+3732291+3732292+3732293+3732294+3732295+3732296+3732297+3732298+3732299	LY	EUS	SNF	EUS	
373230	3732300+3732301+3732302+3732303+3732304+3732305+3732306+3732307+3732308+3732309	LY	EUS	SNF	EUS	
373231	3732310+3732311+3732312+3732313+3732314+3732315+3732316+3732317+3732318+3732319	LY	EUS	SNF	EUS	
373232	3732320+3732321+3732322+3732323+3732324+3732325+3732326+3732327+3732328+3732329	LY	EUS	SNF	EUS	

* Advertising livery - London Virgins.   ‡ de Gaulle 70th branding.   ¤ Operated in France on domestic services.

Regional sets (373/3)

Number	Formation	Depot	Livery	Owner	Operator
373301	3733010+3733011+3733012+3733013+3733015+3733016+3733017+3733019	LY	EUS	EUS	SNF
373302	3733020+3733021+3733022+3733023+3733025+3733026+3733027+3733029	LY	EUS	EUS	SNF
373303(S)	3733030+3733031+3733032+3733033+3733035+3733036+3733037+3733039	LY	EUS	EUS	SNF
373304(S)	3733040+3733041+3733042+3733043+3733045+3733046+3733047+3733049	LY	EUS	EUS	SNF
373305	3733050+3733051+3733052+3733053+3733055+3733056+3733057+3733059	LY	EUS	EUS	SNF
373306	3733060+3733061+3733062+3733063+3733065+3733066+3733067+3733069	LY	EUS	EUS	SNF
373307(S)	3733070+3733071+3733072+3733073+3733075+3733076+3733077+3733079	LY	EUS	EUS	SNF
373308(S)	3733080+3733081+3733082+3733083+3733085+3733086+3733087+3733089	LY	EUS	EUS	SNF
373309	3733090+3733091+3733092+3733093+3733095+3733096+3733097+3733099	LY	EUS	EUS	SNF
373310	3733100+3733101+3733102+3733103+3733105+3733106+3733107+3733109	LY	EUS	EUS	SNF
373311	3733110+3733111+3733112+3733113+3733115+3733116+3733117+3733119	LY	EUS	EUS	SNF
373312	3733120+3733121+3733122+3733123+3733125+3733127+3733129	LY	EUS	EUS	SNF
373313	3733130+3733131+3733132+3733133+3733135+3733136+3733137+3733139	LY	EUS	EUS	SNF
373314	3733140+3733141+3733142+3733143+3733145+3733146+3733147+3733149	LY	EUS	EUS	SNF

Vehicle Length: (DM) 72ft 8in (22.15m), (MS) 71ft 8in (21.84m)
(TS, TBK, TE, TBF) 61ft 4in (18.70m)
Height: 12ft 4½in (3.77m)
Width: 9ft 3in (2.81m)
Horsepower: 16,400hp (12,249kW)
Seats (total/car): 102F/272S, 0/48S/56S/56S/56S/0/39F/39F/24F

■ These 14 short half-sets are loaned to SNCF for domestic duties until 2013.

Above: *The Class 373 Eurostar sets deployed on Anglo-French passenger services have changed little since their introduction in 1993. In 2011 a new Eurostar logo was applied on the cab sides of a blue stylised 'e'. French sets Nos. (37)3218/17 storm through Stratford International with a train from St Pancras International towards the Channel Tunnel.* **Antony Christie**

Spare DM

Number		Depot	Livery	Owner	Operator
3999	(Spare vehicle used as required to cover for maintenance)	TI	EUS	EUS	EUS

● Ten new Eurostar e320 16-car Class 374 sets have been ordered from Siemens for delivery in 2013-14; these will have a 200mph (320km/h) capability and seat 900. The sets will have the ability to operate throughout Europe. Length: 400m, Power: 16,000kW from 25kV ac and 1.5/3kV dc. Driving cars = 25.7m, Intermediate cars = 14.2m, 32 2-axle bogies per train. Numbering wil be in the international series 80 70 **37 40 001** - 80 70 **37 40 010** series.

Class 08

Vehicle Length: 29ft 3in (8.91m)	Engine: English Electric 6K
Height: 12ft 8⅝in (3.87m)	Horsepower: 400hp (298kW)
Width: 8ft 6in (2.59m)	Electrical Equipment: English Electric

Number	Depot	Pool	Livery	Owner	Opt'r
08948	TI	GPSS	TTG	EUS	EUS

Right: *Eurostar stock which requires to be shunted within the depot at Temple Mills has to be either hauled by a diesel locomotive or a remote controlled shunting trolley. To assist this operation, Eurostar own one Class 08 No. 08948. This is a heavily modified loco with drop head Scharfenberg couplers and an extended buffer beam. It is painted in two-tone Channel Tunnel grey livery with wasp warning ends.* **CJM**

First Capital Connect

Address: ✉ Hertford House, 1 Cranwood Street, London, EC1V 9QS

🖱 customer.relations.fcc@firstgroup.com

✆ 0845 026 4700

ⓘ www.firstcapitalconnect.co.uk

Managing Director: Neil Lawson

Franchise Dates: 1 April 2006 - 14 September 2013§

Principal Routes: London King's Cross - King's Lynn,
Peterborough/Cambridge
Moorgate - Hertford Loop and Letchworth
Bedford - Brighton (Thameslink)
Luton - Wimbledon/
Sutton (Thameslink)

Depots: Bedford Cauldwell
Walk (BF),
Hornsey (HE),
Brighton (BI)*
* Stabling point

Parent Company: First Group PLC

§ Might be extended,
re-franchising suspended

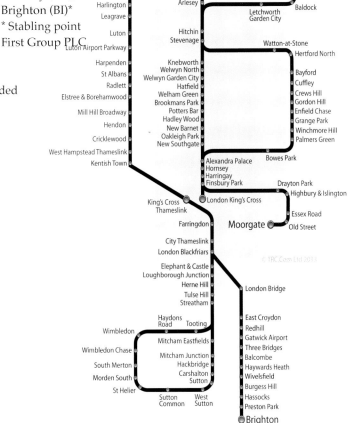

Class 313/0 & 313/1

Vehicle Length: (Driving) 64ft 11½in (20.75m)	Width: 9ft 3in (2.82m)
(Inter) 65ft 4¼in (19.92m)	Horsepower: 880hp (656kW)
Height: 11ft 9in (3.58m)	Seats (total/car): 231S, 74S/83S/74S

Number	Formation DMSO+PTSO+BDMSO	Depot	Livery	Owner	Operator	Name
313018	62546+71230+62160	HE	FCC	EVL	FCC	
313024	62552+71236+62616	HE	FCC	EVL	FCC	
313025	62553+71237+62617	HE	FCC	EVL	FCC	
313026	62554+71238+62618	HE	FCC	EVL	FCC	
313027	62555+71239+62619	HE	FCC	EVL	FCC	
313028	62556+71240+62620	HE	FCC	EVL	FCC	
313029	62557+71241+62621	HE	FCC	EVL	FCC	
313030	62558+71242+62622	HE	FCC	EVL	FCC	
313031	62559+71243+62623	HE	FCC	EVL	FCC	
313032	62560+71244+62643	HE	FCC	EVL	FCC	
313033	62561+71245+62625	HE	FCC	EVL	FCC	
313035	62563+71247+62627	HE	FCC	EVL	FCC	
313036	62564+71248+62628	HE	FCC	EVL	FCC	
313037	62565+71249+62629	HE	FCC	EVL	FCC	
313038	62566+71250+62630	HE	FCC	EVL	FCC	
313039	62567+71251+62631	HE	FCC	EVL	FCC	
313040	62568+71252+62632	HE	FCC	EVL	FCC	
313041	62569+71253+62633	HE	FCC	EVL	FCC	
313042	62570+71254+62634	HE	FCC	EVL	FCC	
313043	62571+71255+62635	HE	FCC	EVL	FCC	
313044	62572+71256+62636	HE	FCC	EVL	FCC	
313045	62573+71257+62637	HE	FCC	EVL	FCC	
313046	62574+71258+62638	HE	FCC	EVL	FCC	
313047	62575+71259+62639	HE	FCC	EVL	FCC	
313048	62576+71260+62640	HE	FCC	EVL	FCC	
313049	62577+71261+62641	HE	FCC	EVL	FCC	
313050	62578+71262+62649	HE	FCC	EVL	FCC	
313051	62579+71263+62624	HE	FCC	EVL	FCC	
313052	62580+71264+62644	HE	FCC	EVL	FCC	
313053	62581+71265+62645	HE	FCC	EVL	FCC	
313054	62582+71266+62646	HE	FCC	EVL	FCC	Captain William Leefe Robinson VC
313055	62583+71267+62647	HE	FCC	EVL	FCC	
313056	62584+71268+62648	HE	FCC	EVL	FCC	
313057	62585+71269+62642	HE	FCC	EVL	FCC	
313058	62586+71270+62650	HE	FCC	EVL	FCC	
313059	62587+71271+62651	HE	FCC	EVL	FCC	
313060	62588+71272+62652	HE	FCC	EVL	FCC	
313061	62589+71273+62653	HE	FCC	EVL	FCC	
313062	62590+71274+62654	HE	FCC	EVL	FCC	
313063	62591+71275+62655	HE	FCC	EVL	FCC	
313064	62592+71276+62656	HE	FCC	EVL	FCC	
313122	62550+71234+61614	HE	FCC	EVL	FCC	
313123	62551+71235+61615	HE	FCC	EVL	FCC	
313134	62562+71246+61626	HE	FCC	EVL	FCC	City of London

Right: *The First Capital Connect Class 313 fleet were the first production of 1972-design high-density EMUs which emerged from the PEP prototypes used on the Southern Region. The FCC '313s' are allocated to Hornsey depot and operate the dual voltage Great Northern Lines into and from Moorgate and King's Cross. All sets are finished in First Group livery. Set No. 313038 is seen at London King's Cross on 28 September 2012.*
Antony Christie

First Capital Connect

Class 317/3

Vehicle Length: (Driving) 65ft 0¾in (19.83m) Width: 9ft 3in (2.82m)
(Inter) 65ft 4¼in (19.92m) Horsepower: 1,000hp (746kW)
Height: 12ft 1½in (3.58m) Seats (total/car): 22F/269S, 74S/79S/22F-46S/70S

Number	Formation	Depot	Livery	Owner	Operator	Name
	DTSO+MSO+TCO+DTSO					
317337	77036+62671+71613+77084	HE	FCC	ANG	FCC	
317338	77037+62698+71614+77085	HE	FCC	ANG	FCC	
317339	77038+62699+71615+77086	HE	FCC	ANG	FCC	
317340	77039+62700+71616+77087	HE	FCC	ANG	FCC	
317341	77040+62701+71617+77088	HE	FCC	ANG	FCC	
317342	77041+62702+71618+77089	HE	FCC	ANG	FCC	
317343	77042+62703+71619+77090	HE	FCC	ANG	FCC	
317344	77029+62690+71620+77091	HE	FCC	ANG	FCC	
317345	77044+62705+71621+77092	HE	FCC	ANG	FCC	*Driver John Webb*
317346	77045+62706+71622+77093	HE	FCC	ANG	FCC	
317347	77046+62707+71623+77094	HE	FCC	ANG	FCC	
317348	77047+62708+71624+77095	HE	FCC	ANG	FCC	*Richard A. Jenner*

Left: *First Capital Connect operate a fleet of 12 Class 317/3s, allocated to Hornsey. The sets are painted in First Group corporate livery and operate on longer distance outer-suburban routes. Set No. 317344 is seen at London King's Cross stabled at one of the suburban FCC platforms.*
Antony Christie

Class 319/0

Vehicle Length: (Driving) 65ft 0¾in (19.83m) Width: 9ft 3in (2.82m)
(Inter) 65ft 4¼in (19.92m) Horsepower: 1,326hp (990kW)
Height: 11ft 9in (3.58m) Seats (total/car): 319S, 82S/82S/77S/78S

Number	Formation	Depot	Livery	Owner	Operator	Name
	DTSO(A)+MSO+TSO+DTSO(B)					
319001	77291+62891+71772+77290	SU	FCC	PTR	FCC	
319002	77293+62892+71773+77292	SU	FCC	PTR	FCC	
319003	77295+62893+71774+77294	SU	FCC	PTR	FCC	
319004	77297+62894+71775+77296	SU	FCC	PTR	FCC	
319005	77299+62895+71776+77298	SU	FCC	PTR	FCC	
319006	77301+62896+71777+77300	SU	FCC	PTR	FCC	
319007	77303+62897+71778+77302	SU	FCC	PTR	FCC	
319008	77305+62898+71779+77304	SU	SOU	PTR	FCC	*Cheriton*
319009	77307+62899+71780+77306	SU	SOU	PTR	FCC	*Coquelles*
319010	77309+62900+71781+77308	SU	FCC	PTR	FCC	
319011	77311+62901+71782+77310	SU	SOU	PTR	FCC	*John Ruskin College*
319012	77313+62902+71783+77312	SU	SOU	PTR	FCC	
319013	77315+62903+71784+77314	SU	SOU	PTR	FCC	*The Surrey Hills*

Class 319/2

Vehicle Length: (Driving) 65ft 0¾in (19.83m) Width: 9ft 3in (2.82m)
(Inter) 65ft 4¼in (19.92m) Horsepower: 1,326hp (990kW)
Height: 11ft 9in (3.58m) Seats (total/car): 18F/212S, 64S/60S/52S/18F-36S

Number	Formation	Depot	Livery	Owner	Operator	Name/Notes
	DTSO+MSO+TSO+DTCO					
319214	77317+62904+71785+77316	SU	SOU	PTR	FCC	
319215	77319+62905+71786+77318	SU	ADV	PTR	FCC	*(Visit Switzerland livery)*
319216	77321+62906+71787+77320	SU	SOU	PTR	FCC	
319217	77323+62907+71788+77322	BF	SOU	PTR	FCC	*Brighton*
319218	77325+62908+71789+77324	BF	ADV	PTR	FCC	*Croydon* *(Lycamobile)*
319219	77327+62909+71790+77326	BF	SOU	PTR	FCC	
319220	77329+62910+71791+77328	BF	SOU	PTR	FCC	

Class 319/3

Vehicle Length: (Driving) 65ft 0¾in (19.83m) Width: 9ft 3in (2.82m)
(Inter) 65ft 4¼in (19.92m) Horsepower: 1,326hp (990kW)
Height: 11ft 9in (3.58m) Seats (total/car): 300S, 70S/78S/74S/78S

Number	Formation	Depot	Livery	Owner	Operator	Name
	DTSO(A)+MSO+TSO+DTSO(B)					
319361	77459+63043+71929+77458	BF	FCC	PTR	FCC	
319362	77461+63044+71930+77460	BF	FCC	PTR	FCC	
319363	77463+63045+71931+77462	BF	FCC	PTR	FCC	
319364	77465+63046+71932+77464	BF	TLP	PTR	FCC	*Transforming Blackfriars*
319365	77467+63047+71933+77466	BF	TLP	PTR	FCC	*Transforming Farringdon*
319366	77469+63048+71934+77468	BF	FCC	PTR	FCC	
319367	77471+63049+71935+77470	BF	FCC	PTR	FCC	
319368	77473+63050+71936+77472	BF	FCC	PTR	FCC	
319369	77475+63051+71937+77474	BF	FCC	PTR	FCC	
317370	77477+63052+71938+77476	BF	FCC	PTR	FCC	
319371	77479+63053+71939+77478	BF	FCC	PTR	FCC	
319372	77481+63054+71940+77480	BF	FCC	PTR	FCC	
319373	77483+63055+71941+77482	BF	FCC	PTR	FCC	
319374	77485+63056+71942+77484	BF	FCC	PTR	FCC	*Bedford Cauldwell Walk TMD*
319375	77487+63057+71943+77486	BF	FCC	PTR	FCC	
319376	77489+63058+71944+77488	BF	FCC	PTR	FCC	
319377	77491+63059+71945+77490	BF	FCC	PTR	FCC	
319378	77493+63060+71946+77492	BF	FCC	PTR	FCC	
319379	77495+63061+71947+77494	BF	FCC	PTR	FCC	
319380	77497+63082+71948+77496	BF	FCC	PTR	FCC	
319381	77973+63093+71978+77974	BF	FCC	PTR	FCC	
319382	77975+63094+71980+77976	BF	FCC	PTR	FCC	
319383	77977+63096+71981+77978	BF	FCC	PTR	FCC	
319384	77979+63096+71982+77980	BF	FCC	PTR	FCC	
319385	77981+63097+71983+77982	BF	FCC	PTR	FCC	
319386	77983+63098+71984+77984	BF	FCC	PTR	FCC	

Right: *At present First Capital Connect operate the north-south Thameslink service, but in the future this is set to change with new stock and revised routes. Today, Class 319s and some 377s are used. Four different sub-classes of 319 exist; the different sub-groups refer to seating variants and some minor design changes. In this view we see Class 319/4 No. 319458 and Class 319/2 No. 319214 side by side at Bedford on 12 January 2012.*
CJM

Class 319/4

Vehicle Length: (Driving) 65ft 0¾in (19.83m) Width: 9ft 3in (2.82m)
(Inter) 65ft 4¼in (19.92m) Horsepower: 1,326hp (990kW)
Height: 11ft 9in (3.58m) Seats (total/car): 12F/277S, 12F-54S/77S/72S/74S

Number	Formation	Depot	Livery	Owner	Operator	Name
	DTCO+MSO+TSO+DTSO					
319421	77331+62911+71792+77330	BF	FCC	PTR	FCC	
319422	77333+62912+71793+77332	BF	FCC	PTR	FCC	
319423	77335+62913+71794+77334	BF	FCC	PTR	FCC	
319424	77337+62914+71795+77336	BF	FCC	PTR	FCC	
319425	77339+62915+71796+77338	BF	FCC	PTR	FCC	*Transforming Travel*
319426	77341+62916+71797+77340	BF	FCC	PTR	FCC	
319427	77343+62917+71798+77342	BF	FCC	PTR	FCC	
319428	77345+62918+71799+77344	BF	FCC	PTR	FCC	
319429	77347+62919+71800+77346	BF	FCC	PTR	FCC	
319430	77349+62920+71801+77348	BF	FCC	PTR	FCC	
319431	77351+62921+71802+77350	BF	FCC	PTR	FCC	
319432	77353+62922+71803+77352	BF	FCC	PTR	FCC	
319433	77355+62923+71804+77354	BF	FCC	PTR	FCC	

First Capital Connect

319434	77357+62924+71805+77356	BF	FCC	PTR	FCC	
319435	77359+62925+71806+77358	BF	FCC	PTR	FCC	*Adrian Jackson-Robbins Chairman 1987-2007 Association of Public Transport Users*
319436	77361+62926+71807+77360	BF	FCC	PTR	FCC	
319437	77363+62927+71808+77362	BF	FCC	PTR	FCC	
319438	77365+62928+71809+77364	BF	FCC	PTR	FCC	
319439	77367+62929+71810+77366	BF	FCC	PTR	FCC	
319440	77369+62930+71811+77368	BF	FCC	PTR	FCC	
319441	77371+62931+71812+77370	BF	FCC	PTR	FCC	*Driver Mick Winnett*
319442	77373+62932+71813+77372	BF	FCC	PTR	FCC	
319443	77375+62933+71814+77374	BF	FCC	PTR	FCC	
319444	77377+62934+71815+77376	BF	FCC	PTR	FCC	
319445	77379+62935+71816+77378	BF	FCC	PTR	FCC	
319446	77381+62936+71817+77380	BF	FCC	PTR	FCC	
319447	77431+62961+71866+77430	BF	FCC	PTR	FCC	
319448	77433+62962+71867+77432	BF	FCC	PTR	FCC	
319449	77435+62963+71868+77434	BF	FCC	PTR	FCC	
319450	77437+62964+71869+77436	BF	FCC	PTR	FCC	
319451	77439+62965+71870+77438	BF	FCC	PTR	FCC	
319452	77441+62966+71871+77440	BF	FCC	PTR	FCC	
319453	77443+62967+71872+77442	BF	FCC	PTR	FCC	
319454	77445+62968+71873+77444	BF	FCC	PTR	FCC	
319455	77447+62969+71874+77446	BF	FCC	PTR	FCC	
319456	77449+62970+71875+77448	BF	FCC	PTR	FCC	
319457	77451+62971+71876+77450	BF	FCC	PTR	FCC	
319458	77453+62972+71877+77452	BF	FCC	PTR	FCC	
319459	77455+62973+71878+77454	BF	FCC	PTR	FCC	
319460	77457+62974+71879+77456	BF	FCC	PTR	FCC	

Class 321/4

Vehicle Length: (Driving) 65ft 0¾in (19.83m)   Width: 9ft 3in (2.82m)
(Inter) 65ft 4¼in (19.92m)   Horsepower: 1,328hp (996kW)
Height: 12ft 4¾in (3.78m)   Seats (total/car): 28F/271S, 28F-40S/79S/74S/78S

Number	Formation DMCO+MSO+TSO+DMSO	Depot	Livery	Owner	Operator	Name
321401	78095+63063+71949+77943	HE	FCC	EVL	FCC	
321402	78096+63064+71950+77944	HE	FCC	EVL	FCC	
321403	78097+63065+71951+77945	HE	FCC	EVL	FCC	*Stewart Fleming Signalman King's Cross*
321404	78098+63066+71952+77946	HE	FCC	EVL	FCC	
321405	78099+63067+71953+77947	HE	FCC	EVL	FCC	
321406	78100+63068+71954+77948	HE	FCC	EVL	FCC	
321407	78101+63069+71955+77949	HE	FCC	EVL	FCC	
321408	78102+63070+71956+77959	HE	FCC	EVL	FCC	
321409	78103+63071+71957+77960	HE	FCC	EVL	FCC	
321410	78104+63072+71958+77961	HE	FCC	EVL	FCC	
321418	78112+63080+71968+77962	HE	FCC	EVL	FCC	
321419	78113+63081+71969+77963	HE	FCC	EVL	FCC	
321420	78114+63082+71970+77964	HE	FCC	EVL	FCC	

Left: *One of the more recent additions to the FCC fleet are 13 Class 321/4 units. Allocated to Hornsey, these sets operate mainly peak hour services. On 3 January 2012, set No. 321419 displaying full FCC livery stands at London King's Cross between duties. These 321/4s were from the original batch used on the Euston-Birmingham route.* **Antony Christie**

Class 365
Networker Express

	Vehicle Length: (Driving) 68ft 6½in (20.89m)	Width: 9ft 2½in (2.81m)
	(Inter) 65ft 9¼in (20.89m)	Horsepower: 1,684hp (1,256kW)
	Height: 12ft 4½in (3.77m)	Seats (total/car): 24F/239S, 12F-56S/59S/68S/12F-56S

Number	Formation DMCO(A)+TSO+PTSO+DMCO(B)	Depot	Livery	Owner	Operator	Name
365501	65894+72241+72240+65935	HE	FCC	EVL	FCC	
365502	65895+72243+72242+65936	HE	FCC	EVL	FCC	
365503	65896+72245+72244+65937	HE	FCC	EVL	FCC	
365504	65897+72247+72246+65938	HE	FCC	EVL	FCC	
365505	65898+72249+72248+65939	HE	FCC	EVL	FCC	
365506	65899+72251+72250+65940	HE	FCC	EVL	FCC	The Royston Express
365507	65900+72253+72252+65941	HE	FCC	EVL	FCC	
365508	65901+72255+72254+65942	HE	FCC	EVL	FCC	
365509	65902+72257+72256+65943	HE	FCC	EVL	FCC	
365510	65903+72259+72258+65944	HE	FCC	EVL	FCC	
365511	65904+72261+72260+65945	HE	FCC	EVL	FCC	
365512	65905+72263+72262+65946	HE	FCC	EVL	FCC	
365513	65906+72265+72264+65947	HE	FCC	EVL	FCC	Hornsey Depot
365514	65907+72267+72266+65948	HE	FCC	EVL	FCC	Captain George Vancouver
365515	65908+72269+72268+65949	HE	FCC	EVL	FCC	
365516	65909+72271+72270+65950	HE	FCC	EVL	FCC	
365517	65910+72273+72272+65951	HE	FCC	EVL	FCC	
365518	65911+72275+72274+65952	HE	FCC	EVL	FCC	The Fenman
365519	65912+72277+72276+65953	HE	FCC	EVL	FCC	
365520	65913+72279+72278+65954	HE	FCC	EVL	FCC	
365521	65914+72281+72280+65955	HE	FCC	EVL	FCC	
365522	65915+72283+72282+65956	HE	FCC	EVL	FCC	
365523	65916+72285+72284+65957	HE	FCC	EVL	FCC	
365524	65917+72287+72286+65958	HE	FCC	EVL	FCC	
365525	65918+72289+72288+65959	HE	FCC	EVL	FCC	
365527	65920+72293+72292+65961	HE	FCC	EVL	FCC	Robert Stripe Passengers' Champion
365528	65921+72296+72294+65962	HE	FCC	EVL	FCC	
365529	65922+72297+72296+65963	HE	FCC	EVL	FCC	
365530	65923+72299+72298+65964	HE	FCC	EVL	FCC	The Interlink Partnership Promoting Integrated Transport Since 1999
365531	65924+72301+72300+65965	HE	FCC	EVL	FCC	
365532	65925+72303+72302+65966	HE	FCC	EVL	FCC	
365533	65926+72305+72304+65967	HE	FCC	EVL	FCC	
365534	65927+72307+72306+65968	HE	FCC	EVL	FCC	
365535	65928+72309+72308+65969	HE	FCC	EVL	FCC	
365536	65929+72311+72310+65970	HE	FCC	EVL	FCC	
365537	65930+72313+72312+65971	HE	FCC	EVL	FCC	Daniel Edwards (1974-2010) Cambridge Driver
365538	65931+72315+72314+65972	HE	FCC	EVL	FCC	
365539	65932+72317+72316+65973	HE	FCC	EVL	FCC	
365540	65933+72319+72318+65974	HE	FCC	EVL	FCC	
365541	65934+72321+72320+65975	HE	FCC	EVL	FCC	

Passenger Train Operating Companies - First Capital Connect

Right: *A fleet of 40 'Networker Express' Class 365 units are allocated to Hornsey and are operated by First Capital Connect on King's Cross outer-suburban services. On 4 July 2012, No. 365541 is seen arriving at London King's Cross. The front ends of these sets were extensively rebuilt, originally having the same front end as a Class 465.* **Antony Christie**

First Capital Connect

Class 377/5
Electrostar

Vehicle Length: (Driving) 66ft 9in (20.40m)
(Inter) 65ft 6in (19.99m)
Height: 12ft 4in (3.77m)

Width: 9ft 2in (2.80m)
Horsepower: 2,012hp (1,500kW) (ac), dual voltage sets
Seats (total/car): 20F-221S, 10F-48S/69S/56S/10F-48S

Number	Formation DMCO(A)+MSO+PTSO+DMCO(B)	Depot	Livery	Owner	Operator
377501	73501+75901+74901+73601	BF	FCC	PTR	FCC *(Sub-lease from Southern)*
377502	73502+75902+74902+73602	BF	FCC	PTR	FCC *(Sub-lease from Southern)*
377503	73503+75903+74903+73603	BF	FCC	PTR	FCC *(Sub-lease from Southern)*
377504	73504+75904+74904+73604	BF	FCC	PTR	FCC *(Sub-lease from Southern)*
377505	73505+75905+74905+73605	BF	FCC	PTR	FCC *(Sub-lease from Southern)*
377506	73506+75906+74906+73606	BF	FCC	PTR	FCC *(Sub-lease from Southern)*
377507	73507+75907+74907+73607	BF	FCC	PTR	FCC *(Sub-lease from Southern)*
377508	73508+75908+74908+73608	BF	FCC	PTR	FCC *(Sub-lease from Southern)*
377509	73509+75909+74909+73609	BF	FCC	PTR	FCC *(Sub-lease from Southern)*
377510	73510+75910+74910+73610	BF	FCC	PTR	FCC *(Sub-lease from Southern)*
377511	73511+75911+74911+73611	BF	FCC	PTR	FCC *(Sub-lease from Southern)*
377512	73512+75912+74912+73612	BF	FCC	PTR	FCC *(Sub-lease from Southern)*
377513	73513+75913+74913+73613	BF	FCC	PTR	FCC *(Sub-lease from Southern)*
377514	73514+75914+74914+73614	BF	FCC	PTR	FCC *(Sub-lease from Southern)*
377515	73515+75915+74915+73615	BF	FCC	PTR	FCC *(Sub-lease from Southern)*
377516	73516+75916+74916+73616	BF	FCC	PTR	FCC *(Sub-lease from Southern)*
377517	73517+75917+74917+73617	BF	FCC	PTR	FCC *(Sub-lease from Southern)*
377518	73518+75918+74918+73618	BF	FCC	PTR	FCC *(Sub-lease from Southern)*
377519	73519+75919+74919+73619	BF	FCC	PTR	FCC *(Sub-lease from Southern)*
377520	73520+75920+74920+73620	BF	FCC	PTR	FCC *(Sub-lease from Southern)*
377521	73521+75921+74921+73621	BF	FCC	PTR	FCC *(Sub-lease from Southern)*
377522	73522+75922+74922+73622	BF	FCC	PTR	FCC *(Sub-lease from Southern)*
377523	73523+75923+74923+73623	BF	FCC	PTR	FCC *(Sub-lease from Southern)*

Technically on sub-lease from train operator Southern, the 23 Class 377/5s are now operated by First Capital Connect, forming express services via the Thameslink route. Units are painted in full FCC livery and allocated to Bedford depot. Following the introduction of new Thameslink stock and upon modernisation of the north-south route through London, these Class 377/5s are likely to return to Southern. Set No. 377512 is seen approaching Gatwick Airport. **Chris Wilson**

First Great Western

Address: ✉ Milford House, 1 Milford Street, Swindon, SN1 1HL
🖅 fgwfeedback@firstgroup.com
✆ 08457 000125 ⓘ www.firstgreatwestern.co.uk

Managing Director: Mark Hopwood

Franchise Dates: 1 April 2006 - 31 March 2013§

Principal Routes: Paddington - Penzance/Paignton, Bristol, Swansea
Thames Valley local lines
Local lines in Bristol, Exeter, Plymouth and Cornwall
Bristol - Weymouth, Portsmouth/Brighton

Depots: Exeter (EX), Old Oak Common (OO), Laira (LA), Landore (LE),
St Philip's Marsh (PM), Penzance (PZ), Reading (RG)

Parent Company: First Group PLC

§ Might be extended, re-franchising suspended

Class 08

Vehicle Length: 29ft 3in (8.91m)	Engine: English Electric 6K	
Height: 12ft 8⅝in (3.87m)	Horsepower: 400hp (298kW)	
Width: 8ft 6in (2.59m)	Electrical Equipment: English Electric	

Number	Depot	Pool	Livery	Owner	Operator
08410	LA	EFSH	FGB	FGP	FGW
08483	OO	EFSH	GWG	FGP	FGW
08641	LA	EFSH	FGB	FGP	FGW
08644	PZ	EFSH	BLU	FGP	FGW
08645	LA	EFSH	GWG	FGP	FGW
08663(S)	PM	EFSH	FGB	FGP	FGW
08795	LE	EFSH	GWG	FGP	FGW
08822	LE	EFSH	FGB	FGP	FGW
08836	OC	EFSH	GWG	FGP	FGW

Names applied
08483 *Dusty - Driver David Miller*
08645 *Mike Baggott*

Below: *An allocation of nine Class 08 350hp diesel-electric shunting locos are on the books of First Great Western. These are based at the depots where HST or loco-hauled stock is required to be re-formed. All are air brake fitted and carry either hinged or drop head knuckle couplers to provide easy attachment to buck-eye fitted HST stock. No. 08410 painted in First Group blue is seen at Penzance, where the resident '08' is frequently used to shunt the stock used on the overnight sleeping car service, as well as haul the stock between Long Rock depot and Penzance station. For this reason the loco is headlight fitted and has OTMR equipment.* **Antony Christie**

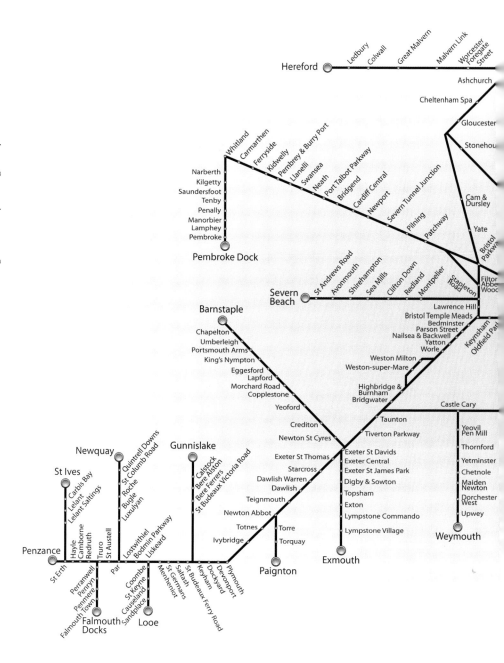

First Great Western

Class 43 – HST

Vehicle Length: 58ft 5in (18.80m)
Height: 12ft 10in (3.90m)
Width: 8ft 11in (2.73m)
Engine: MTU 16V4000 R41R
Horsepower: 2,250hp (1,680kW)
Electrical Equipment: Brush

Passenger Train Operating Companies - First Great Western

Number	Depot	Pool	Livery	Owner	Operator	Number	Depot	Pool	Livery	Owner	Operator
43002	LA	EFPC	FGB	ANG	FGW	43134	LE	EFPC	FGB	ANG	FGW
43003	LA	EFPC	FGB	ANG	FGW	43135	LE	EFPC	FGB	ANG	FGW
43004	LA	EFPC	FGB	ANG	FGW	43136	LE	EFPC	FGB	ANG	FGW
43005	LA	EFPC	FGB	ANG	FGW	43137	LE	EFPC	FGB	ANG	FGW
43009	LA	EFPC	FGB	ANG	FGW	43138	LE	EFPC	FGB	ANG	FGW
43010	LA	EFPC	FGB	ANG	FGW	43139	LE	EFPC	FGB	ANG	FGW
43012	LA	EFPC	FGB	ANG	FGW	43140	LE	EFPC	FGB	ANG	FGW
43015	LA	EFPC	FGB	ANG	FGW	43141	LE	EFPC	FGB	ANG	FGW
43016	LA	EFPC	FGB	ANG	FGW	43142	LE	EFPC	FGB	ANG	FGW
43017	LA	EFPC	FGB	ANG	FGW	43143	LE	EFPC	FGB	ANG	FGW
43018	LA	EFPC	FGB	ANG	FGW	43144	LE	EFPC	FGB	ANG	FGW
43020	LA	EFPC	FGB	ANG	FGW	43145	LE	EFPC	FGB	ANG	FGW
43021	LA	EFPC	FGB	ANG	FGW	43146	LE	EFPC	FGB	ANG	FGW
43022	LA	EFPC	FGB	ANG	FGW	43147	LE	EFPC	FGB	ANG	FGW
43023	LA	EFPC	FGB	ANG	FGW	43148	LE	EFPC	FGB	ANG	FGW
43024	LA	EFPC	FGB	ANG	FGW	43149	LE	EFPC	FGB	ANG	FGW
43025	LA	EFPC	FGB	ANG	FGW	43150	LE	EFPC	FGB	ANG	FGW
43026	LA	EFPC	FGB	ANG	FGW	43151	LE	EFPC	FGB	ANG	FGW
43027	LA	EFPC	FGB	ANG	FGW	43152	LE	EFPC	FGB	ANG	FGW
43028	LA	EFPC	FGB	ANG	FGW	43153	OO	EFPC	FGB	FGP	FGW
43029	LA	EFPC	FGB	ANG	FGW	43154	OO	EFPC	FGB	FGP	FGW
43030	LA	EFPC	FGB	ANG	FGW	43155	OO	EFPC	FGB	FGP	FGW
43031	LA	EFPC	FGB	ANG	FGW	43156	OO	EFPC	FGB	PTR	FGW
43032	LA	EFPC	FGB	ANG	FGW	43158	OO	EFPC	FGB	FGP	FGW
43033	LA	EFPC	FGB	ANG	FGW	43159	OO	EFPC	FGB	PTR	FGW
43034	LA	EFPC	FGB	ANG	FGW	43160	OO	EFPC	FGB	PTR	FGW
43035	LA	EFPC	FGB	ANG	FGW	43161	OO	EFPC	FGB	PTR	FGW
43036	LA	EFPC	FGB	ANG	FGW	43162	OO	EFPC	FGB	ANG	FGW
43037	LA	EFPC	FGB	ANG	FGW	43163	OO	EFPC	FGB	ANG	FGW
43040	LA	EFPC	FGB	ANG	FGW	43164	OO	EFPC	FGB	ANG	FGW
43041	OO	EFPC	FGB	ANG	FGW	43165	OO	EFPC	FGB	ANG	FGW
43042	OO	EFPC	FGB	ANG	FGW	43168	OO	EFPC	FGB	ANG	FGW
43053	LE	EFPC	FGB	PTR	FGW	43169	OO	EFPC	FGB	ANG	FGW
43056	LE	EFPC	FGB	PTR	FGW	43170	OO	EFPC	FGB	ANG	FGW
43063	OO	EFPC	FGB	PTR	FGW	43171	OO	EFPC	FGB	ANG	FGW
43069	OO	EFPC	FGB	PTR	FGW	43172	OO	EFPC	FGB	ANG	FGW
43070	OO	EFPC	FGB	PTR	FGW	43174	OO	EFPC	FGB	ANG	FGW
43071	OO	EFPC	FGB	PTR	FGW	43175	OO	EFPC	FGB	ANG	FGW
43078	OO	EFPC	FGB	PTR	FGW	43176	OO	EFPC	FGB	ANG	FGW
43079	OO	EFPC	FGB	PTR	FGW	43177	OO	EFPC	FGB	ANG	FGW
43086	OO	EFPC	FGB	PTR	FGW	43179	OO	EFPC	FGB	ANG	FGW
43087	OO	EFPC	FGB	PTR	FGW	43180	OO	EFPC	FGB	PTR	FGW
43088	OO	EFPC	FGB	PTR	FGW	43181	OO	EFPC	FGB	ANG	FGW
43091	OO	EFPC	FGB	PTR	FGW	43182	OO	EFPC	FGB	ANG	FGW
43092	OO	EFPC	FGB	PTR	FGW	43183	OO	EFPC	FGB	ANG	FGW
43093	OO	EFPC	FGB	PTR	FGW	43185	OO	EFPC	FGB	ANG	FGW
43094	OO	EFPC	FGB	PTR	FGW	43186	OO	EFPC	FGB‡	ANG	FGW
43097	OO	EFPC	FGB	PTR	FGW	43187	OO	EFPC	FGB	ANG	FGW
43098	OO	EFPC	FGB	PTR	FGW	43188	OO	EFPC	FGB	ANG	FGW
43122	OO	EFPC	FGB	FGP	FGW	43189	OO	EFPC	FGB	ANG	FGW
43124	LE	EFPC	FGB	ANG	FGW	43190	OO	EFPC	FGB	ANG	FGW
43125	LE	EFPC	FGB	ANG	FGW	43191	OO	EFPC	FGB	ANG	FGW
43126	LE	EFPC	FGB	ANG	FGW	43192	OO	EFPC	FGB	ANG	FGW
43127	LE	EFPC	FGB	ANG	FGW	43193	OO	EFPC	FGB	PTR	FGW
43128	LE	EFPC	FGB	ANG	FGW	43194	OO	EFPC	FGB	FGP	FGW
43129	LE	EFPC	FGB	ANG	FGW	43195	OO	EFPC	FGB	PTR	FGW
43130	LE	EFPC	FGB	ANG	FGW	43196	OO	EFPC	FGB	PTR	FGW
43131	LE	EFPC	FGB	ANG	FGW	43197	OO	EFPC	FGB	PTR	FGW
43132	LE	EFPC	FGB	ANG	FGW	43198	OO	EFPC	FGB	FGP	FGW
43133	LE	EFPC	FGB	ANG	FGW						

‡ Queen's Diamond Jubilee livery

Names applied

43003	Isambard Kingdom Brunel
43004	First for the Future / First ar gyfer y dyfodol
43009	First Transforming Travel
43020	MTU Power Passion Partnership
43021	David Austin – Cartoonist
43024	Great Western Society 1961-2011 Didcot Railway Centre
43025	The Institution of Railway Operators
43027	Glorious Devon
43030	Christian Lewis Trust
43033	Driver Brian Cooper 15 June 1947 – 5 October 1999
43037	Penydarren
43040	Bristol St Philip's Marsh
43041	Meningitis Trust Support for Life
43053	University of Worcester
43056	The Royal British Legion
43070	The Corps of Royal Electrical and Mechanical Engineers
43087	11 Explosive Ordnance Disposal Regiment Royal Logistic Corps
43097	Environment Agency
43127	Sir Peter Parker 1924-2002 – Cotswold Line 150
43132	We Save the Children - Will You?
43137	Newton Abbot 150
43139	Driver Stan Martin 25 June 1960 – 6 November 2004
43142	Reading Panel Signal Box 1965 - 2010
43143	Stroud 700
43149	University of Plymouth
43156	Dartington International Summer School
43160	Sir Moir Lockhead OBE
43163	Exeter Panel Signal Box 21st Anniversary 2009
43165	Prince Michael of Kent
43169	The National Trust
43175	GWR 175th Anniversary
43179	Pride of Laira
43185	Great Western
43189	Railway Heritage Trust
43198	Oxfordshire 2007

Below: First Great Western operates the largest fleet of HSTs in the UK, with in late 2012 some 119 on the operator's books. The fleet is responsible for all main line services and will remain in service until replaced by the new IEP stock in 2016-17. All vehicles are painted in FGW blue livery. No. 43070 is seen near Dawlish Warren. **CJM**

Class 57/6

Vehicle Length: 63ft 6in (19.38m)
Height: 12ft 10⅛in (3.91m)
Width: 9ft 2in (2.79m)

Engine: EMD 645-12E3
Horsepower: 2,500hp (1,860kW)
Electrical Equipment: Brush

Number	Depot	Pool	Livery	Owner	Operator	Name
57602 (47337)	OO	EFOO	FGB	PTR	FGW	Restormel Castle
57603 (47349)	OO	EFOO	FGB	PTR	FGW	Tintagel Castle
57604 (47209)	OO	EFOO	GWR	PTR	FGW	Pendennis Castle
57605 (47206)	OO	EFOO	FGB	PTR	FGW	Totnes Castle

Right: Four Class 57/6s are operated by First Great Western, to power the overnight sleeper services between London Paddington and Penzance. If required, a Class 57/6 would also be used to provide power to a defective HST or move HST stock between depots. The FGW Class 57s are painted in FGW blue, with the exception of No. 57604 which is painted in mock Great Western green livery. No. 57603 is seen at Plymouth with the westbound sleeper to Penzance on 17 March 2012. **Antony Christie**

First Great Western

HST Passenger Fleet

Vehicle Length: 75ft 0in (22.86m)   *Width: 8ft 11in (2.71m)*
Height: 12ft 9in (3.88m)   *Bogie Type: BT10*

GN2G - TSRMB *Seating 70S*

Number	Depot	Livery	Owner
40101 (42170)	LA	FGW	PTR
40102 (42223)	LA	FGW	PTR
40103 (42316)	LA	FGW	PTR
40104 (42254)	LA	FGW	PTR
40105 (42084)	LA	FGW	PTR
40106 (42162)	LA	FGW	PTR
40107 (42334)	LA	FGW	PTR
40108 (42314)	LA	FGW	PTR
40109 (42262)	LA	FGW	PTR
40110 (42187)	LA	FGW	PTR
40111 (42248)	LA	FGW	PTR
40112 (42336)	LA	FGW	PTR
40113 (42309)	LA	FGW	PTR
40114 (42086)	LA	FGW	PTR
40115 (42320)	LA	FGW	PTR
40116 (42147)	LA	FGW	PTR
40117 (42249)	LA	FGW	PTR
40118 (42338)	LA	FGW	PTR
40119 (42090)	LA	FGW	PTR

GN1G - TRFB *Seating 23F*

Number	Depot	Livery	Owner
40204	LA	FGW	ANG
40205	LA	FGW	ANG
40207	LA	FGW	ANG
40210	LA	FGW	ANG
40221	LA	FGW	ANG
40231	LA	FGW	ANG

GK1G - TRFB *Seating 17F*

Number	Depot	Livery	Owner
40703	LA	FGW	ANG
40707	LA	FGW	ANG
40710	LA	FGW	ANG
40713	LA	FGW	ANG
40715	LA	FGW	ANG
40716	LA	FGW	ANG
40718	OO	FGW	ANG
40721	LA	FGW	ANG
40722	LA	FGW	ANG
40727	LA	FGW	ANG
40733	LA	FGW	ANG
40734	LA	FGW	ANG
40739	LA	FGW	ANG
40743	LA	FGW	ANG
40752	LA	FGW	ANG
40755	LA	FGW	ANG
40757	LA	FGW	ANG

GL1G - TRFB *Seating 17F*

Number	Depot	Livery	Owner
40801	OO	FGW	PTR
40802	OO	FGW	PTR
40803	OO	FGW	PTR
40806	OO	FGW	PTR
40807	OO	FGW	PTR
40808	OO	FGW	PTR
40809	OO	FGW	PTR
40810	OO	FGW	PTR
40811	OO	FGW	PTR

GN1G - TRB *Seating 23F*

Number	Depot	Livery	Owner
40900	LA	FGW	FGP
40901	LA	FGW	FGP
40902	LA	FGW	FGP
40903	LA	FGW	FGP
40904	LA	FGW	FGP

GH1G - TF *Seating 48F*

Number	Depot	Livery	Owner
41003	LA	FGW	ANG
41004	OO	FGW	ANG
41005	OO	FGW	ANG
41006	OO	FGW	ANG
41007	OO	FGW	ANG
41008	OO	FGW	ANG
41009	LA	FGW	ANG
41010	LA	FGW	ANG
41011	LA	FGW	ANG
41012	LA	FGW	ANG
41015	LA	FGW	ANG
41016	LA	FGW	ANG
41017	OO	FGW	ANG
41018	OO	FGW	ANG
41019	LA	FGW	ANG
41020	LA	FGW	ANG
41021	LA	FGW	ANG
41022	LA	FGW	ANG
41023	LA	FGW	ANG
41024	LA	FGW	ANG
41027	OO	FGW	ANG
41028	OO	FGW	ANG
41029	OO	FGW	ANG
41030	OO	FGW	ANG
41031	LA	FGW	ANG
41032	LA	FGW	ANG
41033	OO	FGW	ANG
41034	OO	FGW	ANG
41037	LA	FGW	ANG
41038	LA	FGW	ANG
41045	LA	FGW	FGP
41051	LA	FGW	ANG
41052	LA	FGW	ANG
41055	OO	FGW	ANG
41056	OO	FGW	ANG
41059	LA	FGW	FGP
41065	OO	FGW	ANG
41081	OO	FGW	PTR
41085	LA	FGW	FGP
41086	LA	FGW	FGP
41089	OO	FGW	ANG
41093	LA	FGW	ANG
41094	LA	FGW	ANG
41096	LA	FGW	PTR
41101	OO	FGW	ANG
41102	OO	FGW	ANG
41103	LA	FGW	ANG
41104	LA	FGW	ANG
41105	OO	FGW	ANG
41106	OO	FGW	ANG
41108	OO	FGW	PTR
41109	OO	FGW	PTR
41110	OO	FGW	ANG
41114	LA	FGW	FGP
41116	LA	FGW	ANG
41119	OO	FGW	PTR
41121	LA	FGW	ANG
41122	LA	FGW	ANG
41123	LA	FGW	ANG
41124	LA	FGW	ANG
41125	OO	FGW	ANG
41126	OO	FGW	ANG

Number	Depot	Livery	Owner
41127	OO	FGW	ANG
41128	OO	FGW	ANG
41129	LA	FGW	ANG
41130	LA	FGW	ANG
41131	OO	FGW	ANG
41132	OO	FGW	ANG
41133	LA	FGW	ANG
41134	LA	FGW	ANG
41135	LA	FGW	ANG
41136	LA	FGW	ANG
41137	OO	FGW	ANG
41138	OO	FGW	ANG
41139	LA	FGW	ANG
41140	OO	FGW	ANG
41141	LA	FGW	ANG
41142	LA	FGW	ANG
41143	LA	FGW	ANG
41144	LA	FGW	ANG
41145	LA	FGW	ANG
41146	LA	FGW	ANG
41147	OO	FGW	PTR
41148	OO	FGW	PTR
41149	OO	FGW	PTR
41155	OO	FGW	PTR
41157	LA	FGW	ANG
41158	LA	FGW	ANG
41160	LA	FGW	FGP
41161	OO	FGW	PTR
41162	LA	FGW	FGP
41163	LA	FGW	FGP
41166	LA	FGW	FGP
41167	LA	FGW	FGP
41168	OO	FGW	PTR
41169	OO	FGW	PTR
41176	OO	FGW	PTR
41179	OO	FGW	ANG
41180	OO	FGW	ANG
41181	OO	FGW	PTR
41182	OO	FGW	PTR
41183	OO	FGW	PTR
41184	OO	FGW	PTR
41186	OO	FGW	PTR
41187	OO	FGW	PTR
41189	OO	FGW	PTR
41191	OO	FGW	PTR
41192	OO	FGW	PTR

GH2G - TS *Seating 68-84S*

Number	Depot	Livery	Owner
42003	OO	FGW	ANG
42004	LA	FGW	ANG
42005 ●	LA	FGW	ANG
42006	LA	FGW	ANG
42007	LA	FGW	ANG
42008	OO	FGW	ANG
42009	LA	FGW	ANG
42010 ●	LA	FGW	ANG
42012	LA	FGW	ANG
42013	LA	FGW	ANG
42014	LA	FGW	ANG
42015	LA	FGW	ANG
42016	LA	FGW	ANG
42019 ●	LA	FGW	ANG
42021	LA	FGW	ANG
42023	LA	FGW	ANG
42024	OO	FGW	ANG
42025	OO	FGW	ANG

42026		OO	FGW	ANG	42143		LA	FGW	ANG	42276		LA	FGW	ANG
42027		OO	FGW	ANG	42144		LA	FGW	ANG	42277		LA	FGW	ANG
42028		LA	FGW	ANG	42145		LA	FGW	ANG	42279		LA	FGW	ANG
42029		LA	FGW	ANG	42166 ●		OO	FGW	PTR	42280		LA	FGW	ANG
42030		LA	FGW	ANG	42167		LA	FGW	FGP	42281		LA	FGW	ANG
42031		LA	FGW	ANG	42168 ●		LA	FGW	FGP	42283		OO	FGW	ANG
42032		LA	FGW	ANG	42169		LA	FGW	FGP	42284		OO	FGW	ANG
42033 ●		LA	FGW	ANG	42173		OO	FGW	PTR	42285		OO	FGW	ANG
42034		LA	FGW	ANG	42174		OO	FGW	PTR	42287		OO	FGW	ANG
42035		LA	FGW	ANG	42175		LA	FGW	FGP	42288		OO	FGW	ANG
42039 ●		OO	FGW	ANG	42176 ●		LA	FGW	FGP	42289		OO	FGW	ANG
42040		OO	FGW	ANG	42177		LA	FGW	FGP	42291		LA	FGW	ANG
42041		OO	FGW	ANG	42178 ●		OO	FGW	PTR	42292		LA	FGW	ANG
42042 ●		OO	FGW	ANG	42183		LA	FGW	ANG	42293		LA	FGW	ANG
42043		OO	FGW	ANG	42184 ●		LA	FGW	ANG	42294		OO	FGW	PTR
42044		OO	FGW	ANG	42185		LA	FGW	ANG	42295		LA	FGW	ANG
42045 ●		LA	FGW	ANG	42195		OO	FGW	PTR	42296		LA	FGW	ANG
42046		LA	FGW	ANG	42196		OO	FGW	ANG	42297		LA	FGW	ANG
42047		LA	FGW	ANG	42197 ●		OO	FGW	ANG	42299		LA	FGW	ANG
42048 ●		OO	FGW	ANG	42200		LA	FGW	ANG	42300		LA	FGW	ANG
42049		OO	FGW	ANG	42201		OO	FGW	ANG	42301		LA	FGW	ANG
42050		OO	FGW	ANG	42202		OO	FGW	ANG	42302		LA	FGW	FGP
42054 ●		LA	FGW	ANG	42203		OO	FGW	ANG	42303 ●		LA	FGW	FGP
42055		LA	FGW	ANG	42204		OO	FGW	ANG	42304		LA	FGW	FGP
42056		LA	FGW	ANG	42206		LA	FGW	ANG	42305		LA	FGW	FGP
42060		OO	FGW	ANG	42207		LA	FGW	ANG	42308 ●		OO	FGW	PTR
42061		OO	FGW	ANG	42208		LA	FGW	ANG	42310		OO	FGW	PTR
42062		OO	FGW	ANG	42209		LA	FGW	ANG	42315 ●		OO	FGW	PTR
42066		OO	FGW	ANG	42211		OO	FGW	ANG	42317		OO	FGW	PTR
42067		OO	FGW	ANG	42212 ●		OO	FGW	ANG	42319 ●		OO	FGW	PTR
42068		OO	FGW	ANG	42213		OO	FGW	ANG	42321		OO	FGW	PTR
42069		OO	FGW	ANG	42214		OO	FGW	ANG	42325 ●		LA	FGW	ANG
42070 ●		OO	FGW	ANG	42216 ●		OO	FGW	ANG	42332 ●		LA	FGW	ANG
42071		OO	FGW	ANG	42217		OO	FGW	PTR	42333		LA	FGW	ANG
42072		LA	FGW	ANG	42218		OO	FGW	PTR	42343 ●		LA	FGW	ANG
42073 ●		OO	FGW	ANG	42221 ●		OO	FGW	ANG	42344		OO	FGW	ANG
42074 ●		OO	FGW	ANG	42222 ●		OO	FGW	PTR	42345		LA	FGW	ANG
42075 ●		LA	FGW	ANG	42224		OO	FGW	PTR	42346		OO	FGW	ANG
42076 ●		LA	FGW	ANG	42231		LA	FGW	FGP	42347		OO	FGW	ANG
42077		LA	FGW	ANG	42232 ●		LA	FGW	FGP	42348		OO	FGW	ANG
42078		LA	FGW	ANG	42233		LA	FGW	FGP	42349 ●		OO	FGW	ANG
42079		OO	FGW	ANG	42236 ●		OO	FGW	ANG	42350 ●		LA	FGW	ANG
42080		OO	FGW	ANG	42245		LA	FGW	ANG	42351 ●		LA	FGW	ANG
42081		OO	FGW	ANG	42247 ●		OO	FGW	PTR	42353		LA	FGW	FGP
42083		OO	FGW	ANG	42250		LA	FGW	ANG	42356		OO	FGW	ANG
42085 ●		OO	FGW	ANG	42251		OO	FGW	ANG	42360 ●		LA	FGW	ANG
42087		OO	FGW	ANG	42252		LA	FGW	ANG	42361		LA	FGW	ANG
42089		OO	FGW	ANG	42253		LA	FGW	ANG	42362 ●		OO	FGW	ANG
42092		LA	FGW	FGP	42255		LA	FGW	ANG	42364		OO	FGW	PTR
42093		LA	FGW	FGP	42256		LA	FGW	ANG	42365		OO	FGW	PTR
42094		LA	FGW	FGP	42257		LA	FGW	ANG	42381 (41058)	OO	FGW	PTR
42095		LA	FGW	FGP	42258 ●		OO	FGW	PTR	42382 (12128)	OO	FGW	PTR
42096 ●		LA	FGW	ANG	42259		LA	FGW	ANG	42383 (12172)	OO	FGW	PTR
42098 ●		OO	FGW	ANG	42260		OO	FGW	ANG	42385 (41153)	OO	FGW	PTR
42099		OO	FGW	ANG	42261		OO	FGW	ANG	42501 (40744)	OO	FGW	ANG
42101		OO	FGW	PTR	42263 ●		LA	FGW	ANG	42502 (40731)	OO	FGW	ANG
42102		OO	FGW	PTR	42264		OO	FGW	ANG	42503 (40712)	OO	FGW	ANG
42103		LA	FGW	FGP	42265 ●		LA	FGW	ANG	42504 (40714)	OO	FGW	ANG
42105		LA	FGW	FGP	42266		OO	FGW	PTR	42505 (40228)	OO	FGW	ANG
42107		LA	FGW	ANG	42267		LA	FGW	ANG	42506 (40724)	OO	FGW	ANG
42108		LA	FGW	FGP	42268		LA	FGW	ANG	42507 (40209)	OO	FGW	ANG
42115 ●		OO	FGW	PTR	42269		LA	FGW	ANG	42508 (40725)	OO	FGW	ANG
42118		OO	FGW	ANG	42271		OO	FGW	ANG	42509 (40736)	OO	FGW	ANG
42126		OO	FGW	ANG	42272		OO	FGW	ANG	42510 (40717)	OO	FGW	ANG
42129 ●		LA	FGW	ANG	42273		OO	FGW	ANG	42511 (40709)	OO	FGW	ANG
42138		OO	FGW	ANG	42275		LA	FGW	ANG	42512 (40208)	OO	FGW	ANG

First Great Western

42513 (40738)	OO	FGW	ANG	44016	OO	FGW	ANG	44049	LA	FGW	ANG
42514 (40726)	OO	FGW	ANG	44018	LA	FGW	ANG	44055	LA	FGW	FGP
42515 (40747)	OO	FGW	ANG	44020	OO	FGW	ANG	44059	LA	FGW	ANG
● Volo Television fitted				44022	OO	FGW	ANG	44060	OO	FGW	PTR
				44023	OO	FGW	ANG	44064	OO	FGW	ANG
				44024	OO	FGW	ANG	44066	LA	FGW	ANG

GJ2G - TGS *Seating 67-71S*

Number	Depot	Livery	Owner								
				44025	LA	FGW	ANG	44067	OO	FGW	ANG
44000	OO	FGW	PTR	44026	OO	FGW	ANG	44068	LA	FGW	FGP
44001	LA	FGW	ANG	44028	LA	FGW	ANG	44069	OO	FGW	PTR
44002	OO	FGW	ANG	44029	LA	FGW	ANG	44074	LA	FGW	FGP
44003	OO	FGW	ANG	44030	OO	FGW	ANG	44076	LA	FGW	FGP
44004	LA	FGW	ANG	44032	LA	FGW	ANG	44078	OO	FGW	PTR
44005	LA	FGW	ANG	44033	OO	FGW	ANG	44079	OO	FGW	PTR
44007	LA	FGW	ANG	44034	LA	FGW	ANG	44081	LA	FGW	FGP
44008	OO	FGW	ANG	44035	LA	FGW	ANG	44083	OO	FGW	PTR
44009	LA	FGW	ANG	44036	OO	FGW	ANG	44086	LA	FGW	ANG
44010	LA	FGW	ANG	44037	OO	FGW	ANG	44090	OO	FGW	PTR
44011	LA	FGW	ANG	44038	LA	FGW	ANG	44091	OO	FGW	PTR
44013	OO	FGW	ANG	44039	LA	FGW	ANG	44093	OO	FGW	ANG
44014	OO	FGW	ANG	44040	LA	FGW	ANG	44097	OO	FGW	PTR
44015	LA	FGW	ANG	44042	OO	FGW	PTR	44100	LA	FGW	FGP
				44043	OO	FGW	ANG	44101	OO	FGW	PTR

Left: *All the FGW Mk3 passenger fleet carry FGW blue livery with 'dynamic lines' branding. Plymouth Laira-allocated TS No. 42269 is illustrated in this broadside view. Both TS and TF vehicles share the same body profile. The FGW HST fleet are usually formed with two first class vehicles at the London end.* **CJM**

Class 143

Vehicle Length: 51ft 0½in (15.55m)
Height: 12ft 2¼in (3.73m)
Width: 8ft 10½in (2.70m)

Engine: 1 x Cummins LTA10-R per vehicle
Horsepower: 460hp (343kW)
Seats (total/car): 92S, 48S/44S

Number	Formation DMS+DMSL	Depot	Livery	Owner	Operator						
						143617	55644+55683	EX	FGL	PTR	FGW
						143618	55659+55684	EX	FGL	PTR	FGW
143603	55658+55689	EX	FGL	PTR	FGW	143619	55660+55685	EX	FGL	PTR	FGW
143611	55652+55677	EX	FGL	PTR	FGW	143620	55661+55686	EX	FGL	PTR	FGW
143612	55653+55678	EX	FGL	PTR	FGW	143621	55662+55687	EX	FGL	PTR	FGW

Left: *Exeter depot is the home for the eight FGW Class 143 'Pacer' sets. These operate on Devon branch line services to Exmouth, Paignton and Barnstaple. The fleet have been fully refurbished and all sport First Great Western 'local lines' livery with names of locations, businesses and structures applied on the bodyside in FGW 'dynamic lines' style. Set No. 143620 is seen approaching Dawlish on 25 May 2012 with the 10.15 Paignton to Exmouth local service.* **CJM**

Class 150/0

Vehicle Length: (Driving) 65ft 9¾in (20.05m), (Inter) 66ft 2½in (20.18m)
Height: 12ft 4½in (3.77m)
Width: 9ft 3⅛in (2.82m)

Engine: 1 x Cummins NT855R4 of 285hp per car
Horsepower: 855hp (638kW)
Seats (total/car): 240S, 72S/92S/76S

Number	Formation DMSL+MS+DMS	Depot	Livery	Owner	Opt'r							
150001	55200+55400+55300	RG	FGB	ANG	FGW	150002	55201+55401+55301	RG		FGB	ANG	FGW

Right: *The two unique Class 150/0 three-car sets which previously operated in the Midlands are now based at Reading and work on the Reading to Basingstoke 'shuttle' service, providing accommodation for 240 passengers on this busy route. Set No. 150001 is seen in the bay platform at Basingstoke on 30 August 2012.* **CJM**

Class 150/1

Vehicle Length: 64ft 9¾in (19.74m)	Engine: 1 x NT855R5 of 285hp per vehicle
Height: 12ft 4½in (3.77m)	Horsepower: 570hp (425kW)
Width: 9ft 3⅛in (2.82m)	Seats (total/car): 141S, 71S/70S

Two-car sets

Number	Formation DMSL+DMS	Depot	Livery	Owner	Operator
150101	52101+57101	PM	FGB	PTR	FGW
150102	52102+57102	PM	FGB	PTR	FGW
150104	52104+57104	PM	FGB	PTR	FGW
150106	52106+57106	PM	FGB	PTR	FGW
150108	52108+57108	PM	FGB	PTR	FGW
150120	52120+57120	EX	FGB	PTR	FGW
150122	52122+57122	EX	FGB	PTR	FGW
150123	52123+57123	EX	FGB	PTR	FGW
150124	52124+57124	EX	FGB	PTR	FGW
150125	52125+57125	EX	FGB	PTR	FGW
150126	52126+57126	EX	FGB	PTR	FGW
150128	52128+57128	EX	FGB	PTR	FGW
150129	52129+57129	EX	FGB	PTR	FGW
150130	52130+57130	EX	FGB	PTR	FGW
150131	52130+57130	EX	FGB	PTR	FGW

Three-car sets - Class 150/9

150921	52121+57212+57121	PM	FGB	PTR	FGW		150927	52127+57209+57127	PM	FGB	PTR	FGW

Names applied
150125 *The Heart of Wessex Line*	**150129** *Devon & Cornwall Rail Partnership*
	150130 *Severnside Community Rail Partnership*

Class 150/2

Vehicle Length: 64ft 9¾in (19.74m)	Engine: 1 x NT855R5 of 285hp per vehicle
Height: 12ft 4½in (3.77m)	Horsepower: 570hp (425kW)
Width: 9ft 3⅛in (2.82m)	Seats (total/car): 116S, 60S/56S

Number	Formation DMSL+DMS	Depot	Livery	Owner	Operator
150202	52202+57202	PM	FGB	ANG	FGW
150216	52216+57216	PM	FGB	ANG	FGW
150219	52219+57219	PM	FGL	PTR	FGW
150221	52221+57221	PM	FGL	PTR	FGW
150232	52232+57232	EX	FGL	PTR	FGW
150233	52233+57233	PM	FGL	PTR	FGW
150234	52234+57234	PM	FGL	PTR	FGW
150238	52238+57238	PM	FGL	PTR	FGW
150239	52239+57239	PM	FGL	PTR	FGW
150243	52243+57243	PM	FGL	PTR	FGW
150244	52244+57244	PM	FGL	PTR	FGW
150246	52246+57246	PM	FGL	PTR	FGW
150247	52247+57247	PM	FGL	PTR	FGW
150248	52248+57248	PM	FGL	PTR	FGW
150249	52249+57249	PM	FGL	PTR	FGW
150261	52261+57261	PM	FGL	PTR	FGW
150263	52263+57263	PM	FGL	PTR	FGW
150265	52265+57265	PM	FGL	PTR	FGW
150266	52266+57266	PM	FGL	PTR	FGW

Right: *Today First Great Western operate a fleet of 19 Class 150/2 two-car corridor-fitted 'Sprinter' sets. These are painted in a mix of FGW 'local lines' livery and FGW blue colours. The sets are allocated to Exeter and St Philip's Marsh depots and can be found throughout the western section of the FGW network. Set No. 150216 is recorded at Newton Abbot in all-over FGW blue livery.* **Antony Christie**

Passenger Train Operating Companies - First Great Western

First Great Western

Class 153

Vehicle Length: 76ft 5in (23.29m)
Height: 12ft 3¹⁄₂in (3.75m)
Width: 8ft 10in (2.70m)

Engine: 1 x NT855R5 of 285hp
Horsepower: 285hp (213kW)
Seats (total/car): 72S

Number	Formation DMSL	Depot	Livery	Owner	Operator	Number	Formation	Depot	Livery	Owner	Operator
						153368	57368	EX	FGL	ANG	FGW
						153369	57369	EX	FGL	ANG	FGW
153305	52305	EX	FGL	ANG	FGW	153370	57370	EX	FGL	ANG	FGW
153318	52318	EX	FGL	ANG	FGW	153372	57372	EX	FGL	ANG	FGW
153329	52329	EX	FGL	ANG	FGW	153373	57373	EX	FGL	ANG	FGW
153325	52325	EX	LMI	PTR	FGW	153377	57377	EX	FGL	ANG	FGW
153333	52333	EX	LMI	PTR	FGW	153380	57380	EX	FGL	ANG	FGW
153361	57361	EX	FGL	ANG	FGW	153382	57382	EX	FGL	ANG	FGW

Left: *First Great Western operates a fleet of 14 single-car Class 153s, allocated to Exeter depot. The '153s' were rebuilt many years ago from two-car Class 155 Leyland 'Sprinter' sets. They are used on Devon and Cornwall branch line services, and frequently strengthen two-car formations at busy periods. Sets often operate in pairs to provide accommodation in line with Class 150/2 or even 158 stock. All vehicles are painted in FGW 'local lines' livery. Car No. 153368 is seen departing from Exeter St Thomas bound for Paignton. This view shows the 'new' driving cab formed during the rebuild work from '155' to '153'.*
Antony Christie

Class 158/0 (2-car)

Vehicle Length: 76ft 1¾in (23.21m)
Height: 12ft 6in (3.81m)
Width: 9ft 3¾in (2.82m)

Engine: 1 x Cummins NTA855R of 350hp per vehicle
Horsepower: 700hp (522kW)
Seats (total/car): 134S, 66S/68S

Number	Formation DMSL+DMSL	Depot	Livery	Owner	Operator	Number	Formation	Depot	Livery	Owner	Operator
158763	52763+57763	PM	FGL	PTR	FGW	158766	52766+57766	PM	FGL	PTR	FGW

Class 158/0 (3-car)

158798
Vehicle Length: 76ft 1¾in (23.21m)
Height: 12ft 6in (3.81m)
Width: 9ft 3¼in (2.82m)

Engine: 1 x Cummins NTA855R of 350hp per vehicle
Horsepower: 1,050hp (783kW)
Seats (total/car): 200S, 66S/66S/68S

158950 - 158959
Vehicle Length: 76ft 1¾in (23.21m)
Height: 12ft 6in (3.81m)
Width: 9ft 3¼in (2.82m)

Engine: 1 x Cummins NTA855R of 350hp per vehicle
Horsepower: 1,050hp (783kW)
Seats (total/car): 204S, 66S/70S/68S

Number	Formation DMSL+MSL+DMSL	Depot	Livery	Owner	Operator
158798	52798+58715+57798	PM	FGL	PTR	FGW

Number	Formation DMSL+DMSL+DMSL		Depot	Livery	Owner	Operator
158950	(158751/761)	57751+52761+57761	PM	FGL	PTR	FGW
158951	(158751/764)	52751+52764+57764	PM	FGL	PTR	FGW
158952	(158745/762)	57745+52762+57762	PM	FGL	PTR	FGW
158953	(158745/750)	52745+52750+57750	PM	FGL	PTR	FGW
158954	(158747/760)	52747+52760+57760	PM	FGL	PTR	FGW
158955	(158747/765)	52747+52765+57765	PM	FGL	PTR	FGW
158956	(158748/768)	57748+52768+57768	PM	FGL	PTR	FGW
158957	(158748/771)	52748+52771+57771	PM	FGL	PTR	FGW
158958	(158746/776)	57746+52776+57776	PM	FGL	PTR	FGW
158959	(158746/778)	52746+52778+57778	PM	FGL	PTR	FGW
158960	(158769/749)	57769+52769+57749	PM	FGL	PTR	FGW
158961	(158767/749)	57767+52767+52749	PM	FGL	PTR	FGW

Right: *First Great Western 'local lines' services are very well patronised on routes such as Cardiff/Bristol to Portsmouth Harbour, and a batch of Class 158 two-car sets have been strengthened to three-car formation by adding a single '158' car at one end. As the sets are fully gangwayed no access restrictions are imposed. Three-car set No. 158954 is seen arriving at Bristol Temple Meads on 26 September 2012, on a Cardiff to Portsmouth Harbour service. This unit is formed of set No. 158760 plus one car from 158747.* **CJM**

Class 165/1 (3-car)
Networker Turbo

Vehicle Length: (Driving) 75ft 2½in (22.91m), (Inter) 74ft 6½in (22.72m)
Height: 12ft 5¼in (3.79m)
Width: 9ft 5½in (2.81m)
Engine: 1 x Perkins 2006TWH of 350hp
Horsepower: 1,050hp (783kW)
Seats (total/car): 16F/270S, 16F-66S/106S/98S

Number	Formation DMCL+MS+DMS	Depot	Livery	Owner	Operator
165101	58953+55415+58916	RG	FGT	ANG	FGW
165102	58954+55416+58917	RG	FGT	ANG	FGW
165103	58955+55417+58918	RG	FGT	ANG	FGW
165104	58956+55418+58919	RG	FGT	ANG	FGW
165105	58957+55419+58920	RG	FGT	ANG	FGW
165106	58958+55420+58921	RG	FGT	ANG	FGW
165107	58959+55421+58922	RG	FGT	ANG	FGW
165108	58960+55422+58923	RG	FGT	ANG	FGW
165109	58961+55423+58924	RG	FGT	ANG	FGW
165110	58962+55424+58925	RG	FGT	ANG	FGW
165111	58963+55425+58926	RG	FGT	ANG	FGW
165112	58964+55426+58927	RG	FGT	ANG	FGW
165113	58965+55427+58928	RG	FGT	ANG	FGW
165114	58966+55428+58929	RG	FGT	ANG	FGW
165116	58968+55430+58931	RG	FGT	ANG	FGW
165117	58969+55431+58932	RG	FGT	ANG	FGW

Right: *During the period of Network SouthEast, a sizeable fleet of 'Networker Turbo' Class 165 sets were built at York to replace heritage DMU and loco-hauled stock on Paddington local services. The first 17 sets of Class 165/1 are three-car units. Set No. 165117 is seen at Reading with its DMCL coach leading. All FGW '165s' carry FGW 'dynamic lines' livery and are allocated to Reading. Only 16 sets remain in operation; set No. 165115 was destroyed in the Ladbroke Grove accident.* **CJM**

Class 165/1 (2-car)
Networker Turbo

Vehicle Length: 75ft 2½in (22.91m)
Height: 12ft 5¼in (3.79m)
Width: 9ft 5½in (2.81m)
Engine: 1 x Perkins 2006TWH of 350hp per car
Horsepower: 700hp (522kW)
Seats (total/car): 16F/170S, 16F-72S/98S

Number	Formation DMCL+DMS	Depot	Livery	Owner	Operator	Number	Formation	Depot	Livery	Owner	Operator
165118	58879+58933	RG	FGT	ANG	FGW	165122	58883+58937	RG	FGT	ANG	FGW
165119	58880+58934	RG	FGT	ANG	FGW	165123	58884+58938	RG	FGT	ANG	FGW
165120	58881+58935	RG	FGT	ANG	FGW	165124	58885+58939	RG	FGT	ANG	FGW
165121	58882+58936	RG	FGT	ANG	FGW	165125	58886+58940	RG	FGT	ANG	FGW
						165126	58887+58941	RG	FGT	ANG	FGW
						165127	58888+58942	RG	FGT	ANG	FGW

Passenger Train Operating Companies - First Great Western

First Great Western

165128	58889+58943	RG	FGT	ANG	FGW	165133	58894+58948	RG	FGT	ANG	FGW
165129	58890+58944	RG	FGT	ANG	FGW	165134	58895+58949	RG	FGT	ANG	FGW
165130	58891+58945	RG	FGT	ANG	FGW	165135	58896+58950	RG	FGT	ANG	FGW
165131	58892+58946	RG	FGT	ANG	FGW	165136	58897+58951	RG	FGT	ANG	FGW
165132	58893+58947	RG	FGT	ANG	FGW	165137	58898+58952	RG	FGT	ANG	FGW

Left: In addition to the three-car Class 165s for Network SouthEast Thames Valley operations, a batch of 20 two-car Class 165/1s were built. Viewed from its standard class vehicle (DMS) set No. 165137 approaches Didcot on a service from Oxford to London Paddington. Each two-car Class 165 seats 16 first and 170 standard class passengers. **Antony Christie**

Class 166
Networker Turbo Express

Vehicle Length: (Driving) 75ft 2½in (22.91m), (Inter) 74ft 6½in (22.72m)
Height: 12ft 5¼in (3.79m)   *Engine: 1 x Perkins 2006TWH of 350hp per car*
Width: 9ft 5½in (2.81m)   *Horsepower: 1,050hp (783kW)*
Seats (total/car): 32F/243S, 16F-75S/96S/16F-72S

Number	Formation DMCL(A)+MS+DMCL(B)	Depot	Livery	Owner	Operator
166201	58101+58601+58122	RG	FGT	ANG	FGW
166202	58102+58602+58123	RG	FGT	ANG	FGW
166203	58103+58603+58124	RG	FGT	ANG	FGW
166204	58104+58604+58125	RG	FGT	ANG	FGW
166205	58105+58605+58126	RG	FGT	ANG	FGW
166206	58106+58606+58127	RG	FGT	ANG	FGW
166207	58107+58607+58128	RG	FGT	ANG	FGW
166208	58108+58608+58129	RG	FGT	ANG	FGW
166209	58109+58609+58130	RG	FGT	ANG	FGW
166210	58110+58610+58131	RG	FGT	ANG	FGW
166211	58111+58611+58132	RG	FGT	ANG	FGW
166212	58112+58612+58133	RG	FGT	ANG	FGW
166213	58113+58613+58134	RG	FGT	ANG	FGW
166214	58114+58614+58135	RG	FGT	ANG	FGW
166215	58115+58615+58136	RG	FGT	ANG	FGW
166216	58116+58616+58137	RG	FGT	ANG	FGW
166217	58117+58617+58138	RG	FGT	ANG	FGW
166218	58118+58618+58139	RG	FGT	ANG	FGW
166219	58119+58619+58140	RG	FGT	ANG	FGW
166220	58120+58620+58141	RG	FGT	ANG	FGW
166221	58121+58621+58142	RG	FGT	ANG	FGW

Left: In conjunction with the Network SouthEast Thames Valley replacement stock order, a batch of 21 'Networker Turbo Express' sets were delivered for longer distance services, fitted with air conditioning and slightly improved interiors. These sets were immediately distinguishable from '165s' by the mix of solid and quarter light fitted body side windows. All sets are allocated to Reading and carry standard First Great Western 'dynamic lines' livery. Set No. 166211 is illustrated at Bedwyn. **John Binch**

Class 180
Adelante

Vehicle Length: (Driving) 75ft 7in (23.71m), (Inter) 75ft 5in (23.03m)
Height: 12ft 4in (3.75m)
Width: 9ft 2in (2.80m)
Engine: 1 x Cummins QSK19 of 750hp per car
Horsepower: 3,750hp (2,796kW)
Seats (total/car): 42F/226S, 46S/42F/68S/56S/56S

Number	Formation	Depot	Livery	Owner	Operator
	DMSL(A)+MFL+MSL+MSLRB+DMSL(B)				
180102	50902+54902+55902+56902+59902	OO	FGW	ANG	FGW
180103	50903+54903+55903+56903+59903	OO	FGW	ANG	FGW
180104	50904+54904+55904+56904+59904	OO	FGW	ANG	FGW
180106	50906+54906+55906+56906+59906	OO	FGW	ANG	FGW
180108	50908+54908+55908+56908+59908	OO	FGW	ANG	FGW

Right: *Originally built for Great Western operation and then transferred away for other duties, First Great Western re-introduced five Class 180 'Adelante' five-car Alstom-built sets for use on the Paddington to Worcester corridor in mid-2012. The sets have been fully refurbished by Wabtec and now have high-quality standard and first class interiors, in some respects better than the HST fleet. In full 'dynamic lines' livery, set No. 180104 basks under the Brunel roof at Paddington in October 2012.*
Antony Christie

Mk3 Hauled Stock

Vehicle Length: 75ft 0in (22.86m)
Height: 12ft 9in (3.88m)
Width: 8ft 11in (2.71m)
Bogie Type: BT10

AJ1G - RFB *Seating 18F*

Number	Depot	Livery	Owner
10219	PZ	FGW	PTR
10225	PZ	FGW	PTR
10232	PZ	FGW	PTR

AU4G - SLEP *Comps 12*

Number	Depot	Livery	Owner
10532	PZ	FGW	PTR
10534	PZ	FGW	PTR
10563	PZ	FGW	PTR

10584	PZ	FGW	PTR
10589	PZ	FGW	PTR
10590	PZ	FGW	PTR
10594	PZ	FGW	PTR
10601	PZ	FGW	PTR
10612	PZ	FGW	PTR
10616	PZ	FGW	PTR

AC2G - TSO *Seating 45S*

Number	Depot	Livery	Owner
12100	PZ	FGW	PTR

12161	PZ	FGW	PTR

AE1H - BFO *Seating 36F*

Number	Depot	Livery	Owner
17173	PZ	FGW	PTR
17174	PZ	FGW	PTR
17175	PZ	FGW	PTR

Right: *FGW operate a fleet of 18 Mk3 loco-hauled vehicles which make up the 'Night Riviera' fleet based at Long Rock, Penzance. All carriages carry full FGW 'dynamic lines' livery with the additional bodyside branding 'Night Riviera Sleeper'. The saloon vehicles have first class design 2+1 seating. SLEP No. 10563 is seen from its berth side in this unusual daytime view at Plymouth.* **Antony Christie**

Service Stock

HST Barrier Vehicles

Number	Depot	Livery	Owner	Former Identity
6330	PM	FGB	ANG	BFK - 14084
6336	LA	FGB	ANG	BG - 81591/92185

6338	LA	FGB	ANG	BG - 81581/92180
6348	PM	FGB	ANG	BG - 81233/92963

First Hull Trains

Address: ✉ Europa House, 184 Ferensway, Kingston-upon-Hull, HU1 3UT
customer.services@hulltrains.co.uk
✆ 0845 676 9905
ⓘ www.hulltrains.co.uk

General Manager: Cath Bellamy
Franchise Dates: Private Open Access Operator, agreement to December 2016
Principal Route: London King's Cross - Hull
Depots: Old Oak Common (OO) [Operated by FGW], Crofton (XW)
Parent Company: First Group PLC

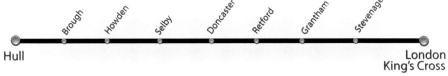

Hull — Brough — Howden — Selby — Doncaster — Retford — Grantham — Stevenage — London King's Cross

Class 180
Adelante

Vehicle Length: (Driving) 75ft 7in (23.71m), (Inter) 75ft 5in (23.03m)
Height: 12ft 4in (3.75m)   Engine: 1 x Cummins QSK19 of 750hp per car
Width: 9ft 2in (2.80m)   Horsepower: 3,750hp (2,796kW)
Seats (total/car): 42F/226S, 46S/42F/68S/56S/56S

Number	Formation	Depot	Livery	Owner	Operator
	DMSL(A)+MFL+MSF+MSLRB+DMSL(B)				
180109	50909+54909+55909+56909+59909	OO/XW	FHT	ANG	FHT
180110	50910+54910+55910+56910+59910	OO/XW	FHT	ANG	FHT
180111	50911+54911+55911+56911+59911	OO/XW	FHT	ANG	FHT
180113	50913+54913+55913+56913+59913	OO/XW	FHT	ANG	FHT

Below: *Open access operator First Hull Trains currently deploys a fleet of four ex-First Great Western Class 180 'Adelante' sets on its London King's Cross to Hull service. All sets carry First Group 'dynamic lines' livery and are sadly now devoid of front end coupling covers. Sets have recently been facelifted. No. 180109 departs from London King's Cross bound for Hull.* **Antony Christie**

First ScotRail

Address: ✉ Atrium Court, 50 Waterloo Street, Glasgow, G2 6HQ

✈ scotrail.enquiries@firstgroup.com

☎ 08700 005151

ⓘ www.firstscotrail.com

Managing Director: Steve Montgomery

Franchise Dates: 17 October 2004 - March 2015

Principal Routes: All Scottish services, plus ScotRail sleeper services

Depots: Corkerhill (CK), Glasgow Shields Road (GW), Haymarket (HA), Inverness (IS)

Parent Company: First Group PLC

Class 156

Vehicle Length: 75ft 6in (23.03m)	Engine: 1 x Cummins NT855R5 of 285hp	
Height: 12ft 6in (3.81m)	Horsepower: 570hp (425kW)	
Width: 8ft 11in (2.73m)	Seats (total/car): 142S, 70 or 72S	

Number	Formation DMSL+DMS	Depot	Livery	Owner	Operator
156430	52430+57430	CK	FSS	ANG	FSR
156431	52431+57431	CK	FSS	ANG	FSR
156432	52432+57432	CK	FSS	ANG	FSR
156433	52433+57433	CK	FSS	ANG	FSR
156434	52434+57434	CK	FSS	ANG	FSR
156435	52435+57435	CK	FSS	ANG	FSR
156436	52436+57436	CK	FSS	ANG	FSR
156437	52437+57437	CK	FSS	ANG	FSR
156439	52439+57439	CK	FSS	ANG	FSR
156442	52442+57442	CK	FSS	ANG	FSR
156445	52445+57445	CK	FSS	ANG	FSR
156446	52446+57446	CK	FSR	ANG	FSR
156447	52447+57447	CK	FSR	ANG	FSR
156449	52449+57449	CK	FSR	ANG	FSR
156450	52450+57450	CK	FSR	ANG	FSR
156453	52453+57453	CK	FSR	ANG	FSR
156456	52456+57456	CK	FSR	ANG	FSR
156457	52457+57457	CK	FSR	ANG	FSR
156458	52458+57458	CK	FSR	ANG	FSR
156462	52462+57462	CK	FSR	ANG	FSR
156465	52465+57465	CK	FSR	ANG	FSR
156467	52467+57467	CK	FSR	ANG	FSR
156474	52474+57474	CK	FSR	ANG	FSR
156476	52476+57476	CK	FSR	ANG	FSR
156477	52477+57477	CK	FSR	ANG	FSR
156478	52478+57478	CK	FSR	ANG	FSR
156485	52485+57485	CK	FSR	ANG	FSR
156492	52492+57492	CK	FSS	ANG	FSR
156493	52493+57493	CK	FSS	ANG	FSR
156494	52494+57494	CK	FSS	ANG	FSR
156495	52495+57495	CK	FSS	ANG	FSR
156496	52496+57496	CK	FSS	ANG	FSR
156499	52499+57499	CK	FSR	ANG	FSR
156500	52500+57500	CK	FSS	ANG	FSR
156501	52501+57501	CK	FSS	ANG	FSR
156502	52502+57502	CK	FSS	ANG	FSR
156503	52503+57503	CK	FSS	ANG	FSR
156504	52504+57504	CK	FSS	ANG	FSR
156505	52505+57505	CK	FSS	ANG	FSR
156506	52506+57506	CK	FSR	ANG	FSR
156507	52507+57507	CK	FSS	ANG	FSR
156508	52508+57508	CK	FSS	ANG	FSR
156509	52509+57509	CK	FSS	ANG	FSR
156510	52510+57510	CK	FSS	ANG	FSR
156511	52511+57511	CK	FSS	ANG	FSR
156512	52512+57512	CK	FSS	ANG	FSR
156513	52513+57513	CK	FSS	ANG	FSR
156514	52514+57514	CK	FSS	ANG	FSR

Right: *A total of 48 Metro-Cammell-built two-car Class 156 'Sprinter' sets are operated by First ScotRail, forming medium distance domestic services. The '156s' are allocated to Corkerhill depot and are painted in a mix of First ScotRail and Scottish Saltire liveries. Set No. 156445 is illustrated near Barassie, forming the 17.12 Glasgow Central to Girvan service on 25 May 2012, showing the latest Scottish Saltire colour scheme, identified by the code FSS in the listing above.*
Robin Ralston

Passenger Train Operating Companies - First ScotRail

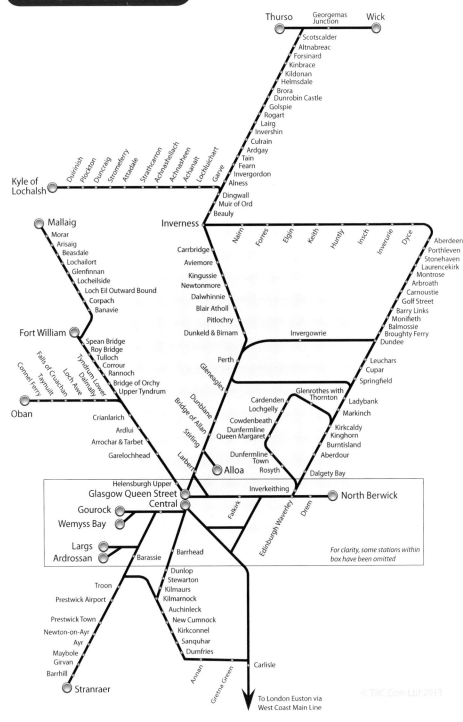

Class 158

	Vehicle Length: 76ft 1¾in (23.21m)	Engine: 1 x Cummins NTA855R of 350hp per vehicle
	Height: 12ft 6in (3.81m)	Horsepower: 700hp (522kW)
	Width: 9ft 3¼in (2.82m)	Seats (total/car): 14F/116S, 14F-46S/70S, * 138S, 68S/70S

Number	Formation DMCL/DMSL*+DMS	Depot	Livery	Owner	Operator
158701	52701+57701	IS	FSR	PTR	FSR
158702	52702+57702	IS	FSR	PTR	FSR
158703	52703+57703	IS	FSR	PTR	FSR
158704	52704+57704	IS	FSR	PTR	FSR
158705	52705+57705	IS	FSR	PTR	FSR
158706	52706+57706	IS	FSR	PTR	FSR
158707	52707+57707	IS	FSR	PTR	FSR
158708	52708+57708	IS	FSR	PTR	FSR
158709	52709+57709	IS	FSR	PTR	FSR
158710	52710+57710	IS	FSR	PTR	FSR
158711	52711+57711	IS	FSR	PTR	FSR
158712	52712+57712	IS	FSR	PTR	FSR
158713	52713+57713	IS	FSR	PTR	FSR
158714	52714+57714	IS	FSR	PTR	FSR
158715	52715+57715	IS	FSR	PTR	FSR
158716	52716+57716	IS	FSR	PTR	FSR
158717	52717+57717	IS	FSR	PTR	FSR
158718	52718+57718	IS	FSR	PTR	FSR
158719	52719+57719	IS	FSR	PTR	FSR
158720	52720+57720	IS	FSR	PTR	FSR
158721	52721+57721	IS	FSR	PTR	FSR
158722	52722+57722	IS	FSR	PTR	FSR
158723	52723+57723	IS	FSR	PTR	FSR
158724	52724+57724	IS	FSR	PTR	FSR
158725	52725+57725	IS	FSR	PTR	FSR
158726	52726+57726	HA	FSR	PTR	FSR
158727	52727+57727	IS	FSR	PTR	FSR
158728	52728+57728	IS	FSR	PTR	FSR
158729	52729+57729	HA	FSR	PTR	FSR
158730	52730+57730	HA	FSR	PTR	FSR
158731	52731+57731	HA	FSR	PTR	FSR
158732	52732+57732	HA	FSR	PTR	FSR
158733	52733+57733	HA	FSR	PTR	FSR
158734	52734+57734	HA	FSR	PTR	FSR
158735	52735+57735	HA	FSR	PTR	FSR
158736	52736+57736	HA	FSR	PTR	FSR
158737	52737+57737	HA	FSR	PTR	FSR
158738	52738+57738	HA	FSR	PTR	FSR
158739	52739+57739	HA	FSR	PTR	FSR
158740	52740+57740	HA	FSR	PTR	FSR
158741	52741+57741	HA	FSR	PTR	FSR
158782	52782*+57782	HA	FSS	ANG	FSR
158786	52786*+57786	HA	FSS	ANG	FSR
158789	52789*+57789	HA	FSS	ANG	FSR
158867	52867*+57867	HA	FSS	ANG	FSR
158868	52868*+57868	HA	FSS	ANG	FSR
158869	52869*+57869	HA	FSS	ANG	FSR
158870	52870*+57870	HA	FSS	ANG	FSR
158871	52871*+57871	HA	FSS	ANG	FSR

Name applied
158707 - Far North Line

Right: *The First ScotRail Scottish Saltire colour scheme is now being applied to Class 158s as they receive overhauls. Set No. 158789 is illustrated at Springburn working a Cumbernauld to Glasgow Queen Street service, sporting a slightly revised front headlight/marker light display.*
Murdoch Currie

Class 170/3
Turbostar

	Vehicle Length: 77ft 6in (23.62m)	Engine: 1 x MTU 6R 183TD13H 422hp per vehicle
	Height: 12ft 4½in (3.77m)	Horsepower: 1,266hp (944kW)
	Width: 8ft 10in (2.69m)	Seats (total/car): 164S, 57S/43S/64S

Number	Formation DMSL+MS+DMSL	Depot	Livery	Owner	Operator	+ Standard class only
170393	50393+55393+79393	HA	FSS	PTR	FSR	
170394+	50394+55394+79394	HA	FSR	PTR	FSR	
170395+	50395+55395+79395	HA	FSR	PTR	FSR	
170396	50396+55396+79396	HA	FSR	PTR	FSR	

Class 170/4
Turbostar

	Vehicle Length: 77ft 6in (23.62m)	Engine: 1 x MTU 6R 183TD13H 422hp per vehicle
	Height: 12ft 4½in (3.77m)	Horsepower: 1,266hp (944kW)
	Width: 8ft 10in (2.69m)	(170431/432 have 3 x 483hp engines giving 1,449hp)
		Seats (total/car): 18F/168S 9F-43S/76S/9F-49S

Number	Formation DMCL+MS+DMCL	Depot	Livery	Owner	Operator	Name
170401	50401+55401+79401	HA	FSR	PTR	FSR	*Sir Moir Lockhead OBE*
170402	50402+55402+79402	HA	FSS	PTR	FSR	
170403	50403+55403+79403	HA	FSR	PTR	FSR	
170404	50404+55404+79404	HA	FSR	PTR	FSR	

First ScotRail

170405	50405+55405+79405	HA	FSR	PTR	FSR	*Riverside Museum*
170406	50406+55406+79406	HA	FSR	PTR	FSR	
170407	50407+55407+79407	HA	FSR	PTR	FSR	*University of Aberdeen*
170408	50408+55408+79408	HA	FSR	PTR	FSR	
170409	50409+55409+79409	HA	FSR	PTR	FSR	
170410	50410+55410+79410	HA	FSR	PTR	FSR	
170411	50411+55411+79411	HA	FSR	PTR	FSR	
170412	50412+55412+79412	HA	FSS	PTR	FSR	
170413	50413+55413+79413	HA	FSR	PTR	FSR	
170414	50414+55414+79414	HA	FSR	PTR	FSR	
170415	50415+55415+79415	HA	FSS	PTR	FSR	
170416	50416+55416+79416	HA	FSR	EVL	FSR	
170417	50417+55417+79417	HA	FSR	EVL	FSR	
170418	50418+55418+79418	HA	FSS	EVL	FSR	
170419	50419+55419+79419	HA	FSR	EVL	FSR	
170420	50420+55420+79420	HA	FSR	EVL	FSR	
170421	50421+55421+79421	HA	FSR	EVL	FSR	
170422	50422+55422+79422	HA	FSR	EVL	FSR	
170423	50423+55423+79423	HA	FSR	EVL	FSR	
170424	50424+55424+79424	HA	FSR	EVL	FSR	
170425	50425+55425+79425	HA	FSS	PTR	FSR	
170426	50426+55426+79426	HA	FSS	PTR	FSR	
170427	50427+55427+79427	HA	FSS	PTR	FSR	
170428	50428+55428+79428	HA	FSS	PTR	FSR	
170429	50429+55429+79429	HA	FSS	PTR	FSR	
170430	50430+55430+79430	HA	FSS	PTR	FSR	
170431	50431+55431+79431	HA	FSS	PTR	FSR	
170432	50432+55432+79432	HA	FSS	PTR	FSR	
170433	50433+55433+79433	HA	FSR	PTR	FSR	*Investor in People*
170434	50434+55434+79434	HA	FSS	PTR	FSR	

Class 170/4
Turbostar

Vehicle Length: 77ft 6in (23.62m)	*Engine: 1 x MTU 6R 183TD13H 422hp per vehicle*	
Height: 12ft 4½in (3.77m)	*Horsepower: 1,266hp (944kW)*	
Width: 8ft 10in (2.69m)	*Seats: 170450-170471 (total/car) 198S, 55S/76S/67S*	
	170472-170478 (total/car) 200S, 57S/76S/67S	

Number Formation   Depot Livery Owner Opt'r

DMSL+MS+DMSL

170450	50450+55450+79450	HA	FSS	PTR	FSR		170460	50460+55460+79460	HA	FSR	PTR	FSR
170451	50451+55451+79451	HA	FSS	PTR	FSR		170461	50461+55461+79461	HA	FSR	PTR	FSR
170452	50452+55452+79452	HA	FSS	PTR	FSR		170470	50470+55470+79470	HA	FSS	PTR	FSR
170453	50453+55453+79453	HA	FSR	PTR	FSR		170471	50471+55471+79471	HA	FSS	PTR	FSR
170454	50454+55454+79454	HA	FSS	PTR	FSR		170472	50472+55472+79472	HA	FSP	PTR	FSR
170455	50455+55455+79455	HA	FSS	PTR	FSR		170473	50473+55473+79473	HA	FSP	PTR	FSR
170456	50456+55456+79456	HA	FSS	PTR	FSR		170474	50474+55474+79474	HA	FSP	PTR	FSR
170457	50457+55457+79457	HA	FSS	PTR	FSR		170475	50475+55475+79475	HA	FSP	PTR	FSR
170458	50458+55458+79458	HA	FSR	PTR	FSR		170476	50476+55476+79476	HA	FSP	PTR	FSR
170459	50459+55459+79459	HA	FSR	PTR	FSR		170477	50477+55477+79477	HA	FSP	PTR	FSR
							170478	50478+55478+79478	HA	FSP	PTR	FSR

Left: *The largest operator of Class 170 'Turbostar' DMU sets in the UK is First ScotRail, who deploy their fleet on longer distance main line services on the Edinburgh/Glasgow to Inverness and Aberdeen corridor as well as on the Edinburgh to Glasgow route. A six-car formation led by set No. 170415 is seen arriving at Edinburgh Haymarket on 21 April 2012.* **Nathan Williamson**

Class 314

Vehicle Length: (Driving) 64ft 11½in (19.80m)
(Inter) 65ft 4¼in (19.92m)
Height: 11ft 6½in (3.58m)
Width: 9ft 3in (2.82m)
Horsepower: 880hp (656kW)
Seats (total/car): 212S, 68S/76S/68S

Number	Formation	Depot	Livery	Owner	Operator	Name
	DMSO(A)+PTSO+DMSO(B)					
314201	64583+71450+64584	GW	FSP	ANG	FSR	
314202	64585+71451+64586	GW	FSP	ANG	FSR	
314203	64587+71452+64588*	GW	FSS	ANG	FSR	
314204	64589+71453+64590	GW	FSS	ANG	FSR	
314205	64591+71454+64592	GW	FSS	ANG	FSR	
314206	64593+71455+64594	GW	FSP	ANG	FSR	
314207	64595+71456+64596	GW	FSP	ANG	FSR	
314208	64597+71457+64598	GW	FSS	ANG	FSR	
314209	64599+71458+64600	GW	FSP	ANG	FSR	
314210	64601+71459+64602	GW	FSP	ANG	FSR	
314211	64603+71460+64604	GW	FSS	ANG	FSR	
314212	64604+71461+64606	GW	FSS	ANG	FSR	
314213	64607+71462+64608	GW	FSP	ANG	FSR	
314214	64609+71463+64610	GW	FSS	ANG	FSR	
314215	64611+71464+64612	GW	FSP	ANG	FSR	
314216	64613+71465+64614	GW	FSP	ANG	FSR	

* 64588 rebuilt from Class 507 car No. 64426 and seats 74S

Right: *The first of the 'new' generation of electric multiple-units based on the 1972-design style are still in frontline service in Scotland. The 16 Class 314s are based at Glasgow Shields and operate suburban electrified services in the Glasgow area. Set No. 314212, painted in the latest Scottish Saltire livery, is seen at Glasgow Central.* **Murdoch Currie**

Class 318

Vehicle Length: (Driving) 65ft 0¾in (19.83m)
(Inter) 65ft 4¼in (19.92m)
Height: 12ft 1½in (3.70m)
Width: 9ft 3in (2.82m)
Horsepower: 1,328hp (996kW)
Seats (total/car): 216S, 66S/79S/71S

Number	Formation	Depot	Livery	Owner	Operator	Name
	DTSO(A)+MSO+DTSO(B)					
318250	77240+62866+77260	GW	FSP	EVL	FSR	
318251	77241+62867+77261	GW	FSP	EVL	FSR	
318252	77242+62868+77262	GW	FSP	EVL	FSR	
318253	77243+62869+77263	GW	FSP	EVL	FSR	
318254	77244+62870+77264	GW	FSP	EVL	FSR	
318255	77245+62871+77265	GW	FSP	EVL	FSR	
318256	77246+62872+77266	GW	FSP	EVL	FSR	
318257	77247+62873+77267	GW	FSP	EVL	FSR	
318258	77248+62874+77268	GW	FSP	EVL	FSR	
318259	77249+62875+77269	GW	FSP	EVL	FSR	Citizens' Network
318260	77250+62876+77270	GW	FSP	EVL	FSR	
318261	77251+62877+77271	GW	FSP	EVL	FSR	
318262	77252+62878+77272	GW	FSP	EVL	FSR	
318263	77253+62879+77273	GW	FSP	EVL	FSR	
318264	77254+62880+77274	GW	FSP	EVL	FSR	
318265	77255+62881+77275	GW	FSP	EVL	FSR	
318266	77256+62882+77276	GW	FSP	EVL	FSR	Strathclyder
318267	77257+62883+77277	GW	FSP	EVL	FSR	
318268	77258+62884+77278	GW	FSP	EVL	FSR	
318269	77259+62885+77279	GW	FSP	EVL	FSR	
318270	77288+62890+77289	GW	FSP	EVL	FSR	

First ScotRail

Left: *The 21 members of Class 318 were originally fitted with end gangways, but these were removed during the sets' latest overhaul. The units are allocated to Glasgow Shields depot, and currently operate on the Argyle line. Painted in fleet standard carmine and cream colours, set No. 318253 is viewed near Carluke, forming a Glasgow Central to Lanark service.* **Brian Morrison**

Class 320

Vehicle Length: (Driving) 65ft 0¾in (19.83m)	Width: 9ft 3in (2.82m)
(Inter) 65ft 4¼in (19.92m)	Horsepower: 1,328hp (996kW)
Height: 12ft 4¾in (3.78m)	Seats (total/car): 227S, 76S/76S/75S

Number	Formation DTSO(A)+MSO+DTSO(B)	Depot	Livery	Owner	Operator	Name
320301	77899+63021+77921	GW	FSS	EVL	FSR	
320302	77900+63022+77922	GW	FSS	EVL	FSR	
320303	77901+63023+77923	GW	FSS	EVL	FSR	
320304	77902+63024+77924	GW	FSS	EVL	FSR	
320305	77903+63025+77925	GW	FSP	EVL	FSR	*Glasgow School of Art* *1845 – 150 – 1995*
320306	77904+63026+77926	GW	FSS	EVL	FSR	
320307	77905+63027+77927	GW	FSS	EVL	FSR	
320308	77906+63028+77928	GW	FSS	EVL	FSR	
320309	77907+63029+77929	GW	FSP	EVL	FSR	*Radio Clyde 25th Anniversary*
320310	77908+63030+77930	GW	FSP	EVL	FSR	
320311	77909+63031+77931	GW	FSS	EVL	FSR	
320312	77910+63032+77932	GW	FSP	EVL	FSR	*Sir William A Smith* *Founder of the Boys' Brigade*
320313	77911+63033+77933	GW	FSS	EVL	FSR	
320314	77912+63034+77934	GW	FSS	EVL	FSR	
320315	77913+63035+77935	GW	FSS	EVL	FSR	
320316	77914+63036+77936	GW	FSS	EVL	FSR	
320317	77915+63037+77937	GW	FSP	EVL	FSR	
320318	77916+63038+77938	GW	FSS	EVL	FSR	
320319	77917+63039+77939	GW	FSP	EVL	FSR	
320320	77918+63040+77940	GW	FSP	EVL	FSR	
320321	77919+63041+77941	GW	FSS	EVL	FSR	
320322	77920+63042+77942	GW	FSP	EVL	FSR	*Festival Glasgow Orchid*

Left: *The overhaul and repainting into ScotRail Saltire livery continued through 2012 for the 22 members of Class 320, as displayed on set No. 320306 at Springburn on a service to Dalmuir.* **Murdoch Currie**

Class 334
Juniper

Vehicle Length: (Driving) 69ft 0¾in (21.04m)			Width: 9ft 2¾in (2.80m)			
	(Inter) 65ft 4½in (19.93m)		Horsepower: 1,448hp (1,080kW)			
Height: 12ft 3in (3.77m)			Seats (total/car): 183S, 64S/55S/64S			

Number	Formation DMSO(A)+PTSO+DMSO(B)	Depot	Livery	Owner	Operator	Name
334001	64101+74301+65101	GW	FSP	EVL	FSR	Donald Dewar
334002	64102+74302+65102	GW	FSP	EVL	FSR	
334003	64103+74303+65103	GW	FSP	EVL	FSR	
334004	64104+74304+65104	GW	FSP	EVL	FSR	
334005	64105+74305+65105	GW	FSP	EVL	FSR	
334006	64106+74306+65106	GW	FSS	EVL	FSR	
334007	64107+74307+65107	GW	FSP	EVL	FSR	
334008	64108+74308+65108	GW	FSP	EVL	FSR	
334009	64109+74309+65109	GW	FSP	EVL	FSR	
334010	64110+74310+65110	GW	FSP	EVL	FSR	
334011	64111+74311+65111	GW	FSP	EVL	FSR	
334012	64112+74312+65112	GW	FSS	EVL	FSR	
334013	64113+74313+65113	GW	FSP	EVL	FSR	
334014	64114+74314+65114	GW	FSP	EVL	FSR	
334015	64115+74315+65115	GW	FSP	EVL	FSR	
334016	64116+74316+65116	GW	FSP	EVL	FSR	
334017	64117+74317+65117	GW	FSP	EVL	FSR	
334018	64118+74318+65118	GW	FSP	EVL	FSR	
334019	64119+74319+65119	GW	FSP	EVL	FSR	
334020	64120+74320+65120	GW	FSS	EVL	FSR	
334021	64121+74321+65121	GW	FSP	EVL	FSR	Larkhill
334022	64122+74322+65122	GW	FSS	EVL	FSR	
334023	64123+74323+65123	GW	FSS	EVL	FSR	
334024	64124+74324+65124	GW	FSP	EVL	FSR	
334025	64125+74325+65125	GW	FSP	EVL	FSR	
334026	64126+74326+65126	GW	FSP	EVL	FSR	
334027	64127+74327+65127	GW	FSS	EVL	FSR	
334028	64128+74328+65128	GW	FSS	EVL	FSR	
334029	64129+74329+65129	GW	FSS	EVL	FSR	
334030	64130+74330+65130	GW	FSP	EVL	FSR	
334031	64131+74331+65131	GW	FSS	EVL	FSR	
334032	64132+74332+65132	GW	FSP	EVL	FSR	
334033	64133+74333+65133	GW	FSP	EVL	FSR	
334034	64134+74334+65134	GW	FSP	EVL	FSR	
334035	64135+74335+65135	GW	FSS	EVL	FSR	
334036	64136+74336+65136	GW	FSS	EVL	FSR	
334037	64137+74337+65137	GW	FSP	EVL	FSR	
334038	64138+74338+65138	GW	FSS	EVL	FSR	
334039	64139+74339+65139	GW	FSP	EVL	FSR	
334040	64140+74340+65140	GW	FSP	EVL	FSR	

Right: *A total of 40 three-car Class 334 'Juniper' sets were built by Alstom. These are allocated to Glasgow Shields Road depot and deployed on the North Clyde services. As sets pass through shops for overhaul, the latest Scottish Saltire livery is being applied, as shown on set No. 334006 at Dalmuir.* **Nathan Williamson**

First ScotRail

Class 380/0
Desiro

Vehicle Length: 77ft 3in (23.57m) Horsepower: 1,341hp (1,000kW)
Height: 12ft 1½in (3.7m) Seats (total/car): 191S, 70S/57S/64S
Width: 9ft 2in (2.7m)

Number	Formation DMSO(A)+PTSO+DMSO(B)	Depot	Livery	Owner	Operator
380001	38501+38601+38701	GW	FSS	EVL	FSR
380002	38502+38602+38702	GW	FSS	EVL	FSR
380003	38503+38603+38703	GW	FSS	EVL	FSR
380004	38504+38604+38704	GW	FSS	EVL	FSR
380005	38505+38605+38705	GW	FSS	EVL	FSR
380006	38506+38606+38706	GW	FSS	EVL	FSR
380007	38507+38607+38707	GW	FSS	EVL	FSR
380008	38508+38608+38708	GW	FSS	EVL	FSR
380009	38509+38609+38709	GW	FSS	EVL	FSR
380010	38510+38610+38710	GW	FSS	EVL	FSR
380011	38511+38611+38711	GW	FSS	EVL	FSR
380012	38512+38612+38712	GW	FSS	EVL	FSR
380013	38513+38613+38713	GW	FSS	EVL	FSR
380014	38514+38614+38714	GW	FSS	EVL	FSR
380015	38515+38615+38715	GW	FSS	EVL	FSR
380016	38516+38616+38716	GW	FSS	EVL	FSR
380017	38517+38617+38717	GW	FSS	EVL	FSR
380018	38518+38618+38718	GW	FSS	EVL	FSR
380019	38519+38619+38719	GW	FSS	EVL	FSR
380020	38520+38620+38720	GW	FSS	EVL	FSR
380021	38521+38621+38721	GW	FSS	EVL	FSR
380022	38522+38622+38722	GW	FSS	EVL	FSR

Class 380/1
Desiro

Vehicle Length: 77ft 3in (23.57m) Horsepower: 1,341hp (1,000kW)
Height: 12ft 1½in (3.7m) Seats (total/car): 265S, 70S/57S/74S/64S
Width: 9ft 2in (2.7m)

Number	Formation DMSO(A)+PTSO+MSO+DMSO(B)	Depot	Livery	Owner	Operator
380101	38551+38651+38851+38751	GW	FSS	EVL	FSR
380102	38552+38652+38852+38752	GW	FSS	EVL	FSR
380103	38553+38653+38853+38753	GW	FSS	EVL	FSR
380104	38554+38654+38854+38754	GW	FSS	EVL	FSR
380105	38555+38655+38855+38755	GW	FSS	EVL	FSR
380106	38556+38656+38856+38756	GW	FSS	EVL	FSR
380107	38557+38657+38857+38757	GW	FSS	EVL	FSR
380108	38558+38658+38858+38758	GW	FSS	EVL	FSR
380109	38559+38659+38859+38759	GW	FSS	EVL	FSR
380110	38560+38660+38860+38760	GW	FSS	EVL	FSR
380111	38561+38661+38861+38761	GW	FSS	EVL	FSR
380112	38562+38662+38862+38762	GW	FSS	EVL	FSR
380113	38563+38663+38863+38763	GW	FSS	EVL	FSR
380114	38564+38664+38864+38764	GW	FSS	EVL	FSR
380115	38565+38665+38865+38765	GW	FSS	EVL	FSR
380116	38566+38666+38866+38766	GW	FSS	EVL	FSR

Left: *The most modern of the ScotRail EMU classes are the 38 Class 380 Siemens 'Desiro' sets. All are allocated to Glasgow Shields Road depot and operate on the Ayrshire and Inverclyde services, displacing Class 318 and 334 fleets to other routes. The fleet was built and tested in Germany before rail delivery to the UK. Four-car set No. 380114, is seen at Paisley Gilmour Street. All sets are painted in the latest Scottish Saltire livery.* **Murdoch Currie**

Mk2 & Mk3 Hauled Stock

Mk2
Vehicle Length: 66ft 0in (20.11m)   Width: 9ft 3in (2.81m)
Height: 12ft 9½in (3.89m)   Seats (total/car): 60S

Mk3
Vehicle Length: 75ft 0in (22.86m)   Width: 8ft 11in (2.71m)
Height: 12ft 9in (3.88m)   Bogie Type: BT10

AN1F (Mk2) - RLO Seating 28-30F

Number	Depot	Livery	Owner
6700 (3347)	IS	FSS	EVL
6701 (3346)	IS	FSR	EVL
6702 (3421)	IS	FSR	EVL
6703 (3308)	IS	FSR	EVL
6704 (3341)	IS	FSR	EVL
6705 (3310)	IS	FSR	EVL
6706 (3283)	IS	FSR	EVL
6707 (3276)	IS	FSR	EVL
6708 (3370)	IS	FSR	EVL

AN1F (Mk2) - BUO Seating 31U

Number	Depot	Livery	Owner
9800 (5751)	IS	FSR	EVL
9801 (5760)	IS	FSR	EVL
9802 (5772)	IS	FSR	EVL
9803 (5799)	IS	FSR	EVL
9804 (5826)	IS	FSR	EVL
9805 (5833)	IS	FSR	EVL
9806 (5840)	IS	FSR	EVL
9807 (5851)	IS	FSS	EVL
9808 (5871)	IS	FSS	EVL
9809 (5890)	IS	FSR	EVL
9810 (5892)	IS	FSR	EVL

AU4G (Mk3) - SLEP Comps 12

Number	Depot	Livery	Owner
10501	IS	FSR	PTR
10502	IS	FSR	PTR
10504	IS	FSR	PTR
10506	IS	FSR	PTR
10507	IS	FSR	PTR
10508	IS	FSR	PTR
10513	IS	FSR	PTR
10516	IS	FSS	PTR
10519	IS	FSR	PTR
10520	IS	FSR	PTR
10522	IS	FSR	PTR
10523	IS	FSR	PTR

10526	IS	FSR	PTR
10527	IS	FSR	PTR
10529	IS	FSR	PTR
10531	IS	FSR	PTR
10542	IS	FSR	PTR
10543	IS	FSR	PTR
10544	IS	FSR	PTR
10548	IS	FSR	PTR
10551	IS	FSR	PTR
10553	IS	FSR	PTR
10561	IS	FSR	PTR
10562	IS	FSS	PTR
10565	IS	FSR	PTR
10580	IS	FSR	PTR
10588	IS	BLG	FSR
10597	IS	FSR	PTR
10598	IS	FSR	PTR
10600	IS	FSR	PTR
10605	IS	FSR	PTR
10607	IS	FSR	PTR
10610	IS	FSR	PTR
10613	IS	FSR	PTR
10614	IS	FSR	PTR
10617	IS	FSR	PTR

AS4G (MK3) - SLE Comps 13

Number	Depot	Livery	Owner
10675	IS	FSR	PTR
10683	IS	FSR	PTR
10688	IS	FSR	PTR
10690	IS	FSR	PTR
10693	IS	FSR	PTR
10703	IS	FSR	PTR

AQ4G (Mk3) - SLED Comps 11

Number	Depot	Livery	Owner
10648	IS	FSR	PTR
10650	IS	FSR	PTR
10666	IS	FSR	PTR
10680	IS	FSR	PTR
10689	IS	FSR	PTR
10699	IS	FSR	PTR
10706	IS	FSR	PTR
10714	IS	FSR	PTR
10718	IS	FSR	PTR
10719	IS	FSR	PTR
10722	IS	FSR	PTR
10723	IS	FSR	PTR

Right: *First ScotRail are responsible for operating sleeping car services from Aberdeen, Inverness, Fort William, Glasgow and Edinburgh to London and return. The 73 Mk2 and Mk3 vehicles are owned by Porterbrook and Eversholt and operated by ScotRail, being based at Inverness. Traction is hired from DBS. In the upper view we see Mk3 SLEP No. 10562. These vehicles have 12 compartments. The illustration is taken from the corridor side. In the lower view we see Mk2 BUO No. 9802. These vehicles have guards, luggage space and seating for 31, which is termed as unclassified.*
Both: **Robin Ralston**

First TransPennine Express

Address: ✉ Floor 7, Bridgewater House, 60 Whitworth Street, Manchester, M1 6LT
✍ tpecustomer.relations@firstgroup.com
☎ 0845 600 1671
ⓘ www.tpexpress.co.uk

Managing Director: Nick Donovan
Franchise Dates: 1 February 2004 - between April 2014 & April 2015
Principal Routes: Newcastle, Middlesbrough, Scarborough, Hull, Cleethorpes to Manchester, Liverpool, Barrow, Carlisle, Edinburgh and Glasgow
Depots: Ardwick (AK) - Siemens-operated, York (YK), Crofton (XW)
Parent Company: First Group, Keolis

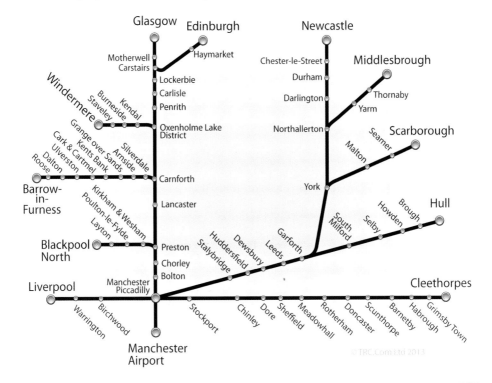

Class 350/3
Desiro

Vehicle Length: 66ft 9in (20.4m)
Height: 12ft 1½in (3.78m)
Width: 9ft 2in (2.7m)

Horsepower: 1,341hp (1,000kW)
Seats (total/car): Not yet available

Number	Formation
	DMSO(A)+TCO+PTSO+DMSO(B)
350301	On order
350302	On order
350303	On order
350304	On order
350305	On order
350306	On order
350307	On order
350308	On order
350309	On order
350310	On order

Class 170/3
Turbostar

Vehicle Length: 77ft 6in (23.62m)
Height: 12ft 4½in (3.77m)
Width: 8ft 10in (2.69m)

Engine: 1 x MTU 6R 183TD13H 422hp per vehicle
Horsepower: 844hp (629kW)
Seats (total/car): 8F/108S 8F-43S/65S

Number	Formation DMCL+DMS	Depot	Livery	Owner	Operator
170301	50301+79301	XW	FTP	PTR	FTP
170302	50302+79302	XW	FTP	PTR	FTP
170303	50303+79303	XW	FTP	PTR	FTP
170304	50304+79304	XW	FTP	PTR	FTP
170305	50305+79305	XW	FTP	PTR	FTP
170306	50306+79306	XW	FTP	PTR	FTP
170307	50307+79307	XW	FTP	PTR	FTP
170308	50308+79308	XW	FTP	PTR	FTP
170309	50399+79399	XW	FTP	PTR	FTP

Right: *Operator First TransPennine Express has a fleet of nine 'Turbostar' Class 170/3 units, allocated to Crofton, near Wakefield. These sets are used on the Manchester to East Coast corridor. Set No. 170306 displaying full FTPE livery is seen at Barnetby. These sets carry 8 first and 108 standard class passengers.* **Antony Christie**

Class 185
Desiro

Vehicle Length: (Driving) 77ft 11in (23.76m), (Inter) 77ft 10½in (23.75m)
Height: 12ft 4in (3.75m)
Width: 9ft 3in (2.81m)

Engine: 1 x Cummins QSK19 of 750hp per car
Horsepower: 2,250hp (1,680kW)
Seats (total/car): 15F/154S, 15F-18S/72S/64S

Number	Formation DMCL+MSL+DMS	Depot	Livery	Owner	Optr
185101	51101+53101+54101	AK	FTP	EVL	FTP
185102	51102+53102+54102	AK	FTP	EVL	FTP
185103	51103+53103+54103	AK	FTP	EVL	FTP
185104	51104+53104+54104	AK	FTP	EVL	FTP
185105	51105+53105+54105	AK	FTP	EVL	FTP
185106	51106+53106+54106	AK	FTP	EVL	FTP
185107	51107+53107+54107	AK	FTP	EVL	FTP
185108	51108+53108+54108	AK	FTP	EVL	FTP
185109	51109+53109+54109	AK	FTP	EVL	FTP
185110	51110+53110+54110	AK	FTP	EVL	FTP
185111	51111+53111+54111	AK	FTP	EVL	FTP
185112	51112+53112+54112	AK	FTP	EVL	FTP
185113	51113+53113+54113	AK	FTP	EVL	FTP
185114	51114+53114+54114	AK	FTP	EVL	FTP
185115	51115+53115+54115	AK	FTP	EVL	FTP
185116	51116+53116+54116	AK	FTP	EVL	FTP
185117	51117+53117+54117	AK	FTP	EVL	FTP
185118	51118+53118+54118	AK	FTP	EVL	FTP
185119	51119+53119+54119	AK	FTP	EVL	FTP
185120	51120+53120+54120	AK	FTP	EVL	FTP
185121	51121+53121+54121	AK	FTP	EVL	FTP
185122	51122+53122+54122	AK	FTP	EVL	FTP
185123	51123+53123+54123	AK	FTP	EVL	FTP
185124	51124+53124+54124	AK	FTP	EVL	FTP
185125	51125+53125+54125	AK	FTP	EVL	FTP
185126	51126+53126+54126	AK	FTP	EVL	FTP
185127	51127+53127+54127	AK	FTP	EVL	FTP
185128	51128+53128+54128	AK	FTP	EVL	FTP
185129	51129+53129+54129	AK	FTP	EVL	FTP
185130	51130+53130+54130	AK	FTP	EVL	FTP
185131	51131+53131+54131	AK	FTP	EVL	FTP
185132	51132+53132+54132	AK	FTP	EVL	FTP
185133	51133+53133+54133	AK	FTP	EVL	FTP
185134	51134+53134+54134	AK	FTP	EVL	FTP
185135	51135+53135+54135	AK	FTP	EVL	FTP
185136	51136+53136+54136	AK	FTP	EVL	FTP
185137	51137+53137+54137	AK	FTP	EVL	FTP
185138	51138+53138+54138	AK	FTP	EVL	FTP
185139	51139+53139+54139	AK	FTP	EVL	FTP
185140	51140+53140+54140	AK	FTP	EVL	FTP
185141	51141+53141+54141	AK	FTP	EVL	FTP
185142	51142+53142+54142	AK	FTP	EVL	FTP
185143	51143+53143+54143	AK	FTP	EVL	FTP
185144	51144+53144+54144	AK	FTP	EVL	FTP
185145	51145+53145+54145	AK	FTP	EVL	FTP
185146	51146+53146+54146	AK	FTP	EVL	FTP
185147	51147+53147+54147	AK	FTP	EVL	FTP
185148	51148+53148+54148	AK	FTP	EVL	FTP
185149	51149+53149+54149	AK	FTP	EVL	FTP
185150	51150+53150+54150	AK	FTP	EVL	FTP
185151	51151+53151+54151	AK	FTP	EVL	FTP

Below: *Core FTPE services are operated by a fleet of 51 three-car Class 185 'Desiro' diesel sets based at Manchester Ardwick depot. Set No. 185108 is seen at York bound for Scarborough, displaying a modified Liverpool '08 livery.* **Antony Christie**

Grand Central

Address:	✉ River House, 17 Museum Street, York, YO1 7DJ
	✍ info@grandcentral.com
	✆ 0845 603 4852
	ⓘ www.grandcentral.co.uk
Managing Director:	Richard McLean
Franchise Dates:	Private Open Access Operator, to December 2016
Principal Routes:	London King's Cross - Sunderland / Bradford
Depots:	Heaton (HT)
Parent Company:	Arriva PLC

Below: *Grand Central services are operated by MTU fitted HSTs or Class 180s. All the Grand Central stock is finished in a distinctive black and orange livery, shown on an HST set led by power car No. 43480 arriving at London King's Cross.*
Antony Christie

Sunderland
Hartlepool
Eaglescliffe
Northallerton
Thirsk
York
Doncaster
Halifax
Wakefield Kirkgate
Brighouse
Pontefract Monkhill
Bradford Interchange
London King's Cross

Class 43 – HST

Vehicle Length: 58ft 5in (18.80m)
Height: 12ft 10in (3.90m)
Width: 8ft 11in (2.73m)
Engine: MTU 16V4000 R41R
Horsepower: 2,250hp (1,680kW)
Electrical Equipment: Brush

Number	Depot	Pool	Livery	Owner	Operator
43423 (43123)	HT	GCHP	GTL	ANG	GTL
43465 (43065)	HT	GCHP	GTL	ANG	GTL
43467 (43067)	HT	GCHP	GTL	ANG	GTL
43468 (43068)	HT	GCHP	GTO	ANG	GTL
43480 (43080)	HT	GCHP	GTO	ANG	GTL
43484 (43084)	HT	GCHP	GTL	ANG	GTL

Name applied
43423 *'Valenta' 1972 - 2010*
43484 *Peter Fox 1942 - 2011*

Class 180
Zephyrs

Vehicle Length: (Driving) 75ft 7in (23.71m), (Inter) 75ft 5in (23.03m)
Height: 12ft 4in (3.75m)
Width: 9ft 2in (2.80m)
Engine: 1 x Cummins QSK19 of 750hp per car
Horsepower: 3,750hp (2,796kW)
Seats (total/car): 42F/226S, 46S/42F/68S/56S/56S

Number	Formation DMSL(A)+MFL+MSL+MSLRB+DMSL(B)	Depot	Livery	Owner	Operator	Name
180101	50901+54901+55901+56901+59901	HT	GTL	ANG	GTL	
180105	50905+54905+55905+56905+59905	HT	GTL	ANG	GTL	*The Yorkshire Artist Ashley Jackson*
180107	50907+54907+55907+56907+59907	HT	GTL	ANG	GTL	*Hart of the North*
180112	50912+54912+55912+56912+59912	HT	GTL	ANG	GTL	*James Herriot*
180114	50914+54914+55914+56914+59914	HT	GTL	ANG	GTL	

Above: *Five former First Great Western Class 180 sets are now operated by Grand Central, who term the stock as 'Zephyrs'. All have been refurbished internally and now sport black and orange livery. Set No. 180112 arrives at York with a northbound service. It is a pity the original front-end hinged doors have been removed from these sets.* **Antony Christie**

Mk3 HST stock

Vehicle Length: 75ft 0in (22.86m)   Width: 8ft 11in (2.71m)
Height: 12ft 9in (3.88m)   Bogie Type: BT10

GK2G - TRSB *Seating 33S*

Number		Depot	Livery	Owner
40424	(40024)	HT	GTO	ANG
40426	(40026)	HT	GTL	ANG
40433	(40033)	HT	GTL	ANG

GH1G - TF *Seating 48F*

Number		Depot	Livery	Owner
41201	(11045)	HT	GTO	ANG
41202	(11017)	HT	GTL	ANG
41203	(11038)	HT	GTL	ANG
41204	(11023)	HT	GTL	ANG
41205	(11036)	HT	GTL	ANG
41206	(11055)	HT	GTL	ANG

GH2G - TS *Seating 64S* *TSD Seating 60S*

Number		Depot	Livery	Owner
42401	(12149)	HT	GTO	ANG
42402	(12155)	HT	GTO	ANG
42403*	(12033)	HT	GTO	ANG
42404	(12152)	HT	GTL	ANG
42405	(12136)	HT	GTL	ANG
42406*	(12112)	HT	GTL	ANG
42407	(12044)	HT	GTL	ANG
42408	(12121)	HT	GTL	ANG
42409*	(12088)	HT	GTL	ANG

GJ2G - TGS *Seating 67S*

Number	Depot	Livery	Owner
44065 (S)	HT/LM	GTL	GTL
44088 (S)	HT/LM	GTL	GTL
44089 (S)	HT/LM	GTL	GTL

■ Grand Central also has Mk2D BSO No. 9488 on its books as a barrier vehicle.

Right: *A total of 21 HST passenger vehicles owned by Angel Trains are operated by Grand Central, all based at Heaton depot in Newcastle. All vehicles carry the latest black and orange GC livery. TRSB No. 40424 is illustrated at King's Cross; note the grey passenger door with the catering symbol* **Antony Christie**

Greater Anglia

Address:	✉ 2nd Floor, East Anglia House, 12-34 Great Eastern Street, London, EC2A 3EH
	✆ contactcentre@greateranglia.co.uk
	✆ 0845 600 7245
	ⓘ www.greateranglia.co.uk
Managing Director:	Ruud Haket
Franchise Dates:	1 February 2012 - 19 July 2014
Principal Routes:	London Liverpool Street to Norwich, Cambridge, Enfield Town, Hertford East, Upminster, Southend Victoria, Southminster, Braintree, Sudbury, Clacton, Walton, Harwich Town, Felixstowe, Lowestoft, Great Yarmouth, Sheringham, Stansted Airport and Peterborough
Depots:	Ilford (IL), Norwich (NC), Clacton (CC)
Parent Company:	Abellio

Passenger Train Operating Companies - Greater Anglia

Class 90/0

Vehicle Length: 61ft 6in (18.74m)	Power Collection: 25kV ac overhead
Height: 13ft 0¼in (3.96m)	Horsepower: 7,860hp (5,860kW)
Width: 9ft 0in (2.74m)	Electrical Equipment: GEC

Number	Depot	Pool	Livery	Owner	Operator	Name
90001	NC	IANA	ORN	PTR	NXA	
90002	NC	IANA	ORN	PTR	NXA	
90003	NC	IANA	NXA	PTR	NXA	Raedwald of East Anglia
90004	NC	IANA	ORN	PTR	NXA	Eastern Daily Press 1870-2010 Serving Norfolk for 140 years
90005	NC	IANA	ORN	PTR	NXA	Vice-Admiral Lord Nelson
90006	NC	IANA	ORN	PTR	NXA	Roger Ford / Modern Railways Magazine
90007	NC	IANA	ORN	PTR	NXA	Sir John Betjeman
90008	NC	IANA	NXA	PTR	NXA	The East Anglian
90009	NC	IANA	ORN	PTR	NXA	Diamond Jubilee
90010	NC	IANA	ORN	PTR	NXA	Bressingham Steam and Gardens
90011	NC	IANA	ORN	PTR	NXA	Let's Go - East of England
90012	NC	IANA	ORN	PTR	NXA	Royal Anglian Regiment
90013	NC	IANA	ORN	PTR	NXA	The Evening Star
90014	NC	IANA	ORN	PTR	NXA	Norfolk and Norwich Festival
90015	NC	IANA	NXA	PTR	NXA	Colchester Castle

Left: *The Greater Anglia franchise is currently operated by Abellio. The short length of the franchise has seen little re-liveried stock emerging, with branding of the older liveries being common. Greater Anglia uses 15 Class 90/0 locomotives on its prime London Liverpool Street to Norwich route. The locos operate in full push-pull mode with Mk3 DVTs on the remote ends of trains, using the Time Division Multiplex (TDM)control system. The Class 90s are usually coupled at the London end of formations. Painted in tatty blue livery with Greater Anglia branding, No. 90004 Eastern Daily Press is seen at Ipswich with a train bound for London Liverpool Street.*
Antony Christie

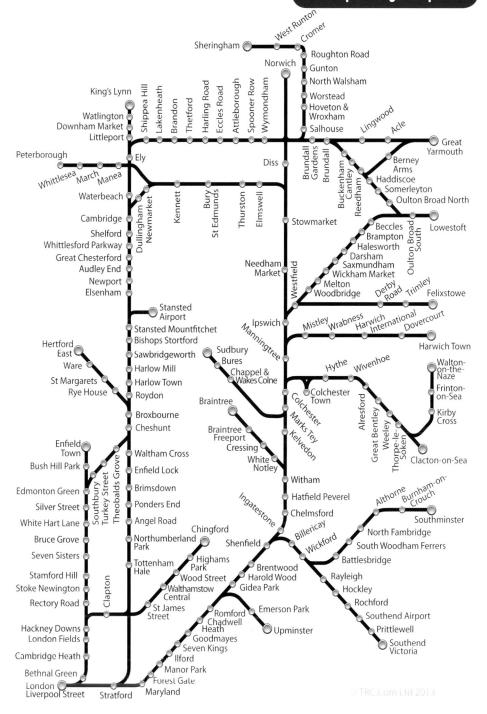

Greater Anglia

Mk 3 Hauled Stock

Vehicle Length: 75ft 0in (22.86m)   Width: 8ft 11in (2.71m)
Height: 12ft 9in (3.88m)   Bogie Type: BT10

AJ1G - RFM *Seating 24F*

Number	Depot	Livery	Owner
10200 (40519)	NC	ORN	PTR
10203 (40506)	NC	NXA	PTR
10206 (40507)	NC	ORN	PTR
10214 (11034)	NC	ORN	PTR
10216 (11041)	NC	ORN	PTR
10223 (11043)	NC	ORN	PTR
10228 (11035)	NC	NXA	PTR
10229 (11059)	NC	AWT	PTR
10247 (10011)	NC	ORN	PTR

AN2G - TSOB *Seating 52S*

10401 (12168)	NC	NXA	PTR
10402 (12010)	NC	ORN	PTR
10403 (12135)	NC	ORN	PTR
10404 (12068)	NC	ORN	PTR
10405 (12137)	NC	ORN	PTR
10406 (12020)	NC	ORN	PTR

AD1G - FO, *FOD Seating 48F/34F**

11021 (S)	NC	VTS	PTR
11066	NC	ORN	PTR
11067	NC	ORN	PTR
11068	NC	NXA	PTR
11069	NC	ORN	PTR
11070	NC	ORN	PTR
11072*	NC	ORN	PTR
11073*	NC	NXA	PTR
11074 (S)	NC	VTS	PTR
11075	NC	ORN	PTR
11076	NC	ORN	PTR
11077	NC	ORN	PTR
11078*	NC	ORN	PTR
11080	NC	ORN	PTR
11081	NC	ORN	PTR
11082	NC	NXA	PTR
11085*	NC	ORN	PTR
11087*	NC	NXA	PTR
11088*	NC	NXA	PTR
11090*	NC	ORN	PTR
11091*	NC	NXA	PTR
11092	NC	ORN	PTR
11093*	NC	ORN	PTR
11094*	NC	ORN	PTR
11095*	NC	ORN	PTR
11096*	NC	ORN	PTR
11098*	NC	ORN	PTR

11099*	NC	ORN	PTR
11100*	NC	NXA	PTR
11101*	NC	ORN	PTR

AC2G - TSO *Seating 80S*

12005	NC	ORN	PTR
12009	NC	ORN	PTR
12012	NC	ORN	PTR
12013	NC	ORN	PTR
12015	NC	ORN	PTR
12016	NC	ORN	PTR
12019	NC	ORN	PTR
12021	NC	NXA	PTR
12024	NC	ORN	PTR
12026	NC	ORN	PTR
12027	NC	NXA	PTR
12030	NC	ORN	PTR
12031	NC	ORN	PTR
12032	NC	ORN	PTR
12034	NC	ORN	PTR
12035	NC	NXA	PTR
12037	NC	ORN	PTR
12040	NC	ORN	PTR
12041	NC	ORN	PTR
12042	NC	ORN	PTR
12046	NC	ORN	PTR
12049	NC	ORN	PTR
12051	NC	NXA	PTR
12056	NC	ORN	PTR
12057	NC	ORN	PTR
12060	NC	ORN	PTR
12061	NC	ORN	PTR
12062	NC	ORN	PTR
12064	NC	ORN	PTR
12066	NC	ORN	PTR
12067	NC	ORN	PTR
12073	NC	ORN	PTR
12079	NC	ORN	PTR
12081	NC	ORN	PTR
12082	NC	ORN	PTR
12084	NC	NXA	PTR
12089	NC	ORN	PTR
12090	NC	ORN	PTR
12091	NC	ORN	PTR
12093	NC	ORN	PTR
12097	NC	NXA	PTR
12098	NC	ORN	PTR
12099	NC	ORN	PTR

12103	NC	ORN	PTR
12105	NC	ORN	PTR
12107	NC	ORN	PTR
12108	NC	NXA	PTR
12109	NC	ORN	PTR
12110	NC	ORN	PTR
12111	NC	NXA	PTR
12114	NC	NXA	PTR
12115	NC	ORN	PTR
12116	NC	ORN	PTR
12118	NC	NXA	PTR
12120	NC	ORN	PTR
12125	NC	ORN	PTR
12126	NC	ORN	PTR
12129	NC	NXA	PTR
12130	NC	ORN	PTR
12132	NC	NXA	PTR
12137	NC	ORN	PTR
12139	NC	ORN	PTR
12141	NC	ORN	PTR
12143	NC	ORN	PTR
12146	NC	NXA	PTR
12147	NC	ORN	PTR
12148	NC	ORN	PTR
12150	NC	ORN	PTR
12151	NC	ORN	PTR
12153	NC	NXA	PTR
12154	NC	ORN	PTR
12159	NC	ORN	PTR
12164	NC	ORN	PTR
12166	NC	ORN	PTR
12167	NC	ORN	PTR
12170	NC	ORN	PTR
12171	NC	ORN	PTR

NZAH - DVT

82102	NC	ORN	PTR
82103§	NC	ORN	PTR
82105	NC	ORN	PTR
82107	NC	NXA	PTR
82112	NC	ORN	PTR
82114	NC	ORN	PTR
82118	NC	NXA	PTR
82121	NC	ORN	PTR
82127	NC	ORN	PTR
82132	NC	ORN	PTR
82133	NC	ORN	PTR
82136	NC	ORN	PTR
82139	NC	ORN	PTR
82143	NC	NXA	PTR
82152	NC	ORN	PTR

§ Fitted with de-icing equipment

Left: *While mass repainting in the new Greater Anglia colours has not been forthcoming, some vehicles due through works have emerged in an all-white livery, offset by red doors and a black window banner. RFM No. 10229 shows the colour scheme at Norwich Crown Point in November 2012. This vehicle was rebuilt from FO No. 11059.*
Antony Christie

Class 153

	Vehicle Length: 76ft 5in (23.29m)	Engine: 1 x NT855R5 of 285hp
	Height: 12ft 3⅜in (3.75m)	Horsepower: 285hp (213kW)
	Width: 8ft 10in (2.70m)	Seats (total/car): 72S

Number	Formation DMSL	Depot	Livery	Owner	Operator	Name
153306	52306	NC	AWT	PTR	NXA	
153309	52309	NC	AWT	PTR	NXA	Gerard Fiennes
153314	52314	NC	ORN	PTR	NXA	
153322	52322	NC	AWT	PTR	NXA	Benjamin Britten
153335	52335	NC	AWT	PTR	NXA	Michael Palin

Above: *Abellio Greater Anglia operate a small fleet of five Class 153 'bubble' cars, allocated to Norwich Crown Point for local rural branch line use. Seen from its original cab end, set No. 153306, painted in Greater Anglia white and red livery, is seen stabled between duties at Ipswich.* **Antony Christie**

Class 156

	Vehicle Length: 75ft 6in (23.03m)	Engine: 1 x Cummins NT855R5 of 285hp
	Height: 12ft 6in (3.81m)	Horsepower: 570hp (425kW)
	Width: 8ft 11in (2.73m)	Seats (total/car): 146S, 70/76S

Number	Formation DMSL+DMS	Depot	Livery	Owner	Operator
156402	52402+57402	NC	AWT	PTR	NXA
156407	52407+57407	NC	ORN	PTR	NXA
156409	52409+57409	NC	ORN	PTR	NXA
156412	52412+57412	NC	ORN	PTR	NXA
156416	52416+57416	NC	ORN	PTR	NXA
156417	52417+57417	NC	ORN	PTR	NXA
156418	52418+57418	NC	ORN	PTR	NXA
156419	52419+57419	NC	NXA	PTR	NXA
156422	52422+57422	NC	AWT	PTR	NXA

Name applied
156409 *Cromer Pier Seaside Special*

Right: *Looking rather tatty and still showing signs of its original 'One Railway' livery, Class 156 No. 156422 carries bodyside branding 'Travel the East Suffolk Lines'. A total of nine Class 156s are operated by Greater Anglia, all allocated to Norwich Crown Point depot.* **Antony Christie**

Class 170/2
Turbostar

Vehicle Length: 77ft 6in (23.62m)			*Engine: 1 x MTU 6R 183TD13H 422hp per vehicle*			
Height: 12ft 4½in (3.77m)			*Horsepower: 1,266hp (944kW)*			
Width: 8ft 10in (2.69m)			*Seats (total/car): 7F-173S 7F-39S/68S/66S*			

Number	Formation	Depot	Livery	Owner	Operator
	DMCL+MSL+DMSL				
170201	50201+56201+79201	NC	ORN	PTR	NXA
170202	50202+56202+79202	NC	ORN	PTR	NXA
170203	50203+56203+79203	NC	ORN	PTR	NXA
170204	50204+56204+79204	NC	ORN	PTR	NXA
170205	50205+56205+79205	NC	ORN	PTR	NXA
170206	50206+56206+79206	NC	ORN	PTR	NXA
170207	50207+56207+79207	NC	ORN	PTR	NXA
170208	50208+56208+79208	NC	ORN	PTR	NXA

Vehicle Length: 77ft 6in (23.62m)			*Engine: 1 x MTU 6R 183TD13H 422hp per vehicle*			
Height: 12ft 4½in (3.77m)			*Horsepower: 844hp (629kW)*			
Width: 8ft 10in (2.69m)			*Seats (total/car): 9F-110S 57S/9F-53S*			

Number	Formation	Depot	Livery	Owner	Operator
	DMSL+DMCL				
170270	50270+79270	NC	ORN	PTR	NXA
170271	50271+79271	NC	ORN	PTR	NXA
170272	50272+79272	NC	ORN	PTR	NXA
170273	50273+79273	NC	ORN	PTR	NXA

Left: Greater Anglia operate both two- and three-car versions of the Class 170/2 'Turbostar'. Eight three-car and four two-car sets are allocated to Norwich Crown Point. Showing its 'as built' green and white colour scheme but with Greater Anglia branding, two-car set No. 170271 is seen departing from Bury St Edmunds on 26 October 2012. **Antony Christie**

Class 315

Vehicle Length: (Driving) 64ft 11½in (19.80m)		*Width: 9ft 3in (2.82m)*	
(Inter) 65ft 4½in (19.92m)		*Horsepower: 880hp (656kW)*	
Height: 11ft 6½in (3.58m)		*Seats (total/car): 318S, 74S/86S/84S/74S*	

Number	Formation	Depot	Livery	Owner	Operator	Name
	DMSO(A)+TSO+PTSO+DMSO(B)					
315801	64461+71281+71389+64462	IL	ORN	EVL	NXA	
315802	64463+71282+71390+64464	IL	ORN	EVL	NXA	
315803	64465+71283+71391+64466	IL	AWT	EVL	NXA	
315804	64467+71284+71392+64468	IL	AWT	EVL	NXA	
315805	64469+71285+71393+64470	IL	ORN	EVL	NXA	
315806	64471+71286+71394+64472	IL	AWT	EVL	NXA	
315807	64473+71287+71395+64474	IL	ORN	EVL	NXA	
315808	64475+71288+71396+64476	IL	ORN	EVL	NXA	
315809	64477+71289+71397+64478	IL	AWT	EVL	NXA	
315810	64479+71290+71398+64480	IL	ORN	EVL	NXA	
315811	64481+71291+71399+64482	IL	ORN	EVL	NXA	
315812	64483+71292+71400+64484	IL	AWT	EVL	NXA	
315813	64485+71293+71401+64486	IL	ORN	EVL	NXA	
315814	64487+71294+71402+64488	IL	ORN	EVL	NXA	
315815	64489+71295+71403+64490	IL	ORN	EVL	NXA	
315816	64491+71296+71404+64492	IL	ORN	EVL	NXA	
315817	64493+71297+71405+64494	IL	ORN	EVL	NXA	*Transport for London*
315818	64495+71298+71406+64496	IL	ORN	EVL	NXA	

315819	64497+71299+71407+64498	IL	ORN	EVL	NXA	
315820	64499+71300+71408+64500	IL	ORN	EVL	NXA	
315821	64501+71301+71409+64502	IL	ORN	EVL	NXA	
315822	64503+71302+71410+64504	IL	ORN	EVL	NXA	
315823	64505+71303+71411+64506	IL	ORN	EVL	NXA	
315824	64507+71304+71412+64508	IL	ORN	EVL	NXA	
315825	64509+71305+71413+64510	IL	ORN	EVL	NXA	
315826	64511+71306+71414+64512	IL	ORN	EVL	NXA	
315827	64513+71307+71415+64514	IL	ORN	EVL	NXA	
315828	64515+71308+71416+64516	IL	ORN	EVL	NXA	
315829	64517+71309+71417+64518	IL	ORN	EVL	NXA	*London Borough of Havering Celebrating 40 Years*
315830	64519+71310+71418+64520	IL	ORN	EVL	NXA	
315831	64521+71311+71419+64522	IL	ORN	EVL	NXA	
315832	64523+71312+71420+64524	IL	ORN	EVL	NXA	
315833	64525+71313+71421+64526	IL	ORN	EVL	NXA	
315834	64527+71314+71422+64528	IL	ORN	EVL	NXA	
315835	64529+71315+71423+64530	IL	ORN	EVL	NXA	
315836	64531+71316+71424+64532	IL	ORN	EVL	NXA	
315837	64533+71317+71425+64534	IL	ORN	EVL	NXA	
315838	64535+71318+71426+64536	IL	ORN	EVL	NXA	
315839	64537+71319+71427+64538	IL	ORN	EVL	NXA	
315840	64539+71320+71428+64540	IL	ORN	EVL	NXA	
315841	64541+71321+71429+64542	IL	ORN	EVL	NXA	
315842	64543+71322+71430+64544	IL	ORN	EVL	NXA	
315843	64545+71323+71431+64546	IL	ORN	EVL	NXA	
315844	64547+71324+71432+64548	IL	ORN	EVL	NXA	
315845	64549+71325+71433+64550	IL	ORN	EVL	NXA	*Herbie Woodward*
315846	64551+71326+71434+64552	IL	ORN	EVL	NXA	
315847	64553+71327+71435+64554	IL	ORN	EVL	NXA	
315848	64555+71328+71436+64556	IL	ORN	EVL	NXA	
315849	64557+71329+71437+64558	IL	ORN	EVL	NXA	
315850	64559+71330+71438+64560	IL	NXU	EVL	NXA	
315851	64561+71331+71439+64562	IL	ORN	EVL	NXA	
315852	64563+71332+71440+64564	IL	ORN	EVL	NXA	
315853	64565+71333+71441+64566	IL	ORN	EVL	NXA	
315854	64567+71334+71442+64568	IL	ORN	EVL	NXA	
315855	64569+71335+71443+64570	IL	ORN	EVL	NXA	
315856	64571+71336+71444+64572	IL	ORN	EVL	NXA	
315857	64573+71337+71445+64574	IL	ORN	EVL	NXA	
315858	64575+71338+71446+64576	IL	ORN	EVL	NXA	
315859	64577+71339+71447+64578	IL	ORN	EVL	NXA	
315860	64579+71340+71448+64580	IL	ORN	EVL	NXA	
315861	64581+71341+71449+64582	IL	ORN	EVL	NXA	

Right: *Abellio Greater Anglia's Great Eastern suburban network from London Liverpool Street is principally operated by a fleet of 61 four-car Class 315 units, based on the 1972-design of electric multiple-unit. The '315s' are allocated to Ilford depot and are scheduled to continue operation until replaced by new stock ordered for the Crossrail project. Set No. 315834 in Greater Anglia branded blue livery is seen at London Liverpool Street.*
Antony Christie

Greater Anglia

Class 317/5

			Vehicle Length: (Driving) 65ft 0¾in (19.83m)		Width: 9ft 3in (2.82m)			
			(Inter) 65ft 4¼in (19.92m)		Horsepower: 1,000hp (746kW)			
			Height: 12ft 1½in (3.58m)		Seats (total/car): 291S, 74S/79S/68S/70S			

Number	Former Number	Formation DTSO(A)+MSO+TCO+DTSO(B)	Depot	Livery	Owner	Operator	Name
317501	(317301)	77024+62661+71577+77048	IL	NXA	ANG	NXA	
317502	(317302)	77001+62662+71578+77049	IL	NXA	ANG	NXA	
317503	(317303)	77002+62663+71579+77050	IL	NXA	ANG	NXA	
317504	(317304)	77003+62664+71580+77051	IL	NXA	ANG	NXA	
317505	(317305)	77004+62665+71581+77052	IL	NXA	ANG	NXA	
317506	(317306)	77005+62666+71582+77053	IL	NXA	ANG	NXA	
317507	(317307)	77006+62667+71583+77054	IL	NXA	ANG	NXA	*University of Cambridge 800 years 1209-2009*
317508	(317311)	77010+62697+71587+77058	IL	NXA	ANG	NXA	
317509	(317312)	77011+62672+71588+77059	IL	NXA	ANG	NXA	
317510	(317313)	77012+62673+71589+77060	IL	NXA	ANG	NXA	
317511	(317315)	77014+62675+71591+77062	IL	NXU	ANG	NXA	
317512	(317316)	77015+62676+71592+77063	IL	NXU	ANG	NXA	
317513	(317317)	77016+62677+71593+77064	IL	NXA	ANG	NXA	
317514	(317318)	77017+62678+71594+77065	IL	NXA	ANG	NXA	
317515	(317320)	77019+62680+71596+77067	IL	NXA	ANG	NXA	

Class 317/6

			Vehicle Length: (Driving) 65ft 0¾in (19.83m)		Width: 9ft 3in (2.82m)			
			(Inter) 65ft 4¼in (19.92m)		Horsepower: 1,000hp (746kW)			
			Height: 12ft 1½in (3.58m)		Seats (total/car): 24F/244S, 64S/70S/62S/24F-48S			

Number	Former Number	Formation DTSO+MSO+TSO+DTCO	Depot	Livery	Owner	Operator	Name
317649	(317349)	77200+62846+71734+77220	IL	NXU	ANG	NXA	
317650	(317350)	77201+62847+71735+77221	IL	NXU	ANG	NXA	
317651	(317351)	77202+62848+71736+77222	IL	NXU	ANG	NXA	
317652	(317352)	77203+62849+71739+77223	IL	NXU	ANG	NXA	
317653	(317353)	77204+62850+71738+77224	IL	NXU	ANG	NXA	
317654	(317354)	77205+62851+71737+77225	IL	NXU	ANG	NXA	*Richard Wells*
317655	(317355)	77206+62852+71740+77226	IL	ORN	ANG	NXA	
317656	(317356)	77207+62853+71742+77227	IL	AWT	ANG	NXA	
317657	(317357)	77208+62854+71741+77228	IL	NXU	ANG	NXA	
317658	(317358)	77209+62855+71743+77229	IL	NXU	ANG	NXA	
317659	(317359)	77210+62856+71744+77230	IL	AWT	ANG	NXA	
317660	(317360)	77211+62857+71745+77231	IL	AWT	ANG	NXA	
317661	(317361)	77212+62858+71746+77232	IL	AWT	ANG	NXA	
317662	(317362)	77213+62859+71747+77233	IL	AWT	ANG	NXA	
317663	(317363)	77214+62860+71748+77234	IL	AWT	ANG	NXA	
317664	(317364)	77215+62861+71749+77235	IL	AWT	ANG	NXA	
317665	(317365)	77216+62862+71750+77236	IL	NXU	ANG	NXA	
317666	(317366)	77217+62863+71752+77237	IL	NXU	ANG	NXA	
317667	(317367)	77218+62864+71751+77238	IL	ORN	ANG	NXA	
317668	(317368)	77219+62865+71753+77239	IL	ORN	ANG	NXA	
317669	(317369)	77280+62886+71762+77284	IL	NXU	ANG	NXA	
317670	(317370)	77281+62887+71763+77285	IL	ORN	ANG	NXA	
317671	(317371)	77282+62888+71764+77286	IL	AWT	ANG	NXA	
317672	(317372)	77283+62889+71765+77287	IL	AWT	ANG	NXA	

Class 317/8

			Vehicle Length: (Driving) 65ft 0¾in (19.83m)		Width: 9ft 3in (2.82m)			
			(Inter) 65ft 4¼in (19.92m)		Horsepower: 1,000hp (746kW)			
			Height: 12ft 1½in (3.58m)		Seats (total/car): 20F/265S, 74S/79S/20F-42S/70S			

Number	Former Number	Formation DTSO(A)+MSO+TCO+DTSO(B)	Depot	Livery	Owner	Operator	Name
317881	(317321)	77020+62681+71597+77068	IL	NXA	ANG	NXA	
317882	(317324)	77023+62684+71600+77071	IL	NXU	ANG	NXA	
317883	(317325)	77000+62685+71601+77072	IL	NXU	ANG	NXA	
317884	(317326)	77025+62686+71602+77073	IL	NXU	ANG	NXA	
317885	(317327)	77026+62687+71603+77074	IL	NXU	ANG	NXA	
317886	(317328)	77027+62688+71604+77075	IL	NXU	ANG	NXA	
317887	(317330)	77043+62704+71606+77077	IL	NXU	ANG	NXA	

317888	(317331)	77030+62691+71607+77078	IL	NXA	ANG	NXA	
317889	(317333)	77032+62693+71609+77080	IL	NXA	ANG	NXA	
317890	(317334)	77033+62694+71610+77081	IL	NXA	ANG	NXA	
317891	(317335)	77034+62695+71611+77082	IL	NXA	ANG	NXA	
317892	(317336)	77035+62696+71612+77083	IL	NXA	ANG	NXA	*Ilford Depot*

Below: *Outer-suburban Greater Anglia services are operated by various sub-classes of Class 317s, with sets of both body style in operation. Set No. 317672 with car 77283 leading displays the latest Greater Anglia white and red livery. The set is seen traversing the East Coast main line while forming a GBRf charter from London to York.* **Ron Cover**

Class 321/3

Vehicle Length: (Driving) 65ft 0¾in (19.83m) Width: 9ft 3in (2.82m)
(Inter) 65ft 4¼in (19.92m) Horsepower: 1,328hp (996kW)
Height: 12ft 4¾in (3.78m) Seats (total/car): 16F/292S, 16F-57S/82S/75S/78S

Number	Formation DTCO+MSO+TSO+DTSO	Depot	Livery	Owner	Operator	Name
321301	78049+62975+71880+77853	IL	NXA	EVL	NXA	
321302	78050+62976+71881+77854	IL	NXA	EVL	NXA	
321303	78051+62977+71882+77855	IL	NXA	EVL	NXA	
321304	78052+62978+71883+77856	IL	NXA	EVL	NXA	
321305	78053+62979+71884+77857	IL	NXA	EVL	NXA	
321306	78054+62980+71885+77858	IL	NXA	EVL	NXA	
321307	78055+62981+71886+77859	IL	NXA	EVL	NXA	
321308	78056+62982+71887+77860	IL	NXA	EVL	NXA	
321309	78057+62983+71888+77861	IL	NXA	EVL	NXA	
321310	78058+62984+71889+77862	IL	NGE	EVL	NXA	
321311	78059+62985+71890+77863	IL	NXA	EVL	NXA	
321312	78060+62986+71891+77864	IL	NXA	EVL	NXA	*Southend-on-Sea*
321313	78061+62987+71892+77865	IL	NXA	EVL	NXA	*University of Essex*
321314	78062+62988+71893+77866	IL	NGE	EVL	NXA	
321315	78063+62989+71894+77867	IL	NXA	EVL	NXA	
321316	78064+62990+71895+77868	IL	NXA	EVL	NXA	
321317	78065+62991+71896+77869	IL	NXA	EVL	NXA	
321318	78066+62992+71897+77870	IL	NXA	EVL	NXA	
321319	78067+62993+71898+77871	IL	NXA	EVL	NXA	
321320	78068+62994+71899+77872	IL	NXA	EVL	NXA	
321321	78069+62995+71900+77873	IL	NXA	EVL	NXA	*NSPCC Essex Full Stop*
321322	78070+62996+71901+77874	IL	NXA	EVL	NXA	
321323	78071+62997+71902+77875	IL	NXA	EVL	NXA	
321324	78072+62998+71903+77876	IL	NXA	EVL	NXA	
321325	78073+62999+71904+77877	IL	NXA	EVL	NXA	
321326	78074+63000+71905+77878	IL	NXA	EVL	NXA	

Greater Anglia

321327	78075+63001+71906+77879	IL	NXU	EVL	NXA		
321328	78076+63002+71907+77880	IL	NXA	EVL	NXA		
321329	78077+63003+71908+77881	IL	NXA	EVL	NXA		
321330	78078+63004+71909+77882	IL	NXU	EVL	NXA		
321331	78079+63005+71910+77883	IL	NXU	EVL	NXA		
321332	78080+63006+71911+77884	IL	NXU	EVL	NXA		
321333	78081+63007+71912+77885	IL	NXU	EVL	NXA	*Amsterdam*
321334	78082+63008+71913+77886	IL	NXU	EVL	NXA		
321335	78083+63009+71914+77887	IL	NXU	EVL	NXA	*Geoffrey Freeman Allen*
321336	78084+63010+71915+77888	IL	NXU	EVL	NXA		
321337	78085+63011+71916+77889	IL	NXU	EVL	NXA		
321338	78086+63012+71917+77890	IL	NXU	EVL	NXA		
321339	78087+63013+71918+77891	IL	NXU	EVL	NXA		
321340	78088+63014+71919+77892	IL	NXU	EVL	NXA		
321341	78089+63015+71920+77893	IL	NXU	EVL	NXA		
321342	78090+63016+71921+77894	IL	NXU	EVL	NXA	*R Barnes*
321343	78091+63017+71922+77895	IL	NXU	EVL	NXA		
321344	78092+63018+71923+77896	IL	NXU	EVL	NXA		
321345	78093+63019+71924+77897	IL	NXU	EVL	NXA		
321346	78094+63020+71925+77898	IL	NGU	EVL	NXA		
321347	78131+63105+71991+78280	IL	NXU	EVL	NXA		
321348	78132+63106+71992+78281	IL	NXU	EVL	NXA		
321349	78133+63107+71993+78282	IL	NGE	EVL	NXA		
321350	78134+63108+71994+78283	IL	NXU	EVL	NXA	*Gurkha*
321351	78135+63109+71995+78284	IL	NXU	EVL	NXA	*London Southend Airport*
321352	78136+63110+71996+78285	IL	NXU	EVL	NXA		
321353	78137+63111+71997+78286	IL	NXU	EVL	NXA		
321354	78138+63112+71998+78287	IL	NXU	EVL	NXA		
321355	78139+63113+71999+78288	IL	NXU	EVL	NXA		
321356	78140+63114+72000+78289	IL	NGU	EVL	NXA		
321357	78141+63115+72001+78290	IL	NGE	EVL	NXA		
321358	78142+63116+72002+78291	IL	NXU	EVL	NXA		
321359	78143+63117+72003+78292	IL	AWT	EVL	NXA		
321360	78144+63118+72004+78293	IL	NXU	EVL	NXA	*Phoenix*
321361	78145+63119+72005+78294	IL	AWT	EVL	NXA		
321362	78146+63120+72006+78295	IL	AWT	EVL	NXA		
321363	78147+63121+72007+78296	IL	AWT	EVL	NXA		
321364	78148+63122+72008+78297	IL	AWT	EVL	NXA		
321365	78149+63123+72009+78298	IL	AWT	EVL	NXA		
321366	78150+63124+72010+78299	IL	AWT	EVL	NXA		

The core fleet for outer-suburban Greater Anglia services are Class 321s, with members of Class 321/3 and 321/4 in service from Ilford. Here we see set No. 321310 in unbranded National Express livery at Clacton in August 2012. The unit's DTSO vehicle is nearest the camera. **John Binch**

Right: *With Greater Anglia branding applied in the middle of the body, base white-liveried MSO No. 63001 from set No. 321327 is illustrated.*
Antony Christie

Class 321/4

Vehicle Length: (Driving) 65ft 0¾in (19.83m)   Width: 9ft 3in (2.82m)
(Inter) 65ft 4¼in (19.92m)   Horsepower: 1,328hp (996kW)
Height: 12ft 4¾in (3.78m)   Seats (total/car): 16F/283S, 16F-52S/79S/74S/78S

Number	Formation DTCO+MSO+TSO+DTSO	Depot	Livery	Owner	Operator	Name
321421	78115+63083+71969+77963	IL	NXU	EVL	NXA	
321422	78116+63084+71970+77964	IL	NXU	EVL	NXA	
321423	78117+63085+71971+77965	IL	NXU	EVL	NXA	
321424	78118+63086+71972+77966	IL	NXA	EVL	NXA	
321425	78119+63087+71973+77967	IL	AWT	EVL	NXA	
321426	78120+63088+71974+77968	IL	NXA	EVL	NXA	
321427	78121+63089+71975+77969	IL	NXA	EVL	NXA	
321428	78122+63090+71976+77970	IL	AWT	EVL	NXA	The Essex Commuter
321429	78123+69031+71977+77971	IL	NXA	EVL	NXA	
321430	78124+63092+71978+77972	IL	NXA	EVL	NXA	
321431	78151+63125+72011+78300	IL	NXA	EVL	NXA	
321432	78152+63126+72012+78301	IL	NXU	EVL	NXA	
321433	78153+63127+72013+78302	IL	NXU	EVL	NXA	
321434	78154+63128+72014+78303	IL	NXU	EVL	NXA	
321435	78155+63129+72015+78304	IL	NXU	EVL	NXA	
321436	78156+63130+72016+78305	IL	NXU	EVL	NXA	
321437	78157+63131+72017+78306	IL	NXU	EVL	NXA	
321438	78158+63132+72018+78307	IL	AWT	EVL	NXA	
321439	78159+63133+72019+78308	IL	AWT	EVL	NXA	
321440	78160+63134+72020+78309	IL	AWT	EVL	NXA	
321441	78161+63135+72021+78310	IL	AWT	EVL	NXA	
321442	78162+63136+72022+78311	IL	AWT	EVL	NXA	
321443	78125+63099+71985+78274	IL	AWT	EVL	NXA	
321444	78126+63100+71986+78275	IL	AWT	EVL	NXA	Essex Lifeboats
321445	78127+63101+71987+78276	IL	AWT	EVL	NXA	
321446	78128+63102+71988+78277	IL	AWT	EVL	NXA	George Mullings
321447	78129+63103+71989+78278	IL	AWT	EVL	NXA	
321448	78130+63104+71990+78279	IL	AWT	EVL	§	

§ To be used for fleet traction development work

Below: *The 2012 works overhaul for the Class 321s has been undertaken at Wabtec Doncaster, with sets emerging in all-over white livery offset by red doors and mid-body Greater Anglia branding. Class 321/4 No. 321443 is seen from its DTCO end.*
Ron Cover

Passenger Train Operating Companies - Greater Anglia

Greater Anglia

Class 360/1
Desiro

Vehicle Length: 66ft 9in (20.4m)
Height: 12ft 1½in (3.7m)
Width: 9ft 2in (2.79m)
Horsepower: 1,341hp (1,000kW)
Seats (total/car): 16F/265S, 8F-59S/69S/78S/8F-59S

Number	Formation	Depot	Livery	Owner	Operator
	DMCO(A)+PTSO+TSO+DMCO(B)				
360101	65551+72551+74551+68551	IL	FNA	ANG	NXA
360102	65552+72552+74552+68552	IL	FNA	ANG	NXA
360103	65553+72553+74553+68553	IL	FNA	ANG	NXA
360104	65554+72554+74554+68554	IL	FNA	ANG	NXA
360105	65555+72555+74555+68555	IL	FNA	ANG	NXA
360106	65556+72556+74556+68556	IL	FNA	ANG	NXA
360107	65557+72557+74557+68557	IL	FNA	ANG	NXA
360108	65558+72558+74558+68558	IL	FNA	ANG	NXA
360109	65559+72559+74559+68559	IL	FNA	ANG	NXA
360110	65560+72560+74560+68560	IL	FNA	ANG	NXA
360111	65561+72561+74561+68561	IL	FNA	ANG	NXA
360112	65562+72562+74562+68562	IL	FNA	ANG	NXA
360113	65563+72563+74563+68563	IL	FNA	ANG	NXA
360114	65564+72564+74564+68564	IL	FNA	ANG	NXA
360115	65565+72565+74565+68565	IL	ENA	ANG	NXA
360116	65566+72566+74566+68566	IL	FNA	ANG	NXA
360117	65567+72567+74567+68567	IL	FNA	ANG	NXA
360118	65568+72568+74568+68568	IL	FNA	ANG	NXA
360119	65569+72569+74569+68569	IL	FNA	ANG	NXA
360120	65570+72570+74570+68570	IL	FNA	ANG	NXA
360121	65571+72571+74571+68571	IL	FNA	ANG	NXA

Left: *Greater Anglia operate a fleet of 21 Class 360/1 Siemens 'Desiro' four-car express EMUs on outer-suburban routes. These high-quality sets based at Ilford were the first of the UK production 'Desiro' EMUs. Painted in as-delivered First Anglia blue livery, now sporting Greater Anglia branding, set No. 360120 passes Pudding Mill Lane station and approaches Stratford with an Ipswich-bound service.* **Antony Christie**

Class 379
Electrostar

Vehicle Length: (Driving) 66ft 9in (20.40m)
(Inter) 65ft 6in (19.99m)
Height: 12ft 4in (3.77m)
Width: 9ft 2in (2.80m)
Horsepower: 2,010hp (1,500kW)
Seats (total/car): 20F/189S, 60S/62S/43S/20F-24S

Number	Formation	Depot	Livery	Owner	Operator	Name
	DMSO(A)+MSO+TSO+DMCO					
379001	61201+61701+61901+62101	IL	NXU	MAG	NXA	
379002	61202+61702+61902+62102	IL	NXU	MAG	NXA	
379003	61203+61703+61903+62103	IL	NXU	MAG	NXA	
379004	61204+61704+61904+62104	IL	NXU	MAG	NXA	
379005	61205+61705+61905+62105	IL	NXU	MAG	NXA	*Stansted Express*
379006	61206+61706+61906+62106	IL	NXU	MAG	NXA	
379007	61207+61707+61907+62107	IL	NXU	MAG	NXA	
379008	61208+61708+61908+62108	IL	NXU	MAG	NXA	
379009	61209+61709+61909+62109	IL	NXU	MAG	NXA	
379010	61210+61710+61910+62110	IL	NXU	MAG	NXA	
379011	61211+61711+61911+62111	IL	NXU	MAG	NXA	*Ely Cathedral*
379012	61212+61712+61912+62112	IL	NXU	MAG	NXA	*The West Anglian*
379013	61213+61713+61913+62113	IL	NXU	MAG	NXA	
379014	61214+61714+61914+62114	IL	NXU	MAG	NXA	

379015	61215+61715+61915+62115	IL	NXU	MAG	NXA	*City of Cambridge*
379016	61216+61716+61916+62116	IL	NXU	MAG	NXA	
379017	61217+61717+61917+62117	IL	NXU	MAG	NXA	
379018	61218+61718+61918+62118	IL	NXU	MAG	NXA	
379019	61219+61719+61919+62119	IL	NXU	MAG	NXA	
379020	61220+61720+61920+62120	IL	NXU	MAG	NXA	
379021	61221+61721+61921+62121	IL	NXU	MAG	NXA	
379022	61222+61722+61922+62122	IL	NXU	MAG	NXA	
379023	61223+61723+61923+62123	IL	NXU	MAG	NXA	
379024	61224+61724+61924+62124	IL	NXU	MAG	NXA	
379025	61225+61725+61925+62125	IL	NXU	MAG	NXA	*Go Discover*
379026	61226+61726+61926+62126	IL	NXU	MAG	NXA	
379027	61227+61727+61927+62127	IL	NXU	MAG	NXA	
379028	61228+61728+61928+62128	IL	NXU	MAG	NXA	
379029	61229+61729+61929+62129	IL	NXU	MAG	NXA	
379030	61230+61730+61930+62130	IL	NXU	MAG	NXA	

Right & Below: *The most modern EMUs operated by Greater Anglia are 30 Bombardier-built 'Electrostar' sets for operation on longer distance services as well as on the Stansted Express service from London Liverpool Street to Stansted Airport. Set No. 379025 is illustrated below, sporting all-over white livery, blue passenger doors and Greater Anglia branding. On the right we see MSO No. 61725 which carries Stansted Express branding. Note the space between the second and third digits of the coach number. Both:* **Antony Christie**

Heathrow Express / Heathrow Connect

Address: ✉ 6th Floor, 50 Eastbourne Terrace, Paddington, London, W2 6LX

📠 queries@heathrowexpress.com or queries@heathrowconnect.com

☎ 020 8750 6600

ⓘ www.heathrowexpress.com or www.heathrowconnect.com

Managing Director: Richard Robinson

Franchise Dates: Private Open Access Operator

Principal Routes: London Paddington - Heathrow Airport

Owned Stations: Heathrow Central, Heathrow Terminal 4, Heathrow Terminal 5

Depots: Old Oak Common HEX (OH)

Parent Company: Heathrow Express - Heathrow Airport Ltd

Heathrow Connect - Heathrow Airport Ltd / First Group

Heathrow Express

Heathrow Airport Terminal 5 —— Heathrow Airport Terminals 1-3 —— London Paddington

Heathrow Connect

Heathrow Airport Terminal 4 —— Heathrow Airport Terminals 1-3 —— Hayes —— Southall —— Hanwell —— West Ealing —— Ealing Broadway —— London Paddington

Shuttle

Left: *The present major campaign for on-train advertising on the Heathrow Airport Ltd Heathrow Express Class 332 stock is with Vodafone. This deal sees one driving car of each Class 332 fully branded in Vodafone colours, plus advertising on the exterior of all coaches, plus interior adverts. Set No. 332013 displays this advertising stabled under the splendid Brunel roof at London Paddington station.*
Antony Christie

Class 332

Vehicle Length: (Driving) 77ft 10¾in (23.74m)   Width: 9ft 1in (2.75m)
(Inter) 75ft 11in (23.143m)   Horsepower: 1,876hp (1,400kW)
Height: 12ft 1½in (3.70m)   Seats 4-car (total/car): 26F-148S, 26F/56S/44S/48S
5-Car (total/car): 26F-204S, 26F/56S/44S/56S/48S

Number	Formation	Depot	Livery	Owner	Operator
	DMFO+TSO+PTSO+(TSO)+DMSO				
332001	78400+72412+63400+ - +78401	OH	HEX	BAA	HEX
332002	78402+72409+63401+ - +78403	OH	HEX‡	BAA	HEX
332003	78404+72407+63402+ - +78405	OH	HEX	BAA	HEX
332004	78406+72406+63403+ - +78407	OH	HEX‡	BAA	HEX
332005	78408+72411+63404+72417+78409	OH	HEX‡	BAA	HEX
332006	78410+72410+63405+72415+78411	OH	HEX‡	BAA	HEX
332007	78412+72401+63406+72414+78413	OH	HEX‡	BAA	HEX

Vehicle Length: (Driving) 77ft 10¾in (23.74m)   Width: 9ft 1in (2.75m)
(Inter) 75ft 11in (23.143m)   Horsepower: 1,876hp (1,400kW)
Height: 12ft 1½in (3.70m)   Seats 4-car (total/car): 14F-148S, 48S/56S/44S/14F
5-Car (total/car): 14F-204S, 48S/56S/44S/56S/14F

Number	Formation	Depot	Livery	Owner	Operator
	DMSO+TSO+PTSO+(TSO)+DMFLO				
332008	78414+72413+63407+72418+78415	OH	HEX‡	BAA	HEX
332009	78416+72400+63408+72416+78417	OH	HEX‡	BAA	HEX
332010	78418+72402+63409+ - +78419	OH	HEX	BAA	HEX
332011	78420+72403+63410+ - +78421	OH	HEX‡	BAA	HEX
332012	78422+72404+63411+ - +78423	OH	HEX	BAA	HEX
332013	78424+72408+63412+ - +78425	OH	HEX	BAA	HEX
332014	78426+72406+63413+ - +78427	OH	HEX‡	BAA	HEX

‡ First class vehicles carry Vodafone advertising livery

Class 360/2
Desiro

Vehicle Length: 66ft 9in (20.4m)   Horsepower: 1,341hp (1,000kW)
Height: 12ft 1½in (3.7m)   Seats (total/car): 340S, 63S/66S/74S/74S/63S
Width: 9ft 2in (2.79m)   (360205 - 280S using 2+2 seats)

Number	Formation	Depot	Livery	Owner	Operator	
	DMSO(A)+PTSO+TSO+TSO+DMSO(B)					**Below:** The half hourly interval
360201	78431+63421+72431+72421+78441	OH	HEC	BAA	HEC	stopping service between
360202	78432+63422+72432+72422+78442	OH	HEC	BAA	HEC	Heathrow Airport is operated by
360203	78433+63423+72433+72423+78443	OH	HEC	BAA	HEC	Class 360/2 sets. No. 360203 is
360204	78434+63424+72434+72424+78444	OH	HEC	BAA	HEC	seen at Paddington.
360205	78435+63425+72435+72425+78445	OH	HEL	BAA	HEC	**Antony Christie**

Island Line

Address: ✉ Ryde St Johns Road Station, Ryde, Isle of Wight, PO33 2BA
　　　　　　　🖳 info@island-line.co.uk
　　　　　　　✆ 01983 812591
　　　　　　　ⓘ www.island-line.co.uk
Managing Director: Tim Shoveller (South West Trains), **General Manager:** Andy Naylor
Franchise Dates:　Part of SWT franchise 2 February 2007 - 3 February 2017
Principal Route:　Ryde Pier Head - Shanklin
Owned Stations:　All
Depots:　Ryde St Johns Road (RY)
Parent Company:　Stagecoach

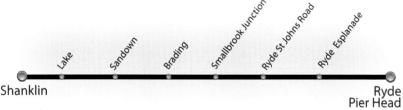

Class 483

Vehicle Length: 52ft 4in (15.95m)	Horsepower: 670hp (500kW)
Height: 9ft 5½in (2.88m)	Seats (total/car): 82S, 40S/42S
Width: 8ft 8½in (2.65m)	

Number	Formation DMSO+DMSO	Depot	Livery	Owner	Operator						
						483006	126+226	RY	LUL	SWT	SIL
						483007	127+227	RY	LUL	SWT	SIL
483002	122+224	RY	LUL	SWT	SIL	483008	128+228	RY	LUL	SWT	SIL
483004	124+224	RY	LUL	SWT	SIL	483009	129+229	RY	LUL	SWT	SIL

Below: *The isolated railway on the Isle of Wight uses six two-car Class 483 units, converted from former London Underground tube stock. Based at Ryde St Johns Road depot, usually only two or occasionally three sets in the high summer operate the daily service. In this view, set No. 006 (483006) traverses Ryde Pier in November 2012.* **Rob Kitley**

London Midland

Address:	✉ 102 New Street, Birmingham, B2 4JB
	✍ comments@londonmidland.com
	☎ 0844 811 0133
	ⓘ www.londonmidland.com
Managing Director:	Patrick Verwer
Franchise Dates:	11 November 2007 - 19 September 2015
Principal Routes:	London Euston - Liverpool Lime Street, West Midlands routes to Stratford, Worcester, Hereford, Shrewsbury, plus Bedford and St Albans Abbey branches
Depots:	Northampton (NN)*, Soho (SI), Tyseley (TS), Stourbridge Junction (SJ) * Operated by Siemens
Parent Company:	Govia

Class 08

Vehicle Length: 29ft 3in (8.91m)
Height: 12ft 8⅝in (3.87m)
Width: 8ft 6in (2.59m)

Engine: English Electric 6K
Horsepower: 400hp (298kW)
Electrical Equipment: English Electric

Number	Depot	Pool	Livery	Owner	Operator
08616 (3785)	TS	EJLO	LMI	LMI	LMI
08805	SI	EJLO	BLU	LMI	LMI

Names applied
08616 *Tyseley 100*   **08805** *Concorde*

Right: *Two Class 08s are owned and operated by London Midland; one is allocated to Tyseley and the other to Soho. The Tyseley loco, No. 08616, carries a version of London Midland livery complete with a cast numberplate 3785 (the loco's pre-TOPS number) and is named* Tyseley 100. **John Stretton**

Class 139

Vehicle Length: 28ft 6in (8.7m)
Width: 7ft 8in (2.4m)

Engine: 1 x MVH420 2.0ltr LPG, flywheel hybrid
Seats (total/car): 18S

Number	Formation DMS	Depot	Livery	Owner	Operator		Number	Formation	Depot	Livery	Owner	Operator
139001	39001	SJ	LMI	LMI	LMI		139002	39002	SJ	LMI	LMI	LMI

Right: *The Stourbridge Junction to Stourbridge Town branch 'shuttle' is operated by two Parry People Mover railcars. The cars are kept in a small single track 'depot' at Stourbridge Junction. The two, painted in full London Midland livery with Stourbridge Shuttle branding, are not allowed off the branch. Vehicle No. 139002 is illustrated at Stourbridge Town.* **Antony Christie**

Passenger Train Operating Companies - London Midland

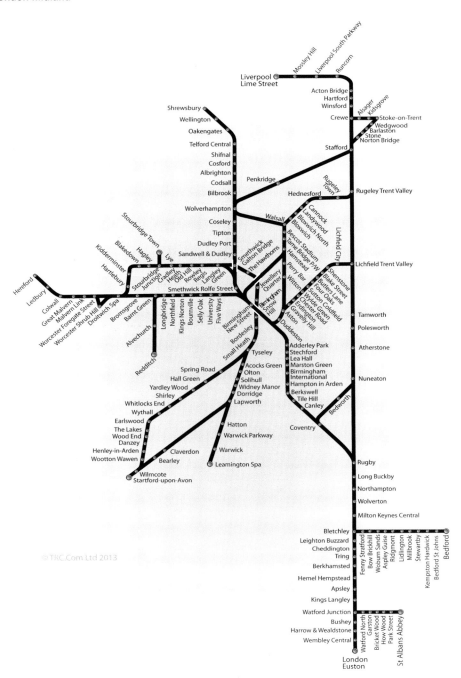

© TRC.Com Ltd 2013

Class 150/1

Vehicle Length: 64ft 9¾in (19.74m)
Height: 12ft 4½in (3.77m)
Width: 9ft 3⅛in (2.82m)

Engine: 1 x NT855R5 of 285hp per vehicle
Horsepower: 855hp (638kW)
Seats (total/car): 148S, 76S/72S

Number	Formation DMSL+DMS	Depot	Livery	Owner	Operator
150105	52105+57105	TS	CTL	ANG	LMI
150107	52107+57107	TS	CTL	ANG	LMI
150109	52109+57109	TS	CTL	ANG	LMI

Right: *London Midland retains three two-car Class 150/1 sets for rural branch line operations, such as the Bedford to Bletchley route. In late 2012 all three sets were refurbished and repainted in the latest London Midland livery by LNWR at Bristol Barton Hill. Set No. 150109 is seen at Woburn Sands on 7 November 2012.*
John Binch

Class 153

Vehicle Length: 76ft 5in (23.29m)
Height: 12ft 3⅛in (3.75m)
Width: 8ft 10in (2.70m)

Engine: 1 x NT855R5 of 285hp
Horsepower: 285hp (213kW)
Seats (total/car): 72S

Number	Formation DMSL	Depot	Livery	Owner	Operator
153334	52334	TS	LMI	PTR	LMI
153354	57354	TS	LMI	PTR	LMI
153356	57356	TS	LMI	PTR	LMI
153364	57364	TS	LMI	PTR	LMI
153365	57365	TS	LMI	PTR	LMI
153366	57366	TS	LMI	PTR	LMI
153371	57371	TS	LMI	PTR	LMI
153375	57375	TS	LMI	PTR	LMI

Right: *London Midland operates a fleet of eight Class 153 'bubble' cars on its lightly used services. All are allocated to Tyseley depot and carry London Midland livery. Set No. 153356 is illustrated at Nuneaton from its small cab end.*
Nathan Williamson

Class 170/5
Turbostar

Vehicle Length: 77ft 6in (23.62m)
Height: 12ft 4½in (3.77m)
Width: 8ft 10in (2.69m)

Engine: 1 x MTU 6R 183TD13H 422hp per vehicle
Horsepower: 844hp (629kW)
Seats (total/car): 122S 55S/67S

Number	Formation DMSL+DMSL	Depot	Livery	Owner	Operator
170501	50501+79501	TS	LMI	PTR	LMI
170502	50502+79502	TS	LMI	PTR	LMI
170503	50503+79503	TS	LMI	PTR	LMI
170504	50504+79504	TS	LMI	PTR	LMI
170505	50505+79505	TS	LMI	PTR	LMI
170506	50506+79506	TS	LMI	PTR	LMI
170507	50507+79507	TS	LMI	PTR	LMI
170508	50508+79508	TS	LMI	PTR	LMI

Passenger Train Operating Companies - London Midland

London Midland

170509	50509+79509	TS	LMI	PTR	LMI		170514	50514+79514	TS	LMI	PTR	LMI
170510	50510+79510	TS	LMI	PTR	LMI		170515	50515+79515	TS	LMI	PTR	LMI
170511	50511+79511	TS	LMI	PTR	LMI		170516	50516+79516	TS	LMI	PTR	LMI
170512	50512+79512	TS	LMI	PTR	LMI		170517	50517+79517	TS	LMI	PTR	LMI
170513	50513+79513	TS	LMI	PTR	LMI							

Class 170/6
Turbostar

			Vehicle Length: 77ft 6in (23.62m)			Engine: 1 x MTU 6R 183TD13H 422hp per vehicle
			Height: 12ft 4½in (3.77m)			Horsepower: 1,266hp (944kW)
			Width: 8ft 10in (2.69m)			Seats (total/car): 196S 55S/74S/67S

Number	Formation	Depot	Livery	Owner	Operator
	DMSL+MS+DMSL				
170630	50630+56630+79630	TS	LMI	PTR	LMI
170631	50631+56631+79631	TS	LMI	PTR	LMI
170632	50632+56632+79632	TS	LMI	PTR	LMI
170633	50633+56633+79633	TS	LMI	PTR	LMI
170634	50634+56634+79634	TS	LMI	PTR	LMI
170635	50635+56635+79635	TS	LMI	PTR	LMI

Left: *London Midland operates a fleet of 23 Class 170 'Turbostar' sets; 17 are formed as two-car units and six as three-car sets. All are allocated to Tyseley and in recent years have been refurbished internally. All units are in full London Midland livery. Three-car set No. 170635 is illustrated at Worcester.* **Antony Christie**

Class 172/2
Turbostar

			Vehicle Length: 73ft 4in (22.37m)			Engine: MTU 6H1800 of 360kW
			Height: 12ft 4½in (3.77m)			Horsepower: 965hp (720kW)
			Width: 8ft 8in (2.69m)			Seats (total/car): 121S, 53S/68S

Number	Formation	Depot	Livery	Owner	Operator							
	DMS+DMS					172216	50216+79216	TS	LMI	PTR	LMI	
						172217	50217+79217	TS	LMI	PTR	LMI	
172211	50211+79211	TS	LMI	PTR	LMI	172218	50218+79218	TS	LMI	PTR	LMI	
172212	50212+79212	TS	LMI	PTR	LMI	172219	50219+59219	TS	LMI	PTR	LMI	
172213	50213+79213	TS	LMI	PTR	LMI	172220	50220+79220	TS	LMI	PTR	LMI	
172214	50214+79214	TS	LMI	PTR	LMI	172221	50221+79221	TS	LMI	PTR	LMI	
172215	50215+79215	TS	LMI	PTR	LMI	172222	50222+79222	TS	LMI	PTR	LMI	

Left: *In 2011-12, London Midland upgraded its local traction fleet with the introduction of two batches of Bombardier 'Turbostar' Class 172 diesel-mechanical sets. Twelve two-car Class 172/2 sets and 15 three-car sets are allocated to Tyseley. The units are gangwayed throughout and after early teething troubles have settled down to perform well. On 26 September 2012, two-car set No. 172222 is viewed at Worcester.* **CJM**

Class 172/3
Turbostar

Vehicle Length: (Driving) 73ft 4in (22.37m)
(Inter): (76ft 7in 23.36m)
Height: 12ft 4½in (3.77m)
Width: 8ft 8in (2.69m)

Engine: MTU 6H1800 of 360kW
Horsepower: 1449hp (1080kW)
Seats (total/car): 193S, 53S/72S/68S

Number	Formation DMSO+MS+DMSO	Depot	Livery	Owner	Operator
172331	50331+56331+79331	TS	LMI	PTR	LMI
172332	50332+56332+79332	TS	LMI	PTR	LMI
172333	50333+56333+79333	TS	LMI	PTR	LMI
172334	50334+56334+79334	TS	LMI	PTR	LMI
172335	50335+56335+79335	TS	LMI	PTR	LMI
172336	50336+56336+79336	TS	LMI	PTR	LMI
172337	50337+56337+79337	TS	LMI	PTR	LMI
172338	50338+56338+79338	TS	LMI	PTR	LMI
172339	50339+56339+79339	TS	LMI	PTR	LMI
172340	50340+56340+79340	TS	LMI	PTR	LMI
172341	50341+56341+79341	TS	LMI	PTR	LMI
172342	50342+56342+79342	TS	LMI	PTR	LMI
172343	50343+56343+79343	TS	LMI	PTR	LMI
172344	50344+56344+79344	TS	LMI	PTR	LMI
172345	50345+56345+79345	TS	LMI	PTR	LMI

Class 321/4

Vehicle Length: (Driving) 65ft 0¾in (19.83m)
(Inter) 65ft 4¼in (19.92m)
Height: 12ft 4¾in (3.78m)

Width: 9ft 3in (2.82m)
Horsepower: 1,328hp (996kW)
Seats (total/car): 28F/271S, 28F-40S/79S/74S/78S

Number	Formation DMCO+MSO+TSO+DMSO	Depot	Livery	Owner	Operator
321411	78105+63073+71959+77953	NN	LMI	EVL	LMI
321412	78106+63074+71960+77954	NN	LMI	EVL	LMI
321413	78107+63075+71961+77955	NN	LMI	EVL	LMI
321414	78108+63076+71962+77956	NN	LMI	EVL	LMI
321415	78109+63077+71963+77957	NN	LMI	EVL	LMI
321416	78110+63078+71964+77958	NN	LMI	EVL	LMI
321417	78111+63079+71965+77959	NN	LMI	EVL	LMI

Right: *Even after the introduction of Class 350 stock, London Midland found a requirement to retain a small fleet of seven Class 321/4s working semi-fast and stopping services over the Northampton-Euston route, mainly during peak hours. Set No. 321411 is seen at London Euston.*
Antony Christie

Class 323

Vehicle Length: (Driving) 76ft 8¼in (23.37m)
(Inter) 76ft 10¾in (23.44m)
Height: 12ft 4¾in (3.78m)

Width: 9ft 2¼in (2.80m)
Horsepower: 1,565hp (1,168kW)
Seats (total/car): 284S, 98S/88S/98S

Number	Formation DMSO(A)+PTSO+DMSO(B)	Depot	Livery	Owner	Operator
323201	64001+72201+65001	SI	LMI	PTR	LMI
323202	64002+72202+65002	SI	LMI	PTR	LMI
323203	64003+72203+65003	SI	LMI	PTR	LMI
323204	64004+72204+65004	SI	LMI	PTR	LMI
323205	64005+72205+65005	SI	LMI	PTR	LMI
323206	64006+72206+65006	SI	LMI	PTR	LMI
323207	64007+72207+65007	SI	LMI	PTR	LMI
323208	64008+72208+65008	SI	LMI	PTR	LMI
323209	64009+72209+65009	SI	LMI	PTR	LMI
323210	64010+72210+65010	SI	LMI	PTR	LMI

London Midland

323211	64011+72211+65011	SI	LMI	PTR	LMI
323212	64012+72212+65012	SI	LMI	PTR	LMI
323213	64013+72213+65013	SI	LMI	PTR	LMI
323214	64014+72214+65014	SI	LMI	PTR	LMI
323215	64015+72215+65015	SI	LMI	PTR	LMI
323216	64016+72216+65016	SI	LMI	PTR	LMI
323217	64017+72217+65017	SI	LMI	PTR	LMI
323218	64018+72218+65018	SI	LMI	PTR	LMI
323219	64019+72219+65019	SI	LMI	PTR	LMI
323220	64020+72220+65020	SI	LMI	PTR	LMI
323221	64021+72221+65021	SI	LMI	PTR	LMI
323222	64022+72222+65022	SI	LMI	PTR	LMI
323240	64040+72340+65040	SI	LMI	PTR	LMI
323241	64041+72341+65041	SI	LMI	PTR	LMI
323242	64042+72342+65042	SI	LMI	PTR	LMI
323243	64043+72343+65043	SI	LMI	PTR	LMI

Left: *Now all painted in full London Midland livery, a fleet of 26 Class 323 three-car electric sets operate on the Birmingham Cross-City line linking Redditch with Lichfield via Birmingham city centre. These standard class only sets seat 284 in three vehicles, providing much of the local commuter network around Birmingham. Set No. 323203 is seen at Selly Oak.* **John Binch**

Class 350/1
Desiro

Vehicle Length: 66ft 9in (20.4m)
Height: 12ft 1½in (3.78m)
Width: 9ft 2in (2.7m)

Horsepower: 1,341hp (1,000kW)
Seats (total/car): 24F-209S, 60S/24F-32S/57S/60S

Number	Formation DMSO(A)+TCO+PTSO+DMSO(B)	Depot	Livery	Owner	Operator
350101	63761+66811+66861+63711	NN	LMI	ANG	LMI
350102	63762+66812+66862+63712	NN	LMI	ANG	LMI
350103	63765+66813+66863+63713	NN	LMI	ANG	LMI
350104	63764+66814+66864+63714	NN	LMI	ANG	LMI
350105	63763+66815+66868+63715	NN	LMI	ANG	LMI
350106	63766+66816+66866+63716	NN	LMI	ANG	LMI
350107	63767+66817+66867+63717	NN	LMI	ANG	LMI
350108	63768+66818+66865+63718	NN	LMI	ANG	LMI
350109	63769+66819+66869+63719	NN	LMI	ANG	LMI
350110	63770+66820+66870+63720	NN	LMI	ANG	LMI
350111	63771+66821+66871+63721	NN	LMI	ANG	LMI
350112	63772+66822+66872+63722	NN	LMI	ANG	LMI
350113	63773+66823+66873+63723	NN	LMI	ANG	LMI
350114	63774+66824+66874+63724	NN	LMI	ANG	LMI
350115	63775+66825+66875+63725	NN	LMI	ANG	LMI
350116	63776+66826+66876+63726	NN	LMI	ANG	LMI
350117	63777+66827+66877+63727	NN	LMI	ANG	LMI
350118	63778+66828+66878+63728	NN	LMI	ANG	LMI
350119	63779+66829+66879+63729	NN	LMI	ANG	LMI
350120	63780+66830+66880+63730	NN	LMI	ANG	LMI
350121	63781+66831+66881+63731	NN	LMI	ANG	LMI
350122	63782+66832+66882+63732	NN	LMI	ANG	LMI
350123	63783+66833+66883+63733	NN	LMI	ANG	LMI
350124	63784+66834+66884+63734	NN	LMI	ANG	LMI

Passenger Train Operating Companies - London Midland

350125	63785+66835+66885+63735	NN	LMI	ANG	LMI
350126	63786+66836+66886+63736	NN	LMI	ANG	LMI
350127	63787+66837+66887+63737	NN	LMI	ANG	LMI
350128	63788+66838+66888+63738	NN	LMI	ANG	LMI
350129	63789+66839+66889+63739	NN	LMI	ANG	LMI
350130	63790+66840+66890+63740	NN	LMI	ANG	LMI

Above: *Siemens Class 350 'Desiro' stock form the main train design operating for London Midland on its prime London Euston to West Midlands corridor. Two sub-classes exist. The 30 Class 350/1 sets are owned by Angel Trains, and have slightly less cramped interiors than the later Porterbrook-owned sets. All are based at Northampton. Set No. 350110 passes Tamworth Low Level on a service bound for London Euston on 16 August 2012.* **Antony Christie**

Class 350/2
Desiro

Vehicle Length: 66ft 9in (20.4m)
Height: 12ft 1½in (3.78m)
Width: 9ft 2in (2.7m)

Horsepower: 1,341hp (1,000kW)
Seats (total/car): 24F-243S, 70S/24F-42S/61S/70S

Number	Formation DMSO(A)+TCO+PTSO+DMSO(B)	Depot	Livery	Owner	Operator	Name
350231	61431+65231+67531+61531	NN	LMI	PTR	LMI	
350232	61432+65232+67532+61532	NN	LMI	PTR	LMI	*Chad Varah*
350233	61433+65233+67533+61533	NN	LMI	PTR	LMI	
350234	61434+65234+67534+61534	NN	LMI	PTR	LMI	
350235	61435+65235+67535+61535	NN	LMI	PTR	LMI	
350236	61436+65236+67536+61536	NN	LMI	PTR	LMI	
350237	61437+65237+67537+61537	NN	LMI	PTR	LMI	
350238	61438+65238+67538+61538	NN	LMI	PTR	LMI	
350239	61439+65239+67539+61539	NN	LMI	PTR	LMI	
350240	61440+65240+67540+61540	NN	LMI	PTR	LMI	
350241	61441+65241+67541+61541	NN	LMI	PTR	LMI	
350242	61442+65242+67542+61542	NN	LMI	PTR	LMI	
350243	61443+65243+67543+61543	NN	LMI	PTR	LMI	
350244	61444+65244+67544+61544	NN	LMI	PTR	LMI	
350245	61445+65245+67545+61545	NN	LMI	PTR	LMI	
350246	61446+65246+67546+61546	NN	LMI	PTR	LMI	
350247	61447+65247+67547+61547	NN	LMI	PTR	LMI	
350248	61448+65248+67548+61548	NN	LMI	PTR	LMI	
350249	61449+65249+67549+61549	NN	LMI	PTR	LMI	
350250	61450+65250+67550+61550	NN	LMI	PTR	LMI	
350251	61451+65251+67551+61551	NN	LMI	PTR	LMI	
350252	61452+65252+67552+61552	NN	LMI	PTR	LMI	

London Midland

350253	61453+65253+67553+61553	NN	LMI	PTR	LMI
350254	61454+65254+67554+61554	NN	LMI	PTR	LMI
350255	61455+65255+67555+61555	NN	LMI	PTR	LMI
350256	61456+65256+67556+61556	NN	LMI	PTR	LMI
350257	61457+65257+67557+61557	NN	LMI	PTR	LMI
350258	61458+65258+67558+61558	NN	LMI	PTR	LMI
350259	61459+65259+67559+61559	NN	LMI	PTR	LMI
350260	61460+65260+67560+61560	NN	LMI	PTR	LMI
350261	61461+65261+67561+61561	NN	LMI	PTR	LMI
350262	61462+65262+67562+61562	NN	LMI	PTR	LMI
350263	61463+65263+67563+61563	NN	LMI	PTR	LMI
350264	61464+65264+67564+61564	NN	LMI	PTR	LMI
350265	61465+65265+67565+61565	NN	LMI	PTR	LMI
350266	61466+65266+67566+61566	NN	LMI	PTR	LMI
350267	61467+65267+67567+61567	NN	LMI	PTR	LMI

Above: *The second batch of 37 Class 350 'Desiro' sets operated by London Midland are owned by Porterbrook and have a higher seating level, more in keeping with a suburban unit. These sets can be identified by having the upper section of the front gangway doors painted in black. Set No. 350262 is seen heading south on the West Coast main line, passing Cathiron north of Rugby.* **Antony Christie**

Class 350/4
Desiro

Vehicle Length: 66ft 9in (20.4m)
Height: 12ft 1½in (3.78m)
Width: 9ft 2in (2.7m)

Horsepower: 1,341hp (1,000kW)
Seats (total/car): 191S/19F

Number	Formation	Depot	Livery	Owner	Operator
	DMSO(A)+TCO+PTSO+DMSO(B)				
350401	On order	NN	LMI	ANG	LMI
350402	On order	NN	LMI	ANG	LMI
350403	On order	NN	LMI	ANG	LMI
350404	On order	NN	LMI	ANG	LMI
350405	On order	NN	LMI	ANG	LMI
350406	On order	NN	LMI	ANG	LMI
350407	On order	NN	LMI	ANG	LMI
350408	On order	NN	LMI	ANG	LMI
350409	On order	NN	LMI	ANG	LMI
350410	On order	NN	LMI	ANG	LMI

London Overground

Address: ✉ 125 Finchley Road, London, NW3 6HY
 ✍ overgroundinfo@tfl.gov.uk
 ✆ 0845 601 4867
 ⓘ www.tfl.gov.uk/overground

Managing Director: Steve Murphy
Principal Routes: Clapham Junction - Willesden, Richmond - Stratford
 Gospel Oak - Barking, Euston - Watford
 East London Line – Dalston - West Croydon
Depots: Willesden (WN) New Cross Gate (NX)
Parent Company: Transport for London

Passenger Train Operating Companies - London Overground

London Overground

Class 09/0

Vehicle Length: 29ft 3in (8.91m)			Engine: English Electric 6K		
Height: 12ft 8⅝in (3.87m)			Horsepower: 400hp (298kW)		
Width: 8ft 6in (2.59m)			Electrical Equipment: English Electric		

Number	Depot	Pool	Livery	Owner	Operator
09007	WN	-	GRN	LOL	LOL

Right: *Transport for London - London Overground own and operate just one diesel loco, Class 09/0 No. 09007, which they purchased from DB Schenker. The loco now repainted in green livery is based at Willesden depot and is frequently used for depot shunting operations.* **Antony Christie**

Class 172/0
Turbostar

Vehicle Length: 73ft 4in (22.37m)		Engine: MTU 6H1800R83 of 360kW (483hp)	
Height: 12ft 4½in (3.77m)		Horsepower: 965hp (720kW)	
Width: 8ft 8in (2.69m)		Seats (total/car): 124S, 60S/64S	

Number	Formation DMS+DMS	Depot	Livery	Owner	Operator
172001	59311+59411	WN	LOG	ANG	LOG
172002	59312+59412	WN	LOG	ANG	LOG
172003	59313+59413	WN	LOG	ANG	LOG
172004	59314+59414	WN	LOG	ANG	LOG
172005	59315+59415	WN	LOG	ANG	LOG
172006	59316+59416	WN	LOG	ANG	LOG
172007	59317+59417	WN	LOG	ANG	LOG
172008	59318+59418	WN	LOG	ANG	LOG

Left: *London Overground operate a fleet of eight two-car Bombardier-built Class 172/0 'Turbostar' diesel-mechanical sets on the Gospel Oak to Barking non-electrified route. The units, with 2+2 low-density seating, do not have corridor ends and are frequently overcrowded. TfL have now gone out to tender for replacement trains with greater capacity. The '172s' will then be displaced. Set No. 172006 is seen in the bay at Gospel Oak with a morning departure to Barking.* **CJM**

Class 378/1
Capitalstar

Vehicle Length: (Driving) (20.46m), (Inter) (20.14m)	Width: 9ft 2in (2.80m)		
Height: 11ft 9in (3.58m)	Horsepower: 4-car (1,500kW)		
750V dc sets	Seats (total/car): 146S, 36S/40S/34S/36S		

Number	Formation DMSO+MSO+TSO+DMSO	Depot	Livery	Owner	Operator
378135	38035+38235+38335+38135	NX	LOG	QWR	LOG
378136	38036+38236+38336+38136	NX	LOG	QWR	LOG
378137	38037+38237+38337+38137	NX	LOG	QWR	LOG
378138	38038+38238+38338+38138	NX	LOG	QWR	LOG
378139	38039+38239+38339+38139	NX	LOG	QWR	LOG
378140	38040+38240+38340+38140	NX	LOG	QWR	LOG
378141	38041+38241+38341+38141	NX	LOG	QWR	LOG
378142	38042+38242+38342+38142	NX	LOG	QWR	LOG
378143	38043+38243+38343+38143	NX	LOG	QWR	LOG
378144	38044+38244+38344+38144	NX	LOG	QWR	LOG
378145	38045+38245+38345+38145	NX	LOG	QWR	LOG
378146	38046+38246+38346+38146	NX	LOG	QWR	LOG
378147	38047+38247+38347+38147	NX	LOG	QWR	LOG
378148	38048+38248+38348+38148	NX	LOG	QWR	LOG
378149	38049+38249+38349+38149	NX	LOG	QWR	LOG
378150	38050+38250+38350+38150	NX	LOG	QWR	LOG
378151	38051+38251+38351+38151	NX	LOG	QWR	LOG
378152	38052+38252+38352+38152	NX	LOG	QWR	LOG
378153	38053+38253+38353+38153	NX	LOG	QWR	LOG
378154	38054+38254+38354+38154	NX	LOG	QWR	LOG

Sets 378150-378154 fitted with de-icing equipment

Class 378/2
Capitalstar

Vehicle Length: (Driving) (20.46m), (Inter) (20.14m)	Width: 9ft 2in (2.80m)			
Height: 11ft 9in (3.58m)	Horsepower: 4-car 2,010hp (1,500kW)			
Dual voltage - 750V dc third rail and 25kV ac overhead	Seats (total/car): 146S, 36S/40S/34S/36S			

Sets built as 3-car units as Class 378/0, MSO added and reclassified as 378/2

Number	Formation DMSO+MSO+PTSO+DMSO	Depot	Livery	Owner	Operator
378201 (378001)	38001+38201+38301+38101	WN	LOG	QWR	LOG
378202 (378002)	38002+38202+38302+38102	WN	LOG	QWR	LOG
378203 (378003)	38003+38203+38303+38103	WN	LOG	QWR	LOG
378204 (378004)	38004+38204+38304+38104	WN	LOG	QWR	LOG
378205 (378005)	38005+38205+38305+38105	WN	LOG	QWR	LOG
378206 (378006)	38006+38206+38306+38106	WN	LOG	QWR	LOG
378207 (378007)	38007+38207+38307+38107	WN	LOG	QWR	LOG
378208 (378008)	38008+38208+38308+38108	WN	LOG	QWR	LOG
378209 (378009)	38009+38209+38309+38109	WN	LOG	QWR	LOG
378210 (378010)	38010+38210+38310+38110	WN	LOG	QWR	LOG
378211 (378011)	38011+38211+38311+38111	WN	ADV‡	QWR	LOG
378212 (378012)	38012+38212+38312+38112	WN	LOG	QWR	LOG
378213 (378013)	38013+38213+38313+38113	WN	LOG	QWR	LOG
378214 (378014)	38014+38214+38314+38114	WN	LOG	QWR	LOG
378215 (378015)	38015+38215+38315+38115	WN	LOG	QWR	LOG
378216 (378016)	38016+38216+38316+38116	WN	LOG	QWR	LOG
378217 (378017)	38017+38217+38317+38117	WN	LOG	QWR	LOG
378218 (378018)	38018+38218+38318+38118	WN	LOG	QWR	LOG
378219 (378019)	38019+38219+38319+38119	WN	LOG	QWR	LOG
378220 (378020)	38020+38220+38320+38120	WN	LOG	QWR	LOG
378221 (378021)	38021+38221+38321+38121	WN	ADV‡	QWR	LOG
378222 (378022)	38022+38222+38322+38122	WN	LOG	QWR	LOG
378223 (378023)	38023+38223+38323+38123	WN	LOG	QWR	LOG
378224 (378024)	38024+38224+38324+38124	WN	LOG	QWR	LOG

Sets 378216-378220 fitted with de-icing equipment

Number	Formation DMSO+MSO+TSO+DMSO	Depot	Livery	Owner	Operator	Name
378225	38025+38225+38325+38125	NX	LOG	QWR	LOG	
378226	38026+38226+38326+38126	NX	LOG	QWR	LOG	
378227	38027+38227+38327+38127	NX	LOG	QWR	LOG	
378228	38028+38228+38328+38128	NX	LOG	QWR	LOG	
378229	38029+38229+38329+38129	NX	LOG	QWR	LOG	
378230	38030+38230+38330+38130	NX	LOG	QWR	LOG	
378231	38031+38231+38331+38131	NX	LOG	QWR	LOG	
378232	38032+38232+38332+38132	NX	LOG	QWR	LOG	
378233	38033+38233+38333+38133	NX	LOG	QWR	LOG	*Ian Brown CBE*
378234	38034+38234+38334+38134	NX	LOG	QWR	LOG	
378255	38055+38255+38355+38155	NX	LOG	QWR	LOG	
378256	38056+38256+38356+38156	NX	LOG	QWR	LOG	
378257	38057+38257+38357+38157	NX	LOG	QWR	LOG	

ADV‡ Lycamobile livery

Right: *The four-car Class 378 stock built by Bombardier are a cross between an Underground train and a suburban unit, with a high-capacity layout offering few seats and lots of standing room. Two types exist: those fitted for only dc third rail operation and those fitted with dual voltage equipment able to operate on 25kV ac overhead and 750V dc third rail. Dual voltage set No. 378214 is seen on a Euston to Watford service at Willesden Junction Low Level.* **Antony Christie**

Passenger Train Operating Companies - London Overground

Merseyrail

Address: ✉ Rail House, Lord Nelson Street, Liverpool, L1 1JF
✍ comment@merseyrail.org
☎ 0151 702 2534
ⓘ www.merseyrail.org

Managing Director: Maarten Spaargaren
Franchise Dates: 20 July 2003 - 19 July 2028
Principal Routes: All non-main line services
in Liverpool area
Depots: Birkenhead North (BD)
Parent Company: Serco / Abellio

Passenger Train Operating Companies - Merseyrail

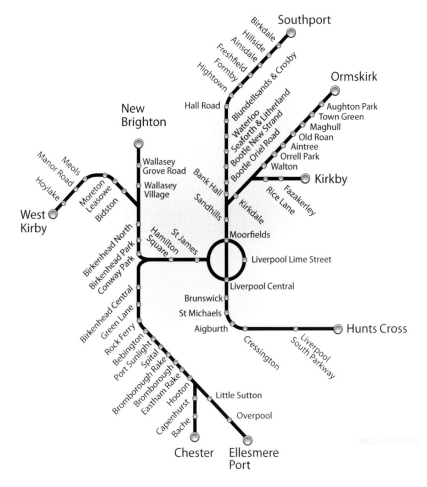

Class 507

Vehicle Length: (Driving) 64ft 11½in (19.80m)	Width: 9ft 3in (2.82m)	
(Inter) 65ft 4¼in (19.92m)	Horsepower: 880hp (656kW)	
Height: 11ft 6½in (3.58m)	Seats (total/car): 186S, 56S/74S/56S	

Number	Formation DMSO+TSO+DMSO	Depot	Livery	Owner	Operator	Name
507001	64367+71342+64405	BD	MER	ANG	MER	
507002	64368+71343+64406	BD	ADV§	ANG	MER	
507003	64369+71344+64407	BD	MER	ANG	MER	
507004	64388+71345+64408	BD	MER	ANG	MER	Bob Paisley
507005	64371+71346+64409	BD	MER	ANG	MER	
507006	64372+71347+64410	BD	MER	ANG	MER	
507007	64373+71348+64411	BD	MER	ANG	MER	
507008	64374+71349+64412	BD	MER	ANG	MER	
507009	64375+71350+64413	BD	MER	ANG	MER	Dixie Dean
507010	64376+71351+64414	BD	MER	ANG	MER	
507011	64377+71352+64415	BD	MER	ANG	MER	
507012	64378+71353+64416	BD	MER	ANG	MER	
507013	64379+71354+64417	BD	MER	ANG	MER	
507014	64380+71355+64418	BD	MER	ANG	MER	
507015	64381+71356+64419	BD	MER	ANG	MER	
507016	64382+71357+64420	BD	MER	ANG	MER	
507017	64383+71358+64421	BD	MER	ANG	MER	
507018	64384+71359+64422	BD	MER	ANG	MER	
507019	64385+71360+64423	BD	MER	ANG	MER	
507020	64386+71361+64424	BD	MER	ANG	MER	John Peel
507021	64387+71362+64425	BD	MER	ANG	MER	Red Rum
507023	64389+71364+64427	BD	MER	ANG	MER	Operating Inspector Stuart Mason
507024	64390+71365+64428	BD	MER	ANG	MER	
507025	64391+71366+64429	BD	MER	ANG	MER	
507026	64392+71367+64430	BD	MER	ANG	MER	
507027	64393+71368+64431	BD	MER	ANG	MER	
507028	64394+71369+64432	BD	MER	ANG	MER	
507029	64395+71370+64433	BD	MER	ANG	MER	
507030	64396+71371+64434	BD	MER	ANG	MER	
507031	64397+71372+64435	BD	MER	ANG	MER	
507032	64398+71373+64436	BD	MER	ANG	MER	
507033	64399+71374+64437	BD	MER	ANG	MER	Councillor Jack Spriggs

§ advertising livery - Hope University

Merseyrail currently operates a fleet of 32 Class 507 three-car third-rail electric sets, all carrying silver and yellow livery. Set No. 507017 is seen at Sandhills with a Kirkby-Liverpool service. **Murdoch Currie**

Merseyrail

Class 508/1

Vehicle Length: (Driving) 64ft 11½in (19.80m)		Width: 9ft 3in (2.82m)		
(Inter) 65ft 4¼in (19.92m)		Horsepower: 880hp (656kW)		
Height: 11ft 6½in (3.58m)		Seats (total/car): 186S, 56S/74S/56S		

Number	Formation DMSO+TSO+DMSO	Depot	Livery	Owner	Operator	Name
508103	64651+71485+64694	BD	MER	ANG	MER	
508104	64652+71486+64964	BD	MER	ANG	MER	
508108	64656+71490+64699	BD	MER	ANG	MER	
508110	64658+71492+64701	BD	MER	ANG	MER	
508111	64659+71493+64702	BD	SPL	ANG	MER	*The Beatles*
508112	64660+71494+64703	BD	MER	ANG	MER	
508114	64662+71496+64705	BD	MER	ANG	MER	
508115	64663+71497+64708	BD	MER	ANG	MER	
508117	64665+71499+64908	BD	MER	ANG	MER	
508120	64668+71502+64711	BD	MER	ANG	MER	
508122	64670+71504+64713	BD	MER	ANG	MER	
508123	64671+71505+64714	BD	MER	ANG	MER	
508124	64672+71506+64715	BD	MER	ANG	MER	
508125	64673+71507+64716	BD	MER	ANG	MER	
508126	64674+71508+64717	BD	MER	ANG	MER	
508127	64675+71509+64718	BD	MER	ANG	MER	
508128	64676+71510+64719	BD	MER	ANG	MER	
508130	64678+71512+64721	BD	MER	ANG	MER	
508131	64679+71513+64722	BD	MER	ANG	MER	
508134	64682+71516+64725	BD	MER	ANG	MER	
508136	64684+71518+64727	BD	MER	ANG	MER	
508137	64685+71519+64728	BD	MER	ANG	MER	
508138	64686+71520+64729	BD	MER	ANG	MER	
508139	64687+71521+64730	BD	MER	ANG	MER	
508140	64688+71522+64731	BD	MER	ANG	MER	
508141	64689+71523+64732	BD	MER	ANG	MER	
508143	64691+71525+64734	BD	MER	ANG	MER	

Above: *Delivered new to the Southern Region, the Class 508 sets were transferred to the Merseyrail network to work alongside the Class 507s. Refurbished with revised cab ends, Class 508/1 No. 508139 is seen at Ellesmere Port with a service to Liverpool.* **Murdoch Currie**

Northern Rail

Address:	✉ Northern House, 9 Rougier Street, York, YO1 6HZ
	✆ customer.relations@northernrail.org
	✆ 0845 000125
	ⓘ www.northernrail.org
Managing Director:	Ian Bevan
Franchise Dates:	12 December 2004 - 31 March 2014
Principal Routes:	Regional services in Merseyside, Greater Manchester, South/ North Yorkshire, Lancashire, Cumbria and the North East
Depots:	Newton Heath (NH), Heaton (HT), Longsight (LG), Neville Hill (NL), Allerton (AN)
Parent Company:	Serco/Abellio

Class 142

Vehicle Length: 51ft 0½in (15.55m)
Height: 12ft 8in (3.86m)
Width: 9ft 2¼in (2.80m)
Engine: 1 x Cummins LTA10-R per vehicle
Horsepower: 460hp (343kW)
Seats (total/car): 106S, 56S/50S

Number	Formation DMS+DMSL	Depot	Livery	Owner	Operator
142001	55542+55592	NH	NOU	ANG	NOR
142003	55544+55594	NH	NOR	ANG	NOR
142004	55545+55595	NH	NOR	ANG	NOR
142005	55546+55596	NH	NOR	ANG	NOR
142007	55548+55598	NH	NOR	ANG	NOR
142009	55550+55600	NH	NOU	ANG	NOR
142011	55552+55602	NH	NOR	ANG	NOR
142012	55553+55603	NH	NOR	ANG	NOR
142013	55554+55604	NH	NOR	ANG	NOR
142014	55555+55605	NH	NOR	ANG	NOR
142015	55556+55606	HT	NOR	ANG	NOR
142016	55557+55607	HT	NOR	ANG	NOR
142017	55558+55608	HT	NOR	ANG	NOR
142018	55559+55609	HT	NOR	ANG	NOR
142019	55560+55610	HT	NOR	ANG	NOR
142020	55561+55611	HT	NOR	ANG	NOR
142021	55562+55612	HT	NOR	ANG	NOR
142022	55563+55613	HT	NOR	ANG	NOR
142023	55564+55614	NH	NOR	ANG	NOR
142024	55565+55615	HT	NOR	ANG	NOR
142025	55566+55616	HT	NOR	ANG	NOR
142026	55567+55617	HT	NOR	ANG	NOR
142027	55568+55618	NH	NOR	ANG	NOR
142028	55569+55619	NH	NOR	ANG	NOR
142029	55570+55620	NH	NOU	ANG	NOR
142030	55571+55621	NH	NOU	ANG	NOR
142031	55572+55622	NH	NOR	ANG	NOR
142032	55573+55623	NH	NOR	ANG	NOR
142033	55574+55624	NH	NOR	ANG	NOR
142034	55575+55625	HT	NOR	ANG	NOR
142035	55576+55626	NH	NOR	ANG	NOR
142036	55577+55627	NH	NOR	ANG	NOR
142037	55578+55628	NH	NOR	ANG	NOR
142038	55579+55629	NH	NOR	ANG	NOR
142039	55580+55630	NH	NOR	ANG	NOR
142040	55581+55631	NH	NOR	ANG	NOR
142041	55582+55632	NH	NOR	ANG	NOR
142042(S)	55583+55633	NH	NOR	ANG	NOR
142043	55584+55634	NH	NOR	ANG	NOR
142044	55585+55635	NH	NOR	ANG	NOR
142045	55586+55636	NH	NOR	ANG	NOR
142046	55587+55637	NH	NOR	ANG	NOR
142047	55588+55638	NH	NOR	ANG	NOR
142048	55589+55639	NH	NOR	ANG	NOR
142049	55590+55640	NH	NOR	ANG	NOR
142050	55591+55641	HT	NOR	ANG	NOR
142051	55701+55747	NH	NOR	ANG	NOR
142052	55702+55748	NH	NOR	ANG	NOR
142053	55703+55749	NH	NOR	ANG	NOR
142054	55704+55750	NH	NOR	ANG	NOR
142055	55705+55751	NH	NOR	ANG	NOR
142056	55706+55752	NH	NOR	ANG	NOR
142057	55707+55753	NH	NOR	ANG	NOR
142058	55708+55754	NH	NOR	ANG	NOR
142060	55710+55756	NH	NOR	ANG	NOR
142061	55711+55757	NH	NOR	ANG	NOR
142062	55712+55758	NH	NOR	ANG	NOR
142063	55713+55759	NH	NOU	ANG	NOR
142064	55714+55760	NH	NOU	ANG	NOR
142065	55715+55761	HT	NOR	ANG	NOR
142066	55716+55762	HT	NOR	ANG	NOR
142067	55717+55763	NH	NOR	ANG	NOR
142068	55718+55764	NH	NOU	ANG	NOR
142070	55720+55766	HT	NOR	ANG	NOR
142071	55721+55767	HT	NOR	ANG	NOR
142078	55728+55768	HT	NOR	ANG	NOR
142079	55729+55769	HT	NOR	ANG	NOR
142084	55764+55780	HT	NOR	ANG	NOR
142086	55736+55782	HT	NOR	ANG	NOR
142087	55737+55783	HT	NOR	ANG	NOR
142088	55738+55784	HT	NOR	ANG	NOR
142089	55739+55785	HT	NOR	ANG	NOR
142090	55740+55786	HT	NOR	ANG	NOR
142091	55741+55787	HT	NOR	ANG	NOR
142092	55742+55788	HT	NOR	ANG	NOR
142093	55743+55789	HT	NOR	ANG	NOR
142094	55744+55790	HT	NOR	ANG	NOR
142095	55745+55791	HT	NOR	ANG	NOR
142096	55746+55792	HT	NOR	ANG	NOR

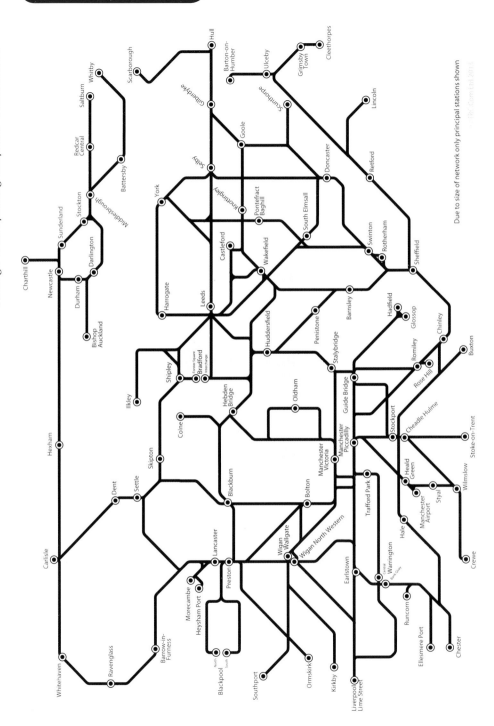

Passenger Train Operating Companies - Northern Rail

Due to size of network only principal stations shown

Right: *Northern Rail is the largest operator of Class 142 'Pacer' stock, with 79 sets based at either Newton Heath (Manchester) or Heaton (Newcastle). All sets carry the standard Northern 'Pacer' livery of base blue onto which mauve and grey vinyls are applied together with the Northern branding. Set No. 142061 is seen at Preston.* **Robin Ralston**

Class 144

					Vehicle Length: 50ft 2in (15.25m)				Engine: 1 x Cummins LTA10-R per vehicle		
					Height: 12ft 2½in (3.73m)				Horsepower: 460hp (343kW)		
					Width: 8ft 10½in (2.70m)				Seats (total/car): 87S, 45S/42S		

Number	Formation DMS+DMSL	Depot	Livery	Owner	Operator
144001	55801+55824	NL	NOR	PTR	NOR
144002	55802+55825	NL	NOR	PTR	NOR
144003	55803+55826	NL	NOR	PTR	NOR
144004	55804+55827	NL	NOR	PTR	NOR
144005	55805+55828	NL	NOR	PTR	NOR
144006	55806+55829	NL	NOR	PTR	NOR
144007	55807+55830	NL	NOR	PTR	NOR
144008	55808+55831	NL	NOR	PTR	NOR
144009	55809+55832	NL	NOR	PTR	NOR
144010	55810+55833	NL	NOR	PTR	NOR
144011	55811+55834	NL	NOR	PTR	NOR
144012	55812+55835	NL	NOR	PTR	NOR
144013	55813+55836	NL	NOR	PTR	NOR

Name applied
144001 *The Penistone Line Partnership*

				Vehicle Length: 50ft 2in (15.25m)			Engine: 1 x Cummins LTA10-R per vehicle	
				Height: 12ft 2½in (3.73m)			Horsepower: 690hp (515kW)	
				Width: 8ft 10½in (2.70m)			Seats (total/car): 145S, 45S/58S/42S	

Number	Formation DMS+MS+DMSL	Depot	Livery	Owner	Operator
144014	55814+55850+55837	NL	NOR	PTR	NOR
144015	55815+55851+55838	NL	NOR	PTR	NOR
144016	55816+55852+55839	NL	NOR	PTR	NOR
144017	55817+55853+55840	NL	NOR	PTR	NOR
144018	55818+55854+55841	NL	NOR	PTR	NOR
144019	55819+55855+55842	NL	NOR	PTR	NOR
144020	55820+55856+55843	NL	NOR	PTR	NOR
144021	55821+55857+55844	NL	NOR	PTR	NOR
144022	55822+55858+55845	NL	NOR	PTR	NOR
144023	55823+55859+55846	NL	NOR	PTR	NOR

Below: *Built by BREL Derby with Walter Alexander supplied bodies, the Class 144s are operated in both two- and three-car formations. All sets are allocated to Leeds Neville Hill and carry standard Northern livery. Two-car set No. 144004 is illustrated.* **Norman E. Preedy**

Northern Rail

Class 150/1

Vehicle Length: 64ft 9¾in (19.74m)
Height: 12ft 4½in (3.77m)
Width: 9ft 3⅛in (2.82m)

Engine: 1 x NT855R5 of 285hp per vehicle
Horsepower: 570hp (425kW)
Seats (total/car): 124S, 59S/65S

Number	Formation DMSL+DMS	Depot	Livery	Owner	Operator
150103§	52103+57103	NH	NOR	ANG	NOR
150110	52110+57110	NH	NOR	ANG	NOR
150111	52111+57111	NH	NOR	ANG	NOR
150112	52112+57112	NH	NOR	ANG	NOR
150113	52113+57113	NH	NOR	ANG	NOR
150114	52114+57114	NH	NOR	ANG	NOR
150115	52115+57115	NH	NOR	ANG	NOR
150116	52116+57116	NH	NOR	ANG	NOR
150117§	52117+57117	NH	NOR	ANG	NOR
150118	52118+57118	NH	NOR	ANG	NOR
150119	52119+57119	NH	NOR	ANG	NOR
150132§	52132+57132	NH	NOR	ANG	NOR
150133	52133+57133	NH	NOR	ANG	NOR
150134	52134+57134	NH	NOR	ANG	NOR
150135	52135+57135	NH	NOR	ANG	NOR
150136	52136+57136	NH	NOR	ANG	NOR
150137	52137+57137	NH	NOR	ANG	NOR
150138	52138+57138	NH	NOR	ANG	NOR
150139	52139+57139	NH	NOR	ANG	NOR
150140	52140+57140	NH	NOR	ANG	NOR
150141	52141+57141	NH	NOR	ANG	NOR
150142	52142+57142	NH	NOR	ANG	NOR
150143	52143+57143	NH	NOR	ANG	NOR
150144	52144+57144	NH	NOR	ANG	NOR
150145	52145+57145	NH	NOR	ANG	NOR
150146	52146+57146	NH	NOR	ANG	NOR
150147	52147+57147	NH	NOR	ANG	NOR
150148	52148+57148	NH	NOR	ANG	NOR
150149	52149+57149	NH	NOR	ANG	NOR
150150	52150+57150	NH	NOR	ANG	NOR

§ Not part of core fleet

Left: *Northern has a fleet of 30 Class 150/1s allocated to Newton Heath depot in Manchester. These units are usually used on North Western routes. Displaying standard Northern livery, set No. 150145 is seen from its DMSL coach.* **Norman E. Preedy**

Class 150/2

Vehicle Length: 64ft 9¾in (19.74m)
Height: 12ft 4½in (3.77m)
Width: 9ft 3⅛in (2.82m)

Engine: 1 x NT855R5 of 285hp per vehicle
Horsepower: 570hp (425kW)
Seats (total/car): 132S, 62S/70S

Number	Formation DMSL+DMS	Depot	Livery	Owner	Operator
150201	52201+57201	NH	NOR	ANG	NOR
150203	52203+57203	NH	NOR ¤	ANG	NOR
150204	52204+57204	NH	NOR	ANG	NOR
150205	52205+57205	NH	NOR ¤	ANG	NOR
150206	52206+57206	NH	NOR	ANG	NOR
150207	52207+57207	NH	NOR ¤	ANG	NOR
150210	52210+57210	NH	NOR	ANG	NOR
150211	52211+57211	NH	NOR ¤	ANG	NOR
150214	52214+57214	NH	NOR	ANG	NOR
150215	52215+57215	NH	NOR ¤	ANG	NOR
150218	52218+57218	NH	NOR ¤	ANG	NOR
150220	52220+57220	NH	NOR	ANG	NOR
150222	52222+57222	NH	NOR ¤	ANG	NOR
150223	52223+57223	NH	NOR	ANG	NOR
150224	52224+57224	NH	NOR	ANG	NOR
150225	52225+57225	NH	NOR	ANG	NOR
150226	52226+57226	NH	NOR	ANG	NOR
150228	52228+57228	NH	NOR ¤	PTR	NOR
150268	52268+57268	NH	NOR ¤	PTR	NOR
150269	52269+57269	NH	NOR ¤	PTR	NOR
150270	52270+57270	NH	NOR ¤	PTR	NOR
150271	52271+57271	NH	NOR ¤	PTR	NOR
150272	52272+57272	NH	NOR ¤	PTR	NOR
150273	52273+57273	NH	NOR ¤	PTR	NOR
150274	52274+57274	NH	NOR ¤	PTR	NOR
150275	52275+57275	NH	NOR ¤	PTR	NOR
150276	52276+57276	NH	NOR ¤	PTR	NOR
150277	52277+57277	NH	NOR ¤	PTR	NOR
150285§	52285+57285	NH	ATW	PTR	NOR

§ On loan from Arriva Trains Wales

¤ Advertising liveries

150203 - Yorkshire
150205 - Yorkshire
150207 - Yorkshire
150211 - Yorkshire
150215 - Yorkshire
150218 - Yorkshire
150222 - Yorkshire
150225 - Yorkshire
150228 - Outdoors
150270 - City Life

150276 - Sport
150268 - Heritage
150269 - Yorkshire
150271 - Arts
150272 - Colne Festival
150273 - Yorkshire
150274 - Events
150275 - Yorkshire
150277 - Yorkshire

Left: *Branded in Yorkshire livery, Class 150/2 No. 150225 departs from Whaley Bridge with a Buxton service.* **John Binch**

Class 153

	Vehicle Length: 76ft 5in (23.29m)	Engine: 1 x NT855R5 of 285hp
	Height: 12ft 3½in (3.75m)	Horsepower: 285hp (213kW)
	Width: 8ft 10in (2.70m)	Seats (total/car): 70S

Number	Formation DMSL	Depot	Livery	Owner	Operator
153301	52301	NL	NOR	ANG	NOR
153304	52304	NL	NOR	ANG	NOR
153307	52307	NL	NOR	ANG	NOR
153315	52315	NL	NOR	ANG	NOR
153316	52316	NL	NOR	PTR	NOR
153317	52317	NL	NOR	ANG	NOR
153324	52324	NL	NOR	PTR	NOR
153328	52328	NL	NOR	ANG	NOR
153330	52330	NL	NOR	PTR	NOR
153331	52331	NL	NOR	ANG	NOR
153332	52332	NL	NOR	ANG	NOR
153351	57351	NL	NOR	ANG	NOR
153352	57352	NL	NOR	ANG	NOR
153358	57358	NL	NOR	PTR	NOR
153359	57359	NL	NOR	PTR	NOR
153360	57360	NL	NOR	PTR	NOR
153363	57363	NL	NOR	PTR	NOR
153378	57378	NL	NOR	ANG	NOR

Right: *For deployment on lesser used routes, Northern has a fleet of 18 single-car Class 153 'bubble' cars. The units are based at Leeds Neville Hill, but can be found throughout the Northern operating area, especially in the North West. In this view, No. 153351 stands attached to a Northern Class 158 at Carlisle.*
Murdoch Currie

Class 155

	Vehicle Length: 76ft 5in (23.29m)	Engine: 1 x NT855R5 of 285hp
	Height: 12ft 3½in (3.75m)	Horsepower: 570hp (425kW)
	Width: 8ft 10in (2.70m)	Seats (total/car): 156S, 76S/80S

Number	Formation DMSL+DMS	Depot	Livery	Owner	Operator
155341	52341+57341	NL	NOR	PTR	NOR
155342	52342+57342	NL	NOR	PTR	NOR
155343	52343+57343	NL	NOR	PTR	NOR
155344	52344+57344	NL	NOR	PTR	NOR
155345	52345+57345	NL	NOR	PTR	NOR
155346	52346+57346	NL	NOR	PTR	NOR
155347	52347+57347	NL	NOR	PTR	NOR

Right: *Of the original sizeable fleet built, only seven of the original Class 155 Leyland 'Super Sprinter' sets are still in traffic. These are owned by Porterbrook and operated by Northern Rail. Until 2011 these sets were officially owned by West Yorkshire PTE, but under control of Porterbrook; however, the sets have now been sold to Porterbrook. Based at Leeds Neville Hill, these units carry pictogram area advertising liveries. Set No. 155342 is illustrated at Leeds.*
Murdoch Currie

Class 156

	Vehicle Length: 75ft 6in (23.03m)	Engine: 1 x Cummins NT855R5 of 285hp
	Height: 12ft 6in (3.81m)	Horsepower: 570hp (425kW)
	Width: 8ft 11in (2.73m)	Seats (total/car): 146S, 70/76S

Number	Formation DMSL+DMS	Depot	Livery	Owner	Operator
156420	52420+57420	AN	NOR	PTR	NOR
156421	52421+57421	AN	NOR	PTR	NOR
156423	52423+57423	AN	NOR	PTR	NOR
156424	52424+57424	AN	NOR	PTR	NOR
156425	52425+57425	AN	NOR	PTR	NOR
156426	52426+57426	AN	NOR	PTR	NOR
156427	52427+57427	AN	NOR	PTR	NOR
156428	52428+57428	AN	NOR	PTR	NOR
156429	52429+57429	AN	NOR	PTR	NOR
156438	52438+57438	HT	NOR	ANG	NOR

Passenger Train Operating Companies - Northern Rail

Northern Rail

156440	52440+57440	AN	NOR	PTR	NOR
156441	52441+57441	AN	§	PTR	NOR
156443	52443+57443	HT	NOR	ANG	NOR
156444	52444+57444	HT	NOR	ANG	NOR
156448	52448+57448	HT	NOR	ANG	NOR
156451	52451+57451	HT	NOR	ANG	NOR
156452	52452+57452	AN	NOR	PTR	NOR
156454	52454+57454	HT	NOR	ANG	NOR
156455	52455+57455	AN	NOR	PTR	NOR
156459	52459+57459	AN	NOR	PTR	NOR
156460	52460+57460	AN	NOR	PTR	NOR
156461	52461+57461	AN	NOR	PTR	NOR
156463	52463+57463	HT	NOR	ANG	NOR
156464	52464+57464	AN	SPL	PTR	NOR
156466	52466+57466	AN	NOR	PTR	NOR
156468	52468+57468	AN	NOR	ANG	NOR
156469	52469+57469	HT	NOR	ANG	NOR
156471	52471+57471	AN	NOR	ANG	NOR
156472	52472+57472	AN	NOR	ANG	NOR
156475	52475+57475	HT	NOR	ANG	NOR
156479	52479+57479	AN	NOR	ANG	NOR
156480	52480+57480	HT	NOR	ANG	NOR
156481	52481+57481	AN	NOR	ANG	NOR
156482	52482+57482	AN	NOR	ANG	NOR
156483	52483+57483	AN	NOR	ANG	NOR
156484	52484+57484	HT	NOR	ANG	NOR
156486	52486+57486	AN	NOR	ANG	NOR
156487	52487+57487	AN	NOR	ANG	NOR
156488	52488+57488	AN	NOR	ANG	NOR
156489	52489+57489	AN	NOR	ANG	NOR
156490	52490+57490	HT	NOR	ANG	NOR
156491	52491+57491	AN	NOR	ANG	NOR

§ - Liverpool & Manchester Railway livery

Names applied
156438 *Timothy Hackworth*
156440 *George Bradshaw*
156441 *William Huskisson MP*
156444 *Councillor Bill Cameron*
156459 *Benny Rothman -*
    The Manchester Rambler
156460 *Driver John Axon GC*
156466 *Gracie Fields*
156464 *Lancashire DalesRail*

Left: *Allocated to Allerton and Heaton the Northern '156s' are used for longer distance services. Set No. 156468 is seen at Preston.* **Murdoch Currie**

Class 158/0

Vehicle Length: 76ft 1¾in (23.21m)	Engine: 1 x Cummins NTA855R of 350hp per vehicle	
Height: 12ft 6in (3.81m)	Horsepower: 1,050hp (783kW)	
Width: 9ft 3¼in (2.82m)	Seats (total/car): 208S, 68S/70S/70S	

Number	Formation DMSL+MSL+DMSL	Depot	Livery	Owner	Operator
158752	52752+58716+57752	NL	NOR	PTR	NOR
158753	52753+58710+57753	NL	NOR	PTR	NOR
158754	52754+58708+57754	NL	NOR	PTR	NOR
158755	52755+58702+57755	NL	NOR	PTR	NOR
158756	52756+58712+57756	NL	NOR	PTR	NOR
158757	52757+58706+57757	NL	NOR	PTR	NOR
158758	52758+58714+57758	NL	NOR	PTR	NOR
158759	52759+58713+57759	NL	NOR	PTR	NOR

Vehicle Length: 76ft 1¾in (23.21m)	Engine: 1 x Cummins NTA855R of 350hp per vehicle	
Height: 12ft 6in (3.81m)	Horsepower: 700hp (522kW)	
Width: 9ft 3¼in (2.82m)	Seats (total/car): 138S, 68S/70S	

Number	Formation DMSL+DMSL	Depot	Livery	Owner	Operator
158784	52784+57784	NH	NOR	ANG	NOR
158787	52787+57787	NH	NOR	ANG	NOR
158790	52790+57790	NH	NOR	ANG	NOR
158791	52791+57791	NH	NOR	ANG	NOR
159792	52792+57792	NH	NOR	ANG	NOR
158793	52793+57793	NH	NOR	ANG	NOR
158794	52794+57794	NH	NOR	ANG	NOR
158795	52795+57795	NH	NOR	ANG	NOR
158796	52796+57796	NH	NOR	ANG	NOR
158797	52797+57797	NH	NOR	ANG	NOR
158815	52815+57815	NL	NOR	ANG	NOR
158816	52816+57816	NL	NOR	ANG	NOR
158817	52817+57817	NL	NOR	ANG	NOR
158842	52842+57842	NL	NOR	ANG	NOR
158843	52843+57843	NL	NOR	ANG	NOR
158844	52844+57844	NL	NOR	ANG	NOR
158845	52845+57845	NL	NOR	ANG	NOR
158848	52848+57848	NL	NOR	ANG	NOR
158849	52849+57849	NL	NOR	ANG	NOR
158850	52850+57850	NL	NOR	ANG	NOR
158851	52851+57851	NL	NOR	ANG	NOR
158853	52853+57853	NL	NOR	ANG	NOR
158855	52855+57855	NL	NOR	ANG	NOR
158859	52859+57859	NL	NOR	ANG	NOR

158860	52860+57860	NL	NOR	ANG	NOR
158861	52861+57861	NL	SPL§	ANG	NOR
158872	52872+57872	NL	NOR	ANG	NOR

§ Carries Welcome to Yorkshire livery

Class 158/9

Vehicle Length: 76ft 1¾in (23.21m) Engine: 1 x Cummins NTA855R of 350hp per vehicle
Height: 12ft 6in (3.81m) Horsepower: 700hp (522kW)
Width: 9ft 3¼in (2.82m) Seats (total/car): 142S, 70S/72S

Number	Formation	Depot	Livery	Owner	Operator
	DMSL+DMS				
158901	52901+57901	NL	NOR	EVL	NOR
158902	52902+57902	NL	NOR	EVL	NOR
158903	52903+57903	NL	NOR	EVL	NOR
158904	52904+57904	NL	NOR	EVL	NOR
158905	52905+57905	NL	NOR	EVL	NOR
158906	52906+57906	NL	NOR	EVL	NOR
158907	52907+57907	NL	NOR	EVL	NOR
158908	52908+57908	NL	NOR	EVL	NOR
158909	52909+57909	NL	NOR	EVL	NOR
158910	52910+57910	NL	NOR	EVL	NOR

Names applied
158784 *Barbara Castle*
158791 *County of Nottinghamshire*
158796 *Fred Trueman - Cricketing Legend*
158797 *Jane Tomlinson*
158860 *Ian Dewhirst*
158910 *William Wilberforce*

Right: *Carrying standard Northern Rail livery, one of the standard 158/0 sets, No. 158817, is illustrated in one of the south-facing bays at York in June 2012.*
Antony Christie

Class 321/9

Vehicle Length: (Driving) 65ft 0¾in (19.83m) Width: 9ft 3in (2.82m)
(Inter) 65ft 4¼in (19.92m) Horsepower: 1,328hp (996kW)
Height: 12ft 4¾in (3.78m) Seats (total/car): 293S, 70S/79S/74S/70S

Number	Formation	Depot	Livery	Owner	Operator
	DTCO+MSO+TSO+DTSO				
321901	77990+63153+72128+77993	NL	NOM	EVL	NOR
321902	77991+63154+72129+77994	NL	NOM	EVL	NOR
321903	77992+63155+72130+77995	NL	NOM	EVL	NOR

Right: *When the Leeds to Doncaster WYPTE electrified route was modernised, three Class 321/9 four-car sets were ordered from BREL York, and allocated to Leeds Neville Hill. The sets remain in service today and rarely operate on the Wharfedale or Airedale lines. All sets are painted in revised Northern Rail livery incorporating Metro branding and lettering with red bodies and blue markings on driving cars. Set No. 321901 is seen at Wakefield Westgate.* **Antony Christie**

Class 322

Vehicle Length: (Driving) 65ft 0¾in (19.83m) Width: 9ft 3in (2.82m)
(Inter) 65ft 4¼in (19.92m) Horsepower: 1,328hp (996kW)
Height: 12ft 4¾in (3.78m) Seats (total/car): 291S, 74S/83S/76S/58S

Number	Formation	Depot	Livery	Owner	Operator
	DTSO(A)+MSO+TSO+DTSO(B)				
322481	78163+62137+72023+77985	NL	NOR	EVL	NOR
322482	78164+62138+72024+77986	NL	NOR	EVL	NOR
322483	78165+62139+72025+77987	NL	NOR	EVL	NOR
322484	78166+63140+72026+77988	NL	NOR	EVL	NOR
322485	78167+63141+72027+77898	NL	NOR	EVL	NOR

Train Operating Companies

Northern Rail

Left: *At the end of 2011, the five former First ScotRail four-car Class 322s , which have operated in a number of different areas, were transferred to Northern Rail at Leeds Neville Hill to supplement its fleet of near-identical Class 321/9s. Sets are in Northern blue with bodyside branding and can usually be found on the Leeds to Doncaster corridor. Set No. 322484 is pictured heading north out of Wakefield Westgate bound for Leeds.*
Antony Christie

Class 323

Vehicle Length: (Driving) 76ft 8¼in (23.37m)
(Inter) 76ft 10¾in (23.44m)
Height: 12ft 4¾in (3.78m)
Width: 9ft 2¼in (2.80m)
Horsepower: 1,565hp (1,168kW)
Seats (total/car) 323223-225: 244S, 82S/80S/82S
323226-239: 284S, 98S/88S/98S

Number	Formation DMSO(A)+PTSO+DMSO(B)	Depot	Livery	Owner	Operator
323223	64023+72223+65023	LG	NOR	PTR	NOR
323224	64024+72224+65024	LG	NOR	PTR	NOR
323225	64025+72225+65025	LG	FSN	PTR	NOR
323226	64026+72226+65026	LG	FSN	PTR	NOR
323227	64027+72227+65027	LG	FSN	PTR	NOR
323228	64028+72228+65028	LG	NOR	PTR	NOR
323229	64029+72229+65029	LG	NOR	PTR	NOR
323230	64030+72230+65030	LG	FSN	PTR	NOR
323231	64031+72231+65031	LG	NOR	PTR	NOR
323232	64032+72232+65032	LG	NOR	PTR	NOR
323233	64033+72233+65033	LG	NOR	PTR	NOR
323234	64034+72234+65034	LG	NOR	PTR	NOR
323235	64035+72235+65035	LG	NOR	PTR	NOR
323236	64036+72236+65036	LG	NOR	PTR	NOR
323237	64037+72237+65037	LG	NOR	PTR	NOR
323238	64038+72238+65038	LG	FSN	PTR	NOR
323239	64039+72239+65039	LG	FSN	PTR	NOR

Below: *For use in the Manchester area, Northern operates a fleet of 17 three-car Class 323s. Two different seating configurations can be found; sets 323223-225 have a reduced seating capacity for use on Manchester Airport services where extra luggage space is required. Conventional set No. 323226 stops at Macclesfield on 27 February 2012 with the 12.48 Manchester Piccadilly to Stoke-on-Trent service.*
Murdoch Currie

Class 333

			Vehicle Length: (Driving) 77ft 10¾in (23.74m)	Width: 9ft 0¼in (2.75m)
			(Inter) 75ft 11in (23.14m)	Horsepower: 1,877hp (1,400kW)
			Height: 12ft 1½in (3.79m)	Seats (total/car): 353S, 90S/73S/100S/90S

Passenger Train Operating Companies - Northern Rail

Number	Formation DMSO(A)+PTSO+TSO+DMSO(B)	Depot	Livery	Owner	Operator	Name
333001	78451+74461+74477+78452	NL	NOM	ANG	NOR	
333002	78453+74462+74478+78454	NL	NOM	ANG	NOR	
333003	78455+74463+74479+78456	NL	NOM	ANG	NOR	
333004	78457+74464+74480+78458	NL	NOM	ANG	NOR	
333005	78459+74465+74481+78460	NL	NOM	ANG	NOR	
333006	78461+74466+74482+78462	NL	NOM	ANG	NOR	
333007	78463+74467+74483+78464	NL	NOM	ANG	NOR	*Alderman J Arthur Godwin - First Lord Mayor of Bradford 1907*
333008	78465+74468+74484+78466	NL	NOM	ANG	NOR	
333009	78467+74469+74485+78468	NL	NOM	ANG	NOR	
333010	78469+74470+74486+78470	NL	NOM	ANG	NOR	
333011	78471+74471+74487+78472	NL	NOM	ANG	NOR	
333012	78473+74472+74488+78474	NL	NOM	ANG	NOR	
333013	78475+74473+74489+78476	NL	NOM	ANG	NOR	
333014	78477+74474+74490+78478	NL	NOM	ANG	NOR	
333015	78479+74475+74491+78480	NL	NOM	ANG	NOR	
333016	78481+74476+74492+78482	NL	NOM	ANG	NOR	

Above & Right: *Built by Siemens and CAF to operate on the newly electrified Aire Valley lines radiating from Leeds to Bradford and Skipton was this fleet of Class 333s, similar in design to the Heathrow Express stock. After introduction as three-car sets, an additional intermediate vehicle – a Trailer Standard (TS) – was added to strengthen sets to four-car formations. All units are based at Leeds Neville Hill and carry a version of Northern livery. In the above view, set No. 333011 is seen at Guiseley with a service bound for Leeds. Right, we see one of the additional TS cars No. /4486 from set No. 333010. All vehicles are set out in the 2+3 high-density style.* Both: **Antony Christie**

Train Operating Companies

South West Trains

Address: Friars Bridge Court, 41-45 Blackfriars Road, London, SE1 8NZ
✉ customerrelations@swtrains.co.uk
✆ 08700 00 5151
ⓘ www.southwesttrains.co.uk

Managing Director: Tim Shoveller
Franchise Dates: 4 December 1996 - 3 February 2017
Principal Routes: London Waterloo - Weymouth, Exeter, Portsmouth and suburban services in Surrey, Berkshire, Hampshire
Depots: Wimbledon Park (WD), Bournemouth (BM), Clapham Junction (CJ)*, Salisbury (SA) * No stock allocated Northam (Siemens Transportation) (NT)
Parent Company: Stagecoach Group

Class 158

Vehicle Length: 76ft 1¾in (23.21m)   Engine: 1 x Cummins NTA855R of 350hp per vehicle
Height: 12ft 6in (3.81m)   Horsepower: 700hp (522kW)
Width: 9ft 3¼in (2.82m)   Seats (total/car): 13F-114S, 13F-44S/70S

Number	Formation DMSL+DMSL	Depot	Livery	Owner	Operator
158880 (158737)	52737+57737	SA	SWM	PTR	SWT
158881 (158742)	52742+57742	SA	SWM	PTR	SWT
158882 (158743)	52743+57743	SA	SWM	PTR	SWT
158883 (158744)	52744+57744	SA	SWM	PTR	SWT
158884 (158772)	52772+57772	SA	SWM	PTR	SWT
158885 (158775)	52775+57775	SA	SWM	PTR	SWT
158886 (158779)	52779+57779	SA	SWM	PTR	SWT
158887 (158781)	52781+57781	SA	SWM	PTR	SWT
158888 (158802)	52802+57802	SA	SWM	PTR	SWT
158889 (158808)	52808+57808	SA	SWM	PTR	SWT
158890 (158814)	52814+57814	SA	SWM	PTR	SWT

Below: *South West Trains operates a fleet of 11 Class 158 two-car sets based at Salisbury and used on local routes as well as supplementing '159' stock on the Yeovil/Salisbury to Waterloo line. All sets are refurbished and were renumbered into a new 158/8 series from their original numbers. Set No. 158890 (the original 158814) is seen at Southampton Central.* **CJM**

Passenger Train Operating Companies - South West Trains

ITRC.Com Ltd 2013

For clarity some stations have been omitted

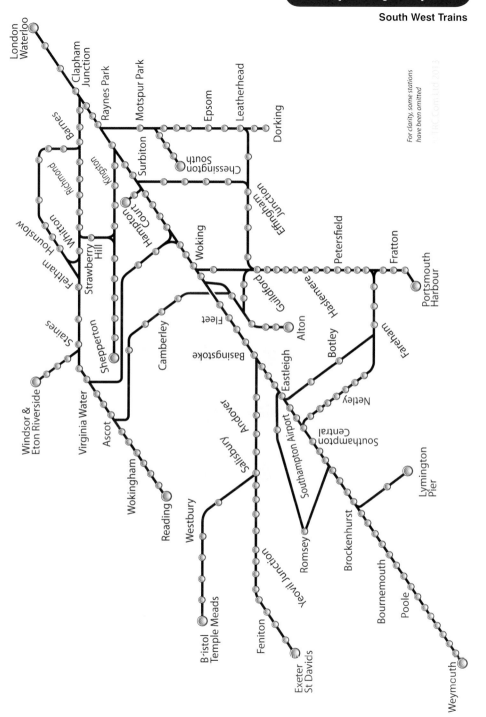

South West Trains

Class 159/0

Vehicle Length: 76ft 1¾in (23.21m) Engine: 1 x Cummins NTA855R of 400hp per vehicle
Height: 12ft 6in (3.81m) Horsepower: 1,200hp (895kW)
Width: 9ft 3¼in (2.82m) Seats (total/car): 24F-172S, 24F-28S/72S/72S

Number	Formation DMCL+MSL+DMSL	Depot	Livery	Owner	Operator	Name
159001	52873+58718+57873	SA	SWM	PTR	SWT	City of Exeter
159002	52874+58719+57874	SA	SWM	PTR	SWT	City of Salisbury
159003	52875+58720+57875	SA	SWM	PTR	SWT	Templecombe
159004	52876+58721+57876	SA	SWM	PTR	SWT	Basingstoke and Deane
159005	52877+58722+57877	SA	SWM	PTR	SWT	West of England Line
159006	52878+58723+57878	SA	SWM	PTR	SWT	
159007	52879+58724+57879	SA	SWM	PTR	SWT	
159008	52880+58725+57880	SA	SWM	PTR	SWT	
159009	52881+58726+57881	SA	SWM	PTR	SWT	
159010	52882+58727+57882	SA	SWM	PTR	SWT	
159011	52883+58728+57883	SA	SWM	PTR	SWT	
159012	52884+58729+57884	SA	SWM	PTR	SWT	
159013	52885+58730+57885	SA	SWM	PTR	SWT	
159014	52886+58731+57886	SA	SWM	PTR	SWT	
159015	52887+58732+57887	SA	SWM	PTR	SWT	
159016	52888+58733+57888	SA	SWM	PTR	SWT	
159017	52889+58734+57889	SA	SWM	PTR	SWT	
159018	52890+58735+57890	SA	SWM	PTR	SWT	
159019	52891+58736+57891	SA	SWM	PTR	SWT	
159020	52892+58737+57892	SA	SWM	PTR	SWT	
159021	52893+58738+57893	SA	SWM	PTR	SWT	
159022	52894+58739+57894	SA	SWM	PTR	SWT	

Above: *A total of 30 Class 159 three-car main line sets are operated by SWT and are used on the Waterloo to Exeter route, being allocated to Salisbury depot. The sets frequently work in two- and three-set formations. All are refurbished and carry the Stagecoach main line white livery, offset by red and orange swirl ends. The 22 original Class 159/0s are represented by set No. 159014 at Exeter St Davids, viewed from its DMCL end.* **CJM**

Class 159/1

Vehicle Length: 76ft 1¾in (23.21m) Engine: 1 x Cummins NTA855R of 350hp per vehicle
Height: 12ft 6in (3.81m) Horsepower: 1,050hp (782kW)
Width: 9ft 3¼in (2.82m) Seats (total/car): 24F-170S, 24F-28S/70S/72S

Number	Formation DMCL+MSL+DMSL	Depot	Livery	Owner	Operator
159101 (158800)	52800+58717+57800	SA	SWM	PTR	SWT
159102 (158803)	52803+58703+57803	SA	SWM	PTR	SWT
159103 (158804)	52804+58704+57804	SA	SWM	PTR	SWT
159104 (158805)	52805+58705+57805	SA	SWM	PTR	SWT
159105 (158807)	52807+58707+57807	SA	SWM	PTR	SWT
159106 (158809)	52809+58709+57809	SA	SWM	PTR	SWT
159107 (158811)	52811+58711+57811	SA	SWM	PTR	SWT
159108 (158801)	52801+58701+57801	SA	SWM	PTR	SWT

Right: *In advance of an expansion of SWT services in 2006-07, an additional batch of Class 159s were converted from Class 158s at the Wabtec Works in Doncaster in 2006. These units are classified as 159/1 and have some minor differences from the original 22 Class 159/0s, the most noticeable being that only two opening quarter lights are provided on each side of each coach, whereas the '159/0s' have four. Set No. 159106 (the original 158809) is seen at Salisbury with a service bound for Exeter.* **CJM**

Class 444
Desiro

Vehicle Length: 77ft 3in (23.57m)
Height: 12ft 1½in (3.7m)
Width: 9ft 2in (2.7m)
Horsepower: 2,682hp (2,000kW)
Seats (total/car): 35F-299S, 35F-24S/47S/76S/76S/76S

Number	Formation DMCO+TSO+TSO+TSRMB+DMSO	Depot	Livery	Owner	Operator	Name
444001	63801+67101+67151+67201+63851	NT	SWM	ANG	SWT	Naomi House
444002	63802+67102+67152+67202+63852	NT	SWM	ANG	SWT	
444003	63803+67103+67153+67203+63853	NT	SWM	ANG	SWT	
444004	63804+67104+67154+67204+63854	NT	SWM	ANG	SWT	
444005	63805+67105+67155+67205+63855	NT	SWM	ANG	SWT	
444006	63806+67106+67156+67206+63856	NT	SWM	ANG	SWT	
444007	63807+67107+67157+67207+63857	NT	SWM	ANG	SWT	
444008	63808+67108+67158+67208+63858	NT	SWM	ANG	SWT	
444009	63809+67109+67159+67209+63859	NT	SWM	ANG	SWT	
444010	63810+67110+67160+67210+63860	NT	SWM	ANG	SWT	
444011	63811+67111+67161+67211+63861	NT	SWM	ANG	SWT	
444012	63812+67112+67162+67212+63862	NT	SWM	ANG	SWT	Destination Weymouth
444013	63813+67113+67163+67213+63863	NT	SWM	ANG	SWT	
444014	63814+67114+67164+67214+63864	NT	SWM	ANG	SWT	
444015	63815+67115+67165+67215+63865	NT	SWM	ANG	SWT	
444016	63816+67116+67166+67216+63866	NT	SWM	ANG	SWT	
444017	63817+67117+67167+67217+63867	NT	SWM	ANG	SWT	
444018	63818+67118+67168+67218+63868	NT	SWM	ANG	SWT	The FAB 444
444019	63819+67119+67169+67219+63869	NT	SWM	ANG	SWT	
444020	63820+67120+67170+67220+63870	NT	SWM	ANG	SWT	
444021	63821+67121+67171+67221+63871	NT	SWM	ANG	SWT	
444022	63822+67122+67172+67222+63872	NT	SWM	ANG	SWT	
444023	63823+67123+67173+67223+63873	NT	SWM	ANG	SWT	
444024	63824+67124+67174+67224+63874	NT	SWM	ANG	SWT	
444025	63825+67125+67175+67225+63875	NT	SWM	ANG	SWT	
444026	63826+67126+67176+67226+63876	NT	SWM	ANG	SWT	
444027	63827+67127+67177+67227+63877	NT	SWM	ANG	SWT	
444028	63828+67128+67178+67228+63878	NT	SWM	ANG	SWT	
444029	63829+67129+67179+67229+63879	NT	SWM	ANG	SWT	
444030	63830+67130+67180+67230+63880	NT	SWM	ANG	SWT	
444031	63831+67131+67181+67231+63881	NT	SWM	ANG	SWT	
444032	63832+67132+67182+67232+63882	NT	SWM	ANG	SWT	
444033	63833+67133+67183+67233+63883	NT	SWM	ANG	SWT	
444034	63834+67134+67184+67234+63884	NT	SWM	ANG	SWT	
444035	63835+67135+67185+67235+63885	NT	SWM	ANG	SWT	
444036	63836+67136+67186+67236+63886	NT	SWM	ANG	SWT	
444037	63837+67137+67187+67237+63887	NT	SWM	ANG	SWT	
444038	63838+67138+67188+67238+63888	NT	SWM	ANG	SWT	
444039	63839+67139+67189+67239+63889	NT	SWM	ANG	SWT	
444040	63840+67140+67190+67240+63890	NT	SWM	ANG	SWT	

South West Trains

444041	63841+67141+67191+67241+63891	NT	SWM	ANG	SWT
444042	63842+67142+67192+67242+63892	NT	SWM	ANG	SWT
444043	63843+67143+67193+67243+63893	NT	SWM	ANG	SWT
444044	63844+67144+67194+67244+63894	NT	SWM	ANG	SWT
444045	63845+67145+67195+67245+63895	NT	SWM	ANG	SWT

Left: *The core long distance main line EMUs of South West Trains' franchise are a fleet of 45 five-car Class 444 Siemens 'Desiro' units, introduced to operate fast services on the Waterloo to Weymouth and Portsmouth lines. All sets are based at the specialist servicing depot operated by Siemens Transportation at Northam near Southampton. Set No. 444038 is seen inside the main servicing shed at Northam.* **CJM**

Class 450/0
Desiro

Vehicle Length: 66ft 9in (20.4m)	Horsepower: 2,682hp (2,000kW)
Height: 12ft 1½in (3.7m)	Seats (total/car): 24F-237S, 70S/24F-36S/61S/70S
Width: 9ft 2in (2.7m)	

Number	Formation DMSO+TCO+TSO+DMSO	Depot	Livery	Owner	Operator	Name
450001	63201+64201+68101+63601	NT	SWO	ANG	SWT	
450002	63202+64202+68102+63602	NT	SWO	ANG	SWT	
450003	63203+64203+68103+63603	NT	SWO	ANG	SWT	
450004	63204+64204+68104+63604	NT	SWO	ANG	SWT	
450005	63205+64205+68205+63605	NT	SWO	ANG	SWT	
450006	63206+64206+68206+63606	NT	SWO	ANG	SWT	
450007	63207+64207+68207+63607	NT	SWO	ANG	SWT	
450008	63208+64208+68108+63608	NT	SWO	ANG	SWT	
450009	63209+64209+68109+63609	NT	SWO	ANG	SWT	
450010	63210+64210+68110+63610	NT	SWO	ANG	SWT	
450011	63211+64211+68111+63611	NT	SWO	ANG	SWT	
450012	63212+64212+68112+63612	NT	SWO	ANG	SWT	
450013	63213+64213+68113+63613	NT	SWO	ANG	SWT	
450014	63214+64214+68114+63614	NT	SWO	ANG	SWT	
450015	63215+64215+68115+63615	NT	SWO	ANG	SWT	Desiro
450016	63216+64216+68116+63616	NT	SWO	ANG	SWT	
450017	63217+64217+68117+63617	NT	SWO	ANG	SWT	
450018	63218+64218+68118+63618	NT	SWO	ANG	SWT	
450019	63219+64219+68119+63619	NT	SWO	ANG	SWT	
450020	63220+64220+68120+63620	NT	SWO	ANG	SWT	
450021	63221+64221+68121+63621	NT	SWO	ANG	SWT	
450022	63222+64222+68122+63622	NT	SWO	ANG	SWT	
450023	63223+64223+68123+63623	NT	SWO	ANG	SWT	
450024	63224+64224+68124+63624	NT	SWO	ANG	SWT	
450025	63225+64225+68125+63625	NT	SWO	ANG	SWT	
450026	63226+64226+68126+63626	NT	SWO	ANG	SWT	
450027	63227+64227+68127+63627	NT	SWO	ANG	SWT	
450028	63228+64228+68128+63628	NT	SWO	ANG	SWT	
450029	63229+64229+68129+63629	NT	SWO	ANG	SWT	
450030	63230+64230+68130+63630	NT	SWO	ANG	SWT	
450031	63231+64231+68131+63631	NT	SWO	ANG	SWT	
450032	63232+64232+68132+63632	NT	SWO	ANG	SWT	
450033	63233+64233+68133+63633	NT	SWO	ANG	SWT	
450034	63234+64234+68134+63634	NT	SWO	ANG	SWT	
450035	63235+64235+68135+63635	NT	SWO	ANG	SWT	
450036	63236+64236+68136+63636	NT	SWO	ANG	SWT	

450037	63237+64237+68137+63637	NT	SWO	ANG	SWT	
450038	63238+64238+68138+63638	NT	SWO	ANG	SWT	
450039	63239+64239+68139+63639	NT	SWO	ANG	SWT	
450040	63240+64240+68140+63640	NT	SWO	ANG	SWT	
450041	63241+64241+68141+63641	NT	SWO	ANG	SWT	
450042	63242+64242+68142+63642	NT	SWO	ANG	SWT	*Treloar College*
450071	63271+64271+68171+63671	NT	SWO	ANG	SWT	
450072	63272+64272+68172+63672	NT	SWO	ANG	SWT	
450073	63273+64273+68173+63673	NT	SWO	ANG	SWT	
450074	63274+64274+68174+63674	NT	SWO	ANG	SWT	
450075	63275+64275+68175+63675	NT	SWO	ANG	SWT	
450076	63276+64276+68176+63676	NT	SWO	ANG	SWT	
450077	63277+64277+68177+63677	NT	SWO	ANG	SWT	
450078	63278+64278+68178+63678	NT	SWO	ANG	SWT	
450079	63279+64279+68179+63679	NT	SWO	ANG	SWT	
450080	63280+64280+68180+63680	NT	SWO	ANG	SWT	
450081	63281+64281+68181+63681	NT	SWO	ANG	SWT	
450082	63282+64282+68182+63682	NT	SWO	ANG	SWT	
450083	63283+64283+68183+63683	NT	SWO	ANG	SWT	
450084	63284+64284+68184+63684	NT	SWO	ANG	SWT	
450085	63285+64285+68185+63685	NT	SWO	ANG	SWT	
450086	63286+64286+68186+63686	NT	SWO	ANG	SWT	
450087	63287+64287+68187+63687	NT	SWO	ANG	SWT	
450088	63288+64288+68188+63688	NT	SWO	ANG	SWT	
450089	63289+64289+68189+63689	NT	SWO	ANG	SWT	
450090	63290+64290+68190+63690	NT	SWO	ANG	SWT	
450091	63291+64291+68191+63691	NT	SWO	ANG	SWT	
450092	63292+64292+68192+63692	NT	SWO	ANG	SWT	
450093	63293+64293+68193+63693	NT	SWO	ANG	SWT	
450094	63294+64294+68194+63694	NT	SWO	ANG	SWT	
450095	63295+64295+68195+63695	NT	SWO	ANG	SWT	
450096	63296+64296+68196+63696	NT	SWO	ANG	SWT	
450097	63297+64297+68197+63697	NT	SWO	ANG	SWT	
450098	63298+64298+68198+63698	NT	SWO	ANG	SWT	
450099	63299+64299+68199+63699	NT	SWO	ANG	SWT	
450100	63300+64300+68200+63700	NT	SWO	ANG	SWT	
450101	63701+66851+66801+63751	NT	SWO	ANG	SWT	
450102	63702+66852+66802+63752	NT	SWO	ANG	SWT	
450103	63703+66853+66803+63753	NT	SWO	ANG	SWT	
450104	63704+66854+66804+63754	NT	SWO	ANG	SWT	
450105	63705+66855+66805+63755	NT	SWO	ANG	SWT	
450106	63706+66856+66806+63756	NT	SWO	ANG	SWT	
450107	63707+66857+66807+63757	NT	SWO	ANG	SWT	
450108	63708+66858+66808+63758	NT	SWO	ANG	SWT	
450109	63709+66859+66809+63759	NT	SWO	ANG	SWT	
450110	63710+66860+66810+63750	NT	SWO	ANG	SWT	
450111	63901+66921+66901+63921	NT	SWO	ANG	SWT	
450112	63902+66922+66902+63922	NT	SWO	ANG	SWT	
450113	63903+66923+66903+63923	NT	SWO	ANG	SWT	
450114	63904+66924+66904+63924	NT	SWO	ANG	SWT	*Fairbridge - investing in the Future*
450115	63905+66925+66905+63925	NT	SWO	ANG	SWT	
450116	63906+66926+66906+63926	NT	SWO	ANG	SWT	
450117	63907+66927+66907+63927	NT	SWO	ANG	SWT	
450118	63908+66928+66908+63928	NT	SWO	ANG	SWT	
450119	63909+66929+66909+63929	NT	SWO	ANG	SWT	
450120	63910+66930+66910+63930	NT	SWO	ANG	SWT	
450121	63911+66931+66911+63931	NT	SWO	ANG	SWT	
450122	63912+66932+66912+63932	NT	SWO	ANG	SWT	
450123	63913+66933+66913+63933	NT	SWO	ANG	SWT	
450124	63914+66934+66914+63934	NT	SWO	ANG	SWT	
450125	63915+66935+66915+63935	NT	SWO	ANG	SWT	
450126	63916+66936+66916+63936	NT	SWO	ANG	SWT	
450127	63917+66937+66917+63937	NT	SWO	ANG	SWT	

South West Trains

Above: *A fleet of 127 four-car Class 450 Siemens 'Desiro' sets form the backbone of South West Trains' outer-suburban service, also undertaking a number of main line duties. All sets are painted in the South West Trains/Stagecoach blue livery. Set No. 450090 is seen on the Windsor side at Clapham Junction, passing an Alstom Class 458.* **Antony Christie**

Class 450/5
Desiro

Vehicle Length: 66ft 9in (20.4m)	Horsepower: 2,682hp (2,000kW)
Height: 12ft 1½in (3.7m)	Seats (total/car): 240S, 64S/56S/56S/64S
Width: 9ft 2in (2.7m)	

Number	Formation DMSO+TSO+TSO+DMSO	Depot	Livery	Owner	Operator
450543 (450043)	63243+64243+68143+63643	NT	SWO	ANG	SWT
450544 (450044)	63244+64244+68144+63644	NT	SWO	ANG	SWT
450545 (450045)	63245+64245+68145+63645	NT	SWO	ANG	SWT
450546 (450046)	63246+64246+68146+63646	NT	SWO	ANG	SWT
450547 (450047)	63247+64247+68147+63647	NT	SWO	ANG	SWT
450548 (450048)	63248+64248+68148+63648	NT	SWO	ANG	SWT
450549 (450049)	63249+64249+68149+63649	NT	SWO	ANG	SWT
450550 (450050)	63250+64250+68150+63650	NT	SWO	ANG	SWT
450551 (450051)	63251+64251+68151+63651	NT	SWO	ANG	SWT
450552 (450052)	63252+64252+68152+63652	NT	SWO	ANG	SWT
450553 (450053)	63253+64253+68153+63653	NT	SWO	ANG	SWT
450554 (450054)	63254+64254+68154+63654	NT	SWO	ANG	SWT
450555 (450055)	63255+64255+68155+63655	NT	SWO	ANG	SWT
450556 (450056)	63256+64256+68156+63656	NT	SWO	ANG	SWT
450557 (450057)	63257+64257+68157+63657	NT	SWO	ANG	SWT
450558 (450058)	63258+64258+68158+63658	NT	SWO	ANG	SWT
450559 (450059)	63259+64259+68159+63659	NT	SWO	ANG	SWT
450560 (450060)	63260+64260+68160+63660	NT	SWO	ANG	SWT
450561 (450061)	63261+64261+68161+63661	NT	SWO	ANG	SWT
450562 (450062)	63262+64262+68162+63662	NT	SWO	ANG	SWT
450563 (450063)	63263+64263+68163+63663	NT	SWO	ANG	SWT
450564 (450064)	63264+64264+68164+63664	NT	SWO	ANG	SWT
450565 (450065)	63265+64265+68165+63665	NT	SWO	ANG	SWT
450566 (450066)	63266+64266+68166+63666	NT	SWO	ANG	SWT
450567 (450067)	63267+64267+68167+63667	NT	SWO	ANG	SWT
450568 (450068)	63268+64268+68168+63668	NT	SWO	ANG	SWT
450569 (450069)	63269+64269+68169+63669	NT	SWO	ANG	SWT
450570 (450070)	63270+64270+68170+63670	NT	SWO	ANG	SWT

Left: *Twenty-eight of the Class 450 'Desiro' fleet have been adapted to high-capacity or HC sets. These form sub-class 450/5 and have the letters HC on the front end. They have had their first class removed and revisions to seating in other carriages to increase standing room. The sets should be deployed on the Waterloo 'Windsor line' routes, where serious capacity issues arise even with eight-car formations. Set No. 450551 is seen passing Basingstoke.* **CJM**

Class 455/7

	Vehicle Length: (Driving) 65ft 0½in (19.83m)	Width: 9ft 3¼in (2.82m)
	(Inter) 65ft 4½in (19.92m)	Horsepower: 1,000hp (746kW)
	Height: 12ft 1½in (3.79m) [TSO- 11ft 6½in (3.58m)]	Seats (total/car): 244S, 54S/68S/68S/54S

Number	Formation	Depot	Livery	Owner	Operator
	DMSO(A)+MSO+TSO+DTSO(B)				
(45)5701	77727+62783+71545+77728	WD	SWS	PTR	SWT
(45)5702	77729+62784+71547+77730	WD	SWS	PTR	SWT
(45)5703	77731+62785+71540+77732	WD	SWS	PTR	SWT
(45)5704	77733+62786+71548+77734	WD	SWS	PTR	SWT
(45)5705	77735+62787+71565+77736	WD	SWS	PTR	SWT
(45)5706	77737+62788+71534+77738	WD	SWS	PTR	SWT
(45)5707	77739+62789+71536+77740	WD	SWS	PTR	SWT
(45)5708	77741+62790+71560+77742	WD	SWS	PTR	SWT
(45)5709	77743+62791+71532+77744	WD	SWS	PTR	SWT
(45)5710	77745+62792+71566+77746	WD	SWS	PTR	SWT
(45)5711	77747+62793+71542+77748	WD	SWS	PTR	SWT
(45)5712	77749+62794+71546+77750	WD	SWS	PTR	SWT
(45)5713	77751+62795+71567+77752	WD	SWS	PTR	SWT
(45)5714	77753+62796+71539+77754	WD	SWS	PTR	SWT
(45)5715	77755+62796+71535+77756	WD	SWS	PTR	SWT
(45)5716	77757+62798+71564+77758	WD	SWS	PTR	SWT
(45)5717	77759+62799+71528+77760	WD	SWS	PTR	SWT
(45)5718	77761+62800+71557+77762	WD	SWS	PTR	SWT
(45)5719	77763+62801+71558+77764	WD	SWS	PTR	SWT
(45)5720	77765+62802+71568+77766	WD	SWS	PTR	SWT
(45)5721	77767+62803+71553+77768	WD	SWS	PTR	SWT
(45)5722	77769+62804+71533+77770	WD	SWS	PTR	SWT
(45)5723	77771+62805+71526+77772	WD	SWS	PTR	SWT
(45)5724	77773+62806+71561+77774	WD	SWS	PTR	SWT
(45)5725	77775+62807+71541+77776	WD	SWS	PTR	SWT
(45)5726	77777+62608+71556+77778	WD	SWS	PTR	SWT
(45)5727	77779+62809+71562+77780	WD	SWS	PTR	SWT
(45)5728	77781+62810+71527+77782	WD	SWS	PTR	SWT
(45)5729	77783+62811+71550+77784	WD	SWS	PTR	SWT
(45)5730	77785+62812+71551+77786	WD	SWS	PTR	SWT
(45)5731	77787+62813+71555+77788	WD	SWS	PTR	SWT
(45)5732	77789+62814+71552+77790	WD	SWS	PTR	SWT
(45)5733	77791+62815+71549+77792	WD	SWS	PTR	SWT
(45)5734	77793+62816+71531+77794	WD	SWS	PTR	SWT
(45)5735	77795+62817+71563+77796	WD	SWS	PTR	SWT
(45)5736	77797+62818+71554+77798	WD	SWS	PTR	SWT
(45)5737	77799+62819+71544+77800	WD	SWS	PTR	SWT
(45)5738	77801+62820+71529+77802	WD	SWS	PTR	SWT
(45)5739	77803+62821+71537+77804	WD	SWS	PTR	SWT
(45)5740	77805+62822+71530+77806	WD	SWS	PTR	SWT
(45)5741	77807+62823+71559+77808	WD	SWS	PTR	SWT
(45)5742	77809+62824+71543+77810	WD	SWS	PTR	SWT
(45)5750*	77811+62825+71538+77812	WD	SWS	PTR	SWT	* Originally numbered (45)5743

Right: *Suburban services on South West Trains are in the hands of three breeds of Class 455, built in the 1980s at BREL York. All sets are painted in the SWT local red livery and are allocated to East Wimbledon depot. The Class 455/7s incorporate one vehicle of a different profile. These were originally marshalled in the Class 508 sets before transfer to Merseyrail. Class 455/7 No. 5704 is seen heading towards Waterloo at Vauxhall.* **Antony Christie**

Passenger Train Operating Companies - South West Trains

South West Trains

Class 455/8

	Vehicle Length: (Driving) 65ft 0½in (19.83m)	Width: 9ft 3¼in (2.82m)
	(Inter) 65ft 4½in (19.92m)	Horsepower: 1,000hp (746kW)
	Height: 12ft 1½in (3.79m)	Seats (total/car): 268S, 50S/84S/84S/50S

Number	Formation DMSO(A)+MSO+TSO+DTSO(B)	Depot	Livery	Owner	Operator
(45)5847	77671+62755+71683+77672	WD	SWS	PTR	SWT
(45)5848	77673+62756+71684+77674	WD	SWS	PTR	SWT
(45)5849	77675+62757+71685+77676	WD	SWS	PTR	SWT
(45)5850	77677+62758+71686+77678	WD	SWS	PTR	SWT
(45)5851	77679+62759+71687+77680	WD	SWS	PTR	SWT
(45)5852	77681+62760+71688+77682	WD	SWS	PTR	SWT
(45)5853	77683+62761+71689+77684	WD	SWS	PTR	SWT
(45)5854	77685+62762+71690+77686	WD	SWS	PTR	SWT
(45)5855	77687+62763+71691+77688	WD	SWS	PTR	SWT
(45)5856	77689+62764+71692+77690	WD	SWS	PTR	SWT
(45)5857	77691+62765+71693+77692	WD	SWS	PTR	SWT
(45)5858	77693+62766+71694+77694	WD	SWS	PTR	SWT
(45)5859	77695+62767+71695+77696	WD	SWS	PTR	SWT
(45)5860	77697+62768+71696+77698	WD	SWS	PTR	SWT
(45)5861	77699+62769+71697+77700	WD	SWS	PTR	SWT
(45)5862	77701+62770+71698+77702	WD	SWS	PTR	SWT
(45)5863	77703+62771+71699+77704	WD	SWS	PTR	SWT
(45)5864	77705+62772+71700+77706	WD	SWS	PTR	SWT
(45)5865	77707+62773+71701+77708	WD	SWS	PTR	SWT
(45)5866	77709+62774+71702+77710	WD	SWS	PTR	SWT
(45)5867	77711+62775+71703+77712	WD	SWS	PTR	SWT
(45)5868	77713+62776+71704+77714	WD	SWS	PTR	SWT
(45)5869	77715+62777+71705+77716	WD	SWS	PTR	SWT
(45)5870	77717+62778+71706+77718	WD	SWS	PTR	SWT
(45)5871	77719+62779+71707+77720	WD	SWS	PTR	SWT
(45)5872	77721+62780+71708+77722	WD	SWS	PTR	SWT
(45)5873	77723+62781+71709+77724	WD	SWS	PTR	SWT
(45)5874	77725+62782+71710+77726	WD	SWS	PTR	SWT

Class 455/9

	Vehicle Length: (Driving) 65ft 0½in (19.83m)	Width: 9ft 3¼in (2.82m)
	(Inter) 65ft 4½in (19.92m)	Horsepower: 1,000hp (746kW)
	Height: 12ft 1½in (3.79m)	Seats (total/car): 236S, 50S/68S/68S/50S

Number	Formation DMSO(A)+MSO+TSO+DTSO(B)	Depot	Livery	Owner	Operator
(45)5901	77813+62826+71714+77814	WD	SWS	PTR	SWT
(45)5902	77815+62827+71715+77816	WD	SWS	PTR	SWT
(45)5903	77817+62828+71716+77818	WD	SWS	PTR	SWT
(45)5904	77819+62829+71717+77820	WD	SWS	PTR	SWT
(45)5905	77821+62830+71725+77822	WD	SWS	PTR	SWT
(45)5906	77823+62831+71719+77824	WD	SWS	PTR	SWT
(45)5907	77825+62832+71720+77826	WD	SWS	PTR	SWT
(45)5908	77827+62833+71721+77828	WD	SWS	PTR	SWT
(45)5909	77829+62834+71722+77830	WD	SWS	PTR	SWT
(45)5910	77831+62835+71723+77832	WD	SWS	PTR	SWT
(45)5911	77833+62836+71724+77834	WD	SWS	PTR	SWT
(45)5912	77835+62837+67400+77836	WD	SWS	PTR	SWT
(45)5913	77837+62838+71726+77838	WD	SWS	PTR	SWT *(62838 stored, collision damage)*
(45)5914	77839+62839+71727+77840	WD	SWS	PTR	SWT
(45)5915	77841+62840+71728+77842	WD	SWS	PTR	SWT
(45)5916	77843+62841+71729+77844	WD	SWS	PTR	SWT
(45)5917	77845+62842+71730+77846	WD	SWS	PTR	SWT
(45)5918	77847+62843+71732+77848	WD	SWS	PTR	SWT
(45)5919	77849+62844+71718+77850	WD	SWS	PTR	SWT
(45)5920	77851+62845+71733+77852	WD	SWS	PTR	SWT

Class 456

In mid-2012, it was announced that following the delivery of new Class 377 stock to train operator Southern in 2013, the operator's 24 two-car Class 456 sets would transfer to South West Trains to enable their franchise commitment of running 10-car formations of the busy 'Windsor line' routes. SWT have announced the sets will be refurbished to be on a par with the Class 455 stock.

Right: *The final batch of Class 455s to be delivered were the 455/9 sub-class. Set No. 5905 approaches Vauxhall with a service from Waterloo to Waterloo via the Kingston loop line. A major refurbishment of the Class 455 fleet was announced in autumn 2012, with work commencing at Bournemouth depot in 2013.* **Antony Christie**

Class 458
Juniper

Vehicle Length: (Driving) 69ft 6in (21.16m) (Inter) 65ft 4in (19.91m)
Height: 12ft 3in (3.73m)
Width: 9ft 2in (2.79m)
Horsepower: 2,172hp (1,620kW)
Seats (total/car): 24F-250S, 12F-63S/49S/75S/12F-63S

Number	Formation DMCO(A)+TSO+MSO+DTCO(B)	Depot	Livery	Owner	Operator
(45)8001	67601+74001+74101+67701	WD	SWM	PTR	SWT
(45)8002	67602+74002+74102+67702	WD	SWM	PTR	SWT
(45)8003	67603+74003+74103+67703	WD	SWM	PTR	SWT
(45)8004	67604+74004+74104+67704	WD	SWM	PTR	SWT
(45)8005	67605+74005+74105+67705	WD	SWM	PTR	SWT
(45)8006	67606+74006+74106+67706	WD	SWM	PTR	SWT
(45)8007	67607+74007+74107+67707	WD	SWM	PTR	SWT
(45)8008	67608+74008+74108+67708	WD	SWM	PTR	SWT
(45)8009	67609+74009+74109+67709	WD	SWM	PTR	SWT
(45)8010	67610+74010+74110+67710	WD	SWM	PTR	SWT
(45)8011	67611+74011+74111+67711	WD	SWM	PTR	SWT
(45)8012	67612+74012+74112+67712	WD	SWM	PTR	SWT
(45)8013	67613+74013+74113+67713	WD	SWM	PTR	SWT
(45)8014	67614+74014+74114+67714	WD	SWM	PTR	SWT
(45)8015	67615+74015+74115+67715	WD	SWM	PTR	SWT
(45)8016	67616+74016+74116+67716	WD	SWM	PTR	SWT
(45)8017	67617+74017+74117+67717	WD	SWM	PTR	SWT
(45)8018	67618+74018+74118+67718	WD	SWM	PTR	SWT
(45)8019	67619+74019+74119+67719	WD	SWM	PTR	SWT
(45)8020	67620+74020+74120+67720	WD	SWM	PTR	SWT
(45)8021	67621+74021+74121+67721	WD	SWM	PTR	SWT
(45)8022	67622+74022+74122+67722	WD	SWM	PTR	SWT
(45)8023	67623+74023+74123+67723	WD	SWM	PTR	SWT
(45)8024	67624+74024+74124+67724	WD	SWM	PTR	SWT
(45)8025	67625+74025+74125+67725	WD	SWM	PTR	SWT
(45)8026	67626+74026+74126+67726	WD	SWM	PTR	SWT
(45)8027	67627+74027+74127+67727	WD	SWM	PTR	SWT
(45)8028	67628+74028+74128+67728	WD	SWM	PTR	SWT
(45)8029	67629+74029+74129+67729	WD	SWM	PTR	SWT
(45)8030	67630+74030+74130+67730	WD	SWM	PTR	SWT

■ A total of 36 five-car Class 458/5s are currently under conversion from the 30 original Class 458/0 sets plus all but two of the Class 460 vehicles. Each 'new' set will be formed of five vehicles, allowing SWT to operate 10-car trains on the outer-suburban routes. The sets will have new front ends with modern gangways and seating will be in the 2+2 style. The sets, to be numbered 458501-458536, will be allocated to East Wimbledon depot.

Right: *The first new trains ordered by Stagecoach for their South West Trains franchise were 30 Alstom Class 458 'Juniper' units. These were delivered between 1999-2002, but were plagued with major problems and at one time were stored. The sets were later confined to the Waterloo to Reading route. A Waterloo-bound train is seen at Reading, with set No. (15)8003 nearest the camera. These sets are now the subject of a major rebuilding programme and will soon emerge as 5-car Class 458/5s with new front ends.* **Antony Christie**

South Eastern

Address: ✉ Friars Bridge Court, 41-45 Blackfriars Road, London, SE1 8NZ

✆ info@southeasternrailway.co.uk

✆ 08700 000 2222

ⓘ www.southeasternrailway.co.uk

Managing Director: Charles Horton

Franchise Dates: 1 April 2006 - 31 March 2014

Principal Routes: London to Kent and parts of East Sussex, domestic services on HS1

Depots: Slade Green (SG), Ramsgate (RM), Ashford (AD*)

Parent Company: Govia

* Operated by Hitachi

Class 375/3
Electrostar

Vehicle Length: (Driving) 66ft 9in (20.3m)   *Width: 9ft 2in (2.79m)*
(Inter) 65ft 6in (19.96m)   *Horsepower: 1,341hp (1,000kW)*
Height: 12ft 4in (3.75m)   *Seats (total/car): 24F-152S, 12F-48S/56S/12F-48S*

Number	Formation DMCO(A)+TSO+DMCO(B)	Depot	Livery	Owner	Operator	Name
375301	67921+74351+67931	RM	SET	EVL	SET	
375302	67922+74352+67932	RM	SET	EVL	SET	
375303	67923+74353+67933	RM	SET	EVL	SET	
375304	67924+74354+67934	RM	SET	EVL	SET	Medway Valley Line 1856-2006
375305	67925+74355+67935	RM	SET	EVL	SET	
375306	67926+74356+67936	RM	SET	EVL	SET	
375307	67927+74357+67937	RM	SET	EVL	SET	
375308	67928+74358+67938	RM	SET	EVL	SET	
375309	67929+74359+67939	RM	SET	EVL	SET	
375310	67930+74360+67940	RM	SET	EVL	SET	

Class 375/6
Electrostar

Vehicle Length: (Driving) 66ft 9in (20.3m)   *Width: 9ft 2in (2.79m)*
(Inter) 65ft 6in (19.96m)   *Horsepower: 2,012hp (1,500kW)*
Height: 12ft 4in (3.75m)   *Seats (total/car): 24F-218S, 12F-48S/66S/56S/12F-48S*

Number	Formation DMCO(A)+MSO+TSO+DMCO(B)	Depot	Livery	Owner	Operator	Name
375601	67801+74251+74201+67851	RM	SET	EVL	SET	
375602	67802+74252+74202+67852	RM	SET	EVL	SET	
375603	67803+74253+74203+67853	RM	SET	EVL	SET	
375604	67804+74254+74204+67854	RM	SET	EVL	SET	
375605	67805+74255+74205+67855	RM	SET	EVL	SET	
375606	67806+74256+74206+67856	RM	SET	EVL	SET	
375607	67807+74257+74207+67857	RM	SET	EVL	SET	
375608	67808+74258+74208+67858	RM	SET	EVL	SET	Bromley Travelwise
375609	67809+74259+74209+67859	RM	SET	EVL	SET	
375610	67810+74260+74210+67860	RM	SET	EVL	SET	Royal Tunbridge Wells
375611	67811+74261+74211+67861	RM	SET	EVL	SET	Dr William Harvey
375612	67812+74262+74212+67862	RM	SET	EVL	SET	
375613	67813+74263+74213+67863	RM	SET	EVL	SET	
375614	67814+74264+74214+67864	RM	SET	EVL	SET	
375615	67815+74265+74215+67865	RM	SET	EVL	SET	
375616	67816+74266+74216+67866	RM	SET	EVL	SET	
375617	67817+74267+74217+67867	RM	SET	EVL	SET	
375618	67818+74268+74218+67868	RM	SET	EVL	SET	
375619	67819+74269+74219+67869	RM	SET	EVL	SET	Driver John Neve

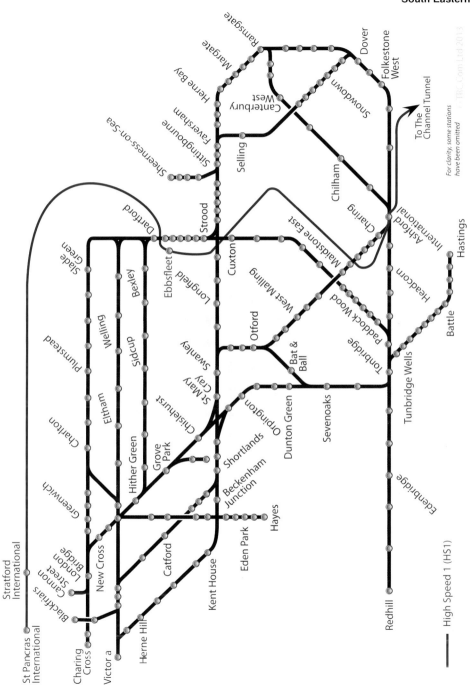

Passenger Train Operating Companies - South Eastern

For clarity, some stations have been omitted

— High Speed 1 (HS1)

South Eastern

375620	67820+74270+74220+67870	RM	SET	EVL	SET	
375621	67821+74271+74221+67871	RM	SET	EVL	SET	
375622	67822+74272+74222+67872	RM	SET	EVL	SET	
375623	67823+74273+74223+67873	RM	SET	EVL	SET	*Hospice in the Weald*
375624	67824+74274+74224+67874	RM	SET	EVL	SET	
375625	67825+74275+74225+67875	RM	SET	EVL	SET	
375626	67826+74276+74226+67876	RM	SET	EVL	SET	
375627	67827+74277+74227+67877	RM	SET	EVL	SET	
375628	67828+74278+74228+67878	RM	SET	EVL	SET	
375629	67829+74279+74229+67879	RM	SET	EVL	SET	
375630	67830+74280+74230+67880	RM	SET	EVL	SET	

Class 375/7
Electrostar

Vehicle Length: (Driving) 66ft 9in (20.3m) — Width: 9ft 2in (2.79m)
(Inter) 65ft 6in (19.96m) — Horsepower: 2,012hp (1,500kW)
Height: 12ft 4in (3.75m) — Seats (total/car): 24F-218S, 12F-48S/66S/56S/12F-48S

Number	Formation DMCO(A)+MSO+TSO+DMCO(B)	Depot	Livery	Owner	Operator	Name
375701	67831+74281+74231+67881	RM	SET	EVL	SET	*Kent Air Ambulance Explorer*
375702	67832+74282+74232+67882	RM	SET	EVL	SET	
375703	67833+74283+74233+67883	RM	SET	EVL	SET	
375704	67834+74284+74234+67884	RM	SET	EVL	SET	
375705	67835+74285+74235+67885	RM	SET	EVL	SET	
375706	67836+74286+74236+67886	RM	SET	EVL	SET	
375707	67837+74287+74237+67887	RM	SET	EVL	SET	
375708	67838+74288+74238+67888	RM	SET	EVL	SET	
375709	67839+74289+74239+67889	RM	SET	EVL	SET	
375710	67840+74290+74240+67890	RM	SET	EVL	SET	
375711	67841+74291+74241+67891	RM	SET	EVL	SET	
375712	67842+74292+74242+67892	RM	SET	EVL	SET	
375713	67843+74293+74243+67893	RM	SET	EVL	SET	
375714	67844+74294+74244+67894	RM	SET	EVL	SET	
375715	67845+74295+74245+67895	RM	SET	EVL	SET	

Class 375/8
Electrostar

Vehicle Length: (Driving) 66ft 9in (20.3m) — Width: 9ft 2in (2.79m)
(Inter) 65ft 6in (19.96m) — Horsepower: 2,012hp (1,500kW)
Height: 12ft 4in (3.75m) — Seats (total/car): 24F-218S, 12F-48S/66S/56S/12F-48S

Number	Formation DMCO(A)+MSO+TSO+DMCO(B)	Depot	Livery	Owner	Operator	Name
375801	73301+79001+78201+73701	RM	SET	EVL	SET	
375802	73302+79002+78202+73702	RM	SET	EVL	SET	
375803	73303+79003+78203+73703	RM	SET	EVL	SET	
375804	73304+79004+78204+73704	RM	SET	EVL	SET	
375805	73305+79005+78205+73705	RM	SET	EVL	SET	
375806	73306+79006+78206+73706	RM	SET	EVL	SET	
375807	73307+79007+78207+73707	RM	SET	EVL	SET	
375808	73308+79008+78208+73708	RM	SET	EVL	SET	
375809	73309+79009+78209+73709	RM	SET	EVL	SET	
375810	73310+79010+78210+73710	RM	SET	EVL	SET	
375811	73311+79011+78211+73711	RM	SET	EVL	SET	
375812	73312+79012+78212+73712	RM	SET	EVL	SET	
375813	73313+79013+78213+73713	RM	SET	EVL	SET	
375814	73314+79014+78214+73714	RM	SET	EVL	SET	
375815	73315+79015+78215+73715	RM	SET	EVL	SET	
375816	73316+79016+78216+73716	RM	SET	EVL	SET	
375817	73317+79017+78217+73717	RM	SET	EVL	SET	
375818	73318+79018+78218+73718	RM	SET	EVL	SET	
375819	73319+79019+78219+73719	RM	SET	EVL	SET	
375820	73320+79020+78220+73720	RM	SET	EVL	SET	
375821	73321+79021+78221+73721	RM	SET	EVL	SET	
375822	73322+79022+78222+73722	RM	SET	EVL	SET	
375823	73323+79023+78223+73723	RM	SET	EVL	SET	
375824	73324+79024+78224+73724	RM	SET	EVL	SET	
375825	73325+79025+78225+73725	RM	SET	EVL	SET	

375826	73326+79026+78226+73726	RM	SET	EVL	SET	
375827	73327+79027+78227+73727	RM	SET	EVL	SET	
375828	73328+79028+78228+73728	RM	SET	EVL	SET	
375829	73329+79029+78229+73729	RM	SET	EVL	SET	
375830	73330+79030+78230+73730	RM	SET	EVL	SET	*City of London*

Set 375812 fitted with De-icing equipment

Class 375/9
Electrostar

Vehicle Length: (Driving) 66ft 9in (20.3m)	Width: 9ft 2in (2.79m)	
(Inter) 65ft 6in (19.96m)	Horsepower: 2,012hp (1,500kW)	
Height: 12ft 4in (3.75m)	Seats (total/car): 24F-250S, 12F-59S/73S/59S/12F-59S	

Number	Formation DMCO(A)+MSO+TSO+DMCO(B)	Depot	Livery	Owner	Operator
375901	73331+79031+79061+73731	RM	SET	EVL	SET
375902	73332+79032+79062+73732	RM	SET	EVL	SET
375903	73333+79033+79063+73733	RM	SET	EVL	SET
375904	73334+79034+79064+73734	RM	SET	EVL	SET
375905	73335+79035+79065+73735	RM	SET	EVL	SET
375906	73336+79036+79066+73736	RM	SET	EVL	SET
375907	73337+79037+79067+73737	RM	SET	EVL	SET
375908	73338+79038+79068+73738	RM	SET	EVL	SET
375909	73339+79039+79069+73739	RM	SET	EVL	SET
375910	73340+79040+79070+73740	RM	SET	EVL	SET
375911	73341+79041+79071+73741	RM	SET	EVL	SET
375912	73342+79042+79072+73742	RM	SET	EVL	SET
375913	73343+79043+79073+73743	RM	SET	EVL	SET
375914	73344+79044+79074+73744	RM	SET	EVL	SET
375915	73345+79045+79075+73745	RM	SET	EVL	SET
375916	73346+79046+79076+73746	RM	SET	EVL	SET
375917	73347+79047+79077+73747	RM	SET	EVL	SET
375918	73348+79048+79078+73748	RM	SET	EVL	SET
375919	73349+79049+79079+73749	RM	SET	EVL	SET
375920	73350+79050+79080+73750	RM	SET	EVL	SET
375921	73351+79051+79081+73751	RM	SET	EVL	SET
375922	73352+79052+79082+73752	RM	SET	EVL	SET
375923	73353+79053+79083+73753	RM	SET	EVL	SET
375924	73354+79054+79084+73754	RM	SET	EVL	SET
375925	73355+79055+79085+73755	RM	SET	EVL	SET
375926	73356+79056+79086+73756	RM	SET	EVL	SET
375927	73357+79057+79087+73757	RM	SET	EVL	SET

Below: *The SouthEastern franchise operates five different sub-classes of the Bombardier 'Electrostar' product range classified as 375. The sets are used on outer-suburban and main line services based at Ramsgate. Four-car Class 375/9 set No. 375914 is seen shunting at Ramsgate depot.* **Antony Christie**

South Eastern

Class 376
Electrostar

Vehicle Length: (Driving) 66ft 9in (20.3m)
(Inter) 65ft 6in (19.96m)
Height: 12ft 4in (3.75m)
Width: 9ft 2in (2.79m)
Horsepower: 2,682hp (2,000kW)
Seats (total/car): 216S, 36S/48S/48S/48S/36S + 116 perch

Number	Formation DMSO(A)+MSO+TSO+MSO+DMSO(B)	Depot	Livery	Owner	Operator
376001	61101+63301+64301+63501+61601	SG	SET	EVL	SET
376002	61102+63302+64302+63502+61602	SG	SET	EVL	SET
376003	61103+63303+64303+63503+61603	SG	SET	EVL	SET
376004	61104+63304+64304+63504+61604	SG	SET	EVL	SET
376005	61105+63305+64305+63505+61605	SG	SET	EVL	SET
376006	61106+63306+64306+63506+61606	SG	SET	EVL	SET
376007	61107+63307+64307+63507+61607	SG	SET	EVL	SET
376008	61108+63308+64308+63508+61608	SG	SET	EVL	SET
376009	61109+63309+64309+63509+61609	SG	SET	EVL	SET
376010	61110+63310+64310+63510+61610	SG	SET	EVL	SET
376011	61111+63311+64311+63511+61611	SG	SET	EVL	SET
376012	61112+63312+64312+63512+61612	SG	SET	EVL	SET
376013	61113+63313+64313+63513+61613	SG	SET	EVL	SET
376014	61114+63314+64314+63514+61614	SG	SET	EVL	SET
376015	61115+63315+64315+63515+61615	SG	SET	EVL	SET
376016	61116+63316+64316+63516+61616	SG	SET	EVL	SET
376017	61117+63317+64317+63517+61617	SG	SET	EVL	SET
376018	61118+63318+64318+63518+61618	SG	SET	EVL	SET
376019	61119+63319+64319+63519+61619	SG	SET	EVL	SET
376020	61120+63320+64320+63520+61620	SG	SET	EVL	SET
376021	61121+63321+64321+63521+61621	SG	SET	EVL	SET
376022	61122+63322+64322+63522+61622	SG	SET	EVL	SET
376023	61123+63323+64323+63523+61623	SG	SET	EVL	SET
376024	61124+63324+64324+63524+61624	SG	SET	EVL	SET
376025	61125+63325+64325+63525+61625	SG	SET	EVL	SET
376026	61126+63326+64326+63526+61626	SG	SET	EVL	SET
376027	61127+63327+64327+63527+61627	SG	SET	EVL	SET
376028	61128+63328+64328+63528+61628	SG	SET	EVL	SET
376029	61129+63329+64329+63529+61629	SG	SET	EVL	SET
376030	61130+63330+64330+63530+61630	SG	SET	EVL	SET
376031	61131+63331+64331+63531+61631	SG	SET	EVL	SET
376032	61132+63332+64332+63532+61632	SG	SET	EVL	SET
376033	61133+63333+64333+63533+61633	SG	SET	EVL	SET
376034	61134+63334+64334+63534+61634	SG	SET	EVL	SET
376035	61135+63335+64335+63535+61635	SG	SET	EVL	SET
376036	61136+63336+64336+63536+61636	SG	SET	EVL	SET

Below: *Traffic levels on the inner-suburban South Eastern network were so high that a revised version of the 'Electrostar' was introduced in 2005-06 with high-capacity interiors and formed of five carriages. These sets have fewer seats than conventional 'Electrostars', with large standing and perching areas. Set No. 376023 approaches Lewisham with a Dartford-bound service.* **Mark V. Pike**

Class 395
Javelin

Vehicle Length: (Driving) 67ft 7in (20.6m)	Width: 9ft 2in (2.79m)	
(Inter) 67ft 6in (20.5m)	Horsepower: 2,252hp (1,680kW)	
Height: 12ft 6in (3.81m)	Seats (total/car): 340S, 28S/66S/66S/66S/66S/48S	

Number	Formation DMSO(A)+MSO(A)+MSO(B)+ MSO(C)+MSO(D)+DMSO(B)	Depot	Livery	Owner	Operator	Name
395001	39011+39012+39013+39014+39015+39016	AD	HS1	EVL	SET	Dame Kelly Holmes
395002	39021+39022+39023+39024+39025+39026	AD	HS1	EVL	SET	Sebastian Coe
395003	39031+39032+39033+39034+39035+39036	AD	HS1	EVL	SET	Sir Steve Redgrave
395004	39041+39042+39043+39044+39045+39046	AD	HS1	EVL	SET	Sir Chris Hoy
395005	39051+39052+39053+39054+39055+39056	AD	HS1	EVL	SET	Dame Tanni Grey-Thompson
395006	39061+39062+39063+39064+39065+39066	AD	HS1	EVL	SET	Daley Thompson
395007	39071+39072+39073+39074+39075+39076	AD	HS1	EVL	SET	Steve Backley
395008	39081+39082+39083+39084+39085+39086	AD	HS1	EVL	SET	Ben Ainslie
395009	39091+39092+39093+39094+39095+39096	AD	HS1	EVL	SET	Rebecca Adlington
395010	39101+39102+39103+39104+39105+39106	AD	HS1	EVL	SET	
395011	39111+39112+39113+39114+39115+39116	AD	HS1	EVL	SET	
395012	39121+39122+39123+39124+39125+39126	AD	HS1	EVL	SET	
395013	39131+39132+39133+39134+39135+39136	AD	HS1	EVL	SET	
395014	39141+39142+39143+39144+39145+39146	AD	HS1	EVL	SET	
395015	39151+39152+39153+39154+39155+39156	AD	HS1	EVL	SET	
395016	39161+39162+39163+39164+39165+39166	AD	HS1	EVL	SET	Jamie Staff
395017	39171+39172+39173+39174+39175+39176	AD	HS1	EVL	SET	
395018	39181+39182+39183+39184+39185+39186	AD	HS1	EVL	SET	
395019	39191+39192+39193+39194+39195+39196	AD	HS1	EVL	SET	
395020	39201+39202+39203+39204+39205+39206	AD	HS1	EVL	SET	
395021	39211+39212+39213+39214+39215+39216	AD	HS1	EVL	SET	
395022	39221+39222+39223+39224+39225+39226	AD	HS1	EVL	SET	
395023	39231+39232+39233+39234+39235+39236	AD	HS1	EVL	SET	
395024	39241+39242+39243+39244+39245+39246	AD	HS1	EVL	SET	
395025	39251+39252+39253+39254+39255+39256	AD	HS1	EVL	SET	
395026	39261+39262+39263+39264+39265+39266	AD	HS1	EVL	SET	Marc Woods
395027	39271+39272+39273+39274+39275+39276	AD	HS1	EVL	SET	
395028	39281+39282+39283+39284+39285+39286	AD	HS1	EVL	SET	
395029	39291+39292+39293+39294+39295+39296	AD	HS1	EVL	SET	

Below: *Following the opening of the first high speed line in the UK, HS1 between St Pancras International and the Channel Tunnel, operator SouthEastern commenced running a domestic service over the route at up to 140mph (225km/h). For this operation a fleet of 29 six-car Class 395 'Javelin' sets were built in Japan by Hitachi Industries and are maintained at Ashford, Kent. The units are painted in SouthEastern dark blue. Class 395s also operate over classic routes in Kent providing through services off the high speed connection. Set No. 395024 is seen arriving at St Pancras International.* **Antony Christie**

South Eastern

Class 465/0
Networker

Vehicle Length: (Driving) 68ft 6½in (20.89m) Width: 9ft 3in (2.81m)
(Inter) 65ft 9¾in (20.05m) Horsepower: 2,252hp (1,680kW)
Height: 12ft 4½in (3.77m) Seats (total/car): 348S, 86S/90S/86S/86S

Number	Formation	Depot	Livery	Owner	Operator
	DMSO(A)+TSO+TSO+DMSO(B)				
465001	64759+72028+72029+64809	SG	SET	EVL	SET
465002	64760+72030+72031+64810	SG	SET	EVL	SET
465003	64761+72032+72033+64811	SG	SET	EVL	SET
465004	64762+72034+72035+64812	SG	SET	EVL	SET
465005	64763+72036+72037+64813	SG	SET	EVL	SET
465006	64764+72038+72039+64814	SG	SET	EVL	SET
465007	64765+72040+72041+64815	SG	SET	EVL	SET
465008	64766+72042+72043+64816	SG	SET	EVL	SET
465009	64767+72044+72045+64817	SG	SET	EVL	SET
465010	64768+72046+72047+64818	SG	SET	EVL	SET
465011	64769+72048+72049+64819	SG	SET	EVL	SET
465012	64770+72050+72051+64820	SG	SET	EVL	SET
465013	64771+72052+72053+64821	SG	SET	EVL	SET
465014	64772+72054+72055+64822	SG	SET	EVL	SET
465015	64773+72056+72057+64823	SG	SET	EVL	SET
465016	64774+72058+72059+64824	SG	SET	EVL	SET
465017	64775+72060+72061+64825	SG	SET	EVL	SET
465018	64776+72062+72063+64826	SG	SET	EVL	SET
465019	64777+72064+72065+64827	SG	SET	EVL	SET
465020	64778+72066+72067+64828	SG	SET	EVL	SET
465021	64779+72068+72069+64829	SG	SET	EVL	SET
465022	64780+72070+72071+64830	SG	SET	EVL	SET
465023	64781+72072+72073+64831	SG	SET	EVL	SET
465024	64782+72074+72075+64832	SG	SET	EVL	SET
465025	64783+72076+72077+64833	SG	SET	EVL	SET
465026	64784+72078+72079+64834	SG	SET	EVL	SET
465027	64785+72080+72081+64835	SG	SET	EVL	SET
465028	64786+72082+72083+64836	SG	SET	EVL	SET
465029	64787+72084+72085+64837	SG	SET	EVL	SET
465030	64788+72086+72087+64838	SG	SET	EVL	SET
465031	64789+72088+72089+64839	SG	SET	EVL	SET
465032	64790+72090+72091+64840	SG	SET	EVL	SET
465033	64791+72092+72093+64841	SG	SET	EVL	SET
465034	64792+72094+72095+64842	SG	SET	EVL	SET
465035	64793+72096+72097+64843	SG	SET	EVL	SET
465036	64794+72098+72099+64844	SG	SET	EVL	SET
465037	64795+72100+72101+64845	SG	SET	EVL	SET
465038	64796+72102+72103+64846	SG	SET	EVL	SET
465039	64797+72104+72105+64847	SG	SET	EVL	SET
465040	64798+72106+72107+64848	SG	SET	EVL	SET
465041	64799+72108+72109+64849	SG	SET	EVL	SET
465042	64800+72110+72111+64850	SG	SET	EVL	SET
465043	64801+72112+72113+64851	SG	SET	EVL	SET
465044	64802+72114+72115+64852	SG	SET	EVL	SET
465045	64803+72116+72117+64853	SG	SET	EVL	SET
465046	64804+72118+72119+64854	SG	SET	EVL	SET
465047	64805+72120+72121+64855	SG	SET	EVL	SET
465048	64806+72122+72123+64856	SG	SET	EVL	SET
465049	64807+72124+72125+64857	SG	SET	EVL	SET
465050	64808+72126+72127+64858	SG	SET	EVL	SET

Class 465/1
Networker

Vehicle Length: (Driving) 68ft 6½in (20.89m) Width: 9ft 3in (2.81m)
(Inter) 65ft 9¾in (20.05m) Horsepower: 2,252hp (1,680kW)
Height: 12ft 4½in (3.77m) Seats (total/car): 348S, 86S/90S/86S/86S

Number	Formation	Depot	Livery	Owner	Operator
	DMSO(A)+TSO+TSO+DMSO(B)				
465151	65800+72900+72901+65847	SG	SET	EVL	SET
465152	65801+72902+72903+65848	SG	SET	EVL	SET

465153	65802+72904+72905+65849	SG	SET	EVL	SET
465154	65803+72906+72907+65850	SG	SET	EVL	SET
465155	65804+72908+72909+65851	SG	SET	EVL	SET
465156	65805+72910+72911+65852	SG	SET	EVL	SET
465157	65806+72912+72913+65853	SG	SET	EVL	SET
465158	65807+72914+72915+65854	SG	SET	EVL	SET
465159	65808+72916+72917+65855	SG	SET	EVL	SET
465160	65809+72918+72919+65856	SG	SET	EVL	SET
465161	65810+72920+72921+65857	SG	SET	EVL	SET
465162	65811+72922+72923+65858	SG	SET	EVL	SET
465163	65812+72924+72925+65859	SG	SET	EVL	SET
465164	65813+72926+72927+65860	SG	SET	EVL	SET
465165	65814+72928+72929+65861	SG	SET	EVL	SET
465166	65815+72930+72931+65862	SG	SET	EVL	SET
465167	65816+72932+72933+65863	SG	SET	EVL	SET
465168	65817+72934+72935+65864	SG	SET	EVL	SET
465169	65818+72936+72937+65865	SG	SET	EVL	SET
465170	65819+72938+72939+65866	SG	SET	EVL	SET
465171	65820+72940+72941+65867	SG	SET	EVL	SET
465172	65821+72942+72943+65868	SG	SET	EVL	SET
465173	65822+72944+72945+65869	SG	SET	EVL	SET
465174	65823+72946+72947+65870	SG	SET	EVL	SET
465175	65824+72948+72949+65871	SG	SET	EVL	SET
465176	65825+72950+72951+65872	SG	SET	EVL	SET
465177	65826+72952+72952+65873	SG	SET	EVL	SET
465178	65827+72954+72955+65874	SG	SET	EVL	SET
465179	65828+72956+72957+65875	SG	SET	EVL	SET
465180	65829+72958+72959+65876	SG	SET	EVL	SET
465181	65830+72960+72961+65877	SG	SET	EVL	SET
465182	65831+72962+72963+65878	SG	SET	EVL	SET
465183	65832+72964+72965+65879	SG	SET	EVL	SET
465184	65833+72966+72967+65880	SG	SET	EVL	SET
465185	65834+72968+72969+65881	SG	SET	EVL	SET
465186	65835+72970+72971+65882	SG	SET	EVL	SET
465187	65836+72972+72973+65883	SG	SET	EVL	SET
465188	65837+72974+72975+65884	SG	SET	EVL	SET
465189	65838+72976+72977+65885	SG	SET	EVL	SET
465190	65839+72978+72979+65886	SG	SET	EVL	SET
465191	65840+72980+72981+65887	SG	SET	EVL	SET
465192	65841+72982+72983+65888	SG	SET	EVL	SET
465193	65842+72984+72985+65889	SG	SET	EVL	SET
465194	65843+72986+72987+65890	SG	SET	EVL	SET
465195	65844+72988+72989+65891	SG	SET	EVL	SET
465196	65845+72990+72991+65892	SG	SET	EVL	SET
465197	65846+72992+72993+65893	SG	SET	EVL	SET

Class 465/2
Networker

Vehicle Length: (Driving) 68ft 6½in (20.89m) Width: 9ft 3in (2.81m)
(Inter) 65ft 9¾in (20.05m) Horsepower: 2,252hp (1,680kW)
Height: 12ft 4½in (3.77m) Seats (total/car): 348S, 86S/90S/86S/86S

Number	Formation DMSO(A)+TSO+TSO+DMSO(B)	Depot	Livery	Owner	Operator
465235	65734+72787+72788+65784	SG	SET	ANG	SET
465236	65735+72789+72790+65785	SG	SET	ANG	SET
465237	65736+72791+72792+65786	SG	SET	ANG	SET
465238	65737+72793+72794+65787	SG	SET	ANG	SET
465239	65738+72795+72796+65788	SG	SET	ANG	SET
465240	65739+72797+72798+65789	SG	SET	ANG	SET
465241	65740+72799+72800+65790	SG	SET	ANG	SET
465242	65741+72801+72802+65791	SG	SET	ANG	SET
465243	65742+72803+72804+65792	SG	SET	ANG	SET
465244	65743+72805+72806+65793	SG	SET	ANG	SET
465245	65744+72807+72808+65794	SG	SET	ANG	SET
465246	65745+72809+72810+65795	SG	SET	ANG	SET
465247	65746+72811+72812+65796	SG	SET	ANG	SET

Train Operating Companies

South Eastern

465248	65747+72813+72814+65797	SG	SET	ANG	SET
465249	65748+72815+72816+65798	SG	SET	ANG	SET
465250	65749+72817+72818+65799	SG	SET	ANG	SET

Class 465/9
Networker

Vehicle Length: (Driving) 68ft 6½in (20.89m)
(Inter) 65ft 9¾in (20.05m)
Height: 12ft 4½in (3.77m)
Width: 9ft 3in (2.81m)
Horsepower: 2,252hp (1,680kW)
Seats (total/car): 24F-302S, 12F-68S/76S/90S/12F-68S

Number	Formation DMCO(A)+TSO+TSO+DMCO(B)	Depot	Livery	Owner	Operator	Name
465901 (465201)	65700+72719+72720+65750	SG	SET	ANG	SET	
465902 (465202)	65701+72721+72722+65751	SG	SET	ANG	SET	
465903 (465203)	65702+72723+72724+65752	SG	SET	ANG	SET	Remembrance
465904 (465204)	65703+72725+72726+65753	SG	SET	ANG	SET	
465905 (465205)	65704+72727+72728+65754	SG	SET	ANG	SET	
465906 (465206)	65705+72729+72730+65755	SG	SET	ANG	SET	
465907 (465207)	65706+72731+72732+65756	SG	SET	ANG	SET	
465908 (465208)	65707+72733+72734+65757	SG	SET	ANG	SET	
465909 (465209)	65708+72735+72736+65758	SG	SET	ANG	SET	
465910 (465210)	65709+72737+72738+65759	SG	SET	ANG	SET	
465911 (465211)	65710+72739+72740+65760	SG	SET	ANG	SET	
465912 (465212)	65711+72741+72742+65761	SG	SET	ANG	SET	
465913 (465213)	65712+72743+72744+65762	SG	SET	ANG	SET	
465914 (465214)	65713+72745+72746+65763	SG	SET	ANG	SET	
465915 (465215)	65714+72747+72748+65764	SG	SET	ANG	SET	
465916 (465216)	65715+72749+72750+65765	SG	SET	ANG	SET	
465917 (465217)	65716+72751+72752+65766	SG	SET	ANG	SET	
465918 (465218)	65717+72753+72754+65767	SG	SET	ANG	SET	
465919 (465219)	65718+72755+72756+65768	SG	SET	ANG	SET	
465920 (465220)	65719+72757+72758+65769	SG	SET	ANG	SET	
465921 (465221)	65720+72759+72760+65770	SG	SET	ANG	SET	
465922 (465222)	65721+72761+72762+65771	SG	SET	ANG	SET	
465923 (465223)	65722+72763+72764+65772	SG	SET	ANG	SET	
465924 (465224)	65723+72765+72766+65773	SG	SET	ANG	SET	
465925 (465225)	65724+72767+72768+65774	SG	SET	ANG	SET	
465926 (465226)	65725+72769+72770+65775	SG	SET	ANG	SET	
465927 (465227)	65726+72771+72772+65776	SG	SET	ANG	SET	
465928 (465228)	65727+72773+72774+65777	SG	SET	ANG	SET	
465929 (465229)	65728+72775+72776+65778	SG	SET	ANG	SET	
465930 (465230)	65729+72777+72778+65779	SG	SET	ANG	SET	
465931 (465231)	65730+72779+72780+65780	SG	SET	ANG	SET	
465932 (465232)	65731+72781+72782+65781	SG	SET	ANG	SET	
465933 (465233)	65732+72783+72784+65782	SG	SET	ANG	SET	
465934 (465234)	65733+72785+72786+65783	SG	SET	ANG	SET	

Left: Suburban services operated by SouthEastern are formed of a sizeable fleet of BREL/ABB and Metro-Cammell Class 465 'Networker' units. All units are based at the large EMU depot at Slade Green. Members of Class 465/0, 465/1 and 465/2 are all standard class units, while the 34 members of Class 465/9, modified by Wabtec, Doncaster from Class 465/2s, have limited first class accommodation in the two driving cars. One of the original batch of BREL sets, No. 465006, is seen at Denmark Hill. **John Binch**

Class 466
Networker

Vehicle Length: (Driving) 68ft 6½in (20.89m)
Height: 12ft 4½in (3.77m)
Width: 9ft 3in (2.81m)
Horsepower: 1,126hp (840kW)
Seats (total/car): 168S, 86S/82S

Number	Formation DMSO+DTSO	Depot	Livery	Owner	Operator
466001	64860+78312	SG	SET	ANG	SET
466002	64861+78313	SG	SET	ANG	SET
466003	64862+78314	SG	SET	ANG	SET
466004	64863+78315	SG	SET	ANG	SET
466005	64864+78316	SG	SET	ANG	SET
466006	64865+78317	SG	SET	ANG	SET
466007	64866+78318	SG	SET	ANG	SET
466008	64867+78319	SG	SET	ANG	SET
466009	64868+78320	SG	SET	ANG	SET
466010	64869+78321	SG	SET	ANG	SET
466011	64870+78322	SG	SET	ANG	SET
466012	64871+78323	SG	SET	ANG	SET
466013	64872+78324	SG	SET	ANG	SET
466014	64873+78325	SG	SET	ANG	SET
466015	64874+78326	SG	SET	ANG	SET
466016	64875+78327	SG	SET	ANG	SET
466017	64876+78328	SG	SET	ANG	SET
466018	64877+78329	SG	SET	ANG	SET
466019	64878+78330	SG	SET	ANG	SET
466020	64879+78331	SG	SET	ANG	SET
466021	64880+78332	SG	SET	ANG	SET
466022	64881+78333	SG	SET	ANG	SET
466023	64882+78334	SG	SET	ANG	SET
466024	64883+78335	SG	SET	ANG	SET
466025	64884+78336	SG	SET	ANG	SET
466026	64885+78337	SG	SET	ANG	SET
466027	64886+78338	SG	SET	ANG	SET
466028	64887+78339	SG	SET	ANG	SET
466029	64888+78340	SG	SET	ANG	SET
466030	64889+78341	SG	SET	ANG	SET
466031	64890+78342	SG	SET	ANG	SET
466032	64891+78343	SG	SET	ANG	SET
466033	64892+78344	SG	SET	ANG	SET
466034	64893+78345	SG	SET	ANG	SET
466035	64894+78346	SG	SET	ANG	SET
466036	64895+78347	SG	SET	ANG	SET
466037	64896+78348	SG	SET	ANG	SET
466038	64897+78349	SG	SET	ANG	SET
466039	64898+78350	SG	SET	ANG	SET
466040	64899+78351	SG	SET	ANG	SET
466041	64900+78352	SG	SET	ANG	SET
466042	64901+78353	SG	SET	ANG	SET
466043	64902+78354	SG	SET	ANG	SET

Above: To give flexibility to operate two-, six- or ten-car trains a batch of 43 two-car 'Networker' sets classified '466' were built by Alstom. Set No. 466042 is illustrated. **Inset:** Networker Class 465 and 466 driving cab layout. These were some of the first sets to use a single power and brake controller operated by the driver's left hand. **John Binch / CJM**

Passenger Train Operating Companies - South Eastern

Southern

Address: Go-Ahead House, 26-28 Addiscombe Road, Croydon, CR9 5GA
 info@southernrailway.com
 08451 272920
 www.southernrailway.com

Managing Director: Chris Burchell
Franchise Dates: 1 March 2003 - 25 July 2015
Principal Routes: London Victoria/London Bridge to Brighton, Coastway route, Uckfield/East Grinstead. Services to Surrey/Sussex, and Brighton to Ashford route
Depots: Brighton (BI), Selhurst (SU)
Parent Company: Govia

Passenger Train Operating Companies - Southern

For clarity, some stations have been omitted

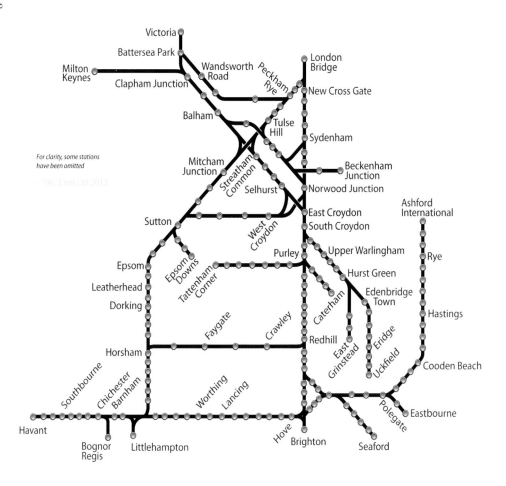

Class 171/7
Turbostar

Vehicle Length: 77ft 6in (23.62m)					Engine: 1 x MTU 6R 183TD13H 422hp per vehicle				
Height: 12ft 4½in (3.77m)					Horsepower: 844hp (629kW)				
Width: 8ft 10in (2.69m)					Seats (total/car): 9F-107S 9F-43S/64S				

Number	Formation	Depot	Livery	Owner	Operator				
	DMCL+DMSL								
171721	50721+79721	SU	SOU	PTR	SOU				
171722	50722+79722	SU	SOU	PTR	SOU				
171723	50723+79723	SU	SOU	PTR	SOU				
171724	50724+79724	SU	SOU	PTR	SOU				
171725	50725+79725	SU	SOU	PTR	SOU				
171726	50726+79726	SU	SOU	PTR	SOU				
171727	50727+79727	SU	SOU	PTR	SOU				
171728	50728+79728	SU	SOU	PTR	SOU				
171729	50729+79729	SU	SOU	PTR	SOU				
171730	50392+79392	SU	SOU	PTR	SOU				

171730 Previously numbered 170392

Class 171/8
Turbostar

Vehicle Length: 77ft 6in (23.62m)		Engine: 1 x MTU 6R 183TD13H 422hp per vehicle		
Height: 12ft 4½in (3.77m)		Horsepower: 1,688hp (1,259kW)		
Width: 8ft 10in (2.69m)		Seats (total/car): 18F-241S 9F-43S/74S/74S/9F-50SS		

Number	Formation	Depot	Livery	Owner	Operator
	DMCL(A)+MS+MS+DMCL(B)				
171801	50801+54801+56801+79801	SU	SOU	PTR	SOU
171802	50802+54802+56802+79802	SU	SOU	PTR	SOU
171803	50803+54803+56803+79803	SU	SOU	PTR	SOU
171804	50804+54804+56804+79804	SU	SOU	PTR	SOU
171805	50805+54805+56805+79805	SU	SOU	PTR	SOU
171806	50806+54806+56806+79806	SU	SOU	PTR	SOU

Right: *A small fleet of two- and four-car Class 171 'Turbostar' diesel sets are operated by Southern for use on non-electrified routes. Four-car set No. 171804 is seen passing beneath the East London Line flyover on the approaches to New Cross Gate, with the 09.08 service from London Bridge to Uckfield on 1 April 2011.*
Brian Morrison

Class 313/2

Vehicle Length: (Driving) 64ft 11½in (20.75m)		Width: 9ft 3in (2.82m)		
(Inter) 65ft 4½in (19.92m)		Horsepower: 880hp (656kW)		
Height: 11ft 9in (3.58m)		Seats (total/car): 202S, 66S/70S/66S		

Number	Formation	Depot	Livery	Owner	Operator	
	DMSO+PTSO+BDMSO					
313201 (313101)*	62529+71213+62593	BI	SOU	BEA	SOU	* DC only
313202 (313102)	62530+71214+62594	BI	SOU	BEA	SOU	
313203 (313103)	62531+71215+62595	BI	SOU	BEA	SOU	
313204 (313104)	62532+71216+62596	BI	SOU	BEA	SOU	
313205 (313105)	62533+71217+62597	BI	SOU	BEA	SOU	
313206 (313106)	62534+71218+62598	BI	SOU	BEA	SOU	
313207 (313107)	62535+71219+62599	BI	SOU	BEA	SOU	
313208 (313108)	62536+71220+62600	BI	SOU	BEA	SOU	
313209 (313109)	62537+71221+62601	BI	SOU	BEA	SOU	
313210 (313110)	62538+71222+62602	BI	SOU	BEA	SOU	
313211 (313111)	62539+71223+62603	BI	SOU	BEA	SOU	
313212 (313112)	62540+71224+62604	BI	SOU	BEA	SOU	
313213 (313113)	62541+71225+62605	BI	SOU	BEA	SOU	
313214 (313114)	62542+71226+62606	BI	SOU	BEA	SOU	
313215 (313115)	62543+71227+62607	BI	SOU	BEA	SOU	
313216 (313116)	62544+71228+62608	BI	SOU	BEA	SOU	
313217 (313117)	62545+71229+61609	BI	SOU	BEA	SOU	
313219 (313119)	62547+71231+61611	BI	SOU	BEA	SOU	
313220 (313120)	62548+71232+61612	BI	SOU	BEA	SOU	

Passenger Train Operating Companies - Southern

Southern

Left: *After introduction of new Class 378 stock on London Overground, 19 of the dual voltage Class 313s were transferred to Brighton for use on the Coastway route. The units have been fully refurbished for their latest role and carry Southern livery, some with route-specific pictograms. Set No. 313220 is seen at Barnham on 26 January 2012.* **Brian Garrett**

Class 377/1
Electrostar

Vehicle Length: (Driving) 66ft 9in (20.3m) Width: 9ft 2in (2.79m)
(Inter) 65ft 6in (19.96m) Horsepower: 2,012hp (1,500kW)
Height: 12ft 4in (3.75m) Seats (total/car): 24F-210S or 244S 12F-48S(56S)/62S(70S)/52S(62S)/12F-48S(56S)

Number	Formation DMCO(A)+MSO+TSO+DMCO(B)	Depot	Livery	Owner	Operator
377101	78501+77101+78901+78701	BI	SOU	PTR	SOU
377102	78502+77102+78902+78702	BI	SOU	PTR	SOU
377103	78503+77103+78903+78703	BI	SOU	PTR	SOU
377104	78504+77104+78904+78704	BI	SOU	PTR	SOU
377105	78505+77105+78905+78705	BI	SOU	PTR	SOU
377106	78506+77106+78906+78706	BI	SOU	PTR	SOU
377107	78507+77107+78907+78707	BI	SOU	PTR	SOU
377108	78508+77108+78908+78708	BI	SOU	PTR	SOU
377109	78509+77109+78909+78709	BI	SOU	PTR	SOU
377110	78510+77110+78910+78710	BI	SOU	PTR	SOU
377111	78511+77111+78911+78711	BI	SOU	PTR	SOU
377112	78512+77112+78912+78712	BI	SOU	PTR	SOU
377113	78513+77113+78913+78713	BI	SOU	PTR	SOU
377114	78514+77114+78914+78714	BI	SOU	PTR	SOU
377115	78515+77115+78915+78715	BI	SOU	PTR	SOU
377116	78516+77116+78916+78716	BI	SOU	PTR	SOU
377117	78517+77117+78917+78717	BI	SOU	PTR	SOU
377118	78518+77118+78918+78718	BI	SOU	PTR	SOU
377119	78519+77119+78919+78719	BI	SOU	PTR	SOU
377120	78520+77120+78920+78720	BI	SOU	PTR	SOU
377121	78521+77121+78921+78721	BI	SOU	PTR	SOU
377122	78522+77122+78922+78722	BI	SOU	PTR	SOU
377123	78523+77123+78923+78723	BI	SOU	PTR	SOU
377124	78524+77124+78924+78724	BI	SOU	PTR	SOU
377125	78525+77125+78925+78725	BI	SOU	PTR	SOU
377126	78526+77126+78926+78726	BI	SOU	PTR	SOU
377127	78527+77127+78927+78727	BI	SOU	PTR	SOU
377128	78528+77128+78928+78728	BI	SOU	PTR	SOU
377129	78529+77129+78929+78729	BI	SOU	PTR	SOU
377130	78530+77130+78930+78730	BI	SOU	PTR	SOU
377131	78531+77131+78931+78731	BI	SOU	PTR	SOU
377132	78532+77132+78932+78732	BI	SOU	PTR	SOU
377133	78533+77133+78933+78733	BI	SOU	PTR	SOU
377134	78534+77134+78934+78734	BI	SOU	PTR	SOU
377135	78535+77135+78935+78735	BI	SOU	PTR	SOU
377136	78536+77136+78936+78736	BI	SOU	PTR	SOU
377137	78537+77137+78937+78737	BI	SOU	PTR	SOU
377138	78538+77138+78938+78738	BI	SOU	PTR	SOU
377139	78539+77139+78939+78739	BI	SOU	PTR	SOU
377140	78540+77140+78940+78740	BI	SOU	PTR	SOU

377141	78541+77141+78941+78741	BI	SOU	PTR	SOU
377142	78542+77142+78942+78742	BI	SOU	PTR	SOU
377143	78543+77143+78943+78743	BI	SOU	PTR	SOU
377144	78544+77144+78944+78744	BI	SOU	PTR	SOU
377145	78545+77145+78945+78745	BI	SOU	PTR	SOU
377146	78546+77146+78946+78746	BI	SOU	PTR	SOU
377147	78547+77147+78947+78747	BI	SOU	PTR	SOU
377148	78548+77148+78948+78748	BI	SOU	PTR	SOU
377149	78549+77149+78949+78749	BI	SOU	PTR	SOU
377150	78550+77150+78950+78750	BI	SOU	PTR	SOU
377151	78551+77151+78951+78751	BI	SOU	PTR	SOU
377152	78552+77152+78952+78752	BI	SOU	PTR	SOU
377153	78553+77153+78953+78753	BI	SOU	PTR	SOU
377154	78554+77154+78954+78754	BI	SOU	PTR	SOU
377155	78555+77155+78955+78755	BI	SOU	PTR	SOU
377156	78556+77156+78956+78756	BI	SOU	PTR	SOU
377157	78557+77157+78957+78757	BI	SOU	PTR	SOU
377158	78558+77158+78958+78758	BI	SOU	PTR	SOU
377159	78559+77159+78959+78759	BI	SOU	PTR	SOU
377160	78560+77160+78960+78760	BI	SOU	PTR	SOU
377161	78561+77161+78961+78761	BI	SOU	PTR	SOU
377162	78562+77162+78962+78762	SU	SOU	PTR	SOU
377163	78563+77163+78963+78763	SU	SOU	PTR	SOU
377164	78564+77164+78964+78764	SU	SOU	PTR	SOU

Class 377/2
Electrostar

Vehicle Length: (Driving) 66ft 9in (20.3m) Width: 9ft 2in (2.79m)
(Inter) 65ft 6in (19.96m) Horsepower: 2,012hp (1,500kW)
Height: 12ft 4in (3.75m) Seats (total/car): 24F-222S, 12F-48S/69S/57S/12F-48S

Number	Formation	Depot	Livery	Owner	Operator
	DMCO(A)+MSO+PTSO+DMCO(B)				
377201	78571+77171+78971+78771	BI	SOU	PTR	SOU
377202	78572+77172+78972+78772	BI	SOU	PTR	SOU
377203	78573+77173+78973+78773	BI	SOU	PTR	SOU
377204	78574+77174+78974+78774	BI	SOU	PTR	SOU
377205	78575+77175+78975+78775	SU	SOU	PTR	SOU
377206	78576+77176+78976+78776	SU	SOU	PTR	SOU
377207	78577+77177+78977+78777	BI	SOU	PTR	SOU
377208	78578+77178+78978+78778	BI	SOU	PTR	SOU
377209	78579+77179+78979+78779	BI	SOU	PTR	SOU
377210	78580+77180+78980+78780	SU	SOU	PTR	SOU
377211	78581+77181+78981+78781	SU	SOU	PTR	SOU
377212	78582+77182+78982+78782	SU	SOU	PTR	SOU
377213	78583+77183+78983+78783	BI	SOU	PTR	SOU
377214	78584+77184+78984+78784	SU	SOU	PTR	SOU
377215	78585+77185+78985+78785	BI	SOU	PTR	SOU

Class 377/3
Electrostar

Vehicle Length: (Driving) 66ft 9in (20.3m) Width: 9ft 2in (2.79m)
(Inter) 65ft 6in (19.96m) Horsepower: 2,012hp (1,500kW)
Height: 12ft 4in (3.75m) Seats (total/car): 24F-152S, 12F-48S/56S/12F-48S

Number		Formation	Depot	Livery	Owner	Operator
		DMCO(A)+TSO+DMCO(B)				
377301	(375311)	68201+74801+68401	SU	SOU	PTR	SOU
377302	(375312)	68202+74802+68402	SU	SOU	PTR	SOU
377303	(375313)	68203+74803+68403	SU	SOU	PTR	SOU
377304	(375314)	68204+74804+68404	SU	SOU	PTR	SOU
377305	(375315)	68205+74805+68405	SU	SOU	PTR	SOU
377306	(375316)	68206+74806+68406	SU	SOU	PTR	SOU
377307	(375317)	68207+74807+68407	SU	SOU	PTR	SOU
377308	(375318)	68208+74808+68408	SU	SOU	PTR	SOU
377309	(375319)	68209+74809+68409	SU	SOU	PTR	SOU
377310	(375320)	68210+74810+68410	SU	SOU	PTR	SOU
377311	(375321)	68211+74811+68411	SU	SOU	PTR	SOU
377312	(375322)	68212+74812+68412	SU	SOU	PTR	SOU

Southern

377313 (375323)	68213+74813+68413	SU	SOU	PTR	SOU
377314 (375324)	68214+74814+68414	SU	SOU	PTR	SOU
377315 (375325)	68215+74815+68415	SU	SOU	PTR	SOU
377316 (375326)	68216+74816+68416	SU	SOU	PTR	SOU
377317 (375327)	68217+74817+68417	SU	SOU	PTR	SOU
377318 (375328)	68218+74818+68418	SU	SOU	PTR	SOU
377319 (375329)	68219+74819+68419	SU	SOU	PTR	SOU
377320 (375330)	68220+74820+68420	SU	SOU	PTR	SOU
377321 (375331)	68221+74821+68421	SU	SOU	PTR	SOU
377322 (375332)	68222+74822+68422	SU	SOU	PTR	SOU
377323 (375333)	68223+74823+68423	SU	SOU	PTR	SOU
377324 (375334)	68224+74824+68424	SU	SOU	PTR	SOU
377325 (375335)	68225+74825+68425	SU	SOU	PTR	SOU
377326 (375336)	68226+74826+68426	SU	SOU	PTR	SOU
377327 (375337)	68227+74827+68427	SU	SOU	PTR	SOU
377328 (375338)	68228+74828+68428	SU	SOU	PTR	SOU

Left: The main motive power for Southern franchise main line services is the Class 377 'Electrostar'. Four and soon to be five sub-classes exist. In this view, a Class 377/2, No. 377204, passes South Kenton on the West Coast main line with a Milton Keynes to Croydon through service. To operate this duty one of the dual voltage 377/2 sets has to be deployed, with the voltage changeover taking place between Kensington Olympia and North Pole Junction. **Antony Christie**

Class 377/4
Electrostar

Vehicle Length: (Driving) 66ft 9in (20.3m) Width: 9ft 2in (2.79m)
(Inter) 65ft 6in (19.96m) Horsepower: 2,012hp (1,500kW)
Height: 12ft 4in (3.75m) Seats (total/car): 20F-221S, 10F-48S/69S/56S/10F-48S

Number	Formation	Depot	Livery	Owner	Operator
	DMCO(A)+MSO+TSO+DMCO(B)				
377401	73401+78801+78601+73801	BI	SOU	PTR	SOU
377402	73402+78802+78602+73802	BI	SOU	PTR	SOU
377403	73403+78803+78603+73803	BI	SOU	PTR	SOU
377404	73404+78804+78604+73804	BI	SOU	PTR	SOU
377405	73405+78805+78605+73805	BI	SOU	PTR	SOU
377406	73406+78806+78606+73806	BI	SOU	PTR	SOU
377407	73407+78807+78607+73807	BI	SOU	PTR	SOU
377408	73408+78808+78608+73808	BI	SOU	PTR	SOU
377409	73409+78809+78609+73809	BI	SOU	PTR	SOU
377410	73410+78810+78610+73810	BI	SOU	PTR	SOU
377411	73411+78811+78611+73811	BI	SOU	PTR	SOU
377412	73412+78812+78612+73812	BI	SOU	PTR	SOU
377413	73413+78813+78613+73813	BI	SOU	PTR	SOU
377414	73414+78814+78614+73814	BI	SOU	PTR	SOU
377415	73415+78815+78615+73815	BI	SOU	PTR	SOU
377416	73416+78816+78616+73816	SU	SOU	PTR	SOU
377417	73417+78817+78617+73817	BI	SOU	PTR	SOU
377418	73418+78818+78618+73818	BI	SOU	PTR	SOU
377419	73419+78819+78619+73819	BI	SOU	PTR	SOU
377420	73420+78820+78620+73820	BI	SOU	PTR	SOU
377421	73421+78821+78621+73821	BI	SOU	PTR	SOU
377422	73422+78822+78622+73822	BI	SOU	PTR	SOU
377423	73423+78823+78623+73823	BI	SOU	PTR	SOU
377424	73424+78824+78624+73824	BI	SOU	PTR	SOU
377425	73425+78825+78625+73825	BI	SOU	PTR	SOU
377426	73426+78826+78626+73826	BI	SOU	PTR	SOU
377427	73427+78827+78627+73827	BI	SOU	PTR	SOU

377428	73428+78828+78628+73828	BI	SOU	PTR	SOU
377429	73429+78829+78629+73829	SU	SOU	PTR	SOU
377430	73430+78830+78630+73830	BI	SOU	PTR	SOU
377431	73431+78831+78631+73831	BI	SOU	PTR	SOU
377432	73432+78832+78632+73832	BI	SOU	PTR	SOU
377433	73433+78833+78633+73833	BI	SOU	PTR	SOU
377434	73434+78834+78634+73834	BI	SOU	PTR	SOU
377435	73435+78835+78635+73835	BI	SOU	PTR	SOU
377436	73436+78836+78636+73836	BI	SOU	PTR	SOU
377437	73437+78837+78637+73837	BI	SOU	PTR	SOU
377438	73438+78838+78638+73838	BI	SOU	PTR	SOU
377439	73439+78839+78639+73839	BI	SOU	PTR	SOU
377440	73440+78840+78640+73840	BI	SOU	PTR	SOU
377441	73441+78841+78641+73841	BI	SOU	PTR	SOU
377442	73442+78842+78642+73842	BI	SOU	PTR	SOU
377443	73443+78843+78643+73843	BI	SOU	PTR	SOU
377444	73444+78844+78644+73844	BI	SOU	PTR	SOU
377445	73445+78845+78645+73845	BI	SOU	PTR	SOU
377446	73446+78846+78646+73846	BI	SOU	PTR	SOU
377447	73447+78847+78647+73847	SU	SOU	PTR	SOU
377448	73448+78848+78648+73848	BI	SOU	PTR	SOU
377449	73449+78849+78649+73849	BI	SOU	PTR	SOU
377450	73450+78850+78650+73850	BI	SOU	PTR	SOU
377451	73451+78851+78651+73851	BI	SOU	PTR	SOU
377452	73452+78852+78652+73852	SU	SOU	PTR	SOU
377453	73453+78853+78653+73853	BI	SOU	PTR	SOU
377454	73454+78854+78654+73854	BI	SOU	PTR	SOU
377455	73455+78855+78655+73855	BI	SOU	PTR	SOU
377456	73456+78856+78656+73856	BI	SOU	PTR	SOU
377457	73457+78857+78657+73857	BI	SOU	PTR	SOU
377458	73458+78858+78658+73858	BI	SOU	PTR	SOU
377459	73459+78859+78659+73859	BI	SOU	PTR	SOU
377460	73460+78860+78660+73860	SU	SOU	PTR	SOU
377461	73461+78861+78661+73861	BI	SOU	PTR	SOU
377462	73462+78862+78662+73862	BI	SOU	PTR	SOU
377463	73463+78863+78663+73863	BI	SOU	PTR	SOU
377464	73464+78864+78664+73864	BI	SOU	PTR	SOU
377465	73465+78865+78665+73865	BI	SOU	PTR	SOU
377466	73466+78866+78666+73866	BI	SOU	PTR	SOU
377467	73467+78867+78667+73867	BI	SOU	PTR	SOU
377468	73468+78868+78668+73868	BI	SOU	PTR	SOU
377469	73469+78869+78669+73869	BI	SOU	PTR	SOU
377470	73470+78870+78670+73870	BI	SOU	PTR	SOU
377471	73471+78871+78671+73871	BI	SOU	PTR	SOU
377472	73472+78872+78672+73872	BI	SOU	PTR	SOU
377473	73473+78873+78673+73873	BI	SOU	PTR	SOU
377474	73474+78874+78674+73874	BI	SOU	PTR	SOU
377475	73475+78875+78675+73875	BI	SOU	PTR	SOU

Right: *The most prolific sub-class of Southern Class 377s are the 75 members of Class 377/4. All '377s' operate in one main pool and can be found throughout the Southern network. Set No. 377402 is seen departing from Clapham Junction bound for London Victoria.* **CJM**

Passenger Train Operating Companies - Southern

Class 377/6
Electrostar

Vehicle Length: (Driving) 66ft 9in (20.3m) Width: 9ft 2in (2.79m)
(Inter) 65ft 6in (19.96m) Horsepower: 2,012hp (1,500kW)
Height: 12ft 4in (3.75m) Seats (total/car): 298S-60S/64S/46S/662S/62S

Number	Formation	Depot	Livery	Owner	Operator
	DMSO(A)+MSO+TSO+MSO+DMSO(B)				
377601	70101+70201+70301+70401+70501	BI	SOU	PTR	SOU (on delivery)
377602	70102+70202+70302+70402+70502	BI	SOU	PTR	SOU (on delivery)
377603	70103+70203+70303+70403+70503	BI	SOU	PTR	SOU (on delivery)
377604	70104+70204+70304+70404+70504	BI	SOU	PTR	SOU (on delivery)
377605	70105+70205+70305+70405+70505	BI	SOU	PTR	SOU (on delivery)
377606	70106+70206+70306+70406+70506	BI	SOU	PTR	SOU (on delivery)
377607	70107+70207+70307+70407+70507	BI	SOU	PTR	SOU (on delivery)
377608	70108+70208+70308+70408+70508	BI	SOU	PTR	SOU (on delivery)
377609	70109+70209+70309+70409+70509	BI	SOU	PTR	SOU (on delivery)
377610	70110+70210+70310+70410+70510	BI	SOU	PTR	SOU (on delivery)
377611	70111+70211+70311+70411+70511	BI	SOU	PTR	SOU (on delivery)
377612	70112+70212+70312+70412+70512	BI	SOU	PTR	SOU (on delivery)
377613	70113+70213+70313+70413+70513	BI	SOU	PTR	SOU (on delivery)
377614	70114+70214+70314+70414+70514	BI	SOU	PTR	SOU (on delivery)
377615	70115+70215+70315+70415+70515	BI	SOU	PTR	SOU (on delivery)
377616	70116+70216+70316+70416+70516	BI	SOU	PTR	SOU (on delivery)
377617	70117+70217+70317+70417+70517	BI	SOU	PTR	SOU (on delivery)
377618	70118+70218+70318+70418+70518	BI	SOU	PTR	SOU (on delivery)
377619	70119+70219+70319+70419+70519	BI	SOU	PTR	SOU (on delivery)
377620	70120+70220+70320+70420+70520	BI	SOU	PTR	SOU (on delivery)
377621	70121+70221+70321+70421+70521	BI	SOU	PTR	SOU (on delivery)
377622	70122+70222+70322+70422+70522	BI	SOU	PTR	SOU (on delivery)
377623	70123+70223+70323+70423+70523	BI	SOU	PTR	SOU (on delivery)
377624	70124+70224+70324+70424+70524	BI	SOU	PTR	SOU (on delivery)
377625	70125+70225+70325+70425+70525	BI	SOU	PTR	SOU (on delivery)
377626	70126+70226+70326+70426+70526	BI	SOU	PTR	SOU (on delivery)
377627	70127+70227+70327+70427+70527	BI	SOU	PTR	SOU (on delivery)
377628	70128+70228+70328+70428+70528	BI	SOU	PTR	SOU (on delivery)
377629	70129+70229+70329+70429+70529	BI	SOU	PTR	SOU (on delivery)
377630	70130+70230+70330+70430+70530	BI	SOU	PTR	SOU (on delivery)

Class 442

Vehicle Length: (Driving) 75ft 11½in (23.15m) Width: 8ft 11½in (2.73m)
(Inter) 75ft 5½in (22.99m) Horsepower: 1,608hp (1,200kW)
Height: 12ft 4in (3.81m) Seats (total/car): 24F-318S, 74S/76S/24F-28S/66S/74S

Number	Formation	Depot	Livery	Owner	Operator
	DTSO(A)+TSO+MBC+TSO+DTSO(B)				
442401	77382+71818+62937+71841+77406	SL	SGX	ANG	SOU
442402	77383+71819+62938+71842+77407	SL	SGX	ANG	SOU
442403	77384+71820+62941+71843+77408	SL	SGX	ANG	SOU
442404	77385+71821+62939+71844+77409	SL	SGX	ANG	SOU
442405	77386+71822+62944+71845+77410	SL	SGX	ANG	SOU
442406	77389+71823+62942+71846+77411	SL	SGX	ANG	SOU
442407	77388+71824+62943+71847+77412	SL	SGX	ANG	SOU
442408	77387+71825+62945+71848+77413	SL	SGX	ANG	SOU
442409	77390+71826+62946+71849+77414	SL	SGX	ANG	SOU
442410	77391+71827+62948+71850+77415	SL	SGX	ANG	SOU
442411	77392+71828+62940+71851+77422	SL	SGX	ANG	SOU
442412	77393+71829+62947+71858+77417	SL	SGX	ANG	SOU
442413	77394+71830+62949+71853+77418	SL	SGX	ANG	SOU
442414	77395+71831+62950+71854+77419	SL	SGX	ANG	SOU
442415	77396+71832+62951+71855+77420	SL	SGX	ANG	SOU
442416	77397+71833+62952+71856+77421	SL	SGX	ANG	SOU
442417	77398+71834+62953+71857+77416	SL	SGX	ANG	SOU
442418	77399+71835+62954+71852+77423	SL	SGX	ANG	SOU
442419	77400+71836+62955+71859+77424	SL	SGX	ANG	SOU
442420	77401+71837+62956+71860+77425	SL	SGX	ANG	SOU
442421	77402+71838+62957+71861+77426	SL	SGX	ANG	SOU
442422	77403+71839+62958+71862+77427	SL	SGX	ANG	SOU
442423	77404+71840+62959+71863+77428	SL	SGX	ANG	SOU
442424	77405+71841+62960+71864+77429	SL	SGX	ANG	SOU

Right: *After the merger of the Southern and Gatwick Express franchise operations, the Class 460 'Juniper' stock, built specifically for the Gatwick Express route, were phased out and replaced with refurbished Class 442 sets displaced from the Waterloo to Weymouth line. The 24 '442s' were all fully rebuilt with a middle Motor Brake Composite vehicle. Sets are finished in a distinctive Express livery. Set No 442407 is seen passing Clapham Junction.* **CJM**

Class 455/8

Vehicle Length: (Driving) 65ft 0½in (19.83m)
(Inter) 65ft 4½in (19.92m)
Height: 12ft 1½in (3.79m)
Width: 9ft 3¼in (2.82m)
Horsepower: 1,000hp (746kW)
Seats (total/car): 310S, 74S/78S/84S/74S

Number	Formation DTSO(A)+MSO+TSO+DTSO(B)	Depot	Livery	Owner	Operator
455801	77627+62709+71657+77580	SU	SOU	EVL	SOU
455802	77581+62710+71664+77582	SU	SOU	EVL	SOU
455803	77583+62711+71639+77584	SU	SOU	EVL	SOU
455804	77585+62712+71640+77586	SU	SOU	EVL	SOU
455805	77587+62713+71641+77588	SU	SOU	EVL	SOU
455806	77589+62714+71642+77590	SU	SOU	EVL	SOU
455807	77591+62715+71643+77592	SU	SOU	EVL	SOU
455808	77637+62716+71644+77594	SU	SOU	EVL	SOU
455809	77623+62717+71648+77602	SU	SOU	EVL	SOU
455810	77597+62718+71646+77598	SU	SOU	EVL	SOU
455811	77599+62719+71647+77600	SU	SOU	EVL	SOU
455812	77595+62720+71645+77626	SU	SOU	EVL	SOU
455813	77603+62721+71649+77604	SU	SOU	EVL	SOU
455814	77605+62722+71650+77606	SU	SOU	EVL	SOU
455815	77607+62723+71651+77608	SU	SOU	EVL	SOU
455816	77609+62724+71652+77633	SU	SOU	EVL	SOU
455817	77611+62725+71653+77612	SU	SOU	EVL	SOU
455818	77613+62726+71654+77632	SU	SOU	EVL	SOU
455819	77615+62727+71637+77616	SU	SOU	EVL	SOU
455820	77617+62728+71656+77618	SU	SOU	EVL	SOU
455821	77619+62729+71655+77620	SU	SOU	EVL	SOU
455822	77621+62730+71658+77622	SU	SOU	EVL	SOU
455823	77601+62731+71659+77596	SU	SOU	EVL	SOU
455824	77593+62732+71660+77624	SU	SOU	EVL	SOU
455825	77579+62733+71661+77652	SU	SOU	EVL	SOU
455826	77630+62734+71662+77629	SU	SOU	EVL	SOU
455827	77610+62735+71663+77614	SU	SOU	EVL	SOU
455828	77631+62736+71638+77634	SU	SOU	EVL	SOU
455829	77635+62737+71665+77636	SU	SOU	EVL	SOU
455830	77625+62743+71666+77638	SU	SOU	EVL	SOU
455831	77639+62739+71667+77640	SU	SOU	EVL	SOU
455832	77641+62740+71668+77642	SU	SOU	EVL	SOU
455833	77643+62741+71669+77644	SU	SOU	EVL	SOU
455834	77645+62742+71670+77646	SU	SOU	EVL	SOU
455835	77647+62738+71671+77648	SU	SOU	EVL	SOU
455836	77649+62744+71672+77650	SU	SOU	EVL	SOU
455837	77651+62745+71673+77652	SU	SOU	EVL	SOU
455838	77653+62746+71674+77654	SU	SOU	EVL	SOU
455839	77655+62747+71675+77656	SU	SOU	EVL	SOU
455840	77657+62748+71676+77658	SU	SOU	EVL	SOU
455841	77659+62749+71677+77660	SU	SOU	EVL	SOU
455842	77661+62750+71678+77662	SU	SOU	EVL	SOU

455843	776636+2751+71679+77664	SU	SOU	EVL	SOU
455844	776656+2752+71680+77666	SU	SOU	EVL	SOU
455845	776676+2753+71681+77668	SU	SOU	EVL	SOU
455846	776696+2754+71682+77670	SU	SOU	EVL	SOU

Left: *Southern operates a fleet of 46 Class 455/8s on its suburban network from London Victoria and London Bridge. The sets are allocated to Selhurst. Set No. 455804 is illustrated at Clapham Junction. The Southern Class 455 stock has been modified from the similar sets operating on South West Trains. The cab ends have lost their gangways and a cab air conditioning module is now fitted in the former central door. Revised light clusters are also fitted with a headlight and dual tail/marker light on each side.* **CJM**

Class 456

Vehicle Length: (Driving) 65ft 3¼in (19.89m)
Height: 12ft 4½in (3.77m)
Width: 9ft 3in (2.81m)
Horsepower: 500hp (370kW)
Seats (total/car): 152S, 79S/73S

Number	*Formation DMSO+DTSO*	*Depot*	*Livery*	*Owner*	*Operator*
456001	64735+78250	SU	SOU	PTR	SOU
456002	64736+78251	SU	SOU	PTR	SOU
456003	64737+78252	SU	SOU	PTR	SOU
456004	64738+78253	SU	SOU	PTR	SOU
456005	64739+78254	SU	SOU	PTR	SOU
456006	64740+78255	SU	SOU	PTR	SOU
456007	64741+78256	SU	SOU	PTR	SOU
456008	64742+78257	SU	SOU	PTR	SOU
456009	64743+78258	SU	SOU	PTR	SOU
456010	64744+78259	SU	SOU	PTR	SOU
456011	64745+78260	SU	SOU	PTR	SOU
456012	64746+78261	SU	SOU	PTR	SOU
456013	64747+78262	SU	SOU	PTR	SOU
456014	64748+78263	SU	SOU	PTR	SOU
456015	64749+78264	SU	SOU	PTR	SOU
456016	64750+78265	SU	SOU	PTR	SOU
456017	64751+78266	SU	SOU	PTR	SOU
456018	64752+78267	SU	SOU	PTR	SOU
456019	64753+78268	SU	SOU	PTR	SOU
456020	64754+78269	SU	SOU	PTR	SOU
456021	64755+78270	SU	SOU	PTR	SOU
456022	64756+78271	SU	SOU	PTR	SOU
456023	64757+78272	SU	SOU	PTR	SOU
456024	64758+78273	SU	SOU	PTR	SOU

Name applied
456024 ***Sir Cosmo Bonsor***

Left: *As part of the original introduction of Class 455 sets on the BR Southern Region Central Division, a batch of 24 two-car Class 456s emerged from York Works, enabling two-, six- or ten-car formations to operate. In 2012, all sets were allocated to Selhurst and operated for Southern, painted in Southern livery. Set No. 456005 is seen from its DMSO end at Denmark Hill.* **John Binch**

■ In mid-2012, it was announced that following the delivery of new Class 377 stock to train operator Southern in 2013, the operator's 24 two-car Class 456 sets would transfer to South West Trains to enable their franchise commitment of running 10-car formations of the busy 'Windsor line' routes. SWT have announced the sets will be refurbished to be on a par with the Class 455 stock.

Class 09/0

	Vehicle Length: 29ft 3in (8.91m)	Engine: English Electric 6K
	Height: 12ft 8⅝in (3.87m)	Horsepower: 400hp (298kW)
	Width: 8ft 6in (2.59m)	Electrical Equipment: English Electric

Number	Depot	Pool	Livery	Owner	Operator	Name
09026	BI	HWSU	GRN	SOU	SOU	*Cedric Wares*

Right: *Southern is one of the few main line operators to still retain a Class 09 0-6-0 diesel-electric shunting locomotive – No. 09026* Cedric Wares. *The loco is allocated to Brighton and carries out shunting duties at Lovers Walk depot and also performs depot de-icing duties. The equipment to keep the tracks of Lovers Walk free from ice in the winter period can be seen by the front foot steps. Painted in mid-green livery, the loco shares depot space at Brighton with various Class 313 units.*
Antony Christie

Class 73/2

	Vehicle Length: 53ft 8in (16.35m)	Power: 750V dc third rail or English Electric 6K
	Height: 12ft 5⁷⁄₁₆in (3.79m)	Horsepower: electric - 1,600hp (1,193kW)
	Width: 8ft 8in (2.64m)	Horsepower: diesel - 600hp (447kW)
		Electrical Equipment: English Electric

Number	Depot	Pool	Livery	Owner	Operator	Name
73202 (73137)	SL	MBED	GAT	PTR	SOU	*Dave Berry*

Below: *One Class 73/2, No. 73202* Dave Berry, *is retained by train operator Southern, based at Stewarts Lane, and is considered as part of the Gatwick Express operation. The loco was retained as a 'Thunderbird' locomotive for the Gatwick Express Class 460 stock, but in more recent times has been used as a driver's route training loco and pilot for hauling stock around the Southern network. No. 73202 is seen at Brighton.* **Antony Christie**

Virgin West Coast

Address: 85 Smallbrook Queensway, Birmingham, B5 4HA

info@virgintrains.co.uk

© 0845 000 8000   ⓘ www.virgintrains.co.uk

Managing Director: Chris Gibb

Franchise Dates: 12 December 2006 - 9 December 2014 - extended from 2012, re-franchising suspended

Principal Routes: London Euston - Birmingham, Holyhead, Manchester Liverpool, Glasgow and Edinburgh

Depots: Edge Hill* (LL), Longsight** (MA), Oxley** (OY), Wembley** (WB), Central Rivers (CZ)
** Operated by Alstom Transportation

Parent Company: Virgin Group

Above: *The present day work horse of the Virgin Trains west coast operation, is the Alstom-built Class 390 'Pendolino' fixed-formation train. Originally delivered as eight-car sets, the fleet were soon expanded to nine-car formations and in 2011-12 some 31 sets were further reformed as eleven-car trains, with each lengthened set providing 147 first and 450 standard class seats. On 12 May 2011, set No. 390049 heads north at Easenhall, north of Rugby.* **Antony Christie**

Virgin West Coast

Class 221
Super Voyager

Vehicle Length: 77ft 6in (23.62m)
Height: 12ft 4in (3.75m)
Width: 8ft 11in (2.73m)
Engine: 1 x Cummins 750hp per vehicle
Horsepower: 5-car - 3,750hp (2,796kW). 4-car - 3,000hp (2,237kW)
Seats (total/car): 26F/214S 42S/60S/60S/52S/26F (*not in 4-car set)*

Passenger Train Operating Companies - Virgin West Coast

Number	Formation	Depot	Livery	Owner	Operator	Name
	221101 - 221118 - DMS+MS+MS+MSRMB+DMF					
221101	60351+60951+60851+60751+60451	CZ	VWC	HBS	VWC	*Louis Bleriot*
221102	60352+60952+60852+60752+60452	CZ	VWC	HBS	VWC	*John Cabot*
221103	60353+60953+60853+60753+60453	CZ	VWC	HBS	VWC	*Christopher Columbus*
221104	60354+60954+60854+60754+60454	CZ	VWC	HBS	VWC	*Sir John Franklin*
221105	60355+60955+60855+60755+60455	CZ	VWC	HBS	VWC	*William Baffin*
221106	60356+60956+60856+60756+60456	CZ	VWC	HBS	VWC	*William Barents*
221107	60357+60957+60857+60757+60457	CZ	VWC	HBS	VWC	*Sir Martin Frobisher*
221108	60358+60958+60858+60758+60458	CZ	VWC	HBS	VWC	*Sir Ernest Shackleton*
221109	60359+60959+60859+60759+60459	CZ	VWC	HBS	VWC	*Marco Polo*
221110	60360+60960+60860+60760+60460	CZ	VWC	HBS	VWC	*James Cook*
221111	60361+60961+60861+60761+60461	CZ	VWC	HBS	VWC	*Roald Amundsen*
221112	60362+60962+60862+60762+60462	CZ	VWC	HBS	VWC	*Ferdinand Magellan*
221113	60363+60963+60863+60763+60463	CZ	VWC	HBS	VWC	*Sir Walter Raleigh*
221114	60364+60964+60864+60764+60464	CZ	VWC	HBS	VWC	
221115	60365+60965+60865+60765+60465	CZ	VWC¤	HBS	VWC	*Polmadie Depot*
221116	60366+60966+60866+60766+60466	CZ	VWC	HBS	VWC	
221117	60367+60967+60867+60767+60467	CZ	VWC	HBS	VWC	
221118	60368+60968+60868+60768+60468	CZ	VWC	HBS	VWC	
221142	60392+60992+60994ø+60792+60492	CZ	VWC	HBS	VWC	*Bombardier Voyager*
221143	60393+60993+60794+60793+60493	CZ	VWC	HBS	VWC	*Auguste Picard*
221144	60394+-+-+-+60494	CZ	VWC	HBS	(Training)	

¤ One driving car carries Bombardier branding. ø MRSMB vehicle

Left: *Of the original Virgin Trains fleet of 'Voyager' and 'Super Voyager' trains, today Virgin operate a fleet of just 20 five-car 'Super Voyager' sets. Based at Central Rivers near Burton, these are deployed on West Coast services operating the North Wales coast services, and under the wires on Anglo-Scottish main line duties. Set No. 221112* Ferdinand Magellan, *passes Tamworth on 16 August 2012 with a London Euston-bound service.*
Antony Christie

Left: *During 2011, Virgin Trains agreed to re-form as many as possible of their four-car 'Super Voyager' fleet into five-car sets thus reducing some overcrowding. This was achieved by disbanding set No. 221144, which donated its two intermediate coaches, one each to sets Nos. 221142/43. The two spare driving cars were then placed in warm store, being available if required. Sometimes the pair are used for training purposes but are usually kept at Central Rivers depot. Class 57/3 No. 57308 is seen departing from Central Rivers with the spare driving cars.*

Class 390
Pendolino

Vehicle Length Driving: 75ft 6in (23.01m)
Height: 11ft 6in (3.50m)
Width: 8ft 11in (2.71m)

Horsepower: 6,840hp (5,100kW)
Seats (total/car): 147F/300S, 18F/39F/44F/46F/74S/76S/76S/66S/48S/64S/46S
31 sets are now formed of 11 vehicles 147F/450S

Formation: DMRFO+MFO+PTFO+MFO+(TSO+MSO)+TSO+MSO+PTSRMB+MSO+DMSO

Number	Formation	Depot	Livery	Owner	Operator	Name
390001	69101+69401+69501+68801+69601+69701+69801+69901+69201	MA	VWC	ANG	VWC	Virgin Pioneer
390002	69102+69402+69502+68802+69602+69702+69802+69902+69202	MA	VWC	ANG	VWC	Virgin Angel
390103	69103+69403+69503+65303+68903+69703+69803+69903+69203	MA	VWC	ANG	VWC	Virgin Hero
390104	69104+69404+69504+65304+68904+69704+69804+69904+69204	MA	VWC	ANG	VWC	Alstom Pendolino
390005	69105+69405+69505+68805+69605+69705+69805+69905+69205	MA	VWC	ANG	VWC	City of Wolverhampton
390006	69106+69406+69506+68806+69606+69706+69806+69906+69206	MA	VWC	ANG	VWC	Tate Liverpool
390107	69107+69407+69507+65307+68907+69707+69807+69907+69207	MA	VWC	ANG	VWC	Virgin Lady (branded Abigail Inozunu)
390008	69108+69408+69508+68808+69608+69708+69808+69908+69208	MA	VWC	ANG	VWC	Virgin King
390009	69109+69409+69509+68809+69609+69709+69809+69909+69209	MA	VWC	ANG	VWC	Treaty of Union
390010	69110+69410+69510+68810+69610+69710+69810+69910+69210	MA	VWC	ANG	VWC	A Decade of Progress
390011	69111+69411+69511+68811+69611+69711+69811+69911+69211	MA	VWC	ANG	VWC	City of Lichfield
390112	69112+69412+69512+65312+68912+69712+69812+69912+69212	MA	VWC	ANG	VWC	Virgin Star
390013	69113+69413+69513+68813+69613+69713+69813+69913+69213	MA	VWC	ANG	VWC	Virgin Spirit
390114	69114+69414+69514+65314+68914+69714+69814+69914+69214	MA	VWC	ANG	VWC	City of Manchester
390115	69115+69415+69515+65315+68915+69715+69815+69915+69215	MA	VWC	ANG	VWC	Virgin Crusader
390016	69116+69416+69516+68816+69616+69716+69816+69916+69216	MA	VWC	ANG	VWC	Virgin Champion
390117	69117+69417+69517+65317+68917+69717+69817+69917+69217	MA	VWC	ANG	VWC	Virgin Prince
390118	69118+69418+69518+65318+68918+69718+69818+69918+69218	MA	VWC	ANG	VWC	Virgin Princess
390119	69119+69419+69519+65319+68919+69719+69819+69919+69219	MA	VWC	ANG	VWC	Virgin Warrior
390020	69120+69420+69520+68820+69620+69720+69820+69920+69220	MA	VWC	ANG	VWC	Virgin Cavalier
390121	69121+69421+69521+65321+68921+69721+69821+69921+69221	MA	VWC	ANG	VWC	Virgin Dream
390122	69122+69422+69522+65322+68922+69722+69822+69922+69222	MA	VWC	ANG	VWC	Penny the Pendolino
390023	69123+69423+69523+68823+69623+69723+69823+69923+69223	MA	VWC	ANG	VWC	Virgin Glory
390124	69124+69424+69524+65324+68924+69724+69824+69924+69224	MA	VWC	ANG	VWC	Virgin Venturer
390125	69125+69425+69525+65325+68925+69725+69825+69925+69225	MA	VWC	ANG	VWC	Virgin Stagecoach
390126	69126+69426+69526+65326+68926+69726+69826+69926+69226	MA	VWC	ANG	VWC	Virgin Enterprise
390127	69127+69427+69527+65327+68927+69727+69827+69927+69227	MA	VWC	ANG	VWC	Virgin Buccaneer
390128	69128+69428+69528+65328+68928+69728+69828+69928+69228	MA	VWC	ANG	VWC	City of Preston
390129	69129+69429+69529+65329+68929+69729+69829+69929+69229	MA	VWC	ANG	VWC	City of Stoke-on-Trent
390130	69130+69430+69530+65330+68930+69730+69830+69930+69230	MA	VWC	ANG	VWC	City of Edinburgh
390131	69131+69431+69531+65331+68931+69731+69831+69931+69231	MA	VWC	ANG	VWC	City of Liverpool
390132	69132+69432+69532+65332+68932+69732+69832+69932+69232	MA	VWC	ANG	VWC	City of Birmingham
390134	69134+69434+69534+65334+68934+69734+69834+69934+69234	MA	VWC	ANG	VWC	City of Carlisle
390035	69135+69435+69535+68835+69635+69735+69835+69935+69235	MA	VWC	ANG	VWC	City of Lancaster
390136	69136+69436+69536+65336+68936+69736+69836+69936+69236	MA	VWC	ANG	VWC	City of Coventry
390137	69137+69437+69537+65337+68937+69737+69837+69937+69237	MA	VWC	ANG	VWC	Virgin Difference
390038	69138+69438+69538+68838+69638+69738+69838+69938+69238	MA	VWC	ANG	VWC	City of London
390039	69139+69439+69539+68839+69639+69739+69839+69939+69239	MA	VWC	ANG	VWC	Virgin Quest
390040	69140+69440+69540+68840+69640+69740+69840+69940+69240	MA	VWC	ANG	VWC	Virgin Pathfinder

Virgin West Coast

Number	Formation				Name
390141	69141+69441+69541+69641+65341+69841+68841+69741+69841+69941+69241	MA	VWC	ANG	City of Chester
390042	69142+69442+69542+69642+69842+69742+69842+69942+69242	MA	VWC	ANG	City of Bangor / Dinas Bangor
390043	69143+69443+69543+68843+69843+69743+69843+69943+69243	MA	VWC	ANG	Virgin Explorer
390044	69144+69444+69544+68844+69744+69844+69944+69244	MA	VWC	ANG	Virgin Lionheart
390045	69145+69445+69545+69645+69845+69745+69845+69945+69245	MA	VWC	ANG	101 Squadron
390046	69146+69446+69546+68846+69746+69846+69946+69246	MA	VWC	ANG	Virgin Soldiers
390047	69147+69447+69547+68847+69747+69847+69947+69247	MA	VWC	ANG	Clic Sargent
390148	69148+69448+69548+65348+69848+68848+69748+69848+69948+69248	MA	VWC	ANG	Virgin Harrier
390049	69149+69449+69549+69649+69849+69749+69849+69949+69249	MA	VWC	ANG	Virgin Express
390050	69150+69450+69550+68850+69750+69850+69950+69250	MA	VWC	ANG	Virgin Invader
390151	69151+69451+69551+69651+63351+68851+69751+69851+69951+69251	MA	VWC	ANG	Virgin Ambassador
390152	69152+69452+69552+65352+68852+69752+69852+69952+69252	MA	VWC	ANG	Alison Waters
390153	69153+69453+69553+69653+68853+69753+69853+69953+69253	MA	VWC	ANG	Mission Accomplished
390154	69154+69454+69554+65354+68854+69754+69854+69954+69254	MA	VWC	ANG	
390155	69155+69455+69555+69655+68355+69755+65855+69955+69255	MA	VWC	ANG	
390156	69156+69456+69556+68356+69756+65856+69956+69256	MA	VWC	ANG	
390157	69157+69457+69557+69657+68357+69757+65857+69957+69257	MA	VWC	ANG	Chad Varah

Above: In 2011-12, Virgin Trains commenced the strengthening of some 30 Class 390 sets to 11-car formation to ease congestion on the busy West Coast route. The lengthened sets have been classified as 390/1 and renumbered in the 3901xx series. Eleven-car set No. 390123 passes Bletchley heading for London Euston on 29 October 2012. **John Binch**

■ Pendolino set No. 390033 *City of Glasgow*, which was involved in the Grayrigg derailment on 23 February 2007, was withdrawn from service. After spending a period stored at Long Marston, some of the vehicles have now seen further use.

Cars 69133 and 69833 have been rebuilt as static training vehicles for use at the Virgin Trains training school in Crewe.

Nos. 69933 and 69733 are in use at the fire training school in Moreton-in-Marsh, while Nos. 69533, 68833 and 69433 remain in store at Long Marston owned by Virgin Group.

Vehicle No. 69233 has been broken up.

Mk3 Hauled Stock

Vehicle Length: 75ft 0in (22.86m)   Width: 8ft 11in (2.71m)
Height: 12ft 9in (3.88m)   Bogie Type: BT10

AJ1G - RFB *Seating 18F*

Number	Depot	Livery	Owner
10212	WB	VWC	PTR
10217	WB	VWC	PTE

AD1G - FO *Seating 48F*

Number	Depot	Livery	Owner
11007	WB	VWC	PTR
11018	WB	VWC	PTR

11048	WB	VWC	PTR

AC2G - TS0 (*TSOD) *Seating 76/70*S*

Number	Depot	Livery	Owner
12011	WB	VWC	PTR
12078	WB	VWC	PTR
12122*	WB	VWC	PTR
12133	WB	VWC	PTR
12138	WB	VWC	PTR

NL - DVT

Number	Depot	Livery	Owner
82101	WB	VWC	PTR§
82126	WB	VWC	PTR

§ Spare vehicle

■ The Virgin West Coast loco-hauled set is operated on an 'as-required' basis to cover for a shortfall in 'Pendolino' stock. Motive power is provided by DBS in the form of a Class 90/0 or a VWC Class 57/3. The regulr use of this train ceased in December 2012.

Right Top: *All of the operational Virgin Trains stand-in loco-hauled set are fully refurbished and all are painted in the silver, black and red livery. The sole TSOD (trailer standard open with disabled access toilet) No. 12122 is illustrated at Carlisle. This vehicle seats 70 passengers.* **Nathan Williamson**

Right Middle : *Three Mk3 FOs are in the Virgin pool. These have a short yellow first class 'flash' applied just above the passenger doors. The FOs seat 48 in the 2+1 style, with the interiors restyled to be in keeping with the 'Pendolino' fleet. No. 11048 is illustrated at Euston.* **Stacey Thew**

Right Bottom: *Standard class interior of Virgin Trains Mk3 TSO No. 12133, showing a mix of airline style and group seating, with moquette in blue and red in a like style to the core 'Pendolino' fleet.* **Nathan Williamson**

Colas Rail Freight

Address: ✉ Dacre House, 19 Dacre Street, London, SW1H 0DJ

✈ enquiries@colasrail.co.uk

☎ 0207 593 5353

ⓘ www.colasrail.co.uk

Chairman: Charles-Albert Giral

Depots: Washwood Heath (AW), Rugby (RU), Eastleigh Works (ZG)

Class 47/7

Vehicle Length: 63ft 6in (19.35m)		Engine: Sulzer 12LDA28C	
Height: 12ft 10⅜in (3.91m)		Horsepower: 2,580hp (1,922kW)	
Width: 9ft 2in (2.79m)		Electrical Equipment: Brush	
Electric Train Heat fitted			

Number		Depot	Pool	Livery	Owner	Operator	Name
47727	(47569)	AW	COLO	COL	COL	COL	*Rebecca*
47739	(47594)	AW	COLO	COL	COL	COL	*Robin of Templecombe*
47749	(47625)	AW	COLO	COL	COL	COL	*Demelza*

Left: *Displaying its distinctive black, orange and lime colours, Colas Rail Freight presently operates three Class 47/7s for general freight operations. These were fully refurbished by Eastleigh and retain full train supply equipment and are fitted with green spot multiple control. The three are based at Washwood Heath. No. 47739* Robin of Templecombe *is seen powering a Washwood Heath to Boston steel train at Water Orton.* **Lee Martin**

Class 56

Vehicle Length: 63ft 6in (19.35m)		Engine: Ruston Paxman 16RK3CT	
Height: 13ft 0in (3.96m)		Horsepower: 3,250hp (2,420kW)	
Width: 9ft 2in (2.79m)		Electrical Equipment: Brush	

Number		Depot	Pool	Livery	Owner	Operator	Notes
56051(S)		WH	COLO	?	COL	-	Awaiting overhaul
56078(S)		WH	COLO	COL	COL	-	
56087		WH	COLO	COL	COL	COL	
56094		WH	COLO	COL	COL	COL	
56105(S)		RU	COLO	FER	COL	-	
56113(S)		WH	COLO	FER	COL	-	
56302	(56124)	WH	COLO	COL	COL	COL	

Left: *In 2012, Colas Rail Freight started to introduce overhauled Class 56s to its freight operations. By the end of the year two of a possible five were in traffic. The locos have been repainted in standard Colas livery and are based at Washwood Heath. The '56s' tend to operate the heavier trains such as the log traffic associated with Kronospan in Chirk. No. 56094 is seen at Newton Abbot while running round to take charge of the Teigngrace to Chirk log train.* **Antony Christie**

Class 66/8

Vehicle Length: 70ft 0½in (21.34m)			*Engine: EMD 12N-710G3B-EC*			
Height: 12ft 10in (3.91m)			*Horsepower: 3,300hp (2,462kW)*			
Width: 8ft 8¼in (2.65m)			*Electrical Equipment: EMD*			

Number		Depot	Pool	Livery	Owner	Operator	Name
66846	(66573)	RU	COLO	COL	COL	COL	
66847	(66574)	RU	COLO	COL	COL	COL	
66848	(66575)	RU	COLO	COL	COL	COL	
66849	(66576)	RU	COLO	COL	COL	COL	*Wylam Dilly*
66850	(66577)	RU	COLO	COL	COL	COL	

Above: *Five former Freightliner Class 66/5s are now operated by Colas and renumbered as 66/8s. The fleet are officially allocated to Rugby, but spend little time at this location, spending most time powering services throughout the country. No. 66850, the original No. 66577, is illustrated from its silencer end.* **CJM**

Right: *Until introduction of the Colas Rail Freight Class 56s in autumn 2012, the Class 66/8s were the mainstay of long distance freight duties, including the log traffic from the West Country. On 18 July 2012, No. 66846 passes Dawlish with empty log wagons bound for Teigngrace.* **CJM**

Class 86/7

Colas Rail Freight also operates Electric Traction Ltd Class 86/7 No. 86701 see ETL listings

Hauled Stock (NPCCS)

Mk1		*Height: 12ft 9½in (3.89m)*
Vehicle Length: 64ft 6in (19.65m)		*Width: 9ft 3in (2.81m)*

Motorail Wagons

96602	(96150)	NV	COL	RU	96604	(96156)	NV	COL	RU	96607	(96215)	NV	COL	RU
96603	(96155)	NV	COL	RU	96605	(96157)	NV	COL	RU	96608	(96216)	NV	COL	RU
					96606	(96213)	NV	COL	RU	96609	(96217)	NV	COL	RU

DB Schenker - EWS

Address (UK): ✉ Lakeside Business Park, Caroline Way, Doncaster, DN4 5PN

✎ info@rail.dbschenker.co.uk

☎ 0870 140 5000

ⓘ www.rail.dbschenker.co.uk

Chief Executive: Alain Thauvette

Class 08

Vehicle Length: 29ft 3in (8.91m)	Engine: English Electric 6K
Height: 12ft 8⅝in (3.87m)	Horsepower: 400hp (298kW)
Width: 8ft 6in (2.59m)	Electrical Equipment: English Electric

Number	Depot	Pool	Livery	Owner	Operator
08405¤	DR	WNYX	EWS	DBS	-
08428	TO	WSSK	EWS	DBS	DBS
08480*	TO	WNYX	EWS	DBS	DBS
08495¤	EH	WSSK	EWS	DBS	DBS
08499(S)	WQ	WSXX	BLU	DBS	PUL
08500(S)	WQ	WNYX	EWS	DBS	-
08567	TO	WSSK	EWS	DBS	DBS
08578¤(S)	TO	WNXX	EWS	DBS	DBS
08580(S)	BS	WNXX	EWS	DBS	-
08593(S)	CE	WNXX	EWS	DBS	-
08605¤	TO	WSSX	EWS	DBS	DBS
08623	TO	WSSL	EWS	DBS	DBS
08630(S)	TO	WNXX	EWS	DBS	-
08632	TO	WSSK	EWS	DBS	DBS
08633¤	CE	WSSK	EWS	DBS	DBS
08653	TO	WNXX	EWS	DBS	-
08676	TO	WSSL	EWS	DBS	
08701¤	TO	WNXX	PCL	DBS	
08703	CE	WSSK	EWS	DBS	-
08706¤(S)	TO	WNYX	EWS	DBS	-
08709	BS	WNXX	EWS	DBS	-
08711(S)	TE	WNXX	PCL	DBS	-
08714(S)	TO	WSXX	EWS	DBS	-
08735¤	EH	WNYX	EWS	DBS	-
08737	TO	WSSI	EWS	DBS	DBS
08738(S)	TO	WNTS	ECR	DBS	-
08742¤	TO	WSSK	PCL	DBS	DBS
08752	TO	WSSK	EWS	DBS	DBS
08757¤(S)	TO	WNYX	RES	DBS	-
08782	MG	WSSI	BLK	DBS	DBS
08784¤	TO	WNTS	EWS	DBS	-
08799	TO	WNYX	EWS	DBS	DBS
08802	TO	WSSL	EWS	DBS	DBS
08804¤	TO	WSSK	EWS	DBS	DBS
08824(S)	WQ	WSXX	BLK	DBS	-
08865	CE	WSSK	EWS	DBS	DBS
08877(S)	WQ	WSXX	BRD	DBS	-
08879¤(S)	TO	WNYX	EWS	DBS	-
08886(S)	BS	WNXX	EWS	DBS	-
08888¤	TO	WSSI	EWS	DBS	DBS
08904(S)	TO	WNYX	EWS	DBS	-
08907	TO	WSSL	EWS	DBS	DBS
08922(S)	TO	WNTS	BRD	DBS	-
08939(S)	TO	WNTS	ECR	DBS	-
08993(S)+	TO	WNTS	EWS	DBS	-
08994(S)+	DR	WNTS	EWS	DBS	DBS
08995+	TO	WSSK	EWS	DBS	DBS

Names applied

08495	*Noel Kirton OBE*	**08630**	*Bob Brown*
		08701	*Type 100*
		08799	*Andy Bower / Fred*

+ Numbered - Toton No. 1, 08993 was previously No. 08592, 08994 was previously No. 08562, 08995 was previously No. 08687.
¤ Remote control fitted.

Left: *Considering how many BR standard 0-6-0 diesel-electric shunting locos were built, only a few remain in traffic today, with the vast number of local shunting operations being carried out by train engines. No. 08633 painted in EWS red and gold is seen at Westbury. This loco sports frontal lights either side of the radiator indicating it is fitted with remote control equipment.* **Antony Christie**

Class 09/0

	Vehicle Length: 29ft 3in (8.91m)	Engine: English Electric 6K
	Height: 12ft 8⅝in (3.87m)	Horsepower: 400hp (298kW)
	Width: 8ft 6in (2.59m)	Electrical Equipment: English Electric

Number	Depot	Pool	Livery	Owner	Operator
09006(S)	TO	WNXX	EWS	DBS	-

Class 09/1

	Vehicle Length: 29ft 3in (8.91m)	Engine: English Electric 6K
	Height: 12ft 8⅝in (3.87m)	Horsepower: 400hp (298kW)
	Width: 8ft 6in (2.59m)	Electrical Equipment: English Electric

Number		Depot	Pool	Livery	Owner	Operator
09106	(08759)	TO	WSSI	BRD	DBS	DBS

Class 09/2

	Vehicle Length: 29ft 3in (8.91m)	Engine: English Electric 6K
	Height: 12ft 8⅝in (3.87m)	Horsepower: 400hp (298kW)
	Width: 8ft 6in (2.59m)	Electrical Equipment: English Electric

Number		Depot	Pool	Livery	Owner	Operator
09201	(08421)	KY	WSSI	BRD	DBS	DBS

Class 58

	Vehicle Length: 62ft 9½in (19.13m)	Engine: Ruston Paxman 12RK3ACT
	Height: 12ft 10in (3.91m)	Horsepower: 3,300hp (2,460kW)
	Width: 9ft 1in (2.72m)	Electrical Equipment: Brush

Number	Hire No.	Depot	Pool	Livery	Owner	Location	Operator	Name
58001		-	WNTS	ETF	DBS	France	ETF	
58004§		-	WNTS	TSO	DBS	France	TSO	
58005		-	WNTS	ETF	DBS	France	ETF	
58006§		-	WNTS	ETF	DBS	France	ETF	
58007		-	WNTS	TSO	DBS	France	TSO	
58008(S)		EH	WNTS	MLF	DBS	UK	-	
58009		-	WNTS	TSO	DBS	France	TSO	
58010		-	WNTS	FER	DBS	France	TSO	
58011§		-	WNTS	TSO	DBS	France	TSO	
58012(S)		TO	WNTS	MLG	DBS	UK	-	
58013		-	WNTS	ETF	DBS	France	ETF	
58015	L54	CON/SS	-	CON	DBS/T	Spain	TRN	
58017(S)		EH	WNTS	MLG	DBS	UK	-	
58018		EH	WNTS	TSO	DBS	France	TSO	
58020	L43	CON/SS	-	CON	DBS/T	Spain	TRN	
58021		-	WNTS	TSO	DBS	France	TSO	
58022(S)		CD	WNTS	MLG	DBS	UK	-	
58023(S)		TO	WNTS	MLF	DBS	UK	-	
58024	L42	CON/SS	-	CON	DBS/T	Spain	TRN	
58025	L41	CON/SS	-	CON	DBS	Spain	CON	
58026§		-	WNTS	TSO	DBS	France	TSO	
58027	L52	CON/SS	-	CON	DBS	Spain	CON	
58029	L44	CON/SS	-	CON	DBS/T	Spain	TRN	
58030	L46	CON/SS	-	CON	DBS/T	Spain	TRN	
58031	L45	CON/SS	-	CON	DBS/T	Spain	TRN	Cabellero Ferroviaro
58032		-	WNTS	ETF	DBS	France	ETF	
58033		-	WNTS	TSO	DBS	France	TSO	
58034		-	WNTS	TSO	DBS	France	TSO	
58035		-	WNTS	TSO	DBS	France	TSO	
58036		-	WNTS	ETF	DBS	France	ETF	
58037(S)		EH	WNTS	EWS	DBS	UK	-	
58038	58-038	-	WNTS	ETF	DBS	France	ETF	
58039	58-039	-	WNTS	ETF	DBS	France	ETF	
58040§		-	WNTS	TSO	DBS	France	TSO	
58041	L36	CON/SS	-	CON	DBS/T	Spain	TRN	
58042		-	WNTS	TSO	DBS	France	TSO	
58043	L37	CON/SS	-	CON	DBS/T	Spain	TRN	
58044	58-044	-	WZFF	ETF	DBS	France	ETF	
58046		-	WNTS	TSO	DBS	France	TSO	
58047	L51	CON/SS	-	CON	DBS/T	Spain	TRN	
58048(S)		CE	WNTS	EWS	DBS	UK	-	

DB Schenker

58049§	-		WNTS	TSO	DBS	France	ETF
58050	L53	CON/SS	-	CON	DBS	Spain	CON

§ Stored at Alizay (Rouen)

Left: *Introduced between 1983-87 and built by BREL Doncaster, the Class 58 modular diesel-electric locos saw only a few years' use in the UK in revenue-earning traffic but subsequently saw considerable operations overseas, working in Belgium, France and Spain. All are currently stored, but further contracts are likely. No. 58021, painted in Fertis colours, is illustrated. This loco is currently stored in France.*
Paul Fuller

Class 59/2

Vehicle Length: 70ft 0½in (21.34m)
Height: 12ft 10in (3.91m)
Width: 8ft 8¼in (2.65m)
Engine: EMD 16-645 E3C
Horsepower: 3,000hp (2,462kW)
Electrical Equipment: EMD

Number	Depot	Pool	Livery	Owner	Operator	Name
59201	TO	WDAK	DBS	DBS	DBS	
59202	TO	WFMU	DBS	DBS	DBS	
59203	TO	WFMU	DBS	DBS	DBS	
59204	TO	WNTR	DBS	DBS	DBS	
59205	TO	WDAK	DBS	DBS	DBS	
59206	TO	WNWX	DBS	DBS	DBS	John F. Yeoman Rail Pioneer

Left: *All six of the original National Power Class 59/2s, now operated by DB-S and maintained by Mendip Rail at Merehead, are now painted in the latest DB-S red and grey livery, which suits the body profile of these locos well. The fleet spend their time powering aggregate trains from the Mendips to a number of locations in the south of England. No. 59206 is seen heading west to the Mendips through Newbury.*
Nathan Williamson

Class 60

Vehicle Length: 70ft 0½in (21.34m)
Height: 12ft 10⅝in (3.92m)
Width: 8ft 8in (2.64m)
Engine: Mirrlees MB275T
Horsepower: 3,100hp (2,240kW)
Electrical Equipment: Brush

Number	Depot	Pool	Livery	Owner	Operator	Name
60001(S)	TO	WNWX	RFE	DBS	-	
60002(S)	TO	WNTR	EWS	DBS	-	High Peak
60003(S)	TO	WNWX	EWS	DBS	-	Freight Transport Association
60004(S)	TO	WNTS	EWS	DBS	-	
60005(S)	TO	WNTS	EWS	DBS	-	
60007‡	TO	WCBI	DBS	DBS	DBS	The Spirit of Tom Kendell

60009(S)	TO	WNTS	EWS	DBS	-	
60010‡	TO	WCBI	DBS	DBS	DBS	
60011‡	TO	WCAI	DBS	DBS	DBS	
60012(S)	TO	WNWX	EWS	DBS	-	
60013(S)	TO	WCAK	RFE	DBS	-	Robert Boyle
60015‡	TO	WCBK	DBS	DBS	DBS	
60017‡	TO	WCAI	DBS	DBS	DBS	
60018(S)	TO	WNTS	EWS	DBS	-	
60019‡	TO	WCAK	DBS	DBS	DBS	Port of Grimsby & Immingham
60020‡	TO	WCBK	DBS	DBS	DBS	
60021(S)	TO	WNWX	EWS	DBS	-	
60022(S)	TO	WNTS	EWS	DBS	-	
60024‡(S)	TO	WNWX	EWS	DBS	-	
60025(S)	TO	WNTS	EWS	DBS	-	
60026(S)	TO	WNTS	EWS	DBS	-	
60027(S)	TO	WNTS	EWS	DBS	-	
60028(S)	TO	WNTS	RFE	DBS	-	John Flamsteed
60029(S)	TO	WNTS	EWS	DBS	-	Clitheroe Castle
60030(S)	TO	WNTS	EWS	DBS	-	
60032(S)	TO	WNWX	EWS	DBS	-	
60033(S)	TO	WNWX	COR	DBS	-	Tees Steel Express
60034(S)	TO	WNTS	RFE	DBS	-	Carnedd Llewelyn
60035	TO	WCAI	EWS	DBS	DBS	
60036(S)	TO	WNTS	EWS	DBS	-	GEFCO
60037(S)	TO	WNWX	EWS	DBS	-	
60039‡(S)	TO	WNTR	EWS	DBS	-	
60040‡	TO	WCAI	DBS	DBS	DBS	The Territorial Army Centenary
60041(S)	TO	WNTS	EWS	DBS	-	
60043(S)	TO	WNWX	EWS	DBS	-	
60044C(S)	TO/BZ	WNWX	MLF	DBS	-	
60045‡	TO	WCAK	EWS	DBS	DBS	The Permanent Way Institution

After a period when it was considered that the Class 60s were all to be phased out of service, 2011-2013 has seen a large number refurbished by Toton and returned to frontline use, powering the heavier DB-S trains. Refurbishment also sees an application of DB-S red and grey livery. On 3 November 2012, No. 60017 is illustrated powering the 07.15 Lindsey Oil Refinery to Kingsbury Oil Sidings block oil train between Willington and Burton-on-Trent. **John Tuffs**

Freight Operating Companies - DB Schenker

Freight Operating Companies - DB Schenker

DB Schenker

60046(S)	TO	WNTS	RFE	DBS	-	William Wilberforce
60047(S)	TO	WNTS	EWS	DBS	-	
60048(S)	TO	WNTS	EWS	DBS	-	
60049‡	TO	WCAK	EWS	DBS	DBS	
60051(S)	TO	WNTS	EWS	DBS	-	
60052(S)	TO	WNTS	EWS	DBS	-	Glofa Twr - The last deep mine in Wales - Tower Colliery
60053(S)	TO	WNTS	EWS	DBS	-	
60054‡	TO	WCBI	DBS	DBS	DBS	
60056(S)	TO	WNTS	RFE	DBS	-	William Beveridge
60057(S)	TO	WNWX	RFE	DBS	-	Adam Smith
60059‡	TO	WFMU	DBS	DBS	DBS	Swinden Dalesman
60060(S)	TO	WNWX	RFE	DBS	-	
60061(S)	TO	WNTS	RFE	DBS	-	
60062(S)	TO	WNTS	EWS	DBS	-	
60063	TO	WCAI	DBS	DBS	DBS	
60064(S)	TO	WNWX	RFE	DBS	-	Back Tor
60065	TO	WCAI	EWS	DBS	DBS	Spirit of Jaguar
60066(S)	TO	WNTR	RFE	DBS	-	John Logie Baird
60067(S)	TO	WNWX	RFE	DBS	-	
60069(S)	TO	WNWX	EWS	DBS	-	Slioch
60071‡	TO	WCBI	DBS	DBS	DBS	Ribblehead Viaduct
60072(S)	TO	WNWX	RFE	DBS	-	Cairn Toul
60073(S)	TO	WNTS	RFE	DBS	-	Cairn Gorm
60074‡	TO	WCAK	DBB	DBS	DBS	Teenage Spirit
60076(S)	TO	WNTR	RFE	DBS	-	
60077(S)	TO	WNWX	RFE	DBS	-	
60079‡	TO	WCAI	DBS	DBS	DBS	
60083(S)	TO	WNTS	EWS	DBS	-	
60084(S)	TO	WNTS	RFE	DBS	-	Cross Fell
60085(S)	TO	WNWX	EWS	DBS	-	Mini - Pride of Oxford
60086(S)	TO	WNWX	RFE	DBS	-	
60087(S)	TO	WNWX	EWS	DBS	-	
60088(S)	TO	WNWX	MLG	DBS	-	
60090(S)	TO	WNTS	RFE	DBS	-	Quinag
60091‡	TO	WCBI	DBS	DBS	DBS	
60092‡	TO	WCBI	DBS	DBS	DBS	
60093(S)	TO	WNTS	EWS	DBS	-	
60094(S)	CD	WNTS	EWS	DBS	-	Rugby Flyer
60095(S)	TO	WNTS	RFE	DBS	-	
60096(S)	TO/BZ	WBAK	EWS	DBS	DBS	
60097(S)	TO	WNTS	EWS	DBS	-	
60099(S)	TO	WCAI	TAT	DBS	-	
60100‡(S)	TO/BZ	WNTS	EWS	DBS	-	
60500(S)*	TO	WNTS	EWS	DBS	-	

* Previously numbered 60016. ‡ Refurbished (Super 60)

In support of the Teenage Cancer Trust, DB-S agreed to paint refurbished No. 60074 Teenage Spirit in mid-blue livery with Teenage Cancer Trust bodyside branding. The loco is viewed at Margam. **Mark Jones**

Class 66

Vehicle Length: 70ft 0½in (21.34m)
Height: 12ft 10in (3.91m)
Width: 8ft 8¼in (2.65m)

Engine: EMD 12N-710G3B-EC
Horsepower: 3,300hp (2,462kW)
Electrical Equipment: EMD

Number	Depot	Pool	Livery	Owner	Operator
66001‡	TO	WNTR	EWS	ANG	DBS
66002‡	TO	WNTR	EWS	ANG	DBS
66003	TO	WBAL	EWS	ANG	DBS
66004	TO	WFMU	EWS	ANG	DBS
66005	TO	WBSN	EWS	ANG	DBS
66006	TO	WFMS	EWS	ANG	DBS
66007	TO	WBAI	EWS	ANG	DBS
66008	TO	WFMU	EWS	ANG	DBS
66009	TO	WFMU	EWS	ANG	DBS
66010 ●	AZ	WBEN	EWS	ANG	DBS
66011	TO	WBAI	EWS	ANG	DBS
66012	TO	WBAL	EWS	ANG	DBS
66013 ●	TO	WFMU	EWS	ANG	DBS
66014	TO	WFMS	EWS	ANG	DBS
66015	TO	WBAK	EWS	ANG	DBS
66016	TO	WFMU	EWS	ANG	DBS
66017	TO	WFMS	EWS	ANG	DBS
66018	TO	WBAI	EWS	ANG	DBS
66019	TO	WBAK	EWS	ANG	DBS
66020	TO	WNTR	EWS	ANG	DBS
66021	TO	WBAK	EWS	ANG	DBS
66022 ●	AZ	WBEN	EWS	ANG	DBS
66023	TO	WBAI	EWS	ANG	DBS
66024	TO	WBAL	EWS	ANG	DBS
66025	TO	WFMU	EWS	ANG	DBS
66026 ●	TO	WBEN	EWS	ANG	ECR
66027	TO	WBAI	EWS	ANG	DBS
66028 ●	AZ	WBEN	EWS	ANG	ECR
66029 ●	AZ	WBEN	EWS	ANG	ECR
66030	TO	WBAL	EWS	ANG	DBS
66031 ●	TO	WFMU	EWS	ANG	DBS
66032 ●	TO	WBES	EWS	ANG	ECR
66033 ●	AZ	WBEN	EWS	ANG	DBS
66034	TO	WFMU	EWS	ANG	DBS
66035	TO	WBSN	EWS	ANG	DBS
66036 ●	AZ	WBEN	EWS	ANG	ECR
66037	TO	WNWX	EWS	ANG	DBS
66038 ●	AZ	WBEN	EWS	ANG	ECR
66039	TO	WSSK	EWS	ANG	DBS
66040	TO	WFMU	EWS	ANG	DBS
66041	TO	WBAK	EWS	ANG	DBS
66042 ●	AZ	WFMS	EWS	ANG	ECR
66043	TO	WBAL	EWS	ANG	DBS
66044	TO	WBSN	EWS	ANG	DBS
66045 ●	AZ	WBEN	EWS	ANG	ECR
66046	TO	WFMU	EWS	ANG	DBS
66047	TO	WBSN	EWS	ANG	DBS
66048(S)	TO	WNTS	STO	ANG	-
66049 ●	TO	WBEN	EWS	ANG	ECR
66050	TO	WFMU	EWS	ANG	DBS
66051	TO	WBAK	EWS	ANG	DBS
66052 ●	AZ	WFMS	EWS	ANG	ECR
66053	TO	WFMU	EWS	ANG	DBS
66054	TO	WBAI	EWS	ANG	DBS
66055	TO	WBAL	EWS	ANG	DBS
66056	TO	WBLI	EWS	ANG	DBS
66057	TO	WBLI	EWS	ANG	DBS
66058	TO	WFMU	EWS	ANG	DBS
66059	TO	WBLI	EWS	ANG	DBS
66060	TO	WNTR	EWS	ANG	DBS
66061	TO	WBAI	EWS	ANG	DBS
66062 ●	AZ	WBEN	EWS	ANG	DBS
66063	TO	WFMS	EWS	ANG	DBS
66064 ●	TO	WBEN	EWS	ANG	DBS
66065	TO	WBAI	EWS	ANG	DBS
66066	TO	WBAI	EWS	ANG	DBS
66067	TO	WBAI	EWS	ANG	DBS
66068	TO	WBAK	EWS	ANG	DBS
66069	TO	WBAI	EWS	ANG	DBS
66070	TO	WSSK	EWS	ANG	DBS
66071 ●	AZ	WSSK	EWS	ANG	DBS
66072 ●	AZ	WBEN	EWS	ANG	DBS
66073 ●	AZ	WBEN	EWS	ANG	ECR
66074	TO	WBAL	EWS	ANG	DBS
66075	TO	WBAI	EWS	ANG	DBS
66076	TO	WBAK	EWS	ANG	DBS
66077	TO	WBEN	EWS	ANG	DBS
66078	TO	WBAI	EWS	ANG	DBS
66079	TO	WBAK	EWS	ANG	DBS
66080	TO	WBAK	EWS	ANG	DBS
66081	TO	WBAK	EWS	ANG	DBS
66082	TO	WNWX	EWS	ANG	DBS
66083	TO	WNTR	EWS	ANG	DBS
66084	TO	WBAK	EWS	ANG	DBS
66085	TO	WBAI	EWS	ANG	DBS
66086	TO	WSSK	EWS	ANG	DBS
66087	TO	WBAI	EWS	ANG	DBS
66088	TO	WFMU	EWS	ANG	DBS
66089	TO	WBAI	EWS	ANG	DBS
66090	TO	WBAI	EWS	ANG	DBS
66091	TO	WBAK	EWS	ANG	DBS
66092	TO	WFMU	EWS	ANG	DBS
66093	TO	WBAI	EWS	ANG	DBS
66094	TO	WBAI	EWS	ANG	DBS
66095	TO	WBAK	EWS	ANG	DBS
66096	TO	WNTR	EWS	ANG	DBS
66097	TO	WBAI	DBS	ANG	DBS
66098	TO	WBAI	EWS	ANG	DBS
66099	TO	WBBK	EWS	ANG	DBS
66100	TO	WNTR	EWS	ANG	DBS
66101	TO	WNTR	DBS	ANG	DBS
66102	TO	WFMS	EWS	ANG	DBS
66103	TO	WFMU	EWS	ANG	DBS
66104	TO	WFMU	EWS	ANG	DBS
66105	TO	WFMS	EWS	ANG	DBS
66106	TO	WBBL	EWS	ANG	DBS
66107	TO	WFMU	EWS	ANG	DBS
66108	TO	WBBL	EWS	ANG	DBS
66109	TO	WBAK	EWS	ANG	DBS
66110	TO	WBAK	EWS	ANG	DBS
66111	TO	WNTR	EWS	ANG	DBS
66112	TO	WBBI	EWS	ANG	DBS
66113	TO	WFMU	EWS	ANG	DBS
66114	TO	WBBI	EWS	ANG	DBS
66115	TO	WBAI	EWS	ANG	DBS
66116	TO	WBAK	EWS	ANG	DBS
66117	TO	WBAK	EWS	ANG	DBS
66118	TO	WFMU	DBS	ANG	DBS
66119	TO	WNTR	EWS	ANG	DBS
66120	TO	WSSK	EWS	ANG	DBS
66121	TO	WBAI	EWS	ANG	DBS
66122	TO	WFMU	EWS	ANG	DBS
66123 ●	AZ	WBES	EWS	ANG	DBS

DB Schenker

66124	TO	WBSN	EWS	ANG	DBS
66125	TO	WNTR	EWS	ANG	DBS
66126	TO	WBAK	EWS	ANG	DBS
66127	TO	WBAI	EWS	ANG	DBS
66128	TO	WBAI	EWS	ANG	DBS
66129	TO	WFMS	EWS	ANG	DBS
66130	TO	WBAI	EWS	ANG	DBS
66131	TO	WBAI	EWS	ANG	DBS
66132	TO	WFMU	EWS	ANG	DBS
66133	TO	WBAI	EWS	ANG	DBS
66134	TO	WFMS	EWS	ANG	DBS
66135	TO	WBAK	EWS	ANG	DBS
66136	TO	WBAK	EWS	ANG	DBS
66137	TO	WBAI	EWS	ANG	DBS
66138	TO	WBAL	EWS	ANG	DBS
66139	TO	WBAI	EWS	ANG	DBS
66140	TO	WBAL	EWS	ANG	DBS
66141	TO	WBAK	EWS	ANG	DBS
66142	TO	WFMU	EWS	ANG	DBS
66143	TO	WBAI	EWS	ANG	DBS
66144	TO	WBAI	EWS	ANG	DBS
66145	TO	WNTR	EWS	ANG	DBS
66146 P	PN	WBEP	EWS	ANG	DBS
66147	TO	WNTR	EWS	ANG	DBS
66148	TO	WBAI	EWS	ANG	DBS
66149	TO	WBAL	EWS	ANG	DBS
66150	TO	WBAK	EWS	ANG	DBS
66151	TO	WBAI	EWS	ANG	DBS
66152	TO	WBAI	DBS	ANG	DBS
66153 P	PN	WBEP	EWS	ANG	DBS
66154	TO	WBAI	EWS	ANG	DBS
66155	TO	WBAL	EWS	ANG	DBS
66156	TO	WNTR	EWS	ANG	DBS
66157 P	PN	WBEP	EWS	ANG	DBS
66158	TO	WNTR	EWS	ANG	DBS
66159 P	PN	WBEP	EWS	ANG	DBS
66160	TO	WBAI	EWS	ANG	DBS
66161	TO	WBAK	EWS	ANG	DBS
66162	TO	WBAK	EWS	ANG	DBS
66163 P	PN	WBEP	DBS	ANG	DBS
66164	TO	WFMU	EWS	ANG	DBS
66165	TO	WBAI	EWS	ANG	DBS
66166 P	PN	WBEP	EWS	ANG	DBS
66167	TO	WBAK	EWS	ANG	DBS
66168	TO	WFMU	EWS	ANG	DBS
66169	TO	WBAK	EWS	ANG	DBS
66170	TO	WFMU	EWS	ANG	DBS
66171	TO	WBAK	EWS	ANG	DBS
66172	TO	WBAK	EWS	ANG	DBS
66173 P	PN	WBEP	EWS	ANG	DBS
66174	TO	WNTR	EWS	ANG	DBS
66175	TO	WBAI	EWS	ANG	DBS
66176	TO	WBAK	EWS	ANG	DBS
66177	TO	WBAK	EWS	ANG	DBS
66178 P	PN	WBEP	EWS	ANG	DBS
66179 ●	TO	WBAK	EWS	ANG	ECR
66180 P	PN	WBEP	EWS	ANG	DBS
66181	TO	WBAK	EWS	ANG	DBS
66182	TO	WBAK	EWS	ANG	DBS
66183	TO	WBAK	EWS	ANG	DBS
66184	TO	WNTR	EWS	ANG	DBS
66185	TO	WBAK	EWS	ANG	DBS
66186	TO	WBAI	EWS	ANG	DBS
66187	TO	WFMU	EWS	ANG	DBS
66188	TO	WBAK	EWS	ANG	DBS
66189 P	PN	WBEP	EWS	ANG	DBS
66190 ●	AZ	WBEN	EWS	ANG	ECR
66191 ●	AZ	WBEN	EWS	ANG	DBS
66192	TO	WBAI	EWS	ANG	DBS
66193	TO	WNTR	EWS	ANG	DBS
66194	TO	WBAK	EWS	ANG	DBS
66195 ●	AZ	WBEN	EWS	ANG	ECR
66196 P	PN	WBEP	EWS	ANG	DBS
66197	TO	WBAK	EWS	ANG	DBS
66198	TO	WBAK	EWS	ANG	DBS
66199	TO	WBAI	EWS	ANG	DBS
66200	TO	WBAK	EWS	ANG	DBS
66201	TO	WBAI	EWS	ANG	DBS
66202 ●	AZ	WBEN	EWS	ANG	ECR
66203 ●	AZ	WBEN	EWS	ANG	ECR
66204	TO	WBAI	EWS	ANG	DBS
66205 ●	AZ	WBEN	EWS	ANG	ECR
66206	TO	WFMU	EWS	ANG	DBS
66207	TO	WBAI	EWS	ANG	DBS
66208 ●	AZ	WBEN	EWS	ANG	ECR
66209 ●	AZ	WBEN	EWS	ANG	ECR
66210 ●	AZ	WBEN	EWS	ANG	ECR
66211 ●	TO	WBEN	EWS	ANG	ECR
66212 ●	AZ	WBEN	EWS	ANG	ECR
66213	TO	WBAK	EWS	ANG	DBS
66214 ●	AZ	WBEN	EWS	ANG	ECR
66215 ●	AZ	WBEN	EWS	ANG	ECR
66216 ●	AZ	WBEN	EWS	ANG	ECR
66217 ●	AZ	WBEN	EWS	ANG	ECR
66218 ●	AZ	WFMU	EWS	ANG	ECR
66219 ●	AZ	WBEN	EWS	ANG	ECR
66220 P	PN	WBEP	DBS	ANG	DBS
66221	TO	WNTR	EWS	ANG	DBS
66222 ●	AZ	WBEN	EWS	ANG	ECR
66223 ●	AZ	WBEN	EWS	ANG	DBS
66224 ●	AZ	WBEN	EWS	ANG	ECR
66225 ●	AZ	WBEN	EWS	ANG	ECR
66226 ●	AZ	WBEN	EWS	ANG	ECR
66227 P	PN	WBEP	EWS	ANG	DBS
66228 ●	AZ	WBEN	EWS	ANG	ECR
66229 ●	AZ	WBEN	EWS	ANG	ECR
66230	TO	WFMU	EWS	ANG	DBS
66231 ●	AZ	WBEN	EWS	ANG	ECR
66232	TO	WFMU	EWS	ANG	DBS
66233 ●	AZ	WBEN	EWS	ANG	ECR
66234 ●	AZ	WBEN	EWS	ANG	ECR
66235 ●	AZ	WBEN	EWS	ANG	ECR
66236 ●	AZ	WBEN	EWS	ANG	ECR
66237 P	PN	WBEP	EWS	ANG	DBS
66238	TO	WNTR	EWS	ANG	DBS
66239 ●	AZ	WBEN	EWS	ANG	ECR
66240 ●	AZ	WBEN	EWS	ANG	ECR
66241 ●	AZ	WBEN	EWS	ANG	ECR
66242 ●	AZ	WBEN	EWS	ANG	ECR
66243 ●	TO	WBEN	EWS	ANG	ECR
66244 ●	AZ	WBEN	EWS	ANG	ECR
66245 ●	AZ	WBEN	EWS	ANG	DBS
66246 ●	AZ	WBEN	EWS	ANG	ECR
66247 ●	AZ	WBEN	EWS	ANG	ECR
66248 P	PN	WBEP	DBS	ANG	DBS
66249 ●	AZ	WBES	EWS	ANG	DBS
66250	TO	WBAK	EWS	ANG	DBS

‡ Not fitted with combination couplers

Names applied

66002	*Lafarge Quorn*
66048	*James the Engine*
66050	*EWS Energy*
66077	*Benjamin Gimbert GC*
66079	*James Nightall GC*
66152	*Derek Holmes Railway Operator*
66172	*Paul Melleney*
66200	*Railway Heritage Committee*
66250	*Robert K. Romak* (not standard nameplate)

● Class 66/0s marked with this symbol are modified and can operate with Euro Cargo Rail in France. Usually around 60 locos are in France at one time, but this figure is reduced in the autumn when a number return to the UK for RHTT operations. Locos working in France operate in the pool WBEN.

P Locomotives marked with a 'P' are operated by DB Schenker in Poland. Only locos from the series 66146-250 can be modified for this contract.

Right: *The mainstay of DB-S freight motive power is the EMD-built Class 66. Originally 250 were introduced in the UK, but following downturns in the UK freight industry, a significant number now operate in France and Poland for Euro Cargo Rail. The locos operating in France do return to the UK via the Channel Tunnel either for autumn/winter RHTT work or extended maintenance, but those exported to Poland have so far remained in that country. No 66065 displaying standard EWS maroon and gold livery is seen at Cardiff, powering a westbound coal train.* **CJM**

Class 67

Vehicle Length: 64ft 7in (19.68m)	Engine: EMD 12N-710G3B-EC
Height: 12ft 9in (3.88m)	Horsepower: 2,980hp (2,223kW)
Width: 8ft 9in (2.66m)	Electrical Equipment: EMD

Number	Depot	Pool	Livery	Owner	Operator	Name
67001	CE	WAAN	ATW	ANG	DBS/ATW	
67002	CE	WAAN	ATW	ANG	DBS/ATW	
67003	CE	WAAN	ATW	ANG	DBS/ATW	
67004	CE	WABN	EWS	ANG	DBS	
67005	CE	WAAN	ROY	ANG	DBS	*Queen's Messenger*
67006	CE	WAAN	ROY	ANG	DBS	*Royal Sovereign*
67007	CE	WABN	EWS	ANG	DBS	
67008	CE	WAAN	EWS	ANG	DBS	
67009	CE	WFMU	EWS	ANG	DBS	
67010	CE	WNTR	WSR	ANG	DBS/CRW	
67011	CE	WABN	EWS	ANG	DBS	
67012	CE	WAWN	WSR	ANG	DBS/CRW	*A Shropshire Lad*
67013	CE	WNTR	WSR	ANG	DBS/CRW	*Dyfrbont Pontcysyllte*
67014	CE	WAAN	WSR	ANG	DBS/CRW	*Thomas Telford*
67015	CE	WAWN	WSR	ANG	DBS/CRW	*David J. Lloyd*
67016	CE	WAFN	EWS	ANG	DBS	
67017	CE	WAFN	EWS	ANG	DBS	*Arrow*
67018	CE	WAFN	DBS	ANG	DBS	*Keith Heller*
67019	CE	WAAN	EWS	ANG	DBS	
67020	CE	WAAN	EWS	ANG	DBS	
67021	CE	WAAN	EWS	ANG	DBS	
67022	CE	WFMU	EWS	ANG	DBS	
67023	CE	WAAN	EWS	ANG	DBS	
67024	CE	WAAN	EWS	ANG	DBS	
67025	CE	WAAN	ANC	ANG	DBS	*Western Star*
67026	CE	WAAN	ROJ	ANG	DBS	*Diamond Jubilee*
67027	CE	WAAN	EWS	ANG	DBS	*Rising Star*
67028	CE	WAAN	EWS	ANG	DBS	
67029	CE	WAAN	EWE	ANG	DBS	*Royal Diamond*
67030	CE	WABN	EWS	ANG	DBS	

DB Schenker

Left: *In addition to the EMD Class 66s ordered by EWS a fleet of 30 Class 67s for passenger and fast freight were ordered, being assembled in Spain. The fleet can be found throughout the country, operating for their booked operator DB-S, as well as Arriva Trains Wales, Chiltern Railways, East Coast, First ScotRail and the charter sector. Several locos sport special liveries including two in Royal Train claret livery and one in silver for the 2012 Queen's Diamond Jubilee. Diamond Jubilee No. 67026 is seen with 'Royal' No. 67006 on a freight at Burton on 20 September 2012.* **John Tuffs**

Class 90

Vehicle Length: 61ft 6in (18.74m)		Power Collection: 25kV ac overhead			
Height: 13ft 0¼in (3.96m)		Horsepower: 7,860hp (5,860kW)			
Width: 9ft 0in (2.74m)		Electrical Equipment: GEC			

Number		Depot	Pool	Livery	Owner	Operator	Name/Notes
90017		CE	WNTS	EWS	DBS	-	
90018		CE	WEFE	DVS	DBS	DBS	
90019		CE	WEFE	FGS	DBS	DBS	
90020		CE	WEFE	EWS	DBS	DBS	*Collingwood*
90021	(90221)	CE	WEFE	FGS	DBS	-	
90022	(90222)	CE	WNTS	RFE	DBS	-	*Freightconnection*
90023	(90223)	CE	WNTS	EWS	DBS	-	
90024(S)	(90224)	CE	WNTR	FGS	DBS	-	
90025	(90225)	CE	WNTS	FGS	DBS	-	
90026		CE	WEFE	EWS	DBS	DBS	
90027(S)	(90227)	CE	WNTS	RFD	DBS	-	*Allerton T&RS Depot Quality Approved*
90028		CE	WEFE	EWS	DBS	DBS	
90029		CE	WNTR	DBS	DBS	DBS	
90030	(90130)	CE	WNTS	EWS	DBS	-	*Crewe Locomotive Works*
90031	(90131)	CE	WNTS	EWS	DBS	-	*The Railway Children Partnership - Working for Street Children Worldwide*
90032	(90132)	CE	WNTS	EWS	DBS	-	
90033	(90233)	CE	WFMU	RFI	DBS	DBS	
90034(S)	(90134)	CE	WNTS	EWS	DBS	-	
90035	(90135)	CE	WEFE	EWS	DBS	DBS	
90036	(90136)	CE	WEFE	RFE	DBS	-	
90037	(90137)	CE	WNTS	EWS	DBS	-	*Spirit of Dagenham*
90038	(90238)	CE	WNTS	RFI	DBS	-	
90039(S)	(90239)	CE	WNTR	EWS	DBS	-	
90040	(90140)	CE	WNTS	EWS	DBS	-	*The Railway Mission*
90050	(90050)	LNWR	WNTS	FLG	DBS	-	*(At LNWR Crewe for spares recovery and scrap)*

Left: *DB-S have a fleet of 24 Class 90s on their books; however, that number of locos will never all be found in traffic. Frequently up to a dozen are stored out of service at Crewe Electric Depot. Painted in EWS maroon and gold livery, No. 90020 Collingwood is seen at Carlisle.* **Nathan Williamson**

Class 92

Vehicle Length: 70ft 1in (21.34m)
Height: 13ft 0in (3.95m)
Width: 8ft 8in (2.66m)
Power Collection: 25kV ac overhead / 750V dc third rail
Horsepower: ac - 6,700hp (5,000kW) / dc 5,360hp (4,000kW)
Electrical Equipment: Brush

Number	Depot	Pool	Livery	Owner	Operator	Name
92001(S)	CE	WNTR	EWS	HAL	-	Victor Hugo
92002(S)	CE	WNWX	RFE	HAL	-	H G Wells
92003	CE	WNTR	RFE	HAL	DBS	Beethoven
92004(S)	CE	WNWX	RFE	HAL	-	Jane Austen
92005(S)	CE	WNTR	RFE	HAL	-	Mozart
92007	CE	WNTR	RFE	HAL	DBS	Schubert
92008(S)	CE	WNWX	RFE	HAL	-	Jules Verne
92009§(S)	CE	WTHE	DBS	HAL	-	Marco Polo
92011	CE	WTAE	RFE	HAL	DBS	Handel
92012	CE	WTAE	RFE	HAL	DBS	Thomas Hardy
92013(S)	CE	WNWX	RFE	HAL	-	Puccini
92015§	CE	WTHE	DBS	HAL	DBS	D H Lawrence
92016§	CE	WTAE	DBS	HAL	DBS	
92017(S)	CE	WNTR	STO	HAL	-	Bart the Engine
92019	CE	WEFE	RFE	HAL	DBS	Wagner
92022(S)	CE	WNTR	RFE	HAL	-	Charles Dickens
92024(S)	CE	WNWX	RFE	HAL	-	J S Bach
92025±	-	WNTR	RFE	HAL	Exported Bulgaria	Oscar Wilde
92026(S)	CE	WNTR	RFE	HAL	-	Britten
92027±	-	WTAE	RFE	HAL	Exported Bulgaria	George Eliot
92029(S)	CE	WNWX	RFE	HAL	-	Dante
92030	CE	WTAE	RFE	HAL	DBS	Ashford
92031§	CE	WTHE	DBS	HAL	DBS	The Institute of Logistics and Transport
92034±	-	WTEB	RFE	HAL	Exported Bulgaria	Kipling
92035(S)	CE	WNWX	RFE	HAL	-	Mendelssohn
92036§	CE	WTAE	RFE	HAL	DBS	Bertolt Brecht
92037(S)	CE	WNTR	RFE	HAL	-	Sullivan
92039	CE	WNWX	RFE	HAL	DBS	Johann Strauss
92041	CE	WNTR	RFE	HAL	DBS	Vaughan Williams
92042§	CE	WTHE	DBS	HAL	DBS	

§ Fitted with equipment to allow operation over HS1

± Exported to Bulgaria for assessment

Right: *The Brush-built Class 92s originally intended for Channel Tunnel freight services are another DB-S asset which spend more time stored than operational. In 2012, a handful sported DB-S red and grey livery, as demonstrated by this view of No. 92016 at Crewe.* **Andrew Royle**

Hauled Stock (Passenger)

	Mk1	Height: 12ft 9½in (3.89m)
	Vehicle Length: 64ft 6in (19.65m)	Width: 9ft 3in (2.81m)
	Mk2	Height: 12ft 9½in (3.89m)
	Vehicle Length: 66ft 0in (20.11m)	Width: 9ft 3in (2.81m)
	Mk 3	Height: 12ft 9in (3.88m)
	Vehicle Length: 75ft 0in (22.86m)	Width: 8ft 11in (2.71m)

AJ41 - RBR

Number	Depot	Livery	Owner
1658(S)	FH	MAR	DBR
1679	EH	LNE	DBR
1680(S)	EH	LNE	DBR
1696(S)	(EH)	GRN	DBR

AD1F - FOT

Number	Depot	Livery	Owner
3255(S) (3525)	(EH)	MAR	DBR
3269(S)	EH	MAR	DBR

DB Schenker

AD1F - FO

Number	Depot	Livery	Owner
3279	MH	MAR	DBR/FSR
3292	CE	MAR	DBR
3303(S)	CE	ANG	DBR
3318	MH	MAR	DBR/FSR
3331	MH	MAR	DBR/FSR
3338(S)	EH	MAR	DBR
3368(S)	(EH)	MAR	DBR
3375(S)	EH	MAR	DBR
3388(S)	EH	MAR	DBR
3399(S)	EH	MAR	DBR
3400	MH	MAR	DBR/FSR
3414(S)	EH	MAR	DBR
3424	MH	MAR	DBR/FSR

AC2A - TSO

Number	Depot	Livery	Owner
5331(S)	(EH)	MAR	DBR
5386(S)	(EH)	MAR	DBR

AC2B - TSO

Number	Depot	Livery	Owner
5482	TO	BLG	DBR

AC2D - TSO

Number	Depot	Livery	Owner
5631	MH	MAR	AUT
5632	MH	MAR	AUT
5657(S)	MH	MAR	AUT

AC2F - TSO

Number	Depot	Livery	Owner
5922	EH	MAR	AUT
5924	EH	MAR	AUT
5954(S)	EH	MAR	AUT
5959(S)	EH	MAR	AUT
6036(S)	EH	MAR	DBR
6110(S)	EH	MAR	DBR
6139(S)	TO	MAR	DBR
6152(S)	EH	MAR	DBR

AX51 - GEN

Number	Depot	Livery	Owner
6311(S) (92911)	TO	BLU	DBR (for sale)

AN1D - RMBF

Number	Depot	Livery	Owner
6720 (6602)	EH	MAR	DBR

AE2D - BSO

Number	Depot	Livery	Owner
9494	MH	MAR	DBR/FSR

AE2F - BSO

Number	Depot	Livery	Owner
9522	MH	MAR	DBR/FSR
9529(S)	EH	MAR	DBR
9531(S)	EH	MAR	DBR

AJ1G - RFM

Number		Depot	Livery	Owner
10201(S)	(40520)	LM	VIR	DBR
10202	(40504)	LM	BLG	DBR/CRW
10211	(40510)	TO	EWE	DBS

10215	(11032)	LM	BLG	DBR/CRW
10222(S)	(11063)	BY	BLG	DBR
10226(S)	(11015)	LM	VIR	DBR
10233(S)	(10013)	LM	VIR	DBR
10235	(10015)	LM	BLG	DBR/CRW
10237(S)	(10022)	BY	DRU	DBR
10242(S)	(10002)	LM	BLG	DBR
10246	(10114)	CF	BLG	DBR/CRW
10250(S)	(10020)	LM	VIR	DBR
10257(S)	(10007)	BY	BLG	DBR

AU4G - SLEP

Number	Depot	Livery	Owner
10540(S)	LM	FGW	DBR
10546	TO	EWE	DBS
10554(S)	LM	ICS	DBR (scrap)

AS4G - SLE

Number	Depot	Livery	Owner
10647(S)	LM	ICS	DBR
10681(S)	LM	-	DBR
10682(S)	LM	ICS	DBR (scrap)
10710(S)	LM	CWR	DBR/CRW
10731(S)	LM	ICS	DBR (scrap)

AD1G - FO

Number	Depot	Livery	Owner
11005(S)	LM	VIR	DBR
11013(S)	LM	DRU	DBR
11019(S)	ZB	DRU	DBR
11027(S)	BY	BLU	DBR
11028(S)	ZB	VIR	DBR
11029	AL	CWR	DBR/CRW
11030(S)	ZB	DRU	DBR
11031	AL	BLG	DBR/CRW
11033(S)	LM	DRU	DBR
11039	TO	EWE	DBS
11044(S)	BY	DRU	DBR
11046(S)	ZB	DRU	DBR
11054(S)	ZB	DRU	DBR
11064(S)	CF	BLG	DBR
11065(S)	CF	BLG	DBR
11071(S)	CF	BLG	DBR
11079(S)	LM	BLG	DBR/CRW
11083(S)	CF	BLG	DBR
11084(S)	CF	BLG	DBR
11086(S)	LM	BLG	DBR
11089	AL	BLG	DBR/CRW
11097(S)	LM	BLG	DBR

AB21 - BSK

Number	Depot	Livery	Owner
35290(S)	CP	CAR	DBR

GK2G - TRSB

Number		Depot	Livery	Owner
40402(S)	(40002)	LM	VIR	DBR
40403(S)	(40003)	LM	VIR	DBR
40416(S)	(40016)	LM	VIR	DBR
40419(S)	(40019)	LM	VIR	DBR
40434(S)	(40234)	LM	VIR	DBR

Saloon

Number	Depot	Livery	Owner
45020(S)	TO	MAR	DBR

Hauled Stock (NPCCS)

Mk 3 (DVT)   Height: 12ft 9in (3.88m)
Vehicle Length: 61ft 9in (18.83m)   Width: 8ft 11in (2.71m)

NZAG - DVT

Number	Depot	Livery	Owner
82104(S)	LM	ORN	DBR
82106(S)	LM	VIR	DBR
82110(S)	LM	VIR	DBR
82113(S)	LM	VIR	DBR
82116(S)	LM	VIR	DBR
82120(S)	LM	VIR	DBR
82122(S)	LM	VIR	DBR
82137(S)	LM	VIR	DBR
82138(S)	LM	VIR	DBR
82141(S)	LM	VIR	DBR
82146	TO	DBE	DBS
82148(S)	LM	VIR	DBR
82150(S)	LM	VIR	DBR

NKA1 - H-GUV

Number		Depot	Livery	Owner
94103 (W)	(95103)	CF	RES	DBS
94104 (S)	(95104)	TO	RES	DBS
94106 (S)	(95106)	MH	RES	DBS
94116 (S)	(95116)	TY	RES	DBS
94121 (S)	(95121)	TO	RES	DBS
94137 (S)	(95137)	MY	RES	DBS
94147 (S)	(95147)	MY	RES	DBS
94153 (S)	(95153)	WE	RES	DBS
94160 (S)	(95160)	MH	RES	DBS
94166 (S)	(95166)	BS	RES	DBS
94170 (S)	(95170)	BS	RES	DBS
94176 (S)	(95176)	MH	RES	DBS
94177 (S)	(95177)	TO	RES	DBS
94192 (S)	(95352)	MY	RES	DBS
94195 (S)	(95355)	BS	RES	DBS
94197 (S)	(95357)	BS	RES	DBS
94207 (S)	(95367)	TO	RES	DBS
94208 (S)	(95368)	TO	RES	DBS
94209 (W)	(95369)	CU	RES	DBS
94213 (S)	(95373)	MY	RES	DBS
94214 (S)	(95374)	MH	RES	DBS
94217 (S)	(93131)	MH	RES	DBS
94221 (S)	(93905)	MY	RES	DBS
94222 (S)	(93474)	MH	RES	DBS
94225 (S)	(93849)	MH	RES	DBS
94227 (S)	(93585)	TE	RES	DBS
94229 (S)	(93720)	MH	RES	DBS

NAA1 - PCV

Number		Depot	Livery	Owner
94302 (S)	(75124)	TY	RES	DBS
94303 (S)	(75131)	TY	RES	DBS
94304 (S)	(75107)	MH	RES	DBS
94306 (S)	(75112)	TY	RES	DBS
94307 (S)	(75127)	CX	RES	DBS
94308 (S)	(75125)	MH	RES	DBS
94310 (S)	(75119)	WE	RES	DBS
94311 (S)	(75105)	WE	RES	DBS
94313 (S)	(75129)	WE	RES	DBS
94316 (S)	(75108)	TO	RES	DBS
94317 (S)	(75117)	TO	RES	DBS
94318 (S)	(75115)	CX	RES	DBS
94322 (S)	(75111)	MH	RES	DBS
94323 (S)	(75110)	TY	RES	DBS
94326 (S)	(75123)	TY	RES	DBS
94331 (S)	(75022)	CX	RES	DBS
94332 (S)	(75011)	TY	RES	DBS
94333 (S)	(75016)	TY	RES	DBS
94334 (S)	(75017)	CD	RES	DBS
94335 (S)	(75032)	TY	RES	DBS
94336 (S)	(75031)	TY	RES	DBS
94340 (S)	(75012)	CD	RES	DBS
94343 (S)	(75027)	MH	RES	DBS
94344 (S)	(75014)	TO	RES	DBS

NBA1, NOA1, NQA, NRA1 - BVHS

Number		Depot	Livery	Owner
94400	(92524)	CX	RES	DBS
94406	(92956)	MH	RES	DBS
94408	(92981)	TY	RES	DBS
94410	(92941)	WE	RES	DBS
94411	(92945)	CX	RES	DBS
94412	(92945)	ML	RES	DBS
94413	(92236)	ML	RES	DBS
94416	(92746)	MY	RES	DBS
94420	(92263)	MH	RES	DBS
94422	(92651)	TO	RES	DBS
94423	(92914)	BS	RES	DBS
94427	(92754)	WE	RES	DBS
94428	(92166)	MY	RES	DBS
94429	(92232)	TE	RES	DBS
94431	(92604)	MH	RES	DBS
94432	(92999)	MY	RES	DBS
94433	(92643)	MH	RES	DBS
94434	(92501)	TY	RES	DBS
94435	(92134)	TO	RES	DBS
94438	(92251)	TO	RES	DBS
94440	(92615)	MY	RES	DBS
94445	(92615)	WE	RES	DBS
94451	(92257)	WE	RES	DBS
94458	(92974)	CX	RES	DBS
94462	(92270)	CD	RES	DBS
94463	(92995)	TY	RES	DBS
94470	(92113)	TO	RES	DBS
94479	(92132)	TO	RES	DBS
94481	(92641)	CX	RES	DBS
94482	(92639)	MH	RES	DBS
94488	(92105)	CD	RES	DBS
94490	(92230)	MH	RES	DBS
94492	(92721)	WE	RES	DBS
94495	(92755)	TY	RES	DBS
94497	(92717)	ML	RES	DBS
94498	(92555)	MH	RES	DBS
94499	(92577)	CD	BLG	DBS
94501	(92725)	TO	RES	DBS
94504	(92748)	TY	RES	DBS
94512	(92582)	TY	RES	DBS
94511	(92122)	MY	RES	DBS
94515	(92513)	EH	DBS	DBS
94518	(92258)	MY	RES	DBS
94519	(92916)	ML	RES	DBS

DB Schenker

94520 (92917)	TY	RES	DBS
94521 (92917)	CD	RES	DBS
94522 (92907)	TY	RES	DBS
94525 (92229)	TY	RES	DBS
94526 (92518)	TY	RES	DBS
94527 (92728)	TY	RES	DBS
94528 (92252)	ML	RES	DBS
94529 (92267)	CD	RES	DBS
94530 (94409)	MY	RES	DBS
94531 (94456)	TY	RES	DBS
94532 (94489)	LM	RES	DBS
94534 (94430)	MY	RES	DBS
94536 (94491)	MY	RES	DBS
94539 (92302)	MH	RES	DBS
94540 (92860)	TJ	RES	DBS
94541 (92316)	ML	RES	DBS
94542 (92330)	TY	RES	DBS
94543 (92389)	MY	RES	DBS
94544 (92345)	MH	RES	DBS
94545 (92329)	TE	RES	DBS
94546 (92804)	TY	RES	DBS
94547 (92392)	MH	RES	DBS
94548 (92344)	TY	RES	DBS

NAA1 - PCV

Number	Depot	Livery	Owner
95300 (94300)	MH	RES	DBS
95301 (94301)	MH	RES	DBS

NRA1 - BAA

Number	Depot	Livery	Owner
95400 (95203)	MH	EWS	DBS
95410 (95213)	MH	EWS	DBS

NOA1 - H-GUV

Number	Depot	Livery	Owner
95727 (95127)	WE	RES	DBS
95754 (95154)	TY	RES	DBS
95761 (95161)	WE	RES	DBS
95763 (95163)	BS	RES	DBS

NX5G - NGV

Number	Depot	Livery	Owner
96371(S) (10545)	WB	EPS	DBS
96372(S) (10564)	LM	EPS	DBS
96373(S) (10568)	LM	EPS	DBS
96375(S) (10587)	LM	EPS	DBS

Right: *Although mainly a freight operator DB-S does provide stock for passenger charter operations and long term hire deals, including the provision of traction and train crew. Painted in EWS maroon, this is Mk2F TSO No. 6110.* **Nathan Williamson**

Below: *The annual 'Torbay Express' steam charters between Bristol and Kingswear are provided by DB-S. A westbound 'TE' is seen passing Dawlish powered by 'Standard' No. 70000 Britannia.* **CJM**

Euro Cargo Rail A part of DB Schenker

Address: ✉ Immeuble la Palacio, 25-29 Place de la Madeleine, Paris, 75008

📠 info@eurocargorail.com

📞 +33 977 400000

ⓘ www.eurocargorail.com

Class 21

Vehicle Length: (21/5) 48ft 2in (14.70m), (21/6) 46ft 3in (14.13m)
Height: (21/5) 13ft 8in (4.16m), (21/6) 13ft 9in (4.19m)
Width: 8ft 8¼in (2.65m)

Engine: (21/5) Caterpillar 3512B DITA of 2,011hp
Engine: (21/6) MTU 8V 4000 R41L of 1,475hp
Hydraulic Equipment: Voith

Number	Depot	Pool	Livery	Owner	Operator
21544	DM	WLAN	MAR	ANG	ECR
21545	DM	WLAN	MAR	ANG	ECR
21546	DM	WLAN	MAR	ANG	ECR
21547	DM	WLAN	MAR	ANG	ECR
21610	DM	WLAN	MAR	ANG	ECR
21611	DM	WLAN	MAR	ANG	ECR

Class 77
(JT42CWRM)

Vehicle Length: 70ft 0½in (21.34m)
Height: 12ft 10in (3.91m)
Width: 8ft 8¼in (2.65m)

Engine: EMD 12N-710G3B-EC
Horsepower: 3,300hp (2,462kW)
Electrical Equipment: EMD

Number	Depot	Livery	Owner	Opt'r
77001	ND	ELR	DBS	ECR
77002	ND	ELR	DBS	ECR
77003	ND	ELR	DBS	ECR
77004	ND	ELR	DBS	ECR
77005	ND	ELR	DBS	ECR
77006	ND	ELR	DBS	ECR
77007‡	ND	ELR	DBS	ECR
77008	ND	ELR	DBS	ECR
77009	ND	ELR	DBS	ECR
77010	ND	ELR	DBS	ECR
77011	ND	ELR	DBS	ECR
77012	ND	ELR	DBS	ECR
77013	ND	ELR	DBS	ECR
77014	ND	ELR	DBS	ECR
77015	ND	ELR	DBS	ECR
77016	ND	ELR	DBS	ECR
77017	ND	ELR	DBS	ECR
77018	ND	ELR	DBS	ECR
77019	ND	ELR	DBS	ECR
77020‡	ND	ELR	DBS	ECR
77021	ND	ELR	DBS	ECR
77022	ND	ELR	DBS	ECR
77023	ND	ELR	DBS	ECR
77024	ND	ELR	DBS	ECR
77025	ND	ELR	DBS	ECR
77026‡	ND	ELR	DBS	ECR
77027	ND	ELR	DBS	ECR
77028	ND	ELR	DBS	ECR
77029‡	ND	ELR	DBS	ECR
77030	ND	ELR	DBS	ECR
77031‡	ND	ELR	DBS	ECR
77032	ND	ELR	DBS	ECR
77033	ND	ELR	DBS	ECR
77034‡	ND	ELR	DBS	ECR
77035	ND	ELR	DBS	ECR
77036	ND	ELR	DBS	ECR
77037†	ND	ELR	DBS	ECR
77038‡	ND	ELR	DBS	ECR
77039‡	ND	ELR	DBS	ECR
77040	ND	ELR	DBS	ECR
77041‡	ND	ELR	DBS	ECR
77042‡	ND	ELR	DBS	ECR
77043‡	ND	ELR	DBS	ECR
77044‡	ND	ELR	DBS	ECR
77045	ND	ELR	DBS	ECR
77046‡	ND	ELR	DBS	ECR
77047	ND	ELR	DBS	ECR
77048	ND	ELR	DBS	ECR
77049‡	ND	ELR	DBS	ECR
77050‡	ND	ELR	DBS	ECR
77051‡	ND	ELR	DBS	ECR
77052‡	ND	ELR	DBS	ECR
77053‡	ND	ELR	DBS	ECR
77054‡	ND	ELR	DBS	ECR
77055‡	ND	ELR	DBS	ECR
77056‡	ND	ELR	DBS	ECR
77057‡	ND	ELR	DBS	ECR
77058	ND	ELR	DBS	ECR
77059	ND	ELR	DBS	ECR
77060	ND	ELR	DBS	ECR

‡ Working for DB-S in Germany, re-classified as Class 247 and running in number range 247 007 onwards; final three digits remain the same.
† Working for MEG in Germany as 247-037.

Euro Cargo Rail operate a fleet of 60 Class 66 design locos, numbered in the 77xxx series and operated in mainland Europe. These were built at the EMD plant in London (Ontario), Canada, in 2008-10. This illustration shows Euro numbered 247 056-5 (77056).
Brian Denton

Direct Rail Services

Address (UK): ✉ Kingmoor Depot, Etterby Road, Carlisle, Cumbria, CA3 9NZ

✆ info@directrailservices.com

✆ 01228 406600

ⓘ www.directrailservices.com

Managing Director: Neil McNicholas

Depots: Carlisle Kingmoor (KM), Crewe Gresty Bridge (CG)

Class 20/3

Vehicle Length: 46ft 9¼in (14.26m)
Height: 12ft 7⅜in (3.84m)
Width: 8ft 9in (2.66m)

Engine: English Electric 8SVT Mk2
Horsepower: 1,000hp (745kW)
Electrical Equipment: English Electric

Number		Depot	Pool	Livery	Owner	Operator	Name
20301	(20047)	KM	XHNC	DRC	DRS	DRS	*Max Joule 1958 - 1999*
20302	(20084)	KM	XHNC	DRU	DRS	DRS	
20303	(20127)	KM	XHNC	DRC	DRS	DRS	
20304	(20120)	KM	XHNC	DRU	DRS	DRS	
20305	(20095)	KM	XHNC	DRC	DRS	DRS	*Gresty Bridge*
20306(S)	(20131)	KM	XHNC	DRS	DRS	-	
20307(S)	(20128)	KM/CS	XHSS	DRS	DRS	-	
20308	(20187)	KM	XHNC	DRC	DRS	DRS	
20309	(20075)	KM	XHSS	DRC	DRS	DRS	
20310(S)	(20190)	KM/CS	XHSS	DRS	DRS	-	
20312(S)	(20042)	KM/CS	XHNC	DRC	DRS	DRS	
20313(S)	(20194)	KM/CS	XHSS	DRS	DRS	-	
20315(S)	(20104)	KM	XHSS	DRS	DRS	-	

At the end of 2012, seven DRS Class 20/3s were still in operation, with a further six stored. These Type 1s, which usually operate in pairs, tend to operate the lighter weight DRS flows, including flask traffic. Nos. 20303 and 20312 are seen on Dainton bank on 1 May 2012, heading west with a MoD flask bound for Devonport.
Antony Christie

Class 37/0

Vehicle Length: 61ft 6in (18.74m)
Height: 13ft 0¼in (3.96m)
Width: 8ft 11⅝in (2.73m)

Engine: English Electric 12CSVT
Horsepower: 1,750hp (1,304kW)
Electrical Equipment: English Electric

Number	Depot	Pool	Livery	Owner	Operator	Name
37038	KM	XHSS	DRS	DRS	DRS	
37059(S)‡	KM	XHSS	DRC	DRS	-	
37069(S)	KM	XHSS	DRC	DRS	-	
37087(S)	KM/BH	XHSS	DRS	DRS	-	
37194	KM	XHNC	DRC	DRS	DRS	
37218	KM	XHNC	DRC	DRS	DBS	
37229§	KM	XHNC	DRC	DRS	DRS	*Jonty Jarvis*
37259	KM	XHNC	DRU	DRS	DRS	
37261	KM	XHNC	DRC	DRS	DRS	

§ For store

‡ At Barrow Hill usedby NewRail, part of Newcastle University, as a research loco into the study of wheel/rail interface issues

Class 37/4

Vehicle Length: 61ft 6in (18.74m)
Height: 13ft 0¼in (3.96m)
Width: 8ft 11⅝in (2.73m)
Electric Train Heat fitted

Engine: English Electric 12CSVT
Horsepower: 1,750hp (1,304kW)
Electrical Equipment: English Electric

Number		Depot	Pool	Livery	Owner	Operator	Name
37401(S)	(37268)	KM	XHHP	EWS	DRS	-	
37402	(37274)	BH	XHHP	DRC	DBS	-	
37405	(37282)	BH	XHHP	DRC	DRS	-	
37406(S)	(37295)	KM	XHHP	EWS	DRS	-	The Saltire Society
37409	(37270)	KM	XHNC	DRC	DRS	DRS	Lord Hinton
37410(S)	(37273)	KM	XHHP	EWS	DRS	-	
37411(S)	(37290)*	KM	XHHP	GRN	DRS	-	
37419	(37291)	KM	XHAC	DRC	DRS	DRS	Carl Haviland 1954-2012
37422(S)	(37266)	KM	XHHP	EWS	DRS	-	
37423	(37296)	KM	XHNC	DRC	DRS	DRS	Spirit of the Lakes
37425	(37292)	BH	XHAC	DRC	DRS	DRS	
37426(S)	(37299)	KM	XHHP	EWS	DRS	-	

Class 37/5

Vehicle Length: 61ft 6in (18.74m)
Height: 13ft 0¼in (3.96m)
Width: 8ft 11⅝in (2.73m)

Engine: English Electric 12CSVT
Horsepower: 1,750hp (1,304kW)
Electrical Equipment: English Electric

Number		Depot	Pool	Livery	Owner	Operator	Name/Notes
37510(S)		KM/BH	XHSS	DRC	DRS	-	
37667	(37151)	KM	XHNC	DRC	DRS	DRS	
37682(S)	(37236)	KM	XHHP	DRC	DRS	-	
37683(S)	(37187)	CG	XHHP	DRS	DRS	-	(At Waterman Railways Crewe – training loco)
37688	(37205)	KM	XHNC	DRC	DRS	DRS	Kingmoor TMD

Class 37/6

Vehicle Length: 61ft 6in (18.74m)
Height: 13ft 0¼in (3.96m)
Width: 8ft 11⅝in (2.73m)

Engine: English Electric 12CSVT
Horsepower: 1,750hp (1,304kW)
Electrical Equipment: English Electric

Number		Depot	Pool	Livery	Owner	Operator	Name
37601	(37501)	KM	XHNC	DRC	DRS	DRS	Class 37 – 'Fifty'
37602	(37502)	KM	XHNC	DRS	DRS	DRS	
37603	(37504)	KM	XHNC	DRC	DRS	DRS	
37604	(37506)	KM	XHNC	DRC	DRS	DRS	
37605	(37507)	KM	XHNC	DRC	DRS	DRS	
37606	(37508)	KM	XHNC	DRS	DRS	DRS	
37607	(37511)	KM	XHNC	DRC	DRS	DRS	
37608	(37512)	KM	XHNC	DRC	DRS	DRS	
37609	(37514)	KM	XHNC	DRC	DRS	DRS	
37610	(37687)	KM	XHNC	DRC	DRS	DRS	T. S. (Ted) Cassady 14.5.61-6.4.08
37611	(37690)	KM	XHNC	DRC	DRS	DRS	
37612	(37691)	KM	XHNC	DRS	DRS	DRS	

Right: Direct Rail Services provide traction and staff to operate a number of the Network Rail track and infrastructure test trains. These services are usually operated in the 'top and tail' mode. On 11 January 2012, Nos. 37607 and 37606 'top and tail' test cars Nos. 72630, 977985, 977997 and 5981 along the Dawlish sea wall, forming train 1Z13, the 12.08 Plymouth to Derby RTC. **CJM**

Direct Rail Services

Class 47/4 & 47/7

Vehicle Length: 63ft 6in (19.35m)
Height: 12ft 10⅜in (3.91m)
Width: 9ft 2in (2.79m)
Electric Train Heat fitted

Engine: Sulzer 12LDA28C
Horsepower: 2,580hp (1,922kW)
Electrical Equipment: Brush

Number		Depot	Pool	Livery	Owner	Operator	Name
47501		KM	XHAC	DRC	DRS	DRS	Craftsman
47703(S)	(47514)	KM	XHSS	FRB	DRS	-	
47712(S)	(47505)	KM	XHAC	DRC	DRS	(at LNWR Crewe)	Pride of Carlisle
47747(S)	(47615)	KM	XHSS	EWS	DRS	-	
47790	(47673)	KM	XHAC	NBP	DRS	DRS	Galloway Princess
47791(S)	(47675)	KM	XHSS	RES	DRS	-	
47802	(47552)	KM	XHAC	DRC	DRS	DRS	Pride of Cumbria
47805	(47650)	KM	XHAC	DRC	DRS	DRS	
47810	(47247/655)	BH	XHAC	DRC	DRS	DRS	Peter Bath MBE 1927-2006
47813	(47129/658)	KM	XHAC	DRC	DRS	DRS	Solent
47818	(47240/663)	BH	XHHP	DRC	DRS	DRS	
47828	(47266/629)	BH	XHAC	DRC	DRS	DRS	
47832	(47560)	KM	XHAC	NBP	DRS	DRS	Solway Princess
47839	(47621)	KM	XHAC	RIV	DRS	DRS	
47841	(47622)	KM	XHNC	DRC	DRS	DRS	
47853	(47614)	KM	XHAC	DRC	DRS	DRS	Rail Express

Left: *In late 2012, 16 Class 47s were operated by Direct Rail Services, but several were not operational and stored or under long term repair. DRS provide the traction power and crews for several charter train operations, including the 'Northern Belle' and the Scotland to Southampton Docks 'Docksaver' services. In full DRS Compass livery No. 47810 Peter Bath MBE 1927-2006 is seen at the head of the VSOE-managed 'Northern Belle' train.* **Mark V. Pike**

Class 57/0

Vehicle Length: 63ft 6in (19.38m)
Height: 12ft 10⅛in (3.91m)
Width: 9ft 2in (2.79m)

Engine: EMD 645-12E3
Horsepower: 2,500hp (1,864kW)
Electrical Equipment: Brush

Number		Depot	Pool	Livery	Owner	Operator	Name/Notes
57002(S)	(47322)	KM	XHSS	DRC*	PTR	-	* with Colas branding
57003	(47317)	KM	XHCK	DRC	PTR	DRS	
57004	(47347)	KM	XHCK	DRC	DRS	DRS	
57007	(47332)	KM	XHCK	DRC	PTR	DRS	
57008	(47060)	KM	XHCK	DRC	PTR	DRS	Telford International Railfreight Park June - 2009
57009	(47079)	KM	XHCK	DRC	PTR	DRS	
57010	(47231)	KM	XHCK	DRC	PTR	DRS	
57011	(47329)	KM	XHCK	DRC	PTR	DRS	
57012(S)	(47204)	KM	XHSS	DRC	PTR	-	

Left: *Direct Rail Services have nine Class 57s under their control, all painted in full DRS Compass livery. The locos work alongside the DRS Class 47 fleet. No. 57007 is seen near Rotherham on 27 July 2012, powering a short container train.* **John Binch**

Class 57/3

				Vehicle Length: 63ft 6in (19.38m)	Engine: EMD 645-12F3B
				Height: 12ft 10½in (3.91m)	Horsepower: 2,750hp (2,051kW)
				Width: 9ft 2in (2.79m)	Electrical Equipment: Brush

Number	Depot	Pool	Livery	Owner	Operator	Name
57302 (47827)	KM	XHHP	DRC	PTR	DRS	Chad Varah
57304 (47807)	KM	XHHP	DRC	PTR	DRS	Pride of Cheshire
57307 (47225)	KM	XHHP	VWC	PBR	DRB	Lady Penelope
57308 (47846)	KM	XHHP	VWC	PBR	VWC	
57309 (47806)	KM	XHAC	DRC	PTR	DRS	Pride of Crewe
57311 (47817)	KM	XHHP	VWC	PBR	VWC	

Right: *Following the reduction in the requirement for Class 57/3s by Virgin Trains, six locos were re-leased by owner Porterbrook to Direct Rail Services for general freight/passenger operation. The locos were overhauled at Eastleigh and now carry DRS livery. All retain their drop head Scharfenberg couplers for emergency use. No. 57309 is seen at York. This loco carries the name* Pride of Crewe *in recognition of the DRS facility in the town.*
Antony Christie

Class 66/3, 66/4

				Vehicle Length: 70ft 0½in (21.34m)	Engine: EMD 12N-710G3B-EC
				Height: 12ft 10in (3.91m)	Horsepower: 3,300hp (2,462kW)
				Width: 8ft 8¼in (2.65m)	Electrical Equipment: EMD

Number	Depot	Pool	Livery	Owner	Operator
66301	KM	XHIM	DRC	BEA	DRS
66302	KM	XHIM	DRC	BEA	DRS
66303	KM	XHIM	DRC	BEA	DRS
66304	KM	XHIM	DRC	BEA	DRS
66305	KM	XHIM	DRC	BEA	DRS
66421	KM	XHIM	DRC	HAL	DRS
66422	KM	XHIM	DRC	HAL	DRS
66423	KM	XHIM	DRC	HAL	DRS
66424	KM	XHIM	DRC	HAL	DRS
66425	KM	XHIM	DRC	HAL	DRS
66426	KM	XHIM	DRC	HAL	DRS
66427	KM	XHIM	DRC	HAL	DRS
66428	KM	XHIM	DRC	HAL	DRS
66429	KM	XHIM	DRC	HAL	DRS
66430	KM	XHIM	DRC	HAL	DRS
66431	KM	XHIM	DRC	HAL	DRS
66432	KM	XHIM	DRC	HAL	DRS
66433	KM	XHIM	DRC	HAL	DRS
66434	KM	XHIM	ADV§	HAL	DRS

§ Malcolm promotional livery

Right: *Direct Rail Services still operate a sizeable fleet of Electro Motive Diesel Class 66s. However, the fleet has been reduced in recent years and might well shrink again following delivery of the new Class 68s in late 2013. Displaying DRS Compass livery, No. 66428 is seen stabled between duties at Cardiff.*
Norman E. Preedy

Direct Rail Services

Class 68 'UK Light'

Vehicle Length: 67ft 3in (20.5m)				Engine: Caterpiller C175-16			
Height: 12ft 6½in (3.82m)				Horsepower: 3,750hp (2,800kW)			
Speed: 100mph (161km/h)				Electrical Equipment: ABB			

Number	Depot	Pool	Livery	Owner	Operator	Name
68001	KM	XH--	DRS	BEA	DRS	
68002	KM	XH--	DRS	BEA	DRS	
68003	KM	XH--	DRS	BEA	DRS	
68004	KM	XH--	DRS	BEA	DRS	
68005	KM	XH--	DRS	BEA	DRS	
68006	KM	XH--	DRS	BEA	DRS	
68007	KM	XH--	DRS	BEA	DRS	
68008	KM	XH--	DRS	BEA	DRS	
68009	KM	XH--	DRS	BEA	DRS	
68010	KM	XH--	DRS	BEA	DRS	
68011	KM	XH--	DRS	BEA	DRS	
68012	KM	XH--	DRS	BEA	DRS	
68013	KM	XH--	DRS	BEA	DRS	
68014	KM	XH--	DRS	BEA	DRS	
68015	KM	XH--	DRS	BEA	DRS	

Left: *Artist's impression of how the new DRS Class 68 will look. A total of 15 of these state-of-the-art 3700hp locos are currently under construction in Spain at the Vossloh factory in Valencia. The first of these Bo-Bo locos is expected to start testing in spring/summer 2013, with production locos arriving in the UK towards the end of the year.* **Vossloh**

Coaching Stock

Mk2	Height: 12ft 9½in (3.89m)	
Vehicle Length: 66ft 0in (20.11m)	Width: 9ft 3in (2.81m)	

Number	Type	Depot	Livery	Operator		Number	Type	Depot	Livery	Operator
1254 (3391)	AJ1F/RFO	KM	BLG	DRS		6046	AC2F/TSO	KM	BLG	DRS
3366	AD1F/FO	KM	BLG	DRS		6064	AC2F/TSO	KM	BLG	DRS
3374	AD1F/FO	KM	BLG	DRS		6117	AC2F/TSO	KM	BLG	DRS
5810	AC2E/TSO	KM	BLG	DRS		6122	AC2F/TSO	KM	BLG	DRS
5901	AC2F/TSO	KM	BLG	DRS		6173	AC2F/TSO	KM	BLG	DRS
5919	AC2F/TSO	KM	BLG	DRS		9419	AC2E/TSO	KM	DRC	DRS
5971	AC2F/TSO	KM	BLG	DRS		9428	AE2E/BSO	KM	DRC	DRS
5995	AC25/TSO	KM	BLG	DRS		9506	AE2E/BSO	KM	BLG	DRS
6001	AC2F/TSO	KM	BLG	DRS		9508	AE2E/BSO	KM	BLG	DRS
6008	AC2F/TSO	KM	BLG	DRS		9525	AE2E/BSO	KM	BLG	DRS
						17159	AB1D/BFK	KM	DRO	DRS

Left: *The MoD flask trains which are operated by DRS sometimes require the attachment of a support coach to carry security staff. These vehicles are modified with their end gangways removed and a window inserted and a small generator located in the original brake van. BSO No. 9428 is illustrated.* **Antony Christie**

Royal Mail (operations contracted to DB-S)

Address: ✉ 148 Old Street, London, EC1V 9HQ
✆ press.office@royalmail.com ✆ 0207 250 2468 ⓘ www.royalmailgroup.com

Class 325

Vehicle Length: (Driving) 65ft 0¾in (19.82m) Width: 9ft 2in (2.82m)
(Inter) 65ft 4¼in (19.92m) Horsepower: 1,278hp (990kW)
Height: 12ft 4¼in (3.76m) Seats (total/car): None - luggage space

Number	Formation	Depot	Livery	Owner	Operator	Name
	DTPMV+MPMV+TPMV+DTPMV					
325001	68300+68340+68360+68301	CE	RML	RML	DBS	
325002	68302+68341+68361+68303	CE	RML	RML	DBS	Royal Mail North Wales & North West
325003	68304+68342+68362+68305	CE	RML	RML	DBS	
325004	68306+68343+68363+68307	CE	RML	RML	DBS	
325005	68308+68344+68364+68309	CE	RML	RML	DBS	John Grierson
325006	68310+68345+68365+68311	CE	RML	RML	DBS	
325007	68312+68346+68366+68313	CE	RML	RML	DBS	Peter Howarth C.B.E
325008	68314+68347+68367+68315	CE	RML	RML	DBS	
325009	68316+68348+68368+68317	CE	RML	RML	DBS	
325011	68320+68350+68370+68321	CE	RML	RML	DBS	
325012	68322+68351+68371+68323	CE	RML	RML	DBS	
325013	68324+68352+68372+68325	CE	RML	RML	DBS	
325014	68326+68353+68373+68327	CE	RML	RML	DBS	
325015	68328+68354+68374+68329	CE	RML	RML	DBS	
325016	68330+68355+68375+68331	CE	RML	RML	DBS	

Above. Of the original fleet of 16 Royal Mail-owned four-car EMU Mail units of Class 325 only 15 remain. One was cut up in 2012. These sets are operated under contract by DB Schenker and work only a limited service over the West Coast main Line, where they use their overhead power equipment. These sets were built as dual ac/dc voltage sets, but the dc third rail equipment is now isolated. Set No. 325003 is seen passing South Kenton, heading north to Warrington. **Nathan Williamson**

Europorte – GB Railfreight (GBRf)

Address: 15-25 Artillery Lane, London, E1 7HA

✉ gbrfinfo@gbrailfreight.com

✆ 0207 983 5177

ⓘ www.gbrailfreight.com

Managing Director: John Smith

Depots: Peterborough (PT), Wembley (SV), St Leonards (SE)
Coquelles (CQ), Ashford Hitachi (AD)

Class 08/0, 09

Vehicle Length: 29ft 3in (8.91m)
Height: 12ft 8⅝in (3.87m)
Width: 8ft 6in (2.59m)

Engine: English Electric 6K
Horsepower: 400hp (298kW)
Electrical Equipment: English Electric

Number	Depot	Pool	Livery	Owner	Operator
08401	CF	GBWM	GRN	HEC	GBF
08925	CF	GBWM	GRN	GBF	GBF
08934	CF	GBWM	GRN	GBF	GBF

Number		Pool	Livery	Owner	Operator
09002	§	GBWM	GRN	GBF	GBF
09009	§	GBWM	GRN	GBF	GBF

§ Working at Barton Dock, Trafford Park

Left: *A total of five Class 08 and 09 350hp diesel-electric shunting locos are on the books of GB Railfreight. Painted in unbranded green livery is No. 08934 seen at Cardiff Tidal Yard. Note the loco's original number D4164 applied in white in the red buffer beam.*
Antony Christie

Class 20

Vehicle Length: 46ft 9¼in (14.26m)
Height: 12ft 7⅜in (3.84m)
Width: 8ft 9in (2.66m)

Engine: English Electric 8SVT Mk2
Horsepower: 1,000hp (745kW)
Electrical Equipment: English Electric

Number		Depot	Pool	Livery	Owner	Operator
20142		PG	GBEE	SPL	PRI	GBR
20189		PG	GBEE	SPL	PRI	GBR
20227		PG	GBEE	SPL	PRI	GBR
20901	(20101)	PG	GBEE	GBN	HNR	GBR
20905	(20225)	PG	GBEE	GBN	HNR	GBR

Class 66/7

Vehicle Length: 70ft 0½in (21.34m)
Height: 12ft 10in (3.91m)
Width: 8ft 8¼in (2.65m)

Engine: EMD 12N-710G3B-EC
Horsepower: 3,300hp (2,462kW)
Electrical Equipment: EMD

Number	Depot	Pool	Livery	Owner	Operator	Name
66701	PT	GBRT	GBR	EVL	GBR	
66702	PT	GBRT	GBR	EVL	GBR	Blue Lightning
66703	PT	GBCM	GBR	EVL	GBR	Doncaster PSB 1981 - 2002
66704	PT	GBCM	GBR	EVL	GBR	Colchester Power Signalbox
66705	PT	GBCM	GBR	EVL	GBR	Golden Jubilee
66706	PT	GBCM	GBR	EVL	GBR	Nene Valley
66707	PT	GBCM	GBR	EVL	GBR	Sir Sam Fay / Great Central Railway
66708	PT	GBRT	GBR	EVL	GBR	Jayne
66709	PT	GBRT	MSC	EVL	GBR	Sorrento
66710	PT	GBCM	GBR	EVL	GBR	Phil Packer

66711	PT	GBCM	GBR	EVL	GBR	Peterborough Power Signalbox
66712	PT	GBCM	GBR	EVL	GBR	Forest City
66713	PT	GBCM	GBR	EVL	GBR	Cromer Lifeboat
66714	PT	GBCM	GBR	EVL	GBR	Valour
66715	PT	GBCM	GBR	EVL	GBR	Locomotive & Carriage Institution Centenary 1911-2011
66716	PT	GBCM	GBR	EVL	GBR	
66717	PT	GBCM	GBR	EVL	GBR	Good Old Boy
66718	PT	GBCM	GBM	EVL	GBR	Gwyneth Dunwoody
66719	PT	GBCM	GBM	EVL	GBR	Metro-Land
66720	PT	GBCM	SPL	EVL	GBR	
66721	PT	GBCM	GBM	EVL	GBR	Harry Beck
66722	PT	GBCM	GBM	EVL	GBR	Sir Edward Watkin
66723	PT	GBSD	GBF	EVL	GBR	Chinook
66724	PT	GBSD	GBF	EVL	GBR	Drax Power Station
66725	PT	GBSD	GBF	EVL	GBR	Sunderland
66726	PT	GBCM	GBF	EVL	GBR	Sheffield Wednesday
66727	PT	GBSD	GBF	EVL	GBR	Andrew Scott CBE
66728	PT	GBMU	GBN	PTR	GBR	Institution of Railway Operators
66729	PT	GBMU	GBN	PTR	GBR	Derby County
66730	PT	GBMU	GBF	PTR	GBR	Whitemoor
66731	PT	GBMU	GBN	PTR	GBR	interhubGB
66732	PT	GBMU	GBN	PTR	GBR	GBRf The First Decade 1999-2009 John Smith - MD
66733‡ (66401)	PT	GBFM	BLU	PTR	GBR	
66734(S) ‡ (66402)	PT	GBZZ	GBN	PTR	GBR	(Loco officially written-off with collision damage)
66735‡ (66403)	PT	GBFM	GBN	PTR	GBR	
66736‡ (66404)	PT	GBFM	GBN	PTR	GBR	Wolverhampton Wanderers
66737‡ (66405)	PT	GBFM	GBN	PTR	GBR	Lesia
66738 (66578)	PT	GBCM	GBN	GBR	GBR	
66739 (66579)	PT	GBCM	FLU	GBR	GBR	
66740 (66580)	PT	GBCM	FLU	GBR	GBR	
66741 (66581)	PT	GBCM	FLU	GBR	GBR	
66742 (66406, 66841)	PT	GBRT	GBN	PTR	GBR	Port of Immingham Centenary 1912 - 2012
66743 (66407, 66842)	PT	GBRT	GBN	PTR	GBR	
66744 (66408, 66843)	PT	GBRT	GBN	PTR	GBR	Crossrail
66745 (66409, 66844)	PT	GBRT	GBN	PTR	GBR	Modern Railways - The First 50 years
66746 (66410, 66845)	PT	GBRT	GBN	PTR	GBR	
66747	PT	GBNF	GBN		GBR	Being converted from EMD 20078968-004
66748	PT	GBNF	GBN		GBR	Being converted from EMD 20078968-006
66749	PT	GBNF	GBN		GBR	Being converted from EMD 20078968-007

‡ Fitted with RETB equipment

Below: *GBRf operate General Motors/EMD-built Class 66s as their primary diesel power, with a total of 46 being on the company register at the end of 2012, but one was stored with huge collision damage at the end of 2011. The locos are officially allocated to Peterborough, but can be found throughout the GBRf operating area. No. 66742 is seen on the West Coast main line at South Kenton.* **Antony Christie**

Freight Operating Companies - Europorte GBRf

Europorte – GBRf

Class 73

	Vehicle Length: 53ft 8in (16.35m)	Power: 750V dc third rail or English Electric 6K
	Height: 12ft 5⅜in (3.79m)	Horsepower: electric - 1,600hp (1,193kW)
	Width: 8ft 8in (2.64m)	Horsepower: diesel - 600hp (447kW)
		Electrical Equipment: English Electric

Number		Depot	Pool	Livery	Owner	Operator	Name
73119		SE	GBED	BLU	GBR	GBR	
73141		SE	GBED	FGF	GBR	GBR	Charlotte
73204	(73125)	SE	GBED	GBR	GBR	GBR	Janice
73205	(73124)	SE	GBED	INT	GBR	GBR	Jeanette
73206	(73123)	SE	GBED	GBR	GBR	GBR	Lisa
73207	(73122)	SE	GBED	BLL	GBR	GBR	
73208	(73121)	SE	GBED	BLU	GBR	GBR	Kirsten
73209§	(73120)	SE	GBZZ	GBR	GBR	GBR	Alison
73212	(73102)	SE	GBED	GBU	GBR	GBR	
73213	(73112)	SE	GBED	FGU	GBR	GBR	

§ To be trial-fitted with new design MTU R43 4000 V8 power unit set to deliver 1,500hp. Five locos are to be converted by Wabtec (Brush Traction) and renumbered in the series 73901 - 73905. The locos should be Nos. 73204/205/206/207/209

Above: *A fleet of 10 dual power electro-diesel Class 73s are operated by GBRf. These are normally used over the former Southern Region area operating under third rail conditions. In multiple, however, these locos can haul quite heavy trains off the juice using their own diesel engines. In all-over blue, No. 73141 is seen at Southampton Docks.* **Steve Stubbs**

Class 92

	Vehicle Length: 70ft 1in (21.34m)	Power Collection: 25kV ac overhead / 750V dc third rail
	Height: 13ft 0in (3.95m)	Horsepower: ac - 6,700hp (5,000kW) / dc 5,360hp (4,000kW)
	Width: 8ft 8in (2.66m)	Electrical Equipment: Brush

Number	Depot	Pool	Livery	Owner	Operator	Name
92006(S)	DM	PTXX	SNF	GBR	-	Louis Armand
92010(S)	CO	PTXX	EU2	GBR	-	Moliere
92014(S)	CE	PTXX	SNF	GBR	-	Emile Zola
92018(S)	DM	PTXX	SNF	GBR	-	Stendhal
92020(S)	DM	PTXX	EU2	GBR	-	Milton
92021(S)	CO	PTXX	EU2	GBR	-	Purcell
92023(S)	CE	PTXX	EU2	GBR	-	Ravel
92028	CO	GBET	EU2	GBR	GBR	Saint Saens
92032	CO	GBET	GBN	GBR	GBR	I Mech E Railway Division
92033(S)	DM	PTXX	SNF	GBR	-	Berlioz
92038(S)	CE	GBET	EU2	GBR	-	Voltaire
92040(S)	CO	PTXX	BLU	GBR	-	Goethe
92043	CO	GBET	EU2	GBR	GBR	Debussy
92044	CO	GBET	EU2	GBR	GBR	Couperin
92045(S)	Brush	PTXX	EU2	GBR	-	Chaucer
92046(S)	Brush	PTXX	EU2	GBR	-	Sweelinck

Right: *Following a merger of GBRf and Europorte, the Europorte-purchased Class 92s were merged into the GBRf traction portfolio. Subsequent to merger, further '92s' have been added to the fleet with the purchase of several off-lease locos. It is still planned to return many but not all to full operation. It has been suggested that a possible rebuilding of a small number with dual power capabilities could be on the cards. No. 92028 carrying Europorte2 branded triple-grey livery is seen at Kensington Olympia.* **Nathan Williamson**

Coaching Stock

Mk1	
Vehicle Length: 64ft 6in (19.65m)	Height: 12ft 9½in (3.89m)
	Width: 9ft 3in (2.81m)

Barrier Vans

AW51

Number	Depot	Livery	Owner
6376 (ADB975973, 1021)	PG	BLU	PTR
6377 (ADB975975, 1042)	PG	BLU	PTR
6378 (ADB975971, 1054)	PG	BLU	PTR
6379 (ADB975972, 1039)	PG	BLU	PTR

Class Di 8

Vehicle Length: 17.38m	Engine: Caterpillar 3516 DITA
Height: 4.01m	Horsepower: 2,100hp (1,570kW)
Width: 2.95m	Electrical Equipment: Siemens

GBRf have purchased 12 former Cargo-Net, Norway, Class Di 8 locos for use within the SSI Lackenby Steelworks in Redcar. The 2,100hp (1,566kW) locos were built in 1996-97 by Mak in Kiel, Germany, as an order for 20 locos. In the UK the fleet classified by the UIC as 308 will be painted in a joint GBRf/SSI livery.

8.701	8.708	8.717
8.702	8.711	8.718
8.703	8.712	8.719
8.704	8.716	8.720

Industrial 0-6-0DH

DH50-1 Works No. TH278V - 0-6-0DH 50-ton design, built 1978, fitted with a Cummins engine
DH50-2 Works No. TH246V - 0-6-0DH 50-ton design, built 1973

The above two industrial locos are operated by GBRf at the Celsa steel plant in Cardiff.

Right: *This rather unusual pair of industrial shunting locos, Nos. DH50-1 and DH50 2, are not certified for main line operation and remain in the Celsa steel plant in Cardiff. Both sport a version of the GBRf livery of blue, orange and yellow. No. DH50-1 is illustrated.* **Antony Christie**

Freightliner

Address:	✉ 3rd Floor, The Podium, 1 Eversholt Street, London, NW1 2FL
	✈ pressoffice@freightliner.co.uk
	☎ 0207 200 3900
	ⓘ www.freightliner.com

Chief Executive:	Peter Maybury
Managing Director Intermodal:	Adam Cunliffe
Managing Director Heavy Haul:	Paul Smart
Depots:	Freightliner Diesels (FD), Freightliner Electrics (FE), Freightliner Shunters (FS), Ipswich* (IP), Leeds Midland Road (LD), Southampton Maritime (SZ)
	* Stabling point
Parent Company:	Arcapita

Class 08/0

Vehicle Length: 29ft 3in (8.91m)
Height: 12ft 8⅝in (3.87m)
Width: 8ft 6in (2.59m)
Engine: English Electric 6K
Horsepower: 400hp (298kW)
Electrical Equipment: English Electric

Number	Depot	Pool	Livery	Owner	Operator
08077(S)	FS/LH	DHLT	FLR	FLR	FLR
08393**	LH				FLR
08530(S)	LH	DFLS	FLR	PTR	FLR
08531	TL	DFLS	FLR	PTR	FLR
08575	SZ	DHLT	FLR	PTR	FLR
08585	FS	DFLS	FLR	PTR	FLR
08624	LH	DFLS	BLU	PTR	FLR
08691 ¤	SZ	DHLT	FLR	FLR	FLR
08785	SZ	DFLS	FLR	PTR	FLR
08891	FD	DFLS	FLR	PTR	FLR

¤ 08691 At L H Group Services
**08393 sold to L H Group Services

Names applied
| 08585 | *Vicky* |
| 08691 | *Terri* |

Left: *For shunting at the main Freightliner-controlled container terminals a small fleet of Class 08s is operated by Freightliner. Most are painted in standard Freightliner colours, as shown on No. 08575 at Southampton.* **Norman W. Preedy**

Class 47/4

Vehicle Length: 63ft 6in (19.35m)
Height: 12ft 10⅜in (3.91m)
Width: 9ft 2in (2.79m)
Electric Train Heat fitted
Engine: Sulzer 12LDA28C
Horsepower: 2,580hp (1,922kW)
Electrical Equipment: Brush

Number		Depot	Pool	Livery	Owner	Operator
47811	(47656)	FD	DFLH	GRN	FLR	FLR (pilot)
47816(S)	(47661)	FD	DFLH	GRN	FLR	-
47830(S)	(47649)	BH	DFLH	GRN	FLR	-

Class 66/4

Vehicle Length: 70ft 0½in (21.34m)
Height: 12ft 10in (3.91m)
Width: 8ft 8¼in (2.65m)
Engine: EMD 12N-710G3B-EC
Horsepower: 3,300hp (2,462kW)
Electrical Equipment: EMD

Number	Depot	Pool	Livery	Owner	Operator	Name
66411 *Exported, working in Poland for Freightliner Poland as 66013TPL*						
66412 *Exported, working in Poland for Freightliner Poland*						
66413 (S)	LD	DFHG	DRC	CBR	-	

66414	LD	DFIN	TES	HAL	FLT	
66415	LD	DFHG	DRC	HAL	FLT	
66416	LD	DFIN	DRC	HAL	FLT	
66417 *Exported, working in Poland for Freightliner Poland as 66014FPL*						
66418	LD	DFIN	DRC	HAL	FLT	
66419	LD	DFHG	DRC	HAL	FLT	
66420	LD	DFIN	DRC	HAL	FLT	

Class 66/5

Vehicle Length: 70ft 0½in (21.34m)
Height: 12ft 10in (3.91m)
Width: 8ft 8¼in (2.65m)

Engine: EMD 12N-710G3B-EC
Horsepower: 3,300hp (2,462kW)
Electrical Equipment: EMD

Number	Depot	Pool	Livery	Owner	Operator	Name
66501	LD	DFGM	FLR	PTR	FLR	*Japan 2001*
66502	LD	DFGM	FLR	PTR	FLR	*Basford Hall Centenary 2001*
66503	LD	DFGM	FLR	PTR	FLR	*The Railway Magazine*
66504	LD	DFGM	FLR	PTR	FLR	
66505	LD	DFRT	FLR	PTR	FLR	
66506	LD	DFHH	FLR	EVL	FLR	*Crewe Regeneration*
66507	LD	DFHH	FLR	EVL	FLR	
66508	LD	DFRT	FLR	EVL	FLR	
66509	LD	DFHH	FLR	EVL	FLR	
66510	LD	DFRT	FLR	EVL	FLR	
66511	LD	DFRT	FLR	EVL	FLR	
66512	LD	DFHH	FLR	EVL	FLR	
66513	LD	DFHH	FLR	EVL	FLR	
66514	LD	DFRT	FLR	EVL	FLR	
66515	LD	DFGM	FLR	EVL	FLR	
66516	LD	DFGM	FLR	EVL	FLR	
66517	LD	DFGM	FLR	EVL	FLR	
66518	LD	DFRT	FLR	EVL	FLR	
66519	LD	DFHH	FLR	EVL	FLR	
66520	LD	DFRT	FLR	EVL	FLR	
66522	LD	DFRT	FLR	EVL	FLR	*east london express*
66523	LD	DFRT	FLR	EVL	FLR	
66524	LD	DFHH	FLR	EVL	FLR	
66525	LD	DFHH	FLR	EVL	FLR	
66526	LD	DFHH	FLR	PTR	FLR	*Driver Steve Dunn (George)*
66527	LD	DFHH	FLR	EVL	FLR	*Don Raider*
66528	LD	DFHH	FLR	PTR	FLR	
66529	LD	DFHH	FLR	PTR	FLR	
66530	LD	DFGM	FLR	PTR	FLR	
66531	LD	DFHH	FLR	PTR	FLR	
66532	LD	DFGM	FLR	PTR	FLR	*P&O Nedlloyd Atlas*
66533	LD	DFGM	FLR	PTR	FLR	*Hanjin Express / Senator Express*
66534	LD	DFGM	FLR	PTR	FLR	*OOCL Express*
66535	LD	DFHH	FLR	PTR	FLR	
66536	LD	DFHH	FLR	PTR	FLR	
66537	LD	DFGM	FLR	PTR	FLR	
66538	LD	DFIM	FLR	EVL	FLR	
66539	LD	DFHH	FLR	EVL	FLR	
66540	LD	DFIM	FLR	EVL	FLR	*Ruby*
66541	LD	DFIM	FLR	EVL	FLR	
66542	LD	DFIM	FLR	EVL	FLR	
66543	LD	DFIM	FLR	EVL	FLR	
66544	LD	DFHG	FLR	PTR	FLR	
66545	LD	DFHG	FLR	PTR	FLR	
66546	LD	DFHG	FLR	PTR	FLR	
66547	LD	DFHG	FLR	PTR	FLR	
66548	LD	DFHG	FLR	PTR	FLR	
66549	LD	DFHG	FLR	PTR	FLR	
66550	LD	DFHG	FLR	PTR	FLR	
66551	LD	DFHG	FLR	PTR	FLR	
66552	LD	DFHG	FLR	PTR	FLR	*Maltby Raider*
66553	LD	DFHG	FLR	PTR	FLR	

Freightliner

66554	LD	DFHG	FLR	EVL	FLR	
66555	LD	DFHG	FLR	EVL	FLR	
66556	LD	DFHG	FLR	EVL	FLR	
66557	LD	DFHG	FLR	EVL	FLR	
66558	LD	DFIM	FLR	EVL	FLR	
66559	LD	DFIM	FLR	EVL	FLR	
66560	LD	DFHG	FLR	EVL	FLR	
66561	LD	DFHG	FLR	EVL	FLR	
66562	LD	DFIM	FLR	EVL	FLR	
66563	LD	DFIM	FLR	EVL	FLR	
66564	LD	DFIM	FLR	EVL	FLR	
66565	LD	DFIM	FLR	EVL	FLR	
66566	LD	DFIM	FLR	EVL	FLR	
66567	LD	DFIM	FLR	EVL	FLR	
66568	LD	DFIM	FLR	EVL	FLR	
66569	LD	DFIM	FLR	EVL	FLR	
66570	LD	DFIM	FLR	EVL	FLR	
66571	LD	DFIM	FLR	EVL	FLR	
66572	LD	DFIM	FLR	EVL	FLR	
66582	*Exported, working in Poland for Freightliner Poland as 66009FPL*					
66583	*Exported, working in Poland for Freightliner Poland as 66010FPL*					
66584	*Exported, working in Poland for Freightliner Poland as 66011FPL*					
66585	LD	DFHG	FLR	HAL	FLR	*The Drax Flyer*
66586	*Exported, working in Poland for Freightliner Poland as 66008FPL*					
66587	LD	DFFT	FLR	HAL	FLR	
66588	LD	DFIN	FLR	HAL	FLR	
66589	LD	DFIN	FLR	HAL	FLR	
66590	LD	DFIN	FLR	HAL	FLR	
66591	LD	DFIN	FLR	MAG	FLR	
66592	LD	DFIN	FLR	MAG	FLR	*Johnson Stevens Agencies*
66593	LD	DFIN	FLR	MAG	FLR	*3MG Mersey Multimodal Gateway*
66594	LD	DFIN	FLR	MAG	FLR	*NYK Spirit of Kyoto*
66595	LD	DFHG	FLR	BEA	FLR	
66596	LD	DFHG	FLR	BEA	FLR	
66597	LD	DFHG	FLR	BEA	FLR	*Viridor*
66598	LD	DFHG	FLR	BEA	FLR	
66599	LD	DFHG	FLR	BEA	FLR	

Today 85 Class 66/5s are operated by Freightliner in the UK, with a further four working in Poland. Owned by Beacon Rail, No. 66598, one of the five-door examples, is seen shunting ballast vehicles at Taunton Fairwater. **Antony Christie**

Freight Operating Companies - Freightliner

Class 66/6

Number	Depot	Pool	Livery	Owner	Operator	Name
66601	LD	DFHH	FLR	PTR	FLR	The Hope Valley
66602	LD	DFHH	FLR	PTR	FLR	
66603	LD	DFHH	FLR	PTR	FLR	
66604	LD	DFHH	FLR	PTR	FLR	
66605	LD	DFHH	FLR	PTR	FLR	
66606	LD	DFHH	FLR	PTR	FLR	
66607	LD	DFHG	FLR	PTR	FLR	
66608	Exported, working in Poland for Freightliner Poland as 66603FPL					
66609	Exported, working in Poland for Freightliner Poland as 66605FPL					
66610	LD	DFHG	FLR	PTR	FLR	
66611	Exported, working in Poland for Freightliner Poland as 66604FPL					
66612	Exported, working in Poland for Freightliner Poland as 66606FPL					
66613	LD	DFTZ	FLR	PTR	-	
66614	LD	DFHG	FLR	PTR	FLR	
66615	LD	DFHG	FLR	PTR	FLR	
66616	LD	DFHG	FLR	PTR	FLR	
66617	LD	DFHG	FLR	PTR	FLR	
66618	LD	DFHG	FLR	PTR	FLR	Railways Illustrated Annual Photographic Awards - Alan Barnes
66619	LD	DFHG	FLR	PTR	FLR	Derek W. Johnson MBE
66620	LD	DFHG	FLR	PTR	FLR	
66621	LD	DFHG	FLR	PTR	FLR	
66622	LD	DFHG	FLR	PTR	FLR	
66623	LD	DFHG	AIN	EVL	FLR	Bill Bolsover
66624	Exported, working in Poland for Freightliner Poland as 66602FPL					
66625	Exported, working in Poland for Freightliner Poland as 66601FPL					

Nineteen of the original 25 Class 66/6 high traction output locos are still operating in the UK and are usually deployed on the heavier trains operated by Freightliner Heavy Haul. No. 66616 is seen passing Totnes with a long sleeper-carrying train. **Nathan Williamson**

Class 66/9

Number	Depot	Pool	Livery	Owner	Operator	Name
66951	LD	DFHG	FLR	EVL	FLR	
66952	LD	DFHG	FLR	EVL	FLR	
66953	LD	DFHG	FLR	BEA	FLR	
66954	LD	DFIN	FLR	BEA	FLR	
66955	LD	DFIN	FLR	BEA	FLR	
66956	LD	DFHH	FLR	BEA	FLR	
66957	LD	DFIN	FLR	BEA	FLR	Stephenson Locomotive Society 1909-2009

Freightliner

Class 70 - PH37ACmi

Vehicle Length: 71ft 2½in (21.71m)
Height: 12ft 10in (3.91m)
Width: 8ft 8in (2.64m)

Engine: GE V16-cyliner PowerHaul 616
Horsepower: 3,700hp (2,750kW)
Electrical Equipment: General Electric

Number	Depot	Pool	Livery	Owner	Operator	Name/Notes
70001	FD	DFGI	FLP	MAG	FLR	*PowerHaul*
70002	FD	DFGH	FLP	MAG	FLR	
70003	FD	DFGH	FLP	MAG	FLR	
70004	FD	DFGH	FLP	MAG	FLR	*The Coal Industry Society*
70005	FD	DFGH	FLP	MAG	FLR	
70006	FD	DFGH	FLP	MAG	FLR	
70007	FD	DFGI	FLP	MAG	FLR	
70008	FD	DFGI	FLP	MAG	FLR	
70009	FD	DFGI	FLP	MAG	FLR	
70010	FD	DFGH	FLP	MAG	FLR	
70011	FD	DFGH	FLP	MAG	FLR	
(70012	-	-	FLP	GE	-)	*Returned to General Electric, Erie, PA, USA*
70013	FD	DFGH	FLP	MAG	FLR	
70014	FD	DFGH	FLP	MAG	FLR	
70015	FD	DFGH	FLP	MAG	FLR	
70016	FD	DFGH	FLP	MAG	FLR	
70017	FD	DFGI	FLP	MAG	FLR	
70018	FD	DFGI	FLP	MAG	FLR	
70019	FD	DFGI	FLP	MAG	FLR	
70020	FD	DFGI	FLP	MAG	FLR	
70099	HQ	MBDL	GRN	GE	-	

Above: *In 2012, the UK's most modern fleet of main line diesel locos were the Freightliner-operated General Electric Class 70s. Delivery of these rather ugly machines was protracted, with 19 out of an original order for 30 working for Freightliner at the end of 2012. The locos are used on a mix of Heavy Haul and Intermodal duties with performance not as good as expected. No. 70016 is seen at Burton.* **John Binch**

■ Originally 30 locomotives were ordered in 2007 for delivery in 2009-10. Ninteen locos were delivered by February 2012; no further deliveries are due at this stage.

Class 86/5 & 86/6

Vehicle Length: 58ft 6in (17.83m)
Height: 13ft 0⅝in (3.97m)
Width: 8ft 8¼in (2.64m)

Power Collection: 25kV ac overhead
Horsepower: 5,900hp (4,400kW)
Electrical Equipment: GEC

Number		Depot	Pool	Livery	Owner	Operator
86501	(86608/86408)	FE	DFGC	FLR	FLR	FLR
86604	(86404)	FE	DFNC	FLR	FLR	FLR
86605	(86405)	FE	DFNC	FLR	FLR	FLR
86607	(86407)	FE	DFNC	FLR	FLR	FLR
86609	(86409)	FE	DFNC	FLR	PTR	FLR

86610	(86410)	FE	DFNC	FLR	PTR	FLR
86612	(86412)	FE	DFNC	FLR	PTR	FLR
86613	(86413)	FE	DFNC	FLR	PTR	FLR
86614	(86414)	FE	DHNC	FLR	PTR	FLR
86622	(86422)	FE	DFNC	FLP	PTR	FLR
86627	(86427)	FE	DFNC	FLR	PTR	FLR
86628	(86428)	FE	DFNC	FLR	PTR	FLR
86632	(86432)	FE	DFNC	FLR	PTR	FLR
86637	(86437)	FE	DFNC	FLP	PTR	FLR
86638	(86438)	FE	DFNC	FLR	PTR	FLR
86639	(86439)	FE	DFNC	FLR	PTR	FLR

86247 at LNWR Crewe in pool DHLT

Below: *Freightliner Intermodal operate a fleet of 16 Class 86/5 and 86/6 locos. These are based at Crewe and are usually deployed on the services traversing the West Coast route working through to Ipswich on the Felixstowe corridor. No. 86609 is seen double-heading No. 86627 through South Kenton on 2 April 2012 with a northbound container service.* **Antony Christie**

Class 90

Vehicle Length: 61ft 6in (18.74m)	Power Collection: 25kV ac overhead
Height: 13ft 0¼in (3.96m)	Horsepower: 7,860hp (5,860kW)
Width: 9ft 0in (2.74m)	Electrical Equipment: GEC

Number	Depot	Pool	Livery	Owner	Operator
90016	CP	DFLC	FLR	PTR	FLR
90041	CP	DFLC	FLR	PTR	FLR
90042	CP	DFLC	FLY	PTR	FLR
90043	CP	DFLC	FLY	PTR	FLR
90044	CP	DFLC	FLY	PTR	FLR
90045	CP	DFLC	FLP	PTR	FLR

Number	Depot	Pool	Livery	Owner	Operator
90046	CP	DFLC	FLR	PTR	FLR
90047	CP	DFLC	FLY	PTR	FLR
90048	CP	DFLC	FLR	PTR	FLR
90049	CP	DFLC	FLP	PTR	FLR

Name applied

90043 *Freightliner Coatbridge*

Right: *Freightliner Intermodal operate a fleet of 10 Class 90/0s for longer distance electric freight services over the West Coast route and to/from Ipswich. Until December 2012 they were frequently hired to Virgin Trains to operate the Virgin loco-hauled stand-in set. Painted in a version of the Freightliner Power Haul livery, No. 90049 is seen with the Virgin Mk3 set at Euston.* **Nathan Williamson**

Freight Operating Companies - Mendip Rail

Mendip Rail

Address: ✉ Torr Works, East Cranmore, Shepton Mallet, Somerset, BA4 5SQ
📠 info@mendip-rail.co.uk ✆ 01749 880672 ⓘ www.mendip-rail.co.uk

Managing Director: Alan Taylor
Depots: Merehead (MD), Whatley (WH)
Parent Company: Aggregate Industries and Hanson

Class 08

Vehicle Length: 29ft 3in (8.91m)
Height: 12ft 8⅝in (3.87m)
Width: 8ft 6in (2.59m)

Engine: English Electric 6K
Horsepower: 400hp (298kW)
Electrical Equipment: English Electric

Number	Depot	Pool	Livery	Owner	Operator						
08643	MD	MBDL	GRN	FOS	MRL	08652	WH	MBDL	HAN	HAN	MRL
08650	MD	MBDL	FOS	FOS	MRL	08731	MD	MBDL	BLU	FOS	MRL
						08947	WH	MBDL	BLU	FOS	MRL

Class 59/0 & 59/1

Vehicle Length: 70ft 0½in (21.34m)
Height: 12ft 10in (3.91m)
Width: 8ft 8¼in (2.65m)

Engine: EMD 16-645 E3C
Horsepower: 3,000hp (2,462kW)
Electrical Equipment: EMD

Number	Depot	Pool	Livery	Owner	Operator	Name
59001	MD	XYPO	AGI	FOS	MRL	Yeoman Endeavour
59002	MD	XYPO	FOS	FOS	MRL	Alan J Day
59003	-	-	HHP	HHP	HHP	Yeoman Highlander
59004	MD	XYPO	FOS	FOS	MRL	Paul A Hammond
59005	MD	XYPO	AGI	FOS	MRL	Kenneth J Painter
59101	MD	XYPA	HAN	HAN	MRL	Village of Whatley
59102	MD	XYPA	HAN	HAN	MRL	Village of Chantry
59103	MD	XYPA	HAN	HAN	MRL	Village of Mells
59104	MD	XYPA	HAN	HAN	MRL	Village of Great Elm

■ Loco No. 59003 *Yeoman Highlander*, originally used by Foster Yeoman in the UK, is now owned and operated by Heavy Haul Power International and based in Germany.

Left: *Mendip Rail operate the combined fleets of the original Foster Yeoman and Hanson Class 59s. The Foster Yeoman locos, 59001-59005, were the first General Motors main line locos to operate in England and were built in Chicago by General Motors. No. 59002* Alan J Day *is seen in Foster Yeoman livery stabled in Acton Yard.* **Nathan Williamson**

Left: *By the time ARC Southern, later part of Hanson, ordered their Class 59s, the General Motors primary site for loco building had moved to London, Ontario, Canada, where the four members of Class 59/1, 59101-59104, were constructed. These locos had a very slight revision to the front end styling. All '59s' are fitted with AAR multiple jumpers, so up to three locos can operate in multiple together. Nos. 59101 and 59103 are seen passing Newbury with an Acton-bound 'Jumbo' train.* **Stacey Thew**

SW1001 'Switcher'

Vehicle Length: 40ft 6in (12.34m)
Height: 14ft 3in (4.34m)
Width: 10ft 0in (3.04m)

Engine: GM 8-645E
Horsepower: 1,000hp (746kW)
Electrical Equipment: EMD

Number	Depot	Pool	Livery	Owner	Operator	Name
44	MD	-	FOS	FOS	MRL	Western Yeoman II
120	WH	-	HAN	HAN	MRL	

Eurotunnel

Address (UK): ✉ The Channel Tunnel Group Ltd, Ashford Road, Folkestone, CT18 8XX
✐ info@eurotunnel.com ✆ 01303 282222 ⓘ www.eurotunnel.com

Chairman & CEO: Jacques Gounon
Depot: Coquelles, France (CO)

Shuttle

All locomotives are allocated to the Eurotunnel Maintenance Facility in Coquelles, France, but can be stabled and receive light repair at Cheriton terminal in the UK.

Class 9/0

Vehicle Length: 72ft 2in (22m)	Power Collection: 25kV ac overhead
Height: 13ft 9in (4.20m)	Horsepower: 7,720hp (5,760kW)
Width: 9ft 9in (3.01m)	Electrical Equipment: Brush

Original loco order, many now rebuilt and upgraded to Class 9/8.

9005	*Jessye Norman*	9018	*Wilhelmena Fernandez*	9033	*Montserrat Caballé*
9007	*Dame Joan Sutherland*	9022	*Dame Janet Baker*	9036	*Alain Fondary*
9011	*José Van Dam*	9024	*Gotthard 1882*	9037	*Gabriel Bacquier*
9013	*Maria Callas*	9026	*Furkatunnel 1982*		
9015	*Lötschberg 1913*	9029	*Thomas Allen*		

Class 9/7

Vehicle Length: 72ft 2in (22m)	Power Collection: 25kV ac overhead
Height: 13ft 9in (4.20m)	Horsepower: 9,387hp (7,000kW)
Width: 9ft 9in (3.01m)	Electrical Equipment: Brush

9701	9704	9707	9713 (9103)	9716 (9106)	9719 (9109)	9722 (9112)
9702	9705	9711 (9101)	9714 (9104)	9717 (9107)	9720 (9110)	9723 (9113)
9703	9706	9712 (9102)	9715 (9105)	9718 (9108)	9721 (9111)	

Class 9/8

Rebuilt from Class 9/0 locos, 800 added to original running number on conversion.

Vehicle Length: 72ft 2in (22m)	Power Collection: 25kV ac overhead
Height: 13ft 9in (4.20m)	Horsepower: 9,387hp (7,000kW)
Width: 9ft 9in (3.01m)	Electrical Equipment: Brush

9801	*Lesley Garrett*	9814	*Lucia Popp*	9827	*Barbara Hendricks*
9802	*Stuart Burrows*	9816	*Willard White*	9828	*Dame Kiri Te Kanawa*
9803	*Benjamin Luxon*	9817(S)	*José Carreras*	9831	
9804	*Victoria de Los Angeles*	9819	*Maria Ewing*	9832	*Renata Tebaldi*
9806	*Régine Crespin*	9820	*Nicolai Ghiaurov*	9834	*Mirella Freni*
9808	*Elisabeth Soderstrom*	9821	*Teresa Berganza*	9835	*Nicolai Gedda*
9809	*François Pollet*	9823	*Dame Elisabeth Legge-*	9838	*Hildegard Behrens*
9810	*Jean-Philippe Courtis*		*Schwarzkopf*	9840	
9812	*Luciano Pavarotti*	9825			

Right: *Class 9/8 'shuttle' No. 9821 Teresa Berganza is seen on the rear of a lorry shuttle arriving at the UK terminal of the Channel Tunnel at Cheriton, Folkestone. All Channel Tunnel 'shuttle' trains are powered by a loco at each end of the train to ensure trains can be brought out of the tunnel in the case of an emergency.*
Alisdair Anderson

MaK DE1004

Vehicle Length: 54ft 2in (16.50m)	Diesel Engine: MTU 12V396tc
	Horsepower: 1,260hp (939.5kW)
	Electrical Equipment: BBC

0001 (21901)	0003 (21903)	0005 (21905)	0007 (21907) [6457]
0002 (21902)	0004 (21904)	0006 (21906) [6456]	

Hunslet/Schöma

| Diesel Engine: Deutz |
| Horsepower: 200hp (270kW) |
| Mechanical Equipment: Hunslet |

0031	0033	0035	0037	0039	0041
0032	0034	0036	0038	0040	0042

Network Rail

Address: Kings Place, 90 York Way, London, N1 9AG

✉ enquiries@networkrail.co.uk

☎ Helpline: 08457 114141, Switchboard: 0203 356 9595

ⓘ www.networkrail.co.uk

Chief Executive: David Higgins   **Director Operations:** Robin Gisby

Depots: Heaton (HT), Barrow Hill (BH), Derby (DF), Rugby (RU), Eastleigh (ZG)

Class 08

Vehicle Length: 29ft 3in (8.91m)	Engine: English Electric 6K		
Height: 12ft 8⅝in (3.87m)	Horsepower: 400hp (298kW)		
Width: 8ft 6in (2.59m)	Electrical Equipment: English Electric		

Number	Depot	Pool	Livery	Owner	Operator		Number	Depot	Pool	Livery	Owner	Operator
08417	DF	QADD	NRL	NRL	NRL		08956	DF	QADD	BLU	NRL	NRL

Left: *The Network Rail pool QADD contains two Class 08s, Nos. 08417 and 08956, both based at the Railway Technical Centre (RTC), Derby, where they are used to form and shunt test train stock. No. 08417, painted in all-over Network Rail yellow with wasp ends and a red buffer beam, is seen in the RTC yard.* **Antony Christie**

Class 31/1 & 31/4

Vehicle Length: 56ft 9in (17.29m)	Engine: English Electric 12SVT		
Height: 12ft 7in (3.91m)	Horsepower: 1,470hp (1,097kW)		
Width: 8ft 9in (2.65m)	Electrical Equipment: Brush		
31/4 Fitted with Electric Train Heat			

Number	Depot	Pool	Livery	Owner	Operator		Number	Depot	Pool	Livery	Owner	Operator
31105	DF	QADD	NRL	NRL	NRL		31285	DF	QADD	NRL	NRL	NRL
31233	DF	QADD	NRL	NRL	NRL		31465*	DF	QADD	NRL	NRL	NRL

* Previously numbered 31565, 31213

Left: *Today, one of the most important safety-led operations of Network Rail is the ongoing inspection of its network in terms of track condition and surrounding infrastructure. To fulfil this role, a number of test trains are based at Derby. To power some of these trains, a fleet of four Class 31s painted in Network Rail yellow are retained. All are based at the RTC, Derby. The locos have received many modifications from their normal traffic days; this mainly involves front lights and mounting brackets for extra equipment. No. 31285 is seen at the head of the structure gauging train at Newton Abbot on 13 March 2012.* **Antony Christie**

Class 43

Vehicle Length: 58ft 5in (18.80m)				Engine: MTU 16V4000 R31R			
Height: 12ft 10in (3.90m)				Horsepower: 2,250hp (1,680kW)			
Width: 8ft 11in (2.73m)				Electrical Equipment: Brush			

Number	Depot	Pool	Livery	Owner	Operator	Name
43013	HT	QCAR	NRL	PTR	NRL	
43014	HT	QCAR	NRL	PTR	NRL	
43062	HT	QCAR	NRL	PTR	NRL	John Armitt

Right: *Three of the Porterbrook Leasing HST power cars are operated by Network Rail and provide power to operate the New Measurement Train (NMT), which, formed of Mk3 stock, operates over most main lines in the UK on a timetabled basis to review track condition. The train's formation can be varied depending on the tests being undertaken. With No. 43062 on the front, the train passes Dawlish on a run from Plymouth to London.* **CJM**

Class 57/3

Vehicle Length: 63ft 6in (19.38m)				Engine: EMD 645-12F3B		
Height: 12ft 10½in (3.91m)				Horsepower: 2,750hp (2,051kW)		
Width: 9ft 2in (2.79m)				Electrical Equipment: Brush		

Number	Depot	Pool	Livery	Owner	Operator	Name
57301 (47845)	ZG	QADD	NRL	PBR	NRL	
57303 (47705)	ZG	QADD	NRL	PBR	NRL	
57305 (47822)	ZG	QADD	NRL	PBR	NRL	
57306 (47814)	ZG	QADD	NRL	PBR	NRL	
57310 (47831)	ZG	QADD	NRL	PBR	NRL	
57312 (47330)	ZG	QADD	NRL	PBR	NRL	Peter Henderson

57301 & 57303 fitted with Tightlock couplings, 57310 & 57312 fitted with modified Dellner couplings

Right: *Commissioned by Network Rail at the end of 2011 is a fleet of six Class 57/3s previously used by Virgin Trains. The locos, painted in Network Rail yellow, can be used to power any Network Rail train, especially the snow train and RHTT services. Originally all six were fitted with drop head Scharfenberg couplers, but to allow easier coupling to various stock modifications have been made in 2012 which has seen two locos fitted with drop head Tightlock couplings, as shown on No. 57301 at Eastleigh.* **Antony Christie**

Class 73/1

Vehicle Length: 53ft 8in (16.35m)			Power: 750V dc third rail or English Electric 6K		
Height: 12ft 5⅜in (3.79m)			Horsepower: electric - 1,600hp (1,193kW)		
Width: 8ft 8in (2.64m)			Horsepower: diesel - 600hp (447kW)		
			Electrical Equipment: English Electric		

Number	Depot	Pool	Livery	Owner	Operator
73138	DF	QADD	NRL	NRL	NRL

Right: *One of the most universal locos on the Network Rail books is Class 73/1 electro-diesel No. 73138. This loco is usually deployed powering test trains involving operation over third rail electrified areas. The loco's on-board 600hp diesel engine is then used to power the train away from the electric supply between its base in Derby and test sites. Showing its revised front end equipment with modified head/marker lights and a forward-facing camera, No. 73138 is seen passing Eastleigh in October 2012.* **Antony Christie**

Network Rail

Class 86/9

Vehicle Length: 58ft 6in (17.83m) Power Collection: 25kV ac overhead
Height: 13ft 0⅝in (3.97m) Horsepower: 2,950hp (2,200kW)
Width: 8ft 8¼in (2.64m) Electrical Equipment: GEC

Number		Depot	Pool	Livery	Owner	Operator	Name
86901	(86253)	ZA	QACL	NRL	NRL	NRL	Chief Engineer
86902	(86210)	ZA	QACL	NRL	NRL	NRL	Rail Vehicle Engineering

Class 97/3 & 37

Vehicle Length: 61ft 6in (18.74m) Engine: English Electric 12CSVT
Height: 13ft 0¼in (3.96m) Horsepower: 1,750hp (1,304kW)
Width: 8ft 11⅝in (2.73m) Electrical Equipment: English Electric

Number		Depot	Pool	Livery	Owner	Operator	Name
37198		BH	MBDL	NRL	NRL	NRL	
97301	(37100)	ZA	QETS	NRL	NRL	NRL	
97302	(37170)	ZA	QETS	NRL	NRL	NRL	
97303	(37178)	ZA	QETS	NRL	NRL	NRL	
97304	(37217)	ZA	QETS	NRL	NRL	NRL	John Tiley

Network Rail operate a fleet of five Class 37s. Four are classified as Class 97/3, and have been modified for use in the development of the UK ERTMS cab signalling now used on the Cambrian Line. However, when not required in this role, the fleet can be seen powering other Network Rail trains, including autumn Rail Head Treatment Trains, track test trains or route training runs. With a four-coach test train, No. No. 97301 is seen near Dawlish on 22 June 2012. **CJM**

Class 313/1

Vehicle Length: (Driving) 64ft 11½in (20.75m) Width: 9ft 3in (2.82m)
(Inter) 65ft 4¼in (19.92m) Horsepower: 880hp (656kW)
Height: 11ft 9in (3.58m) Seats (total/car): 202S, 66S/70S/66S

Great Northern Route - ERTMS development unit

Number	Formation	Depot	Livery	Owner	Operator
	DMSO+PTSO+BDMSO				
313121	62549+71233+61613	-	SIL	BEA	NRL (at Wembly)

Class 950

Vehicle Length: 64ft 9¾in (19.74m) Engine: 1 x NT855R5 of 285hp per vehicle
Height: 12ft 4½in (3.77m) Horsepower: 570hp (425kW)
Width: 9ft 3⅛in (2.82m) Seats (total/car): 124S, 59S/65S

Number	Formation	Depot	Livery	Owner	Operator	Note
950001	999600+999601	ZA	NRL	NRL	NRL	Track assessment train (Class 150 outline)

Right: *One of the most commonly
seen track test trains is the Class 150
outline DMU, seen throughout the
Network Rail system, visiting most
parts of the country and branch lines
at least once a year. The test equipment
is housed in one coach (left in the
illustration) while the other coach is
basically a Class 150/1 DMS. Note the
modifications and additional equipment
on the front end. No. 950001 is seen
traversing the Newquay branch.*
Antony Christie

De-Icing Cars

Vehicle Length: 66ft 4in (20.22m)		Horsepower: 500hp (370kW)
Height: 12ft 4in (3.75m)		Seats (total/car): None
Width: 9ft 2in (2.82m)		

Number	Vehicle	Depot	Livery	Owner	Operator	Notes
489102	68501 (977975)	TN	NRL	NRL	NRL	De-icing vehicle modified from Class 489 DMBS
489105	68504	TN	NRL	NRL	GBR	De-icing vehicle modified from Class 489 DMBS
489106	68505	TN	NRL	NRL	GBR	De-icing vehicle modified from Class 489 DMBS

Hauled Stock

Mk2		
Vehicle Length: 66ft 0in (20.11m)	Height: 12ft 9½in (3.89m)	
	Width: 9ft 3in (2.81m)	

Royal Train

Mk 3		
Vehicle Length: 75ft 0in (22.86m)	Height: 12ft 9in (3.88m)	
	Width: 8ft 11in (2.71m)	

Number		Type	Depot	Livery	Operator	Use
2903	(11001)	AT5G	ZN	ROY	NRL/DBS	HM The Queen's Saloon
2904	(12001)	AT5G	ZN	ROY	NRL/DBS	HRH The Duke of Edinburgh's Saloon
2915	(10735)	AT5G	ZN	ROY	NRL/DBS	Royal Household Sleeping Coach
2916	(40512)	AT5G	ZN	ROY	NRL/DBS	HRH The Prince of Wales's Dining Coach
2917	(40514)	AT5G	ZN	ROY	NRL/DBS	Kitchen Car and Royal Household Dining Coach
2918	(40515)	AT5G	ZN	ROY	NRL/DBS	Royal Household Coach
2919	(40518)	AT5G	ZN	ROY	NRL/DBS	Royal Household Coach
2920	(17109)	AT5B	ZN	ROY	NRL/DBS	Generator Coach and Household Sleeping Coach
2921	(17107)	AT5B	ZN	ROY	NRL/DBS	Brake, Coffin Carrier and Household Accommodation
2922		AT5G	ZN	ROY	NRL/DBS	HRH The Prince of Wales's Sleeping Coach
2923		AT5G	ZN	ROY	NRL/DBS	Royal Passenger Saloon

Below: *Network Rail is responsible for the operation of the Royal Train stock, which is usually powered by DB-S locos and
staff. The train is usually kept at Wolverton Works. Car No. 2917, a former HST kitchen car No. 40514, is seen in the full Royal
consist passing Totnes. This vehicle is used for food preparation and looking after the Royal household staff.* **Nathan Williamson**

Infrastructure Companies - Network Rail

Network Rail

Hauled Stock

Number		Type	Depot	Livery	Operator	Use
1205	(6348)	AJIF/RFO	ZA	VIR	NRL	Out of use
1256	(3296)	AJIF/RFO	ZA	NRL	NRL	Special vehicle
5981		AC2F/TSO	ZA	NRL	NRL	Special vehicle
6260	(92116)	AX51/GEN	ZA	RTK	NRL/LUL	Generator (owned by DBS)
6261	(92988)	AX51/GEN	ZA	NRL	NRL	Generator (owned by DBS)
6262	(92928)	AX51/GEN	ZA	NRL	NRL	Generator (owned by DBS)
6263	(92961)	AX51/GEN	ZA	NRL	NRL	Generator (owned by DBS)
6264	(92923)	AX51/GEN	ZA	NRL	NRL	Generator (owned by DBS)
9481		AE2D/BSO	ZA	NRL	NRL	Radio Survey coach
9516		AE2D/BSO	ZA	NRL	-	Under conversion at RVEL
9523		AE2D/BSO	ZA	NRL	-	Under conversion at RVEL
9701	(9528)	AF2F/DBSO	ZA	NRL	NRL	Remote driving car (Mentor train)
9702	(9510)	AF2F/DBSO	ZA	NRL	NRL	Remote driving car
9703	(9517)	AF2F/DBSO	ZA	NRL	NRL	Remote driving car
9708	(9530)	AF2F/DBSO	ZA	NRL	NRL	Remote driving car (Structure Gauging)
9714	(9536)	AF2F/DBSO	ZA	NRL	NRL	Remote driving car
62384		MBS	ZA	NRL	NRL	Ultrasonic test car (under conversion)
72612	(6156)	Mk2f/TSO	ZA	NRL	NRL	Brake force runner
72616	(6007)	Mk2f/TSO	ZA	NRL	NRL	Brake force runner
72630	(6094)	Mk2f/TSO	ZA	NRL	NRL	Brake force runner
72631	(6096)	Mk2f/TSO	ZA	NRL	NRL	Brake force runner
72639	(6070)	Mk2f/TSO	ZA	NRL	NRL	Brake force runner
82111		MK3/DVT	ZA	VIR	NRL	Driving Van Trailer
82115		MK3/DVT	ZA	VIR	NRL	Driving Van Trailer
82124		MK3/DVT	ZA	VIR	NRL	Driving Van Trailer
82129		MK3/DVT	ZA	VIR	NRL	Driving Van Trailer
82145		MK3/DVT	ZA	VIR	NRL	Driving Van Trailer
92114	(81443)	Mk1/BG	ZA	NRL	NRL	Special vehicle
92939	(92039)	Mk1/BG	ZA	INT	NRL	Special vehicle
99666	(3250)	Mk2e/FO	ZA	NRL	NRL	Ultrasonic Test Train
971001	(94150)	Mk1/NKA	BS	NRL	NRL	Tool Van
971002	(94190)	Mk1/NKA	WT	NRL	NRL	Tool Van
971003	(94191)	Mk1/NKA	BS	NRL	NRL	Tool Van
971004	(94168)	Mk1/NKA	KY	NRL	NRL	Tool Van
975025	(60755)	6B Buffet	ZA	GRN	NRL	Control Inspection Saloon *Caroline*
975081	(35313)	Mk1/BSK	ZA	NRL	NRL	Structure Gauging Train
975091	(34615)	Mk1/BSK	ZA	NRL	NRL	Overhead line test coach - *Mentor*
975280	(21263)	Mk1/BCK	ZA	NRL	NRL	Staff coach
975464	(35171)	Mk1/BSK	IS	NRL	NRL	Snowblower coach *Ptarmigan*
975486	(34100)	Mk1/BSK	IS	NRL	NRL	Snowblower coach *Polar Bear*
975814	(41000)	HST/TF	EC	NRL	NRL	NMT Conference coach
975984	(40000)	HST/TRUB	EC	NRL	NRL	NMT Lecture coach
977337	(9395)	Mk2/BSO	ZA	NRL	NRL	Track recording - Staff coach
977868	(5846)	Mk2e/TSO	ZA	NRL	NRL	Radio Survey coach
977869	(5858)	Mk2e/TSO	ZA	NRL	NRL	Radio Survey coach
977969	(14112)	Mk2/BFK	ZA	NRL	NRL	Staff coach (Former Royal Saloon 2906)
977974	(5854)	Mk2e/TSO	ZA	NRL	NRL	Laboratory coach (Owned by Delta Rail)
977983	(3407)	Mk2f/FO	ZA	NRL	NRL	Hot Box Detection coach
977984	(40501)	HST/TRFK	EC	NRL	NRL	NMT Staff coach
977985	(6019)	Mk2f/TSO	ZA	NRL	NRL	Structure Gauging Train
977986	(3189)	Mk2d/FO	ZA	NRL	NRL	Track Recording coach

Left: *A large number of former revenue-earning passenger or parcels/mail vehicles are now operated by Network Rail as Departmental vehicles for various operations. This vehicle No. 6262 is a former BG No. 92928 which has been heavily adapted and is now a generator van for supplying hotel power to Network Rail track test trains. Two generators are located one at each end. Note the ventilation grilles in the bodyside and additional power jumpers on the coach end.* **Antony Christie**

977993	(44053)	HST/TGS	EC	NRL	NRL	NMT Overhead Line Test coach
977994	(44087)	HST/TGS	EC	NRL	NRL	NMT Recording coach
977995	(40719)	HST/TRFM	EC	NRL	NRL	NMT Generator coach
977996	(44062)	HST/TGS	EC	NRL	NRL	NMT Battery coach
977997	(72613)	Mk2f/TSO	ZA	NRL	NRL	Radio Survey Test Vehicle (originally TSO 6126)
999508		Saloon	ZA	NRL	NRL	Track Recording coach - UTU3
999550		Mk2	ZA	NRL	NRL	Track Recording coach (Purpose built)
999602	(62483)	Mk1/REP	ZA	NRL	SEC	Ultrasonic Test coach - UTU3
999605	(62482)	Mk1/REP	ZA	NRL	NRL	Ultrasonic Test coach - UTU2
999606	(62356)	Mk1/REP	ZA	NRL	NRL	Ultrasonic Test coach - UTU4

Snowploughs
Independent Drift Ploughs – ZZA

Number	*Allocation*
ADB965203	Tees
ADB965206	Doncaster
ADB965208	Inverness
ADB965209	Bristol Barton H
ADB965210	Tonbridge
ADB965211	Peterborough
ADB965217	Slateford
ADB965219	Mossend
ADB965223	Margam
ADB965224	Carlisle
ADB965230	Carlisle
ADB965231	Bristol Barton H
ADB965232	Peterborough
ADB965233	Peterborough
ADB965234	Carlisle
ADB965235	Margam
ADB965236	Tonbridge

ADB965237	Peterborough
ADB965240	Inverness
ADB965241	Doncaster
ADB965242	Tees
ADB965243	Slateford

Right: *At the end of 2012, 22 heavy independent drift snowploughs were in traffic, stationed around the country. No. ADB965231 is illustrated at Bristol Barton Hill.* **Antony Christie**

Beilhack Patrol Ploughs (ex-Class 40 bogies) – ZZA

Number	*Allocation*
ADB965576	Doncaster
ADB965577	Doncaster
ADB965578	Carlisle
ADB965579	Carlisle
ADB965580	Wigan
ADB965581	Wigan
ADB966098	Doncaster
ADB966099	Doncaster

Right: *Four pairs of ex-Class 40 bogie snowploughs are still available to Network Rail. No. ADB965577 allocated to Doncaster is illustrated.* **Antony Christie**

Beilhack Snow Blowers – ZWA

Number	*Allocation*
ADB968500	Rutherglen
ADB968501	Rutherglen

Right: *For the most difficult snowdrifts a pair of Beilhack snow blowers are on the books of Network Rail. Based in Scotland at Rutherglen, these self propelled vehicles cut their way into snow and eject it by blower to the side of the track. No. 968501 is illustrated.* **Antony Christie**

Track Machines (On-Track Plant)

Plasser & Theurer DTS-62-N – Dynamic Track Stabiliser – ZWA

DR72211	Balfour Beatty
DR72213	Balfour Beatty

Plasser & Theurer 09-16-CSM – Tamper/Liner – ZWA

DR73103	Colas	DR73105(S)	Colas

Left: *Plasser & Theurer 09-16-CSM machine No. DR73103 painted in Colas livery at Didcot.*
Antony Christie

Plasser & Theurer 09-32-RT – Tamper/Liner – ZWA

DR73108	*Tiger*	Amey

Plasser & Theurer 09-3X – Tamper/Liner – ZWA

DR73109		SB Rail	DR73110	*Peter White*	SB Rail

Plasser & Theurer 09-3X-D-RT – Tamper/Liner ZWA

DR73111 *Reading Panel 1965 - 2005*	Network Rail	DR73116	Network Rail
DR73113	Network Rail	DR73117	Network Rail
DR73114 *Ron Henderson*	Network Rail	DR73118	Network Rail
DR73115	Network Rail		

Left: *Plasser & Theurer 09-3X-D-RT tamper 7 liner No. DR73111 coupled to Plasser & Theurer USP5000RT ballast regulator, passing through Totnes station.*
Nathan Williamson

Plasser & Theurer 07-275 – Switch/Crossing Tamper – ZWA

DR73311	*Cyril Dryland*	Balfour Beatty

Plasser & Theurer 07-32 – Duomatic Tamper/Liner – ZWA

DR73428	J H Russell
DR73434(S)	Balfour Beatty

Plasser & Theurer 08-16/90 – Tamper/Liner – ZWA

DR73502	Balfour Beatty	DR73503 (S)	Balfour Beatty

Plasser & Theurer 08-32U RT – Plain Line Tamper – ZWA

DR73803 *Alexander Graham Bell*   SBRail

Plasser & Theurer 08-16U RT – Plain Line Tamper – ZWA

DR73804 *James Watt* SBRail

Plasser & Theurer 08-16(32)U RT – Plain Line Tamper – ZWA

DR73805   Colas   DR73806 *Karine* Colas

Plasser & Theurer 08-4x4/4S - RT – Switch/Crossing Tamper – ZWA

DR73904	*Thomas Telford*	SBRail	DR73908		Colas
DR73905	*Eddie King*	Amey	DR73909	*Saturn*	Colas
DR73906	*Panther*	Amey	DR73910	*Jupiter*	Colas
DR73907		Colas			

Right: *Colas-operated Plasser & Theurer 08-4x4/4S switch and crossing tamper No. DR73910* Jupiter *is seen at Preston.* **Antony Christie**

Plasser & Theurer 08-16/4x4C - RT – Switch/Crossing Tamper – ZWA

DR73911 (S)	*Puma*	Amey	DR73913	Colas
DR73912 (S)	*Lynx*	Amey		

Right: *Plasser & Theurer 08-16/4x4C switch and crossing tamper No. DR73913 operated by Colas is seen stabled between work at Banbury.* **John Wills**

Plasser & Theurer 08-4x4S - RT – Switch/Crossing Tamper – ZWA

DR73914   *Robert McAlpine*   SBRail

Plasser & Theurer 08-16/4x4C - RT – Switch/Crossing Tamper – ZWA

DR73915 *William Arrol*   SBRail   DR73916 *First Engineering*   SBRail

Infrastructure Companies - Network Rail

Plasser & Theurer 08-4x4S - RT – Switch/Crossing Tamper – ZWA
DR73917   Balfour Beatty   DR93918   Balfour Beatty

Plasser & Theurer 08-16/4x4 C100 - RT – Tamper – ZWA
DR73919   Colas

Plasser & Theurer 08-16/4x4C80 - RT – Tamper – ZWA
DR73920	Amey	DR73922 *John Snowdon*	Amey
DR73921	Amey		

Left: *Painted in Amey Railways livery, DR73920, a Plasser & Theurer 08-16/4x4C80 tamper, is seen stabled at Didcot.* **Antony Christie**

Plasser & Theurer 08-4x4S - RT – Switch/Crossing Tamper – ZWA
DR73923   *Mercury*   Colas

Plasser & Theurer 08-16/4x4C100 - RT – Tamper – ZWA
DR73924	*Atlas*	Colas	DR73927	Balfour Beatty
DR73925	*Europa*	Colas	DR73928	Balfour Beatty
DR73926	*Stephen Keith Blanchard*	Balfour Beatty		

Plasser & Theurer 08-4x4S - RT – Switch/Crossing Tamper – ZWA
DR73929   Colas   DR73930   Colas

Left: *Carrying Colas branding, one of two Plasser & Theurer 08-4x4S switch and crossing tampers No. DR73930 passes South Kenton while heading for Wembley.* **Antony Christie**

Plasser & Theurer 08-16/4x4C100 - RT – Tamper – ZWA
DR73931   Colas

Plasser & Theurer 08-4x4/4S - RT – Switch/Crossing Tamper
DR73932   SBRail

Plasser & Theurer 08-16/4x4C100 - RT – Tamper – ZWA
DR73933   SBRail   DR73934   SB Rail

Right: Displaying Colas orange livery No. DR73931, a Plasser & Theurer 08-16/4x4C100 tamper, is viewed stabled at Westbury. **Antony Christie**

Plasser & Theurer 08-4x4/4S - RT – Switch/Crossing Tamper – ZWA

DR73935	Colas	DR73936	Colas

Plasser & Theurer 08-16/4x4C100 - RT – Tamper – ZWA

DR73937	Balfour Beatty	DR73938	Balfour Beatty	DR73939	Balfour Beatty

Plasser & Theurer 08-4x4/4S - RT – Switch/Crossing Tamper – ZWA

DR73940	SBRail	DR73941	SBRail	DR73942	Colas

Above: *One of three Plasser & Theurer 08-4x4/4S switch and crossing tampers, No. DR73942 awaits work in Chester yard on 29 July 2012.* **John Binch**

Plasser & Theurer 08-16/4x4C100 - RT – Tamper – ZWA

DR73943	Balfour Beatty	DR73944	Balfour Beatty	DR73945	Balfour Beatty

Plasser & Theurer Euromat 08-4x4/4S – ZWA

DR73946	VolkerRail

Plasser & Theurer 08-4x4/4S - RT – Switch/Crossing Tamper ZWA

DR73947	Colas	DR73948	Colas

Plasser & Theurer 08-16/90 275 – Switch/Crossing Tamper – ZWA

DR75201	Balfour Beatty	DR75202	Balfour Beatty

Plasser & Theurer 08-16/90 SP-T – Switch/Crossing Tamper – ZWA

DR75203	MLP Maintenance

Plasser & Theurer 08-275ZW – Switch/Crossing Tamper – ZWY

DR75204	Trackwork

Matisa B45 Tamper – ZWA

DR75301	VolkerRail	DR75302	VolkerRail	DR75303	VolkerRail

Matisa B41UE Tamper – ZWA

DR75401	VolkerRail	DR75405	VolkerRail	DR75408	Balfour Beatty
DR75402	VolkerRail	DR75406	Colas	DR75409	Balfour Beatty
DR75403	VolkerRail		Eric Machell	DR75410	Balfour Beatty
DR75404	VolkerRail	DR75407	Colas	DR75411	Balfour Beatty

Network Rail

Left: One of 11 Matisa B41UE
tamping machines operated by
VolkerRail, Colas and Balfour Beatty.
No. 75408, one of the Balfour Beatty-
operated machines, is seen at Ely.
Antony Christie

Matisa B66UC Tamper – ZWA

DR75501	Balfour Beatty	DR75502	Balfour Beatty

Plasser & Theurer RM74 – Ballast Cleaner – ZWB

DR76304(S)	Plasser	DR76318(S)	Plasser

Plasser & Theurer RM95RT – Ballast Cleaner – ZWA

DR76323	Network Rail	DR76324	Network Rail

Plasser & Theurer RM900RT Ballast Cleaner – ZWA / ZWQ

DR76501 (HOBC-1)	Network Rail	DR76503 (HOBC-3)	Network Rail
DR76502 (HOBC-2)	Network Rail		

*An excellent location to see many track machines and the high output ballast
train is in the Taunton area. The RM900RT vehicle No. DR76501 from High
Output Ballast Cleaning train No. 1 is seen formed in a train consist passing
Taunton.* **Nathan Williamson**

Plasser & Theurer VM80 NR – ZWA

DR76701	(HOBC-3)	Network Rail	DR76710	(HOTRT-2)	Network Rail
DR76702	(HOBC-2)	Network Rail	DR76711	(HOTRT-1)	Network Rail
DR76703	(HOBC-1)	Network Rail			

Matisa D75 Undercutter – ZWA

DR76750	(HRTRT-2)	Network Rail	DR76751	(HRTRT-1)	Network Rail

Plasser & Theurer 09-16 CM NR – ZWA

DR76801	(HOBC-3)	Network Rail

Plasser & Theurer AFM 2000 RT – Rail Finishing Machine – ZWA

DR77001	SBRail	DR77002	SBRail

Infrastructure Companies - Network Rail

Right: *Two of these three-vehicle rail finishing trains, built by Plasser & Theurer and operated by SB Rail, are in service. Machine No. DR77001 is viewed at Carlisle Currock.*
Anthony Christie

Plasser & Theurer USP 5000C – Ballast Regulator – ZWA

DR77315(S)	Balfour Beatty	DR77322	Balfour Beatty	DR77336	Balfour Beatty
DR77316(S)	Balfour Beatty	DR77327	Colas		
DR77319(S)	Colas	DR77335	Colas		

Matisa R24S – Ballast Regulator – ZWA

DR77801	VolkerRail	DR77802	VolkerRail

Plasser & Theurer USP 5000RT – Ballast Regulator – ZWA

DR77901		Colas	
DR77903	*Frank Jones*	Network Rail	
DR77904		Network Rail	
DR77905		Network Rail	
DR77906		Network Rail	
DR77907		Network Rail	
DR77908*		SBRail	
* Previously DR77902			

Right: *Stabled at Exeter St Davids, Plasser & Theurer USP5000RT ballast regulator No. DR77901 displays Colas orange and yellow livery.*
Antony Christie

Plasser & Theurer Self-Propelled Heavy Duty Twin Jib Crane – YJB

DR78211	Network Rail	DR78216	Balfour Beatty	DR78221	Balfour Beatty
DR78212	Network Rail	DR78217	SB Rail	DR78222	Balfour Beatty
DR78213	VolkerRail	DR78218	Balfour Beatty	DR78223	Balfour Beatty
DR78215	SB Rail	DR78219	SB Rail	DR78224	Balfour Beatty

Cowens Sheldon Self-Propelled Heavy Duty Twin Jib Crane – YJB

DR78226	Colas	DR78231	(stored)	DR78235	Colas
DR78229	Network Rail	DR78234	(stored)	DR78237	(stored)

Donelli PD350 Single Line Track Relayer

DR78116	Balfour Beatty	DR78417	Balfour Beatty	DR78490	VolkerRail

Harsco Track Technologies NTC Power Wagon – YJA

DR78701	Balfour Beatty	DR78702	Balfour Beatty

Network Rail

Matisa P95 Track Renewal Train – YJA

DR78801	Network Rail	DR78812	Network Rail	DR78831	Network Rail
DR78802	Network Rail	DR78821	Network Rail	DR78832	Network Rail
DR78811	Network Rail	DR78822	Network Rail		

Left: *Matisa P95 No. DR78831, part of the Track Renewal Train, which in 2012 was based at Taunton Fairwater, where this illustration was recorded.*
Antony Christie

Schweebau SPML15 – Rail Grinder – ZWA

| DR79200 | Loram |

Loram/Barclay SPML17 – Rail Grinder – ZWA

| DR79201 | Loram |

Speno RPS 32-2 – Rail Grinder – ZWA

| DR79221 | Speno | DR79223 | Speno | DR79225 | Speno |
| DR79222 | Speno | DR79224 | Speno | DR79226 | Speno |

Loram C21 – Rail Grinder – ZWA

Set 01		Set 02		Set 03	
DR79231	Loram	DR79241	Loram	DR79251	Loram
DR79232	Loram	DR79242	Loram	DR79252	Loram
DR79233	Loram	DR79243	Loram	DR79253	Loram
DR79234	Loram	DR79244	Loram	DR79254	Loram
DR79235	Loram	DR79245	Loram	DR79255	Loram
DR79236	Loram	DR79246	Loram	DR79256	Loram
DR79237	Loram	DR79247 *Roger Smith*	Loram	DR79257	Loram

Harsco Track Technologies RGH-20C Switch/Crossing Rail Grinder – ZWA

DR79261 + DR79271	Network Rail	DR79264 + DR79274	Network Rail
DR79262 + DR79272	Network Rail	DR79265 + DR79275	Network Rail
DR79263 + DR79273	Network Rail		

Left: *The presentation of the rail heads in a perfect condition with the correct profile is achieved by the use of a fleet of rail grinding trains, which traverse the main line network on a programmed basis. Harsco Track Technologies RGH-20C two-vehicle set No. DR79273 and DR79263 pass west through Totnes.*
Nathan Williamson

Pandrol Jackson – Stoneblower – YZA

DR80201	Network Rail	DR80207(S)	Network Rail	DR80212	Network Rail
DR80202(S)	Network Rail	DR80208	Network Rail		
DR80203(S)	Network Rail	DR80209	Network Rail		
DR80205	Network Rail	DR80210	Network Rail		
DR80206	Network Rail	DR80211	Network Rail		

Harsco Track Technologies – Stoneblower – YZA

DR80213	Network Rail	DR80215	Network Rail	DR80217	Network Rail
DR80214	Network Rail	DR80216	Network Rail		

Harsco Track Technologies – Switch/Crossing Stoneblower – YZA

DR80301	*Stephen Cornish*	Network Rail	DR80303	Network Rail
DR80302		Network Rail		

Plasser & Theurer Heavy Duty Diesel Hydraulic Crane – YOB

DR81505	Balfour Beatty	DR81513	Balfour Beatty	DR81525	Balfour Beatty
DR81507	Balfour Beatty	DR51517	Balfour Beatty	DR81532	Balfour Beatty
DR81508	Balfour Beatty	DR81519	Balfour Beatty		
DR81511(S)	Balfour Beatty	DR81522	Balfour Beatty		

Cowans Sheldon Heavy Duty Diesel Hydraulic Crane

DR81541	Corus	DR81545	Corus

Kirow KRC810UK 100 tonne Diesel Hydraulic Crane – ZOA

DR81601	*Nigel Chester*	VolkerRail	DR81602		Balfour Beatty

Kirow KRC1200UK 125 tonne Diesel Hydraulic Crane – ZOA

DR81611	*Malcolm L Pearce*	Balfour Beatty	DR81613	VolkerRail
DR81612		Colas		

Right: *One of the largest rail-mounted cranes in operation in the UK is this Kirow KRC1200UK No. DR81612 operated by Colas. The crane has a maximum lift capacity of 125 tonnes and always operates with several escort vehicles carrying weight block and other equipment. In this view the crane and its associated vehicles pass Eastleigh in October 2012.*
Brian Garrett

Kirow KRC250UK Heavy Duty Diesel Hydraulic Crane – ZOA

DR81621	VolkerRail	DR81623	SBRail	DR81625	SBRail
DR81622	VolkerRail	DR81624	SBRail		

Right: *With a safe lifting capacity of 25 tonnes, this view shows Kirow crane No. DR81621, operated by VolkerRail and used for track replacement work. In this view it is seen re-laying track and crossings in Acton Yard, West London, in October 2012.* **Antony Christie**

Infrastructure Companies - Network Rail

Network Rail

Plasser & Theurer 08-16 Universal Tamper/Liner

DR86101(S)	Balfour Beatty

Plasser & Theurer Loading Station

DR88101	Network Rail

Starfer Single Line Spoil Handling System Train

DR92201	Network Rail	DR92205	Network Rail	DR92209	Network Rail
DR92202	Network Rail	DR92206	Network Rail	DR92210	Network Rail
DR92203	Network Rail	DR92207	Network Rail	DR92211	Network Rail
DR92204	Network Rail	DR92208	Network Rail	DR92212	Network Rail

Skako Ballast Distribution Train – YDA 'Octopus'

DR92213	Network Rail	DR92217	Network Rail	DR92221	Network Rail
DR92214	Network Rail	DR92218	Network Rail	DR92222	Network Rail
DR92215	Network Rail	DR92219	Network Rail		
DR92216	Network Rail	DR92220	Network Rail		

Plasser & Theurer NFS-D Ballast Distribution Train Hopper – YDA

DR92223	Network Rail	DR92229	Network Rail	DR92235	Network Rail
DR92224	Network Rail	DR92230	Network Rail	DR92236	Network Rail
DR92225	Network Rail	DR92231	Network Rail	DR92237	Network Rail
DR92226	Network Rail	DR92232	Network Rail	DR92238	Network Rail
DR92227	Network Rail	DR92233	Network Rail	DR92239	Network Rail
DR92228	Network Rail	DR92234	Network Rail	DR92240	Network Rail

Plasser & Theurer MFS-D Ballast Distribution Train Hopper – YDA

DR92241	Network Rail	DR92246	Network Rail	DR92251	Network Rail
DR92242	Network Rail	DR92247	Network Rail	DR92252	Network Rail
DR92243	Network Rail	DR92248	Network Rail	DR92253	Network Rail
DR92244	Network Rail	DR92249	Network Rail	DR92254	Network Rail
DR92245	Network Rail	DR92250	Network Rail		

Plasser & Theurer MFS-SB Swivel Conveyer Wagon – YDA

DR92259	Network Rail	DR92261	Network Rail
DR92260	Network Rail	DR92262	Network Rail

Plasser & Theurer MFS-PW Single Line Handling Train Power Wagon – YOA

DR92263	Network Rail

Plasser & Theurer NB-PW Ballast Distribution Train Power Wagon – YOA

DR92264	Network Rail

Plasser & Theurer MFS-D Ballast Distribution Train Hopper – YDA

DR92265	Network Rail	DR92270	Network Rail	DR92275	Network Rail
DR92266	Network Rail	DR92271	Network Rail	DR92276	Network Rail
DR92267	Network Rail	DR92272	Network Rail	DR92277	Network Rail
DR92268	Network Rail	DR92273	Network Rail	DR92278	Network Rail
DR92269	Network Rail	DR92274	Network Rail	DR92279	Network Rail

Plasser & Theurer MFS-SB Swivel Conveyer Wagon – YDA

DR92280	Network Rail	DR92281	Network Rail

Plasser & Theurer MFS-A Materials Handling Train Interface Wagon – YDA

DR92282	Network Rail	DR92283	Network Rail

Plasser & Theurer PW-RT Materials Handling Train Power Wagon – YOA

DR92285	Network Rail

Plasser & Theurer NPW-RT Materials Handling Train Power Wagon – YOA

DR92286	Network Rail

Plasser & Theurer MFS-SB Swivel Conveyer Wagon – YDA

DR92287	Network Rail	DR92290	Network Rail	DR92293	Network Rail
DR92288	Network Rail	DR92291	Network Rail	DR92294	Network Rail
DR92289	Network Rail	DR92292	Network Rail		

Plasser & Theurer MFS-D Ballast Distribution Train Hopper – YDA

DR92295	Network Rail	DR92307	Network Rail	DR92319	Network Rail
DR92296	Network Rail	DR92308	Network Rail	DR92320	Network Rail
DR92297	Network Rail	DR92309	Network Rail	DR92321	Network Rail
DR92298	Network Rail	DR92310	Network Rail	DR92322	Network Rail
DR92299	Network Rail	DR92311	Network Rail	DR92323	Network Rail
DR92300	Network Rail	DR92312	Network Rail	DR92324	Network Rail
DR92301	Network Rail	DR92313	Network Rail	DR92325	Network Rail
DR92302	Network Rail	DR92314	Network Rail	DR92326	Network Rail
DR92303	Network Rail	DR92315	Network Rail	DR92327	Network Rail
DR92304	Network Rail	DR92316	Network Rail	DR92328	Network Rail
DR92305	Network Rail	DR92317	Network Rail	DR92329	Network Rail
DR92306	Network Rail	DR92318	Network Rail	DR92330	Network Rail

Plasser & Theurer PW-RT Materials Handling Train Power Wagon – YOA

DR92331	Network Rail

Plasser & Theurer NPW-RT Materials Handling Train Power Wagon – YOA

DR92332	Network Rail

Plasser & Theurer MFS-SB Swivel Conveyer Wagon – YDA

DR92333	Network Rail	DR92336	Network Rail	DR92339	Network Rail
DR92334	Network Rail	DR92337	Network Rail	DR92340	Network Rail
DR92335	Network Rail	DR92338	Network Rail		

Plasser & Theurer MFS-D Ballast Distribution Train Hopper – YDA

DR92341	Network Rail	DR92354	Network Rail	DR92367	Network Rail
DR92342	Network Rail	DR92355	Network Rail	DR92368	Network Rail
DR92343	Network Rail	DR92356	Network Rail	DR92369	Network Rail
DR92344	Network Rail	DR92357	Network Rail	DR92370	Network Rail
DR92345	Network Rail	DR92358	Network Rail	DR92371	Network Rail
DR92346	Network Rail	DR92359	Network Rail	DR92372	Network Rail
DR92347	Network Rail	DR92360	Network Rail	DR92373	Network Rail
DR92348	Network Rail	DR92361	Network Rail	DR92374	Network Rail
DR92349	Network Rail	DR92362	Network Rail	DR92375	Network Rail
DR92350	Network Rail	DR92363	Network Rail	DR92376	Network Rail
DR92351	Network Rail	DR92364	Network Rail	DR92377	Colas
DR92352	Network Rail	DR92365	Network Rail		
DR92353	Network Rail	DR92366	Network Rail		

Plasser & Theurer MFS-A Materials Handling Train Interface Wagon – YDA

DR92400	Colas

Plasser & Theurer PW-RT Materials Handling Train Power Wagon

DR92431	Network Rail

Plasser & Theurer NPW-RT Materials Handling Train Power Wagon

DR92432	Network Rail

Plasser & Theurer MFS-SB Swivel Conveyer Wagon

DR92433	Network Rail	DR92437	Network Rail
DR92434	Network Rail	DR92438	Network Rail
DR92435	Network Rail	DR92439	Network Rail
DR92436	Network Rail	DR92440	Network Rail

Infrastructure Companies - Network Rail

Network Rail

Plasser & Theurer MFS-D Ballast Distribution Train Hopper – YDA

DR92441	Network Rail	DR92453	Network Rail	DR92465	Network Rail
DR92442	Network Rail	DR92454	Network Rail	DR92466	Network Rail
DR92443	Network Rail	DR92455	Network Rail	DR92467	Network Rail
DR92444	Network Rail	DR92456	Network Rail	DR92468	Network Rail
DR92445	Network Rail	DR92457	Network Rail	DR92469	Network Rail
DR92446	Network Rail	DR92458	Network Rail	DR92470	Network Rail
DR92447	Network Rail	DR92459	Network Rail	DR92471	Network Rail
DR92448	Network Rail	DR92460	Network Rail	DR92472	Network Rail
DR92449	Network Rail	DR92461	Network Rail	DR92473	Network Rail
DR92450	Network Rail	DR92462	Network Rail	DR92474	Network Rail
DR92451	Network Rail	DR92463	Network Rail	DR92475	Network Rail
DR92452	Network Rail	DR92464	Network Rail	DR92476	Network Rail

Sleeper Delivery Train – Generator Wagon – YFA

DR92501	(Stored)	DR92502	(Stored)	DR92503	(Stored)

Twin Jib Rail Recovery Train 'Slinger' – YFA

DR92504	(Stored)	DR92507	(Stored)	DR92510	(Stored)
DR92505	(Stored)	DR92508	(Stored)	DR92511	(Stored)
DR92506	(Stored)	DR92509	(Stored)	DR92512	(Stored)

Single Jib Rail Recovery Train 'Slinger' – YFA

DR92513	(Stored)	DR92515	(Stored)	DR92517	(Stored)
DR92514	(Stored)	DR92516	(Stored)	DR92518	(Stored)

Sleeper Delivery Train – Twin Crane 'Slinger' – YFA

DR92519	(Stored)

Sleeper Delivery Train – Generator Wagon 'Slinger' – YFA

DR92520	(Stored)	DR92522	(Stored)	DR92524	(Stored)
DR92521	(Stored)	DR92523	(Stored)	DR92525	(Stored)

Sleeper Delivery Train – Twin Crane 'Slinger' – YFA

DR92526	(Stored)	DR92529	(Stored)	DR92532	(Stored)
DR92527	(Stored)	DR92530	(Stored)		
DR92528	(Stored)	DR92531	(Stored)		

Sleeper Delivery Train – Generator Wagon 'Slinger' – YFA

DR92533	(Stored)	DR92534	(Stored)

Sleeper Delivery Train – Twin Crane 'Slinger' – YFA

DR92535	(Stored)	DR92539	(Stored)	DR92543	(Stored)
DR92536	(Stored)	DR92540	(Stored)	DR92544	(Stored)
DR92537	(Stored)	DR92541	(Stored)	DR92545	(Stored)
DR92538	(Stored)	DR92542	(Stored)	DR92546	(Stored)

Sleeper Delivery Train – Generator Wagon 'Slinger' – YFA

DR92547	(Stored)	DR92548	(Stored)	DR92549	(Stored)

Sleeper Delivery Train – Twin Crane 'Slinger' – YFA

DR92550	(Stored)	DR92558	(Stored)	DR92566	(Stored)
DR92551	(Stored)	DR92559	(Stored)	DR92567	(Stored)
DR92552	(Stored)	DR92560	(Stored)	DR92568	(Stored)
DR92553	(Stored)	DR92561	(Stored)	DR92569	(Stored)
DR92554	(Stored)	DR92562	(Stored)	DR92570	(Stored)
DR92555	(Stored)	DR92563	(Stored)	DR92571	(Stored)
DR92556	(Stored)	DR92564	(Stored)		
DR92557	(Stored)	DR92565	(Stored)		

W H Davis Sleeper Wagons – YXA

DR92601	Network Rail	DR92623	Network Rail	DR92645	Network Rail
DR92602	Network Rail	DR92624	Network Rail	DR92646	Network Rail
DR92603	Network Rail	DR92625	Network Rail	DR92647	Network Rail
DR92604	Network Rail	DR92626	Network Rail	DR92648	Network Rail
DR92605	Network Rail	DR92627	Network Rail	DR92649	Network Rail
DR92606	Network Rail	DR92628	Network Rail	DR92650	Network Rail
DR92607	Network Rail	DR92629	Network Rail	DR92651	Network Rail
DR92608	Network Rail	DR92630	Network Rail	DR92652	Network Rail
DR92609	Network Rail	DR92631	Network Rail	DR92653	Network Rail
DR92610	Network Rail	DR92632	Network Rail	DR92654	Network Rail
DR92611	Network Rail	DR92633	Network Rail	DR92655	Network Rail
DR92612	Network Rail	DR92634	Network Rail	DR92656	Network Rail
DR92613	Network Rail	DR92635	Network Rail	DR92657	Network Rail
DR92614	Network Rail	DR92636	Network Rail	DR92658	Network Rail
DR92615	Network Rail	DR92637	Network Rail	DR92659	Network Rail
DR92616	Network Rail	DR92638	Network Rail	DR92660	Network Rail
DR92617	Network Rail	DR92639	Network Rail	DR92661	Network Rail
DR92618	Network Rail	DR92640	Network Rail	DR92662	Network Rail
DR92619	Network Rail	DR92641	Network Rail	DR92663	Network Rail
DR92620	Network Rail	DR92642	Network Rail	DR92664	Network Rail
DR92621	Network Rail	DR92643	Network Rail	DR92665	Network Rail
DR92622	Network Rail	DR92644	Network Rail		

International Sleeper Wagons – YXA

31 70 4629 001 9	629001	Network Rail	31 70 4629 026 6	629026	Network Rail
31 70 4629 002 7	629002	Network Rail	31 70 4629 027 4	629027	Network Rail
31 70 4629 003 5	629003	Network Rail	31 70 4629 028 2	629028	Network Rail
31 70 4629 004 3	629004	Network Rail	31 70 4629 029 0	629029	Network Rail
31 70 4629 005 0	629005	Network Rail	31 70 4629 030 8	629030	Network Rail
31 70 4629 006 8	629006	Network Rail	31 70 4629 031 6	629031	Network Rail
31 70 4629 007 6	629007	Network Rail	31 70 4629 032 4	629032	Network Rail
31 70 4629 008 4	629008	Network Rail	31 70 4629 033 2	629033	Network Rail
31 70 4629 009 2	629009	Network Rail	31 70 4629 034 0	629034	Network Rail
31 70 4629 010 0	629010	Network Rail	31 70 4629 035 7	629035	Network Rail
31 70 4629 011 8	629011	Network Rail	31 70 4629 036 5	629036	Network Rail
31 70 4629 012 6	629012	Network Rail	31 70 4629 037 3	629037	Network Rail
31 70 4629 013 4	629013	Network Rail	31 70 4629 038 1	629038	Network Rail
31 70 4629 014 2	629014	Network Rail	31 70 4629 039 9	629039	Network Rail
31 70 4629 015 9	629015	Network Rail	31 70 4629 040 7	629040	Network Rail
31 70 4629 016 7	629016	Network Rail	31 70 4629 041 5	629041	Network Rail
31 70 4629 017 5	629017	Network Rail	31 70 4629 042 3	629042	Network Rail
31 70 4629 018 3	629018	Network Rail	31 70 4629 043 1	629043	Network Rail
31 70 4629 019 1	629019	Network Rail	31 70 4629 044 9	629044	Network Rail
31 70 4629 020 9	629020	Network Rail	31 70 4629 045 6	629045	Network Rail
31 70 4629 021 7	629021	Network Rail	31 70 4629 046 4	629046	Network Rail
31 70 4629 022 5	629022	Network Rail	31 70 4629 047 2	629047	Network Rail
31 70 4629 023 3	629023	Network Rail	31 70 4629 048 0	629048	Network Rail
31 70 4629 024 1	629024	Network Rail	31 70 4629 049 8	629049	Network Rail
31 70 4629 025 8	629025	Network Rail	31 70 4629 050 6	629050	Network Rail

W H Davis Flat/Workshop/Barrier Wagons – YSA

DR92701	Network Rail	DR92703	Network Rail	DR92705	Network Rail
DR92702	Network Rail	DR92704	Network Rail	DR92706	Network Rail

Cowans Sheldon 75 tonne Diesel Hydraulic Recovery Crane – ZIA* ZIB¤

ARDC96710¤ Network Rail (BS)   ARDC96714* Network Rail (MG)
ARDC96713¤ Network Rail (SP)   ARDC96715¤ Network Rail (TO)

Eiv de Brieve DU94BA – TRAMM – ZWA

DR97001   High Speed 1 (HS1)

Network Rail

Windhoff Overhead Line – MPV – YXA

DR97011	High Speed 1 (HS1)	DR97013	High Speed 1 (HS1)
DR97012	High Speed 1 (HS1)	DR97014	High Speed 1 (HS1)

Windhoff Overhead Line – MPV – YXA

DR98001 Network Rail	DR98004 Network Rail	DR98007 Network Rail	DR98010 Network Rail
DR98002 Network Rail	DR98005 Network Rail	DR98008 Network Rail	DR98011 Network Rail
DR98003 Network Rail	DR98006 Network Rail	DR98009 Network Rail	DR98014 Network Rail

Left: *Three of the Windhoff MPVs are seen powering a Network Rail overhead power equipment maintenance train at Tamworth. The leading vehicle is No. DR98009.* **Lee Martin**

Plasser & Theurer General Purpose Machine (GP-TRAMM) – ZWA

DR98215 Balfour Beatty	DR98217 Balfour Beatty	DR98219 Balfour Beatty
DR98216 Balfour Beatty	DR98218 Balfour Beatty	DR98220 Balfour Beatty

Geismar General Purpose Machine (GP-TRAMM)

DR98303   BAR

Geismar VMT860 PL/UM – ZWA

DR98305	Network Rail	DR98307(S)	Colas
DR98306	Network Rail	DR98308(S)	Colas

Below: *Geismar VMT860 maintenance trolley Nos. DR98305 and DR98306 are seen at Eastleigh.* **Antony Christie**

Rail Head Treatment Train (RHTT) FEA-F

642001 Network Rail	642011 Network Rail	642021 Network Rail	642031 Network Rail
642002 Network Rail	642012 Network Rail	642022 Network Rail	642032 Network Rail
642003 Network Rail	642013 Network Rail	642023 Network Rail	642033 Network Rail
642004 Network Rail	642014 Network Rail	642024 Network Rail	642034 Network Rail
642005 Network Rail	642015 Network Rail	642025 Network Rail	642035 Network Rail
642006 Network Rail	642016 Network Rail	642026 Network Rail	642036 Network Rail
642007 Network Rail	642017 Network Rail	642027 Network Rail	642037 Network Rail
642008 Network Rail	642018 Network Rail	642028 Network Rail	642038 Network Rail
642009 Network Rail	642019 Network Rail	642029 Network Rail	642039 Network Rail
642010 Network Rail	642020 Network Rail	642030 Network Rail	642040 Network Rail

642041	Network Rail	642044	Network Rail	642047	Network Rail	642050	Network Rail
642042	Network Rail	642045	Network Rail	642048	Network Rail		
642043	Network Rail	642046	Network Rail	642049	Network Rail		

Right: *Of the 50 Rail Head Treatment Trains (RHTT) wagons owned by Network Rail, 47 are rostered to be in traffic during the autumn leaf fall season working throughout the country in areas of known low adhesion to improve the performance of passenger and freight services. All vehicles are based at York and were introduced in 2008. Car No. 642042 is illustrated passing Totnes. For the 2012 leaf-fall season this was one of the vehicles based at St Blazey.* **Antony Christie**

Windhoff Multi Purpose Vehicle (MPV) – YXA

DR98901 + DR98951	Network Rail	DR98912 + DR98962	Network Rail	DR98923 + DR98973	Network Rail
DR98902 + DR98952	Network Rail	DR98913 + DR98963	Network Rail	DR98924 + DR98974	Network Rail
DR98903 + DR98953	Network Rail	DR98914 + DR98964	Network Rail	DR98925 + DR98975	Network Rail
DR98904 + DR98954	Network Rail	DR98915 + DR98965	Network Rail	DR98926 + DR98976	Network Rail
DR98905 + DR98955	Network Rail	DR98916 + DR98966	Network Rail	DR98927 + DR98977	Network Rail
DR98906 + DR98956	Network Rail	DR98917 + DR98967	Network Rail	DR98928 + DR98978	Network Rail
DR98907 + DR98957	Network Rail	DR98918 + DR98968	Network Rail	DR98929 + DR98979	Network Rail
DR98908 + DR98958	Network Rail	DR98919 + DR98969	Network Rail	DR98930 + DR98980	Network Rail
DR98909 + DR98959	Network Rail	DR98920 + DR98970	Network Rail	DR98931 + DR98981	Network Rail
DR98910 + DR98960	Network Rail	DR98921 + DR98971	Network Rail	DR98932 + DR98982	Network Rail
DR98911 + DR98961	Network Rail	DR98922 + DR98972	Network Rail		

Right: *A fleet of 32 Multi Purpose Vehicle twin-sets (MPVs) are operated by Network Rail. These are to be found all over the rail network and carry different equipment pods depending on the type of work being undertaken. This can range from general maintenance needs to the application of weed control liquid. MPV set Nos. DR98908 and DR98958 are illustrated approaching the crossing at Teigngrace on the Newton Abbot to Heathfield freight branch, where the set was involved in vegetation control.* **Antony Christie**

Rail Wagon – YEA 'Perch'

DR979001	Network Rail	DR979009	Network Rail	DR979017	Network Rail	DR979025	Network Rail
DR979002	Network Rail	DR979010	Network Rail	DR979018	Network Rail	DR979026	Network Rail
DR979003	Network Rail	DR979011	Network Rail	DR979019	Network Rail	DR979027	Network Rail
DR979004	Network Rail	DR979012	Network Rail	DR979020	Network Rail	DR979028	Network Rail
DR979005	Network Rail	DR979013	Network Rail	DR979021	Network Rail	DR979029	Network Rail
DR979006	Network Rail	DR979014	Network Rail	DR979022	Network Rail	DR979030	Network Rail
DR979007	Network Rail	DR979015	Network Rail	DR979023	Network Rail	DR979031	Network Rail
DR979008	Network Rail	DR979016	Network Rail	DR979024	Network Rail	DR979032	Network Rail

Network Rail

DR979033 Network Rail	DR979068 Network Rail	DR979103 Network Rail
DR979034 Network Rail	DR979069 Network Rail	DR979104 Network Rail
DR979035 Network Rail	DR979070 Network Rail	DR979105 Network Rail
DR979036 Network Rail	DR979071 Network Rail	DR979106 Network Rail
DR979037 Network Rail	DR979072 Network Rail	DR979107 Network Rail
DR979038 Network Rail	DR979073 Network Rail	DR979108 Network Rail
DR979039 Network Rail	DR979074 Network Rail	DR979109 Network Rail
DR979040 Network Rail	DR979075 Network Rail	DR979110 Network Rail
DR979041 Network Rail	DR979076 Network Rail	DR979111 Network Rail
DR979042 Network Rail	DR979077 Network Rail	DR979112 Network Rail
DR979043 Network Rail	DR979078 Network Rail	DR979113 Network Rail
DR979044 Network Rail	DR979079 Network Rail	DR979114 Network Rail
DR979045 Network Rail	DR979080 Network Rail	DR979115 Network Rail
DR979046 Network Rail	DR979081 Network Rail	DR979116 Network Rail
DR979047 Network Rail	DR979082 Network Rail	DR979117 Network Rail
DR979048 Network Rail	DR979083 Network Rail	DR979118 Network Rail
DR979049 Network Rail	DR979084 Network Rail	DR979119 Network Rail
DR979050 Network Rail	DR979085 Network Rail	DR979120 Network Rail
DR979051 Network Rail	DR979086 Network Rail	DR979121 Network Rail
DR979052 Network Rail	DR979087 Network Rail	DR979122 Network Rail
DR979053 Network Rail	DR979088 Network Rail	DR979123 Network Rail
DR979054 Network Rail	DR979089 Network Rail	DR979124 Network Rail
DR979055 Network Rail	DR979090 Network Rail	DR979125 Network Rail
DR979056 Network Rail	DR979091 Network Rail	DR979126 Network Rail
DR979057 Network Rail	DR979092 Network Rail	DR979127 Network Rail
DR979058 Network Rail	DR979093 Network Rail	DR979128 Network Rail
DR979059 Network Rail	DR979094 Network Rail	DR979129 Network Rail
DR979060 Network Rail	DR979095 Network Rail	DR979130 Network Rail
DR979061 Network Rail	DR979096 Network Rail	DR979131 Network Rail
DR979062 Network Rail	DR979097 Network Rail	DR979132 Network Rail
DR979063 Network Rail	DR979098 Network Rail	DR979133 Network Rail
DR979064 Network Rail	DR979099 Network Rail	DR979134 Network Rail
DR979065 Network Rail	DR979100 Network Rail	
DR979066 Network Rail	DR979101 Network Rail	
DR979067 Network Rail	DR979102 Network Rail	

Continuous Welded Rail Clamping Wagon – YEA 'Perch'

DR979409 Network Rail	DR979412 Network Rail	DR979415 Network Rail

Continuous Welded Rail End of Train Wagon – YEA 'Porpoise'

DR979505 Network Rail	DR979509 Network Rail	DR979513 Network Rail	DR979515 Network Rail
DR979506 Network Rail	DR979511 Network Rail	DR979514 Network Rail	

Left: *Continuous welded rail end of train wagon No. DR979585 – a YEA 'Porpoise' is seen empty, passing along the Dawlish sea wall.* **CJM**

Continuous Welded Rail 'Chute' Wagon – YEA 'Porpoise'

DR979500 Network Rail	DR979502 Network Rail	DR979507 Network Rail	DR979510 Network Rail
DR979501 Network Rail	DR979503 Network Rail	DR979508 Network Rail	DR979512 Network Rail

Continuous Welded Rail Gantry Wagon – YEA 'Perch'

DR979604	Network Rail	DR979611	Network Rail	DR979614	Network Rail
DR979607	Network Rail	DR979612	Network Rail		
DR979609	Network Rail	DR979613	Network Rail		

Plasser & Theurer EM-SAT RT900 Survey Vehicle

DR999800	*Richard Spoors*	Network Rail
DR999801		Network Rail

Above: *One of the more unusual track maintenance vehicles is this Plasser & Theurer EM-SAT RT900 survey vehicle No. DR999800 Richard Spoors. The vehicle is seen stabled between duties at Watford Junction.* **Stacey Thew**

Swedish Rail Vacuum

99709	Railcare, Sweden*	*operated in the UK

Winter Development Train 'Perch'

99709594014-1 IS	977986 IS

Balfour Beatty Rail Services

Address: ✉ 130 Wilton Road, London, SW1V 4LQ
   ✍ info@bbrail.com
   ✆ 0207 216 6800
   ⓘ www.bbrail.com

Managing Director: Peter Anderson   **Depot:** Ashford (AD)

Hauled Stock

Mk1	Height: 12ft 9½in (3.89m)	
Vehicle Length: 64ft 6in (19.65m)	Width: 9ft 3in (2.81m)	

Number	Type	Depot	Livery	Operator	Use
977163 (35487)	Mk1/BSK	AD	BBR	BBR	Staff & Generator coach
977165 (35408)	Mk1/BSK	AD	BBR	BBR	Staff & Generator coach
977166 (35419)	Mk1/BSK	AD	BBR	BBR	Staff & Generator coach
977167 (35400)	Mk1/BSK	AD	BBR	BBR	Staff & Generator coach
977168 (35289)	Mk1/BSK	AD	BBR	BBR	Staff & Generator coach

Alstom Transport

Address: ✉ PO Box 70, Newbold Road, Rugby, Warwickshire, CV21 2WR

✉ info@transport.alstom.com © 01788 577111, ⓘ www.transport.alstom.com

Managing Director: Paul Robinson

Facilities: Following the assembly of the Virgin Trains Class 390 'Pendolino' stock, Alstom closed down its UK production facility at Washwood Heath, Birmingham. However, the company still operates from many specialist sites in mainland Europe and if Alstom win further new-build contracts in the UK, these will be assembled in Europe.

Depots: Chester (CH), Liverpool - Edge Hill (LL), Manchester - Longsight (MA), Wolverhampton - Oxley (OY), Wembley (WB)

Class 08

Vehicle Length: 29ft 3in (8.91m)
Height: 12ft 8⅝in (3.87m)
Width: 8ft 6in (2.59m)
Engine: English Electric 6K
Horsepower: 400hp (298kW)
Electrical Equipment: English Electric

Number	Depot	Pool	Livery	Owner	Operator
08451	AT	ATZZ	BLK	ALS	ALS
08454	WB	ATLO	BLK	ALS	ALS
08611	MA	ATLO	VT1	ALS	ALS
08617	WB	ATLO	BLK	ALS	ALS
08696	AT	ATLO	GRN	ALS	ALS
08721	AT	ATLO	BLU	ALS	ALS
08790	AT	ATLO	BLU	ALS	ALS
08887	AT	ATZZ	BLK	ALS	ALS

Names applied
08451 *M A Smith*
08790 *Starlet*
08721 *Downside CS*

Bombardier Transportation

Address: ✉ Litchurch Lane, Derby, DE24 8AD

✉ info@bombardier.com © 01332 344666, ⓘ www.bombardier.com

Chief Country Representative: Paul Roberts

Works: Derby (ZD), Crewe (ZC)

Facilities: Bombardier Transportation is one of the largest transport builders in the world, with offices and building facilities in many countries. Its product range extends well beyond rail vehicles and includes aircraft, boats and leisure equipment.

In terms of the UK, two main sites are located in Derby (Litchurch Lane) and Crewe. New-build work is undertaken at the Derby site, which mainly concentrates on electric and diesel multiple-unit designs.

Class 08

Vehicle Length: 29ft 3in (8.91m)
Height: 12ft 8⅝in (3.87m)
Width: 8ft 6in (2.59m)
Engine: English Electric 6K
Horsepower: 400hp (298kW)
Electrical Equipment: English Electric

Number	Depot	Pool	Livery	Owner	Operator	Name
08682 (D3849)	ZD	INDL	GRN	BOM	BOM	Lionheart
08846 (No. 3)	ZD	INDL	BOM	BOM	BOM	

Left: The Bombardier Works in Litchurch Lane, Derby, is one of the only sites in the UK where new train construction can be undertaken. The works has in recent years been responsible for the design and building of the 'Electrostar' and 'Turbostar' product ranges and it is hoped further new orders will be awarded to the site. This view shows a Class 377 under assembly.
CJM

ABC Rail Guide 2013

Electro-Motive Diesels (EMD)

Address: ✉ Electro-Motive Diesels Inc, 9301 West 55th Street, LaGrange, Illinois, USA, 60525

Electro-Motive Diesels Inc, Muncie, Indiana, USA

🖷 info@emdiesels.com ✆ +1 (800) 255 5355, ⓘ www.emdiesels.com

Facilities: Formerly part of General Motors, Electro-Motive is one of the two largest loco builders in the world. Its main production facility is in Muncie, Indiana, USA. Production from this site took over from the London, Ontario, Canada, plant in 2012. In terms of the UK, the JT42CWRM or Class 66 were all built at the Canadian facility. EMD is now owned by Progress Rail, a part of the Caterpillar Group.

General Electric (GE)

Address: ✉ GE Transportation Rail, 2901 East Lake Road, Erie, Pennsylvania, USA, 16531

UK office: Inspira House, Martinfield, Welwyn Garden City, Herts, AL7 1GW

🖷 info@getransportation.com ✆ 01707 383700 ⓘ www.getransportation.com

Chief Executive Officer: Lorenzo Simonelli

Facilities: General Electric have only recently entered the UK loco arena, and are currently fulfilling an order for 'PowerHaul' locomotives for Freightliner. The company operates a huge construction facility in Erie, Pennsylvania, USA where the UK locos are being built.

Class 70 - PH37ACmi

Vehicle Length: 71ft 2½in (21.71m)				Engine: GE V16-cylinder PowerHaul 616			
Height: 12ft 10in (3.91m)				Horsepower: 3,700hp (2,750kW)			
Width: 8ft 8in (2.64m)				Electrical Equipment: General Electric			

Number	Depot	Pool	Livery	Owner	Operator	Name/Notes
70099 (DE37001)	HQ	MBDL	GRN	GE	GBR	To operate under trials for GBRf

Above: *The General Electric Company of Erie, Pennsylvania, USA, broke into the UK loco building market in 2009 with the delivery of the first Class 70 for Freightliner. The company had hopes of further significant orders but by 2012 these had not been forthcoming. In late 2012, a Turkish-built Class 70 identified as No. 70099 was delivered to the UK for trial and demonstration work. It is seen in this illustration at Crewe, awaiting transfer to Brush Traction of Loughborough.*
Cliff Beeton

Hitachi Europe Ltd

Address: ✉ 16 Upper Woburn Place, London, WC1H 0AF
      ✍ hirofumi.ojima@hitachi-eu.com
      ✆ 0207 970 2700,
      ⓘ www.hitachi-rail.com

Facilities: Hitachi Rail, one of the newer names to the UK rail scene, won the contract to design, build, test and manage the fleet of Class 395 EMUs used for domestic services on HS1. In 2009, the company formed the construction arm of Aglity Trains awarded the IEP project to design, build and introduce the next generation of high speed passenger trains in the UK.

Hitachi are now building construction facilities in the UK at Newton Aycliffe, County Durham.

In 2012, it was announced that the DfT required 596 IEP vehicles for the Great Western franchise and Phase 1 of the East Coast operation, equating to 92 trains. A further 498 vehicles would be needed for the second phase of East Coast, Great Western, West Coast and Cambridge line operations. For the core routes of Phase 1, Great Western will operate a mix of five-car bi-mode and eight-car electric sets on a daily basis plus spare sets, while East Cast will operate 10 five-car electric sets, eight bi-mode sets and 10 nine-car bi-mode sets on a daily basis. This equates to a total of 77 sets being in passenger service every day. 250 vehicles will incorporate one MTU 12V 1600R80L underfloor engine

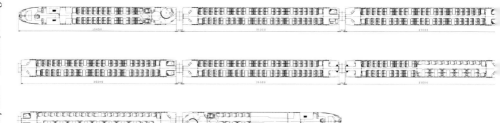

Above: *Drawing of the proposed Hitachi InterCity Express train. The above shows the layout of an eight-car electric and bi-mode set. This shows the set formed DPTS with 48 standard class seats, two wheelchair spaces and one disabled access toilet, MS with 88 standard class seats one toilet, MS with 88 seats and two toilets, TS with 88 seats and two toilets, TS with 88 seats with no toilets, MC with 30 first class and 38 standard class seats with no toilets, MF with 56 first class seats and two toilets and DF with 15 first class seats, two wheelchair sets one catering facility and 1 disabled access toilet.* **DfT**

Arlington Fleet Services

Address: ✉ Eastleigh Rail Works, Campbell Road, Eastleigh, Hampshire, SO50 5AD
      ✍ info@Arlington-fleet.co.uk   ✆ 02380 698789, ⓘ www.arlington-fleet.com

Managing Director: Barry Stephens

Facilities: Arlington Fleet Group offer high-quality rail engineering services to all vehicle owners. They are based in the former loco/carriage works at Eastleigh.

Depots: Eastleigh (ZG), Shoeburyness (SN)

Class 07

						Vehicle Length: 26ft 9½in (8.16m)	Engine: Paxman 6RPHL MkIII
						Height: 12ft 10in (3.91m)	Horsepower: 275hp (205kW)
						Width: 8ft 6in (2.59m)	Electrical Equipment: AEI

Number	Depot	Pool	Livery	Owner	Operator
07007 (D2991)	ZG	MBDL	BLU	AFG	AFG

Right: *Knights Rail Services sold their Eastleigh business operation to Arlington Fleet Services in 2012 and the loco assets transferred to the new owner. One of the most popular locos on the Eastleigh site is original Southampton Docks Class 07 diesel-electric 0-6-0 shunting loco No. 07007 (D2991). This loco is used for much of the shunting of vehicles and locomotives around the extensive workshop area. It is seen in the works yard coupled to a withdrawn Metropolitan Line London Transport unit, with a Silverlink-liveried Class 508 behind.* **Antony Christie**

Ex-DB (Germany) Class 323

Former German shunting locos, built by Gmeinder and now owned by Northumbria Rail and used at Eastleigh Works by Arlington Fleet Services for pilotage.

Number	Depot	Pool	Livery	Owner	Operator
323-539-7	ZG	-	-	NHR	AFS
323-674-2	ZG	-	-	NHR	AFS

Right: *Two former German 0-4-0 diesel shunting locos of Class 323 are now at Arlington Fleet Services, Eastleigh. Officially owned by Northumbria Rail, the two share depot shunting duties with the Class 07. No, 323-674-2 is seen in the works yard coupled to a former SouthEastern Class 508 unit.* **Antony Christie**

London & North Western Railway Company (LNWR)

Address: ✉ LNWR Co Ltd, PO Box 111, Crewe, Cheshire. CW1 2FB

📠 allservicedeliverymanagers@lnwr.com   ☎ 01270 508000,   ⓘ www.lnwr.com

Managing Director: Mark Knowles

Facilities: LNWR is a high-quality engineering company, owned by Arriva and based at Crewe, with outbased facilities at Bristol, Eastleigh, Cambridge and Tyne.

Depot: Crewe (CO), Bristol Barton Hill (BK), Eastleigh (EH), Cambridge (CA), Tyne (TY)

Train Engineering Companies – Arlington Fleet Services, LNWR

Number	Depot	Pool	Livery	Owner	Operator	Name
08442	EH	MBDL	BRT	LNW	LNW	Richard J Wenham Eastleigh Depot December 1989 - July 1999
08516	BK	MBDL	LNW	LNW	LNW	Rory
08810	CO	MBDL	LNW	LNW	LNW	
08830	CO	MBDL	BLK	LNW	LNW	
09204	CC	MBDL	BRD	LNW	LNW	

Left: Owned by Arriva, the London & North Western Railway workshops at Crewe, Eastleigh, Bristol Barton Hill, Cambridge and Tyne offer high-quality specialist engineering services to the rail industry. To shunt vehicles within the sites a small number of Class 08s are operated under the LNWR banner. One is No. 08810, seen at Crewe sporting full LNWR livery.
Brian Morrison

Pullman Group (Colas Rail Freight)

Address: ✉ Train Maintenance Depot, Leckwith Road, Cardiff, CF11 8HP
📠 sales@pullmans.net ☎ 029 2036 8850, ⓘ www.pullmans.net
Managing Director: Colin Robinson
Facilities: Pullman Rail operates from part of the former Canton depot in Cardiff and provides a quality engineering service to all types of rail vehicles.
Depot: Cardiff Canton (CF)

Class 08

Vehicle Length: 29ft 3in (8.91m)	Engine: English Electric 6K
Height: 12ft 8⅝in (3.87m)	Horsepower: 400hp (298kW)
Width: 8ft 6in (2.59m)	Electrical Equipment: English Electric

Number	Depot	Pool	Livery	Owner	Operator
08499	CF	WSXX	BLU	DBS	PUL

The Pullman Group based at Cardiff Canton, now part of the GBRf operation, has one Class 08 on its books, No. 08499, which is painted in all-over mid-blue and offset by white numbers and yellow/black wasp ends. The loco is seen with a shunting truck in the yard at the depot.
Brian Morrison

Railcare Ltd

Address: ✉ Wolverton Works, Stratford Road, Wolverton, Milton Keynes, MK12 5NT
☏ info@railcare.co.uk ✆ 08000 741122, ⓘ www.railcare.co.uk
Managing Director: Colin Love, **Depots:** Glasgow (ZH), Wolverton (ZN)
Owner: Ombros Group

Class 08

Vehicle Length: 29ft 3in (8.91m)				Engine: English Electric 6K		
Height: 12ft 8⅝in (3.87m)				Horsepower: 400hp (298kW)		
Width: 8ft 6in (2.59m)				Electrical Equipment: English Electric		

Number	Depot	Pool	Livery	Owner	Operator	Name
08568	ZH	RCZH	ALS	RCL	RCL	St Rollox
08629	ZN	RCZN	RCL	RCL	RCL	
08649	ZN	RCZN	WEX	RCL	RCL	
08730	ZH	RCZH	ALS	RCL	RCL	The Caley

Right: *Railcare, the operators of the large railway works in Wolverton and Glasgow, operate four standard Class 08 0-6-0 shunting locos, two at each site. One of the pair allocated to Wolverton, No. 08629, sports this bright red, white and blue colour scheme, offset by yellow/black wasp ends. The loco is seen here while operating on a preserved railway, complete with a 'Gronks on Tour' headboard.* **Norman E. Preedy**

Rail Vehicle Engineering Ltd

Address: ✉ Vehicles Workshop, RTC Business Park, London Road, Derby, DE24 8UP
☏ enquiries@rvel.co.uk ✆ 01332 331210, ⓘ www.rvel.co.uk
Managing Director: Andy Lynch
Depot: Derby (DF)

Class 08

Vehicle Length: 29ft 3in (8.91m)			Engine: English Electric 6K		
Height: 12ft 8⅝in (3.87m)			Horsepower: 400hp (298kW)		
Width: 8ft 6in (2.59m)			Electrical Equipment: English Electric		

Number	Depot	Pool	Livery	Owner	Operator
08536	DF	RVLS	-	RVE	RVE
08697	DF	RVLS	EMT	RVE	RVE

Class 31/1, 31/4

Vehicle Length: 56ft 9in (17.29m)			Engine: English Electric 12SVT		
Height: 12ft 7in (3.91m)			Horsepower: 1,470hp (1,097kW)		
Width: 8ft 9in (2.65m)			Electrical Equipment: Brush		
Class 31/4 - Fitted with Electric Train Heat. Class 31/6 - Fitted with through wiring					

Number		Depot	Pool	Livery	Owner	Operator	Name
31106		DF	RVLO	BLU	HJA	RVE	
31422	(31310)	DF	RVLS	INT	RVE	RVE	Cerberus
31459	(31256)	DF	RVLO	BLK	RVE	RVE	Hydra
31468(S)	(31568, 31321)	DF	RVLS	BLK	RVE	RVE	

Left: *Rail Vehicle Engineering Ltd, which operate from the former vehicle workshop within the Railway Technical Centre, Derby, employ and manage a fleet of Class 31s which are generally used to power Network Rail test trains. Class 31/1 No. 31106, painted in rail blue and owned by Howard Johnson, is seen with a Network Rail test train at Newton Abbot.* **Antony Christie**

Class 73/1

Vehicle Length: 53ft 8in (16.35m)				*Power:* 750V dc third rail or English Electric 6K		
Height: 12ft 5⅜in (3.79m)				*Horsepower:* electric - 1,600hp (1,193kW)		
Width: 8ft 8in (2.64m)				*Horsepower:* diesel - 600hp (447kW)		
				Electrical Equipment: English Electric		

Number	Depot	Pool	Livery	Owner	Operator	Notes
73101	DF	RVLO	PUL	RVE	RVE	Super ED project
73104	DF	RVLO	(NRL)	RVE	NRL	Super ED project
73139	DF	RVLO	PUL	RVE	RVE	
73211	DF	RVLO	(NRL)	RVE	NRL	Super ED project (loco 1)

73104/211 to be rebuilt with 2 x Cummins CSK19 750hp engines to provide high output electro-diesel loco, due in 2013.

Siemens Transportation

Address: ✉ Kings Heath Traincare Facility, Heathfield Way, Kings Heath, Northampton, NN5 7QP

enquiries@siemenstransportation.co.uk ✆ 01604 594500

ⓘ www.siemenstransportation.co.uk

Managing Director UK: Steve Scrimshaw

Depots: Ardwick, Manchester (AK), Kings Heath, Northampton (NN), Northam, Southampton (NT)

Class 01.5

Number	Depot	Pool	Livery	Owner	Operator	Name
01551 (H016)	AK	MBDL	WAB	WAB	SIE	*Lancelot*

Barrier Wagons

Number	Depot	Pool	Livery	Owner	Operator	Notes
6321 (96385, 86515)	NN	SIEM	BLU	SIE	-	Desiro stock barrier wagon
6322 (93686, 86859)	NN	SIEM	BLU	SIE	-	Desiro stock barrier wagon
6323 (96387, 86973)	NN	SIEM	BLU	SIE	-	Desiro stock barrier wagon
6324 (96388, 86562)	CP	SIEM	BLU	SIE	-	Desiro stock barrier wagon
6325 (96389, 86135)	NN	SIEM	BLU	SIE	-	Desiro stock barrier wagon

Address: ✉ Ashby Park, Ashby de la Zouch, Leicestershire, LE65 1JD

✆ uk.mobility@siemens.com ✆ 01530 258000

ⓘ www.siemens.co.uk/mobility

Managing Director UK: Steve Scrimshaw

Facilities: Siemens is now an established provider of UK EMU and DMU rolling stock with various derivatives of its 'Desiro' product line. While having maintenance facilities in the UK, Siemens performs all new-build work in mainland Europe at its Krefeld/Uerdingen factory in Germany. Testing of vehicles is performed in Germany before delivery at the world-famous test track at Wildenrath.

Wabtec

Brush Traction, Loughborough

Address: ✉ PO Box 17, Loughborough, Leicestershire, LE11 1HS

📠 sales@brushtraction.com ✆ 01509 617000, ⓘ www.brushtraction.com

Managing Director: John Bidewell

Facilities: The world-famous name of Brush Traction, based in Loughborough, is now part of the Wabtec Group. In recent years the site has been responsible for the majority of UK loco building. The company has been synonymous with loco building for the UK and overseas markets for many years. Although recent main line loco builds have been awarded overseas, the facilities at the Loughborough plant where the Class 31, 47, 60, Eurotunnel Shuttle locos and the Class 57s emerged are still available for new-build work. Recently the site has concentrated on re-build operations including the highly successful re-engining of the HST fleet with MTU power units for First Group, East Coast, Grand Central and Network Rail. In 2012-13 the site was undertaking work for General Electric/Freightliner, Arriva, First Group, as well as the re-engineering of a Class 73 with an MTU power unit. The site is fully rail connected. In late 2012, Wabtec purchased L H Group Services.

Doncaster

Address: ✉ PO Box 400, Doncaster Works, Hexthorpe Road, Doncaster, DN1 1SL

📠 wabtecrail@wabtec.com ✆ 01302 340700, ⓘ www.wabtecrail.co.uk

Managing Director: John Meehan

Depot: Doncaster (ZB)

Class 08

Vehicle Length: 29ft 3in (8.91m)			Engine: English Electric 6K			
Height: 12ft 8⅝in (3.87m)			Horsepower: 400hp (298kW)			
Width: 8ft 6in (2.59m)			Electrical Equipment: English Electric			

Number	Depot	Pool	Livery	Owner	Operator	Name
08472	EC	RFSH	BLK	WAB	ICE	
08571	ZB	RFSH	WAB	WAB	ICE	
08596(S)	ZB	RFSH	WAB	WAB	NXE	
08615	ZB	RFSH	WAB	WAB	NXE	
08669	ZB	RFSH	WAB	WAB	WAB	Bob Machin
08724	ZB	RFSH	WAB	WAB	WAB	
08764	ZB	MBDL	BLU	WAB	TRN	Old Tom
08853	ZB	RFSH	BLU	WAB	WAB	
08871	ZB	MBDL	COT	WAB	‡	

‡ Working as Teesport

Coaching Stock

Vehicle Length: 75ft 0in (22.86m)		Width: 8ft 11in (2.71m)
Height: 12ft 9in (3.88m)		Bogie Type: BT10

NX5G - NGV

Number	Depot	Livery	Owner
96374(S) (10585)	ZB	EPS	WAB

Right: *Used to provide a train supply for the testing of overhauled loco-hauled and HST passenger stock at Wabtec, Doncaster, this former European Night Star generator carriage looks the worse for wear.* **Derek Porter**

Scotland (Previously Brush Barclay)

Address: ✉ Caledonia Works, West Langlands Street, Kilmarnock, Ayrshire, KA1 2QD

📠 sales@brushtraction.com ✆ 01563 523573, ⓘ www.brushtraction.com

Managing Director: John Bidewell

Facilities: The Wabtec site in Scotland concentrates on vehicle overhaul and refurbishment, including EMU, DMU and loco-hauled vehicles as well as HST stock.

Europhoenix Ltd

Address: ✉ 58A High Street, Stony Stratford, Milton Keynes, MK11 1AX

📠 info@europhoenix.eu © 01467 624366, ① www.europhoenix.eu

Facilities: Europhoenix have purchased redundant Class 56, 86 and 87 locos; these are offered to Continental European operators fully refurbished and modified to suit customer needs.

Class 56

Vehicle Length: 63ft 6in (19.35m)	Engine: Ruston Paxman 16RK3CT
Height: 13ft 0in (3.96m)	Horsepower: 3,250hp (2,420kW)
Width: 9ft 2in (2.79m)	Electrical Equipment: Brush

Number	Owner	Location	Livery	Operator
56086	EPX	WH	BLU	EPX
56096	EPX	WH	FER	EPX
56101 (92 55 0659 001-5)	EPX	-	BLK	Hire to Floyd, Hungary
56115 (92 55 0659 002-3)	EPX	-	BLK	Hire to Floyd, Hungary
56117 (92 55 0659 003-1)	EPX	-	BLK	Hire to Floyd, Hungary
56301 (56045)	EPX	-	FLF	EPX

Left: *The Europhoenix company has masterminded a number of overseas hire contracts involving Class 86 electric locos and Class 56 diesel-electric locos, mainly for Hungarian operator Floyd. In 2012, three Class 56s, Nos. 56101/115/117 were overhauled at Burton and exported to Hungary. No. 92 55 0659 002-3 is seen departing from the Nemesis Rail facility at Burton en route to Hungary.* **Stuart Hillis**

Class 86

Vehicle Length: 58ft 6in (17.83m)	Power Collection: 25kV ac overhead
Height: 13ft 0⅝in (3.97m)	Horsepower: 5,900hp (4,400kW)
Width: 8ft 8¼in (2.64m)	Electrical Equipment: GEC

Number	Location	Hire to						
86215	EXP	Floyd (Hungary)	86232	LM	-	86250	XX	Floyd (Hungary)
86217	EXP	Floyd (Hungary)	86233	EXP	Floyd (Hungary)	86251	LM	-
86218	EXP	Floyd (Hungary)	86234	LM	-	86424	LM	-
86226	LM	-	86235	LM	-	(Now with AC Loco Group)		
86228	EXP	Floyd (Hungary)	86242	LM	-	86621	CC	-
86229	LM	-	86246	LM	-	86633	CC	-
86231	LM	-	86247	LNWR	(Spares)±	86635	CC	-
			86248	EXP	Floyd (Hungary)	± DHLT pool		

Class 87

Vehicle Length: 58ft 6in (17.83m)	Power Collection: 25kV ac overhead
Height: 13ft 1¼in (3.99m)	Horsepower: 7,860hp (5,680kW)
Width: 8ft 8¼in (2.64m)	Electrical Equipment: GEC

Number	Owner	Status	Location	Livery	Name
87009	EPX	Stored	EXP	VIR	
87017	EPX	Operational	EXP	EPX	*Iron Duke*
87023	EPX	Operational	EXP	EPX	*Velocity*
87025	EPX	Stored	EXP	VIR	

(Hire locomotives in Bulgaria working for short line operator Bulmarket)

Above: *Europhoenix-based at Long Marston overhauled a number of Class 87s for use in Bulgaria by operator BZK, which have operated freight services for several years. In 2012, four further '87s' were exported to Bulgaria, Nos. 87009/017/ 023/025, of which Nos. 87017/023 were fully refurbished with dual pantographs and fully operational, painted in grey and blue Europhoenix livery. The other two were shipped unrefurbished. These locomotives are used by Bulgarian open access operator Bulmarket. Prior to shipment, No. 87023 Velocity is seen at Long Marston.* **Antony Christie**

Porterbrook

Address: ✉ Burdett House, Becket Street, Derby, DE1 1JP

✐ enquiries@porterbrook.co.uk ✆ 01332 262405, ⓘ www.porterbrook.co.uk

Managing Director: Paul Francis

Facilities: Porterbrook Leasing have made available the off-lease Class 87s to mainland European operators, with a significant number being exported to operate in Bulgaria.

Exported

Number	Present operator						
87003	BZK Bulgaria	87007	BZK Bulgaria	87014	BZK Bulgaria	87028	BZK Bulgaria
87004	BZK Bulgaria	87008	BZK Bulgaria	87019	BZK Bulgaria	87029	BZK Bulgaria
	Britannia	87010	BZK Bulgaria	87020	BZK Bulgaria	87033	BZK Bulgaria
87006	BZK Bulgaria	87012	BZK Bulgaria	87022	BZK Bulgaria	87034	BZK Bulgaria
		87013	BZK Bulgaria	87026	BZK Bulgaria		

Right: *Painted in standard Bulgarian Railways green and yellow livery, Class 87 No. 87010 is seen at Senovo on 5 October 2010. A number of different liveries are carried by these Class 87s, including blue, green, Network SouthEast, LNWR black and Cotswold grey.* **A. P. Sayer**

Angel Trains

Address: ✉ Portland House, Bressenden Place, London, SW1E 5BH

✉ reception@angeltrains.co.uk ✆ 0207 592 0500, ⓘ www.angeltrains.co.uk

Chief Executive: Malcolm Brown

Owned by: Babcock Brown, AMP Capital & Deutsche Bank

British American Railway Services

Incorporating: RMS Locotec, RT Rail, Dartmoor Railway, Devon & Cornwall Railways, Weardale Railway, Ealing Community Transport and Hanson Rail

Address: ✉ London Riverside, London, SE1 2AQ

President: Ed Ellis

Depots: RMS Wakefield (ZS), Washwood Heath (WH)

UK operation is part of Iowa Pacific Holdings. BARS is also a Train Operating Company.

Class 08

Vehicle Length: 29ft 3in (8.91m)				Engine: English Electric 6K						
Height: 12ft 8⅝in (3.87m)				Horsepower: 400hp (298kW)						
Width: 8ft 6in (2.59m)				Electrical Equipment: English Electric						

Number	Depot	Pool	Livery	Owner	Operator					
08308	IS	MRSO	FSR	ECT	FSR	08750	ZB	MRSO	BLK	ECT	IND
08423	ZS	INDL	RMS	RMS	IND	08754	±	MRSO	BLU	ECT	IND
08573	ZB	MRSO	BLK	ECT	BOM	08756	MR	MRSO	GRY	ECT	GBR
08588	WH	MRSO	BLK	ECT	IND	08762	ZB	MRSO	BLK	ECT	CEM
08613	§	MOLO	BLU	RMS	IND	08870	ZS	MBDL	BLG	RMS	IND
08622	ZS	INDL	BLU	RMS	IND	08873	ZB	MRSO	HUN	ECT	FLR
08648	ZB	INDL	YEL	BAR	IND	08885	ZS	INDL	GBR	RMS	GBR
						08936	ZS	MBDL	BLU	RMS	IND

§ at Onllwyn
± at Allelys, Studley

Left: *Looking rather the worse for wear, ex-BR Class 08 No. 08588 in black livery with a grey roof is seen shunting at Washwood Heath.*
Antony Christie

Class 20

Vehicle Length: 46ft 9¼in (14.26m)				Engine: English Electric 8SVT Mk2		
Height: 12ft 7⅝in (3.84m)				Horsepower: 1,000hp (745kW)		
Width: 8ft 9in (2.66m)				Electrical Equipment: English Electric		

Number	Depot	Pool	Livery	Owner	Operator
20189	BH	MOLO	GRN	C20	BAR
20227	LUL	MOLO	RFG	C20	BAR

To be repainted in LUL liveries

Right: *The two British American Railway-operated Class 20s are both privately owned but have a full main line certificate. The pair are sometimes used on the GBRf contract to haul London Underground 'S' stock between Derby and Old Dalby or between Old Dalby and London. The locos are seen passing Barton under Needwood near Burton.* **Matt Clarke**

Class 31/1, 31/4 & 31/6

Vehicle Length: 56ft 9in (17.29m)	Engine: English Electric 12SVT
Height: 12ft 7in (3.91m)	Horsepower: 1,470hp (1,097kW)
Width: 8ft 9in (2.65m)	Electrical Equipment: Brush
31/4 Fitted with Electric Train Heat, 31/6 through wired	

Number		Depot	Pool	Livery	Owner	Operator
31190		WH	HTLX	GRN	BAR	- (Spot hire)
31452	(31552/279)	WH	HTLX	DCG	ECT	ECT
31454	(31554, 31228)	WH	HTLX	ICS	BAR	Weardale
31601	(31186)	WH	HTLX	DCG	BAR	RVE
31602	(31191)	WH	HTLX	NRL	BAR	RVE

Right: *Five Class 31s, from sub-classes 31/1, 31/4 and 31/6, are operated by British American Railways, based at Washwood Heath, Birmingham. The locos are available for spot hire work and two are operated by Devon & Cornwall Railways. No. 31454 is seen at Ruddington.* **Antony Christie**

Class 56

Vehicle Length: 63ft 6in (19.35m)	Engine: Ruston Paxman 16RK3CT
Height: 13ft 0in (3.96m)	Horsepower: 3,250hp (2,420kW)
Width: 9ft 2in (2.79m)	Electrical Equipment: Brush

Number		Depot	Pool	Livery	Owner	Operator
56060(S)		WH	-	-	PRI	- (owned by Zweig Ltd)
56065(S)		WH	-	-	PRI	-
56081(S)		BU	-	-	PRI	- (owned by Zweig Ltd)
56091(S)		WH	HTLX	-	BAR	-
56103(S)		WH	HTLX	-	BAR	-
56303	(56125)	WH	HTLX	GRN	BAR	BAR
56311	(56057)	WH	HTLX	GRY	BAR	BAR
56312	(56003)	WH	HTLX	GRY	BAR	BAR
(56313) (S)	56128	WH	HTLX	FRB	BAR	-

Right: *Several Class 56s are on the books of British American Railway; three are fully operational and certified for main line operation, others are likely to follow in 2013. Devon & Cornwall Railways-branded No. 56312 painted in light grey livery is seen passing Dawlish Warren, hauling refurbished Mk3 stock to Laira depot. The loco was operating on a spot hire basis.* **CJM**

Class 73

Vehicle Length: 53ft 8in (16.35m)
Height: 12ft 5½in (3.79m)
Width: 8ft 8in (2.64m)

Power: 750V dc third rail or English Electric 6K
Horsepower: electric - 1,600hp (1,193kW)
Horsepower: diesel - 600hp (447kW)
Electrical Equipment: English Electric

Number	Depot	Pool	Livery	Owner	Operator	Name
73107	SE	MBED	GRY	RTR	ECT	Redhill 1844 - 1994
73201 (73142)	SE	MBED	BLU	PTR	ECT	Broadlands

Above: *Looking immaculate in 1970s BR rail blue, complete with its* Broadlands *nameplates, No. 73201 is seen at Eastleigh. For accuracy this loco carried the number 73142 when named* Broadlands *in BR blue.* **Darren Ford**

Coaching Stock

Mk2
Vehicle Length: 66ft 0in (20.11m)
Height: 12ft 9½in (3.89m)
Width: 9ft 3in (2.81m)

AF2F - DBSO

Number	Depot	Livery	Owner
9704	EH	-	BAR
9705	EH	-	BAR
9707	EH	-	BAR
9709	EH	-	BAR
9710	EH	-	BAR

Ed Stevenson, Mark Zweig

Class 56

Vehicle Length: 63ft 6in (19.35m)
Height: 13ft 0in (3.96m)
Width: 9ft 2in (2.79m)

Engine: Ruston Paxman 16RK3CT
Horsepower: 3,250hp (2,420kW)
Electrical Equipment: Brush

Number	Depot	Pool	Livery	Owner	Operator
56007(S)	P	-	BLU	ES/MZ	-
56018(S)	P	-		ES/MZ	-
56038(S)	P	-		ES/MZ	-
56060(S)	WH	-	-	ES/MZ	-
56065(S)	WH	-	-	ES/MZ	-
56081(S)	BU	-	-	ES/MZ	-
56098(S)	P	-	-	ES/MZ	-

Spot hire locos to be introduced; six from the above list should be returned to traffic

Electric Traction Limited

Address: ✉ Woodlands, Manse Road, Inverurie, Aberdeenshire, Scotland, AB51 3UJ
Depot: Long Marston (LM)
Electric Traction Ltd provide spot hire of Class 86 and 87 traction, as well as providing engineering and graphic design services to the rail industry.

Class 86

Vehicle Length: 58ft 6in (17.83m)   *Power Collection: 25kV ac overhead*
Height: 13ft 0⅝in (3.97m)   *Horsepower: 5,900hp (4,400kW)*
Width: 8ft 8¼in (2.64m)   *Electrical Equipment: GEC*

Number		Depot	Pool	Livery	Owner	Operator	Name
86101		WA	ACAC	BLU	ETL	ETL	
86213		WA	ETLO	INS	ETL	ETL	Lancashire Witch
86401		WA	ETLO	NSE	ETL	ETL	Northampton Town
86701	(86205)	WH	COLO	COL	ETL	COL	Orion
86702	(86260)	WN	ETLO	ETL	ETL	ETL	Cassiopeia

Right: *In late 2012, Electric Traction Ltd hired Class 86/7 No. 86701 to Colas Rail Freight to operate a new service into London Euston, using the former First Great Western side-loading Motorail wagons. No. 86701 is seen on a test run, approaching Northampton.* **Andrew Cripps**

Class 87

Vehicle Length: 58ft 6in (17.83m)   *Power Collection: 25kV ac overhead*
Height: 13ft 1¼in (3.99m)   *Horsepower: 7,860hp (5,680kW)*
Width: 8ft 8¼in (2.64m)   *Electrical Equipment: GEC*

Number	Depot	Pool	Livery	Owner	Operator	Name
87002	WA	ETLO	BLU	ETL	ETL	Royal Sovereign

Above: *The sole UK main line certified Class 87, No. 87002, is owned by Electric Traction Ltd and is available for spot hire and charter work. On 15 July 2012, No. 87002 and Class 86 No. 86101 are seen near Retford with empty stock.* **Lindsay Atkinson**

Eversholt Rail Group (Previously HSBC Rail)

Address: ✉ PO Box 29499, 1 Eversholt Street, London, NW1 2ZF
✉ info@eversholtrail.co.uk   ✆ 0207 380 5040,   ⓘ www.eversholtrail.co.uk
Chief Operating Officer: Mary Kenny

Rolling Stock Hire Companies – Electric Traction, Eversholt

Harry Needle Railroad Company

Address: ✉ Harry Needle Railway Shed, Barrow Hill Roundhouse, Campbell Drive, Chesterfield, Derbyshire, S43 2PR

Managing Director: Harry Needle

Depot: Barrow Hill (BH)

Harry Needle Railroad Company also operates as a scrap dealer in dismantling locomotives and rolling stock. ∅ Reported for sale

Class 01.5

Number		Depot	Pool	Livery	Owner	Operator	
01552	(TH167V)	BH	HNRL	IND	HNR	IND	
01564	(12088)	-	HNRL	BLK	HNR	IND	*Preserved at Aln Valley Railway*

Class 07

Vehicle Length: 26ft 9½in (8.16m)
Height: 12ft 10in (3.91m)
Width: 8ft 6in (2.59m)
Engine: Paxman 6RPHL MkIII
Horsepower: 275hp (205kW)
Electrical Equipment: AEI

Number	Depot	Pool	Livery	Owner	Operator
07001	BH	HNRS	HNR	HNR	IND
07013	BH	HNRS	BLU	HNR	HNR

Class 08 & 09

Vehicle Length: 29ft 3in (8.91m)
Height: 12ft 8⅝in (3.87m)
Width: 8ft 6in (2.59m)
Engine: English Electric 6K
Horsepower: 400hp (298kW)
Electrical Equipment: English Electric

Number	Depot	Pool	Livery	Owner	Operator
08389	BH	HNRL	EWS	HNR	BUR
08502	BH	HNRL	NOR	HNR	NOR
08507	BH	HNRL	HNR	HNR	POB
08527(S)	BH	HNRL	JAR	HNR	IND
08685	BH	HNRL	EWS	HNR	HNR
08704	EL	HNRL	BLU	HNR	ELR
08765	BU	HNRL	EWS	HNR	HNR
08786	BH	HNRL	BRD	HNR	HNR
08818	BH	HNRL	HNR	HNR	IND
08834	BH	HNRL	DRS	HNR	OLD
08868	CP	HNRL	LNW	HNR	LNW
08892	BU	HNRL	DRS	HNR	HNR
08905	BH	HNRL	EWS	HNR	IND
08918	BH	HNRL	EWS	HNR	BUR
08924	BH	HNRL	EWS	HNR	HNR
08929(S)	LM	HNRS	BLK	HNR	-
08943	CZ	MBDL	HNR	HNR	NRM
08954	BU	HNRS	TGG	HNR	BUR
09012‡	BH	HNRS	EWS	HNT	-
09014	BU	HNRS	EWS	HNR	-
09018	BU	HNRS	HNR	HNR	LAF
09019	BU	HNRS	EWS	HNR	-

08507 also carries international No. 98 70 0008507-4
09012 also carries international No. 98 70 0009012-4

Class 20

Vehicle Length: 46ft 9¼in (14.26m)
Height: 12ft 7⅝in (3.84m)
Width: 8ft 9in (2.66m)
Engine: English Electric 8SVT Mk2
Horsepower: 1,000hp (745kW)
Electrical Equipment: English Electric

Number	Depot	Pool	Livery	Owner	Operator
20016(S) ∅	BH	HNRS	BLU	HNR	-
20056	BH	HNRL	COR	HNR	TAT
20057(S) ∅	LM	HNRS	BLU	HNR	-
20066	BH	HNRL	TAT	HNR	TAT
20081(S) ∅	LM	HNRS	BLU	HNR	-
20088(S) ∅	LM	HNRS	RFG	HNR	-
20092(S)	BH	HNRS	LAF	HNR	-
20096	BH	GBEE	BLU	HNR	HNR
20107‡	BH	GBEE	ORG	HNR	HNR
20118	BH	HNRS	GRY	HNR	HNR
20121(S)	WEN	HNRS	BLU	HNR	HNR
20132	BH	HNRS	RFG	HNR	HNR
20138(S)	LM	HNRS	RFT	HNR	-
20166	WEN	HNRS	GRN	HNR	HNR
20168	EA	HNRL	LAF	HNR	LAF

‡ Main line certified

Number		Depot	Pool	Livery	Owner	Operator	Name
20311	(20102)	BH	GBEE	ORG	HNR	HNR	
20314 ‡	(20117)	BH	GBEE	ORG	HNR	HNR	‡ Allocated number 92 70 0020314-5
20901	(20101)	BH	GBEE	GBN	HNR	HNR	
20903(S)	(20083)	LM	HNRS	DRS	HNR	-	
20904(S)	(20041)	LM	HNRS	DRS	HNR	-	
20905	(20225)	BH	GBEE	GBN	HNR	HNR	*Roger Whip*
20906	(20219)	LAF	HNRL	WHT	HNR	LAF	

Right Top: *The remaining Class 20s still continue to provide entertainment for enthusiasts with yet more new liveries emerging in 2012. Two locos operated under contract with GBRf to power the London Underground 'S' stock from Derby to Old Dalby and from Old Dalby to London Underground have emerged in full GBRf colours, the repainting work being carried out at Barrow Hill. No. 20901 is seen on the turntable at Barrow Hill.* **Derek Wilson**

Right Below: *The Harry Needle Railroad Company have started to apply the company orange livery to some of their Class 20 fleet, which looks very smart on the profile of this class. Still sporting its DRS jumper cable arrangement, No. 20314 is seen in orange livery and carries HNRC branding at Barrow Hill.*

Name applied
20168 *Sir George Earle*

20056 carries Tata Steel No. 81.
20066 carries Tata Steel No. 82.

Class 37/0

Vehicle Length: 61ft 6in (18.74m)
Height: 13ft 0¼in (3.96m)
Width: 8ft 11⅝in (2.73m)

Engine: English Electric 12CSVT
Horsepower: 1,750hp (1,304kW)
Electrical Equipment: English Electric

Number	Depot	Pool	Livery	Owner	Operator/Notes
37029	BH	HNRS	GRN	HNR	HNR *(At Epping & Ongar Railway)*
37057(S)	BH	HNRS	BLU	HNR	- (spares)
37165(S) (37374)	CS	HNRS	CIV	HNR	-

Class 37/4

Vehicle Length: 61ft 6in (18.74m)
Height: 13ft 0¼in (3.96m)
Width: 8ft 11⅝in (2.73m)
Electric Train Heat fitted

Engine: English Electric 12CSVT
Horsepower: 1,750hp (1,304kW)
Electrical Equipment: English Electric

Number	Depot	Pool	Livery	Owner	Operator
37415 (37277)	LM	HNRS	EWS	HNR	-

Class 37/5

Vehicle Length: 61ft 6in (18.74m)
Height: 13ft 0¼in (3.96m)
Width: 8ft 11⅝in (2.73m)

Engine: English Electric 12CSVT
Horsepower: 1,750hp (1,304kW)
Electrical Equipment: English Electric

Number		Depot	Pool	Livery	Owner	Operator
37503	(37017)	BH	HNRL	EWS	HNR	HNR
37521(S)	(37117)	BH	HNRL	EWS	HNR	-
37696(S)	(37228) ø	BH	HNRS	TGG	HNR	-

Class 37/7

Vehicle Length: 61ft 6in (18.74m)
Height: 13ft 0¼in (3.96m)
Width: 8ft 11⅝in (2.73m)

Engine: English Electric 12CSVT
Horsepower: 1,750hp (1,304kW)
Electrical Equipment: English Electric

Number		Depot	Pool	Livery	Owner	Operator
37703	(37067)	BH	HNRS	CON	HNR	-
37714	(37024)	BH	HNRS	CON	HNR	-
37716	(37094)	BH	HNRS	CON	HNR	-
37718	(37084)	BH	HNRS	CON	HNR	-
37800	(37143)	BH	HNRS	CON	HNR	-

Class 47

Vehicle Length: 63ft 6in (19.35m)			Engine: Sulzer 12LDA28C		
Height: 12ft 10⅜in (3.91m)			Horsepower: 2,580hp (1,922kW)		
Width: 9ft 2in (2.79m)			Electrical Equipment: Brush		
Electric Train Heat fitted to Class 47/4 and 47/7					

Number	Depot	Pool	Livery	Owner	Opertor
47714 (47511)	OD	HNRL	ANG	HNR	SEC*
47761 (47038/564)	BH	HNRL	RES	HNR	-

* Operating at Old Dalby

Nemesis Rail

Address: ✉ Nemesis Rail Ltd,   Burton Depot, Burton-on-Trent

⌨ enquiries@ nemesisrail.com   ℂ 01246 472331,   ⓘ www.nemesisrail.com

Formed from the demise of FM Rail

Depot: Burton (BU)

Left: *A newer name to the railway engineering operations is Nemesis Rail, which has taken over the long- closed depot buildings at Burton and in 2012 turned them into a hub of engineering activity, This is a general view of the north end of the depot and shows one of the Floyd Class 56s under test.*
Stuart Hillis

Class 31/1

Vehicle Length: 56ft 9in (17.29m)			Engine: English Electric 12SVT		
Height: 12ft 7in (3.91m)			Horsepower: 1,470hp (1,097kW)		
Width: 8ft 9in (2.65m)			Electrical Equipment: Brush		

Number	Depot	Pool	Livery	Owner	Operator	Name
31128	BU	NRLO	BLU	NEM	NYM	*Charybdis*

Class 33/1

Vehicle Length: 50ft 9in (15.47m)			Engine: Sulzer 8LDA28A		
Height: 12ft 8in (3.86m)			Horsepower: 1,550hp (1,156kW)		
Width: 9ft 3in (2.81m)			Electrical Equipment: Crompton Parkinson		

Number	Depot	Pool	Livery	Owner	Operator	Name
33103	BU	MBDL	BLU	NEM	WER	*Swordfish*

Class 37/5

Vehicle Length: 61ft 6in (18.74m)			Engine: English Electric 12CSVT		
Height: 13ft 0¼in (3.96m)			Horsepower: 1,750hp (1,304kW)		
Width: 8ft 11⅝in (2.73m)			Electrical Equipment: English Electric		

Number	Depot	Pool	Livery	Owner	Operator
37679(S) (37123)	BU	MBDL	TGG	NEM	-

Class 45/1

Vehicle Length: 67ft 11in (20.70m)			Engine: Sulzer 12LDA28B		
Height: 12ft 10½in (3.91m)			Horsepower: 2,500hp (1,862kW)		
Width: 9ft 1½in (2.78m)			Electrical Equipment: Crompton Parkinson		

Number	Depot	Pool	Livery	Owner	Operator	Name
45112	BH (at Meldon)	MBDL	BLU	NEM	NEM	*Royal Army Ordnance Corps*

Class 47

							Vehicle Length: 63ft 6in (19.35m)	Engine: Sulzer 12LDA28C
Height: 12ft 10¾in (3.91m)	Horsepower: 2,580hp (1,922kW)
Width: 9ft 2in (2.79m)	Electrical Equipment: Brush
Electric Train Heat fitted to Class 47/4 and 47/7

Number	Depot	Pool	Livery	Owner	Operator			Number	Depot	Pool	Livery	Owner	Operator
47375	BH	MBDL	BLU	NEM	NEM			47716	BH	MBDL	RES	NEM	NEM
47488	BH	MBDL	GRN	NEM	NEM			47744	BH	MBDL	EWS	NEM	NEM

Above: *Painted in BR rail blue but devoid of BR double arrow logo, No. 47375 and Class 56 No. 56302 in the remains of Fastline Freight livery pass Newton Abbot en route to Burngullow.* **Antony Christie**

Porterbrook

Address: ✉ Ivatt House, The Point, Pinnacle Way, Pride Park, Derby, DE24 8ZS
📠 enquiries@porterbrook.co.uk ✆ 01332 285050, ⓘ www.porterbrook.co.uk
Managing Director: Paul Francis
Owned by: Antin Infrastructure Partners, Deutsche Bank & OP Trust

Transmart Trains

Address: ✉ Green Farm House, Falfield, Wootton-under-Edge, Gloucestershire, GL12 8DL
Managing Director: Oliver Buxton
Depots: Selhurst (SU), Stewarts Lane (SL)
Part of Cambrian Transport

Class 73

							Vehicle Length: 53ft 8in (16.35m)	Power: 750V dc third rail or English Electric 6K
Height: 12ft 5⅝in (3.79m)	Horsepower: electric - 1,600hp (1,193kW)
Width: 8ft 8in (2.64m)	Horsepower: diesel - 600hp (447kW)
Electrical Equipment: English Electric

‡ At Barry Railway
• Not main line certified

Number	Depot	Pool	Livery	Owner	Operator	Name
73109	SU	MBED	SWT	TTS	TTS	
73118	‡	-	GRY	TTS	TTS	
73133•	‡	-	GRN	TTS	TTS	
73136	SU	MBED	GRN	TTS	TTS	*Perseverance*

■ Former Gatwick Express
Class 488 vehicles Nos. 72505,
72620, 72621, 72629, 72710 from
sets 488206 and 488311 are also
owned by Transmart Trains.

Listings provide details of locomotives and stock authorised for operation on the UK National Rail network and that can be seen operating special and charter services.
Preserved locomotives authorised for main line operation are found in the preserved section.

Bo'ness and Kinneil Railway

Number	Type	Depot	Livery	Operator	Use
464	AO3/BCK	BT	CAL	BOK	Charter train use
1375 (99803)	AO2/TK	BT	CAL	BOK	Charter train use
3096 (99827)	AD11/FO	BT	MAR	BOK	Charter train use
3115	AD11/FO	BT	MAR	BOK	Charter train use
3150	AD11/FO	BT	MAR	BOK	Charter train use
4831 (99824)	AC21/TSO	BT	MAR	BOK	Charter train use
4832 (99823)	AC21/TSO	BT	CHC	BOK	Charter train use
4836 (99831)	AC21/TSO	BT	MAR	BOK	Charter train use
4856 (99829)	AC21/TSO	BT	MAR	BOK	Charter train use
5028 (99830)	AC21/TSO	BT	CAR	BOK	Charter train use
5412	AC2A/TSO	BT	MAR	BOK	Charter train use
13229 (99826)	AA11/FK	BT	MAR	BOK	Charter train use
13230 (99828)	AA11/FK	BT	MAR	BOK	Charter train use

Flying Scotsman Railway Ltd

Number	Type	Depot	Livery	Operator	Notes/Name
316 (S) (975608)	AO11/PFK	CS	PUL	FSL	Pullman *Magpie*
321 (S)	AO11/PFK	CS	PUL	FSL	Pullman *Swift*
337 (S)	AO11/PSK	CS	PUL	FSL	Pullman Car No. 337

Great Scottish & Western Railway Co

Number	Type	Depot	Livery	Operator	Notes/Name
313 (S) (99964)	AO11/PFK	CS	MAR	GSW	Royal Scotsman - *Finch*
317 (99967)	AO11/PFK	CS	MAR	GSW	Royal Scotsman - *Raven*
319 (99965)	AO11/PFK	CS	MAR	GSW	Royal Scotsman - *Snipe*
324 (99961)	AO11/PFP	CS	MAR	GSW	Royal Scotsman - *Amber*
329 (99962)	AO11/PFP	CS	MAR	GSW	Royal Scotsman - *Pearl*
331 (99963)	AO11/PFP	CS	MAR	GSW	Royal Scotsman - *Topaz*
1999 (99131)	AO10/SAL	CS	MAR	GSW	Royal Scotsman - *Lochaber*

Hastings Diesels Limited

The following vehicles are owned by Hastings Diesels Ltd and kept at St Leonards. Usually a six-car train is formed which is fitted with central door locking and is main line certified (original class numbers shown in brackets).
60000 (201), 60019 (202), 60116 (202), 60018 (202), 60501 (201), 60528 (202), 60529 (202), 69337 (422 EMU), 70262 (411 EMU).
In autumn 2012, the set **1001** was formed **60116+60529+70262+69337+60501+60118**

Ian Riley

		Vehicle Length: 61ft 6in (18.74m)		Engine: English Electric 12CSVT
		Height: 13ft 0¼in (3.96m)		Horsepower: 1,750hp (1,304kW)
		Width: 8ft 11⅝in (2.73m)		Electrical Equipment: English Electric

Number	Depot	Livery	Pool	Owner	Operator	Name
37518 (37076)	BQ	ICS	MBDL	IRY	IRY	Fort William/An Gearasden

Mid-Hants Railway

Number	Type	Depot	Livery	Operator
1105 (99531/302)	AJ41/RG	RL	GRN	MHR
21252	AB31/BCK	RL	GRN	MHR

Northumbria Rail

Number	Type	Depot	Livery	Operator
9497	AC2E/BSO	-	BLG	NOT

North Yorkshire Moors Railway

Class 08

Vehicle Length: 29ft 3in (8.91m)
Height: 12ft 8⅝in (3.87m)
Width: 8ft 6in (2.59m)

Engine: English Electric 6K
Horsepower: 400hp (298kW)
Electrical Equipment: English Electric

Number	Depot	Pool	Livery	Owner	Operator	Notes
08850	NY	MBDL	BLU	NYM	NYM	Restricted main line use

Class 25

Vehicle Length: 50ft 6in (15.39m)
Height: 12ft 8in (3.86m)
Width: 9ft 1in (2.76m)

Engine: Sulzer 6LDA28B
Horsepower: 1,250hp (932kW)
Electrical Equipment: Brush

Number	Depot	Pool	Livery	Owner	Operator	Name	Notes
25278	NY	MBDL	GRN	NYM	NYM	Sybilia	Restricted main line use

Coaching Stock

Number	Type	Depot	Livery	Operator	
1823	AN21/RMB	NY	MAR	NYM	
3860	AC21/TSO	NY	MAR	NYM	
3872	AC21/TSO	NY	CAR	NYM	
3948	AC2I/TSO	NY	CAR	NYM	Spare vehicle
4198	AC21/TSO	NY	CAR	NYM	
4252	AC21/TSO	NY	CAR	NYM	
4290	AC21/TSO	NY	MAR	NYM	
4455	AC21/TSO	NY	CAR	NYM	
4786	AC21/TSO	NY	MAR	NYM	
4817	AC21/TSO	NY	CHC	NYM	
5000	AC21/TSO	NY	MAR	NYM	
5029	AC21/TSO	NY	CHC	NYM	
9267	AE21/BSO	NY	CHC	NYM	
9274	AE21/BSO	NY	CHC	NYM	
16156 (7156)	AA31/CK	NY	MAR	NYM	
21100	AB31/BCK	NY	CHC	NYM	
35089	AB2I/BSK	NY	MAR	NYM	

Railfilms Limited / Statesman Rail

Number	Type	Depot	Livery	Operator	Name
84 (99884)		EH	PUL	RAF	
310 (99107)	AO11/PFL	EH	PUL	RAF	Pegasus
1659 (16509)	AJ41/RBR	EH	PUL	RAF	
3188	AD1D/FO	EH	PUL	RAF	Sovereign
3231	AD1E/FO	EH	PUL	RAF	Apollo
5067 (99993)	AC21/TSO	CP	MAR	RAF	
5797	AD2E/TSO	BH	BLG	RAF	
9004	GWR	EH	GWR	RAF	
13508 (S)	AA1B/FK	CS	MAR	RAF	
17080	AO3/BCK	EH	PUL	RAF	

Ridings Railtours

Number	Type	Depot	Livery	Operator
5520 (S)	AC2C/TSO	SV	PUL	RRS
13581 (S)	AA1D/FK	SV	ICS	RRS
13583 (S)	AA1D/FK	SV	ICS	RRS

Riviera Trains

Class 47

Vehicle Length: 63ft 6in (19.35m)				Engine: Sulzer 12LDA28C		
Height: 12ft 10⅜in (3.91m)				Horsepower: 2,580hp (1,922kW)		
Width: 9ft 2in (2.79m)				Electrical Equipment: Brush		
Electric Train Heat fitted						

Number	Depot	Pool	Livery	Owner	Operator	Name
47769 (47491)	CP	RTLO	VIR	RIV	RIV	
47812 D1916 (47657)	CP	RTLO	GRN	RIV	RIV	
47815 D1748 (47660)	CP	RTLO	GRN	RIV	RIV	*Great Western*
47843 (47623)	CP	RTLO	RIV	RIV	RIV	*Vulcan*
47847 (47577)	CP	RTLO	RIV	RIV	RIV	
47848 (47632)	CP	RTLO	RIV	RIV	RIV	*Titan Star*

Left: *Riviera Trains, based at Crewe, operate a fleet of six Class 47s. All are equipped with electric train supply and are used on charter or spot hire work. Carrying the Riviera Trains Cheshire Cat motif, No. 47843* Vulcan *is seen stabled at Didcot.*
Nathan Williamson

Coaching Stock

Number	Type	Depot	Livery	Operator	Notes/Name
1200 (6459)	AJ1F/RFO	EH	RIV	RIV	Set 04 - The Great Briton - *Amber*
1203 (3291)	AJ1F/RFO	EH	RIV	RIV	
1212 (6453)	AJ1F/RFO	EH	VIR	RIV	Set 05 - The Norfolkman
1250 (3372)	AJ1F/RFO	EH	RIV	RIV	Set 07 - The West Coast Set
1651	AJ41/RBR	EH	RIV	RIV	Set 02 - The Royal Scot Set
1657	AJ41/RBR	EH	CHC	RIV	
1671	AJ41/RBR	EH	CHC	RIV	
1683	AJ41/RBR	BH	BLU	RIV	Set 04 - The Great Briton - *Carol*
1691	AJ41/RBR	CP	CCM	RIV	Set 02 - The Royal Scot Set
1692	AJ41/RBR	CP	CHC	RIV	Set 01 - The British Classic Set
1699	AJ41/RBR	CP	BLU	RIV	Set 04 - The Great Briton
1813	AN21/RMB	CP	MAR	RIV	Set 03
1832	AN21/RMB	EH	CCM	RIV	
1842	AN21/RMB	EH	CCM	RIV	Set 02 - The Royal Scot Set
1863	AN21/RMB	EH	CHC	RIV	Set 01 - The British Classic Set
2834 (21267)	AU51/SLSC	EH	LNR	RIV	
3066 (99566)	AD11/FO	EH	CCM	RIV	Set 02 - The Royal Scot Set
3068 (99568)	AD11/FO	EH	CCM	RIV	Set 02 - The Royal Scot Set
3069 (99540)	AD11/FO	EH	CCM	RIV	Set 02 - The Royal Scot Set
3097	AD11/FO	EH	CCM	RIV	Set 02 - The Royal Scot Set
3098	AD11/FO	EH	CHC	RIV	Set 01 - The British Classic Set
3100	AD11/FO	EH	CHC	RIV	
3107	AD11/FO	EH	CHC	RIV	Set 01 - The British Classic Set
3110 (99124)	AD11/FO	EH	CHC	RIV	Set 01 - The British Classic Set
3112 (99357)	AD11/FO	EH	CHC	RIV	Set 01 - The British Classic Set
3114 (S)	AD11/FO	EH	GRN	RIV	
3119	AD11/FO	EH	CCM	RIV	Set 02 - The Royal Scot Set

3120	AD11/FO	EH	CCM	RIV	Set 03
3121	AD11/FO	EH	CHC	RIV	Set 02 - The Royal Scot Set
3122	AD11/FO	EH	CHC	RIV	Set 01 - The British Classic Set
3123	AD11/FO	EH	CHC	RIV	Set 03
3124 (S)	AD11/FO	EH	GRN	RIV	
3127 (S)	AD11/FO	EH	GRN	RIV	
3131 (S) (99190)	AD11/FO	EH	MAR	RIV	
3132 (S) (99191)	AD11/FO	EH	MAR	RIV	
3133 (S) (99192)	AD11/FO	EH	MAR	RIV	
3140	AD11/FO	EH	CHC	RIV	Set 01 - The British Classic Set
3141 (3608)	AD11/FO	EH	MRN	RIV	Set 03
3144 (3602)	AD11/FO	EH	MRN	RIV	Set 03
3146	AD11/FO	EH	MRN	RIV	Set 03
3147 (3604)	AD11/FO	EH	LNE	RIV	Set 03
3149	AD11/FO	EH	CCM	RIV	Set 02 - The Royal Scot Set
3181 (S)	AD1D/FO	EH	RIV	RIV	*Topaz*
3223 (S)	AD1E/FO	BU	RIV	RIV	*Diamond*
3227	AD1E/FO	EH	RIV	RIV	
3240 (S)	AD1E/FO	BU	RIV	RIV	*Sapphire*
3277	AD1F/FO	EH	ANG	RIV	Set 05 - The Norfolkman
3278	AD1F/FO	EH	RIV	RIV	
3279	AD1F/FO	EH	MAR	RIV	Set 05 - The Norfolkman
3295	AD1F/FO	EH	ANG	RIV	Set 05 - The Norfolkman
3304	AD1F/FO	EH	VIR	RIV	Set 07 - The West Coast Set
3314	AD1F/FO	EH	VIR	RIV	Set 07 - The West Coast Set
3325	AD1F/FO	EH	VIR	RIV	Set 07 - The West Coast Set
3330	AD1F/FO	EH	RIV	RIV	Set 04 - The Great Briton - *Brunel*
3333	AD1F/FO	EH	VIR	RIV	Set 07 - The West Coast Set
3334	AD1F/FO	EH	ANG	RIV	Set 05 - The Norfolkman
3336	AD1F/FO	CD	RIV	RIV	Set 05 - The Norfolkman
3340	AD1F/FO	EH	VIR	RIV	Set 07 - The West Coast Set
3344	AD1F/FO	EH	RIV	RIV	Set 07 - The West Coast Set
3345	AD1F/FO	EH	VIR	RIV	Set 07 - The West Coast Set
3348	ADIF/FO	EH	RIV	RIV	Set 04 - The Great Briton - *Gainsborough*
3356	AD1F/FO	EH	RIV	RIV	Set 04 - The Great Briton - *Tennyson*
3358	AD1F/FO	EH	RIV	RIV	
3364	AD1F/FO	EH	RIV	RIV	Set 04 - The Great Briton - *Shakespeare*
3379	AD1F/FO	EH	ANG	RIV	
3384	AD1F/FO	EH	RIV	RIV	Set 04 - The Great Briton - *Dickens*
3386	AD1F/FO	EH	VIR	RIV	Set 07 - The West Coast Set
3390	AD1F/FO	EH	RIV	RIV	Set 04 - The Great Briton - *Constable*
3397	AD1F/FO	EH	RIV	RIV	Set 04 - The Great Briton - *Wordsworth*
3417	AD1F/FO	EH	ANG	RIV	
3426	AD1F/FO	EH	RIV	RIV	Set 04 - The Great Briton - *Elgar*
4927	AC21/TSO	EH	CHC	RIV	Set 01 - The British Classic Set
4946 (S) (99000)	AC21/TSO	EH	MAR	RIV	
4949	AC21/TSO	EH	CHC	RIV	Set 03
4959	AC21/TSO	ZA	CHC	RIV	
4986	AC21/TSO	EH	GRN	RIV	Set 03
4991	AC21/TSO	EH	CHC	RIV	
4996 (99001)	AC21/TSO	CD	MAR	RIV	
4998	AC21/TSO	EH	CHC	RIV	Set 03
5007 (S)	AC21/TSO	EH	GRN	RIV	
5008 (99002)	AC21/TSO	CD	MAN	RIV	
5009	AC21/TSO	EH	CHC	RIV	Set 01 - The British Classic Set
5023	AC21/TSO	EH	RIV	RIV	Set 03
5027 (S)	AC21/TSO	EH	GRN	RIV	
5040	AC21/TSO	EH	CHC	RIV	Set 01 - The British Classic Set
5276	AC2A/TSO	EH	RIV	RIV	Set 02 - The Royal Scot Set
5292	AC2A/TSO	EH	CHC	RIV	Set 02 - The Royal Scot Set
5309 (S)	AC2A/TSO	EH	CHC	RIV	
5322	AC2A/TSO	EH	RIV	RIV	Set 02 - The Royal Scot Set
5341	AC2A/TSO	EH	CCM	RIV	Set 02 - The Royal Scot Set
5350	AC2A/TSO	EH	CHC	RIV	Set 01 - The British Classic Set - *Dawn*
5366	AC2A/TSO	EH	CHC	RIV	Set 02 - The Royal Scot Set
5494 (S)	AC2B/TSO	SV	NSE	RIV	
5647 (S)	AC2D/TSO	EH	RIV	RIV	

Riviera

5739 (S)	AC2D/TSO	SV	NWM	RIV	
5748	AC2E/TSO	EH	RIV	RIV	
5769	AC2E/TSO	EH	INT	RIV	
5792	AC2E/TSO	EH	VIR	RIV	
5910	AC2F/TSO	EH	VIR	RIV	Set 07 - The West Coast Set
5921	AC2F/TSO	EH	RIV	RIV	Set 05 - The Norfolkman
5929	AC2F/TSO	EH	ANG	RIV	Set 05 - The Norfolkman
5937	AC2F/TSO	EH	VIR	RIV	
5945	AC2F/TSO	EH	VIR	RIV	Set 07 - The West Coast Set
5946	AC2F/TSO	EH	VIR	RIV	Set 07 - The West Coast Set
5950	AC2F/TSO	EH	RIV	RIV	
5952 (S)	AC2F/TSO	EH	VIR	RIV	
5955 (S)	AC2F/TSO	EH	VIR	RIV	
5961	AC2F/TSO	EH	VIR	RIV	Set 07 - The West Coast Set
5964	AC2F/TSO	EH	ANG	RIV	
5985	AC2F/TSO	EH	ANG	RIV	Set 05 - The Norfolkman
5987	AC2F/TSO	EH	VIR	RIV	Set 07 - The West Coast Set
5997	AC2F/TSO	EH	VIR	RIV	Set 07 - The West Coast Set
5998	AC2F/TSO	EH	ANG	RIV	Set 05 - The Norfolkman
6006	AC2F/TSO	CF	ANG	RIV	Set 05 - The Norfolkman
6024 (S)	AC2F/TSO	EH	VIR	RIV	
6027	AC2F/TSO	EH	RIV	RIV	Set 07 - The West Coast Set
6042	AC2F/TSO	EH	ANG	RIV	Set 05 - The Norfolkman
6051	AC2F/TSO	EH	VIR	RIV	Set 07 - The West Coast Set
6054	AC2F/TSO	EH	VIR	RIV	Set 07 - The West Coast Set
6067 (S)	AC2F/TSO	EH	VIR	RIV	
6141	AC2F/TSO	EH	RIV	RIV	Set 07 - The West Coast Set
6158	AC2F/TSO	EH	VIR	RIV	Set 07 - The West Coast Set
6176 (S)	AC2F/TSO	EH	VIR	RIV	
6177	AC2F/TSO	EH	RIV	RIV	
6310 (81448)	AX51/GEN	EH	CHC	RIV	
6320	AZ5Z/SAL	SK	MRN	RIV	
6720 (6602)	AN1D/RMBF	EH	MRN	RIV	
6722 (6611)	AN1D/RMBF	LM	FSW	RIV	
9504	AC2E/BSO	EH	RIV	RIV	Set 07 - The West Coast Set
9507	AC2E/BSO	EH	VIR	RIV	
9520	AE2F/BSO	EH	RIV	RIV	Set 07 - The West Coast Set
9526	AC2F/BSO	EH	RIV	RIV	
9527	AC2F/BSO	EH	ANG	RIV	
9537	AE2F/BSO	EH	ADV	RIV	Boat Train saver
17015 (14015)	AB11/BFK	EH	CHC	RIV	Set 02 - The Royal Scot Set
17056 (S) (14056)	AB1A/BFK	EH	MAR	RIV	
17077 (14077)	AB1A/BFK	EH	RIV	RIV	Set 04 - The Great Briton - *Catherine*
17105 (2905)	AX5B/BFK	EH	RIV	RIV	Set 02 - Staff Couchette
21224	AB31/BCK	EH	MAR	RIV	Directors saloon
21245 (99356)	AB31/BCK	EH	MAR	RIV	Set 03
21269	AB31/BCK	EH	LNE	RIV	
21272 (99129)	AB31/BCK	EH	CHC	RIV	Set 01 - The British Classic Set
35469 (99763)	AB21/BSK	EH	CCM	RIV	Set 03
80041 (1690)	AK51/RK	EH	MAR	RIV	Set 03 - Pride of the Nation
80042 (1646)	AJ41/RK	EH	BLG	RIV	
94538 (94426)	BG	EH	RES	DBS	

Left: *Riviera Trains are one of the main suppliers of coaching stock to the charter market, and have some superbly turned out coaches. In this view we see Mk1 TSO No. 4998 restored to BR Western Region chocolate & cream livery. Many of the Riviera coaches are based at Eastleigh depot.*
Nathan Williamson

Right: *Carrying non-authentic Great Western-style livery, Mk2A TSO No. 5366 is seen attached to a Class 60 while forming a railtour. From its original BR days, this vehicle like many in the charter fleet has had its central door sealed up.* **Nathan Williamson**

Scottish Railway Preservation Society

Number	Type	Depot	Livery	Operator
1859 (99822)	AN21/RMB	BT	MAR	SRP
21241	AB31/BCK	BT	CHC	SRP
35185	AB21/BSK	BT	MAR	SRP

Stratford Class 47 Group

Vehicle Length: 63ft 6in (19.35m)	Engine: Sulzer 12LDA28C
Height: 12ft 10⅜in (3.91m)	Horsepower: 2,580hp (1,922kW)
Width: 9ft 2in (2.79m)	Electrical Equipment: Brush
Electric Train Heat fitted	

Number	Depot	Pool	Livery	Owner	Operator	Name
47580 (47732)	MNR	MBDL	LLB	S4G	S4G	*County of Essex*

Right: *The Stratford Class 47 Group have one of the best maintained Class 47s in the UK, with No. 47580* County of Essex *fully maintained to main line standards and used for charter and spot hire work. On 29 June 2012, the loco is seen powering a charter through Lea Marston in the West Midlands. During 2012, to mark the Queen's Diamond Jubilee, a Stratford-style Union Jack was applied to the bodysides.* **Stacey Thew**

Venice Simplon Orient Express (VSOE)

Number	Name	Type	Depot	Livery	Operator	Notes
213 (99535)	*Minerva*	AO40/PFP	SL	PUL	VSO	
239 (S)	*Agatha*	AO40/PFP	SL	PUL	VSO	
243 (99541)	*Lucille*	AO40/PFP	SL	PUL	VSO	
245 (99534)	*Ibis*	AO40/PFK	SL	PUL	VSO	
254 (99536)	*Zena*	AO40/PFP	SL	PUL	VSO	
255 (99539)	*Ione*	AO40/PFK	SL	PUL	VSO	
261 (S)	Car No. 83	AO40/PTP	SL	PUL	VSO	
264 (S)	*Ruth*	AO40/PCK	SL	PUL	VSO	

VSOE

280 (99537)	*Audrey*	AO40/PFK	SL	PUL	VSO	
281 (99546)	*Gwen*	AO40/PFK	SL	PUL	VSO	
283 (S)	*Mona*	AO40/PFK	SL	PUL	VSO	
284 (99543)	*Vera*	AO40/PFK	SL	PUL	VSO	
285 (S)	Car No. 85	AO40/PTP	SL	PUL	VSO	
286 (S)	Car No. 86	AO40/PTP	SL	PUL	VSO	
288 (S)	Car No. 88	AO40/PTB	SL	PUL	VSO	
292 (S)	Car No. 92	AO40/PTB	SL	PUL	VSO	
293 (S)	Car No. 93	AO40/PTB	SL	PUL	VSO	
301 (99530)	*Perseus*	AO41/PFP	SL	PUL	VSO	
302 (99531)	*Phoenix*	AO41/PFP	SL	PUL	VSO	
307 (S)	*Carina*	AO41/PFK	SL	PUL	VSO	
308 (99532)	*Cygnus*	AO41/PFP	SL	PUL	VSO	
325 (2907)		AJ11/RFO	CP	PUL	VSO	
1207 (6422)		AJ11/RFO	CP	-	VSO	
1221 (3371)		AJ11/RFO	CP	-	VSO	
1566		AK51/RKB	CP	VSN	VSO	
1953		AJ41/RBR	CP	VSN	VSO	
3174	*Glamis*	AD1D/FO	CP	VSN	VSO	
3182	*Warwick*	AD1D/FO	CP	VSN	VSO	
3232		AD1E/FO	CD	RIV	CAD	
3247	*Chatsworth*	AD1E/FO	CP	VSN	VSO	
3267	*Belvoir*	AD1E/FO	CP	VSN	VSO	
3273	*Alnwick*	AD1E/FO	CP	VSN	VSO	
3275	*Harlech*	AD1E/FO	CP	VSN	VSO	
6313 (92167)		AX51/GEN	SL	PUL	VSO	
9502		AE2E/BSO	SL	PUL	VSO	
10541 (99968)		AO4G/SSV	CS	MRN	VSO	Royal Scotsman - State Car 5
10556 (99969)		AO4G/SSV	CS	MRN	VSO	Royal Scotsman - Service Car
10569 (S)	*Leviathan*	AU4G/SLEP	CP	PUL	VSO	
10729	*Crewe*	AS4G/SLE	CP	VSN	VSO	
10734 (2914)	*Balmoral*	AS4G/SLE	CP	VSN	VSO	
17167 (14167)		AB1D/BFK	CP	VSN	VSO	
35466 (99545)		AB21/BSK	SL	PUL	VSO	
92904		NBA	CP	PUL	VSO	

Above: *One of the finest maintained trains in the world is the VSOE Pullman, used almost daily for luxury train travel around the UK. Maintained at Stewarts Lane, the coaching stock is kept in superb condition. Pullman Car Minerva No. 213 or TOPS number 99535 is illustrated.* **CJM**

Vintage Trains

Class 47

			Vehicle Length: 63ft 6in (19.35m)		Engine: Sulzer 12LDA28C
			Height: 12ft 10⅜in (3.91m)		Horsepower: 2,580hp (1,922kW)
			Width: 9ft 2in (2.79m)		Electrical Equipment: Brush
			Electric Train Heat fitted		

Number	Depot	Pool	Livery	Owner	Operator
47773 (47541)	TM	MBDL	GRN	VTN	VTN

Coaching Stock

Number	Type	Depot	Livery	Owner	Operator
335 (99361)	AO11/PSK	TM	PUL	VTN	VTN
349 (99349)	AO11/PSP	TM	PUL	VTN	VTN
353 (99353)	AO11/PSP	TM	PUL	VTN	VTN
1201 (6445)	AJ1F/RFO	TM	CHC	VTN	VTN
3309	AD1F/FO	CS	ICS	VTN	-
3351	AD1F/FO	TM	CHC	VTN	VTN
3416	AD1F/FO	CS	ICS	VTN	-
5148(S)	AC2Z/TSO	TM	REG	VTN	-
5157	AC2Z/TSO	TM	CHC	VTN	VTN
5177	AC2Z/TSO	TM	CHC	VTN	VTN
5179(S)	AC2Z/TSO	TM	REG	VTN	-
5183(S)	AC2Z/TSO	TM	REG	VTN	-
5186(S)	AC2Z/TSO	TM	REG	VTN	-
5191	AC2Z/TSO	TM	CHC	VTN	VTN
5193(S)	AC2Z/TSO	TM	LNE	VTN	-
5194(S)	AC2Z/TSO	TM	REG	VTN	-
5198	AC2Z/TSO	TM	CHC	VTN	VTN
5212(S)	AC2Z/TSO	TM	LNE	VTN	-
5221(S)	AC2Z/TSO	TM	REG	VTN	-
5928	AC2F/TSO	TM	CHC	VTN	VTN
9101 (9398)	AH2Z/BSOT	TM	CHC	VTN	VTN
9496	AE2E/BSO	TM	CHC	VTN	VTN
9711	AF2F/DBSO	TM	?	VTN	VTN
17018 (99108)	AB11/BFK	TM	CHC	VTN	VTN
17090	AB1A/BFK	TM	CHC	VTN	VTN

West Coast Railway Company

Class 03

			Vehicle Length: 26ft 3in (7.92m)		Engine: Gardner 8L3
			Height: 12ft 7¹⁰⁄₁₆in (3.72m)		Horsepower: 204hp (149kW)
			Width: 8ft 6in (2.59m)		Mechanical Equipment: Wilson-Drewry

Number	Depot	Pool	Livery	Owner	Operator	Name
03196(S)	CS	MBDL	GRN	WCR	WCR	Joyce
D2381(S)	CS	MBDL	BLK	WCR	WCR	

Class 08

			Vehicle Length: 29ft 3in (8.91m)		Engine: English Electric 6K
			Height: 12ft 8⅝in (3.87m)		Horsepower: 400hp (298kW)
			Width: 8ft 6in (2.59m)		Electrical Equipment: English Electric

Number	Depot	Pool	Livery	Owner	Operator	Name
08418	CS	MBDL	EWS	WCR	WCR	
08485	CS	MBDL	BLU	WCR	WCR	
08678	CS	MBDL	GLX	WCR	WCR	Artila

Class 33

			Vehicle Length: 50ft 9in (15.47m)		Engine: Sulzer 8LDA28A
			Height: 12ft 8in (3.86m)		Horsepower: 1,550hp (1,156kW)
			Width: 33/0, 33/1 9ft 3in (2.81m),		Electrical Equipment: Crompton P'n
			33/2 8ft 8in (2.64m)		

Number	Depot	Pool	Livery	Owner	Operator	Name
33025	CS	AWCA	WCR	WCR	WCR	Glen Falloch
33029	CS	AWCX	WCR	WCR	WCR	Glen Roy
33207	CS	AWCA	WCR	WCR	WCR	Jim Martin

WCRC

Class 37

					Engine: English Electric 12CSVT
Vehicle Length: 61ft 6in (18.74m)					Horsepower: 1,750hp (1,304kW)
Height: 13ft 0¼in (3.96m)					Electrical Equipment: English Electric
Width: 8ft 11⅝in (2.73m)					

Number	Depot	Pool	Livery	Owner	Operator	Name
37214	CS	AWCX	WCR	WCR	WCR	Loch Laidon
37248 (S)	CS	MBDL	WCR	TTT	WCR	
37516 (S) (37086)	CS	AWCA	WCR	WCR	-	
37517 (S) (37018)	CS	MBDL	LHL	WCR	-	
37668 (S) (37257)	CS	MBDL	EWS	WCR	-	
37669 (S) (37129)	CS	AWCX	EWS	WCR	-	
37676 (37126)	CS	AWCA	WCR	WCR	WCR	Loch Rannoch
37685 (37234)	CS	AWCA	WCR	WCR	WCR	Loch Arkaig
37706 (37016)	CS	AWCA	WCR	WCR	WCR	
37710 (S) (37044)	CS	MBDL	LHL	WCR	-	
37712 (37102)	CS	AWCX	WCR	WCR	WCR	

Above: West Coast Railway, based in Carnforth, have a few Class 37s in their operational fleet. These are painted in the rather drab dark maroon livery, offset by West Coast branding. No. 37685 is seen crossing Cockwood Harbour on 18 September 2010 with a charter stock transit move bound for Plymouth. **CJM**

Class 47

					Engine: Sulzer 12LDA28C
Vehicle Length: 63ft 6in (19.35m)					Horsepower: 2,580hp (1,922kW)
Height: 12ft 10⅜in (3.91m)					Electrical Equipment: Brush
Width: 9ft 2in (2.79m)					
Electric Train Heat fitted to Class 47/4, 47/7 and 47/8					

Number	Depot	Pool	Livery	Owner	Operator	Name
47194 (S)	CS	AWCX	TLF	WCR	-	
47237	CS	AWCA	WCR	WCR	WCR	
47245	CS	AWCA	WCR	WCR	WCR	
47270	CS	AWCA	BLU	WCR	WCR	Swift
47355 (S)	CS	AWCX	WCR	WCR	-	
47492	CS	AWCX	RES	WCR	WCR	
47500 (47770)	CS	AWCA	WCR	WCR	WCR	
47746 (47605)	CS	AWCX	WCR	WCR	WCR	
47760 (47562)	CS	AWCA	WCR	WCR	WCR	
47768 (47490)	CS	AWCX	EWS	WCR	WCR	
47772 (S) (47537)	CS	AWCX	RES	WCR	-	
47776 (S) (47578)	CS	AWCX	RES	WCR	-	
47786 (47821)	CS	AWCA	WCR	WCR	WCR	Roy Castle OBE
47787 (47823)	CS	AWCX	WCR	WCR	WCR	Windsor Castle
47804 (47792)	CS	AWCA	WCR	WCR	WCR	
47826 (47637)	CS	AWCA	WCR	WCR	WCR	
47851/D1648 (47639)	CS	AWCA	WCR	WCR	WCR	
47854 (47674)	CS	AWCA	WCR	WCR	WCR	Diamond Jubilee

Class 57

Vehicle Length: 63ft 6in (19.38m)			Engine: EMD 645-12E3		
Height: 12ft 10⅛in (3.91m)			Horsepower: 2,500hp (1,860kW)		
Width: 9ft 2in (2.79m)			Electrical Equipment: Brush		

Number	Depot	Pool	Livery	Owner	Operator
57001 (47356)	CS	AWCA	WCR	WCR	WCR
57005 (47350)	CS	AWCX	WCR	WCR	WCR
57006 (47187)	CS	AWCA	WCR	WCR	WCR
57313 (47371)	CS	AWCA	BLU	PBR	ATW
57314 (47372)	CS	AWCA	ATE	PBR	ATW
57315 (47234)	CS	AWCA	ATE	PBR	ATW
57316 (47290)	CS	AWCA	BLU	PBR	ATW
57601 (47825)	CS	AWCA	WCR	WCR	WCR

Right: *Three Class 57/0s, four Class 57/3s and one Class 57/6 are operated by West Coast Railway and usually work alongside their Class 47 fleet on passenger charters. The Class 57/0s do not have train heating and are thus seldom seen in charge of passenger services. The '57/0s' carry standard West Coast livery. The '57/3s' are yet to be repainted. No. 57001 is seen at Bristol Temple Meads.*
Antony Christie

Coaching Stock

Number	Name	Type	Depot	Livery	Operator	Notes
159 (99980)		AO10/SAL	CS	SPL	WCR*	LNWR saloon (ex-Q of Scots)
326 (S) (99402)	Emerald	AO11/PFP	CS	PUL	WCR	
347 (99347)	Car No. 347	AO11/PSO	CS	WCR	WCR	
348 (99348)	Car No. 348	AO11/PSP	CS	WCR	WCR	
350 (99350)	Car No. 350	AO11/PSP	CS	GRN	WCR	
352 (99352)	Amethyst	AO11/PSP	CS	PUL	WCR	
354 (99354)	The Hadrian Bar	AO11/PSP	CS	PUL	WCR	
504 (99678)	Ullswater	AP1Z/PFK	CS	PUL	WCR	
506 (99679)	Windermere	AP1Z/PFK	CS	PUL	WCR	
546 (S) (99670)	City of Manchester	AQ1Z/PFP	CS	PUL	WCR	
548 (99671)	Grasmere	AQ1Z/PFP	CS	PUL	WCR	
549 (99672)	Bassenthwaite	AQ1Z/PFP	CS	PUL	WCR	
550 (99673)	Rydal Water	AQ1Z/PFP	CS	PUL	WCR	
551 (99674)	Buttermere	AQ1Z/PFP	CS	PUL	WCR	
552 (99675)	Ennerdale Water	AQ1Z/PFP	CS	PUL	WCR	
553 (99676)	Crummock Water	AQ1Z/PFP	CS	PUL	WCR	
586 (99677)	Derwent Water	AR1Z/PFB	CS	PUL	WCR	
807 (99881)		AO10/SAL	CS	SPL	WCR*	GNR Saloon (ex-Q of Scots)
1252 (3280)		AJ1F/RFO	LM	VIR	WCR	
1253 (3432)		AJ1F/RFO	CS	VIR	WCR	
1644 (S)		AJ41/RBR	CS	ICS	WCR	
1650 (S)		AJ41/RBR	CS	ICS	WCR	
1652 (S)		AJ41/RBR	CS	ICS	WCR	
1655 (S)		AJ41/RBR	CS	ICS	WCR	
1663 (S)		AJ41/RBR	CS	ICS	WCR	
1670 (S)		AJ41/RBR	CS	ICS	WCR	
1730		AJ41/RBR	CS	WCR	WCR	
1800 (5970)		AN2F/RSS	CS	WCR	WCR	
1840		AN21/RMB	CS	WCR	WCR	Set - The Green Train
1860		AN21/RMB	CS	WCR	WCR	
1861 (99132)		AN21/RMB	CS	WCR	WCR	
1882 (99311)		AN21/RMB	CS	WCR	WCR	

Private Train Operators – WCRC

WCRC

1961		AJ41/RBR	CS	GRN	WCR	Set - The Green Train
2127 (S)		AO11/SLF	CS	MAR	WCR	
2833 (21270)		AU51/SLSC	CS	WCR	WCR	
3058	Florence	AD11/FO	CS	WCR	WCR	
3093 (977594)	Paula	AD11/FO	CS	WCR	WCR	
3105 (99121)	Julia	AD11/FO	CS	WCR	WCR	
3106 (99122)	Alexandra	AD11/FO	CS	WCR	WCR	
3113 (99125)	Jessica	AD11/FO	CS	WCR	WCR	
3117 (99127)	Christina	AD11/FO	CS	WCR	WCR	
3128 (99371)	Victoria	AD11/FO	CS	WCR	WCR	
3130 (99128)	Pamela	AD11/FO	CS	WCR	WCR	
3136 (3605)	Diana	AD11/FO	CS	WCR	WCR	
3143 (3609)	Patricia	AD11/FO	CS	WCR	WCR	
3241		AD1F/FO	CS	BLG	CAD	
3313		AD1F/FO	CS	WCR	WCR	
3326		AD1F/FO	CS	WCR	WCR	
3350		AD1F/FO	CS	WCR	WCR	
3352		AD1F/FO	CS	WCR	WCR	
3359		AD1F/FO	CS	WCR	WCR	
3360		AD1F/FO	CS	ICS	WCR	
3362		AD1F/FO	CS	ICS	WCR	
3392 (S)		AD1F/FO	CS	BPM	WCR	Blue Pullman vehicle
3395		AD1F/FO	CS	WCR	WCR	
3408		AD1F/FO	CS	WCR	WCR	
3431		AD1F/FO	CS	WCR	WCR	
3766 (99317)		AC21/SO	CS	WCR	WCR	
4860 (S) (99193)		AC21/TSO	CS	MAR	WCR	
4905		AC21/TSO	CS	WCR	WCR	
4912 (99318)		AC21/TSO	CS	WCR	WCR	
4931 (99329)		AC21/TSO	CS	WCR	WCR	
4932 (S)		AC21/TSO	CS	BLG	WCR	
4940		AC21/TSO	CS	WCR	WCR	
4951		AC21/TSO	CS	WCR	WCR	
4954 (99326)		AC21/TSO	CS	WCR	WCR	
4958		AC21/TSO	CS	WCR	WCR	
4960		AC21/TSO	CS	WCR	WCR	
4973		AC21/TSO	CS	WCR	WCR	
4984		AC21/TSO	CS	WCR	WCR	
4994		AC21/TSO	CS	WCR	WCR	
4997 (S)		AC21/TSO	CS	BLG	WCR	
5032 (99194)		AC21/TSO	CS	WCR	WCR	
5033 (99328)		AC21/TSO	CS	WCR	WCR	
5035 (99195)		AC21/TSO	CS	WCR	WCR	
5044 (99327)		AC21/TSO	CS	WCR	WCR	
5125 (S)		AC2Z/TSO	BH	GRN	WCR	
5171		AC2Z/TSO	CS	MAR	WCR	
5200		AC2Z/TSO	CS	GRN	WCR	
5216		AC2Z/TSO	CS	MAR	WCR	
5222		AC2Z/TSO	CS	MAR	WCR	
5229	The Green Knight	AC2Z/SO	CS	MAR	WTN	
5236		AC2Z/SO	CS	MAR	WCR	
5237		AD2Z/SO	CS	MAR	WCR	
5239	The Red Knight	AD2Z/SO	CS	MAR	WTN	
5249		AD2Z/SO	CS	GRN	WCR	
5278	Melisande	AC2A/TSO	CS	CHC	WTN	
5419		AC2A/TSO	CS	WCR	WTN	
5453		AC2B/TSO	SH	WCR	WCR	
5463 (S)		AC2B/TSO	CS	WCR	WCR	
5478		AC2B/TSO	SH	WCR	WCR	
5487		AC2B/TSO	SH	WCR	WCR	
5491		AC2B/TSO	CS	WCR	WCR	
5569		AC2C/TSO	CS	WCR	WCR	
5756 (S)		AC2E/TSO	CS	WCR	WCR	
5815		AC2E/TSO	CS	WCR	WCR	
5876		AC2E/TSO	BH	BLG	WCR	
5888		AC2E/TSO	SH	MAR	WCR	
5925		AC2F/TSO	BH	BLG	WCR	
5958		AC2F/TSO	SH	BLG	WCR	
6000		AC2F/TSO	CS	WCR	WCR	

6012		AC2F/TSO	CS	WCR	WCR
6014 (S)		AC2F/TSO	CS	ICS	WCR	At Hellifield
6021		AC3F/TSO	CS	WCR	WCR
6022		AC2F/TSO	CS	WCR	WCR
6041		AC2F/TSO	CS	WCR	WCR
6045		AC2F/TSO	SH	VIR	WCR
6073		AC2F/TSO	CS	VIR	WCR
6103		AC2F/TSO	CS	WCR	WCR
6115 (S)		AC2F/TSO	CS	WCR	WCR
6134		AC2F/TSO	SH	ICS	WCR
6135 (S)		AC2F/TSO	CS	ICS	WCR	At Hellifield
6151		AC2F/TSO	CS	BLG	WCR
6154		AC2F/TSO	CS	WCR	WCR
6312 (92925)		AX51/GEN	CS	WCR	WCR
6528 (5592)		AG2C/TSOT	CS	WCR	WCR
6723		AN1D/RMBF	CS	WCR	WCR
6724		AN1D/RMBF	CS	WCR	WCR
9104 (S) (9401)		AH2Z/BSOT	CS	WCR	WCR
9391	Pendragon	AE2Z/BSO	CS	PUL	WTN
9392		AE2Z/BSO	CS	WCR	WCR	Set - The Green Train
9440		AE2C/BSO	CS	WCR	WCR
9448 (S)		AE2C/BSO	CS	WCR	WCR
9493		AE2D/BSO	CS	WCR	CWR	Blue Pullman vehicle
10245 (10019)		AJ1G/RFM	AL	BLG	WCR
13227		AA11/FK	CS	WCR	WCR
13306 (S)		AA11/FK	CS	WCR	WCR
13320 (S)		AA11/FK	CS	WCR	WCR
13321 (99316)		AA11/FK/RBR	CS	WCR	WCR
13440 (S)		AA1A/FK	CS	GRN	WCR	Set - The Green Train
17102 (99680)		AB1A/BFK	CS	MAB	WCR
17168 (S) (99319)		AB1D/BFK	CS	WCR	WCR
18756 (99721)		AA21/SK	SH	WCR	WCR
18767 (99710)		AA21/SK	SH	WCR	WCR
18806 (99722)		AA21/SK	CS	WCR	WCR
18808 (99706)		AA21/SK	SH	WCR	WCR
18862 (99718)		AA21/SK	SH	WCR	WCR
18893 (99712)		Kitchen	CS	WCR	WCR
19208 (99884)	Car No. 84	AA21/SK	CS	WCR	WCR
21256 (99304)		AB31/BCK	CS	WCR	WCR
21266		AB31/BCK	CS	WCR	WCR
34525 (S) (99966)		AR51/GEN	CS	WCR	WCR
35407 (99886)		AB21/BSK	CS	SPL	WCR	LNWR livery (Q of Scots)
45018 (99052)		AO10/SAL	CS	QOS	WCR
45026 (S)		SAL	CS	MAR	WCR	LMS Inspection Saloon
96175		GUV	CS	MAR	WCR	Water carrier
99723 (35459)		AB21/BSK	CS	WCR	WCR

WCR* - Owned by Scottish Highland Railway Co

Right: *Many of the original Mk2 BR Manchester/Liverpool Pullman coaches are now operated by West Coast Railway. These have been largely restored into Pullman umber & cream livery as depicted on car No. 552, a Pullman First Parlor allocated TOPS number 99675 and now named* Ennerdale Water. **Robin Ralston**

Private Train Operators – WCRC

Loco Support Coaches

Most preserved locomotives authorised for main line operation, either steam or diesel, operate with a support coach conveying owners' representatives, engineering staff and light maintenance equipment. Support coaches can be allocated to a specific locomotive or operate with a pool of locos.

Number	Type	Depot	Livery	Support Coach for
14007 (99782) *Mercator*	AB11/BSK	BH	MAR	61264 or 60163
14064	AB11/BSK	CS	MAR	30777, 45305, 70013
14099 (17099)	AB11/BSK	BQ	MAR	44871, 45305 or 70013
17013 (14013) *Botaurus*	AB11/BFK	SH	PUL	60019
17019 (14019)	AB11/BFK	CS	MAR	61994
17025 (14025)	AB11/BFK	CS	MAR	45690
17041 (99141)	AB1Z/BFK	BQ	MAR	71000
17096	AB1B/BFK	SL	CHC	35028
21096 (99080)	AB31/BCK	NY	MAR	60007
21232 (99040)	AB31/BCK	CQ	MAR	6201
21236 (99120)	AB31/BCK	ZG	GRN	30828
21249 (S)	AB21/BCK	-	MAR	60163
21268	AB31/BCK	YK	MAR	6100
35317	AD21/BSK	BQ	GRN	30850
35322 (99035)	AB21/BSK	CS	MAR	70000 and WCRC traction
35329	AB21/BSK	RL	GRN	Mid Hants fleet
35333 (99180)	AB21/BSK	DI	CHC	60163
35449 (99241)	AB21/BSK	BQ	MAR	45231
35457 (99995)	AB21/BSK	NY	MAR	60532
35461 (99720)	AB21/BSK	TM	CHC	5029
35463 (99312)	AB21/BSK	CS	WCR	WCR fleet
35464	AB21/BSK	PR	MAR	Swanage Railway
35465 (99991)	AB21/BSK	BQ	CCM	Jeremy Hosking / 70000
35468 (99953)	AB21/BSK	NY	MAR	NYMR fleet
35470	AB21/BSK	TM	CHC	Vintage Trains fleet
35476 (99041)	AB21/BSK	SK	MAR	46233
35486 (99405)	AB21/BSK	--	MAR	60009 or 61994
35508	AB1C/BSK	BQ	MAR	East Lancs fleet
35517 (17088)	ABIK/BSKk	BQ	MAR	East Lancs fleet
35518 (17097)	AB11/BFK	SH	GRN	34067
80204 (35297)	NNX	CS	MAR	WCRC fleet
80217 (35299)	NNX	CS	MAR	WCRC fleet
80220 (35276)	NNX	NY	MAR	62005

Below: *All main line certified steam locomotives have an allocated support coach, which is usually attached to steam-powered services to act as a staff coach for the loco support crew and a brake van to house some emergency repair items. Painted in Pullman colours is BFK No. 17013* Botaurus *which is allocated to operate with ex-LNER A4 Pacific No. 60019.*
Nathan Williamson

Locomotives

No locos were off lease at the time of going to press

Diesel Multiple-Units

No DMUs were off lease at the time of going to press

Electric Multiple-Units

Number	Class	Owner	Location
365526	365	EVL	ZC*
* Collision damage			
317708	317	ANG	KT
317709	317	ANG	KT
317710	317	ANG	KT
317714	317	ANG	KT
317719	317	ANG	KT
317722	317	ANG	IL
317723	317	ANG	IL
317729	317	ANG	KT
317732	317	ANG	KT
460001	460	PTR (for SWT)	

Number	Class	Owner	Location
460002	460	PTR (for SWT)	
460003	460	PTR (for SWT)	
460004	460	PTR (for SWT)	
460005	460	PTR (for SWT)	
460006	460	PTR (for SWT)	
460007	460	PTR (for SWT)	
460008	460	PTR (for SWT)	
508201	508	ANG	ZG
508202	508	ANG	ZG
508203	508	ANG	ZG
508204	508	ANG	ZG
508205	508	ANG	ZG
508206	508	ANG	ZG

Number	Class	Owner	Location
508207	508	ANG	ZG
508208	508	ANG	ZG
508209	508	ANG	ZG
508210	508	ANG	ZG
508211	508	ANG	ZG
508212	508	-	§
508301	508	ANG	ZG
508302	508	ANG	ZG
508303	508	ANG	ZG

§ Fire training set at Moreton-in-Marsh

Coaching Stock - Passenger

Number	Type	Owner	Location
1209 (6457)	RFO	EVL	ZH
1211 (3305)	RFO	EVL	BU
1219 (3418)	RFO	EVL	KT
1258 (3322)	RFO	EVL	CS
3229	FO	EVL	KT
3434	FO	EVL	OY
3438	FO	EVL	LM
5636	TSO	EVL	PM
5737	TSO	EVL	CS
5740	TSO	EVL	CS
5888	TSO	EVL	CS
5900	TSO	EVL	CS
5903	TSO	EVL	CS
5947	TSO	EVL	ZG¤
5981	TSO	EVL	ZA
5991	TSO	EVL	KT
6059	TSO	EVL	KT
6061	TSO	EVL	ZG¤
6121	TSO	EVL	KT
6160	TSO	EVL	LM
6164	TSO	EVL	KT

¤ For export to New Zealand

Number	Type	Owner	Location
9500	BSO	EVL	LM
9505	BSO	EVL	LM
9516	BSO	EVL	KT
9522	BSO	EVL	CE
9523	BSO	EVL	KT
9713	DBSO	EVL	KT
10204 (40502)	RFM	PTR	3M
10231 (10016)	RFM	PTR	§
10240 (10003)	RFM	PTR	LM
10241 (10009)	RFM	PTR	IL
10253 (10026)	RFM	PTR	LM
10256 (10028)	RFM	PTR	YO¶
10260 (10001)	RFM	PTR	YO¶

¶ Instruction vehicle - Yoker
§ Fire Training School

Number	Type	Owner	Location
10547	SLE	PTR	IS
10596	SLE	PTR	LM
10661 Concept vehicle at Wolverton			
10667	SLE	-	LM
10682	SLE	PTR	TO
10698	SLE	-	LM
10733	SLE	-	MM
11006	FO	PTR	LM

Number	Type	Owner	Location
11011	FO	PTR	LM
11026	FO	PTR	LM
12008	TSO	PTR	ZB
12022	TSO	PTR	ZB
12029	TSO	PTR	LM
12036	TSO	PTR	LM
12047	TSO	PTR	LM
12063	TSO	PTR	LM
12065	TSO	PTR	LM
12083	TSO	PTR	LM
12087	TSO	PTR	LM
12092	TSO	PTR	LM
12095	TSO	PTR	LM
12101	TSO	PTR	LM
12134	TSO	PTR	LM
12142	TSO	PTR	LM
12144	TSO	PTR	LM
12156	TSO	PTR	LM
12158	TSO	PTR	BN
12160	TSO	PTR	LM
12163	TSO	PTR	BN

Coaching Stock - HST

Number	Type	Owner	Location
40402 (40002)	TRSB	DBR	LM
40403 (40003)	TRSB	DBR	LM
40416 (40016)	TRSB	DBR	LM
40417 (40017)	TRSB	DBR	ZK
40419 (40019)	TRSB	DBR	LM
40425 (40025)	TRSB	DBR	ZK
40434 (40034)	TRSB	DBR	LM
40745 (40345)	TRSB	ANG	ZG

42324 owned by East Midlands Trains now at Birkenshaw Fire Training School

Coaching Stock - NPCCS

Number	Type	Owner	Location
82109	DVT	PTR	ZB
82125	DVT	PTR	LM
82140	DVT	PTR	LM
82149	DVT	PTR	FC
92159 (81534)	BG	EVL	KT
92901 (92001)	BG	EVL	WB
92931 (92031)	BG	EVL	PY
96100 (93734)	GUV	EVL	TM
96139 (93751)	GUV	EVL	WB
96181 (93875)	GUV	EVL	LM
96602 (96150)	NV	EVL	RU
96606 (96213)	NV	EVL	RU
96608 (96216)	NV	EVL	RU
96609 (96217)	NV	EVL	RU

Off-lease Rolling Stock

Preserved motive power is listed in this section. Those in a red typeface are authorised for main line operation. For information on preserved steam traction and railway centres, please refer to our sister publication *Railways Restored*, edited by Alan Butcher and published by Ian Allan Publishing.

Locomotives

Main line certified shown in red

Number	Operator/Base	Status
Prototype Locomotives		
LMS7050	NRM	STC
LMS7051	MID	OPR
LMS7069	GWR	RES
D0226	KWV	OPR
18000	DID	STC
DELTIC	NRM	STC
Non-Classified		
D2511	KWV	OPR
D2767	BKR	OPR
D2774	STR	RES
DS75	NRS	STC
Class 01		
D2953	PRL	OPR
D2956	ELR	OPR
Class 02		
D2854	PRL	OPR
D2858	MRC	RES
D2860	NRM	OPR
D2866	PRL	RES
D2867	BAT	OPR
D2868	MSM	OPR
Class 03		
03018	MFM	RES
03020	LDL	STO
03022	SWI	OPR
D2023	KES	OPR
D2024	KES	STO
03027	PRL	RES
03037	-	OPR
D2041	COL	OPR
D2046	PVR	RES
D2051	NNR	STO
03059	IOW	OPR
03062	ELR	OPR
03063	NNR	OPR
03066	BHR	OPR
03069	GWR	OPR
03072	LHR	OPR
03073	RAC	OPR
03078	TYN	OPR
03079	DER	OPR
03081	MFM	RES
03084	ECC	OPR
03089	MFM	OPR
03090	NRS	OPR
03094	CRT	OPR
03099	PRL	OPR
03112	KES	OPR
03113	PRL	RES
D2117	LHR	OPR
D2118	PRL	RES
03119	EPO	OPR
03120	FHL	OPR
03128	APF	STO
D2133	WSR	OPR
03134	DEE	OPR
D2138	MRC	OPR
D2139	PRL	RES
03141	PRB	RES
03144	WEN	OPR
03145	MOL	OPR
D2148	RIB	OPR
03152	SWI	OPR
03158	LWR	OPR
03162	LAN	OPR
03170	BAT	OPR
D2178	GWI	OPR
03180	PRL	OPR
D2182	GWR	OPR
D2184	COL	OPR
03189	RIB	RES
D2192	PDR	OPR
03197	LDL	RES
03199	PRL	OPR
03371	ROW	OPR
03399	MFM	OPR
Class 04		
D2203	EMB	OPR
D2205	WSR	STO
D2207	NYM	OPR
D2229	PRL	RES
D2245	BAT	STO
D2246	SDR	OPR
D2271	WSR	STO
D2272	PRL	RES
D2279	EAR	OPR
D2280	NNR	RES
D2284	PRL	OPR
D2298	BRC	OPR
D2302	BHR	OPR
D2310	BAT	OPR
D2324	PRL	STO
D2325	MFM	OPR
D2334	CVR	OPR
D2337	PRL	RES
Class 05		
05001	IOW	OPR
D2578	BHR	OPR
D2587	PRL	RES
D2595	RIB	OPR
Class 06		
06003	MSM	OPR
Class 07		
07005	GCR	RES
07010	AVR	OPR
07011	SEL	OPR
07012	APF	RES
07013	BHR	RES
Class 08		
D3000	PRL	RES
D3002	PVR	OPR
D3014	PDR	OPR
08011	CPR	OPR
08012	CRT	OPR
08015	SVR	OPR
08016	PRL	OPR
08021	BRM	OPR
08022	CWR	OPR
08032	MHR	OPR
08046	CRB	OPR
08054	EMB	OPR
08060	CWR	OPR
08064	NRS	OPR
D3101	GCR	OPR
08102	LWR	OPR
08108	KES	OPR
08114	GCR	OPR
08123	CWR	OPR
08133	SVR	OPR
D3255	CVR	STO
08164	ELR	OPR
08168	BAT	OPR
D3261	SWI	RES
08195	LAN	OPR
08220	NHC	STO
08238	DFR	OPR
08266	KWV	OPR
08288	MHR	OPR
08331	MRC	OPR
08359	TSR	OPR
08377	WSR	OPR
08388	NHD	STO
08436	SWN	OPR
08443	BKR	RES
08444	BWR	OPR
08471	SVR	OPR
08473	DFR	STO
08476	SWN	OPR
08479	ELR	OPR
08490	STR	OPR
08528	BAT	OPR
08556	NYM	OPR
08590	MRC	OPR
08598	IND	OPR
08604	DID	OPR
08628	RIB	OPR
08631	MNR	OPR
08635	SVR	RES
08683	GWR	RES
08694	GCR	RES
08700	ELR	OPR
08767	NNR	OPR
08769	SVR	OPR
08772	NNR	OPR
08773	EMB	OPR
08780	SOU	OPR
08830	RAC	OPR
08850	NYM	OPR§
08881	MSR	OPR
08891	SVR	RES
08896	SVR	OPR
08911	NRM	OPR
08927	GWR	OPR

Preserved Motive Power

No.	Depot	Status	No.	Depot	Status	No.	Depot	Status
08937	DAR	OPR	20059	BRM	RES	27056	GCR	OPR
08944	ELR	OPR	20063	GWR	STO	27059	SVR	RES
§ Battersby-Whitby only			20069	MNR	OPR	27066	DFR	OPR
			20087	ELR	OPR			
Class 09			20098	GCR	RES	**Class 28**		
09001	PRL	RES	20110	SDR	OPR	D5705	ELR	RES
09004	SPV	OPR	20137	GWR	OPR			
09010	SDR	RES	20142	BAR	OPR	**Class 31**		
09015	PRI	STO	20154	GCR	OPR	D5500	NRM	OPR
09017	NRM	OPR	20169	SRC	RES	31101	BAT	RES
09024	PRI	RES	20177	SVR	STO	31108	MRC	OPR
09025	SWI	OPR	20188	SVR	OPR	31119	EMB	OPR
			20189	MRC	OPR	31130	BAT	OPR
Class 10			20205	MRC	RES	31162	EHC	OPR
D3452	BWR	OPR	20214	LHR	OPR	31163	CPR	OPR
D3489	SPV	OPR	20227	MRC	OPR	31203	PBR(Nem)	OPR
D4067	GCR	OPR	20228	BIR	OPR	31206	RST	OPR
D4092	BHR	RES				31207	NNR	OPR
			Class 24			31210	DFR	RES
Class 11			24032	NYM	RES	31235	MNR	OPR
12052	CRB	STO	24054	ELR	OPR	31255	COL	OPR
12061	PRL	RES	24061	NYM	RES	31270	PRL	OPR
12077	MRC	OPR	24082	GWR	OPR	31271	NVR	OPR
12082	MHR	OPR				31289	NLR	OPR
(Runs as 12049)			**Class 25**			31327	STR	OPR
12093	CRB	OPR	25035	GCR	OPR	31410	SRC	RES
12099	SVR	OPR	25057	NNR	OPR	31414	ECC	OPR
12131	NNR	OPR	25059	KWV	OPR	31415	BHR	RES
			25067	BAT	OPR	31418	MRC	RES
Class 12			25072	CRB	RES	31435	EMB	OPR
15224	SPV	OPR	25083	CRB	RES	31438	EPO	OPR
			25173	EPO	OPR	31461	NEM	STO
Class 14			25185	PDR	OPR	31463	GCR	OPR
D9500	PRL	RES	25191	SDR	STO	31466	DFR	OPR
D9502	PRL	STO	25235	BKR	RES	31530	MNR	RES
D9504	NVR	OPR	25244	EKR	STO			
D9513	EMB	OPR	25262	SDR	OPR	**Class 33**		
D9516	WEN	OPR	25265	GCR	RES	33002	SDR	OPR
D9518	WSR	OPR	25278	NYM	OPR	33008	BAT	RES
D9520	NVR	OPR	25279	GCR	OPR	33012	SWN	OPR
D9521	DFR	OPR	25283	DFR	RES	33019	BAT	OPR
D9523	DVR	OPR	25309	WCR	RES	33021	BRM	RES
D9524	EHC	RES	25313	WEN	RES	33030	BAT	RES
D9525	PRL	OPR	25321	MRC	OPR	33034	SWN	Scrap
D9526	WSR	OPR	25322	CVR	RES	33035	ECC	OPR
D9529	NVR	OPR				33046	MRC	STO
D9531	ELR	RES	**Class 26**			33048	WSR	OPR
D9537	RIP	RES	26001	CRB	OPR	33052	KES	OPR
D9539	RIB	OPR	26002	STR	RES	33053	MHR	OPR
D9551	DEE	OPR	26004	BKR	STO	33057	WSR	RES
D9553	GWR	STO	26007	GCR	OPR	33063	SPV	OPR
D9555	DFR	OPR	26010	LAN	OPR	33065	SPV	RES
			26011	BHR	RES	33102	CVR	RES
Class 15			26014	CRB	OPR	33108	BHR	RES
D8233	ELR	RES	26024	BKR	OPR	33109	ELR	OPR
			26025	STR	RES	33110	BWR	RES
Class 17			26035	CRB	RES	33111	SWN	OPR
D8568	CPR	RES	26038	BKR	RES	33116	GCR	OPR
			26040	MET	RES	33117	ELR	RES
Class 20			26043	GWR	RES	33201	MRC	OPR
D8000	NRM	OPR				33202	MFM	OPR
20001	BAR	OPR	**Class 27**			33208	MHR	OPR
20007	GCR	OPR	27001	BKR	OPR			
20020	BKR	RES	27005	BKR	STO	**Class 35**		
20031	KWV	OPR	27007	MHR	RES	D7017	WSR	OPR
20035	CVR	STO	27024	LHR	OPR	D7018	WSR	RES
20048	MRC	RES	27050	STR	RES	D7029	SVR	RES

No.	Operator	Status	No.	Operator	Status	No.	Operator	Status
D7076	ELR	OPR	**Class 44**			50030	PRL	RES
Class 37			D4	MRC	RES	50031	SVR	RES
D6700	NRM	OPR	44008	PRL	OPR	50033	SBC	STO
						50135	EHD	OPR
37003	MNR	OPR	**Class 45**			50042	BWR	OPR
37009	GCR	RES	45014	BAT	STO	50044	MRC	OPR
37023	ALY	RES	45041	MRC	OPR	50049	SVR (CF)	OPR
37025	BKR	RES	45060	BHR	OPR	50050	YEO	RES
37032	NNR	RES	45105	BHR	RES			
37037	MNR	OPR	45108	MRC	RES	**Class 52**		
37042	EVR	OPR	45118	NLR	RES	D1010	WSR	OPR
37075	CVR	OPR	45125	GCR	OPR	D1013	SVR	OPR
37097	CRB	OPR	45132	MHR	RES	D1015	BRM	OPR
37108	RAC	OPR	45133	MRC	RES	D1023	NRM	OPR
37109	ELR	OPR	45135	ELR	RES	D1041	ELR	STO
37116	CPR	OPR	45149	GWR	RES	D1048	MRC	RES
37142	BWR	OPR				D1062	SVR	OPR
37146	SRC	RES	**Class 46**					
37152	PRL	RES	46010	GCN	OPR	**Class 55**		
37175	BKR	RES	46035	RAC	STO	55002	NRM	RES
37188	PRL	RES	46045	MRC	OPR	55009	BHR	OPR
37207	PVR	RES				55015	BHR	RES
37215	GWR	OPR	**Class 47**			55016	BHR	OPR
37216	PBR	OPR	47004	EMB	OPR	55019	BHR	OPR
37219	PBR	OPR	47105	GWR	OPR	55022	ELR	OPR
37227	BAT	OPR	47117	GCR	OPR			
37240	LAN	OPR	47192	DAR	OPR	**Class 56**		
37250	WED	RES	47205	NLR	OPR	56006	BHR	OPR
37254	SPV	OPR	47292	GCR	OPR	56007	BUR	RES
37255	GCR	OPR	47306	BWR	OPR	56097	GCR	OPR
37263	DFR	RES	47367	NNR	OPR	56098	BAT	RES
37264	BRM	RES	47376	GWR	RES	56301	BHR	OPR
37275	BHR	OPR	47401	MRC	OPR			
37294	EMB	RES	47402	ELR	OPR	**Class 58**		
37308	EHD	RES	47417	MRC	RES	58016	BHR	RES
37314	MRC	OPR	47449	LAN	OPR			
37324	GWR	OPR	47484	BHR	RES	**Class 97**		
37372	BHR	RES	47524	CVR	RES	97650	LWR	OPR
37403	BKR	RES	47540	WEN	STO	97651	STR	OPR
37407	CVR	STO	47596	MNR	RES	97654	PRL	OPR
37413	NEM	RES	47635	BAT	OPR			
37418	ELR	RES	47640	BAT	OPR	**Class 71**		
37421	PBR	RES	47643	BKR	OPR	71001	NRS	STO
37424	CVR	STO	47701	DAR	OPR			
37518	ELR	OPR	47703	WEN	OPR	**Class 73**		
37674	SRC	RES	47715	WEN	OPR	73001	DFR	OPR
37679	NLR	RES	47763	MFM	OPR	73003	SWI	OPR
37901	ELR	OPR	47765	GCR	RES	73005	SVR(EH)	RES
37905	BUR	OPR	47771	COL	RES	73006	RAC	OPR
37906	SVR	OPR	47773	BRM	OPR			
			47785	ECC	RES	73103	THK	STO
Class 40			47793	MFM	OPR	73110	GCR	OPR
D200	NRM	RES	47798	NRM	OPR	73114	BAT	OPR
40012	MRC	OPR	47799	EVR	RES	73117	BHR	OPR
40013	BHR	OPR	47840	WST	OPR	73128	PBR	OPR
40106	WAS	OPR				73129	GWR	OPR
40118	BRM	RES	**Class 50**			73130	FIN	OPR
40135	ELR	OPR	50002	SDR	RES	73134	BHR	OPR
40145	ELR	OPR	50007	MRC	OPR	73140	SPV	OPR
			50008	ELR	OPR	73210	MNR	OPR
Class 41			50015	ELR	OPR			
41001	NRM	STC	50017	PVR	RES	**Class 76**		
			50019	MNR	OPR	E26020	NRM	STC
Class 42			50021	BRM	RES			
D821	SVR	OPR	50026	EHD	RES	**Class 77**		
D832	WSR	OPR	50027	MHR	OPR	E27000	MRC	STC
			50029	PRL	STO	E27001	MSM	STC

Preserved Motive Power

Below: *The quite superb condition of many of the UK preserved diesel and electric locomotives is a credit to the owners and groups, many of which have spent thousands of pounds restoring locos to as near perfect condition as possible. In immaculate condition is InterCity-liveried Class 73/2 No. 73210 Selhurst which is preserved on the Mid-Norfolk Railway.* **Antony Christie**

Class 81		
81002	BHR	STC

Class 82		
82008	BHR	STC

Class 83		
83012	BHR	STC

Class 84		
84001	BHR	STC

Class 85		
85101	BHR	STC

Class 86		
86101	BHR	OPR
86259	BRM	OPR

Class 87		
87001	NRM	STC
87002	MLM	OPR
87035	RAC	RES

Class 89		
89001	BHR	STC

London Transport		
12	LUL	OPR

Diesel Units

Number	Base							
Unclassified		51247	WEN	**Class 104**		50632	PBR
APT-E	NRS	51427	GCR	50447	LAN	50929	KWV
LEV1	NNR	51432	SWN	50454	LAN	50980	BWR
RB004	TEL	51434	MNR	50455	TEL	51562	ELR
		51498	SWN	50479	TEL	51565	KWV
79018	MRC	51499	MNR	50494	CVR	51566	DFR
79612	MRC	51503	MNR	50517	CVR	51567	MRC
79900	ECC	51505	EAR	50528	LAN	51568	KEI
79960	NNR	51511	NYM	50531	TEL	51571	KES
79962	KWV	51512	CRT	50547	CVR	51572	WEN
79963	NNR	51213	EAR	50556	TEL	51907	LAN
79964	KWV	51803	KWV	56182	CVR	51909	MSR
79976	GCR	53160	MRC	59137	CVR	51914	DFR
79978	COL	53164	CHS	59228	TEL	51919	BVR
		53170	ECC			51922	ELR
Class 100		53193	GCR	**Class 105**		51933	DFR
56301	MNR	53203	GCR	51485	ELR	51941	SVR
		53204	NYM	56121	ELR	51942	PBR
Class 101		53253	MRC	56456	LAN	51947	BWR
50222	BIR	53266	GCR			51950	GWR
50256	EKR	53321	GCR	**Class 107**		51973	MRC
50338	BIR	53746	WEN	51990	STR	52044	PBR
51505	ECC	54055	CRT	52005	NVR	52048	BVR
51187	CRT	54062	NNR	52006	AVR	52053	KEI
51188	ECC	54365	EAR	52008	STR	52054	BWR
51189	KWV	54408	SPV	52025	AVR	52062	GWR
51192	ELR	56343	EKR	52030	STR	52064	SVR
51205	CRT	56352	ELR	59791	NVR	53628	KEI
51210	WEN	56358	EAR			53645	GCR
51226	MNR			**Class 108**		53926	GCR
51228	NNR	59117	MNR	50599	EAR	53971	KES
		59539	NYM	50619	DFR	54223	EAR

54270	PBR	59678	-	59508	GWI	55966	MRC
54279	LDL	59719	SDR	59509	WEN	55976	MRC
54490	LAN	59740	SDR	59510	GWR	59609	MRC
54504	SWN	59761	BRC	59513	PDR		
56208	SVR			59514	SWI	**Class 140**	
56224	ECC	**Class 116**		59516	SWN	140001 - 55500/01 KEI	
56271	MSR	51131	BAT	59517	PDR		
56484	MRC	51138	GCR	59520	PBR	**Class 141**	
56491	KEI	51151	GCR	59521	MRC	141103	WED
56492	DFR	51321	BAT	59522	CHS	141108	COL
56495	KLR	59003	PDR	59603	CHS	141110	WED
59245	APF	59004	PDR			141113	MRC
59250	SVR	59444	CHS	**Class 119**			
59387	DFR			51073	ECC	**Class 201, 202 & 203**	
59389	GCR	**Class 117**		51074	SWI	60116	HAD
		51339	GWR	51104	SWI	60118	HAD
Class 109		51342	EPO			60501	HAD
50416	LAN	51346	SWN	**Class 120**		60529	HAD
56171	LAN	51347	GWI	59276	GCR	60750	WPH
		51351	PBR			201001	HAD
Class 110		51353	MRC	**Class 121**			
51813	WEN	51356	SWN	55019	BRM	**Class 205**	
51842	WEN	51359	NLR	55023	CPR	60117	PBR
52071	LHR	51360	ECC	55024	BRM	60822	LDL
52077	LHR	51363	GWR	55028	SWN	60828	PBR
59701	CVR	51365	GWR	55029	RST	60154 X 1101 EKR	
		51367	STR	55033	COL	60800 X 1101 EKR	
Class 111		51372	TIT	54289	ECC	70549	ELR
59575	MRC	51381	MFM	56287	COL	Set 205009 EDR	
		51382	GWR			Set 205025 MHR	
Class 114		51384	EPO	**Class 122**		Set 205028 DAR	
50015	MRC	51388	SWN	55000	SDR	Set 205032 DAR	
50019	MRC	51392	SWN	55001	ELR	Set 205033 LDL	
54057	STR	51395	MRC	55003	GWR	Set 205205 EPO	
56006	MRC	51397	PBR	55005	BAT		
56015	MRC	51398	MRC	55006	ECC	**Class 207**	
		51400	WEN	55009	MNR	60127	SWI
Class 115		51401	GWI	55012	SHI	60130 X 207202 ELR	
51655	(BIR)	51402	STR			60138	WPH
51663	WSR	51405	GWR	**Class 126**		60142	SPV
51669	SPV	51407	GWR	51017	BKR	60145	SEL
51677	(BIR)	59486	SWN	51043	BKR	60149	SEL
51859	WSR	59488	PDR	59404	BKR	60616	SPV
51880	WSR	59492	SWN	79443	BKR	60901	SWI
51886	BRC	59494	PDR			60904 X 207202 ELR	
51887	WSR	59500	WEN	**Class 127**		60916	SPV
51899	BRC	59503	PDR	51616	GCR		
59659	SDR	59506	WSR	51618	LAN	901001	CVR
59664	(BIR)	59507	PDR	51622	GCR		

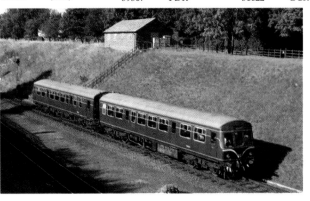

Left: *Looking just as it did when introduced in the 1960s, here is a Met-Cam power twin formed of vehicles 50321 and 51427 operating on the Great Central Railway.*
Nathan Williamson

Electric Units

Unclassified

28249	NRM
29666	MRC
29670	MRC
79998	DEE
79999	DEE

BEL

85	SOU
87	KEI
91	RAM

BIL

10656 (2090)	NRS
12123 (2090)	NRS

COR

10096	EKR
11161	EKR
11179	NRM
11201	BLU
11825	EKR

DD

13004	NIR

Class 302

75033	MFM
75250	MFM

Class 303

303032	SHP

Class 306

306017	EAR

Class 307

75023	ERM

Class 308

75881	ERM

Class 309

309616	COV
309624	COV

Class 405 (SUB)

S8143S	NRM
4732	COV

Class 411/412 (CEP)

61742	DAR
61743	DAR
61798	EVR
61799	EVR
61804	EVR
61805	EVR
70229	EVR
70257	GCR
70273	DFR
70284	NIR
70292	SMP
70296	NIR
70354	EVR
70527	WRN
70531	SMP
70539	EVR
70576	SNI
70607	EVR
Set 1198	PBR
Set 7105	EKR

Class 414 (HAP)

61275	NRM
61287 (4311)	COV
75395	NRM
75407 (4311)	COV

Class 415 (EPB)

14351 (5176)	NIR
14352 (5176)	NIR
15345	COV
15396 (5176)	NIR

Class 416 (EPB)

65302	FIN
65304	FIN
65373 (5759)	EKR
77558 (5759)	EKR
14573 (6307)	COV
16117 (6307)	COV
65321 (5791)	COV
77112 (5793)	COV

Class 419 (MLV)

68001	EKR
68002	EKR
68003	EVR
68004	MNR
68005	EVR
68008	EKR
68009	EKR

Class 421 (CIG)

62364	DFR
62378	DFR
62887	LWR
69339	GCR
76726	DFR
76740	DFR
76797	DFR
76811	DFR
76812	DAR
Set 1496	DAR
Set 1497	MNR
Set 1498	EPO
Set 1399	PBR
Set 1881	BEL

Class 422 (BEP)

69304	NIR
69310	DAR
69318	COL
69332	DAR
69333	LDL

69337	HAD

Class 423 (VEP)

(42)3417	BLU
76875	NRM

Class 457

67300	COV

Class 488

72501	ECC
72617	ECC

Class 489

68500	ECC
68506	ECC

Class 501

61183	COV
75186	COV

Class 502

28361	TEB
29896	TEB

Class 503

28690	COV
29298	COV
29720	COV

Class 504

65451	ELR
77172	ELR

Right: *Although there is no live rail for many miles around, the Dartmoor Railway at Okehampton has a driving car from former Class 411 4-CEP No. 1589, which operates in push-pull mode with diesel-powered services. The vehicle has been restored to 1970s BR blue/grey livery.* **Antony Christie**

Over the years a number of former BR locomotives have, after withdrawal from normal duties, taken up use for industrial operators. The list below represents those which are understood to still be in existence in late 2012. Some locos operated at preservation sites are deemed to be 'industrial' but these are grouped in the preserved section.

Class 03
03179 *Clive*	First Capital Connect, Hornsey Depot

Class 08
08202	The Potter Group, Ely
08375	P D Ports, Teesport No. 21
08411	LH Group, Burton – owned by Classic Traction
08441	Colne Valley Railway
08445	Daventry International Railfreight Terminal (DIRFT) – at LH Group, Burton
08447	John G. Russell Transit, Hillington, Glasgow
08460	Colne Valley Railway
08484 *Captain Nathaniel Darell*	Felixstowe Dock & Railway
08503	Rye Farm, Wishaw
08511	Felixstowe Dock & Railway
08523	Weardale Railway (H061)
08535	Corus, Shotton Works
08598	The Potter Group, Ely
08600	LH Group Services, Barton-under-Needwood
08613	Hanson Traction, Washwood Heath
08622 (H028) (7)	Weardale Railway
08643	Aggregate Industries, Whatley
08648	P D Ports, Teesport No. 20
08650 *Isle of Grain*	Aggregate Industries, Isle of Grain
08652	Hanson Aggregates, Whatley Quarry
08670	Colne Valley Railway
08699	Corus, Shotton Works
08728	St Modwen Storage, Long Marston
08731	Aggregate Industries, Merehead
08743 *Bryan Turner*	LH Group Services, Barton under Needwood
08774 *Arthur Vernon Dawson*	AV Dawson, Middlesbrough
08787	Hanson Aggregates, Machen
08807	AV Dawson, Middlesbrough
08809	Corus, Shotton (at Washwood Heath 12/10)
08818 *Molly*	Faber Prest Ports, Flixborough Wharf
08823 (D3991)	Daventry International Railfreight Terminal
08847	Stored at Norwich Crown Point (Cotswold Rail - for sale)
08870 (H024)	Castle Cement, Ketton
08872	European Metal Reprocessing, Attercliffe
08873	Freightliner Terminal, Southampton
08903 *John W. Antill*	SembCorp Utilities Teesside, Wilton
08912	AV Dawson, Middlesbrough
08913	Daventry International Railfreight Terminal (Malcolm Rail)
08915	Stephenson Railway Museum
08933	Aggregate Industries, Merehead
08936	Corus, Shotton Works
08937 *Bluebell Mel*	Aggregate Industries, Meldon Quarry
08947	Aggregate Industries, Merehead
09022	Boston Docks Co
09023	European Metal Reprocessing, Kingsbury

Class 11
12088	Butterwell

Class 14
D9529 (14029)	Aggregate Industries, Bardon Quarry

Class 56
56009 (56201)	Brush Traction, Loughborough

These lists give details of former UK diesel and electric locos exported for further use overseas and understood to still be operational.

Class 03
D2013	Italy
D2032	Italy
D2033	Italy
D2036	Italy

Class 04
D2216	Italy
D2232	Italy
D2289	Italy
D2295	Italy

Class 08
D3047	Lamco Liberia
D3092	Lamco Liberia
D3094	Lamco Liberia
D3098	Lamco Liberia
D3100	Lamco Liberia

Class 10
D3639	Conakry (Guinea)
D3649	Conakry (Guinea)

Class 14
D9534	Bruges

Class 56
56101	Floyd, Hungary 92 55 0659-001-5
56115	Floyd, Hungary 92 55 0659-002-3
56117	Floyd, Hungary 92 55 0659-003-1

Class 58
58001	ETF France
58004	TSO France
58005	ETF France
58006	ETF France
58007	TSO France
58009	TSO France
58010	TSO France
58011	TSO France
58013	ETF France
58015	Transfesa, Spain
58018	TSO France
58020	Transfesa, Spain
58021	TSO France
58024	Transfesa, Spain
58025	Continental Rail, Spain
58026	TSO France
58027	Continental Rail, Spain
58029	Transfesa, Spain
58030	Transfesa, Spain
58031	Transfesa, Spain
58032	ETF France
58033	TSO France
58034	TSO France
58035	TSO France
58036	ETF France
58038	ETF France
58039	ETF France
58040	TSO France
58041	Transfesa, Spain
58042	TSO France
58043	Transfesa, Spain
58044	ETF France
58046	TSO France
58047	Transfesa, Spain
58049	ETF France
58050	Continental Rail, Spain

Class 59
59003	HHPI, Germany

Class 66
66010	ECR, France
66022	ECR, France
66026	ECR, France
66032	ECR, France
66036	ECR, France
66038	ECR, France
66042	ECR, France
66045	ECR, France
66049	ECR, France
66052	ECR, France
66064	ECR, France
66072	ECR, France
66073	ECR, France
66123	ECR, France
66146	ECR, Poland
66153	ECR, Poland
66157	ECR, Poland
66159	ECR, Poland
66163	ECR, Poland
66166	ECR, Poland
66173	ECR, Poland
66178	ECR, Poland
66179	ECR, France
66180	ECR, Poland
66189	ECR, Poland
66190	ECR, France
66195	ECR, France
66196	ECR, France
66202	ECR, France
66203	ECR, France
66205	ECR, France
66208	ECR, France
66209	ECR, France
66210	ECR, France
66211	ECR, France
66212	ECR, France
66214	ECR, France
66215	ECR, France
66216	ECR, France
66217	ECR, France
66218	ECR, France
66219	ECR, France
66220	ECR, Poland
66222	ECR, France
66223	ECR, France
66224	ECR, France
66225	ECR, France
66226	ECR, France
66228	ECR, France
66229	ECR, France
66231	ECR, France
66233	ECR, France
66234	ECR, France
66235	ECR, France
66236	ECR, France
66237	ECR, Poland
66240	ECR, France
66241	ECR, France
66242	ECR, France
66244	ECR, France
66246	ECR, France
66247	ECR, France
66248	ECR, Poland
66411	Freightliner PL, As 66013FPL
66412	Freightliner PL, As 660xxFPL
66417	Freightliner PL, As 66014FPL
66582	Freightliner PL, As 66009FPL
66583	Freightliner PL, As 66010FPL
66584	Freightliner PL, As 66011FPL
66586	Freightliner PL, As 66008FPL
66608	Freightliner PL, As 66603FPL
66609	Freightliner PL, As 66605FPL
66611	Freightliner PL, As 66604FPL
66612	Freightliner PL, As 66606FPL
66624	Freightliner PL, As 66602FPL
66625	Freightliner PL, As 66601FPL

Class 86
86215	Floyd, Hungary 91 55 0450-005-8
86217	Floyd, Hungary 91 55 0450-006-?
86218	Floyd, Hungary 91 55 0450-004-1
86228	Floyd, Hungary 91 55 0450-007-
86233	Bulgaria (spares)
86232	Floyd, Hungary 91 55 0450-003-3
86248	Floyd, Hungary 91 55 0450-001-7
86250	Floyd, Hungary 91 55 0450-002-5

Class 87
87003	BZK Bulgaria
87004	BZK Bulgaria
87006	BZK Bulgaria
87007	BZK Bulgaria
87008	BZK Bulgaria
87009	BUL Bulgaria
87010	BZK Bulgaria
87012	BZK Bulgaria
87013	BZK Bulgaria
87014	BZK Bulgaria (spares)
87017	BUL Bulgaria
87019	BZK Bulgaria
87020	BZK Bulgaria
87022	BZK Bulgaria
87023	BUL Bulgaria
87025	BUL Bulgaria
87026	BZK Bulgaria
87028	BZK Bulgaria
87029	BZK Bulgaria
87033	BZK Bulgaria
87034	BZK Bulgaria

Class 92
92034	DBS Bulgaria

A number of preserved modern traction locomotives have been allocated five-digit Class 89 TOPS numbers to allow their operation either under power or dead over the National Network. The numbers allocated are shown below; not all locos may currently be authorised for use on Network Rail metals.

The first two digits are the class, the third is the power type, while the final two digits are the final two of the original running number. If two locos clash with the same number, the second to be registered will have 1 added to the number.

Class 89 TOPS No.	BR No.	Type	Name
89100	20050	Class 20	-
89101	20001	Class 20	-
89110	20110	Class 20	-
89127	20227	Class 20	-
89166	20166	Class 20	-
89188	20188	Class 20	-
89200	31018	Class 31	-
89204	26004	Class 26	-
89210	27059	Class 27	-
89212	LT 12	Met Loco	Sarah Siddons
89223	25173	Class 25	-
89233	25283	Class 25	-
89247	27001	Class 27	-
89254	24054	Class 24	-
89259	25309	Class 25	-
89261	24061	Class 24	-
89262	25262	Class 25	-
89280	31162	Class 31	-
89317	D7017	Class 35	-
89376	D7076	Class 35	-
89400	E27000	Class 77	Electra
89401	47401	Class 47	North Eastern
89402	50002	Class 50	Superb
89403	71001	Class 71	-
89404	44004	Class 44	Great Gable
89405	47105	Class 47	-
89407	50007	Class 50	Sir Edward Elgar
89408	50008	Class 50	Thunderer
89412	40012	Class 40	Aureol
89413	D1013	Class 52	Western Ranger
89415	50015	Class 50	Valiant
89416	D1015	Class 52	Western Champion
89417	50017	Class 50	Royal Oak
89420	45108	Class 45	-
89421:1	D821	Class 42	Greyhound
89421:2	50021	Class 50	Rodney
89423	45125	Class 45	-
89424	D1023	Class 52	Western Fusilier
89427	50027	Class 50	Lion
89431	50031	Class 50	Hood
89432	D832	Class 42	Onslaught
89435	40135	Class 40	-
89440	45133	Class 45	-
89441	D1041	Class 52	Western Prince
89442	47192	Class 47	-
89443	50042	Class 50	Triumph
89444	50044	Class 50	Exeter
89445	40145	Class 40	-
89448	D1048	Class 52	Western Lady
89449	50049	Class 50	Defiance
89453	45041	Class 45	Royal Tank Regiment
89460	45060	Class 45	Sherwood Forester
89462	D1062	Class 52	Western Courier
89466	47449	Class 47	-
89472	46035	Class 46	Ixion
89500	55022	Class 55	Royal Scots Grey
89502	55002	Class 55	The King's Own Yorkshire Light Infantry
89503	81002	Class 81	-
89509	55009	Class 55	Alycidon
89515	55015	Class 55	Tulyar
89516	55016	Class 55	Gordon Highlander
89519	55019	Class 55	Royal Highland Fusilier
89523	DP1	Proto	Deltic
89535	83012	Class 83	-
89561	85101	Class 85	-

To allow operation over the National Network, preserved or privately owned locomotives must be allocated a five digit TOPS number. Modern traction locos use the 89xxx series. Class 50 No. 50044 (D444) has the identity 89444 allocated. The loco is seen near Dainton on 21 July 2012, powering a Paignton to Plymouth charter. **CJM**

TOPS Numbered Diesel/Electric

Several preserved steam locomotives have been allocated five-digit TOPS numbers to allow their operation over the National Network. The numbers allocated are shown below; not all locos may currently be authorised for use on Network Rail metals.

TOPS No.	Railway No.	Type	Name
98150	1450	GWR 14xx	
98166	1466	GWR 14xx	
98186	686	0-6-0T	Lady Armaghdale
98212	41312	LMS 2MT	
98219	55189	CR 0-4-4T	
98221	46521	LMS 2MT	
98238	1638	GWR 16xx	
98240	3440	GWR 34xx	City of Truro
98241	46441	LMS 2MT	
98243	46443	LMS 2MT	
98253	30053	SR M7	
98254	58926	LNWR 2F	
98273	65243	NBR J36	Maude
98315	7715	GWR 57xx	
98321	69621	GER N7	A. J. Hill
98372	30072	SR USA	
98400	41000	LMS 4P	
98406	43106	LMS 4MT	
98414	75014	BR 4MT	
98425	7325	GWR 7321	
98426	31625	SR U	
98427	44027	LMS 4F	
98435	80135	BR 4MT	
98455	4555	GWR 45xx	
98457	9600	GWR 8750	
98460	7760	GWR 57xx	
98466	9466	GWR 94xx	
98469	75069	BR 4MT	
98472	5572	GWR 4575	
98476	76079	BR 4MT	
98478	68078	WD 4F	
98479	80079	BR 4MT	
98480	80080	BR 4MT	
98482	3882	0-6-0ST	Barbara
98488	4588	GWR 4575	
98494	65894	LNER J27	
98498	80098	BR 4MT	
98500	45000	LMS 5MT	
98502	7802	GWR 78xx	Bradley Manor
98505	45305	LMS 5MT	Alderman A E Draper
98507	45407	LMS 5MT	Lancashire Fusilier
98510	45110	LMS 5MT	
98512	7812	GWR 78xx	Erlestoke Manor
98519	7819	GWR 78xx	Hinton Manor
98525	45025	LMS 5MT	
98526	30925	SR V	Cheltenham
98529	73129	BR 5MT	
98530	4930	GWR 49xx	Hagley Hall
98531	45231	LMS 5MT	Sherwood Forester
98532	44932	LMS 5MT	
98536	4936	GWR 49xx	Kinlet Hall
98549	4965	GWR 49xx	Rood Ashton Hall
98553	4953	GWR 49xx	Pitchford Hall
98560	6960	GWR 6959	Raveningham Hall
98564	61264	LNER B1	
98565	42765	LMS 6P5F	
98567	44767	LMS 5MT	George Stephenson
98568	42968	LMS 5MT	
98571	44871	LMS 5MT	
98572	5972	GWR 49xx	Olton Hall
98577	30777	SR N15	Sir Lamiel
98596	73096	BR 5MT	
98598	6998	GWR 6959	Burton Agnes Hall
98605	62005	LNER K1	
98628	30828	SR S15	
98641	30841	SR S15	
98642	61994	LNER K4	The Great Marquess
98690	45690	LMS 6P5F	Leander
98693	45593	LMS 6P5F	Kolhapur
98696	45596	LMS 6P5F	Bahamas
98700	70000	BR 7P	Britannia
98701	34101	SR WC	Hartland
98709	53809	SDJR 7F	
98713	70013	BR 7P	Oliver Cromwell
98715	46115	LMS 7P	Scots Guardsman
98716	34016	SR WC	Bodmin
98727	34027	SR WC	Taw Valley
98728	5029	GWR 4073	Nunney Castle
98729	7029	GWR 4073	Clun Castle
98750	30850	SR LN	Lord Nelson
98751	5051	GWR 4073	Earl Bathurst
98767	34067	SR BB	Tangmere
98771	60800	LNER V2	Green Arrow
98772	34072	SR BB	257 Squadron
98780	5080	GWR 4073	Defiant
98792	34092	SR WC	City of Wells
98800	6000	GWR 60xx	King George V
98801	46201	LMS 8P	Princess Elizabeth
98802	71000	BR 8P	Duke of Gloucester
98803	46203	LMS 8P	Princess Margaret Rose
98805	35005	SR MN	Canadian Pacific
98809	60009	LNER A4	Union of South Africa
98824	6024	GWR 60xx	King Edward I
98828	35028	SR MN	Clan Line
98829	46229	LMS 8P	Duchess of Hamilton
98832	60532	LNER A2	Blue Peter
98834	46233	LMS 8P	Duchess of Sutherland
98851	48151	LMS 8F	
98857	2857	GWR 28xx	
98863	60163	LNER A1	Tornado
98868	60022	LNER A4	Mallard
98872	60103	LNER A3	Flying Scotsman
98873	48773	LMS 8F	
98898	60007	LNER A4	Sir Nigel Gresley
98920	92220	BR 9F	Evening Star

Above: Steam locos use the 98xxx numbering series. Here we see No. 98466 (GWR No. 9466) working a charter train over the Liskeard to Looe branch. **Stacey Thew**

Coupling Codes & Couplings

With the introduction of modern traction from the 1950s a number of different methods of multiple operation were introduced, covering the different control principles of locomotives, for example those using electro-pneumatic or electro-magnetic systems.

Six main systems are in operation today:

Blue Star ★ using the electro-pneumatic system and fitted to Classes 20, 25, 31, 33, 37, 40 and 73.

Green Spot ● a unique system installed on some Class 47s operated by the freight sector.

Orange Square ■ an English Electric system used only on the Class 50s.

Red Diamond ◆ a 1970s system developed for the modern freight locos of Classes 56 and 58.

In addition to the above coded systems, the American-developed main line locos of Classes 59, 66, 67 and 70 use the US standard AAR (Association of American Railroads) system. Direct Rail Services (DRS) have also developed a unique system which is installed on some of the company's Class 20, 37, 47 and 57 locos.

A number of locomotives have either been built with or modified to incorporate Time Division Multiplex (TDM) remote operation equipment, which uses coach lighting type Railway Clearing House (RCH) nose end jumper cables.

Some of the surviving first generation DMMU sets carry a **Blue Square** ■ multiple operation system.

Details of the main coupling systems in operation in the UK are included in the accompanying illustrations.

Standard Coupling

Above: *Class 59 and 66 front end layout (non-DB-S operated). 1-Coupling hook, 2-Coupling shackle, 3-Air brake pipe (red), 4-Main reservoir pipe (yellow), 5-Buffer, 6-Association of American Railroads (AAR) jumper socket. No. 66726 illustrated.* **CJM**

Standard Coupling

Above: *Standard coupling arrangement to be found on many classes of UK loco. 1-Electric Train Supply (ETS) jumper socket, 2-Main reservoir air pipe (yellow), 3-Vacuum brake pipe, 4-Coupling hook and shackle, 5-Air brake pipe (red), 6-Electric Train Supply (ETS) jumper cable. Loco No. 47580 illustrated.* **CJM**

Drop Head Buck-Eye with TDM Coupling

Above: *The unique front end layout of the Royal Mail Class 325. 1-Brake pipe (red), 2-Main reservoir pipe (yellow), 3-Electric Train Supply (ETS) socket, 4-Time Division Multiplex (TDM) jumper socket, 5-Drop head buck-eye coupling, 6-Electric Train Supply (ETS) cable.* **CJM**

Couplings

Drop Head Dellner Coupling

Above: *Following the introduction of Virgin Trains 'Voyager' and 'Pendolino' stock, a fleet of 16 Class 57/3s were introduced with drop head Dellner couplers and cabling to provide 'hotel power'. The coupling is seen in this illustration in the raised position. 1-Electric Train Supply (ETS) jumper socket, 2-Main reservoir pipe (yellow), 3-Air brake pipe (red), 4-Coupling hook, 5-Dellner coupling face, 6-Electric Train Supply (ETS) jumper cable.* **CJM**

BSI Coupling

Above: *With the birth of modern multiple-unit trains came the Bergische Stahl Industrie (BSI) automatic coupling, first seen in the UK on the Tyne & Wear Metro vehicles in 1978. The modern generation of UK DMUs now concentrate on the Compact BSI coupler with a CK2 coupling interface. The couplers are engaged by the compression of the two coupling faces, which completes a physical connection and also opens a watertight cover to an electrical connection box. The full train air connection is made during the coupling compression process. The coupling is complete by the driver pressing a 'couple' button in the driving cab. 1-Emergency air connection, 2-Coupling face, 3-Electric connection (behind plate), 4-Air connection. The coupling shown is on a Class 166.* **CJM**

Tightlock with Drum Connection

Above: *The Tightlock coupler is a derivative of the Association of American Railroads (AAR) Type H coupler, later under the control of American Public Transportation Association (APTA). A modified Type H coupler was introduced in the UK from the early 1970s and has become a standard fitting on many of the later BR and several post-privatisation EMUs. The UK Tightlock design can be supplied with or without an electrical connection box and with or without a pneumatic connection. This view shows a fully automated version as fitted to the 'Networker' fleet. Attachment is achieved by driving the two vehicles together which physically connects the vehicles, while a 'roll-cover' box opens to connect electric and pneumatic services. 1-Emergency air connector, 2-Manual release handle, 3-Semi-rotary electric/pneumatic cover, 4-Physical coupler.* **CJM**

Tightlock with Nose End Connections

Above: *The BR Southern Region-designed Class 455 and 456 units have a semi-automatic Tightlock used for physical connections, while air and electrical connections are made by waist height flexible pipes. 1-Main reservoir pipe (yellow), 2-Control jumper, 3-Tightlock coupler, 4-Couple/Uncouple drum switch, 5-Manual release handle, 6-Control jumper receptacle.* **CJM**

Dellner Coupling with Drum Connector

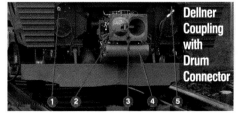

Above: *Dellner couplers have become the standard in the UK and much of Europe; these are fully automatic and come in various forms. 1-Emergency air supply, 2-Dellner coupling plate, 3-Pneumatic connection, 4-Roll-cover to electrical connections, 5-Air supply. Coupling of Class 360 illustrated.* **CJM**

Coup¹ings

Dellner Coupling

Dellner Coupling

Above: *A large number of different designs of Dellner couplers exist on UK rolling stock. Some feature full automatic operation including pneumatic and electrical connections, while others only provide physical coupling. This view shows a pair of Voyager units coupled together with Dellner couplers. The electrical connection box is above the physical coupler. After trains are 'pushed' together the driver operates a 'couple' button in the cab to complete the attachment. Uncoupling is achieved by the driver pressing an 'uncouple' button and driving the trains apart.* **CJM**

Left: *The Virgin Trains 'Pendolino' stock use Dellner couplers with a rotary covered electrical connector plate above. These couplers are supplemented by electric train supply connections either side to provide 'hotel power' to Class 390 sets from attached Class 57 locos. 1-Electric Train Supply (ETS) socket, 2-Emergency air connector, 3-Electrical connector plate under semi-rotary cover, 4-Dellner physical coupler, 5-Pneumatic connections. In normal use the Dellner coupler on 'Pendolino' stock is covered by a front fairing.* **CJM**

Dellner Coupling Without Electric Connector

Above: *Under the front end fairing of the Eurostar Class 373 stock a standard Scharfenberg coupler is located for assistance purposes and shunting. No electrical provision is made and the couplers are seldom used. 1-Scharfenberg coupling face, 2-Pneumatic connections, 3-Manual uncoupling handle.* **CJM**

Dellner Coupling With Electric Connector

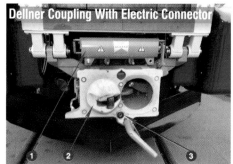

Above: *In as-installed condition and having never been coupled to another set, a Class 380 Scharfenberg coupler is viewed, showing the auto opening electrical connection box above. 1-Electrical connection box, 2-Coupling face plate, 3-Pneumatic connection.* **CJM**

Couplings

Emergency HST Bar Coupling

Above: *If High Speed Trains are required to be coupled to conventional hook couplings an adaptor coupling is carried on the HST for this purpose. It has to be first attached to the front of the HST by opening the front panel and attaching the aluminium bar to a coupling lug. The other end is then at the right level and length to attach to a standard loco hook coupling without the loco's buffers touching the HST's bodywork. Standard air connection is provided. Locos fitted with swing-head or combination couplers cannot be used to assist HST stock. A Class 59/1 is seen attached to HST power car No. 43150 in this view at Westbury.* **Greg Welsh**

Right: *All DB-S Class 66s (except 66001/002) and all Class 67s are fitted with swing-head combination couplers allowing attachment to other like-fitted locos or rolling stock using a knuckle coupling. Two Class 66s are seen here attached using the swing-head coupler. Note that the buffers do not touch and that all traction and breaking forces are transmitted through the coupler. Standard buffer beam air connections are provided on one main reservoir and one brake pipe. The auto coupler can be disconnected by using the white uncoupling handle seen on the left.* **Antony Christie**

DBS Combination Coupler

Couplings

Transport for London
London Underground

Address: ✉ Floor 11, Windsor House, 50 Victoria Street, London SW1H 0TL
       ✆ pressoffice@tfl.gov.uk
       ✆ 0845 604 4141
       ⓘ www.tfl.gov.uk
Managing Director: Mike Brown

Operations: The London Underground system, now operated by Transport for London (TfL), operates services on 10 lines in and around the capital and uses a mix of surface and tunnel stock.

Bakerloo Line
Tube Line. Operates services between Elephant & Castle and Harrow & Wealdstone.
Rolling Stock: 1972 Mk2, livery - red, white and blue, allocated to Stonebridge Park. Scheduled for replacement in 2018.

Central Line
Tube Line. Operates services between West Ruislip/Ealing and Epping
Rolling Stock: 1992, livery - red, white and blue, allocated to Hainault.

Sub-Surface Line. Operates circle network in Central London and the branch from Edgware Road to Hammersmith.
Rolling Stock: 'C' stock, introduced 1969-78, livery - red, white and blue, allocated to Hammersmith.

District Line
Sub-Surface Line. Operates services between Wimbledon, Richmond, Ealing, Edgware Road, Kensington Olympia and Upminster.
Rolling Stock: 'C' and 'D' stock, livery - red, white and blue, allocated to Ealing Common and Upminster.

Jubilee Line
Tube Line. Operates services between Stanmore and Stratford.
Rolling Stock: 1996, livery - red, white and blue, allocated to Wembley Park.

Metropolitan Line
Sub-Surface Line. Operates services from Amersham, Chesham, Watford and Uxbridge to Aldgate.
Rolling Stock: 'S' stock, livery - red, white and blue, allocated to Wembley Park.

Northern Line
Tube Line. Operates services between Morden and Edgware, Mill Hill East and High Barnet.
Rolling Stock: 1995 Stock, livery - red, white and blue, allocated to Morden.

Piccadilly Line
Tube Line. Operates services between Heathrow Airport / Uxbridge and Cockfosters.
Rolling Stock: 1973 Stock, livery - red, white and blue, allocated to Northfields and Cockfosters. Stock due for replacement in 2014.

Victoria Line
Tube Line. Operates services between Brixton and Walthamstow Central
Rolling Stock: 2009 Stock, livery - red, white and blue, allocated to Northumberland Park.

Waterloo & City Line
Tube Line. Operates services between Waterloo and Bank
Rolling Stock: 1992 Stock, livery - red, white and blue, allocated to Waterloo.

Above: *The northern extremity of the Bakerloo Line operated over former BR metals, now operated by Transport for London as far as Harrow. The Bakerloo line uses 1972 stock and car No. 3238 leads a southbound formation into South Kenton. On the right are the tracks of the West Coast main line.* **Antony Christie**

Below: *The new Bombardier 'S' stock has now taken over operations on the Metropolitan Line and in 2013 will commence operation of the Circle Line. A set of 'A' stock, with vehicle No. 21070 nearest the camera, is seen at Moorgate.* **Antony Christie**

For space reasons, we are unable in this publication to provide vehicle numbers for London Underground stock.

Light Rail

Blackpool Tramway

Address: ✉ Blackpool Transport, Rigby Road, Blackpool, FY1 5DD
✈ jean.cox@blackpooltransport.com
📞 01253 473001　ⓘ www.blackpooltrams.info

Blackpool Tramway is operated by Blackpool Transport.
Operations: Blackpool Tramway operates frequent services between Fleetwood and Starr Gate.

Flexity 2

Train Length: 105ft 9in (32.23m) | Seating: 74 + 148 standing
Width: 8ft 8in (2.65m) | Horsepower: 4 x 160hp (120kW) three phase TMs
Power Supply: 600V dc overhead | Electrical Equipment: Bombardier

001	003	005	007	009	011	013	015
002	004	006	008	010	012	014	016

Left: *New Bombardier-built 'Flexity-2' trams now operate on the Blackpool tram system. Tram No. 002 is seen on display at InnoTrans 2012 held in Berlin.* **CJM**

Transport for London
Docklands Light Railway

Contact details as London Underground.

Operations: The Docklands Light Railway operates between Bank and Tower Gateway and Woolwich Arsenal, Beckton and Stratford, as well as a Lewisham to Stratford service.

Class B90 (twin)

Train Length: 94ft 5in (28.80m)　Seating: 52 + 4 tip-up
Width: 8ft 7in (2.65m)　Horsepower: 375hp (280kW)
Power Supply: 750V dc third rail　Electrical Equipment: Brush

22	25	28	31	34	37	40	43
23	26	29	32	35	38	41	44
24	27	30	33	36	39	42	

Class B92 (twin)

Train Length: 94ft 5in (28.80m)　Seating: 54 + 4 tip-up
Width: 8ft 7in (2.65m)　Horsepower: 375hp (280kW)
Power Supply: 750V dc third rail　Electrical Equipment: Brush

45	51	57	63	69	75	81	87
46	52	58	64	70	76	82	88
47	53	59	65	71	77	83	89
48	54	60	66	72	78	84	90
49	55	61	67	73	79	85	91
50	56	62	68	74	80	86	

Class B2K (twin)

				Train Length: 94ft 5in (28.80m) Width: 8ft 7in (2.65m) Power Supply: 750V dc third rail				Seating: 52 + 4 tip-up Horsepower: 375hp (280kW) Electrical Equipment: Brush			

01	03	05	07	09	11	13	15	92	94	96	98
02	04	06	08	10	12	14	16	93	95	97	99

Class B07 (twin)

				Train Length: 94ft 5in (28.80m) Width: 8ft 7in (2.65m) Power Supply: 750V dc third rail				Seating: 52 + 4 tip-up Horsepower: 375hp (280kW) Electrical Equipment: Bombardier			

101	106	111	116	121	126	131	136	141	146	151
102	107	112	117	122	127	132	137	142	147	152
103	108	113	118	123	128	133	138	143	148	153
104	109	114	119	124	129	134	139	144	149	154
105	110	115	120	125	130	135	140	145	150	155

Right: *Taken from the London Cable-car which offers excellent views of the Docklands Light Railway, B07 cars Nos. 104 and 126 approach West Silvertown station with a service bound for Woolwich Arsenal.* **CJM**

Transport for London Croydon Tramlink

Contact details as London Underground.
Operations: The Croydon Tramlink operates between Croydon and Wimbledon, New Addington, Beckenham and Elmers End.

CR4000 stock

				Train Length: 98ft 9in (30.1m) Width: 8ft 7in (2.65m) Power Supply: 750V dc overhead			Seating: 70 Horsepower: 643hp (480kW) Electrical Equipment: Bombardier		

2530	2533	2536	2539	2542	2545	2548	2551
2531	2534	2537	2540	2543	2546	2549	2552
2532	2535	2538	2541	2544	2547	2550	2553

Stadler Variobahn

			Train Length: 106ft 2½in (32.37m) Width: 8ft 7in (2.65m) Power Supply: 750V dc overhead		Seating: 70 Horsepower: 650hp (483kW) Electrical Equipment: Stadler	

2554	2555	2556	2557	2558	2559

Name applied
2535   Stephen Parascandolo
         1980-2007

Right: *Six new Stadler trams have now entered service on the Croydon Tramlink, operating in addition to the original stock. Car No. 2554 is illustrated.*
Antony Christie

Manchester Metrolink

Address: ✉ Greater Manchester PTE, 2 Piccadilly Gardens, Manchester, M1 3BG
RATP Metrolink, Metrolink House, Queens Road, Manchester, M8 0RY
✆ customerservices@metrolink.co.uk
℡ 0161 205 2000 ⓘ www.metrolink.co.uk
Metrolink is operated for GMPTE by Metrolink RATP Dev UK Ltd.
Operations: Manchester Metrolink operates a street and dedicated track tram system around
Manchester. Services operate from the city centre to Bury, Altrincham, Eccles via MediaCity UK and
St Werburgh's Road.

T-68 Six-axle stock

Train Length: 95ft 1in (29m)
Width: 8ft 7in (2.65m)
Power Supply: 750V dc overhead

Seating: 82 + 4 tip-up
Horsepower: 697hp (520kW)
Electrical Equipment: Firema

1002	1012	1016	1023
1003	1013	1017	1024
1007	1014	1021	1025
1009	1015	1022	1026

T-68 Six-axle stock

Train Length: 95ft 1in (29m)
Width: 8ft 7in (2.65m)
Power Supply: 750V dc overhead

Seating: 82 + 4 tip-up
Horsepower: 697hp (520kW)
Electrical Equipment: Ansaldo

2001	2002	2003	2004	2005	2006

M5000 stock

Train Length: 93ft 1in (28.4m)
Width: 8ft 7in (2.65m)
Power Supply: 750V dc overhead

Seating: 52 + 8 tip-up
Horsepower: 643hp (480kW)
Electrical Equipment: Bombardier

3001	3012	3023	3034	3045	3056	3067
3002	3013	3024	3035	3046	3057	3068
3003	3014	3025	3036	3047	3058	3069
3004	3015	3026	3037	3048	3059	3070
3005	3016	3027	3038	3049	3060	3071
3006	3017	3028	3039	3050	3061	3072
3007	3018	3029	3040	3051	3062	3073
3008	3019	3030	3041	3052	3063	3074
3009	3020	3031	3042	3053	3064	
3010	3021	3032	3043	3054	3064	
3011	3022	3033	3044	3055	3066	

Name carried
3009   50th Anniversary
       Coronation Street 1960-2010
3020   Lancashire Fusilier

At the start of 2013, vehicles up to
3047 had been delivered and sets
3001-3036 were in daily use.

Left: *M5000 tram No. 3016 is seen
working on the Manchester Metrolink
system. When all vehicles of this design
are in traffic the older T-68 vehicles
will all be withdrawn.*
Murdoch Currie

Nottingham Express Transit

Address: Transdev Tram UK Ltd, Garrick House, 74 Chiswick High Road, London, W4 1SY
Nottingham City Transport Ltd, Lower Parliament Street, Nottingham, NG1 1GG
info@thetram.net 0115 942 7777, www.thetram.net

Operations: Nottingham Express Transit (NET) operate trams between Hucknall and Nottingham.

Incentro AT6/5

Train Length: 108ft 3in (29m)
Width: 7ft 9in (2.4m)
Power Supply: 750V dc overhead
Seating: 54 + 4 tip-up
Horsepower: 697hp (520kW)
Electrical Equipment: Bombardier

201
202 *DH Lawrence*
203 *Bendigo Thompson*
204 *Erica Beardsmore*
205 *Lord Byron*
206 *Angela Alcock*
207 *Mavis Worthington*
208 *Dinah Minton*
209 *Sid Standard*
210 *Sir Jesse Boot*
211 *Robin Hood*
212 *William Booth*
213 *Mary Potter*
214 *Dennis McCarthy*
215 *Brian Clough*

Right: *NET tram No. 204 painted in NET promotional livery.* **John Binch**

Midland Metro

Address: Travel West Midlands, PO Box 3565, Birmingham, B1 3JR
info@travelmetro.co.uk 0121 254 7272, www.travelmetro.co.uk

Operations: Midland Metro operates trams between Birmingham Snow Hill and Wolverhampton.

T-69 Six-axle stock

Train Length: 108ft 3in (29m)
Width: 7ft 9in (2.4m)
Power Supply: 750V dc overhead
Seating: 54 + 4 tip-up
Horsepower: 697hp (520kW)
Electrical Equipment: Bombardier

01(S) *Sir Frank Whittle*
02
03 *Ray Lewis*
04
05 *Sister Dora*
06 *Alan Garner*
07 *Billy Wright*
08 *Joseph Chamberlain*
09 *Jeff Astle*
10 *John Stanley Webb*
11 *Theresa Stewart*
12
13 *Anthony Nolan*
14 *Jim Eames*
15 *Agenoria*
16 *Gerwyn John*

Right: *A total of 16 trams operate on the Birmingham-Wolverhampton Midland Metro system. This number is scheduled to increase with the arrival of new vehicles and route extensions. Tram No. 09 is illustrated at the St Pauls stop.* **John Binch**

Sheffield Super Tram

Address: ✉ Stagecoach Supertram, Nunnery Depot, Woodburn Road, Sheffield, S9 3LS

      ✍ enquiries@supertram.com

      ☎ 0114 272 8282

      ⓘ www.supertram.com

Operations: Sheffield Super Tram operates services within Sheffield city centre and to Herdings Park, Halfway, Meadowhall Interchange, Middlewood and Malin Bridge.

Six-axle stock

Train Length: 113ft 6in (34.75m)   Seating: 80 + 6 tip-up
Width: 8ft 7in (2.65m)   Horsepower: 800hp (596kW)
Power Supply: 750V dc overhead   Electrical Equipment: Siemens

101	105	109	113	117	121	125
102	106	110	114	118	122	
103	107	111	115	119	123	
104	108	112	116	120	124	

Left: *Twenty-five three-section trams operate on the Sheffield Super Tram system. Today some vehicles are finished in stunning 'wraps' giving a very European style to the busy city centre network. Tram No. 116 is seen at Park Grange Road in Genting Club livery advertising a new casino.*
John Binch

Tyne & Wear Metro

Address: ✉ Tyne & Wear Passenger Transport Executive (NEXUS), Nexus House, 33 St James Boulevard, Newcastle upon Tyne, NE1 4AX

      ✍ enquiries@nexus.co.uk

      ☎ 0191 203 3333

      ⓘ www.nexus.org.uk

Operations: Tyne & Wear Metro operates tram services within Newcastle city centre and to Whitley Bay, Newcastle Airport, South Shields, Sunderland and South Hylton.

Six-axle stock

Train Length: 91ft 3in (27.80m)   Seating: 68 tip-up
Width: 8ft 7in (2.65m)   Horsepower: 500hp (374kW)
Power Supply: 1500V dc overhead   Electrical Equipment: Siemens

4001	4011	4021	4031	4041	4051	4061
4002	4012	4022	4032	4042	4052	4062
4003	4013	4023	4033	4043	4053	4063
4004	4014	4024	4034	4044	4054	4064
4005	4015	4025	4035	4045	4055	4065
4006	4016	4026	4036	4046	4056	4066
4007	4017	4027	4037	4047	4057	4067
4008	4018	4028	4038	4048	4058	4068
4009	4019	4029	4039	4049	4059	4069
4010	4020	4030	4040	4050	4060	4070

4071	4074	4077	4080	4083	4086	4089
4072	4075	4078	4081	4084	4087	4090
4073	4076	4079	4082	4085	4088	

Names applied
4026 *George Stephenson*
4041 *Harry Cowans*
4060 *Thomas Bewick*
4064 *Michael Campbell*
4065 *Dame Catherine Cookson*
4073 *Danny Marshall*
4077 *Robert Stephenson*
4078 *Ellen Wilkinson*

Right: *The first true 'light rail' system in the UK was the Newcastle Metro. Here we see fully refurbished car No. 4042 at Benton on 6 June 2012.*
Antony Christie

Glasgow Subway

Address: ✉ SPT, Consort House, 12 West George Street, Glasgow, G2 1HN

🖰 enquiry@spt.co.uk

☎ 0141 332 6811

ⓘ www.spt.co.uk

Glasgow Subway is operated by Strathclyde Partnership for Transport (SPT).
Operations: Circular network around Glasgow city centre.

Single Power Cars

Length: 42ft 2in (12.81m)
Width: 7ft 7in (2.34m)
Power Supply: 600V dc third rail
Seating: 36S
Horsepower: 190hp (142.4kW)
Electrical Equipment: GEC

101	105	109	113	117	121	125	129	133
102	106	110	114	118	122	126	130	
103	107	111	115	119	123	127	131	
104	108	112	116	120	124	128	132	

Trailer Cars

Length: 41ft 6in (12.70m)
Width: 7ft 7in (2.34m)
Seating: 40S

201	202	203	204	205	206	207	208

Right: *The 'Clockwork orange' Underground system around the city of Glasgow continues to operate and provide an essential travel mode within the city. Cars Nos. 103, 207 and 120 are seen at Govan on 27 October 2012.*
Murdoch Currie

Light Rail

Livery Codes

ABL	Arriva Trains Blue
ADV	Advenza Freight, blue with yellow branding
AGI	Aggregate Industries green, silver and green
AIN	Aggregate Industries - blue
ALS	Alstom Transportation
ANG	Anglia - mid blue
ANN	Anglia - turquoise/white with National Express East Anglia branding
ATE	Arriva Trains Executive - turquoise/cream with branding
ATT	Arriva Trains Wales - two-tone turquoise
ATW	Arriva Trains Wales - turquoise/cream
AWT	Abellio white Greater Anglia
AXC	Arriva Cross Country - brown, silver, pink
BBR	Balfour Beatty Rail blue/white
BLG	Blue and Grey
BLK	Black
BLL	BR rail blue with large logo
BLU	Blue
BLW	Carillion Rail blue/white
BOM	Bombardier Transportation
BPM	Blue Pullman - Nankin blue and white
BRD	BR Departmental mid grey
BRT	BR Trainload two-tone grey
C2C	c2c - blue/pink
CAL	Caledonian Railway
CAR	Carmine & Cream
CEN	Central Trains blue and two-tone green
CHC	Chocolate & Cream
CIV	BR Civil Engineers - grey and yellow
COL	Colas - Orange, lime green and black
CON	Continental Rail - light/mid blue
COR	Corus Steel - light blue or yellow
COX	Connex white and yellow
CRG	Chilton Railways - grey
CRW	Chilton Railways - white/blue
CTL	Central Trains blue, green with yellow doors
CWR	Cotswold Rail - silver with branding
DBB	DB Schenker - light blue
DBM	DB Schenker - maroon
DBS	DB Schenker - red
DCG	Devon & Cornwall Railways - green
DRC	Direct Rail Services - blue Compass branding
DRO	Direct Rail Services - Ocean Liner blue
DRS	Direct Rail Services - blue
DRU	Direct Rail Services - unbranded blue
ECG	East Coast - grey
ECR	European Cargo Rail - grey
ECS	East Coast - silver
ECW	East Coast - white
ECT	East Coast branded National Express livery
EMT	East Midlands Trains, white, blue, swirl cab ends
EPS	European Passenger Services
EPX	Europhoenix red/silver
ETF	ETF Rail - yellow with green band
EU2	Eurotunnel - Europorte2
EUS	Eurostar - white, yellow and blue
EWE	DBS Executive
EWS	English Welsh Scottish - red with gold band
FCC	First Capital Connect, First Group Urban Lights - mauve/blue with pink, blue and white lower branding
FER	Fertis - grey with branding
FGB	First Great Western blue
FGF	First Group - GBRf (Barbie)
FGL	First Great Western local lines
FGN	First Great Western branded Northern blue
FGS	First Group ScotRail with EWS branding
FGT	First Great Western, Thames/London area branding
FGW	First Great Western, as FST with FGW branding
FHT	First Hull Trains, as FST with Hull Trains branding
FLF	Fastline Freight - grey with yellow/white chevrons
FLG	Freightliner green unbranded
FLP	Freightliner - green/yellow - PowerHaul
FLR	Freightliner - green/yellow - original
FLU	Freightliner - green/yellow - unbranded
FLY	Freightliner grey
FNA	First livery with National Express East Anglia branding
FOS	Foster Yeoman
FRB	Fragonset black
FSN	Northern branded First Group
FSP	First ScotRail Strathclyde carmine and cream (some with turquoise band)
FSR	First ScotRail, as FST with FSR branding
FSS	First ScotRail, blue with white Saltire branding
FST	First Group - dark blue, pink and white swirl
FSW	First Group - green and white with gold branding
FTP	First TransPennine, as FST with FTP branding
GAT	Gatwick Express, white, mid-grey and red with red doors
GBE	GB Railfreight - Europorte branding
GBF	GB Railfreight - swirl
GBM	GB Railfreight Metronet
GBN	GB Railfreight/Eurotunnel new livery
GBR	GB Railfreight - blue
GBU	GB Railfreight swirl (no First branding)
GLX	Glaxochem - grey, blue and black
GNE	Great North Eastern Railway - blue
GRN	Green
GRY	Grey
GSW	Great Scottish & Western Railway - maroon
GTL	Grand Central Railway - black
GTO	Grand Central Railway - black with orange
GWG	First Great Western - green
GWR	Great Western Railway - green
HAN	Hanson
HEC	Heathrow Connect - grey, orange
HEL	Heathrow Connect - Terminal 4 'Link'
HEX	Heathrow Express - silver, grey

Data Tables

HNR	Harry Needle Railroad - yellow/grey		RFT	BR Railfreight - grey, red and yellow, with large logo and numbers
HS1	High Speed 1 - blue with powder blue doors		RIV	Riviera Trains - maroon
HUN	Hunslet		RML	Royal Mail Limited - red
ICS	InterCity Swallow - two-tone grey off-set with red and white body band		ROJ	Royal Diamond Jubilee
IND	Industrial colours of operator		ROY	Royal Train - claret
INT	InterCity two-tone grey off-set with red and white body band		RTB	Railtrack - blue
JAR	Jarvis maroon		RTK	Railtrack - grey/brown
LAF	Lafarge Aggregates - green/white		SCE	Stagecoach - white with East Midlands branding
LHL	Loadhaul Freight - black and orange		SCT	ScotRail Caledonian Sleeper - mauve/ white
LLB	Large Logo Blue		SEC	Serco
LMI	London Midland grey, green and black		SET	South Eastern Trains - white with branding
LNE	LNER tourist green/cream		SGK	Southern Gatwick Express - blue, white and red with swirl ends
LOG	London Overground, white and blue with orange doors		SIL	Silver
LUL	London Underground red		SKL	Silverlink London Overground, SLK with London Overground branding
MAB	Statesman Pullman - maroon/beige		SLF	Silverlink, with First Great Western branding
MAI	MainTrain - blue with branding		SLK	Silverlink, mauve, green and white
MAL	Malcolm Rail		SNF	Railfreight grey with SNCF branding
MAR	Maroon		SNT	SNCF domestic on Eurostar, silver, while and yellow
MER	Merseyrail - silver and yellow		SOU	Southern - white, black and green
MLF	Mainline Freight - aircraft blue		SPL	Special livery
MLG	Mainline Freight - branded double grey		STN	Stansted Express
MML	Midland Main Line - turquoise/white		STO	Stobart Rail
MSC	Mediterranean Shipping Company		SWM	South West Trains main line white and blue
NBP	Northern Belle Pullman cream/umber		SWO	South West Trains outer suburban blue
NE2	National Express with c2c branding		SWS	South West Trains suburban red
NGE	First Great Eastern grey/blue with cab end swirl, branded National Express		SWT	South West Trains blue, red, grey
NOM	Northern Rail - blue Metro branded		TAT	Tata Steel - blue
NOR	Northern - blue, purple, grey		TES	Tesco
NOU	Northern unbranded		TEX	TransPennine Express - As FST with TPE brand
NRL	Network Rail - yellow with branding		TGG	Transrail Grey with 'T' branding
NSE	Network SouthEast - red, white and blue		THM	Thameslink - blue, white, yellow
NUB	Northern Rail blue - unbranded ScotRail		TLF	Trainload Freight - grey
NWT	North West Trains - dark blue		TLL	Trainload grey with Loadhaul branding
NXA	National Express East Anglia (Now Abellio)		TLP	Thameslink promotional multi-coloured stripes
NXE	National Express East Coast		TPD	Trans Pennine/Central Trains logo
NXG	National Express East Coast branding on GNER blue livery		TSO	Travaux du Sud Ouest - yellow
NXS	National Express brand on Silverlink		TTG	Two-tone grey
NXU	National Express unbranded white/grey		VIR	Virgin - red/grey
ONE	One Anglia mid-blue (Now Abellio)		VSN	VSOE Northern
ORG	HNRC Orange		VT1	Virgin - red/grey unbranded
ORN	One Railway with National Express branding (Now Abellio)		VWC	Virgin West Coast, silver, red, white and black
PCL	BR Parcels red/grey		WAB	Wabtec Rail - black
POL	Police livery		WAG	West Anglia Great Northern - purple
PTR	Porterbrook		WAL	Wales & Borders 'Alphaline' silver/grey
PUL	Pullman - umber/cream		WCR	West Coast Railway - maroon
PUR	Artemis purple		WES	Wessex Trains - maroon
QOS	Queen of Scots Pullman		WET	Wessex Trains - silver, maroon/pink doors
REG	Regional Railways blue, white		WEX	Wessex Rail Engineering
RES	Rail express systems - red and graphite		WHT	White
RFD	Railfreight Distribution		WMD	West Midlands Network, light blue and green
RFE	Railfreight grey with EWS branding		WSR	Wrexham & Shropshire two-tone grey
RFG	Railfreight grey		YEL	Yellow
RFI	Railfreight International			
RFP	Railfreight with Petroleum branding			

Data Tables

Rail Data Tables

Operational Pool Codes

ADFL	Advenza Freight - Freight locos
ATLO	West Coast Traincare - Locomotives
ATTB	West Coast Traincare - Class 57/3 with Dellner
ATZZ	West Coast Traincare - Locos for disposal
CDJD	Serco Railtest - Shunting locos
COLO	Colas Rail - Operational locomotives
CREL	Cotswold Rail - Locomotives
DFFT	Freightliner - Restricted duties
DFGC	Freightliner Class 86/5 trials locomotive
DFGH	Freightliner - Heavy Haul Class 70
DFGI	Freightliner - Intermodal Class 70
DFGM	Freightliner - Intermodal Class 66/5
DFHG	Freightliner - Heavy Haul Class 66/5 & 66/6
DFHH	Freightliner - Heavy Haul Class 66/5 & 66/6
DFIM	Freightliner - Intermodal Class 66/5
DFIN	Freightliner - Intermodal - low emission
DFLC	Freightliner - Class 90
DFLS	Freightliner - Class 08
DFNC	Freightliner - Class 86/6
DFRT	Freightliner - Class 66 Infrastructure contracts
DFTZ	Freightliner - Stored Class 66
DHLT	Freightliner - Awaiting repairs
EFOO	First Great Western - Class 57
EFPC	First Great Western - HST power cars
EFSH	First Great Western - Class 08
EHPC	CrossCountry Trains - HST power cars
EJLO	London Midland - Class 08
EMPC	East Midlands Trains - HST power cars
EMSL	East Midlands Trains - Class 08
EPXX	Europhoenix Class 86
GBCM	Europorte/GBRf - Class 66 commercial contracts
GBED	Europorte/GBRf - Class 66
GBET	Europorte/GBRf - Class 92
GBFM	Europorte/GBRf - Class 66 modified with RETB
GBMU	Europorte/GBRf - Class 66 modified for MU
GBRT	Europorte/GBRf - Class 66 Infrastructure
GBSD	Europorte/GBRf - Class 66 RETB
GBWM	Europorte/GBRf - Class 08
GBZZ	Europorte/GBRf - Stored locomotives
GCHP	Grand Central - HST power cars
GPSS	Eurostar UK - Class 08
HNRL	Harry Needle Railroad - Class 08, 20 hire locos
HNRS	Harry Needle Railroad - Stored locomotives
HTCX	Hanson Traction - Class 56
HYWD	South West Trains - Class 73
IANA	National Express East Anglia - Class 90
IECA	National Express East Coast - Class 91
IECP	National Express East Coast - HST power cars
INDL	Industrial (unofficial code)
IWCA	Virgin West Coast - Class 57/3
MBDL	Private operators - Diesel traction
MBED	Private operators - Class 73
MRSO	Mainline Rail - Class 08
PTXX	Eurotunnel - Europorte2 Class 92
QACL	Network Rail - Class 86 load banks
QADD	Network Rail - Class 31
QCAR	Network Rail - HST power cars
QETS	Network Rail - Class 97/3
RCZH	Railcare Springburn - Class 08
RCZN	Railcare Wolverton - Class 08
RFSH	Wabtec Rail Doncaster - Class 08
RVLO	Rail Vehicle Engineering Derby - Locos
RVLS	Rail Vehicle Engineering Derby - Stored locos
SIEM	Siemens Transportation - Barriers
TTLS	Traditional Traction - Locomotives
WAAN	DB Schenker - Class 67
WABN	DB Schenker - Class 67 RETB fitted
WATN	DB Schenker - Class 67 hire to Arriva T W
WBAI	DB Schenker - Class 66 Industrial
WBAK	DB Schenker - Class 66 Construction
WBAM	DB Schenker - Class 66 Energy
WBAN	DB Schenker - Class 66 Network
WBBI	DB Schenker - Class 66 Industrial RETB fitted
WBBM	DB Schenker - Class 66 Energy RETB fitted
WBBN	DB Schenker - Class 66 Network RETB fitted
WBEI	DB Schenker - Class 66 Euro in the UK
WBEN	DB Schenker - Class 66 Euro Cargo Rail
WBEP	DB Schenker - Class 66 Poland
WBES	DB Schenker - Class 66 ECR RHTT
WBLI	DB Schenker - Class 66 Industrial auto coupler
WCAI	DB Schenker - Class 60 Industrial 990 gal fuel
WCAK	DB Schenker - Class 60 Construction 990 gal fuel
WCAM	DB Schenker - Class 60 Energy 990 gal fuel
WCBI	DB Schenker - Class 60 Industrial 1150 gal fuel
WCBK	DB Schenker - Class 60 Construct'n 1150 gal fuel
WDAI	DB Schenker - Class 59/2 Industrial
WDAK	DB Schenker - Class 59/2 Construction
WDAM	DB Schenker - Class 59/2 Liverpool Bulk
WEFE	DB Schenker - Class 90
WFMS	DB Schenker - Class 60 Fleet Management
WFMU	DB Schenker - Fleet Management
WKBN	DB Schenker - Class 37 Network RETB fitted
WLAN	DB Schenker - Euro Cargo Rail Class 21
WNTR	DB Schenker - Stored locos - reserve
WNTS	DB Schenker - Stored locos - serviceable
WNXX	DB Schenker - Stored locos - unserviceable
WNYX	DB Schenker - Stored locos - parts recovery
WNZX	DB Schenker - Awaiting disposal
WRLN	DB Schenker - Class 08, 09 - North London
WSEN	DB Schenker - Euro Cargo Rail - Class 08
WSSA	DB Schenker - Class 08, 09 - Axiom Rail
WSSI	DB Schenker - Class 08, 09 Industrial
WSSL	DB Schenker - Class 08, 09 Logistics
WSSM	DB Schenker - Class 08, 09 Energy
WSSK	DB Schenker - Class 08, 09 Network/Const'n
WSXX	DB Schenker - Class 08, 09 Stored
WTAE	DB Schenker - Class 92 Network
WTHE	DB Schenker - Class 92 HS1 authorised
WZFF	DB Schenker - Class 58 France
WZGF	DB Schenker - Class 56, 92 France
WZTS	DB Schenker - Class 08, 56, 58 Stored (hire pool)
XHAC	Direct Rail Services - Class 47
XHCK	Direct Rail Services - Class 57
XHHP	Direct Rail Services - Holding Pool
XHIM	Direct Rail Services - Class 66 - Intermodal
XHNC	Direct Rail Services - Nuclear Traffic
XHSS	Direct Rail Services - Stored
XYPA	Mendip Rail - Hanson Group
XYPO	Mendip Rail - Foster Yeoman (Aggregate Inds)

■ Pools are given only for locomotive groups which are included in this book. Pool codes for multiple-units are not included.

Data Tables

Preserved site codes

ACL	AC Locomotive Group	MID	Middleton Railway
ALY	Allelys, Studley	MLM	Motorail - Long Marston
APF	Appleby-Frodingham RPS	MNF	Mid-Norfolk Railway
AVR	Avon Valley Railway	MOR	Moreton-on-Lugg
BAT	Battlefield Line	MRC	Middleton Railway Centre
BEL	5Bel Trust Barrow Hill	MSM	Museum of Science & Industry, Manchester
BHR	Barrow Hill Roundhouse	MSR	Midsomer Norton
BIR	Barry Island Railway	NHD	Newton Heath Depot
BKR	Bo'ness & Kinneil Railway	NIR	Northamptonshire Ironstone Railway
BLU	Bluebell Railway	NLR	Northampton & Lamport Railway
BRC	Buckinghamshire Railway Centre	NNR	North Norfolk Railway
BRM	Birmingham Railway Museum, Tyseley	NRM	National Railway Museum, York
BVR	Bridgend Valleys Railway	NRS	National Railway Museum, Shildon
BWR	Bodmin & Wenford Railway	NYM	North Yorkshire Moors Railway
CAN	Canton (Pullman Rail)	PBR	Pontypool & Blaenavon Railway
CHS	Chasewater Railway	PDR	Paignton & Dartmouth Railway
COL	Colne Valley Railway	PRL	Peak Rail
COV	Coventry Electric Railway Museum	PVR	Plym Valley Railway
CPR	Chinnor & Princes Risborough Railway	RAC	Railway Age, Crewe
CRB	Caledonian Railway, Brechin	RAM	Rampart, Derby
CRT	Cambrian Railway Trust	RIB	Ribble Steam Railway
CVR	Churnet Valley Railway	RIP	Rippingdale Station
CWR	Cholsey & Wallingford Railway	ROW	Rowley Mill
DAR	Dartmoor Railway	RST	Rushden Station Transport Museum
DEE	Royal Deeside Railway	SEL	St Leonards Railway Engineering
DER	Derwent Valley Railway	SHP	Summerlee Heritage Park
DFR	Dean Forest Railway	SLN	Stewarts Lane Depot
DID	Didcot Railway Centre	SNI	Snibston Railway
EAR	East Anglian Railway Museum	SPV	Spa Valley Railway
ECC	Ecclesbourne Valley Railway	SRC	Stainmore Railway Co
EDR	Eden Valley Railway	STR	Strathspey Railway
EHC	Elsecar Heritage Centre	SVR	Severn Valley Railway
EHD	Eastleigh DBS Depot	SWI	Swindon & Cricklade Railway
EKR	East Kent Railway	SWN	Swanage Railway
ELR	East Lancashire Railway	TEB	Friends of 502 Group, Tebay
EMB	Embsay Steam Railway	TEL	Telford Horsehay Steam Trust
EPO	Epping - Ongar Railway	THK	Throckmorton Airfield
FHL	Fawley Hall (Private)	TIT	Titley Junction
FIN	Finmere Station, Oxfordshire	TSR	Telford Steam Railway
GCN	Great Central Railway (North)	TYN	North Tyneside Railway
GCR	Great Central Railway	VOG	Vale of Glamorgan Railway
GKR	Graham Kirk Rail	WAS	Washwood Heath
GWI	Gwili Railway	WCR	West Coast Railway Co
GWR	Gloucestershire & Warwickshire Railway	WED	Weardale Railway
HAD	Hastings Diesels	WEN	Wensleydale Railway
IOW	Isle of Wight Railway	WPH	Walthamstow Pump House
KEI	Keith & Dufftown Railway	WSR	West Somerset Railway
KES	Kent & East Sussex Railway	XXX	Private unspecified site
KIN	MoD Kineton	YEO	Yeovil Railway Centre
KWV	Keighley & Worth Valley Railway		
LAN	Llangollen Railway		
LDL	Lavender Line	Status	
LHG	L H Group Services, Burton	OPR	Operational
LHR	Lakeside & Haverthwaite Railway	OPR	Operational Main Line certified
LNW	London & North Western, Crewe	RES	Under restoration
LWR	Lincolnshire Wolds Railway	STC	Static exhibit
MET	Methill (Private)	STO	Stored
MFM	Mangapps Farm Railway Museum		
MHR	Mid Hants Railway		

Data Tables

Depot Codes

Code	Facility	Name	Operator
AB	SD	Aberdeen Guild Street	DBS
AC	CSD	Aberdeen Clayhills	ICE
AD	EMUD	Ashford Hitachi	HIT/SET
AF	T&RSMD	Ashford Chart Leacon	BOM
AH	MoD	Ashchurch	MoD
AK	DMUD	Ardwick	SIE/FTP
AL	DMUD	Aylesbury	CRW
AN	TMD/WRD	Allerton, Liverpool	DBS/NOR
AP	TMD	Ashford Rail Plant	BBR
AS	Store	Allelys	ALL
AT	TMD	Various sites	ALS
AW	SD	Washwood Heath	Hanson
AY	SD	Ayr	DBS
AZ	TMD	Ashford	BBR
AZ	TMD	Alizay (France)	ECR (DBS)
BA	TMD	Crewe Basford Hall	FLR, DBS
BC	MoD	Bicester	MoD
BD	T&RSMD	Birkenhead North	MER
BF	EMUD	Bedford Cauldwell Walk	FCC
BG	SD	Hull Botanic Gardens	NOR
BH	Eng	Barrow Hill Roundhouse	BHE
BI	EMUD	Brighton	SOU
BK	T&RSMD	Barton Hill	LNWR
BM	T&RSMD	Bournemouth	SWT
BN	T&RSMD	Bounds Green	ICE
BO	T&RSMD	Burton	Nemesis
BP	SD	Blackpool CS	NOR
BQ	TMD	Bury	ELR
BR	SD	Bristol Kingsland Road	NRL, FLR
BS	TMD	Bescot	DBS
BT	TMD	Bo'ness	BOK
BW	SD	Barrow-in-Furness	NOR
BZ	T&RSMD	St Blazey	DBS
CA	SD	Cambridge Coldhams Ln	AXI
CB	STORE	Crewe Brook Sidings	DBS
CC	T&RSMD	Clacton	NXA
CD	SD	Crewe Diesel	RIV, DBS
CE	IEMD	Crewe Electric	DBS
CF	DMUD	Cardiff Canton	PUL, ATW
CG	TMD	Crewe Gresty Bridge	DRS
CH	DMUD	Chester	ALS, ATW
CJ	SD	Clapham Junction	SWT
CK	DMUD	Corkerhill	FSR
CL	Store	Carlisle Upperby	DBS
CM	SD	Camden	LMI
CO	IEMD	Coquelles (France)	EUR
CP	CARMD	Crewe Carriage Shed	LNW
CQ	T&RSMD	Crewe Railway Age	CHC
CR	SD	Colchester	NXA
CS	T&RSMD	Carnforth	WCR
CT	SD	Cleethorpes	FTP
CW	MoD	Caerwent	MoD
CX	Store	Cardiff Tidal	DBS
CY	Store	Crewe Coal/South Yards	DRS
CZ	TMD	Central Rivers	BOM
DD	SD	Doncaster Wood Yard	DBS
DF	T&RSMD	Rail Vehicle Engineering	RVE
DI	Pres	Didcot Railway Centre	GWS
DM	TMD	Dollands Moor	DBS
DO	Store	Donnington Railfreight	-
DR	TMD	Doncaster Carr	DBS
DT	SD	Didcot Triangle	DBS
DV	SD	Dover	SET
DW	SD	Doncaster West Yard	NRL, WAB
DY	T&RSMD	Derby Etches Park	EMT
EA	SD	Earles Sidings	DBS
EC	T&RSMD	Craigentinny (Edinburgh)	ICE
ED	DMUD	Eastfield	FSR
EF	MPVD	Effingham Junction	AMS
EH	SD	Eastleigh	DBS
EM	EMUD	East Ham	c2c
EN	CARMD	Euston Downside	NRL
EU	SD	Euston Station Sidings	VWC
EZ	DMUD	Exeter	FGW
FB	Store	Ferrybridge	DBS
FC*		Fire College (Moreton-in-Marsh)	
FD	Mobile	Diesel loco	FLR
FE	Mobile	Electric loco	FLR
FF	TRSMD	Forest - Brussels	SNCB, NMBS, EUS
FH	TRACK	Frodingham	GRP
FN	Hire	France	ECR
FP	CSD	Ferme Park	ICE
FR	EMUD	Fratton	SWT
FS	Mobile	Diesel Shunter	FLR
FW	SD	Fort William	DBS
FX	TMD	Felixstowe	FDH
GI	EMUD	Gillingham	SET
GL	TMD	Gloucester	CWR, ADV
GP	SD	Grove Park	SET
GW	EMUD	Glasgow Shields	FSR
HA	TMD	Haymarket	FSR
HD	SD	Holyhead	ATW
HE	EMUD	Hornsey	FCC
HF	SD	Hereford	DBS
HG	Store	Hither Green	DBS
HI	TM	Hitchin	BBR
HJ	SD	Hoo Junction	DBS
HM	SD/WRD	Healey Mills	DBS
HT	T&RSMD	Heaton	NOR, GTL
HY	SD	Oxford Hinksey Yard	NRL
IL	T&RSMD	Ilford	NXA
IM	SD	Immingham	DBS
IP	SD	Ipswich	FLR
IS	TMD	Inverness	FSR
KC	Store	Carlisle Currock WRD	DBS
KD	SD	Kingmoor Yard	DRS
KK	EMUD	Kirkdale	MER
KM	TMD	Carlisle Kingmoor	DRS
KR	T&RSMD	Kidderminster	SVR
KT	SD	Kineton	MoD
KY	SD/WRD	Knottingley	DBS
LA	T&RSMD	Laira	FGW
LB	Eng	Loughborough	BTL
LD	TMD	Leeds Midland Road	FLR
LE	T&RSMD	Landore	FGW
LG	T&RSMD	Longsight Electric	ALT
LH	Eng	LH Group	LHG
LL	CSD	Liverpool Edge Hill	ALS
LM	Store	Long Marston	MLS
LO	T&RSMD	Longsight Diesel	NOR

Data Tables

Code	Type	Name	Operator
LP*	Eng	EMD Longport	EMD
LR	Eng	Leicester	EMD
LT	MoD	Longtown	MoD
LU	MoD	Ludgershall	MoD
LY	T&RSMD	Le Landy - Paris	SNCF, EUS
MA	CARMD	Manchester International	ALS
MD	TMD	Merehead	MRL
MG	TMD	Margam	DBS
MH	SD	Millerhill	DBS
ML	SD	Motherwell	DRS
MM	Store	Moreton-in-Marsh	-
MN	DMUD	Machynlleth	ATW
MQ	Store	Meldon Quarry	BAR
MR	SD	March	GBR
MW	MoD	Marchwood Military Port	MoD
MY	SD/Store	Mossend Yard	DBS, FLR
NB	SD	New Brighton	MER
NC	T&RSMD	Norwich Crown Point	NXA
ND	Works	NedTrans, Tilburg	NDZ
NG	T&RSMD	New Cross Gate	LOL
NH	DMUD	Newton Heath	NOR
NL	T&RSMD	Neville Hill (Leeds)	EMT, ICE
NM	SD	Nottingham Eastcroft	EMT
NN	EMUD	Northampton, Kings Heath	SIE, LMI
NT	EMUD	Northam	SIE, SWT
NY	T&RSMD	Grosmont	NYM
OD	Eng	Old Dalby	ALS
OH	EMUD	Old Oak Common Electric	ICE
ON	SD	Orpington	SET
OO	HSTMD	Old Oak Common HST	FGW
OX	CSD	Oxford Carriage Sidings	FGW
OY	CARMD	Oxley	ALS
PB	SD	Peterborough	DBS
PC	TRSMD	Polmadie	ALS
PE	SD	Peterborough Nene	FCC
PF	SD	Peak Forest	DBS
PG	TRSMD	Peterborough	GBR
PH	SD	Perth	FSR
PM	TRSMD	St Philip's Marsh (Bristol)	FGW
PN	SD	Preston Station	NOR
PN	TMD	Poznan (Poland)	ECR (DBS)
PQ	SD	Harwich Parkeston Quay	DBS
PT	SD	Peterborough	GBR
PY	MoD	Shoeburyness (Pigs Bay)	MoD, KRS
PZ	TRSMD	Penzance (Long Rock)	FGW
RE	EMUD	Ramsgate	SET
RG	DMUD	Reading	FGW
RH	SD	Redhill	DBS
RL	TRSMD	Ropley	MHR
RO	SD	Rotherham Steel	DBS
RU	TMD	Rugby Rail Plant	GRP
RY	EMUD	Ryde	SWT
SA	DMUD	Salisbury	SWT
SB	TMD	Shrewsbury	NOR
SE	TRSMD	St Leonards	SLR
SG	EMUD	Slade Green	SET
SH	CARMD	Southall Railway Centre	WCR
SI	EMUD	Soho	LMI
SJ	TRSMD	Stourbridge Junction	LMI
SK	TRSMD	Swanwick	MRC
SL	TRSMD	Stewarts Lane	DBS, VSO, SOU
SM	SD	Sheffield Station	NOR
SN	SD	Shoeburyness	c2c
SO*	SD	Southend	
SP	CRDC	Springs Branch	DBS
SQ	SD	Stockport	NOR
ST	SD	Southport	MER
SU	TRSMD	Selhurst	SOU
SX	SD	Shrewsbury	ATW
SZ	TMD	Southampton Maritime	FLR
TB	SD	Three Bridges	DBS
TE	TMD	Thornaby/Tees Yard	DBS
TF	SD	Orient Way	NXA
TG	SD	Tonbridge	GBR
TI	TRSMD	Temple Mills	EUS
TJ	TMD	Tavistock Junction	COL
TM	SD	Tyseley Loco Works	BRM
TN	SD	Taunton Fairwater	NRL, FLR
TO	TMD	Toton	DBS
TS	DMUD	Tyseley	LMI
TT	Store	Toton Training Compound	DBS
TY	Store	Tyne Yard	DBS
VI	SD	Victoria	SET
VR	SD	Aberystwyth	ATW
VZ	EMUD	Strawberry Hill	SIE, SWT
WA	SD	Warrington Arpley	DBS
WB	TRSMD	Wembley	ALS
WD	EMUD	East Wimbledon	SWT
WE	SD	Willesden Brent	DBS
WF	SD	Wansford	NVR
WH	Eng	Whatley	MRL
WH*	TMD	Washwood Heath	HAN
WK	SD	West Kirby	MER
WN	EMUD	Willesden	LOG
WO	TMD	Wolsingham	WER
WP	SD	Worksop	DBS
WS	SD	Worcester	LMI
WW	SD	West Worthing	SOU
WY	SD/CSD	Westbury Yard	DBS
WZ*	TRSMD	Washwood Heath	HAN
XW	TMD	Crofton	BOM
XX	-	Exported	-
YK	DMUD	Siemens York	SIE, FTP
YL	TMD	York Leeman Road	JAR, FLF
YM	Store	National Railway Museum	NRM
YN	SD	York North Yard	DBS
YO	SD	Yoker	FSR
ZA	Eng	RTC Derby	SER, NRL, AEA
ZB	Eng	Doncaster	WAB
ZC	Eng	Crewe	BOM
ZD	Eng	Derby Litchurch Lane	BOM
ZG	Eng	Eastleigh Works	KRS
ZH	Eng	Glasgow	RCL
ZI	Eng	Ilford	BOM
ZK	Eng	Kilmarnock	BTL
ZL	Eng	Cardiff Canton	PUL
ZN	Eng	Wolverton	RCL
ZS	Eng	Locotech Wakefield	BAR
ZW	Eng	Stoke-on-Trent (Marcroft)	AXI
WZ	Eng	Warsaw (Poland)	DBS
3M*		3M Industries, Bracknell	

* Unofficial code

Data Tables

Rail Data Tables

Operator Codes

AFG	Arlington Fleet Group
ALL	Allelys Heavy Haul
ALS	Alstom
AMS	Amec Spie Rail
ATW	Arriva Trains Wales
AXC	Arriva Cross Country
AXI	Axiom Rail
BAR	British American Railway Services
BBR	Balfour Beatty
BHE	Barrow Hill Roundhouse
BOK	Bo'ness & Kinneil
BOM	Bombardier
BRM	Birmingham Railway Museum
BTL	Brush Traction Limited
C2C	c2c Rail
CAR	Carillion
CHS	Crewe Heritage Centre
COL	Colas Rail
CON	Continental Rail (Spain)
COR	Corus Steel
CRW	Chiltern Railways
DBA	DB Arriva
DBR	DB Regio
DBS	DB Schenker West
DRS	Direct Rail Services
ECR	Euro Cargo Rail (DBS)
ELR	East Lancashire Railway
EMT	East Midlands Trains
ETF	ETF Freight (France)
ETL	Electric Traction Ltd
EU2	Eurotunnel Europorte2
EUR	Eurotunnel
EUS	Eurostar
FCC	First Capital Connect
FDH	Felixstowe Dock & Harbour
FGW	First Great Western
FHT	First Hull Trains
FLR	Freightliner
FSL	Flying Scotsman Railway Ltd
FSR	First ScotRail
FTP	First TransPennine

GBR	GB Railfreight
GRP	Grant Rail Plant
GTL	Grand Central Railway
GWS	Great Western Society
HEC	Heathrow Connect
HEX	Heathrow Express
HIT	Hitachi
HNR	Harry Needle Railroad
ICE	Inter City East Coast
IND	Industrial operator
IRY	Ian Riley
JHS	Jeremy Hoskins
KRS	Knights Rail Services
LAF	Lafarge Aggregates
LMI	London Midland
LNW	L&NWR Railway Co
LOG	London Overground
LUL	London Underground Ltd
MER	Merseyrail
MHR	Mid Hants Railway
MoD	Ministry of Defence
MRC	Midland Railway Centre
MRL	Mendip Rail Ltd
MRS	Motorail Logistics
NDZ	NedTrains
NOR	Northern Rail
NOT	Northumbria Rail
NRL	Network Rail
NRM	National Railway Museum
NVR	Nene Valley Railway
NYM	North Yorkshire Moors Railway
OLD	Old Dalby Test Track
POB	Port of Boston
PUL	Pullman Group
RAF	Railfilms Ltd
RCL	Railcare Ltd
RIV	Riviera Trains
RRS	Ridings Railtours
RVE	Rail Vehicle Engineering
S4G	Stratford 47 Group
SET	SouthEastern Trains
SIE	Siemens
SIL	Stagecoach Island Line
SLR	St Leonards Rail Engineering
SNB	Société Nationale des Chemins de fer Belges
SNF	Société Nationale des Chemins de fer Français
SOU	Southern
SRP	Scottish Railway Preservation Society
SVR	Severn Valley Railway
SWT	South West Trains
TRN	Transfesa
TSO	Travaux du Sud Ouest (France)
TTS	Transmart Trains
VSO	Venice Simplon Orient Express
VTN	Vintage Trains
VWC	Virgin West Coast
WAB	Wabtec
WCR	West Coast Railway Co

Below: *South West Trains Class 450 No. 450032 arrives at Virginia Water on 1 March 2012 with a Waterloo to Weybridge service.* **CJM**

Data Tables

Owner Codes

AEA	AEA Rail Technology
ALS	Alstom
ANG	Angel Trains
ATW	Arriva Trains Wales
AUT	Arriva UK Trains
BAA	British Airports Authority
BCC	Bridgend County Council
BEA	Beacon Rail
BOM	Bombardier
BOT	Bank of Tokyo (Mitsubishi)
BTM	BTMU Capital Corporation
C20	Class 20 Locomotive Ltd
CAD	Cargo-D
CBR	CB Rail
CCC	Cardiff County Council
COL	Colas Rail
CRW	Chiltern Railways
CWR	Cotswold Rail
DBR	DB Regio
DBS	DB Schenker West
DBS/T	DB Schenker/Transfesa
DRS	Direct Rail Services
ECR	Euro Cargo Rail (DBS)
ECT	ECT Main Line Rail
EMT	East Midlands Trains
ETL	Electric Traction Ltd
EU2	Eurotunnel Europorte2
EUR	Eurotunnel
EUS	Eurostar
EVL	Eversholt Leasing
FGP	First Group
FLF	Fastline Freight

FLR	Freightliner
FOS	Foster Yeoman
GBR	GB Railfreight
GTL	Grand Central Railway Ltd
HAL	Halifax Assets Finance Ltd
HAN	Hanson Traction
HEC	Hunslet Engine Co
HBS	Halifax-Bank of Scotland
HJA	Howard Johnson Associates
HNR	Harry Needle Railroad
IRY	Ian Riley
JAR	Jarvis
KRS	Knights Rail Services
MAG	Macquarie Group
NRL	Network Rail
NYM	North Yorkshire Moors Railway
PTR	Porterbrook
QWR	QW Rail Leasing
RCL	Railcare Limited
RIV	Riviera Trains
RML	Royal Mail
RMS	RMS Locotech
RTR	RT Rail
RVE	Rail Vehicle Engineering
S4G	Stratford Class 47 Group
SEC	Serco
SIE	Siemens
SNB	Société Nationale des Chemins de fer Belges
SNF	Société Nationale des Chemins de fer Français
SOU	Southern (Govia)
SWT	South West Trains (Stagecoach)
TTS	Transmart Trains
VTN	Vintage Trains
WAB	Wabtec
WCR	West Coast Railway Co
WYP	West Yorkshire PTE

Below: *The new order of the day on the Birmingham area local diesel services are either two- or three-car Class 172s, with a total of 27 sets in traffic allocated to Tyseley. On 26 September 2012, set No. 172222 arrives at Worcester with a service from Whitlocks End.* **CJM**

Data Tables

Rail Data Tables

Station three-letter Codes

Station	Code	Station	Code	Station	Code	Station	Code
Abbey Wood	ABW	Appley Bridge	APB	Banstead	BAD	Bere Alston	BAS
Aber	ABE	Apsley	APS	Barassie	BSS	Bere Ferrers	BFE
Abercynon	ACY	Arbroath	ARB	Barbican	ZBB	Berkhamsted	BKM
Aberdare	ABA	Ardgay	ARD	Bardon Mill	BLL	Berkswell	BKW
Aberdeen	ABD	Ardlui	AUI	Bare Lane	BAR	Berney Arms	BYA
Aberdour	AUR	Ardrossan Harbour	ADS	Bargeddie	BGI	Berry Brow	BBW
Aberdovey	AVY	Ardrossan South Beach	ASB	Bargoed	BGD	Berrylands	BRS
Abererch	ABH	Ardrossan Town	ADN	Barking	BKG	Berwick	BRK
Abergavenny	AGV	Ardwick	ADK	Barking Underground	ZBK	Berwick-upon-Tweed	BWK
Abergele & Pensarn	AGL	Argyle Street	AGS	Barlaston	BRT	Bescar Lane	BES
Aberystwyth	AYW	Arisaig	ARG	Barming	BMG	Bescot Stadium	BSC
Accrington	ACR	Arlesey	ARL	Barmouth	BRM	Betchworth	BTO
Achanalt	AAT	Armathwaite	AWT	Barnehurst	BNH	Bethnal Green	BET
Achnasheen	ACN	Arnside	ARN	Barnes	BNS	Betws-y-Coed	BYC
Achnashellach	ACH	Arram	ARR	Barnes Bridge	BNI	Beverley	BEV
Acklington	ACK	Arrochar & Tarbet	ART	Barnetby	BTB	Bexhill	BEX
Acle	ACL	Arundel	ARU	Barnham	BAA	Bexley	BXY
Acocks Green	ACG	Ascot	ACT	Barnhill	BNL	Bexleyheath	BXH
Acton Bridge	ACB	Ascott-u-Wychwood	AUW	Barnsley	BNY	Bicester North	BCS
Acton Central	ACC	Ash	ASH	Barnstaple	BNP	Bicester Town	BIT
Acton Main Line	AML	Ash Vale	AHV	Barnt Green	BTG	Bickley	BKL
Adderley Park	ADD	Ashburys	ABY	Barrhead	BRR	Bidston	BID
Addiewell	ADW	Ashchurch	ASC	Barrhill	BRL	Biggleswade	BIW
Addlestone	ASN	Ashfield	ASF	Barrow Haven	BAV	Bilbrook	BBK
Adisham	ADM	Ashford International	AFK	Barrow upon Soar	BWS	Billericay	BIC
Adlington (Cheshire)	ADC	Ashford (Eurostar)	ASI	Barrow-in-Furness	BIF	Billingham	BIL
Adlington (Lancs)	ADL	Ashford (Surrey)	AFS	Barry	BRY	Billingshurst	BIG
Adwick	AWK	Ashley	ASY	Barry Docks	BYD	Bingham	BIN
Aigburth	AIG	Ashtead	AHD	Barry Island	BYI	Bingley	BIY
Ainsdale	ANS	Ashton-under-Lyne	AHN	Barry Links	BYL	Birchgrove	BCG
Aintree	AIN	Ashurst	AHS	Barton-on-Humber	BAU	Birchington-on-Sea	BCH
Airbles	AIR	Ashurst New Forest	ANF	Basildon	BSO	Birchwood	BWD
Airdrie	ADR	Ashwell & Morden	AWM	Basingstoke	BSK	Birkbeck	BIK
Albany Park	AYP	Askam	ASK	Bat & Ball	BBL	Birkdale	BDL
Albrighton	ALB	Aslockton	ALK	Bath Spa	BTH	Birkenhead Central	BKC
Alderley Edge	ALD	Aspatria	ASP	Bathgate	BHG	Birkenhead North	BKN
Aldermaston	AMT	Aspley Guise	APG	Batley	BTL	Birkenhead Park	BKP
Aldershot	AHT	Aston	AST	Battersby	BTT	Birmingham Int	BHI
Aldrington	AGT	Atherstone	ATH	Battersea Park	BAK	Birmingham Moor St	BMO
Alexandra Palace	AAP	Atherton	ATN	Battle	BAT	Birmingham New St	BHM
Alexandra Parade	AXP	Attadale	ATT	Battlesbridge	BLB	Birmingham Snow Hill	BSW
Alexandria	ALX	Attenborough	ATB	Bayford	BAY	Bishop Auckland	BIA
Alfreton	ALF	Attleborough	ATL	Beaconsfield	BCF	Bishopbriggs	BBG
Allens West	ALW	Auchinleck	AUK	Bearley	BER	Bishops Stortford	BIS
Alloa	ALO	Audley End	AUD	Bearsden	BRN	Bishopstone	BIP
Alness	ASS	Aughton Park	AUG	Bearsted	BSD	Bishopton	BPT
Alnmouth	ALM	Aviemore	AVM	Beasdale	BSL	Bitterne	BTE
Alresford	ALR	Avoncliff	AVF	Beaulieu Road	BEU	Blackburn	BBN
Alsager	ASG	Avonmouth	AVN	Beauly	BEL	Blackheath	BKH
Althorne	ALN	Axminster	AXM	Bebington	BEB	Blackhorse Road	BHO
Althorpe	ALP	Aylesbury	AYS	Beccles	BCC	Blackpool North	BPN
Altnabreac	ABC	Aylesbury Parkway	AVP	Beckenham Hill	BEC	Blackpool P Beach	BPB
Alton	AON	Aylesford	AYL	Beckenham Junction	BKJ	Blackpool South	BPS
Altrincham	ALT	Aylesham	AYH	Bedford	BDM	Blackrod	BLK
Alvechurch	ALV	Ayr	AYR	Bedford St Johns	BSJ	Blackwater	BAW
Ambergate	AMB	Bache	BAC	Bedhampton	BDH	Blaenau Ffestiniog	BFF
Amberley	AMY	Baglan	BAJ	Bedminster	BMT	Blair Atholl	BLA
Amersham	AMR	Bagshot	BAG	Bedworth	BEH	Blairhill	BAI
Ammanford	AMF	Baildon	BLD	Bedwyn	BDW	Blake Street	BKT
Ancaster	ANC	Baillieston	BIO	Beeston	BEE	Blakedown	BKD
Anderston	AND	Balcombe	BAB	Bekesbourne	BKS	Blantyre	BLT
Andover	ADV	Baldock	BDK	Belle Vue	BLV	Blaydon	BLO
Anerley	ANZ	Balham	BAL	Bellgrove	BLG	Bleasby	BSB
Angel Road	AGR	Balloch	BHC	Bellingham	BGM	Bletchley	BLY
Angmering	ANG	Balmossie	BSI	Bellshill	BLH	Bloxwich	BLX
Annan	ANN	Bamber Bridge	BMB	Belmont	BLM	Bloxwich North	BWN
Anniesland	ANL	Bamford	BAM	Belper	BLP	Blundellsands & Crosby	BLN
Ansdell & Fairhaven	AFV	Banavie	BNV	Beltring	BEG	Blythe Bridge	BYB
Appleby	APP	Banbury	BAN	Belvedere	BVD	Bodmin Parkway	BOD
Appledore (Kent)	APD	Bangor (Gwynedd)	BNG	Bempton	BEM	Bodorgan	BOR
Appleford	APF	Bank Hall	BAH	Ben Rhydding	BEY	Bognor Regis	BOG
				Benfleet	BEF	Bogston	BGS
				Bentham	BEN	Bolton	BON
				Bentley	BTY	Bolton-on-Dearne	BTD
				Bentley (South Yorks)	BYK	Bookham	BKA

Data Tables

Station	Code	Station	Code	Station	Code	Station	Code
Bootle	BOC	Brora	BRA	Carlisle	CAR	Chorley	CRL
Bootle New Strand	BNW	Brough	BUH	Carlton	CTO	Chorleywood	CLW
Bootle Oriel Road	BOT	Broughty Ferry	BYF	Carluke	CLU	Christchurch	CHR
Bordesley	BBS	Broxbourne	BXB	Carmarthen	CMN	Christs Hospital	CHH
Borough Green	BRG	Bruce Grove	BCV	Carmyle	CML	Church & Oswaldtwistle	CTW
Borth	BRH	Brundall	BDA	Carnforth	CNF	Church Fenton	CHF
Bosham	BOH	Brundall Gardens	BGA	Carnoustie	CAN	Church Stretton	CTT
Boston	BSN	Brunstane	BSU	Carntyne	CAY	Cilmeri	CIM
Botley	BOE	Brunswick	BRW	Carpenders Park	CPK	City Thameslink	CTK
Bottesford	BTF	Bruton	BRU	Carrbridge	CAG	Clacton on Sea	CLT
Bourne End	BNE	Bryn	BYN	Carshalton	CSH	Clandon	CLA
Bournemouth	BMH	Buckenham	BUC	Carshalton Beeches	CSB	Clapham High Street	CLP
Bournville	BRV	Buckley	BCK	Carstairs	CRS	Clapham Junction	CLJ
Bow Brickhill	BWB	Bucknell	BUK	Cartsdyke	CDY	Clapham (Yorkshire)	CPY
Bowes Park	BOP	Bugle	BGL	Castle Bar Park	CBP	Clapton	CPT
Bowling	BWG	Builth Road	BHR	Castle Cary	CLC	Clarbeston Road	CLR
Boxhill & Westhumble	BXW	Bulwell	BLW	Castleford	CFD	Clarkston	CKS
Bracknell	BCE	Bures	BUE	Castleton	CAS	Claverdon	CLV
Bradford Forster Sq	BDQ	Burgess Hill	BUG	Castleton Moor	CSM	Claygate	CLG
Bradford Interchange	BDI	Burley Park	BUY	Caterham	CAT	Cleethorpes	CLE
Bradford-on-Avon	BOA	Burley-in-Wharfedale	BUW	Catford	CTF	Cleland	CEA
Brading	BDN	Burnage	BNA	Catford Bridge	CFB	Clifton	CLI
Braintree	BTR	Burneside	BUD	Cathays	CYS	Clifton Down	CFN
Braintree Freeport	BTP	Burnham	BNM	Cathcart	CCT	Clitheroe	CLH
Bramhall	BML	Burnham-on-Crouch	BUU	Cattal	CTL	Clock House	CLK
Bramley	BLE	Burnley Barracks	BUB	Causeland	CAU	Clunderwen	CUW
Bramley (Hants)	BMY	Burnley Central	BNC	Cefn-y-Bedd	CYB	Clydebank	CYK
Brampton (Cumbria)	BMP	Burnley Manchester Rd	BYM	Chadwell Heath	CTH	Coatbridge Central	CBC
Brampton (Suffolk)	BRP	Burnside	BUI	Chafford Hundred	CFH	Coatbridge Sunnyside	CBS
Branchton	BCN	Burntisland	BTS	Chalfont & Latimer	CFO	Coatdyke	COA
Brandon	BND	Burscough Bridge	BCB	Chalkwell	CHW	Cobham & Stoke d'An	CSD
Branksome	BSM	Burscough Junction	BCJ	Chandlers Ford	CFR	Codsall	CSL
Braystones	BYS	Bursledon	BUO	Chapel-en-le-Frith	CEF	Cogan	CGN
Bredbury	BDY	Burton Joyce	BUJ	Chapelton	CPN	Colchester	COL
Breich	BRC	Burton-on-Trent	BUT	Chapeltown	CLN	Colchester Town	CET
Brentford	BFD	Bury St Edmunds	BSE	Chappel & Wakes Colne	CWC	Coleshill Parkway	CEH
Brentwood	BRE	Busby	BUS	Charing	CHG	Collingham	CLM
Bricket Wood	BWO	Bush Hill Park	BHK	Charing Cross (FSR)	CHC	Collington	CLL
Bridge of Allan	BEA	Bushey	BSH	Charlbury	CBY	Colne	CNE
Bridge of Orchy	BRO	Butlers Lane	BUL	Charlton	CTN	Colwall	CWL
Bridgend	BGN	Buxted	BXD	Chartham	CRT	Colwyn Bay	CWB
Bridgeton	BDG	Buxton	BUX	Chassen Road	CSR	Combe	CME
Bridgwater	BWT	Byfleet & New Haw	BFN	Chatelherault	CTE	Commondale	COM
Bridlington	BDT	Bynea	BYE	Chatham	CTM	Congleton	CNG
Brierfield	BRF	Cadoxton	CAD	Chathill	CHT	Conisbrough	CNS
Brigg	BGG	Caergwrle	CGW	Cheadle Hulme	CHU	Connel Ferry	CON
Brighouse	BGH	Caerphilly	CPH	Cheam	CHE	Cononley	CEY
Brighton	BTN	Caersws	CWS	Cheddington	CED	Conway Park	CNP
Brimsdown	BMD	Caldicot	CDT	Chelford	CEL	Conwy	CNW
Brinnington	BNT	Caledonian Rd & Bby	CIR	Chelmsford	CHM	Cooden Beach	COB
Bristol Parkway	BPW	Calstock	CSK	Chelsfield	CLD	Cookham	COO
Bristol Temple Meads	BRI	Cam & Dursley	CDU	Cheltenham Spa	CNM	Cooksbridge	CBR
Brithdir	BHD	Camberley	CAM	Chepstow	CPW	Coombe Halt	COE
British Steel Redcar	RBS	Camborne	CBN	Cherry Tree	CYT	Copplestone	COP
Briton Ferry	BNF	Cambridge	CBG	Chertsey	CHY	Corbridge	CRB
Brixton	BRX	Cambridge Heath	CBH	Cheshunt	CHN	Corby	COR
Broad Green	BGE	Cambuslang	CBL	Chessington North	CSN	Corkerhill	CKH
Broadbottom	BDB	Camden Road	CMD	Chessington South	CSS	Corkickle	CKL
Broadstairs	BSR	Camelon	CMO	Chester	CTR	Corpach	CPA
Brockenhurst	BCU	Canley	CNL	Chester Road	CRD	Corrour	CRR
Brockholes	BHS	Cannock	CAO	Chesterfield	CHD	Coryton	COY
Brockley	BCY	Canonbury	CNN	Chester-le-Street	CLS	Coseley	CSY
Brockley Whins	BNR	Canterbury East	CBE	Chestfield & Swalecliffe	CSW	Cosford	COS
Bromborough	BOM	Canterbury West	CBW	Chetnole	CNO	Cosham	CSA
Bromborough Rake	BMR	Cantley	CNY	Chichester	CCH	Cottingham	CGM
Bromley Cross	BMC	Capenhurst	CPU	Chilham	CIL	Cottingley	COT
Bromley North	BMN	Carbis Bay	CBB	Chilworth	CHL	Coulsdon South	CDS
Bromley South	BMS	Cardenden	CDD	Chingford	CHI	Coventry	COV
Bromsgrove	BMV	Cardiff Bay	CDB	Chinley	CLY	Cowden	CWN
Brondesbury	BSY	Cardiff Central	CDF	Chippenham	CPM	Cowdenbeath	COW
Brondesbury Park	BSP	Cardiff Queen Street	CDQ	Chipstead	CHP	Cradley Heath	CRA
Brookmans Park	BPK	Cardonald	CDO	Chirk	CRK	Craigendoran	CGD
Brookwood	BKO	Cardross	CDR	Chislehurst	CIT	Cramlington	CRM
Broome	BME	Carfin	CRF	Chiswick	CHK	Craven Arms	CRV
Broomfleet	BMF	Cark & Cartmel	CAK	Cholsey	CHO	Crawley	CRW

Data Tables

Station	Code	Station	Code	Station	Code	Station	Code
Crayford	CRY	Denmark Hill	DMK	Durrington-on-Sea	DUR	Exeter St Thomas	EXT
Crediton	CDI	Dent	DNT	Dyce	DYC	Exhibition Centre	EXG
Cressing	CES	Denton	DTN	Dyffryn Ardudwy	DYF	Exmouth	EXM
Cressington	CSG	Deptford	DEP	Eaglescliffe	EAG	Exton	EXN
Creswell	CWD	Derby	DBY	Ealing Broadway	EAL	Eynsford	EYN
Crewe	CRE	Derby Road	DBR	Earlestown	ERL	Failsworth	FLS
Crewkerne	CKN	Derker	DKR	Earley	EAR	Fairbourne	FRB
Crews Hill	CWH	Devonport	DPT	Earlsfield	EAD	Fairfield	FRF
Crianlarich	CNR	Dewsbury	DEW	Earlswood (Surrey)	ELD	Fairlie	FRL
Criccieth	CCC	Didcot Parkway	DID	Earlswood (Midlands)	EWD	Fairwater	FRW
Cricklewood	CRI	Digby & Sowton	DIG	East Boldon	EBL	Falconwood	FCN
Croftfoot	CFF	Dilton Marsh	DMH	East Croydon	ECR	Falkirk Grahamston	FKG
Crofton Park	CFT	Dinas Powys	DNS	East Didsbury	EDY	Falkirk High	FKK
Cromer	CMR	Dinas Rhondda	DMG	East Dulwich	EDW	Falls of Cruachan	FOC
Cromford	CMF	Dingle Road	DGL	East Farleigh	EFL	Falmer	FMR
Crookston	CKT	Dingwall	DIN	East Garforth	EGF	Falmouth Docks	FAL
Cross Gates	CRG	Dinsdale	DND	East Grinstead	EGR	Falmouth Town	FMT
Crossflatts	CFL	Dinting	DTG	East Kilbride	EKL	Fareham	FRM
Crosshill	COI	Disley	DSL	East Malling	EML	Farnborough (Main)	FNB
Crosskeys	CKY	Diss	DIS	East Midlands Parkway	EMD	Farnborough North	FNN
Crossmyloof	CMY	Dockyard	DOC	East Tilbury	ETL	Farncombe	FNC
Croston	CSO	Dodworth	DOD	East Worthing	EWR	Farnham	FNH
Crouch Hill	CRH	Dolau	DOL	Eastbourne	EBN	Farningham Road	FNR
Crowborough	COH	Doleham	DLH	Eastbrook	EBK	Farnworth	FNW
Crowhurst	CWU	Dolgarrog	DLG	Easterhouse	EST	Farringdon	ZFD
Crowle	CWE	Dolwyddelan	DWD	Eastham Rake	ERA	Fauldhouse	FLD
Crowthorne	CRN	Doncaster	DON	Eastleigh	ESL	Faversham	FAV
Croy	CRO	Dorchester South	DCH	Eastrington	EGN	Faygate	FGT
Crystal Palace	CYP	Dorchester West	DCW	Ebbw Vale Parkway	EBV	Fazakerley	FAZ
Cuddington	CUD	Dore	DOR	Eccles	ECC	Fearn	FRN
Cuffley	CUF	Dorking	DKG	Eccles Road	ECS	Featherstone	FEA
Culham	CUM	Dorking Deepdene	DPD	Eccleston Park	ECL	Fellgate	FEG
Culrain	CUA	Dorking West	DKT	Edale	EDL	Felixstowe	FLX
Cumbernauld	CUB	Dormans	DMS	Eden Park	EDN	Feltham	FEL
Cupar	CUP	Dorridge	DDG	Edenbridge	EBR	Feniton	FNT
Curriehill	CUH	Dove Holes	DVH	Edenbridge Town	EBT	Fenny Stratford	FEN
Cuxton	CUX	Dover Priory	DVP	Edge Hill	EDG	Fernhill	FER
Cwmbach	CMH	Dovercourt	DVC	Edinburgh Park	EDP	Ferriby	FRY
Cwmbran	CWM	Dovey Junction	DVY	Edinburgh Waverley	EDB	Ferryside	FYS
Cynghordy	CYN	Downham Market	DOW	Edmonton Green	EDR	Ffairfach	FFA
Dagenham Dock	DDK	Drayton Green	DRG	Effingham Junction	EFF	Filey	FIL
Daisy Hill	DSY	Drayton Park	DYP	Eggesford	EGG	Filton Abbey Wood	FIT
Dalgety Bay	DAG	Drem	DRM	Egham	EGH	Finchley Rd & Frognal	FNY
Dalmally	DAL	Driffield	DRF	Egton	EGT	Finsbury Park	FPK
Dalmarnock	DAK	Drigg	DRI	Elephant & Castle	EPH	Finstock	FIN
Dalmeny	DAM	Droitwich Spa	DTW	Elgin	ELG	Fishbourne (Sussex)	FSB
Dalmuir	DMR	Dronfield	DRO	Ellesmere Port	ELP	Fishersgate	FSG
Dalreoch	DLR	Drumchapel	DMC	Elmers End	ELE	Fishguard Harbour	FGH
Dalry	DLY	Drumfrochar	DFR	Elmstead Woods	ESD	Fiskerton	FSK
Dalston	DLS	Drumgelloch	DRU	Elmswell	ESW	Fitzwilliam	FZW
Dalston Kingsland	DLK	Drumry	DMY	Elsecar	ELR	Five Ways	FWY
Dalton	DLT	Dublin Ferryport	DFP	Elsenham	ESM	Fleet	FLE
Dalwhinnie	DLW	Dublin Port - Stena	DPS	Elstree & Borehamwood	ELS	Flimby	FLM
Danby	DNY	Duddeston	DUD	Eltham	ELW	Flint	FLN
Danescourt	DCT	Dudley Port	DDP	Elton & Orston	ELO	Flitwick	FLT
Danzey	DZY	Duffield	DFI	Ely	ELY	Flixton	FLI
Darlington	DAR	Duirinish	DRN	Emerson Park	EMP	Flowery Field	FLF
Darnall	DAN	Duke Street	DST	Emsworth	EMS	Folkestone Central	FKC
Darsham	DSM	Dullingham	DUL	Enfield Chase	ENC	Folkestone West	FKW
Dartford	DFD	Dumbarton Central	DBC	Enfield Lock	ENL	Ford	FOD
Darton	DRT	Dumbarton East	DBE	Enfield Town	ENF	Forest Gate	FOG
Darwen	DWN	Dumbreck	DUM	Entwistle	ENT	Forest Hill	FOH
Datchet	DAT	Dumfries	DMF	Epsom	EPS	Formby	FBY
Davenport	DVN	Dumpton Park	DMP	Epsom Downs	EPD	Forres	FOR
Dawlish	DWL	Dunbar	DUN	Erdington	ERD	Forsinard	FRS
Dawlish Warren	DWW	Dunblane	DBL	Eridge	ERI	Fort Matilda	FTM
Deal	DEA	Duncraig	DCG	Erith	ERH	Fort William	FTW
Dean	DEN	Dundee	DEE	Esher	ESH	Four Oaks	FOK
Dean Lane	DNN	Dunfermline Q'n Margaret	DFL	Essex Road	EXR	Foxfield	FOX
Deansgate	DGT	Dunfermline Town	DFE	Etchingham	ETC	Foxton	FXN
Deganwy	DGY	Dunkeld & Birnam	DKD	Euxton Balshaw Lane	EBA	Frant	FRT
Deighton	DHN	Dunlop	DNL	Evesham	EVE	Fratton	FTN
Delamere	DLM	Dunrobin Castle	DNO	Ewell East	EWE	Freshfield	FRE
Denby Dale	DBD	Dunston	DOT	Ewell West	EWW	Freshford	FFD
Denham	DNM	Dunton Green	DNG	Exeter Central	EXC	Frimley	FML
Denham Golf Club	DGC	Durham	DHM	Exeter St Davids	EXD	Frinton on Sea	FRI

Frizinghall	FZH	Great Bentley	GRB	Harpenden	HPD	Heyford	HYD
Frodsham	FRD	Great Chesterford	GRC	Harrietsham	HRM	Heysham Port	HHB
Frome	FRO	Great Coates	GCT	Harringay	HGY	High Brooms	HIB
Fulwell	FLW	Great Malvern	GMV	Harringay Green Lanes	HRY	High St (Glasgow)	HST
Furness Vale	FNV	Great Missenden	GMN	Harrington	HRR	High Street Kensington	ZHS
Furze Platt	FZP	Great Yarmouth	GYM	Harrogate	HGT	High Wycombe	HWY
Gainsborough Central	GNB	Green Lane	GNL	Harrow & Wealdstone	HRW	Higham	HGM
Gainsborough Lea Rd	GBL	Green Road	GNR	Harrow-on-the-Hill	HOH	Highams Park	HIP
Garelochhead	GCH	Greenbank	GBK	Hartford	HTF	Highbridge & Burnham	HIG
Garforth	GRF	Greenfaulds	GRL	Hartlebury	HBY	Highbury & Islington	HHY
Gargrave	GGV	Greenfield	GNF	Hartlepool	HPL	Hightown	HTO
Garrowhill	GAR	Greenford	GFD	Hartwood	HTW	Hildenborough	HLB
Garscadden	GRS	Greenhithe for Bluewater	GNH	Harwich International	HPQ	Hillfoot	HLF
Garsdale	GSD	Greenock Central	GKC	Harwich Town	HWC	Hillington East	HLE
Garston (Hertfordshire)	GSN	Greenock West	GKW	Haslemere	HSL	Hillington West	HLW
Garswood	GSW	Greenwich	GNW	Hassocks	HSK	Hillside	HIL
Gartcosh	GRH	Gretna Green	GEA	Hastings	HGS	Hilsea	HLS
Garth (Bridgend)	GMG	Grimsby Docks	GMD	Hatch End	HTE	Hinchley Wood	HYW
Garth (Powys)	GTH	Grimsby Town	GMB	Hatfield	HAT	Hinckley	HNK
Garve	GVE	Grindleford	GRN	Hatfield & Stainforth	HFS	Hindley	HIN
Gathurst	GST	Grosmont	GMT	Hatfield Peverel	HAP	Hinton Admiral	HNA
Gatley	GTY	Grove Park	GRP	Hathersage	HSG	Hitchin	HIT
Gatwick Airport	GTW	Guide Bridge	GUI	Hattersley	HTY	Hither Green	HGR
Georgemas Junction	GGJ	Guildford	GLD	Hatton	HTN	Hockley	HOC
Gerrards Cross	GER	Guiseley	GSY	Havant	HAV	Hollingbourne	HBN
Gidea Park	GDP	Gunnersbury	GUN	Havenhouse	HVN	Hollinwood	HOD
Giffnock	GFN	Gunnislake	GSL	Haverfordwest	HVF	Holmes Chapel	HCH
Giggleswick	GIG	Gunton	GNT	Hawarden	HWD	Holmwood	HLM
Gilberdyke	GBD	Gwersyllt	GWE	Hawarden Bridge	HWB	Holton Heath	HOL
Gilfach Fargoed	GFF	Gypsy Lane	GYP	Hawkhead	HKH	Holyhead	HHD
Gillingham (Dorset)	GIL	Habrough	HAB	Haydon Bridge	HDB	Holytown	HLY
Gillingham (Kent)	GLM	Hackbridge	HCB	Haydons Road	HYR	Homerton	HMN
Gilshochill	GSC	Hackney Central	HKC	Hayes & Harlington	HAY	Honeybourne	HYB
Gipsy Hill	GIP	Hackney Downs	HAC	Hayes (Kent)	HYS	Honiton	HON
Girvan	GIR	Hackney Wick	HKW	Hayle	HYL	Honley	HOY
Glaisdale	GLS	Haddenham & T Parkway	HDM	Haymarket	HYM	Honor Oak Park	HPA
Glan Conwy	GCW	Haddiscoe	HAD	Haywards Heath	HHE	Hook	HOK
Glasgow Central	GLC	Hadfield	HDF	Hazel Grove	HAZ	Hooton	HOO
Glasgow Queen Street	GLQ	Hadley Wood	HDW	Headcorn	HCN	Hope (Derbyshire)	HOP
Glasshoughton	GLH	Hag Fold	HGF	Headingley	HDY	Hope (Flintshire)	HPE
Glazebrook	GLZ	Hagley	HAG	Headstone Lane	HDL	Hopton Heath	HPT
Gleneagles	GLE	Hairmyres	HMY	Heald Green	HDG	Horley	HOR
Glenfinnan	GLF	Hale	HAL	Healing	HLI	Hornbeam Park	HBP
Glengarnock	GLG	Halesworth	HAS	Heath High Level	HHL	Hornsey	HRN
Glenrothes with Thornton	GLT	Halewood	HED	Heath Low Level	HLL	Horsforth	HRS
Glossop	GLO	Halifax	HFX	Heathrow Airport T123	HXX	Horsham	HRH
Gloucester	GCR	Hall Green	HLG	Heathrow Airport T4	HAF	Horsley	HSY
Glynde	GLY	Hall-i'-th'-Wood	HID	Heathrow Terminal 5	HWV	Horton-in-Ribblesdale	HIR
Gobowen	GOB	Hall Road	HLR	Heaton Chapel	HTC	Horwich Parkway	HWI
Godalming	GOD	Halling	HAI	Hebden Bridge	HBD	Hoscar	HSC
Godley	GDL	Haltwhistle	HWH	Heckington	HEC	Hough Green	HGN
Godstone	GDN	Ham Street	HMT	Hedge End	HDE	Hounslow	HOU
Goldthorpe	GOE	Hamble	HME	Hednesford	HNF	Hove	HOV
Golf Street	GOF	Hamilton Central	HNC	Heighington	HEI	Hoveton & Wroxham	HXM
Golspie	GOL	Hamilton Square	BKQ	Helensburgh Central	HLC	How Wood	HWW
Gomshall	GOM	Hamilton West	HNW	Helensburgh Upper	HLU	Howden	HOW
Goodmayes	GMY	Hammerton	HMM	Hellifield	HLD	Howwood (Renfrew)	HOZ
Goole	GOO	Hampden Park	HMD	Helmsdale	HMS	Hoylake	HYK
Goostrey	GTR	Hampstead Heath	HDH	Helsby	HSB	Hubberts Bridge	HBB
Gordon Hill	GDH	Hampton	HMP	Hemel Hempstead	HML	Hucknall	HKN
Goring & Streatley	GOR	Hampton Court	HMC	Hendon	HEN	Huddersfield	HUD
Goring-by-Sea	GBS	Hampton Wick	HMW	Hengoed	HNG	Hull Paragon	HUL
Gorton	GTO	Hampton-in-Arden	HIA	Henley-in-Arden	HNL	Humphrey Park	HUP
Gospel Oak	GPO	Hamstead	HSD	Henley-on-Thames	HOT	Huncoat	HCT
Gourock	GRK	Hamworthy	HAM	Hensall	HEL	Hungerford	HGD
Gowerton	GWN	Hanborough	HND	Hereford	HFD	Hunmanby	HUB
Goxhill	GOX	Handforth	HTH	Herne Bay	HNB	Huntingdon	HUN
Grange Park	GPK	Hanwell	HAN	Herne Hill	HNH	Huntly	HNT
Grange-Over-Sands	GOS	Hapton	HPN	Hersham	HER	Hunts Cross	HNX
Grangetown	GTN	Harlech	HRL	Hertford East	HFE	Hurst Green	HUR
Grantham	GRA	Harlesden	HDN	Hertford North	HFN	Hutton Cranswick	HUT
Grateley	GRT	Harling Road	HRD	Hessle	HES	Huyton	HUY
Gravelly Hill	GVH	Harlington	HLN	Heswall	HSW	Hyde Central	HYC
Gravesend	GRV	Harlow Mill	HWM	Hever	HEV	Hyde North	HYT
Grays	GRY	Harlow Town	HWN	Heworth	HEW	Hykeham	HKM
Great Ayton	GTA	Harold Wood	HRO	Hexham	HEX	Hyndland	HYN

Data Tables

Station	Code	Station	Code	Station	Code	Station	Code
Hythe	HYH	Kings Park	KGP	Lenzie	LNZ	London Cannon Street	CST
IBM	IBM	Kings Sutton	KGS	Leominster	LEO	London Charing Cross	CHX
Ifield	IFI	Kingsknowe	KGE	Letchworth Garden City	LET	London Euston	EUS
Ilford	IFD	Kingston	KNG	Leuchars (St Andrews)	LEU	London Fenchurch St	FST
Ilkley	ILK	Kingswood	KND	Levenshulme	LVM	London Fields	LOF
Imperial Wharf	IMW	Kingussie	KIN	Lewes	LWS	London King's Cross	KGX
Ince	INC	Kintbury	KIT	Lewisham	LEW	London Liverpool St	LST
Ince & Elton	INE	Kirby Cross	KBX	Leyland	LEY	London Marylebone	MYB
Ingatestone	INT	Kirk Sandall	KKS	Leyton Midland Road	LEM	London Paddington	PAD
Insch	INS	Kirkby	KIR	Leytonstone High Road	LER	London Road (Brighton)	LRB
Invergordon	IGD	Kirkby-in-Ashfield	KKB	Lichfield City	LIC	London Road (Guildford)	LRD
Invergowrie	ING	Kirkby Stephen	KSW	Lichfield Trent Valley	LTV	London St Pancras	STP
Inverkeithing	INK	Kirkby-in-Furness	KBF	Lidlington	LID	London Victoria	VIC
Inverkip	INP	Kirkcaldy	KDY	Limehouse	LHS	London Waterloo	WAT
Inverness	INV	Kirkconnel	KRK	Lincoln Central	LCN	London Waterloo East	WAE
Invershin	INH	Kirkdale	KKD	Lingfield	LFD	Long Buckby	LBK
Inverurie	INR	Kirkham & Wesham	KKM	Lingwood	LGD	Long Eaton	LGE
Ipswich	IPS	Kirkhill	KKH	Linlithgow	LIN	Long Preston	LPR
Irlam	IRL	Kirknewton	KKN	Liphook	LIP	Longbeck	LGK
Irvine	IRV	Kirkwood	KWD	Liskeard	LSK	Longbridge	LOB
Isleworth	ISL	Kirton Lindsey	KTL	Liss	LIS	Longcross	LNG
Islip	ISP	Kiveton Bridge	KIV	Lisvane & Thornhill	LVT	Longfield	LGF
Iver	IVR	Kiveton Park	KVP	Little Kimble	LTK	Longniddry	LND
Ivybridge	IVY	Knaresborough	KNA	Little Sutton	LTT	Longport	LPT
Jewellery Quarter	JEQ	Knebworth	KBW	Littleborough	LTL	Longton	LGN
Johnston	JOH	Knighton	KNI	Littlehampton	LIT	Looe	LOO
Johnstone	JHN	Knockholt	KCK	Littlehaven	LVN	Lostock	LOT
Jordanhill	JOR	Knottingley	KNO	Littleport	LTP	Lostock Gralam	LTG
Kearsley	KSL	Knucklas	KNU	Liverpool Central	LVC	Lostock Hall	LOH
Kearsney	KSN	Knutsford	KNF	Liverpool James Street	LVJ	Lostwithiel	LOS
Keighley	KEI	Kyle of Lochalsh	KYL	Liverpool Lime Street	LIV	Loughborough	LBO
Keith	KEH	Ladybank	LDY	Liverpool South Parkway	LPY	Loughborough Junction	LGJ
Kelvedon	KEL	Ladywell	LAD	Livingston North	LSN	Lowdham	LOW
Kelvindale	KVD	Laindon	LAI	Livingston South	LVG	Lower Sydenham	LSY
Kemble	KEM	Lairg	LRG	Llanaber	LLA	Lowestoft	LWT
Kempston Hardwick	KMH	Lake	LKE	Llanbedr	LBR	Ludlow	LUD
Kempton Park	KMP	Lakenheath	LAK	Llanbister Road	LLT	Luton	LUT
Kemsing	KMS	Lamphey	LAM	Llanbradach	LNB	Luton Airport Parkway	LTN
Kemsley	KML	Lanark	LNK	Llandaf	LLN	Luxulyan	LUX
Kendal	KEN	Lancaster	LAN	Llandanwg	LDN	Lydney	LYD
Kenley	KLY	Lancing	LAC	Llandecwyn	LLC	Lye	LYE
Kennett	KNE	Landywood	LAW	Llandeilo	LLL	Lymington Pier	LYP
Kennishead	KNS	Langbank	LGB	Llandovery	LLV	Lymington Town	LYT
Kensal Green	KNL	Langho	LHO	Llandrindod	LLO	Lympstone Commando	LYC
Kensal Rise	KNR	Langley	LNY	Llandudno	LLD	Lympstone Village	LYM
Kensington Olympia	KPA	Langley Green	LGG	Llandudno Junction	LLJ	Lytham	LTM
Kent House	KTH	Langley Mill	LGM	Llandybie	LLI	Macclesfield	MAC
Kentish Town	KTN	Langside	LGS	Llanelli	LLE	Machynlleth	MCN
Kentish Town West	KTW	Langwathby	LGW	Llanfairfechan	LLF	Maesteg	MST
Kenton	KNT	Langwith-Whaley Thorns	LAG	Llanfairpwll	LPG	Maesteg (Ewenny Rd)	MEW
Kents Bank	KBK	Lapford	LAP	Llangadog	LLG	Maghull	MAG
Kettering	KET	Lapworth	LPW	Llangammarch	LLM	Maiden Newton	MDN
Kew Bridge	KWB	Larbert	LBT	Llangennech	LLH	Maidenhead	MAI
Kew Gardens	KWG	Largs	LAR	Llangynllo	LGO	Maidstone Barracks	MDB
Keyham	KEY	Larkhall	LRH	Llanharan	LLR	Maidstone East	MDE
Keynsham	KYN	Lawrence Hill	LWH	Llanhilleth	LTH	Maidstone West	MDW
Kidbrooke	KDB	Layton	LAY	Llanishen	LLS	Malden Manor	MAL
Kidderminster	KID	Lazonby & Kirkoswald	LZB	Llanrwst	LWR	Mallaig	MLG
Kidsgrove	KDG	Lea Green	LEG	Llansamlet	LAS	Malton	MLT
Kidwelly	KWL	Lea Hall	LEH	Llantwit Major	LWM	Malvern Link	MVL
Kilburn High Road	KBN	Leagrave	LEA	Llanwrda	LNR	Manchester Airport	MIA
Kildale	KLD	Lealholm	LHM	Llanwrtyd	LNW	Manchester Oxford Rd	MCO
Kildonan	KIL	Leamington Spa	LMS	Llwyngwril	LLW	Manchester Piccadilly	MAN
Kilgetty	KGT	Leasowe	LSW	Llwynypia	LLY	Manchester United FC	MUF
Kilmarnock	KMK	Leatherhead	LHD	Loch Awe	LHA	Manchester Victoria	MCV
Kilmaurs	KLM	Ledbury	LED	Loch Eil Outward Bound	LHE	Manea	MNE
Kilpatrick	KPT	Lee	LEE	Lochailort	LCL	Manningtree	MNG
Kilwinning	KWN	Leeds	LDS	Locheilside	LCS	Manor Park	MNP
Kinbrace	KBC	Leicester	LEI	Lochgelly	LCG	Manor Road	MNR
Kingham	KGM	Leigh (Kent)	LIH	Lochluichart	LCC	Manorbier	MRB
Kinghorn	KGH	Leigh-on-Sea	LES	Lochwinnoch	LHW	Manors	MAS
Kings Langley	KGL	Leighton Buzzard	LBZ	Lockerbie	LOC	Mansfield	MFT
King's Lynn	KLN	Lelant	LEL	Lockwood	LCK	Mansfield Woodhouse	MSW
Kings Norton	KNN	Lelant Saltings	LTS	London Blackfriars	BFR	March	MCH
Kings Nympton	KGN	Lenham	LEN	London Bridge	LBG	Marden	MRN

Data Tables

Station	Code	Station	Code	Station	Code	Station	Code
Margate	MAR	Moreton (Dorset)	MTN	Newton Abbot	NTA	Palmers Green	PAL
Market Harborough	MHR	Moreton (Merseyside)	MRT	Newton Aycliffe	NAY	Pangbourne	PAN
Market Rasen	MKR	Moreton-in-Marsh	MIM	Newton for Hyde	NWN	Pannal	PNL
Markinch	MNC	Morfa Mawddach	MFA	Newton (Lanarks)	NTN	Pantyffynnon	PTF
Marks Tey	MKT	Morley	MLY	Newton St Cyres	NTC	Par	PAR
Marlow	MLW	Morpeth	MPT	Newton-le-Willows	NLW	Parbold	PBL
Marple	MPL	Mortimer	MOR	Newtonmore	NWR	Park Street	PKT
Marsden	MSN	Mortlake	MTL	Newton-on-Ayr	NOA	Parkstone (Dorset)	PKS
Marske	MSK	Moses Gate	MSS	Newtown (Powys)	NWT	Parson Street	PSN
Marston Green	MGN	Moss Side	MOS	Ninian Park	NNP	Partick	PTK
Martin Mill	MTM	Mossley	MSL	Nitshill	NIT	Parton	PRN
Martins Heron	MAO	Mossley Hill	MSH	Norbiton	NBT	Patchway	PWY
Marton	MTO	Mosspark	MPK	Norbury	NRB	Patricroft	PAT
Maryhill	MYH	Moston	MSO	Normans Bay	NSB	Patterton	PTT
Maryland	MYL	Motherwell	MTH	Normanton	NOR	Peartree	PEA
Maryport	MRY	Motspur Park	MOT	North Berwick	NBW	Peckham Rye	PMR
Matlock	MAT	Mottingham	MTG	North Camp	NCM	Pegswood	PEG
Matlock Bath	MTB	Mottisfont & Dunbridge	DBG	North Dulwich	NDL	Pemberton	PEM
Mauldeth Road	MAU	Mouldsworth	MLD	North Fambridge	NFA	Pembrey & Burry Port	PBY
Maxwell Park	MAX	Moulsecoomb	MCB	North Llanrwst	NLR	Pembroke	PMB
Maybole	MAY	Mount Florida	MFL	North Queensferry	NQU	Pembroke Dock	PMD
Maze Hill	MZH	Mount Vernon	MTV	North Road	NRD	Penally	PNA
Meadowhall	MHS	Mountain Ash	MTA	North Sheen	NSH	Penarth	PEN
Meldreth	MEL	Muir of Ord	MOO	North Walsham	NWA	Pencoed	PCD
Melksham	MKM	Muirend	MUI	North Wembley	NWB	Pengam	PGM
Melton	MES	Musselburgh	MUB	Northallerton	NTR	Penge East	PNE
Melton Mowbray	MMO	Mytholmroyd	MYT	Northampton	NMP	Penge West	PNW
Menheniot	MEN	Nafferton	NFN	Northfield	NFD	Penhelig	PHG
Menston	MNN	Nailsea & Backwell	NLS	Northfleet	NFL	Penistone	PNS
Meols	MEO	Nairn	NRN	Northolt Park	NLT	Penkridge	PKG
Meols Cop	MEC	Nantwich	NAN	Northumberland Park	NUM	Penmaenmawr	PMW
Meopham	MEP	Narberth	NAR	Northwich	NWI	Penmere	PNM
Merrytown	MEY	Narborough	NBR	Norton Bridge	NTB	Penrhiwceiber	PER
Merstham	MHM	Navigation Road	NVR	Norwich	NRW	Penrhyndeudraeth	PRH
Merthyr Tydfil	MER	Neath	NTH	Norwood Junction	NWD	Penrith	PNR
Merthyr Vale	MEV	Needham Market	NMT	Nottingham	NOT	Penryn	PYN
Metheringham	MGM	Neilston	NEI	Nuneaton	NUN	Pensarn (Gwynedd)	PES
MetroCentre	MCE	Nelson	NEL	Nunhead	NHD	Penshurst	PHR
Mexborough	MEX	Neston	NES	Nunthorpe	NNT	Pentre-Bach	PTB
Micheldever	MIC	Netherfield	NET	Nutbourne	NUT	Pen-y-Bont	PNY
Micklefield	MIK	Nethertown	NRT	Nutfield	NUF	Penychain	BPC
Middlesbrough	MBR	Netley	NTL	Oakengates	OKN	Penyffordd	PNF
Middlewood	MDL	New Barnet	NBA	Oakham	OKM	Penzance	PNZ
Midgham	MDG	New Beckenham	NBC	Oakleigh Park	OKL	Perranwell	PRW
Milford Haven	MFH	New Brighton	NBN	Oban	OBN	Perry Barr	PRY
Milford (Surrey)	MLF	New Clee	NCE	Ockendon	OCK	Pershore	PSH
Mill Hill Broadway	MIL	New Cross	NWX	Ockley	OLY	Perth	PTH
Mill Hill (Lancashire)	MLH	New Cross Gate	NXG	Old Hill	OHL	Peterborough	PBO
Millbrook (Bedfordshire)	MLB	New Cumnock	NCK	Old Roan	ORN	Petersfield	PTR
Millbrook (Hants)	MBK	New Eltham	NEH	Old Street	OLD	Petts Wood	PET
Milliken Park	MIN	New Hey	NHY	Oldfield Park	OLF	Pevensey & Westham	PEV
Millom	MLM	New Holland	NHL	Oldham Mumps	OLM	Pevensey Bay	PEB
Mills Hill	MIH	New Hythe	NHE	Oldham Werneth	OLW	Pewsey	PEW
Milngavie	MLN	New Lane	NLN	Olton	OLT	Pilning	PIL
Milnrow	MLR	New Malden	NEM	Ore	ORE	Pinhoe	PIN
Milton Keynes Central	MKC	New Mills Central	NMC	Ormskirk	OMS	Pitlochry	PIT
Minffordd	MFF	New Mills Newtown	NMN	Orpington	ORP	Pitsea	PSE
Minster	MSR	New Milton	NWM	Orrell	ORR	Pleasington	PLS
Mirfield	MIR	New Pudsey	NPD	Orrell Park	OPK	Plockton	PLK
Mistley	MIS	New Southgate	NSG	Otford	OTF	Pluckley	PLC
Mitcham Eastfields	MTC	Newark Castle	NCT	Oulton Broad North	OUN	Plumley	PLM
Mitcham Junction	MIJ	Newark North Gate	NNG	Oulton Broad South	OUS	Plumpton	PMP
Mobberley	MOB	Newbridge	NBE	Outwood	OUT	Plumstead	PLU
Monifieth	MON	Newbury	NBY	Overpool	OVE	Plymouth	PLY
Monks Risborough	MRS	Newbury Racecourse	NRC	Overton	OVR	Pokesdown	POK
Montpelier	MTP	Newcastle	NCL	Oxenholme Lake District	OXN	Polegate	PLG
Montrose	MTS	Newcraighall	NEW	Oxford	OXF	Polesworth	PSW
Moorfields	MRF	Newhaven Harbour	NVH	Oxshott	OXS	Pollokshaws East	PWE
Moorgate	ZMG	Newhaven Town	NVN	Oxted	OXT	Pollokshaws West	PWW
Moorside	MSD	Newington	NGT	Paddock Wood	PDW	Pollokshields East	PLE
Moorthorpe	MRP	Newmarket	NMK	Padgate	PDG	Pollokshields West	PLW
Morar	MRR	Newport (Essex)	NWE	Paignton	PGN	Polmont	PMT
Morchard Road	MRD	Newport (S. Wales)	NWP	Paisley Canal	PCN	Polsloe Bridge	POL
Morden South	MDS	Newquay	NQY	Paisley Gilmour Street	PYG	Ponders End	PON
Morecambe	MCM	Newstead	NSD	Paisley St James	PYJ	Pontarddulais	PTD

Data Tables

Station	Code	Station	Code	Station	Code	Station	Code
Pontefract Baghill	PFR	Reddish North	RDN	Salwick	SLW	Shoreham (Kent)	SEH
Pontefract Monkhill	PFM	Reddish South	RDS	Sandal & Agbrigg	SNA	Shoreham-by-Sea	SSE
Pontefract Tanshelf	POT	Redditch	RDC	Sandbach	SDB	Shortlands	SRT
Pontlottyn	PLT	Redhill	RDH	Sanderstead	SNR	Shotton	SHT
Pontyclun	PYC	Redland	RDA	Sandhills	SDL	Shotts	SHS
Pont-y-Pant	PYP	Redruth	RED	Sandhurst	SND	Shrewsbury	SHR
Pontypool & New Inn	PPL	Reedham (Norfolk)	REE	Sandling	SDG	Sidcup	SID
Pontypridd	PPD	Reedham (Surrey)	RHM	Sandown	SAN	Sileby	SIL
Poole	POO	Reigate	REI	Sandplace	SDP	Silecroft	SIC
Poppleton	POP	Renton	RTN	Sandwell & Dudley	SAD	Silkstone Common	SLK
Port Glasgow	PTG	Retford	RET	Sandwich	SDW	Silver Street	SLV
Port Sunlight	PSL	Rhiwbina	RHI	Sandy	SDY	Silverdale	SVR
Port Talbot Parkway	PTA	Rhoose Cardiff Int Airport	RIA	Sankey for Penketh	SNK	Singer	SIN
Portchester	PTC	Rhosneigr	RHO	Sanquhar	SQH	Sittingbourne	SIT
Porth	POR	Rhyl	RHL	Sarn	SRR	Skegness	SKG
Porthmadog	PTM	Rhymney	RHY	Saundersfoot	SDF	Skewen	SKE
Portlethen	PLN	Ribblehead	RHD	Saunderton	SDR	Skipton	SKI
Portslade	PLD	Rice Lane	RIL	Sawbridgeworth	SAW	Slade Green	SGR
Portsmouth & Southsea	PMS	Richmond	RMD	Saxilby	SXY	Slaithwaite	SWT
Portsmouth Arms	PMA	Rickmansworth	RIC	Saxmundham	SAX	Slateford	SLA
Portsmouth Harbour	PMH	Riddlesdown	RDD	Scarborough	SCA	Sleaford	SLR
Possilpark & Parkhouse	PPK	Ridgmont	RID	Scotscalder	SCT	Sleights	SLH
Potters Bar	PBR	Riding Mill	RDM	Scotstounhill	SCH	Slough	SLO
Poulton-le-Fylde	PFY	Risca & Pontymister	RCA	Scunthorpe	SCU	Small Heath	SMA
Poynton	PYT	Rishton	RIS	Seaburn	SEB	Smallbrook Junction	SAB
Prees	PRS	Robertsbridge	RBR	Sea Mills	SML	Smethwick Galton Bridge	SGB
Prescot	PSC	Roby	ROB	Seaford	SEF	Smethwick Rolfe Street	SMR
Prestatyn	PRT	Rochdale	RCD	Seaforth & Litherland	SFL	Smitham	SMI
Prestbury	PRB	Roche	ROC	Seaham	SEA	Smithy Bridge	SMB
Preston	PRE	Rochester	RTR	Seamer	SEM	Snaith	SNI
Preston Park	PRP	Rochford	RFD	Seascale	SSC	Snodland	SDA
Prestonpans	PST	Rock Ferry	RFY	Seaton Carew	SEC	Snowdown	SWO
Prestwick Int Airport	PRA	Rogart	ROG	Seer Green & Jordans	SRG	Sole Street	SOR
Prestwick Town	PTW	Rogerstone	ROR	Selby	SBY	Solihull	SOL
Priesthill & Darnley	PTL	Rolleston	ROL	Selhurst	SRS	Somerleyton	SYT
Princes Risborough	PRR	Roman Bridge	RMB	Sellafield	SEL	South Acton	SAT
Prittlewell	PRL	Romford	RMF	Selling	SEG	South Bank	SBK
Prudhoe	PRU	Romiley	RML	Selly Oak	SLY	South Bermondsey	SBM
Pulborough	PUL	Romsey	ROM	Settle	SET	South Croydon	SCY
Purfleet	PFL	Roose	ROO	Seven Kings	SVK	South Elmsall	SES
Purley	PUR	Rose Grove	RSG	Seven Sisters	SVS	South Greenford	SGN
Purley Oaks	PUO	Rose Hill Marple	RSH	Sevenoaks	SEV	South Gyle	SGL
Putney	PUT	Rosyth	ROS	Severn Beach	SVB	South Hampstead	SOH
Pwllheli	PWL	Rotherham Central	RMC	Severn Tunnel Junction	STJ	South Kenton	SOK
Pyle	PYL	Roughton Road	RNR	Shalford	SFR	South Merton	SMO
Quakers Yard	QYD	Rowlands Castle	RLN	Shanklin	SHN	South Milford	SOM
Queenborough	QBR	Rowley Regis	ROW	Shaw & Crompton	SHA	South Ruislip	SRU
Queens Park (Glasgow)	QPK	Roy Bridge	RYB	Shawford	SHW	South Tottenham	STO
Queens Park (London)	QPW	Roydon	RYN	Shawlands	SHL	South Wigston	SWS
Queens Road, Peckham	QRP	Royston	RYS	Sheerness-on-Sea	SSS	South Woodham Ferrers	SOF
Queenstown Road	QRB	Ruabon	RUA	Sheffield	SHF	Southall	STL
Quintrell Downs	QUI	Rufford	RUF	Shelford	SED	Southampton Airport	SOA
Radcliffe (Notts)	RDF	Rugby	RUG	Shenfield	SNF	Southampton Central	SOU
Radlett	RDT	Rugeley Town	RGT	Shenstone	SEN	Southbourne	SOB
Radley	RAD	Rugeley Trent Valley	RGL	Shepherd's Bush	SPB	Southbury	SBU
Radyr	RDR	Runcorn	RUN	Shepherds Well	SPH	Southease	SEE
Rainford	RNF	Runcorn East	RUE	Shepley	SPY	Southend Central	SOC
Rainham (Essex)	RNM	Ruskington	RKT	Shepperton	SHP	Southend East	SOE
Rainham (Kent)	RAI	Ruswarp	RUS	Shepreth	STH	Southend Victoria	SOV
Rainhill	RNH	Rutherglen	RUT	Sherborne	SHE	Southminster	SMN
Ramsgate	RAM	Ryde St Johns Road	RYR	Sherburn-in-Elmet	SIE	Southport	SOP
Ramsgreave & Wilpshire	RGW	Ryde Esplanade	RYD	Sheringham	SHM	Southwick	SWK
Rannoch	RAN	Ryde Pier Head	RYP	Shettleston	SLS	Sowerby Bridge	SOW
Rauceby	RAU	Ryder Brow	RRB	Shieldmuir	SDM	Spalding	SPA
Ravenglass for Eskdale	RAV	Rye	RYE	Shifnal	SFN	Spean Bridge	SBR
Ravensbourne	RVB	Rye House	RYH	Shildon	SHD	Spital	SPI
Ravensthorpe	RVN	Salford Central	SFD	Shiplake	SHI	Spondon	SPO
Rawcliffe	RWC	Salford Crescent	SLD	Shipley	SHY	Spooner Row	SPN
Rayleigh	RLG	Salfords	SAF	Shippea Hill	SPP	Spring Road	SRI
Raynes Park	RAY	Salhouse	SAH	Shipton	SIP	Springburn	SPR
Reading	RDG	Salisbury	SAL	Shirebrook	SHB	Springfield	SPF
Reading West	RDW	Saltaire	SAE	Shirehampton	SHH	Squires Gate	SQU
Rectory Road	REC	Saltash	STS	Shireoaks	SRO	St Albans	SAC
Redbridge	RDB	Saltburn	SLB	Shirley	SRL	St Albans Abbey	SAA
Redcar Central	RCC	Saltcoats	SLT	Shoeburyness	SRY	St Andrews Road	SAR
Redcar East	RCE	Saltmarshe	SAM	Sholing	SHO	St Annes-on-the-Sea	SAS

Data Tables

Station	Code	Station	Code	Station	Code	Station	Code
St Austell	SAU	Strood	SOO	Three Oaks	TOK	Wakefield Kirkgate	WKK
St Bees	SBS	Stroud	STD	Thurgarton	THU	Wakefield Westgate	WKF
St Budeaux Ferry Road	SBF	Sturry	STU	Thurnscoe	THC	Walkden	WKD
St Budeaux Victoria Rd	SBV	Styal	SYA	Thurso	THS	Wallasey Grove Road	WLG
St Columb Road	SCR	Sudbury	SUY	Thurston	TRS	Wallasey Village	WLV
St Denys	SDN	Sudbury & Harrow Road	SUD	Tilbury Town	TIL	Wallington	WLT
St Erth	SER	Sudbury Hill Harrow	SDH	Tile Hill	THL	Wallyford	WAF
St Germans	SGM	Sugar Loaf	SUG	Tilehurst	TLH	Walmer	WAM
St Helens Central	SNH	Summerston	SUM	Tipton	TIP	Walsall	WSL
St Helens Junction	SHJ	Sunbury	SUU	Tir-Phil	TIR	Walsden	WDN
St Helier	SIH	Sunderland	SUN	Tisbury	TIS	Waltham Cross	WLC
St Ives (Cornwall)	SIV	Sundridge Park	SUP	Tiverton Parkway	TVP	Walthamstow Central	WHC
St James Park	SJP	Sunningdale	SNG	Todmorden	TOD	Walthamstow Queen's Rd	WMW
St James Street	SJS	Sunnymeads	SNY	Tolworth	TOL	Walton (Merseyside)	WAO
St Johns	SAJ	Surbiton	SUR	Ton Pentre	TPN	Walton-on-the-Naze	WON
St Keyne	SKN	Sutton Coldfield	SUT	Tonbridge	TON	Walton-on-Thames	WAL
St Leonards Warrior Sq	SLQ	Sutton Common	SUC	Tondu	TDU	Wanborough	WAN
St Margarets (London)	SMG	Sutton Parkway	SPK	Tonfanau	TNF	Wandsworth Common	WSW
St Margarets (Herts)	SMT	Sutton (Surrey)	SUO	Tonypandy	TNP	Wandsworth Road	WWR
St Mary Cray	SMY	Swale	SWL	Tooting	TOO	Wandsworth Town	WNT
St Michaels	STM	Swanley	SAY	Topsham	TOP	Wanstead Park	WNP
St Neots	SNO	Swanscombe	SWM	Torquay	TQY	Warblington	WBL
St Pancras International	SPX	Swansea	SWA	Torre	TRR	Ware	WAR
St Peter's	STZ	Swanwick	SNW	Totnes	TOT	Wareham	WRM
Stadium of Light	STI	Sway	SWY	Tottenham Hale	TOM	Wargrave	WGV
Stafford	STA	Swaythling	SWG	Totton	TTN	Warminster	WMN
Staines	SNS	Swinderby	SWD	Town Green	TWN	Warnham	WNH
Stallingborough	SLL	Swindon	SWI	Trafford Park	TRA	Warrington Bank Quay	WBQ
Stalybridge	SYB	Swineshead	SWE	Trefforest	TRF	Warrington Central	WAC
Stamford	SMD	Swinton (Gr Manchester)	SNN	Trefforest Estate	TRE	Warwick	WRW
Stamford Hill	SMH	Swinton (Yorks)	SWN	Trehafod	TRH	Warwick Parkway	WRP
Stanford-le-Hope	SFO	Sydenham	SYD	Treherbert	TRB	Water Orton	WTO
Stanlow & Thornton	SNT	Sydenham Hill	SYH	Treorchy	TRY	Waterbeach	WBC
Stansted Airport	SSD	Syon Lane	SYL	Trimley	TRM	Wateringbury	WTR
Stansted Mountfitchet	SST	Syston	SYS	Tring	TRI	Waterloo (Merseyside)	WLO
Staplehurst	SPU	Tackley	TAC	Troed-y-rhiw	TRD	Watford High Street	WFH
Stapleton Road	SRD	Tadworth	TAD	Troon	TRN	Watford Junction	WFJ
Starbeck	SBE	Taffs Well	TAF	Trowbridge	TRO	Watford North	WFN
Starcross	SCS	Tain	TAI	Truro	TRU	Watlington	WTG
Staveley (Cumbria)	SVL	Talsarnau	TAL	Tulloch	TUL	Watton-at-Stone	WAS
Stechford	SCF	Talybont	TLB	Tulse Hill	TUH	Waun-Gron Park	WNG
Steeton & Silsden	SON	Tal-y-Cafn	TLC	Tunbridge Wells	TBW	Wavertree Tech Park	WAV
Stepps	SPS	Tame Bridge Parkway	TAB	Turkey Street	TUR	Wedgwood	WED
Stevenage	SVG	Tamworth	TAM	Tutbury & Hatton	TUT	Weeley	WEE
Stevenston	STV	Taplow	TAP	Twickenham	TWI	Weeton	WET
Stewartby	SWR	Tattenham Corner	TAT	Twyford	TWY	Welham Green	WMG
Stewarton	STT	Taunton	TAU	Ty Croes	TYC	Welling	WLI
Stirling	STG	Taynuilt	TAY	Ty Glas	TGS	Wellingborough	WEL
Stockport	SPT	Teddington	TED	Tygwyn	TYG	Wellington (Shropshire)	WLN
Stocksfield	SKS	Teesside Airport	TEA	Tyndrum Lower	TYL	Welshpool	WLP
Stocksmoor	SSM	Teignmouth	TGM	Tyseley	TYS	Welwyn Garden City	WGC
Stockton	STK	Telford Central	TFC	Tywyn	TYW	Welwyn North	WLW
Stoke Mandeville	SKM	Templecombe	TMC	Uckfield	UCK	Wem	WEM
Stoke Newington	SKW	Tenby	TEN	Uddingston	UDD	Wembley Central	WMB
Stoke-on-Trent	SOT	Teynham	TEY	Ulceby	ULC	Wembley Stadium	WCX
Stone	SNE	Thames Ditton	THD	Ulleskelf	ULL	Wemyss Bay	WMS
Stone Crossing	SCG	Thatcham	THA	Ulverston	ULV	Wendover	WND
Stonebridge Park	SBP	Thatto Heath	THH	Umberleigh	UMB	Wennington	WNN
Stonegate	SOG	The Hawthorns	THW	University	UNI	West Allerton	WSA
Stonehaven	STN	The Lakes	TLK	Uphall	UHA	West Brompton	WBP
Stonehouse	SHU	Theale	THE	Upholland	UPL	West Byfleet	WBY
Stoneleigh	SNL	Theobalds Grove	TEO	Upminster	UPM	West Calder	WCL
Stourbridge Junction	SBJ	Thetford	TTF	Upper Halliford	UPH	West Croydon	WCY
Stourbridge Town	SBT	Thirsk	THI	Upper Holloway	UHL	West Drayton	WDT
Stowmarket	SMK	Thornaby	TBY	Upper Tyndrum	UTY	West Dulwich	WDU
Stranraer	STR	Thorne North	TNN	Upper Warlingham	UWL	West Ealing	WEA
Stratford (London)	SRA	Thorne South	TNS	Upton	UPT	West Ham	WEH
Stratford-upon-Avon	SAV	Thornford	THO	Upwey	UPW	West Hampstead	WHD
Strathcarron	STC	Thornliebank	THB	Urmston	URM	West Hampstead T'link	WHP
Strawberry Hill	STW	Thornton Abbey	TNA	Uttoxeter	UTT	West Horndon	WHK
Streatham	STE	Thornton Heath	TTH	Valley	VAL	West Kilbride	WKB
Streatham Common	SRC	Thorntonhall	THI	Vauxhall	VXH	West Kirby	WKI
Streatham Hill	SRH	Thorpe Bay	TPB	Virginia Water	VIR	West Malling	WMA
Streethouse	SHC	Thorpe Culvert	TPC	Waddon	WDO	West Norwood	WNW
Strines	SRN	Thorpe-le-Soken	TLS	Wadhurst	WAD	West Ruislip	WRU
Stromeferry	STF	Three Bridges	TBD	Wainfleet	WFL	West Runton	WRN

Data Tables

West St Leonards	WLD	Whitley Bridge	WBD	Winnersh	WNS	Workington	WKG
West Sutton	WSU	Whitlocks End	WTE	Winnersh Triangle	WTI	Worksop	WRK
West Wickham	WWI	Whitstable	WHI	Winsford	WSF	Worle	WOR
West Worthing	WWO	Whittlesea	WLE	Wishaw	WSH	Worplesdon	WPL
Westbury (Wilts)	WSB	Whittlesford Parkway	WLF	Witham	WTM	Worstead	WRT
Westcliff	WCF	Whitton	WTN	Witley	WTY	Worthing	WRH
Westcombe Park	WCB	Whitwell	WWL	Witton	WTT	Wrabness	WRB
Westenhanger	WHA	Whyteleafe	WHY	Wivelsfield	WVF	Wraysbury	WRY
Wester Hailes	WTA	Whyteleafe South	WHS	Wivenhoe	WIV	Wrenbury	WRE
Westerfield	WFI	Wick	WCK	Woburn Sands	WOB	Wressle	WRS
Westerton	WES	Wickford	WIC	Woking	WOK	Wrexham Central	WXC
Westgate-on-Sea	WGA	Wickham Market	WCM	Wokingham	WKM	Wrexham General	WRX
Westhoughton	WHG	Widdrington	WDD	Woldingham	WOH	Wye	WYE
Weston Milton	WNM	Widnes	WID	Wolverhampton	WVH	Wylam	WYM
Weston-super-Mare	WSM	Widney Manor	WMR	Wolverton	WOL	Wylde Green	WYL
Wetheral	WRL	Wigan North Western	WGN	Wombwell	WOM	Wymondham	WMD
Weybridge	WYB	Wigan Wallgate	WGW	Wood End	WDE	Wythall	WYT
Weymouth	WEY	Wigton	WGT	Wood Street	WST	Yalding	YAL
Whaley Bridge	WBR	Wildmill	WMI	Woodbridge	WDB	Yardley Wood	YRD
Whalley	WHE	Willesden Junction	WIJ	Woodgrange Park	WGR	Yarm	YRM
Whatstandwell	WTS	Williamwood	WLM	Woodhall	WDL	Yate	YAE
Whifflet	WFF	Willington	WIL	Woodhouse	WDH	Yatton	YAT
Whimple	WHM	Wilmcote	WMC	Woodlesford	WDS	Yeoford	YEO
Whinhill	WNL	Wilmslow	WML	Woodley	WLY	Yeovil Junction	YVJ
Whiston	WHN	Wilnecote	WNE	Woodmansterne	WME	Yeovil Pen Mill	YVP
Whitby	WTB	Wimbledon	WIM	Woodsmoor	WSR	Yetminster	YET
Whitchurch (Cardiff)	WHT	Wimbledon Chase	WBO	Wool	WOO	Ynyswen	YNW
Whitchurch (Hants)	WCH	Winchelsea	WSE	Woolston	WLS	Yoker	YOK
Whitchurch (Shropshire)	WTC	Winchester	WIN	Woolwich Arsenal	WWA	York	YRK
White Hart Lane	WHL	Winchfield	WNF	Woolwich Dockyard	WWD	Yorton	YRT
White Notley	WNY	Winchmore Hill	WIH	Wootton Wawen	WWW	Ystrad Mynach	YSM
Whitecraigs	WCR	Windermere	WDM	Worcester Foregate St	WOF	Ystrad Rhondda	YSR
Whitehaven	WTH	Windsor & Eton Central	WNC	Worcester Park	WCP		
Whitland	WTL	Windsor & Eton Riverside	WNR	Worcester Shrub Hill	WOS		

Left: *CrossCountry Trains 'Voyager' set No. 220006 slows for the Basingstoke stop on 30 August 2012, forming the 10.45 Bournemouth to Manchester Piccadilly service. The set's first class coach is leading.* **CJM**

DMU and EMU Vehicle Codes

BDMSO	Battery Driving Motor Standard Open	MFL	Motor First Lavatory
DM	Driving Motor	MPMV	Motor Parcels Mail Van
DMBO	Driving Motor Brake Open	MS	Motor Standard
DMBS	Driving Motor Brake Standard	MSL	Motor Standard Lavatory
DMCL	Driving Motor Composite Lavatory	MSLRB	Motor Standard Lavatory Restaurant Buffet
DMCO	Driving Motor Composite Open	MSO	Motor Standard Open
DMF	Driving Motor First	MSRMB	Motor Standard Restaurant Micro Buffet
DMFLO	Driving Motor First Luggage Open	PTSO	Pantograph Trailer Standard Open
DMRFO	Driving Motor Restaurant First Open	RB	Restaurant Buffet
DMS	Driving Motor Standard	TBFO	Trailer Brake First Open
DMSL	Driving Motor Standard Lavatory	TCO	Trailer Composite Open
DMSO	Driving Motor Standard Open	TFO	Trailer First Open
DTCO	Driving Trailer Composite Open	TPMV	Trailer Parcels Mail Van
DTPMV	Driving Trailer Parcels Mail Van	TSO	Trailer Standard Open
DTSO	Driving Trailer Standard Open	TSRMB	Trailer Standard Restaurant Micro Buffet
MBC	Motor Brake Composite		
MBSO	Motor Brake Standard Open	(A) - A Car	
MC	Motor Composite	(B) - B Car	

Data Tables

This cross number checklist indicates in which section of the ABC Rail Guide 2013 full details of rolling stock can be found.

Number Cross-Link Codes

3MP	3M Productions
AEA	Abellio East Anglia
AFG	Arlington Fleet Group
ALS	Alstom
ATW	Arriva Trains Wales
AXC	Arriva CrossCountry
BAR	British American Railway
BOK	Bo'ness & Kinneil Railway
BOM	Bombardier Transportation
C2C	c2c Railway
COL	Colas
CRW	Chiltern Railways
DBR	DB Regio
DBS	DB Schenker
DRS	Direct Rail Services
ECR	Euro Cargo Rail
EMT	East Midlands Trains
EPX	Europhoenix Ltd
ETL	Electric Traction Ltd
EUR	Eurotunnel
EUR	Europorte2
EUS	Eurostar UK
EXP	Exported
FCC	First Capital Connect
FGW	First Great Western
FHT	First Hull Trains
FLR	Freightliner
FSL	Flying Scotsman Railway Ltd
FSR	First ScotRail
FTP	First TransPennine
GBR	GB Railfreight
GSW	Great Scottish & Western Rly
GTL	Grand Central Railway
HAN	Hanson Traction
HEC	Heathrow Connect
HEX	Heathrow Express
HNR	Harry Needle Railroad Co
ICE	InterCity East Coast
IND	Industrial
JHS	Jeremy Hoskins
LMI	London Midland
LNW	London North Western
LOG	London Overground
MER	Merseyrail
MHR	Mid Hants Railway
MRL	Mendip Rail Ltd
NEM	Nemesis Rail
NOR	Northern
NRL	Network Rail Limited
NYM	North Yorkshire Moors Railway
OLS	Off Lease
PRE	Preserved
PUL	Pullman Rail
RAF	Railfilms
RCL	Railcare
RIV	Riviera
RRS	Ridings Railtours
RVE	Rail Vehicle Engineering
S47	Stratford Class 47 Group
SEC	Serco Railtest
SET	SouthEastern Trains
SIE	Siemens
SIL	Stagecoach Island Line
SNF	SNCF (French Railways)
SOU	Southern
SRP	Scottish Railway Preservation Soc
SUP	Support Coaches
SWT	South West Trains
TTS	Transmart Trains
VSO	Venice Simplon Orient Express
VTN	Vintage Trains
VWC	Virgin West Coast
WAB	Wabtec
WCR	West Coast Railway

Locomotives – Diesel & Electric

No	Code	No	Code	No	Code	No	Code	No	Code
D0226	PRE	D2139	PRE	D2854	PRE	D8000	PRE	E5001	PRE
		D2148	PRE	D2858	PRE			E26020	PRE
D4	PRE	D2178	PRE	D2860	PRE	D8233	PRE	E27000	PRE
		D2182	PRE	D2866	PRE			E27001	PRE
12	PRE	D2184	PRE	D2867	PRE	D8568	PRE		
		D2192	PRE	D2868	PRE			9005	EUR
		D2199	PRE			D9500	PRE	9006	EUR
44	MRL			D2953	PRE	D9502	PRE	9007	EUR
120	MRL	D2203	PRE	D2956	PRE	D9504	PRE	9011	EUR
		D2205	PRE			D9513	PRE	9013	EUR
		D2207	PRE	D3000	PRE	D9516	PRE	9015	EUR
D200	PRE	D2229	PRE	D3002	PRE	D9518	PRE	9018	EUR
		D2245	PRE	D3014	PRE	D9520	PRE	9022	EUR
D821	PRE	D2246	PRE	D3101	PRE	D9521	PRE	9023	EUR
D832	PRE	D2271	PRE	D3255	PRE	D9523	PRE	9024	EUR
		D2272	PRE	D3261	PRE	D9524	PRE	9026	EUR
D1010	PRE	D2279	PRE	D3452	PRE	D9525	PRE	9027	EUR
D1013	PRE	D2280	PRE	D3489	PRE	D9526	PRE	9029	EUR
D1015	PRE	D2284	PRE			D9529	IND	9031	EUR
D1023	PRE	D2298	PRE	D4067	PRE	D9531	PRE	9033	EUR
D1041	PRE	D2302	PRE	D4092	PRE	D9537	PRE	9036	EUR
D1048	PRE	D2310	PRE	D4095	PRE	D9539	PRE	9037	EUR
D1062	PRE	D2324	PRE			D9551	PRE	9101	EUR
		D2325	PRE	D5500	PRE	D9553	PRE	9103	EUR
D2023	PRE	D2334	PRE			D9555	PRE	9105	EUR
D2024	PRE	D2337	PRE	D5705	PRE			9106	EUR
D2041	PRE					DELTIC	PRE	9107	EUR
D2046	PRE	D2511	PRE	D6700	PRE			9108	EUR
D2051	PRE	D2578	PRE			DS75	PRE	9109	EUR
D2117	PRE	D2587	PRE	D7017	PRE			9110	EUR
D2118	PRE	D2595	PRE	D7018	PRE	LMS7050	PRE	9111	EUR
D2133	PRE	D2767	PRE	D7029	PRE	LMS7051	PRE	9112	EUR
D2138	PRE	D2774	PRE	D7076	PRE	LMS7069	PRE		

Data Tables

No.	Code	No.	Code	No.	Code	No.	Code	No.	Code
9701	EUR	03144	PRE	08418	WCR	08624	FLR	08782	DBS
9702	EUR	03145	PRE	08423	BAR	08629	RCL	08784	DBS
9703	EUR	03152	PRE	08428	DBS	08628	PRE	08785	FLR
9704	EUR	03158	PRE	08436	PRE	08630	DBS	08786	HNR
9705	EUR	03162	PRE	08441	IND	08631	PRE	08787	IND
9706	EUR	03170	PRE	08442	LNW	08632	DBS	08790	ALS
9707	EUR	03179	IND	08443	PRE	08633	DBS	08795	FGW
9712	EUR	03189	PRE	08444	PRE	08635	PRE	08799	DBS
9714	EUR	03196	WCR	08445	IND	08641	FGW	08802	DBS
9723	EUR	03371	PRE	08447	IND	08643	MRL	08804	DBS
9801	EUR	03381	WCR	08451	ALS	08644	FGW	08805	LMI
9802	EUR	03399	PRE	08454	ALS	08645	FGW	08807	IND
9803	EUR			08460	IND	08648	BAR	08809	IND
9804	EUR	05001	PRE	08471	PRE	08649	RCL	08810	LNW
9808	EUR			08472	WAB	08650	MRL	08818	HNR
9809	EUR	06003	PRE	08473	PRE	08652	MRL	08822	FGW
9810	EUR			08476	PRE	08653	DBS	08823	IND
9812	EUR	07001	HNR	08479	PRE	08663	FGW	08824	DBS
9814	EUR	07005	PRE	08480	DBS	08669	WAB	08830	PRE
9816	EUR	07007	AFG	08483	FGW	08670	IND	08834	HNR
9817	EUR	07010	PRE	08484	IND	08676	DBS	08836	FGW
9819	EUR	07011	PRE	08485	WCR	08678	WCR	08846	BOM
9820	EUR	07012	PRE	08490	PRE	08682	BOM	08847	IND
9821	EUR	07013	HNR	08495	DBS	08683	PRE	08850	PRE
9825	EUR			08499	PUL	08685	HNR	08853	WAB
9828	EUR	08011	PRE	08500	DBS	08690	EMT	08865	DBS
9832	EUR	08012	PRE	08502	HNR	08691	FLR	08868	HNR
9834	EUR	08015	PRE	08503	IND	08694	PRE	08870	BAR
9835	EUR	08016	PRE	08507	HNR	08696	ALS	08871	WAB
9838	EUR	08021	PRE	08511	IND	08697	RVE	08872	IND
9840	EUR	08022	PRE	08516	LNW	08699	IND	08873	BAR
		08032	PRE	08523	IND	08700	PRE	08877	DBS
01509	CRW	08046	PRE	08525	EMT	08701	DBS	08879	DBS
01551	SIE	08054	PRE	08527	HNR	08703	DBS	08885	BAR
01552	HNR	08060	PRE	08528	PRE	08704	HNR	08886	DBS
01564	HNR	08064	PRE	08530	FLR	08706	DBS	08887	ALS
		08077	FLR	08531	FLR	08709	DBS	08888	DBS
03018	PRE	08102	PRE	08535	IND	08711	DBS	08891	FLR
03020	PRE	08108	PRE	08536	RVE	08714	DBS	08892	HNR
03022	PRE	08114	PRE	08556	PRE	08721	ALS	08896	PRE
03027	PRE	08123	PRE	08567	DBS	08724	WAB	08899	EMT
03037	PRE	08133	PRE	08568	RCL	08728	IND	08903	IND
03059	PRE	08164	PRE	08571	WAB	08730	RCL	08904	DBS
03062	PRE	08168	PRE	08573	BAR	08731	MRL	08905	HNR
03066	PRE	08195	PRE	08575	FLR	08735	DBS	08907	DBS
03069	PRE	08202	IND	08578	DBS	08737	DBS	08908	EMT
03072	PRE	08220	PRE	08580	DBS	08738	DBS	08911	PRE
03073	PRE	08238	PRE	08585	FLR	08742	DBS	08912	IND
03078	PRE	08266	PRE	08588	BAR	08743	IND	08913	IND
03079	PRE	08288	PRE	08590	PRE	08750	BAR	08915	IND
03081	PRE	08308	BAR	08593	DBS	08752	DBS	08918	HNR
03084	PRE	08331	PRE	08596	WAB	08754	BAR	08922	DBS
03089	PRE	08359	PRE	08598	IND	08756	BAR	08924	HNR
03090	PRE	08375	IND	08600	IND	08757	DBS	08925	GBR
03094	PRE	08377	PRE	08604	PRE	08762	BAR	08927	PRE
03099	PRE	08388	PRE	08605	DBS	08764	WAB	08929	HNR
03112	PRE	08389	HNR	08611	ALS	08765	HNR	08933	IND
03113	PRE	08393	LHG	08613	BAR	08767	PRE	08934	ALS
03119	PRE	08401	GBR	08615	WAB	08769	PRE	08936	BAR
03120	PRE	08405	DBS	08616	LMI	08772	PRE	08937	PRE
03128	PRE	08410	FGW	08617	ALS	08773	PRE	08939	DBS
03134	PRE	08411	IND	08622	BAR	08774	IND	08943	HNR
03141	PRE	08417	NRL	08623	DBS	08780	PRE	08944	PRE

No.	Code	No.	Code	No.	Code	No.	Code	No.	Code
08947	MRL	20107	HNR	25083	PRE	31418	PRE	37116	PRE
08948	EUS	20110	PRE	25173	PRE	31422	RVE	37142	PRE
08950	EMT	20118	HNR	25185	PRE	31435	PRE	37146	PRE
08954	HNR	20121	HNR	25191	PRE	31438	PRE	37152	PRE
08956	NRL	20132	HNR	25235	PRE	31452	BAR	37165	HNR
08993	DBS	20137	PRE	25244	PRE	31454	BAR	37175	PRE
08994	DBS	20138	HNR	25262	PRE	31459	RVE	37188	PRE
08995	DBS	20142	PRE	25265	PRE	31461	PRE	37194	DRS
		20154	PRE	25278	NYM	31463	PRE	37198	NRL
09001	PRE	20166	PRE	25279	PRE	31465	NRL	37207	PRE
09002	GBR	20168	HNR	25283	PRE	31466	PRE	37214	WCR
09004	PRE	20169	PRE	25309	PRE	31468	RVE	37215	PRE
09006	DBS	20177	PRE	25311	PRE	31530	PRE	37216	PRE
09007	LOG	20188	PRE	25321	PRE	31601	BAR	37218	DRS
09009	GBR	20189	BAR	25322	PRE	31602	RVE	37219	PRE
09010	PRE	20205	PRE					37227	PRE
09012	HNR	20214	PRE	26001	PRE	33002	PRE	37229	DRS
09014	HNR	20227	BAR	26002	PRE	33008	PRE	37240	PRE
09015	PRE	20228	PRE	26004	PRE	33012	PRE	37248	WCR
09017	PRE	20301	DRS	26007	PRE	33018	PRE	37250	PRE
09018	HNR	20302	DRS	26010	PRE	33019	PRE	37254	PRE
09019	PRE	20303	DRS	26011	PRE	33021	PRE	37255	PRE
09022	IND	20304	DRS	26014	PRE	33025	WCR	37259	DRS
09023	IND	20305	DRS	26024	PRE	33029	WCR	37261	DRS
09024	PRE	20306	DRS	26025	PRE	33030	PRE	37263	PRE
09025	PRE	20307	DRS	26035	PRE	33035	PRE	37264	PRE
09026	SOU	20308	DRS	26038	PRE	33046	PRE	37275	PRE
09106	DBS	20309	DRS	26040	PRE	33048	PRE	37294	PRE
09201	DBS	20310	DRS	26043	PRE	33052	PRE	37308	PRE
09204	LNW	20311	HNR			33053	PRE	37314	PRE
		20312	DRS	27001	PRE	33057	PRE	37324	PRE
12052	PRE	20313	PRE	27005	PRE	33063	PRE	37372	PRE
12061	PRE	20314	HNR	27007	PRE	33065	PRE	37401	DRS
12077	PRE	20315	DRS	27024	PRE	33102	PRE	37402	DRS
12082	PRE	20901	HNR	27050	PRE	33103	NEM	37403	PRE
12088	IND	20903	HNR	27056	PRE	33108	PRE	37405	DRS
12093	PRE	20904	HNR	27059	PRE	33109	PRE	37406	DRS
12099	PRE	20905	HNR	27066	PRE	33110	PRE	37407	PRE
12131	PRE	20906	HNR			33111	PRE	37409	DRS
				31101	PRE	33116	PRE	37410	DRS
15224	PRE	21544	ECR	31105	NRL	33117	PRE	37411	DRS
		21545	ECR	31106	RVE	33201	PRE	37413	NEM
18000	PRE	21546	ECR	31108	PRE	33202	PRE	37415	HNR
		21547	ECR	31119	PRE	33207	WCR	37418	PRE
20001	PRE			31128	NEM	33208	PRE	37419	DRS
20007	PRE	21610	ECR	31130	PRE			37421	PRE
20016	HNR	21611	ECR	31162	PRE	37003	PRE	37422	DRS
20020	PRE	21901	EUR	31163	PRE	37009	PRE	37423	DRS
20031	PRE	21902	EUR	31190	BAR	37023	PRE	37424	PRE
20035	PRE	21903	EUR	31203	PRE	37025	PRE	37425	DRS
20048	PRE	21904	EUR	31206	PRE	37029	HNR	37426	DRS
20056	HNR	21905	EUR	31207	PRE	37032	PRE	37502	FLR
20057	HNR			31210	PRE	37037	PRE	37503	HNR
20059	PRE	24032	PRE	31233	NRL	37038	DRS	37510	DRS
20063	PRE	24054	PRE	31235	PRE	37042	DRS	37516	WCR
20066	HNR	24061	PRE	31270	PRE	37057	PRE	37517	WCR
20069	PRE	24081	PRE	31271	PRE	37059	DRS	37518	PRE
20081	HNR			31285	NRL	37069	DRS	37521	HNR
20087	PRE	25035	PRE	31289	PRE	37075	PRE	37601	DRS
20088	HNR	25057	PRE	31327	PRE	37087	DRS	37602	DRS
20092	HNR	25059	PRE	31410	PRE	37097	PRE	37603	DRS
20096	HNR	25067	PRE	31414	PRE	37108	PRE	37604	DRS
20098	PRE	25072	PRE	31415	PRE	37109	PRE	37605	DRS

Data Tables

No.	Code	No.	Code	No.	Code	No.	Code	No.	Code
37606	DRS	43036	FGW	43139	FGW	43277	ICE	47194	WCR
37607	DRS	43037	FGW	43140	FGW	43285	AXC	47205	PRE
37608	DRS	43040	FGW	43141	FGW	43290	ICE	47237	WCR
37609	DRS	43041	FGW	43142	FGW	43295	ICE	47245	WCR
37610	DRS	43042	FGW	43143	FGW	43296	ICE	47270	WCR
37611	DRS	43043	EMT	43144	FGW	43299	ICE	47292	PRE
37612	DRS	43044	EMT	43145	FGW	43300	ICE	47306	PRE
37667	DRS	43045	EMT	43146	FGW	43301	AXC	47355	WCR
37668	WCR	43046	EMT	43147	FGW	43302	ICE	47367	PRE
37669	WCR	43047	EMT	43148	FGW	43303	AXC	47375	NEM
37674	PRE	43048	EMT	43149	FGW	43304	AXC	47376	PRE
37676	WCR	43049	EMT	43150	FGW	43305	ICE	47401	PRE
37679	PRE	43050	EMT	43151	FGW	43306	ICE	47402	PRE
37682	DRS	43052	EMT	43152	FGW	43307	ICE	47417	PRE
37683	DRS	43053	FGW	43153	FGW	43308	ICE	47449	PRE
37685	WCR	43054	EMT	43154	FGW	43309	ICE	47484	PRE
37688	DRS	43055	EMT	43155	FGW	43310	ICE	47488	NEM
37696	HNR	43056	FGW	43156	FGW	43311	ICE	47492	WCR
37706	WCR	43058	EMT	43158	FGW	43312	ICE	47500	WCR
37710	WCR	43059	EMT	43159	FGW	43313	ICE	47501	DRS
37712	WCR	43060	EMT	43160	FGW	43314	ICE	47524	PRE
37901	PRE	43061	EMT	43161	FGW	43315	ICE	47526	WCR
37905	PRE	43062	NRL	43162	FGW	43316	ICE	47580	S47
37906	PRE	43063	FGW	43163	FGW	43317	ICE	47596	PRE
		43064	EMT	43164	FGW	43318	ICE	47635	PRE
40012	PRE	43066	EMT	43165	FGW	43319	ICE	47640	PRE
40013	PRE	43069	FGW	43168	FGW	43320	ICE	47643	PRE
40106	PRE	43070	FGW	43169	FGW	43321	AXC	47701	PRE
40118	PRE	43071	FGW	43170	FGW	43357	AXC	47703	HNR
40135	PRE	43073	EMT	43171	FGW	43366	AXC	47712	DRS
40145	PRE	43075	EMT	43172	FGW	43367	ICE	47714	HNR
		43076	EMT	43174	FGW	43378	AXC	47715	PRE
41001	PRE	43078	FGW	43175	FGW	43384	AXC	47716	NEM
		43079	FGW	43176	FGW	43423	GTL	47727	COL
43002	FGW	43081	EMT	43177	FGW	43465	GTL	47739	COL
43003	FGW	43082	EMT	43179	FGW	43467	GTL	47744	NEM
43004	FGW	43083	EMT	43180	FGW	43468	GTL	47746	WCR
43005	FGW	43086	FGW	43181	FGW	43480	GTL	47747	DRS
43009	FGW	43087	FGW	43182	FGW	43484	GTL	47749	COL
43010	FGW	43088	FGW	43183	FGW			47760	WCR
43012	FGW	43089	EMT	43185	FGW	44008	PRE	47761	HNR
43013	NRL	43091	FGW	43186	FGW			47763	PRE
43014	NRL	43092	FGW	43187	FGW	45015	PRE	47765	PRE
43015	FGW	43093	FGW	43188	FGW	45041	PRE	47768	WCR
43016	FGW	43094	FGW	43189	FGW	45060	PRE	47769	RIV
43017	FGW	43097	FGW	43190	FGW	45105	PRE	47771	PRE
43018	FGW	43098	FGW	43191	FGW	45108	PRE	47772	WCR
43020	FGW	43122	FGW	43192	FGW	45112	NEM	47773	VTN
43021	FGW	43124	FGW	43193	FGW	45118	PRE	47776	WCR
43022	FGW	43125	FGW	43194	FGW	45125	PRE	47785	PRE
43023	FGW	43126	FGW	43195	FGW	45132	PRE	47786	WCR
43024	FGW	43127	FGW	43196	FGW	45133	PRE	47787	WCR
43025	FGW	43128	FGW	43197	FGW	45135	PRE	47790	DRS
43026	FGW	43129	FGW	43198	FGW	45149	PRE	47791	DRS
43027	FGW	43130	FGW	43206	ICE			47793	PRE
43028	FGW	43131	FGW	43207	AXC	46010	PRE	47798	PRE
43029	FGW	43132	FGW	43208	ICE	46035	PRE	47799	PRE
43030	FGW	43133	FGW	43238	ICE	46045	PRE	47802	DRS
43031	FGW	43134	FGW	43239	ICE			47804	WCR
43032	FGW	43135	FGW	43251	ICE	47004	PRE	47805	DRS
43033	FGW	43136	FGW	43257	ICE	47105	PRE	47810	DRS
43034	FGW	43137	FGW	43272	ICE	47117	PRE	47811	FLR
43035	FGW	43138	FGW	43274	ICE	47192	PRE	47812	RIV

Data Tables

Number	Code	Number	Code	Number	Code	Number	Code	Number	Code
47813	DRS	56103	BAR	58022	DBS	60024	DBS	66001	DBS
47815	RIV	56105	COL	58023	DBS	60025	DBS	66002	DBS
47816	FLR	56113	COL	58024	DBS	60026	DBS	66003	DBS
47818	DRS	56115	EXP	58025	DBS	60027	DBS	66004	DBS
47826	WCR	56117	EXP	58026	DBS	60028	DBS	66005	DBS
47828	DRS	56301	PRE	58027	DBS	60029	DBS	66006	DBS
47830	FLR	56302	COL	58029	DBS	60030	DBS	66007	DBS
47832	DRS	56303	BAR	58030	DBS	60032	DBS	66008	DBS
47839	DRS	56311	BAR	58031	DBS	60033	DBS	66009	DBS
47840	PRE	56312	BAR	58032	DBS	60034	DBS	66010	DBS
47841	DRS	56313	BAR	58033	DBS	60035	DBS	66011	DBS
47843	RIV			58034	DBS	60036	DBS	66012	DBS
47847	RIV	57001	WCR	58035	DBS	60037	DBS	66013	DBS
47848	RIV	57002	DRS	58036	DBS	60039	DBS	66014	DBS
47851	WCR	57003	DRS	58037	DBS	60040	DBS	66015	DBS
47853	DRS	57004	DRS	58038	DBS	60041	DBS	66016	DBS
47854	WCR	57005	WCR	58039	DBS	60043	DBS	66017	DBS
		57006	WCR	58040	DBS	60044	DBS	66018	DBS
50002	PRE	57007	DRS	58041	DBS	60045	DBS	66019	DBS
50007	PRE	57008	DRS	58042	DBS	60046	DBS	66020	DBS
50008	PRE	57009	DRS	58043	DBS	60047	DBS	66021	DBS
50015	PRE	57010	DRS	58044	DBS	60048	DBS	66022	DBS
50017	PRE	57011	DRS	58046	DBS	60049	DBS	66023	DBS
50019	PRE	57012	DRS	58047	DBS	60051	DBS	66024	DBS
50021	PRE	57301	NRL	58048	DBS	60052	DBS	66025	DBS
50026	PRE	57302	DRS	58049	DBS	60053	DBS	66026	DBS
50027	PRE	57303	NRL	58050	DBS	60054	DBS	66027	DBS
50029	PRE	57304	DRS			60056	DBS	66028	DBS
50030	PRE	57305	NRL	59001	MRL	60057	DBS	66029	DBS
50031	PRE	57306	NRL	59002	MRL	60059	DBS	66030	DBS
50033	PRE	57307	DRS	59003	EXP	60060	DBS	66031	DBS
50135	PRE	57308	DRS	59004	MRL	60061	DBS	66032	DBS
50042	PRE	57309	DRS	59005	MRL	60062	DBS	66033	DBS
50044	PRE	57310	NRL	59101	MRL	60063	DBS	66034	DBS
50049	PRE	57311	DRS	59102	MRL	60064	DBS	66035	DBS
50050	PRE	57312	NRL	59103	MRL	60065	DBS	66036	DBS
		57313	WCR	59104	MRL	60066	DBS	66037	DBS
55002	PRE	57314	WCR			60067	DBS	66038	DBS
55009	PRE	57315	WCR	59201	DBS	60069	DBS	66039	DBS
55015	PRE	57316	WCR	59202	DBS	60071	DBS	66040	DBS
55016	PRE	57601	WCR	59203	DBS	60072	DBS	66041	DBS
55019	PRE	57602	FGW	59204	DBS	60073	DBS	66042	DBS
55022	PRE	57603	FGW	59205	DBS	60074	DBS	66043	DBS
		57604	FGW	59206	DBS	60076	DBS	66044	DBS
56006	PRE	57605	FGW			60077	DBS	66045	DBS
56007	PRE			60001	DBS	60079	DBS	66046	DBS
56009	IND	58001	DBS	60002	DBS	60083	DBS	66047	DBS
56018	PRE	58004	DBS	60003	DBS	60084	DBS	66048	DBS
56038	PRE	58005	DBS	60004	DBS	60085	DBS	66049	DBS
56051	COL	58006	DBS	60005	DBS	60086	DBS	66050	DBS
56060	PRE	58007	DBS	60007	DBS	60087	DBS	66051	DBS
56065	PRE	58008	DBS	60009	DBS	60088	DBS	66052	DBS
56078	COL	58009	DBS	60010	DBS	60090	DBS	66053	DBS
56081	PRE	58010	DBS	60011	DBS	60091	DBS	66054	DBS
56086	EPX	58011	DBS	60012	DBS	60092	DBS	66055	DBS
56087	COL	58012	DBS	60013	DBS	60093	DBS	66056	DBS
56091	BAR	58013	DBS	60015	DBS	60094	DBS	66057	DBS
56060	PRE	58015	DBS	60017	DBS	60095	DBS	66058	DBS
56094	COL	58016	PRE	60018	DBS	60096	DBS	66059	DBS
56096	EPX	58017	DBS	60019	DBS	60097	DBS	66060	DBS
56097	PRE	58018	DBS	60020	DBS	60099	DBS	66061	DBS
56098	PRE	58020	DBS	60021	DBS	60100	DBS	66062	DBS
56101	EXP	58021	DBS	60022	DBS	60500	DBS	66063	DBS

Data Tables

Number	Code	Number	Code	Number	Code	Number	Code	Number	Code
66064	DBS	66127	DBS	66190	DBS	66302	DRS	66535	FLR
66065	DBS	66128	DBS	66191	DBS	66303	DRS	66536	FLR
66066	DBS	66129	DBS	66192	DBS	66304	DRS	66537	FLR
66067	DBS	66130	DBS	66193	DBS	66305	DRS	66538	FLR
66068	DBS	66131	DBS	66194	DBS			66539	FLR
66069	DBS	66132	DBS	66195	DBS	66411	EXP	66540	FLR
66070	DBS	66133	DBS	66196	DBS	66412	EXP	66541	FLR
66071	DBS	66134	DBS	66197	DBS	66413	FLR	66542	FLR
66072	DBS	66135	DBS	66198	DBS	66414	FLR	66543	FLR
66073	DBS	66136	DBS	66199	DBS	66415	FLR	66544	FLR
66074	DBS	66137	DBS	66200	DBS	66416	FLR	66545	FLR
66075	DBS	66138	DBS	66201	DBS	66417	EXP	66546	FLR
66076	DBS	66139	DBS	66202	DBS	66418	FLR	66547	FLR
66077	DBS	66140	DBS	66203	DBS	66419	FLR	66548	FLR
66078	DBS	66141	DBS	66204	DBS	66420	FLR	66549	FLR
66079	DBS	66142	DBS	66205	DBS	66421	DRS	66550	FLR
66080	DBS	66143	DBS	66206	DBS	66422	DRS	66551	FLR
66081	DBS	66144	DBS	66207	DBS	66423	DRS	66552	FLR
66082	DBS	66145	DBS	66208	DBS	66424	DRS	66553	FLR
66083	DBS	66146	DBS	66209	DBS	66425	DRS	66554	FLR
66084	DBS	66147	DBS	66210	DBS	66426	DRS	66555	FLR
66085	DBS	66148	DBS	66211	DBS	66427	DRS	66556	FLR
66086	DBS	66149	DBS	66212	DBS	66428	DRS	66557	FLR
66087	DBS	66150	DBS	66213	DBS	66429	DRS	66558	FLR
66088	DBS	66151	DBS	66214	DBS	66430	DRS	66559	FLR
66089	DBS	66152	DBS	66215	DBS	66431	DRS	66560	FLR
66090	DBS	66153	DBS	66216	DBS	66432	DRS	66561	FLR
66091	DBS	66154	DBS	66217	DBS	66433	DRS	66562	FLR
66092	DBS	66155	DBS	66218	DBS	66434	DRS	66563	FLR
66093	DBS	66156	DBS	66219	DBS			66564	FLR
66094	DBS	66157	DBS	66220	DBS	66501	FLR	66565	FLR
66095	DBS	66158	DBS	66221	DBS	66502	FLR	66566	FLR
66096	DBS	66159	DBS	66222	DBS	66503	FLR	66567	FLR
66097	DBS	66160	DBS	66223	DBS	66504	FLR	66568	FLR
66098	DBS	66161	DBS	66224	DBS	66505	FLR	66569	FLR
66099	DBS	66162	DBS	66225	DBS	66506	FLR	66570	FLR
66100	DBS	66163	DBS	66226	DBS	66507	FLR	66571	FLR
66101	DBS	66164	DBS	66227	DBS	66508	FLR	66572	FLR
66102	DBS	66165	DBS	66228	DBS	66509	FLR	66582	EXP
66103	DBS	66166	DBS	66229	DBS	66510	FLR	66583	EXP
66104	DBS	66167	DBS	66230	DBS	66511	FLR	66584	EXP
66105	DBS	66168	DBS	66231	DBS	66512	FLR	66585	FLR
66106	DBS	66169	DBS	66232	DBS	66513	FLR	66586	EXP
66107	DBS	66170	DBS	66233	DBS	66514	FLR	66587	FLR
66108	DBS	66171	DBS	66234	DBS	66515	FLR	66588	FLR
66109	DBS	66172	DBS	66235	DBS	66516	FLR	66589	FLR
66110	DBS	66173	DBS	66236	DBS	66517	FLR	66590	FLR
66111	DBS	66174	DBS	66237	DBS	66518	FLR	66591	FLR
66112	DBS	66175	DBS	66238	DBS	66519	FLR	66592	FLR
66113	DBS	66176	DBS	66239	DBS	66520	FLR	66593	FLR
66114	DBS	66177	DBS	66240	DBS	66522	FLR	66594	FLR
66115	DBS	66178	DBS	66241	DBS	66523	FLR	66595	FLR
66116	DBS	66179	DBS	66242	DBS	66524	FLR	66596	FLR
66117	DBS	66180	DBS	66243	DBS	66525	FLR	66597	FLR
66118	DBS	66181	DBS	66244	DBS	66526	FLR	66598	FLR
66119	DBS	66182	DBS	66245	DBS	66527	FLR	66599	FLR
66120	DBS	66183	DBS	66246	DBS	66528	FLR		
66121	DBS	66184	DBS	66247	DBS	66529	FLR	66601	FLR
66122	DBS	66185	DBS	66248	DBS	66530	FLR	66602	FLR
66123	DBS	66186	DBS	66249	DBS	66531	FLR	66603	FLR
66124	DBS	66187	DBS	66250	DBS	66532	FLR	66604	FLR
66125	DBS	66188	DBS			66533	FLR	66605	FLR
66126	DBS	66189	DBS	66301	DRS	66534	FLR	66606	FLR

Data Tables

Number Cross-Link

66607	FLR	66744	GBR	70013	FLR	77017	ECR	86231	EPX
66608	EXP	66745	GBR	70014	FLR	77018	ECR	86232	EPX
66609	EXP	66746	GBR	70015	FLR	77019	ECR	86233	EXP
66610	FLR	66747	GBR	70016	FLR	77020	ECR	86234	EPX
66611	EXP	66748	GBR	70017	FLR	77021	ECR	86235	EPX
66612	EXP	66749	GBR	70018	FLR	77022	ECR	86242	EPX
66613	EXP			70019	FLR	77023	ECR	86246	EPX
66614	FLR	66846	COL	70020	FLR	77024	ECR	86247	EPX
66615	FLR	66847	COL			77025	ECR	86248	EXP
66616	FLR	66848	COL	70099	GBR	77026	ECR	86250	EXP
66617	FLR	66849	COL			77027	ECR	86251	EPX
66618	FLR	66850	COL	73001	PRE	77028	ECR	86259	PRE
66619	FLR			73003	PRE	77029	ECR	86401	ETL
66620	FLR	66951	FLR	73005	PRE	77030	ECR	86424	ETL
66621	FLR	66952	FLR	73006	PRE	77031	ECR	86501	FLR
66622	FLR	66953	FLR	73101	RVE	77032	ECR	86604	FLR
66623	FLR	66954	FLR	73103	PRE	77033	ECR	86605	FLR
66624	EXP	66955	FLR	73104	RVE	77034	ECR	86607	FLR
66625	EXP	66956	FLR	73107	BAR	77035	ECR	86609	FLR
		66957	FLR	73109	TTS	77036	ECR	86610	FLR
66701	GBR			73110	PRE	77037	ECR	86612	FLR
66702	GBR	67001	ATW	73114	PRE	77038	ECR	86613	FLR
66703	GBR	67002	ATW	73117	PRE	77039	ECR	86614	FLR
66704	GBR	67003	ATW	73118	TTS	77040	ECR	86622	FLR
66705	GBR	67004	DBS	73119	GBR	77041	ECR	86627	FLR
66706	GBR	67005	DBS	73128	PRE	77042	ECR	86628	FLR
66707	GBR	67006	DBS	73129	PRE	77043	ECR	86632	FLR
66708	GBR	67007	DBS	73130	PRE	77044	ECR	86637	FLR
66709	GBR	67008	DBS	73133	TTS	77045	ECR	86638	FLR
66710	GBR	67009	DBS	73134	PRE	77046	ECR	86639	FLR
66711	GBR	67010	CRW	73136	TTS	77047	ECR	86701	ETL
66712	GBR	67011	DBS	73138	NRL	77048	ECR	86702	ETL
66713	GBR	67012	CRW	73139	RVE	77049	ECR	86901	NRL
66714	GBR	67013	CRW	73140	PRE	77050	ECR	86902	NRL
66715	GBR	67014	CRW	73141	GBR	77051	ECR		
66716	GBR	67015	CRW	73201	BAR	77052	ECR	87001	PRE
66717	GBR	67016	DBS	73202	SOU	77053	ECR	87002	ETL
66718	GBR	67017	DBS	73204	GBR	77054	ECR	87003	EXP
66719	GBR	67018	DBS	73205	GBR	77055	ECR	87004	EXP
66720	GBR	67019	DBS	73206	GBR	77056	ECR	87006	EXP
66721	GBR	67020	DBS	73207	GBR	77057	ECR	87007	EXP
66722	GBR	67021	DBS	73208	GBR	77058	ECR	87008	EXP
66723	GBR	67022	DBS	73209	GBR	77059	ECR	87009	EXP
66724	GBR	67023	DBS	73210	PRE	77060	ECR	87010	EXP
66725	GBR	67024	DBS	73211	RVL			87012	EXP
66726	GBR	67025	DBS	73212	GBR			87013	EXP
66727	GBR	67026	DBS	73213	GBR	81002	PRE	87014	EXP
66728	GBR	67027	DBS					87017	EXP
66729	GBR	67028	DBS	77001	ECR	82008	PRE	87019	EXP
66730	GBR	67029	DBS	77002	ECR			87020	EXP
66731	GBR	67030	DBS	77003	ECR	83012	PRE	87022	EXP
66732	GBR			77004	ECR			87023	EXP
66733	GBR	70001	FLR	77005	ECR	84001	PRE	87025	EXP
66734	GBR	70002	FLR	77006	ECR			87026	EXP
66735	GBR	70003	FLR	77007	ECR	85101	PRE	87028	EXP
66736	GBR	70004	FLR	77008	ECR			87029	EXP
66737	GBR	70005	FLR	77009	ECR	86101	ETL	87033	EXP
66738	GBR	70006	FLR	77010	ECR	86213	ETL	87034	EXP
66739	GBR	70007	FLR	77011	LCR	86215	LXP	87035	PRE
66740	GBR	70008	FLR	77012	ECR	86217	EPX		
66741	GBR	70009	FLR	77013	ECR	86218	EXP	89001	PRE
66742	GBR	70010	FLR	77014	ECR	86226	EPX		
66743	GBR	70011	FLR	77015	ECR	86228	EPX	90001	AEA
				77016	ECR	86229	EPX		

Data Tables

No.	Code	No.	Code	No.	Code	No.	Code	No.	Code
90002	AEA	91114	ICE	92045	GBR	51131	PRE	51663	PRE
90003	AEA	91115	ICE	92046	GBR	51138	PRE	51669	PRE
90004	AEA	91116	ICE			51151	PRE	51677	PRE
90005	AEA	91117	ICE	97301	NRL	51187	PRE	51803	PRE
90006	AEA	91118	ICE	97302	NRL	51188	PRE	51813	PRE
90007	AEA	91119	ICE	97303	NRL	51189	PRE	51842	PRE
90008	AEA	91120	ICE	97304	NRL	51192	PRE	51859	PRE
90009	AEA	91121	ICE			51205	PRE	51880	PRE
90010	AEA	91122	ICE	97650	PRE	51210	PRE	51886	PRE
90011	AEA	91124	ICE	97651	PRE	51226	PRE	51887	PRE
90012	AEA	91125	ICE	97654	PRE	51228	PRE	51899	PRE
90013	AEA	91126	ICE			51247	PRE	51907	PRE
90014	AEA	91127	ICE	323 539-7	AFG	51321	PRE	51909	PRE
90015	AEA	91128	ICE	323 674-2	AFG	51339	PRE	51914	PRE
90016	FLR	91129	ICE			51342	PRE	51919	PRE
90017	DBS	91130	ICE	DH50-1	GBR	51346	PRE	51922	PRE
90018	DBS	91131	ICE	DH50-2	GBR	51347	PRE	51933	PRE
90019	DBS	91132	ICE			51351	PRE	51941	PRE
90020	DBS			8.701	GBR	51353	PRE	51942	PRE
90021	DBS	92001	DBS	8.702	GBR	51356	PRE	51947	PRE
90022	DBS	92002	DBS	8.703	GBR	51359	PRE	51950	PRE
90023	DBS	92003	DBS	8.704	GBR	51360	PRE	51973	PRE
90024	DBS	92004	DBS	8.708	GBR	51363	PRE	51990	PRE
90025	DBS	92005	DBS	8.711	GBR	51365	PRE		
90026	DBS	92006	GBR	8.712	GBR	51367	PRE	52005	PRE
90027	DBS	92007	DBS	8.716	GBR	51372	PRE	52006	PRE
90028	DBS	92008	DBS	8.718	GBR	51381	PRE	52008	PRE
90029	DBS	92009	DBS	8.719	GBR	51382	PRE	52025	PRE
90030	DBS	92010	GRB	8.720	GBR	51384	PRE	52030	PRE
90031	DBS	92011	DBS			51388	PRE	52044	PRE
90032	DBS	92012	DBS	**Diesel Multiple–**		51392	PRE	52048	PRE
90033	DBS	92013	DBS	**Units**		51395	PRE	52053	PRE
90034	DBS	92014	GBR	APT-E	PRE	51397	PRE	52054	PRE
90035	DBS	92015	DBS	LEV1	PRE	51398	PRE	52062	PRE
90036	DBS	92016	DBS			51400	PRE	52064	PRE
90037	DBS	92017	DBS	RB004	PRE	51401	PRE	52071	PRE
90038	DBS	92018	GBR			51402	PRE	52077	PRE
90039	DBS	92019	DBS	50015	PRE	51405	PRE		
90040	DBS	92020	GBR	50019	PRE	51407	PRE	53160	PRE
90041	FLR	92021	GBR	50222	PRE	51427	PRE	53164	PRE
90042	FLR	92022	DBS	50256	PRE	51432	PRE	53170	PRE
90043	FLR	92023	GBR	50338	PRE	51434	PRE	53193	PRE
90044	FLR	92024	DBS	50416	PRE	51485	PRE	53203	PRE
90045	FLR	92025	DBS	50447	PRE	51498	PRE	53204	PRE
90046	FLR	92026	DBS	50454	PRE	51499	PRE	53253	PRE
90047	FLR	92027	DBS	50455	PRE	51503	PRE	53266	PRE
90048	FLR	92028	GBR	50479	PRE	51505	PRE	53321	PRE
90049	FLR	92029	DBS	50517	PRE	51511	PRE	53628	PRE
90050	DBS	92030	DBS	50528	PRE	51512	PRE	53645	PRE
		92031	DBS	50531	PRE	51513	PRE	53746	PRE
91101	ICE	92032	GBR	50547	PRE	51562	PRE	53926	PRE
91102	ICE	92033	GBR	50556	PRE	51565	PRE	53971	PRE
91103	ICE	92034	EXP	50599	PRE	51566	PRE		
91104	ICE	92035	DBS	50619	PRE	51567	PRE	54055	PRE
91105	ICE	92036	DBS	50632	PRE	51568	PRE	54057	PRE
91106	ICE	92037	DBS	50929	PRE	51571	PRE	54062	PRE
91107	ICE	92038	GBR	50980	PRE	51572	PRE	54223	PRE
91108	ICE	92039	DBS			51592	PRE	54270	PRE
91109	ICE	92040	GBR	51017	PRE	51604	PRE	54279	PRE
91110	ICE	92041	DBS	51043	PRE	51616	PRE	54289	PRE
91111	ICE	92042	DBS	51073	PRE	51618	PRE	54365	PRE
91112	ICE	92043	GBR	51074	PRE	51622	PRE	54408	PRE
91113	ICE	92044	GBR	51104	PRE	51655	PRE	54490	PRE

Number	Code
54504	PRE
55000	PRE
55001	PRE
55003	PRE
55005	PRE
55006	PRE
55009	PRE
55012	PRE
55020	CRW
55023	PRE
55028	PRE
55029	PRE
55032	ATW
55033	PRE
55034	CRW
55966	PRE
55976	PRE
56006	PRE
56015	PRE
56121	PRE
56171	PRE
56208	PRE
56224	PRE
56271	PRE
56287	PRE
56301	PRE
56343	PRE
56352	PRE
56358	PRE
56456	PRE
56484	PRE
56491	PRE
56492	PRE
56495	PRE
59003	PRE
59004	PRE
59117	PRE
59228	PRE
59245	PRE
59250	PRE
59276	PRE
59387	PRE
59389	PRE
59404	PRE
59444	PRE
59486	PRE
59488	PRE
59492	PRE
59494	PRE
59500	PRE
59503	PRE
59506	PRE
59507	PRE
59508	PRE
59509	PRE
59510	PRE
59513	PRE
59514	PRE
59516	PRE
59517	PRE
59520	PRE

Number	Code
59521	PRE
59522	PRE
59539	PRE
59575	PRE
59603	PRE
59609	PRE
59659	PRE
59664	PRE
59678	PRE
59701	PRE
59719	PRE
59740	PRE
59761	PRE
59791	PRE
60116	PRE
60117	PRE
60118	PRE
60127	PRE
60130	PRE
60138	PRE
60142	PRE
60145	PRE
60149	PRE
60154	PRE
60501	PRE
60529	PRE
60616	PRE
60750	PRE
60800	PRE
60822	PRE
60828	PRE
60901	PRE
60904	PRE
60916	PRE
70549	PRE
79018	PRE
79612	PRE
79900	PRE
79960	PRE
79962	PRE
79963	PRE
79964	PRE
79976	PRE
79978	PRE
121019	PRE
121020	CRW
121024	PRE
121032	ATW
121034	CRW
139001	LMI
139002	LMI
140001	PRE
141103	PRE
141108	PRE
141110	PRE
141113	PRE

Number	Code
142001	NOR
142002	ATW
142003	NOR
142004	NOR
142005	NOR
142006	ATW
142007	NOR
142009	NOR
142010	ATW
142011	NOR
142012	NOR
142013	NOR
142014	NOR
142015	NOR
142016	NOR
142017	NOR
142018	NOR
142019	NOR
142020	NOR
142021	NOR
142022	NOR
142023	NOR
142024	NOR
142025	NOR
142026	NOR
142027	NOR
142028	NOR
142029	NOR
142030	NOR
142031	NOR
142032	NOR
142033	NOR
142034	NOR
142035	NOR
142036	NOR
142037	NOR
142038	NOR
142039	NOR
142040	NOR
142041	NOR
142042	NOR
142043	NOR
142044	NOR
142045	NOR
142046	NOR
142047	NOR
142048	NOR
142049	NOR
142050	NOR
142051	NOR
142052	NOR
142053	NOR
142054	NOR
142055	NOR
142056	NOR
142057	NOR
142058	NOR
142060	NOR
142061	NOR
142062	NOR
142063	NOR
142064	NOR
142065	NOR

Number	Code
142066	NOR
142067	NOR
142068	NOR
142069	ATW
142070	NOR
142071	NOR
142072	ATW
142073	ATW
142074	ATW
142075	ATW
142076	ATW
142077	ATW
142078	NOR
142079	NOR
142080	ATW
142081	ATW
142082	ATW
142083	ATW
142084	NOR
142085	ATW
142086	NOR
142087	NOR
142088	NOR
142089	NOR
142090	NOR
142091	NOR
142092	NOR
142093	NOR
142094	NOR
142095	NOR
142096	NOR
143601	ATW
143602	ATW
143603	FGW
143604	ATW
143605	ATW
143606	NOR
143607	ATW
143608	ATW
143609	ATW
143610	ATW
143611	FGW
143612	FGW
143614	ATW
143616	ATW
143617	FGW
143618	FGW
143619	FGW
143620	FGW
143621	FGW
143622	ATW
143623	ATW
143624	ATW
143625	ATW
144001	NOR
144002	NOR
144003	NOR
144004	NOR
144005	NOR
144006	NOR
144007	NOR

Number	Code
144008	NOR
144009	NOR
144010	NOR
144011	NOR
144012	NOR
144013	NOR
144014	NOR
144015	NOR
144016	NOR
144017	NOR
144018	NOR
144019	NOR
144020	NOR
144021	NOR
144022	NOR
144023	NOR
150001	FGW
150002	FGW
150101	FGW
150102	FGW
150103	NOR
150104	FGW
150105	LMI
150106	FGW
150107	LMI
150108	FGW
150109	LMI
150110	NOR
150111	NOR
150112	NOR
150113	NOR
150114	NOR
150115	NOR
150116	NOR
150117	NOR
150118	NOR
150119	NOR
150120	FGW
150122	FGW
150123	FGW
150124	FGW
150125	FGW
150126	FGW
150128	FGW
150129	FGW
150130	FGW
150131	FGW
150132	NOR
150133	NOR
150134	NOR
150135	NOR
150136	NOR
150137	NOR
150138	NOR
150139	NOR
150140	NOR
150141	NOR
150142	NOR
150143	NOR
150144	NOR
150145	NOR
150146	NOR

Data Tables

Number		Number		Number		Number		Number	
150147	NOR	150263	FGW	153352	NOR	156421	NOR	156484	NOR
150148	NOR	150264	ATW	153353	ATW	156422	AEA	156485	FSR
150149	NOR	150265	FGW	153354	LMI	156423	NOR	156486	NOR
150150	NOR	150266	FGW	153355	EMT	156424	NOR	156487	NOR
		150267	ATW	153356	LMI	156425	NOR	156488	NOR
150201	NOR	150268	NOR	153357	EMT	156426	NOR	156489	NOR
150202	FGW	150269	NOR	153358	NOR	156427	NOR	156490	NOR
150203	NOR	150270	NOR	153359	NOR	156428	NOR	156491	NOR
150205	NOR	150271	NOR	153360	NOR	156429	NOR	156492	FSR
150207	NOR	150272	NOR	153361	FGW	156430	FSR	156493	FSR
150208	ATW	150273	NOR	153362	ATW	156431	FSR	156494	FSR
150210	NOR	150274	NOR	153363	NOR	156432	FSR	156495	FSR
150211	NOR	150275	NOR	153364	LMI	156433	FSR	156496	FSR
150213	ATW	150276	NOR	153365	LMI	156434	FSR	156497	EMT
150214	NOR	150277	NOR	153366	LMI	156435	FSR	156498	EMT
150215	NOR	150278	ATW	153367	ATW	156436	FSR	156499	FSR
150216	FGW	150279	ATW	153368	FGW	156437	FSR	156500	FSR
150217	ATW	150280	ATW	153369	FGW	156438	NOR	156501	FSR
150218	NOR	150281	ATW	153370	FGW	156439	FSR	156502	FSR
150219	FGW	150282	ATW	153371	LMI	156440	NOR	156503	FSR
150220	NOR	150283	ATW	153372	FGW	156441	NOR	156504	FSR
150221	FGW	150284	ATW	153373	FGW	156442	FSR	156505	FSR
150222	NOR	150285	ATW	153374	EMT	156443	NOR	156506	FSR
150223	NOR			153375	LMI	156444	NOR	156507	FSR
150224	NOR	150921	FGW	153376	EMT	156445	FSR	156508	FSR
150226	NOR	150927	FGW	153377	FGW	156446	FSR	156509	FSR
150225	NOR			153378	NOR	156447	FSR	156510	FSR
150227	ATW	153301	NOR	153379	EMT	156448	NOR	156511	FSR
150228	NOR	153302	EMT	153380	FGW	156449	FSR	156512	FSR
150229	ATW	153303	ATW	153381	EMT	156450	FSR	156513	FSR
150230	ATW	153304	NOR	153382	FGW	156451	NOR	156514	FSR
150231	ATW	153305	FGW	153383	EMT	156452	NOR		
150232	FGW	153306	AEA	153384	EMT	156453	FSR	158701	FSR
150233	FGW	153307	NOR	153385	EMT	156454	NOR	158702	FSR
150234	FGW	153308	EMT			156455	NOR	158703	FSR
150235	ATW	153309	AEA	155341	NOR	156456	FSR	158704	FSR
150236	ATW	153310	EMT	155342	NOR	156457	FSR	158705	FSR
150237	ATW	153311	EMT	155343	NOR	156458	FSR	158706	FSR
150238	FGW	153312	ATW	155344	NOR	156459	NOR	158707	FSR
150239	FGW	153313	EMT	155345	NOR	156460	NOR	158708	FSR
150240	ATW	153314	AEA	155346	NOR	156461	NOR	158709	FSR
150241	ATW	153315	NOR	155347	NOR	156462	FSR	158710	FSR
150242	ATW	153316	NOR			156463	NOR	158711	FSR
150243	FGW	153317	NOR	156401	EMT	156464	NOR	158712	FSR
150244	FGW	153318	FGW	156402	AEA	156465	FSR	158713	FSR
150245	ATW	153319	EMT	156403	EMT	156466	NOR	158714	FSR
150246	FGW	153320	ATW	156404	EMT	156467	FSR	158715	FSR
150247	FGW	153321	EMT	156405	EMT	156468	NOR	158716	FSR
150248	FGW	153322	AEA	156406	EMT	156469	NOR	158717	FSR
150249	FGW	153323	ATW	156407	AEA	156470	EMT	158718	FSR
150250	ATW	153324	NOR	156408	EMT	156471	NOR	158719	FSR
150251	ATW	153325	FGW	156409	AEA	156472	NOR	158720	FSR
150252	ATW	153326	EMT	156410	EMT	156473	EMT	158721	FSR
150253	ATW	153327	ATW	156411	EMT	156474	FSR	158722	FSR
150254	ATW	153328	NOR	156412	AEA	156475	NOR	158723	FSR
150255	ATW	153329	FGW	156413	EMT	156476	FSR	158724	FSR
150256	ATW	153330	NOR	156414	EMT	156477	FSR	158725	FSR
150257	ATW	153331	NOR	156415	EMT	156478	FSR	158726	FSR
150258	ATW	153332	NOR	156416	AEA	156479	NOR	158727	FSR
150259	ATW	153333	FGW	156417	AEA	156480	NOR	158728	FSR
150260	ATW	153334	LMI	156418	AEA	156481	NOR	158729	FSR
150261	FGW	153335	AEA	156419	AEA	156482	NOR	158730	FSR
150262	ATW	153351	NOR	156420	NOR	156483	NOR	158731	FSR

Data Tables

Number	Code	Number	Code	Number	Code	Number	Code	Number	Code
158732	FSR	158831	ATW	158910	NOR	165018	CRW	166204	FGW
158733	FSR	158832	ATW	158950	FGW	165019	CRW	166205	FGW
158734	FSR	158833	ATW	158951	FGW	165020	CRW	166206	FGW
158735	FSR	158834	ATW	158952	FGW	165021	CRW	166207	FGW
158736	FSR	158835	ATW	158953	FGW	165022	CRW	166208	FGW
158737	FSR	158836	ATW	158954	FGW	165023	CRW	166209	FGW
158738	FSR	158837	ATW	158955	FGW	165024	CRW	166210	FGW
158739	FSR	158838	ATW	158956	FGW	165025	CRW	166211	FGW
158740	FSR	158839	ATW	158957	FGW	165026	CRW	166212	FGW
158741	FSR	158840	ATW	158958	FGW	165027	CRW	166213	FGW
158752	NOR	158841	ATW	158959	FGW	165028	CRW	166214	FGW
158753	NOR	158842	NOR	158960	FGW	165029	CRW	166215	FGW
158754	NOR	158843	NOR	158961	FGW	165030	CRW	166216	FGW
158755	NOR	158844	NOR			165031	CRW	166217	FGW
158756	NOR	158845	NOR	159001	SWT	165032	CRW	166218	FGW
158757	NOR	158846	EMT	159002	SWT	165033	CRW	166219	FGW
158758	NOR	158847	EMT	159003	SWT	165034	CRW	166220	FGW
158759	NOR	158848	NOR	159004	SWT	165035	CRW	166221	FGW
158763	FGW	158849	NOR	159005	SWT	165036	CRW		
158766	FGW	158850	NOR	159006	SWT	165037	CRW	168001	CRW
158770	EMT	158851	NOR	159007	SWT	165038	CRW	168002	CRW
158773	EMT	158852	EMT	159008	SWT	165039	CRW	168003	CRW
158774	EMT	158853	NOR	159009	SWT			168004	CRW
158777	EMT	158854	EMT	159010	SWT	165101	FGW	168005	CRW
158780	EMT	158855	NOR	159011	SWT	165102	FGW	168106	CRW
158782	FSR	158856	EMT	159012	SWT	165103	FGW	168107	CRW
158783	EMT	158857	EMT	159013	SWT	165104	FGW	168108	CRW
158784	NOR	158858	EMT	159014	SWT	165105	FGW	168109	CRW
158785	EMT	158859	NOR	159015	SWT	165106	FGW	168110	CRW
158786	FSR	158860	NOR	159016	SWT	165107	FGW	168111	CRW
158787	NOR	158861	NOR	159017	SWT	165108	FGW	168112	CRW
158788	EMT	158862	EMT	159018	SWT	165109	FGW	168113	CRW
158789	FSR	158863	EMT	159019	SWT	165110	FGW		
158790	NOR	158864	EMT	159020	SWT	165111	FGW	168214	CRW
158791	NOR	158865	EMT	159021	SWT	165112	FGW	168215	CRW
158792	NOR	158866	EMT	159022	SWT	165113	FGW	168216	CRW
158793	NOR	158867	FSR			165114	FGW	168217	CRW
158794	NOR	158868	FSR	159101	SWT	165116	FGW	168218	CRW
158795	NOR	158869	FSR	159102	SWT	165117	FGW	168219	CRW
158796	NOR	158870	FSR	159103	SWT	165118	FGW		
158797	NOR	158871	FSR	159104	SWT	165119	FGW	170101	AXC
158798	FGW	158872	NOR	159105	SWT	165120	FGW	170102	AXC
158799	EMT			159106	SWT	165121	FGW	170103	AXC
158806	EMT	158880	SWT	159107	SWT	165122	FGW	170104	AXC
158810	EMT	158881	SWT	159108	SWT	165123	FGW	170105	AXC
158812	EMT	158882	SWT			165124	FGW	170106	AXC
158813	EMT	158883	SWT	165001	CRW	165125	FGW	170107	AXC
158815	NOR	158884	SWT	165002	CRW	165126	FGW	170108	AXC
158816	NOR	158885	SWT	165003	CRW	165127	FGW	170109	AXC
158817	NOR	158886	SWT	165004	CRW	165128	FGW	170110	AXC
158818	ATW	158887	SWT	165005	CRW	165129	FGW	170111	AXC
158819	ATW	158888	SWT	165006	CRW	165130	FGW	170112	AXC
158820	ATW	158889	SWT	165007	CRW	165131	FGW	170113	AXC
158821	ATW	158890	SWT	165008	CRW	165132	FGW	170114	AXC
158822	ATW			165009	CRW	165133	FGW	170115	AXC
158823	ATW	158901	NOR	165010	CRW	165134	FGW	170116	AXC
158824	ATW	158902	NOR	165011	CRW	165135	FGW	170117	AXC
158825	ATW	158903	NOR	165012	CRW	165136	FGW	170201	AEA
158826	ATW	158904	NOR	165013	CRW	165137	FGW	170202	AEA
158827	ATW	158905	NOR	165014	CRW			170203	AEA
158828	ATW	158906	NOR	165015	CRW	166201	FGW	170204	AEA
158829	ATW	158907	NOR	165016	CRW	166202	FGW	170205	AEA
158830	ATW	158908	NOR	165017	CRW	166203	FGW	170206	AEA
		158909	NOR						

Data Tables

170207	AEA	170458	FSR	172001	LOG	175110	ATW	185141	FTP
170208	AEA	170459	FSR	172002	LOG	175111	ATW	185142	FTP
170270	AEA	170460	FSR	172003	LOG	175112	ATW	185143	FTP
170271	AEA	170461	FSR	172004	LOG	175113	ATW	185144	FTP
170272	AEA	170470	FSR	172005	LOG	175114	ATW	185145	FTP
170273	AEA	170471	FSR	172006	LOG	175115	ATW	185146	FTP
170301	FTP	170472	FSR	172007	LOG	175116	ATW	185147	FTP
170302	FTP	170473	FSR	172008	LOG			185148	FTP
170303	FTP	170474	FSR			180101	GTL	185149	FTP
170304	FTP	170475	FSR	172101	CRW	180102	FGW	185150	FTP
170305	FTP	170476	FSR	172102	CRW	180103	FGW	185151	FTP
170306	FTP	170477	FSR	172103	CRW	180104	FGW		
170307	FTP	170478	FSR	172104	CRW	180105	GTL	201001	PRE
170308	FTP	170501	LMI			180106	FGW		
170309	FTP	170502	LMI	172211	LMI	180107	GTL	202202	PRE
170393	FSR	170503	LMI	172212	LMI	180108	FGW		
170394	FSR	170504	LMI	172213	LMI	180109	FHT	205009	PRE
170395	FSR	170505	LMI	172214	LMI	180110	FHT	205025	PRE
170396	FSR	170506	LMI	172215	LMI	180111	FHT	205028	PRE
170397	AXC	170507	LMI	172216	LMI	180112	GTL	205032	PRE
170398	AXC	170508	LMI	172217	LMI	180113	FHT	205033	PRE
170401	FSR	170509	LMI	172218	LMI	180114	GTL	205101	PRE
170402	FSR	170510	LMI	172219	LMI			205205	PRE
170403	FSR	170511	LMI	172220	LMI	185101	FTP		
170404	FSR	170512	LMI	172221	LMI	185102	FTP	220001	AXC
170405	FSR	170513	LMI	172222	LMI	185103	FTP	220002	AXC
170406	FSR	170514	LMI			185104	FTP	220003	AXC
170407	FSR	170515	LMI	172331	LMI	185105	FTP	220004	AXC
170408	FSR	170516	LMI	172332	LMI	185106	FTP	220005	AXC
170409	FSR	170517	LMI	172333	LMI	185107	FTP	220006	AXC
170410	FSR	170518	AXC	172334	LMI	185108	FTP	220007	AXC
170411	FSR	170519	AXC	172335	LMI	185109	FTP	220008	AXC
170412	FSR	170520	AXC	172336	LMI	185110	FTP	220009	AXC
170413	FSR	170521	AXC	172337	LMI	185111	FTP	220010	AXC
170414	FSR	170522	AXC	172338	LMI	185112	FTP	220011	AXC
170415	FSR	170523	AXC	172339	LMI	185113	FTP	220012	AXC
170416	FSR	170630	LMI	172340	LMI	185114	FTP	220013	AXC
170417	FSR	170631	LMI	172341	LMI	185115	FTP	220014	AXC
170418	FSR	170632	LMI	172342	LMI	185116	FTP	220015	AXC
170419	FSR	170633	LMI	172343	LMI	185117	FTP	220016	AXC
170420	FSR	170634	LMI	172344	LMI	185118	FTP	220017	AXC
170421	FSR	170635	LMI	172345	LMI	185119	FTP	220018	AXC
170422	FSR	170636	AXC			185120	FTP	220019	AXC
170423	FSR	170637	AXC	175001	ATW	185121	FTP	220020	AXC
170424	FSR	170638	AXC	175002	ATW	185122	FTP	220021	AXC
170425	FSR	170639	AXC	175003	ATW	185123	FTP	220022	AXC
170426	FSR			175004	ATW	185124	FTP	220023	AXC
170427	FSR	171721	SOU	175005	ATW	185125	FTP	220024	AXC
170428	FSR	171722	SOU	175006	ATW	185126	FTP	220025	AXC
170429	FSR	171723	SOU	175007	ATW	185127	FTP	220026	AXC
170430	FSR	171724	SOU	175008	ATW	185128	FTP	220027	AXC
170431	FSR	171725	SOU	175009	ATW	185129	FTP	220028	AXC
170432	FSR	171726	SOU	175010	ATW	185130	FTP	220029	AXC
170433	FSR	171727	SOU	175011	ATW	185131	FTP	220030	AXC
170434	FSR	171728	SOU	175101	ATW	185132	FTP	220031	AXC
170450	FSR	171729	SOU	175102	ATW	185133	FTP	220032	AXC
170451	FSR	171730	SOU	175103	ATW	185134	FTP	220033	AXC
170452	FSR	171801	SOU	175104	ATW	185135	FTP	220034	AXC
170453	FSR	171802	SOU	175105	ATW	185136	FTP		
170454	FSR	171803	SOU	175106	ATW	185137	FTP	221101	VWC
170455	FSR	171804	SOU	175107	ATW	185138	FTP	221102	VWC
170456	FSR	171805	SOU	175108	ATW	185139	FTP	221103	VWC
170457	FSR	171806	SOU	175109	ATW	185140	FTP	221104	VWC

Data Tables

221105	VWC	222023	EMT
221106	VWC		
221107	VWC	222101	EMT
221108	VWC	222102	EMT
221109	VWC	222103	EMT
221110	VWC	222104	EMT
221111	VWC		
221112	VWC		
221113	VWC		
221114	VWC		
221115	VWC		
221116	VWC		
221117	VWC		
221118	VWC		
221119	AXC		
221120	AXC		
221121	AXC		
221122	AXC		
221123	AXC		
221124	AXC		
221125	AXC		
221126	AXC		
221127	AXC		
221128	AXC		
221129	AXC		
221130	AXC		
221131	AXC		
221132	AXC		
221133	AXC		
221134	AXC		
221135	AXC		
221136	AXC		
221137	AXC		
221138	AXC		
221139	AXC		
221140	AXC		
221141	AXC		
221142	VWC		
221143	VWC		
221144	OLS		

222001	EMT
222002	EMT
222003	EMT
222004	EMT
222005	EMT
222006	EMT
222007	EMT
222008	EMT
222009	EMT
222010	EMT
222011	EMT
222012	EMT
222013	EMT
222014	EMT
222015	EMT
222016	EMT
222017	EMT
222018	EMT
222019	EMT
222020	EMT
222021	EMT
222022	EMT

Electric Multiple–Units

85	PRE
87	PRE
91	PRE
2090	PRE
4732	PRE
5176	PRE
5759	PRE
5791	PRE
5793	PRE
6307	PRE
7105	PRE
8143	PRE
10096	PRE
11161	PRE
11179	PRE
11201	PRE
11825	PRE
13004	PRE
15345	PRE
28249	PRE
28361	PRE
28690	PRE
29298	PRE
29666	PRE
29670	PRE
29720	PRE
29896	PRE
61183	PRE
61275	PRE
61287	PRE
61742	PRE
61743	PRE
61798	PRE
61799	PRE
61804	PRE
61805	PRE
62364	PRE
62384	NRL
62378	PRE
62887	PRE
65302	PRE
65304	PRE
65451	PRE
67300	PRE
68001	PRE
68002	PRE

68003	PRE
68004	PRE
68005	PRE
68008	PRE
68009	PRE
68500	PRE
68506	PRE
69304	PRE
69310	PRE
69318	PRE
69332	PRE
69333	PRE
69337	PRE
69339	PRE
70229	PRE
70257	PRE
70273	PRE
70284	PRE
70292	PRE
70296	PRE
70354	PRE
70527	PRE
70531	PRE
70539	PRE
70576	PRE
70607	PRE
72501	PRE
72617	PRE
75033	PRE
75186	PRE
75250	PRE
75395	PRE
75407	PRE
76726	PRE
76740	PRE
76746	PRE
76797	PRE
76811	PRE
76812	PRE
76875	PRE
77172	PRE
79998	PRE
79999	PRE
303032	PRE
306017	PRE
309616	PRE
309624	PRE
313018	FCC
313024	FCC
313025	FCC
313026	FCC

313027	FCC	314203	FSR
313028	FCC	314204	FSR
313029	FCC	314205	FSR
313030	FCC	314206	FSR
313031	FCC	314207	FSR
313032	FCC	314208	FSR
313033	FCC	314209	FSR
313035	FCC	314210	FSR
313036	FCC	314211	FSR
313037	FCC	314212	FSR
313038	FCC	314213	FSR
313039	FCC	314214	FSR
313040	FCC	314215	FSR
313041	FCC	314216	FSR
313042	FCC		
313043	FCC	315801	AEA
313044	FCC	315802	AEA
313045	FCC	315803	AEA
313046	FCC	315804	AEA
313047	FCC	315805	AEA
313048	FCC	315806	AEA
313049	FCC	315807	AEA
313050	FCC	315808	AEA
313051	FCC	315809	AEA
313052	FCC	315810	AEA
313053	FCC	315811	AEA
313054	FCC	315812	AEA
313055	FCC	315813	AEA
313056	FCC	315814	AEA
313057	FCC	315815	AEA
313058	FCC	315816	AEA
313059	FCC	315817	AEA
313060	FCC	315818	AEA
313061	FCC	315819	AEA
313062	FCC	315820	AEA
313063	FCC	315821	AEA
313064	FCC	315822	AEA
313121	NRL	315823	AEA
313122	FCC	315824	AEA
313123	FCC	315825	AEA
313134	FCC	315826	AEA
313201	SOU	315827	AEA
313202	SOU	315828	AEA
313203	SOU	315829	AEA
313204	SOU	315830	AEA
313205	SOU	315831	AEA
313206	SOU	315832	AEA
313207	SOU	315833	AEA
313208	SOU	315834	AEA
313209	SOU	315835	AEA
313210	SOU	315836	AEA
313211	SOU	315837	AEA
313212	SOU	315838	AEA
313213	SOU	315839	AEA
313214	SOU	315840	AEA
313215	SOU	315841	AEA
313216	SOU	315842	AEA
313217	SOU	315843	AEA
313219	SOU	315844	AEA
313220	SOU	315845	AEA
		315846	AEA
314201	FSR	315847	AEA
314202	FSR	315848	AEA

Data Tables

315849	AEA	317669	AEA	319214	FCC	319449	FCC	321328	AEA
315850	AEA	317670	AEA	319215	FCC	319450	FCC	321329	AEA
315851	AEA	317671	AEA	319216	FCC	319451	FCC	321330	AEA
315852	AEA	317672	AEA	319217	FCC	319452	FCC	321331	AEA
315853	AEA	317708	OLS	319218	FCC	319453	FCC	321332	AEA
315854	AEA			319219	FCC	319454	FCC	321333	AEA
315855	AEA	317709	OLS	319220	FCC	319455	FCC	321334	AEA
315856	AEA	317710	OLS			319456	FCC	321335	AEA
315857	AEA	317714	OLS	319361	FCC	319457	FCC	321336	AEA
315858	AEA	317719	OLS	319362	FCC	319458	FCC	321337	AEA
315859	AEA	317722	OLS	319363	FCC	319459	FCC	321338	AEA
315860	AEA	317723	OLS	319364	FCC	319460	FCC	321339	AEA
315861	AEA	317729	OLS	319365	FCC			321340	AEA
		317732	OLS	319366	FCC	320301	FSR	321341	AEA
317337	FCC			319367	FCC	320302	FSR	321342	AEA
317338	FCC	317881	AEA	319368	FCC	320303	FSR	321343	AEA
317339	FCC	317882	AEA	319369	FCC	320304	FSR	321344	AEA
317340	FCC	317883	AEA	319370	FCC	320305	FSR	321345	AEA
317341	FCC	317884	AEA	319371	FCC	320306	FSR	321346	AEA
317342	FCC	317885	AEA	319372	FCC	320307	FSR	321347	AEA
317343	FCC	317886	AEA	319373	FCC	320308	FSR	321348	AEA
317344	FCC	317887	AEA	319374	FCC	320309	FSR	321349	AEA
317345	FCC	317888	AEA	319375	FCC	320310	FSR	321350	AEA
317346	FCC	317889	AEA	319376	FCC	320311	FSR	321351	AEA
317347	FCC	317890	AEA	319377	FCC	320312	FSR	321352	AEA
317348	FCC	317891	AEA	319378	FCC	320313	FSR	321353	AEA
		317892	AEA	319379	FCC	320314	FSR	321354	AEA
317501	AEA			319380	FCC	320315	FSR	321355	AEA
317502	AEA	318250	FSR	319381	FCC	320316	FSR	321356	AEA
317503	AEA	318251	FSR	319382	FCC	320317	FSR	321357	AEA
317504	AEA	318252	FSR	319383	FCC	320318	FSR	321358	AEA
317505	AEA	318253	FSR	319384	FCC	320319	FSR	321359	AEA
317506	AEA	318254	FSR	319385	FCC	320320	FSR	321360	AEA
317507	AEA	318255	FSR	319386	FCC	320321	FSR	321361	AEA
317508	AEA	318256	FSR			320322	FSR	321362	AEA
317509	AEA	318257	FSR	319421	FCC			321363	AEA
317510	AEA	318258	FSR	319422	FCC	321301	AEA	321364	AEA
317511	AEA	318259	FSR	319423	FCC	321302	AEA	321365	AEA
317512	AEA	318260	FSR	319424	FCC	321303	AEA	321366	AEA
317513	AEA	318261	FSR	319425	FCC	321304	AEA		
317514	AEA	318262	FSR	319426	FCC	321305	AEA	321401	FCC
317515	AEA	318263	FSR	319427	FCC	321306	AEA	321402	FCC
		318264	FSR	319428	FCC	321307	AEA	321403	FCC
317649	AEA	318265	FSR	319429	FCC	321308	AEA	321404	FCC
317650	AEA	318266	FSR	319430	FCC	321309	AEA	321405	FCC
317651	AEA	318267	FSR	319431	FCC	321310	AEA	321406	FCC
317652	AEA	318268	FSR	319432	FCC	321311	AEA	321407	FCC
317653	AEA	318269	FSR	319433	FCC	321312	AEA	321408	FCC
317654	AEA	318270	FSR	319434	FCC	321313	AEA	321409	FCC
317655	AEA			319435	FCC	321314	AEA	321410	FCC
317656	AEA	319001	FCC	319436	FCC	321315	AEA	321411	LMI
317657	AEA	319002	FCC	319437	FCC	321316	AEA	321412	LMI
317658	AEA	319003	FCC	319438	FCC	321317	AEA	321413	LMI
317659	AEA	319004	FCC	319439	FCC	321318	AEA	321414	LMI
317660	AEA	319005	FCC	319440	FCC	321319	AEA	321415	LMI
317661	AEA	319006	FCC	319441	FCC	321320	AEA	321416	LMI
317662	AEA	319007	FCC	319442	FCC	321321	AEA	321417	LMI
317663	AEA	319008	FCC	319443	FCC	321322	AEA	321418	FCC
317664	AEA	319009	FCC	319444	FCC	321323	AEA	321419	FCC
317665	AEA	319010	FCC	319445	FCC	321324	AEA	321420	FCC
317666	AEA	319011	FCC	319446	FCC	321325	AEA	321421	AEA
317667	AEA	319012	FCC	319447	FCC	321326	AEA	321422	AEA
317668	AEA	319013	FCC	319448	FCC	321327	AEA	321423	AEA

Number	Code	Number	Code	Number	Code	Number	Code	Number	Code	Number	Code
321424	AEA	323228	NOR	333016	NOR	350121	LMI	357016	C2C		
321425	AEA	323229	NOR			350122	LMI	357017	C2C		
321426	AEA	323230	NOR	334001	FSR	350123	LMI	357018	C2C		
321427	AEA	323231	NOR	334002	FSR	350124	LMI	357019	C2C		
321428	AEA	323232	NOR	334003	FSR	350125	LMI	357020	C2C		
321429	AEA	323233	NOR	334004	FSR	350126	LMI	357021	C2C		
321430	AEA	323234	NOR	334005	FSR	350127	LMI	357022	C2C		
321431	AEA	323235	NOR	334006	FSR	350128	LMI	357023	C2C		
321432	AEA	323236	NOR	334007	FSR	350129	LMI	357024	C2C		
321433	AEA	323237	NOR	334008	FSR	350130	LMI	357025	C2C		
321434	AEA	323238	NOR	334009	FSR	350231	LMI	357026	C2C		
321435	AEA	323239	NOR	334010	FSR	350232	LMI	357027	C2C		
321436	AEA	323240	LMI	334011	FSR	350233	LMI	357028	C2C		
321437	AEA	323241	LMI	334012	FSR	350234	LMI	357029	C2C		
321438	AEA	323242	LMI	334013	FSR	350235	LMI	357030	C2C		
321439	AEA	323243	LMI	334014	FSR	350236	LMI	357031	C2C		
321440	AEA			334015	FSR	350237	LMI	357032	C2C		
321441	AEA	325001	DBS	334016	FSR	350238	LMI	357033	C2C		
321442	AEA	325002	DBS	334017	FSR	350239	LMI	357034	C2C		
321443	AEA	325003	DBS	334018	FSR	350240	LMI	357035	C2C		
321444	AEA	325004	DBS	334019	FSR	350241	LMI	357036	C2C		
321445	AEA	325005	DBS	334020	FSR	350242	LMI	357037	C2C		
321446	AEA	325006	DBS	334021	FSR	350243	LMI	357038	C2C		
321447	AEA	325007	DBS	334022	FSR	350244	LMI	357039	C2C		
321448	AEA	325008	DBS	334023	FSR	350245	LMI	357040	C2C		
		325009	DBS	334024	FSR	350246	LMI	357041	C2C		
321901	NOR	325011	DBS	334025	FSR	350247	LMI	357042	C2C		
321902	NOR	325012	DBS	334026	FSR	350248	LMI	357043	C2C		
321903	NOR	325013	DBS	334027	FSR	350249	LMI	357044	C2C		
		325014	DBS	334028	FSR	350250	LMI	357045	C2C		
322481	NOR	325015	DBS	334029	FSR	350251	LMI	357046	C2C		
322482	NOR	325016	DBS	334030	FSR	350252	LMI	357201	C2C		
322483	NOR			334031	FSR	350253	LMI	357202	C2C		
322484	NOR	332001	HEX	334032	FSR	350254	LMI	357203	C2C		
322485	NOR	332002	HEX	334033	FSR	350255	LMI	357204	C2C		
		332003	HEX	334034	FSR	350256	LMI	357205	C2C		
323201	LMI	332004	HEX	334035	FSR	350257	LMI	357206	C2C		
323202	LMI	332005	HEX	334036	FSR	350258	LMI	357207	C2C		
323203	LMI	332006	HEX	334037	FSR	350259	LMI	357208	C2C		
323204	LMI	332007	HEX	334038	FSR	350260	LMI	357209	C2C		
323205	LMI	332008	HEX	334039	FSR	350261	LMI	357210	C2C		
323206	LMI	332009	HEX	334040	FSR	350262	LMI	357211	C2C		
323207	LMI	332010	HEX			350263	LMI	357212	C2C		
323208	LMI	332011	HEX	350101	LMI	350264	LMI	357213	C2C		
323209	LMI	332012	HEX	350102	LMI	350265	LMI	357214	C2C		
323210	LMI	332013	HEX	350103	LMI	350266	LMI	357215	C2C		
323211	LMI	332014	HEX	350104	LMI	350267	LMI	357216	C2C		
323212	LMI			350105	LMI			357217	C2C		
323213	LMI	333001	NOR	350106	LMI	357001	C2C	357218	C2C		
323214	LMI	333002	NOR	350107	LMI	357002	C2C	357219	C2C		
323215	LMI	333003	NOR	350108	LMI	357003	C2C	357220	C2C		
323216	LMI	333004	NOR	350109	LMI	357004	C2C	357221	C2C		
323217	LMI	333005	NOR	350110	LMI	357005	C2C	357222	C2C		
323218	LMI	333006	NOR	350111	LMI	357006	C2C	357223	C2C		
323219	LMI	333007	NOR	350112	LMI	357007	C2C	357224	C2C		
323220	LMI	333008	NOR	350113	LMI	357008	C2C	357225	C2C		
323221	LMI	333009	NOR	350114	LMI	357009	C2C	357226	C2C		
323222	LMI	333010	NOR	350115	LMI	357010	C2C	357227	C2C		
323223	NOR	333011	NOR	350116	LMI	357011	C2C	357228	C2C		
323224	NOR	333012	NOR	350117	LMI	357012	C2C				
323225	NOR	333013	NOR	350118	LMI	357013	C2C	360101	AEA		
323226	NOR	333014	NOR	350119	LMI	357014	C2C	360102	AEA		
323227	NOR	333015	NOR	350120	LMI	357015	C2C	360103	AEA		

Data Tables

360104	AEA	365539	FCC	373231	EUS	375706	SET	375924	SET
360105	AEA	365540	FCC	373232	EUS	375707	SET	375925	SET
360106	AEA	365541	FCC	373301	EUS	375708	SET	375926	SET
360107	AEA	373001	EUS	373302	EUS	375709	SET	375927	SET
360108	AEA	373002	EUS	373303	EUS	375710	SET		
360109	AEA	373003	EUS	373304	EUS	375711	SET	376001	SET
360110	AEA	373004	EUS	373305	EUS	375712	SET	376002	SET
360111	AEA	373005	EUS	373306	EUS	375713	SET	376003	SET
360112	AEA	373006	EUS	373307	EUS	375714	SET	376004	SET
360113	AEA	373007	EUS	373308	EUS	375715	SET	376005	SET
360114	AEA	373008	EUS	373309	EUS	375801	SET	376006	SET
360115	AEA	373009	EUS	373310	EUS	375802	SET	376007	SET
360116	AEA	373010	EUS	373311	EUS	375803	SET	376008	SET
360117	AEA	373011	EUS	373312	EUS	375804	SET	376009	SET
360118	AEA	373012	EUS	373313	EUS	375805	SET	376010	SET
360119	AEA	373013	EUS	373314	EUS	375806	SET	376011	SET
360120	AEA	373014	EUS	373999	EUS	375807	SET	376012	SET
360121	AEA	373015	EUS			375808	SET	376013	SET
		373016	EUS	375301	SET	375809	SET	376014	SET
360201	HEC	373017	EUS	375302	SET	375810	SET	376015	SET
360202	HEC	373018	EUS	375303	SET	375811	SET	376016	SET
360203	HEC	373019	EUS	375304	SET	375812	SET	376017	SET
360204	HEC	373020	EUS	375305	SET	375813	SET	376018	SET
360205	HEC	373021	EUS	375306	SET	375814	SET	376019	SET
		373022	EUS	375307	SET	375815	SET	376020	SET
365501	FCC	373101	EUS	375308	SET	375816	SET	376021	SET
365502	FCC	373102	EUS	375309	SET	375817	SET	376022	SET
365503	FCC	373103	EUS	375310	SET	375818	SET	376023	SET
365504	FCC	373104	EUS	375601	SET	375819	SET	376024	SET
365505	FCC	373105	EUS	375602	SET	375820	SET	376025	SET
365506	FCC	373106	EUS	375603	SET	375821	SET	376026	SET
365507	FCC	373107	EUS	375604	SET	375822	SET	376027	SET
365508	FCC	373108	EUS	375605	SET	375823	SET	376028	SET
365509	FCC	373201	EUS	375606	SET	375824	SET	376029	SET
365510	FCC	373202	EUS	375607	SET	375825	SET	376030	SET
365511	FCC	373203	EUS	375608	SET	375826	SET	376031	SET
365512	FCC	373204	EUS	375609	SET	375827	SET	376032	SET
365513	FCC	373205	EUS	375610	SET	375828	SET	376033	SET
365514	FCC	373206	EUS	375611	SET	375829	SET	376034	SET
365515	FCC	373207	EUS	375612	SET	375830	SET	376035	SET
365516	FCC	373208	EUS	375613	SET	375901	SET	376036	SET
365517	FCC	373209	EUS	375614	SET	375902	SET		
365518	FCC	373210	EUS	375615	SET	375903	SET	377101	SOU
365519	FCC	373211	EUS	375616	SET	375904	SET	377102	SOU
365520	FCC	373212	EUS	375617	SET	375905	SET	377103	SOU
365521	FCC	373213	EUS	375618	SET	375906	SET	377104	SOU
365522	FCC	373214	EUS	375619	SET	375907	SET	377105	SOU
365523	FCC	373215	EUS	375620	SET	375908	SET	377106	SOU
365524	FCC	373216	EUS	375621	SET	375909	SET	377107	SOU
365525	FCC	373217	EUS	375622	SET	375910	SET	377108	SOU
365526	OLS	373218	EUS	375623	SET	375911	SET	377109	SOU
365527	FCC	373219	EUS	375624	SET	375912	SET	377110	SOU
365528	FCC	373220	EUS	375625	SET	375913	SET	377111	SOU
365529	FCC	373221	EUS	375626	SET	375914	SET	377112	SOU
365530	FCC	373222	EUS	375627	SET	375915	SET	377113	SOU
365531	FCC	373223	EUS	375628	SET	375916	SET	377114	SOU
365532	FCC	373224	EUS	375629	SET	375917	SET	377115	SOU
365533	FCC	373225	EUS	375630	SET	375918	SET	377116	SOU
365534	FCC	373226	EUS	375701	SET	375919	SET	377117	SOU
365535	FCC	373227	EUS	375702	SET	375920	SET	377118	SOU
365536	FCC	373228	EUS	375703	SET	375921	SET	377119	SOU
365537	FCC	373229	EUS	375704	SET	375922	SET	377120	SOU
365538	FCC	373230	EUS	375705	SET	375923	SET	377121	SOU

❏ 377122	SOU	❏ 377306	SOU	❏ 377441	SOU	❏ 378138	LOG	❏ 379009	AEA
❏ 377123	SOU	❏ 377307	SOU	❏ 377442	SOU	❏ 378139	LOG	❏ 379010	AEA
❏ 377124	SOU	❏ 377308	SOU	❏ 377443	SOU	❏ 378140	LOG	❏ 379011	AEA
❏ 377125	SOU	❏ 377309	SOU	❏ 377444	SOU	❏ 378141	LOG	❏ 379012	AEA
❏ 377126	SOU	❏ 377310	SOU	❏ 377445	SOU	❏ 378142	LOG	❏ 379013	AEA
❏ 377127	SOU	❏ 377311	SOU	❏ 377446	SOU	❏ 378143	LOG	❏ 379014	AEA
❏ 377128	SOU	❏ 377312	SOU	❏ 377447	SOU	❏ 378144	LOG	❏ 379015	AEA
❏ 377129	SOU	❏ 377313	SOU	❏ 377448	SOU	❏ 378145	LOG	❏ 379016	AEA
❏ 377130	SOU	❏ 377314	SOU	❏ 377449	SOU	❏ 378146	LOG	❏ 379017	AEA
❏ 377131	SOU	❏ 377315	SOU	❏ 377450	SOU	❏ 378147	LOG	❏ 379018	AEA
❏ 377132	SOU	❏ 377316	SOU	❏ 377451	SOU	❏ 378148	LOG	❏ 379019	AEA
❏ 377133	SOU	❏ 377317	SOU	❏ 377452	SOU	❏ 378149	LOG	❏ 379020	AEA
❏ 377134	SOU	❏ 377318	SOU	❏ 377453	SOU	❏ 378150	LOG	❏ 379021	AEA
❏ 377135	SOU	❏ 377319	SOU	❏ 377454	SOU	❏ 378151	LOG	❏ 379022	AEA
❏ 377136	SOU	❏ 377320	SOU	❏ 377455	SOU	❏ 378152	LOG	❏ 379023	AEA
❏ 377137	SOU	❏ 377321	SOU	❏ 377456	SOU	❏ 378153	LOG	❏ 379024	AEA
❏ 377138	SOU	❏ 377322	SOU	❏ 377457	SOU	❏ 378154	LOG	❏ 379025	AEA
❏ 377139	SOU	❏ 377323	SOU	❏ 377458	SOU	❏ 378201	LOG	❏ 379026	AEA
❏ 377140	SOU	❏ 377324	SOU	❏ 377459	SOU	❏ 378202	LOG	❏ 379027	AEA
❏ 377141	SOU	❏ 377325	SOU	❏ 377460	SOU	❏ 378203	LOG	❏ 379028	AEA
❏ 377142	SOU	❏ 377326	SOU	❏ 377461	SOU	❏ 378204	LOG	❏ 379029	AEA
❏ 377143	SOU	❏ 377327	SOU	❏ 377462	SOU	❏ 378205	LOG	❏ 379030	AEA
❏ 377144	SOU	❏ 377328	SOU	❏ 377463	SOU	❏ 378206	LOG		
❏ 377145	SOU	❏ 377401	SOU	❏ 377464	SOU	❏ 378207	LOG	❏ 380001	FSR
❏ 377146	SOU	❏ 377402	SOU	❏ 377465	SOU	❏ 378208	LOG	❏ 380002	FSR
❏ 377147	SOU	❏ 377403	SOU	❏ 377466	SOU	❏ 378209	LOG	❏ 380003	FSR
❏ 377148	SOU	❏ 377404	SOU	❏ 377467	SOU	❏ 378210	LOG	❏ 380004	FSR
❏ 377149	SOU	❏ 377405	SOU	❏ 377468	SOU	❏ 378211	LOG	❏ 380005	FSR
❏ 377150	SOU	❏ 377406	SOU	❏ 377469	SOU	❏ 378212	LOG	❏ 380006	FSR
❏ 377151	SOU	❏ 377407	SOU	❏ 377470	SOU	❏ 378213	LOG	❏ 380007	FSR
❏ 377152	SOU	❏ 377408	SOU	❏ 377471	SOU	❏ 378214	LOG	❏ 380008	FSR
❏ 377153	SOU	❏ 377409	SOU	❏ 377472	SOU	❏ 378215	LOG	❏ 380009	FSR
❏ 377154	SOU	❏ 377410	SOU	❏ 377473	SOU	❏ 378216	LOG	❏ 380010	FSR
❏ 377155	SOU	❏ 377411	SOU	❏ 377474	SOU	❏ 378217	LOG	❏ 380011	FSR
❏ 377156	SOU	❏ 377412	SOU	❏ 377475	SOU	❏ 378218	LOG	❏ 380012	FSR
❏ 377157	SOU	❏ 377413	SOU	❏ 377501	FCC	❏ 378219	LOG	❏ 380013	FSR
❏ 377158	SOU	❏ 377414	SOU	❏ 377502	FCC	❏ 378220	LOG	❏ 380014	FSR
❏ 377159	SOU	❏ 377415	SOU	❏ 377503	FCC	❏ 378221	LOG	❏ 380015	FSR
❏ 377160	SOU	❏ 377416	SOU	❏ 377504	FCC	❏ 378222	LOG	❏ 380016	FSR
❏ 377161	SOU	❏ 377417	SOU	❏ 377505	FCC	❏ 378223	LOG	❏ 380017	FSR
❏ 377162	SOU	❏ 377418	SOU	❏ 377506	FCC	❏ 378224	LOG	❏ 380018	FSR
❏ 377163	SOU	❏ 377419	SOU	❏ 377507	FCC	❏ 378225	LOG	❏ 380019	FSR
❏ 377164	SOU	❏ 377420	SOU	❏ 377508	FCC	❏ 378226	LOG	❏ 380020	FSR
❏ 377201	SOU	❏ 377421	SOU	❏ 377509	FCC	❏ 378227	LOG	❏ 380021	FSR
❏ 377202	SOU	❏ 377422	SOU	❏ 377510	FCC	❏ 378228	LOG	❏ 380022	FSR
❏ 377203	SOU	❏ 377423	SOU	❏ 377511	FCC	❏ 378229	LOG	❏ 380101	FSR
❏ 377204	SOU	❏ 377424	SOU	❏ 377512	FCC	❏ 378230	LOG	❏ 380102	FSR
❏ 377205	SOU	❏ 377425	SOU	❏ 377513	FCC	❏ 378231	LOG	❏ 380103	FSR
❏ 377206	SOU	❏ 377426	SOU	❏ 377514	FCC	❏ 378232	LOG	❏ 380104	FSR
❏ 377207	SOU	❏ 377427	SOU	❏ 377515	FCC	❏ 378233	LOG	❏ 380105	FSR
❏ 377208	SOU	❏ 377428	SOU	❏ 377516	FCC	❏ 378234	LOG	❏ 380106	FSR
❏ 377209	SOU	❏ 377429	SOU	❏ 377517	FCC	❏ 378255	LOG	❏ 380107	FSR
❏ 377210	SOU	❏ 377430	SOU	❏ 377518	FCC	❏ 378256	LOG	❏ 380108	FSR
❏ 377211	SOU	❏ 377431	SOU	❏ 377519	FCC	❏ 378257	LOG	❏ 380109	FSR
❏ 377212	SOU	❏ 377432	SOU	❏ 377520	FCC			❏ 380110	FSR
❏ 377213	SOU	❏ 377433	SOU	❏ 377521	FCC	❏ 379001	AEA	❏ 380111	FSR
❏ 377214	SOU	❏ 377434	SOU	❏ 377522	FCC	❏ 379002	AEA	❏ 380112	FSR
❏ 377215	SOU	❏ 377435	SOU	❏ 377523	FCC	❏ 379003	AEA	❏ 380113	FSR
❏ 377301	SOU	❏ 377436	SOU			❏ 379004	AEA	❏ 380114	FSR
❏ 377302	SOU	❏ 377437	SOU	❏ 378135	LOG	❏ 379005	AEA	❏ 380115	FSR
❏ 377303	SOU	❏ 377438	SOU	❏ 378135	LOG	❏ 379006	AEA	❏ 380116	FSR
❏ 377304	SOU	❏ 377439	SOU	❏ 378136	LOG	❏ 379007	AEA		
❏ 377305	SOU	❏ 377440	SOU	❏ 378137	LOG	❏ 379008	AEA	❏ 390001	VWC

Data Tables

No.	Code	No.	Code	No.	Code	No.	Code	No.	Code	No.	Code
390002	VWC	395007	SET	444008	SWT	450025	SWT	450116	SWT		
390103	VWC	395008	SET	444009	SWT	450026	SWT	450117	SWT		
391004	VWC	395009	SET	444010	SWT	450027	SWT	450118	SWT		
390005	VWC	395010	SET	444011	SWT	450028	SWT	450119	SWT		
390006	VWC	395011	SET	444012	SWT	450029	SWT	450120	SWT		
390107	VWC	395012	SET	444013	SWT	450030	SWT	450121	SWT		
390008	VWC	395013	SET	444014	SWT	450031	SWT	450122	SWT		
390009	VWC	395014	SET	444015	SWT	450032	SWT	450123	SWT		
390010	VWC	395015	SET	444016	SWT	450033	SWT	450124	SWT		
390011	VWC	395016	SET	444017	SWT	450034	SWT	450125	SWT		
390112	VWC	395017	SET	444018	SWT	450035	SWT	450126	SWT		
390013	VWC	395018	SET	444019	SWT	450036	SWT	450127	SWT		
390114	VWC	395019	SET	444020	SWT	450037	SWT				
390115	VWC	395020	SET	444021	SWT	450038	SWT	450543	SWT		
390016	VWC	395021	SET	444022	SWT	450039	SWT	450544	SWT		
390117	VWC	395022	SET	444023	SWT	450040	SWT	450545	SWT		
390118	VWC	395023	SET	444024	SWT	450041	SWT	450546	SWT		
390119	VWC	395024	SET	444025	SWT	450042	SWT	450547	SWT		
390020	VWC	395025	SET	444026	SWT	450071	SWT	450548	SWT		
390121	VWC	395026	SET	444027	SWT	450072	SWT	450549	SWT		
390122	VWC	395027	SET	444028	SWT	450073	SWT	450550	SWT		
390023	VWC	395028	SET	444029	SWT	450074	SWT	450551	SWT		
390124	VWC	395029	SET	444030	SWT	450075	SWT	450552	SWT		
390125	VWC			444031	SWT	450076	SWT	450553	SWT		
390126	VWC	411198	PRE	444032	SWT	450077	SWT	450554	SWT		
390127	VWC			444033	SWT	450078	SWT	450555	SWT		
390128	VWC	421399	PRE	444034	SWT	450079	SWT	450556	SWT		
390129	VWC	421496	PRE	444035	SWT	450080	SWT	450557	SWT		
390130	VWC	421497	PRE	444036	SWT	450081	SWT	450558	SWT		
390131	VWC	421498	PRE	444037	SWT	450082	SWT	450559	SWT		
390132	VWC			444038	SWT	450083	SWT	450560	SWT		
390033	OLS	442401	SOU	444039	SWT	450084	SWT	450561	SWT		
390134	VWC	442402	SOU	444040	SWT	450085	SWT	450562	SWT		
390035	VWC	442403	SOU	444041	SWT	450086	SWT	450563	SWT		
390136	VWC	442404	SOU	444042	SWT	450087	SWT	450564	SWT		
390137	VWC	442405	SOU	444043	SWT	450088	SWT	450565	SWT		
390038	VWC	442406	SOU	444044	SWT	450089	SWT	450566	SWT		
390039	VWC	442407	SOU	444045	SWT	450090	SWT	450567	SWT		
390040	VWC	442408	SOU			450091	SWT	450568	SWT		
390141	VWC	442409	SOU	450001	SWT	450092	SWT	450569	SWT		
390042	VWC	442410	SOU	450002	SWT	450093	SWT	450570	SWT		
390043	VWC	442411	SOU	450003	SWT	450094	SWT				
390044	VWC	442412	SOU	450004	SWT	450095	SWT	455701	SWT		
390045	VWC	442413	SOU	450005	SWT	450096	SWT	455702	SWT		
390046	VWC	442414	SOU	450006	SWT	450097	SWT	455703	SWT		
390047	VWC	442415	SOU	450007	SWT	450098	SWT	455704	SWT		
390148	VWC	442416	SOU	450008	SWT	450099	SWT	455705	SWT		
390049	VWC	442417	SOU	450009	SWT	450100	SWT	455706	SWT		
390050	VWC	442418	SOU	450010	SWT	450101	SWT	455707	SWT		
390151	VWC	442419	SOU	450011	SWT	450102	SWT	455708	SWT		
390152	VWC	442420	SOU	450012	SWT	450103	SWT	455709	SWT		
390153	VWC	442421	SOU	450013	SWT	450104	SWT	455710	SWT		
390154	VWC	442422	SOU	450014	SWT	450105	SWT	455711	SWT		
390155	VWC	442423	SOU	450015	SWT	450106	SWT	455712	SWT		
390156	VWC	442424	SOU	450016	SWT	450107	SWT	455713	SWT		
390157	VWC			450017	SWT	450108	SWT	455714	SWT		
		444001	SWT	450018	SWT	450109	SWT	455715	SWT		
395001	SET	444002	SWT	450019	SWT	450110	SWT	455716	SWT		
395002	SET	444003	SWT	450020	SWT	450111	SWT	455717	SWT		
395003	SET	444004	SWT	450021	SWT	450112	SWT	455718	SWT		
395004	SET	444005	SWT	450022	SWT	450113	SWT	455719	SWT		
395005	SET	444006	SWT	450023	SWT	450114	SWT	455720	SWT		
395006	SET	444007	SWT	450024	SWT	450115	SWT	455721	SWT		

Number		Number		Number		Number		Number	
455722	SWT	455842	SOU	456010	SOU	465017	SET	465179	SET
455723	SWT	455843	SOU	456011	SOU	465018	SET	465180	SET
455724	SWT	455844	SOU	456012	SOU	465019	SET	465181	SET
455725	SWT	455845	SOU	456013	SOU	465020	SET	465182	SET
455726	SWT	455846	SOU	456014	SOU	465021	SET	465183	SET
455727	SWT	455847	SWT	456015	SOU	465022	SET	465184	SET
455728	SWT	455848	SWT	456016	SOU	465023	SET	465185	SET
455729	SWT	455849	SWT	456017	SOU	465024	SET	465186	SET
455730	SWT	455850	SWT	456018	SOU	465025	SET	465187	SET
455731	SWT	455851	SWT	456019	SOU	465026	SET	465188	SET
455732	SWT	455852	SWT	456020	SOU	465027	SET	465189	SET
455733	SWT	455853	SWT	456021	SOU	465028	SET	465190	SET
455734	SWT	455854	SWT	456022	SOU	465029	SET	465191	SET
455735	SWT	455855	SWT	456023	SOU	465030	SET	465192	SET
455736	SWT	455856	SWT	456024	SOU	465031	SET	465193	SET
455737	SWT	455857	SWT			465032	SET	465194	SET
455738	SWT	455858	SWT	458001	SWT	465033	SET	465195	SET
455739	SWT	455859	SWT	458002	SWT	465034	SET	465196	SET
455740	SWT	455860	SWT	458003	SWT	465035	SET	465197	SET
455741	SWT	455861	SWT	458004	SWT	465036	SET		
455742	SWT	455862	SWT	458005	SWT	465037	SET	465235	SET
455750	SWT	455863	SWT	458006	SWT	465038	SET	465236	SET
455801	SOU	455864	SWT	458007	SWT	465039	SET	465237	SET
455802	SOU	455865	SWT	458008	SWT	465040	SET	465238	SET
455803	SOU	455866	SWT	458009	SWT	465041	SET	465239	SET
455804	SOU	455867	SWT	458010	SWT	465042	SET	465240	SET
455805	SOU	455868	SWT	458011	SWT	465043	SET	465241	SET
455806	SOU	455869	SWT	458012	SWT	465044	SET	465242	SET
455807	SOU	455870	SWT	458013	SWT	465045	SET	465243	SET
455808	SOU	455871	SWT	458014	SWT	465046	SET	465244	SET
455809	SOU	455872	SWT	458015	SWT	465047	SET	465245	SET
455810	SOU	455873	SWT	458016	SWT	465048	SET	465246	SET
455811	SOU	455874	SWT	458017	SWT	465049	SET	465247	SET
455812	SOU	455901	SWT	458018	SWT	465050	SET	465248	SET
455813	SOU	455902	SWT	458019	SWT			465249	SET
455814	SOU	455903	SWT	458020	SWT	465151	SET	465250	SET
455815	SOU	455904	SWT	458021	SWT	465152	SET		
455816	SOU	455905	SWT	458022	SWT	465153	SET	465901	SET
455817	SOU	455906	SWT	458023	SWT	465154	SET	465902	SET
455818	SOU	455907	SWT	458024	SWT	465155	SET	465903	SET
455819	SOU	455908	SWT	458025	SWT	465156	SET	465904	SET
455820	SOU	455909	SWT	458026	SWT	465157	SET	465905	SET
455821	SOU	455910	SWT	458027	SWT	465158	SET	465906	SET
455822	SOU	455911	SWT	458028	SWT	465159	SET	465907	SET
455823	SOU	455912	SWT	458029	SWT	465160	SET	465908	SET
455824	SOU	455913	SWT	458030	SWT	465161	SET	465909	SET
455825	SOU	455914	SWT			465162	SET	465910	SET
455826	SOU	455915	SWT	465001	SET	465163	SET	465911	SET
455827	SOU	455916	SWT	465002	SET	465164	SET	465912	SET
455828	SOU	455917	SWT	465003	SET	465165	SET	465913	SET
455829	SOU	455918	SWT	465004	SET	465166	SET	465914	SET
455830	SOU	455919	SWT	465005	SET	465167	SET	465915	SET
455831	SOU	455920	SWT	465006	SET	465168	SET	465916	SET
455832	SOU			465007	SET	465169	SET	465917	SET
455833	SOU	456001	SOU	465008	SET	465170	SET	465918	SET
455834	SOU	456002	SOU	465009	SET	465171	SET	465919	SET
455835	SOU	456003	SOU	465010	SET	465172	SET	465920	SET
455836	SOU	456004	SOU	465011	SET	465173	SET	465921	SET
455837	SOU	456005	SOU	465012	SET	465174	SET	465922	SET
455838	SOU	456006	SOU	465013	SET	465175	SET	465923	SET
455839	SOU	456007	SOU	465014	SET	465176	SET	465924	SET
455840	SOU	456008	SOU	465015	SET	465177	SET	465925	SET
455841	SOU	456009	SOU	465016	SET	465178	SET	465926	SET

Data Tables

Data Tables

465927	SET	507001	MER	508204	OLS	548	WCR	2127	WCR
465928	SET	507002	MER	508205	OLS	549	WCR	2833	WCR
465929	SET	507003	MER	508206	OLS	550	WCR	2834	RIV
465930	SET	507004	MER	508207	OLS	551	WCR	2903	NRL
465931	SET	507005	MER	508208	OLS	552	WCR	2904	NRL
465932	SET	507006	MER	508209	OLS	553	WCR	2915	NRL
465933	SET	507007	MER	508210	OLS	586	WCR	2916	NRL
465934	SET	507008	MER	508211	OLS	807	WCR	2917	NRL
466001	SET	507009	MER	508212	OLS	1105	MHR	2918	NRL
466002	SET	507010	MER	508301	OLS			2919	NRL
466003	SET	507011	MER	508302	OLS	1200	RIV	2920	NRL
466004	SET	507012	MER	508303	OLS	1201	VTN	2921	NRL
466005	SET	507013	MER			1203	RIV	2922	NRL
466006	SET	507014	MER	901001	PRE	1204	OLS	2923	NRL
466007	SET	507015	MER			1205	NRL		
466008	SET	507016	MER	**Coaching Stock**		1207	VSO	3058	WCR
466009	SET	507017	MER	84	RAF	1209	OLS	3066	RIV
466010	SET	507018	MER	159	WCR	1211	OLS	3068	RIV
466011	SET	507019	MER			1212	RIV	3069	RIV
466012	SET	507020	MER	213	VSO	1219	OLS	3093	WCR
466013	SET	507021	MER	239	VSO	1221	VSO	3096	BOK
466014	SET	507023	MER	243	VSO	1250	RIV	3097	RIV
466015	SET	507024	MER	245	VSO	1252	WCR	3098	RIV
466016	SET	507025	MER	254	VSO	1253	WCR	3100	RIV
466017	SET	507026	MER	255	VSO	1254	DRS	3105	WCR
466018	SET	507027	MER	261	VSO	1256	NRL	3106	WCR
466019	SET	507028	MER	264	VSO	1258	OLS	3107	RIV
466020	SET	507029	MER	280	VSO	1375	BOK	3110	RIV
466021	SET	507030	MER	281	VSO	1566	VSO	3112	RIV
466022	SET	507031	MER	283	VSO	1644	WCR	3113	WCR
466023	SET	507032	MER	284	VSO	1650	WCR	3114	RIV
466024	SET	507033	MER	285	VSO	1651	RIV	3115	BOK
466025	SET			286	VSO	1652	WCR	3117	WCR
466026	SET	508103	MER	288	VSO	1655	WCR	3119	RIV
466027	SET	508104	MER	292	VSO	1657	RIV	3120	RIV
466028	SET	508108	MER	293	VSO	1658	DBS	3121	RIV
466029	SET	508110	MER	301	VSO	1659	RAF	3122	RIV
466030	SET	508111	MER	302	VSO	1663	WCR	3123	RIV
466031	SET	508112	MER	307	VSO	1670	WCR	3124	RIV
466032	SET	508114	MER	308	VSO	1671	RIV	3127	RIV
466033	SET	508115	MER	310	RAF	1679	DBS	3128	WCR
466034	SET	508117	MER	313	GSW	1680	DBS	3130	WCR
466035	SET	508120	MER	316	FSL	1683	RIV	3131	RIV
466036	SET	508122	MER	317	GSW	1691	RIV	3132	RIV
466037	SET	508123	MER	319	GSW	1692	RIV	3133	RIV
466038	SET	508124	MER	321	FSL	1696	DBR	3136	WCR
466039	SET	508125	MER	324	GSW	1699	RIV	3140	RIV
466040	SET	508126	MER	325	VSO	1730	WCR	3141	RIV
466041	SET	508127	MER	326	WCR	1800	WCR	3143	WCR
466042	SET	508128	MER	329	GSW	1813	RIV	3144	RIV
466043	SET	508130	MER	331	GSW	1823	NYM	3146	RIV
		508131	MER	335	VTN	1832	RIV	3147	RIV
483002	SIL	508134	MER	337	FSL	1840	WCR	3149	RIV
483004	SIL	508136	MER	348	WCR	1842	RIV	3150	BOK
483006	SIL	508137	MER	349	VTN	1859	SRP	3174	VSO
483007	SIL	508138	MER	350	WCR	1860	WCR	3181	RIV
483008	SIL	508139	MER	352	WCR	1861	WCR	3182	VSO
483009	SIL	508140	MER	353	VTN	1862	WCR	3188	RAF
		508141	MER	354	WCR	1863	RIV	3223	RIV
489102	NRL	508143	MER	464	BOK	1882	WCR	3227	RIV
489105	NRL	508201	OLS	504	WCR	1953	VSO	3229	OLS
489106	NRL	508202	OLS	506	WCR	1961	WCR	3231	RAF
		508203	OLS	546	WCR	1999	GSW	3232	VSO

No.	Code	No.	Code	No.	Code	No.	Code	No.	Code
3240	RIV	3766	WCR	5198	VTN	5929	RIV	6158	RIV
3241	WCR	3860	NYM	5200	WCR	5937	RIV	6160	OLS
3247	VSO	3872	NYM	5212	VTN	5945	RIV	6162	ATW
3255	DBS	3948	NYM	5216	WCR	5946	RIV	6164	OLS
3267	VSO			5221	VTN	5947	OLS	6170	ATW
3269	DBS	4198	NYM	5222	WCR	5950	RIV	6173	DRS
3273	VSO	4252	NYM	5229	WCR	5952	RIV	6176	RIV
3275	VSO	4290	NYM	5236	WCR	5954	DBS	6177	RIV
3277	RIV	4455	NYM	5237	WCR	5955	RIV	6183	ATW
3278	RIV	4786	NYM	5239	WCR	5958	WCR	6310	RIV
3279	DBR	4817	NYM	5249	WCR	5959	DBS	6311	DBR
3292	DBS	4831	BOK	5276	RIV	5961	RIV	6312	WCR
3295	RIV	4832	BOK	5278	WCR	5964	RIV	6313	VSO
3303	DBR	4836	BOK	5292	RIV	5965	ATW	6320	RIV
3304	RIV	4856	BOK	5309	RIV	5971	DRS	6528	WCR
3309	VTN	4860	WCR	5322	RIV	5976	ATW	6700	FSR
3313	WCR	4905	WCR	5331	DBS	5981	OLS	6701	FSR
3314	RIV	4912	WCR	5341	RIV	5985	RIV	6702	FSR
3318	DBR	4927	RIV	5350	RIV	5987	RIV	6703	FSR
3325	RIV	4931	WCR	5366	RIV	5991	OLS	6704	FSR
3326	WCR	4932	WCR	5386	DBS	5995	DRS	6705	FSR
3330	RIV	4940	WCR	5412	BOK	5997	RIV	6706	FSR
3331	DBR	4946	RIV	5419	WCR	5998	RIV	6707	FSR
3333	RIV	4949	RIV	5453	WCR			6708	FSR
3334	RIV	4951	WCR	5463	WCR	6000	WCR	6720	RIV
3336	RIV	4954	WCR	5478	WCR	6001	DRS	6722	RIV
3338	DBS	4958	WCR	5482	DBS	6006	RIV	6723	WCR
3340	RIV	4959	RIV	5487	WCR	6008	DRS	6724	WCR
3344	RIV	4960	WCR	5491	WCR	6012	WCR		
3345	RIV	4973	WCR	5494	RIV	6013	ATW	9004	RAF
3348	RIV	4984	WCR	5520	RRS	6014	WCR	9101	VTN
3350	WCR	4986	RIV	5569	WCR	6022	WCR	9104	WCR
3351	VTN	4991	RIV	5631	DBS	6024	RIV	9267	NYM
3352	WCR	4994	WCR	5632	DBS	6027	RIV	9274	NYM
3356	RIV	4996	RIV	5636	OLS	6035	ATW	9391	WCR
3358	DBS	4997	WCR	5647	RIV	6036	DBR	9392	WCR
3359	RIV	4998	RIV	5657	DBS	6041	WCR	9419	DRS
3360	WCR			5737	OLS	6042	RIV	9428	DRS
3362	WCR	5000	NYM	5739	RIV	6045	CAD	9440	WCR
3364	RIV	5007	RIV	5740	OLS	6046	DRS	9448	WCR
3366	DRS	5008	RIV	5748	RIV	6051	RIV	9481	NRL
3368	DBS	5009	RIV	5750	OLS	6054	RIV	9488	GTL
3374	DRS	5023	RIV	5756	WCR	6055	OLS	9493	WCR
3375	DBS	5027	RIV	5769	RIV	6059	OLS	9494	DBR
3379	RIV	5028	BOK	5792	RIV	6061	OLS	9496	VTN
3384	RIV	5029	NYM	5797	RAF	6064	DRS	9497	NOT
3386	RIV	5032	WCR	5810	DRS	6067	RIV	9500	OLS
3388	DBS	5033	WCR	5815	WCR	6073	WCL	9502	VSO
3390	RIV	5035	WCR	5853	ATW	6103	WCR	9503	ATW
3392	WCR	5040	RIV	5876	WCR	6110	DBR	9504	RIV
3395	WCR	5044	WCR	5869	ATW	6115	WCR	9505	OLS
3397	RIV	5067	RAF	5888	OLS	6117	DRS	9506	DRS
3399	DBS	5125	WCR	5900	OLS	6119	ATW	9507	RIV
3400	DBS	5148	VTN	5901	DRS	6121	OLS	9508	DRS
3408	WCR	5157	VTN	5903	OLS	6122	DRS	9509	ATW
3414	DBS	5171	WCR	5910	RIV	6134	WCR	9516	NRL
3416	VTN	5177	VTN	5913	ATW	6135	WCR	9520	RIV
3417	RIV	5179	VTN	5919	DRS	6137	ATW	9521	ATW
3424	DBS	5183	VTN	5921	RIV	6139	DBR	9522	OLS
3426	RIV	5186	VTN	5922	DBS	6141	RIV	9523	NRL
3431	WCR	5191	VTN	5924	DBS	6151	WCR	9524	ATW
3434	OLS	5193	VTN	5925	WCR	6152	DBR	9525	DRS
3438	OLS	5194	VTN	5928	VTN	6154	WCR	9526	RIV

Data Tables

No.	Code	No.	Code	No.	Code	No.	Code	No.	Code
9527	RIV	10274	DBR	10551	FSR	11026	OLS	11283	ICE
9528	DRS	10300	ICE	10553	FSR	11027	DBR	11284	ICE
9529	DBR	10301	ICE	10556	VSO	11028	DBR	11285	ICE
9531	DBR	10302	ICE	10561	FSR	11029	DBR	11286	ICE
9537	RIV	10303	ICE	10562	FSR	11030	DBR	11287	ICE
9539	ATW	10304	ICE	10563	FGW	11031	DBS	11288	ICE
9704	BAR	10305	ICE	10565	FSR	11033	DBR	11289	ICE
9705	BAR	10306	ICE	10569	VSO	11039	DBS	11290	ICE
9707	BAR	10307	ICE	10580	FSR	11044	DBR	11291	ICE
9709	BAR	10308	ICE	10584	FGW	11046	DBR	11292	ICE
9710	BAR	10309	ICE	10588	FSR	11048	VWC	11293	ICE
9711	VTN	10310	ICE	10589	FGW	11054	DBR	11294	ICE
9713	OLS	10311	ICE	10590	FGW	11064	DBR	11295	ICE
9801	FSR	10312	ICE	10594	FGW	11065	DBR	11298	ICE
9802	FSR	10313	ICE	10596	OLS	11066	AEA	11299	ICE
9803	FSR	10315	ICE	10597	FSR	11067	AEA	11301	ICE
9804	FSR	10317	ICE	10598	FSR	11068	AEA	11302	ICE
9805	FSR	10318	ICE	10600	FSR	11069	AEA	11303	ICE
9806	FSR	10319	ICE	10601	FGW	11070	AEA	11304	ICE
9807	FSR	10320	ICE	10605	FSR	11071	DBR	11305	ICE
9808	FSR	10321	ICE	10607	FSR	11072	AEA	11306	ICE
9809	FSR	10323	ICE	10610	FSR	11073	AEA	11307	ICE
9810	FSR	10324	ICE	10612	FGW	11074	AEA	11308	ICE
		10325	ICE	10613	FSR	11075	AEA	11309	ICE
10200	AEA	10326	ICE	10614	FSR	11076	AEA	11310	ICE
10202	DBR	10328	ICE	10616	FGW	11077	AEA	11311	ICE
10203	AEA	10329	ICE	10617	FSR	11078	AEA	11312	ICE
10204	3MP	10330	ICE	10647	DBR	11079	DBR	11313	ICE
10206	AEA	10331	ICE	10648	FSR	11080	AEA	11314	ICE
10211	DBS	10332	ICE	10650	FSR	11081	AEA	11315	ICE
10212	VWC	10333	ICE	10661	OLS	11082	AEA	11316	ICE
10214	AEA	10401	AEA	10666	FSR	11083	DBR	11317	ICE
10215	DBS	10402	AEA	10667	OLS	11084	DBR	11318	ICE
10216	AEA	10403	AEA	10675	FSR	11085	AEA	11319	ICE
10217	VWC	10404	AEA	10680	FSR	11086	DBR	11320	ICE
10219	FGW	10405	AEA	10682	OLS	11087	AEA	11321	ICE
10222	DBS	10406	AEA	10683	FSR	11088	AEA	11322	ICE
10223	AEA	10501	FSR	10688	FSR	11089	DBR	11323	ICE
10225	FGW	10502	FSR	10689	FSR	11090	AEA	11324	ICE
10226	DBS	10504	FSR	10690	FSR	11091	AEA	11325	ICE
10228	AEA	10506	FSR	10693	FSR	11092	AEA	11326	ICE
10229	AEA	10507	FSR	10698	OLS	11093	AEA	11327	ICE
10231	OLS	10508	FSR	10699	FSR	11094	AEA	11328	ICE
10232	FGW	10513	FSR	10703	FSR	11095	AEA	11329	ICE
10233	DBS	10516	FSR	10706	FSR	11096	AEA	11330	ICE
10235	DBR	10519	FSR	10710	DBR	11097	DBR	11401	ICE
10237	DBS	10520	FSR	10714	FSR	11098	AEA	11402	ICE
10240	OLS	10522	FSR	10718	FSR	11099	AEA	11403	ICE
10241	OLS	10523	FSR	10719	FSR	11100	AEA	11404	ICE
10242	DBR	10526	FSR	10722	FSR	11101	AEA	11405	ICE
10245	WCR	10527	FSR	10723	FSR	11201	ICE	11406	ICE
10246	DBR	10529	FSR	10729	VSO	11219	ICE	11407	ICE
10247	AEA	10531	FSR	10731	DBR	11229	ICE	11408	ICE
10249	ATW	10532	FGW	10733	OLS	11237	ICE	11409	ICE
10250	DBS	10534	FGW	10734	VSO	11241	ICE	11410	ICE
10253	OLS	10540	DBR			11244	ICE	11411	ICE
10256	OLS	10541	VSO	11006	OLS	11273	ICE	11412	ICE
10257	DBS	10542	FSR	11007	VWC	11277	ICE	11413	ICE
10259	ATW	10543	FSR	11011	OLS	11278	ICE	11414	ICE
10260	OLS	10544	FSR	11013	DBR	11279	ICE	11415	ICE
10271	DBR	10546	DBR	11018	VWC	11280	ICE	11416	ICE
10272	DBR	10547	OLS	11019	DBR	11281	ICE	11417	ICE
10273	DBR	10548	FSR	11021	AEA	11282	ICE	11418	ICE

No.		No.		No.		No.		No.	
11419	ICE	12090	AEA	12208	ICE	12410	ICE	12481	ICE
11420	ICE	12091	AEA	12209	ICE	12411	ICE	12483	ICE
11421	ICE	12092	OLS	12210	ICE	12414	ICE	12484	ICE
11422	ICE	12093	AEA	12211	ICE	12415	ICE	12485	ICE
11423	ICE	12095	OLS	12212	ICE	12417	ICE	12486	ICE
11424	ICE	12097	AEA	12213	ICE	12419	ICE	12488	ICE
11425	ICE	12098	AEA	12214	ICE	12420	ICE	12489	ICE
11426	ICE	12099	AEA	12215	ICE	12421	ICE	12513	ICE
11427	ICE	12100	FGW	12216	ICE	12422	ICE	12514	ICE
11428	ICE	12101	OLS	12217	ICE	12423	ICE	12515	ICE
11429	ICE	12103	AEA	12218	ICE	12424	ICE	12518	ICE
11430	ICE	12105	AEA	12219	ICE	12425	ICE	12519	ICE
11998	ICE	12107	AEA	12220	ICE	12426	ICE	12520	ICE
11999	ICE	12108	AEA	12222	ICE	12427	ICE	12522	ICE
		12109	AEA	12223	ICE	12428	ICE	12526	ICE
12005	AEA	12110	AEA	12224	ICE	12429	ICE	12533	ICE
12008	OLS	12111	AEA	12225	ICE	12430	ICE	12534	ICE
12009	AEA	12114	AEA	12226	ICE	12431	ICE	12538	ICE
12011	VWC	12115	AEA	12227	ICE	12432	ICE		
12012	AEA	12116	AEA	12228	ICE	12433	ICE	12602	DBR
12013	AEA	12118	AEA	12229	ICE	12434	ICE	12603	DBR
12015	AEA	12120	AEA	12230	ICE	12436	ICE	12604	DBR
12016	AEA	12122	VWC	12231	ICE	12437	ICE	12605	DBR
12019	AEA	12125	AEA	12232	ICE	12438	ICE	12606	DBR
12021	AEA	12126	AEA	12300	ICE	12439	ICE	12607	DBR
12022	OLS	12129	AEA	12301	ICE	12440	ICE	12608	DBR
12024	AEA	12130	AEA	12302	ICE	12441	ICE	12609	DBR
12026	AEA	12132	AEA	12303	ICE	12442	ICE	12612	DBR
12027	AEA	12133	VWC	12304	ICE	12443	ICE	12613	DBR
12029	OLS	12134	OLS	12305	ICE	12444	ICE	12614	DBR
12030	AEA	12137	AEA	12307	ICE	12445	ICE	12615	DBR
12031	AEA	12138	VWC	12308	ICE	12446	ICE	12617	DBR
12032	AEA	12139	AEA	12309	ICE	12447	ICE	12618	DBR
12034	AEA	12141	AEA	12310	ICE	12448	ICE	12619	DBR
12035	AEA	12142	OLS	12311	ICE	12449	ICE		
12036	OLS	12143	AEA	12312	ICE	12450	ICE	13227	WCR
12037	AEA	12144	OLS	12313	ICE	12452	ICE	13229	BOK
12040	AEA	12146	AEA	12315	ICE	12453	ICE	13230	BOK
12041	AEA	12147	AEA	12316	ICE	12454	ICE	13306	WCR
12042	AEA	12148	AEA	12317	ICE	12455	ICE	13320	WCR
12046	AEA	12150	AEA	12318	ICE	12456	ICE	13321	WCR
12047	OLS	12151	AEA	12319	ICE	12457	ICE	13440	WCR
12049	AEA	12153	AEA	12320	ICE	12458	ICE	13508	RAF
12051	AEA	12154	AEA	12321	ICE	12459	ICE	13581	RRS
12056	AEA	12156	OLS	12322	ICE	12460	ICE	13583	RRS
12057	AEA	12158	OLS	12323	ICE	12461	ICE		
12060	AEA	12159	AEA	12324	ICE	12462	ICE	14007	SUP
12061	AEA	12160	OLS	12325	ICE	12463	ICE	14099	SUP
12062	AEA	12161	FGW	12326	ICE	12464	ICE		
12063	OLS	12163	OLS	12327	ICE	12465	ICE	16156	NYM
12064	AEA	12164	AEA	12328	ICE	12466	ICE		
12065	OLS	12166	AEA	12329	ICE	12467	ICE	17013	SUP
12066	AEA	12167	AEA	12330	ICE	12468	ICE	17015	RIV
12067	AEA	12170	AEA	12331	ICE	12469	ICE	17018	VTN
12073	AEA	12171	AEA	12400	ICE	12470	ICE	17025	SUP
12078	VWC			12401	ICE	12471	ICE	17041	SUP
12079	AEA	12200	ICE	12402	ICE	12472	ICE	17056	RIV
12081	AEA	12201	ICE	12403	ICE	12473	ICE	17077	RIV
12082	AEA	12202	ICE	12404	ICE	12474	ICE	17080	RAF
12083	OLS	12203	ICE	12405	ICE	12476	ICE	17090	VTN
12084	AEA	12204	ICE	12406	ICE	12477	ICE	17096	SUP
12087	OLS	12205	ICE	12407	ICE	12478	ICE	17102	WCR
12089	AEA	12207	ICE	12409	ICE	12480	ICE	17105	RIV

Data Tables

Number	Operator
17159	DRS
17167	VSO
17168	WCR
17173	FGW
17174	FGW
17175	FGW
18756	WCR
18767	WCR
18806	WCR
18808	WCR
18862	WCR
18893	WCR
19208	WCR
21096	SUP
21100	NMR
21224	RIV
21232	SUP
21236	SUP
21241	SRP
21245	RIV
21249	SUP
21252	MHR
21256	WCR
21266	WCR
21268	SUP
21269	RIV
21272	RIV
34525	WCR
35089	NYM
35185	SRP
35290	DBR
35317	SUP
35322	SUP
35329	SUP
35333	SUP
35407	WCR
35449	SUP
35457	SUP
35459	WCR
35461	SUP
35463	SUP
35464	SUP
35465	SUP
35466	VSO
35468	SUP
35469	RIV
35470	SUP
35476	SUP
35486	SUP
35508	SUP
35517	SUP
35518	SUP
40101	FGW
40102	FGW
40103	FGW
40104	FGW
40105	FGW
40106	FGW
40107	FGW
40108	FGW
40109	FGW
40110	FGW
40111	FGW
40112	FGW
40113	FGW
40114	FGW
40115	FGW
40116	FGW
40117	FGW
40118	FGW
40119	FGW
40204	FGW
40205	FGW
40207	FGW
40210	FGW
40221	FGW
40231	FGW
40402	DBR
40403	DBR
40416	OLS
40417	OLS
40419	OLS
40424	GTL
40425	OLS
40426	GTL
40433	GTL
40434	OLS
40700	EMT
40701	ICE
40702	ICE
40703	FGW
40704	ICE
40705	ICE
40706	ICE
40707	FGW
40708	ICE
40710	FGW
40711	ICE
40713	FGW
40715	FGW
40716	FGW
40718	FGW
40720	ICE
40721	FGW
40722	FGW
40727	FGW
40728	EMT
40730	EMT
40732	ICE
40733	FGW
40734	FGW
40735	ICE
40737	ICE
40739	FGW
40740	ICE
40741	EMT
40742	ICE
40743	FGW
40745	OLS
40746	EMT
40748	ICE
40749	EMT
40750	ICE
40751	EMT
40752	FGW
40753	EMT
40754	EMT
40755	FGW
40756	EMT
40757	FGW
40801	FGW
40802	FGW
40803	FGW
40805	ICE
40806	FGW
40807	FGW
40808	FGW
40809	FGW
40810	FGW
40811	FGW
40900	FGW
40901	FGW
40902	FGW
40903	FGW
40904	FGW
41003	FGW
41004	FGW
41005	FGW
41006	FGW
41007	FGW
41008	FGW
41009	FGW
41010	FGW
41011	FGW
41012	FGW
41015	FGW
41016	FGW
41017	FGW
41018	FGW
41019	FGW
41020	FGW
41021	FGW
41022	FGW
41023	FGW
41024	FGW
41026	AXC
41027	FGW
41028	FGW
41029	FGW
41030	FGW
41031	FGW
41032	FGW
41033	FGW
41034	FGW
41035	AXC
41037	FGW
41038	FGW
41039	ICE
41040	ICE
41041	EMT
41043	ICE
41044	ICE
41045	FGW
41046	EMT
41051	FGW
41052	FGW
41055	FGW
41056	FGW
41057	EMT
41058	ICE
41059	FGW
41061	EMT
41062	ICE
41063	EMT
41064	EMT
41065	FGW
41066	ICE
41067	EMT
41068	EMT
41069	EMT
41070	EMT
41071	EMT
41072	EMT
41075	EMT
41076	EMT
41077	EMT
41079	EMT
41081	FGW
41083	ICE
41084	EMT
41085	FGW
41086	FGW
41087	ICE
41088	ICE
41089	FGW
41090	ICE
41091	ICE
41092	ICE
41093	FGW
41094	FGW
41095	ICE
41096	FGW
41097	ICE
41098	ICE
41099	ICE
41100	ICE
41101	FGW
41102	FGW
41103	FGW
41104	FGW
41105	FGW
41106	FGW
41108	FGW
41109	FGW
41110	FGW
41111	EMT
41112	EMT
41113	EMT
41114	FGW
41115	ICE
41116	FGW
41117	EMT
41118	ICE
41119	FGW
41120	ICE
41121	FGW
41122	FGW
41123	FGW
41124	FGW
41125	FGW
41126	FGW
41127	FGW
41128	FGW
41129	FGW
41130	FGW
41131	FGW
41132	FGW
41133	FGW
41134	FGW
41135	FGW
41136	FGW
41137	FGW
41138	FGW
41139	FGW
41140	FGW
41141	FGW
41142	FGW
41143	FGW
41144	FGW
41145	FGW
41146	FGW
41147	FGW
41148	FGW
41149	FGW
41150	ICE
41151	ICE
41152	ICE
41154	ICE
41155	FGW
41156	EMT
41157	FGW
41158	FGW
41159	ICE
41160	FGW
41161	FGW
41162	FGW
41163	FGW
41164	ICE
41165	ICE
41166	FGW
41167	FGW
41168	FGW
41169	FGW
41170	ICE
41176	FGW
41179	FGW
41180	FGW
41181	FGW
41182	FGW
41183	FGW
41184	FGW
41185	ICE
41186	FGW
41187	FGW
41189	FGW
41190	ICE
41191	FGW
41192	FGW

Data Tables

41193	AXC	42061	FGW	42132	EMT	42199	ICE	42267	FGW
41194	AXC	42062	FGW	42133	EMT	42200	FGW	42268	FGW
41195	AXC	42063	ICE	42134	ICE	42201	FGW	42269	FGW
41201	GTL	42064	ICE	42135	EMT	42202	FGW	42271	FGW
41202	GTL	42065	ICE	42136	EMT	42203	FGW	42272	FGW
41203	GTL	42066	FGW	42137	EMT	42204	FGW	42273	FGW
41204	GTL	42067	FGW	42138	FGW	42205	ICE	42275	FGW
41205	GTL	42068	FGW	42139	EMT	42206	FGW	42276	FGW
41206	GTL	42069	FGW	42140	EMT	42207	FGW	42277	FGW
		42070	FGW	42141	EMT	42208	FGW	42279	FGW
42003	FGW	42071	FGW	42143	FGW	42209	FGW	42280	FGW
42004	FGW	42072	FGW	42144	FGW	42210	ICE	42281	FGW
42005	FGW	42073	FGW	42145	FGW	42211	FGW	42283	FGW
42006	FGW	42074	FGW	42146	ICE	42212	FGW	42284	FGW
42007	FGW	42075	FGW	42147	ICE	42213	FGW	42285	FGW
42008	FGW	42076	FGW	42148	EMT	42214	FGW	42286	ICE
42009	FGW	42077	FGW	42149	EMT	42215	ICE	42287	FGW
42010	FGW	42078	FGW	42150	ICE	42216	FGW	42288	FGW
42012	FGW	42079	FGW	42151	EMT	42217	FGW	42289	FGW
42013	FGW	42080	FGW	42152	EMT	42218	FGW	42290	AXC
42014	FGW	42081	FGW	42153	EMT	42219	ICE	42291	FGW
42015	FGW	42083	FGW	42154	ICE			42292	FGW
42016	FGW	42085	FGW	42155	EMT	42220	EMT	42293	FGW
42019	FGW	42087	FGW	42156	EMT	42221	FGW	42294	FGW
42021	FGW	42089	FGW	42157	EMT	42222	FGW	42295	FGW
42023	FGW	42091	ICE	42158	ICE	42224	FGW	42296	FGW
42024	FGW	42092	FGW	42159	ICE	42225	EMT	42297	FGW
42025	FGW	42093	FGW	42160	ICE	42226	ICE	42299	FGW
42026	FGW	42094	FGW	42161	ICE	42227	EMT	42300	FGW
42027	FGW	42095	FGW	42163	ICE	42228	ICE	42301	FGW
42028	FGW	42096	FGW	42164	EMT	42229	EMT	42302	FGW
42029	FGW	42097	AXC	42165	EMT	42230	EMT	42303	FGW
42030	FGW	42098	FGW	42166	FGW	42231	FGW	42304	FGW
42031	FGW	42099	FGW	42167	FGW	42232	FGW	42305	FGW
42032	FGW	42100	EMT	42168	FGW	42233	FGW	42306	ICE
42033	FGW	42101	FGW	42169	FGW	42234	AXC	42307	ICE
42034	FGW	42102	FGW	42171	ICE	42235	ICE	42308	FGW
42035	FGW	42103	FGW	42172	ICE	42236	FGW	42310	FGW
42036	AXC	42105	FGW	42173	FGW	42237	ICE	42315	FGW
42037	AXC	42106	ICE	42174	FGW	42238	ICE	42317	FGW
42038	AXC	42107	FGW	42175	FGW	42239	ICE	42319	FGW
42039	FGW	42108	FGW	42176	FGW	42240	ICE	42321	FGW
42040	FGW	42109	ICE	42177	FGW	42241	ICE	42322	ICE
42041	FGW	42110	ICE	42178	FGW	42242	ICE	42323	ICE
42042	FGW	42111	EMT	42179	ICE	42243	ICE	42325	FGW
42043	FGW	42112	EMT	42180	ICE	42244	ICE	42326	ICE
42044	FGW	42113	EMT	42181	ICE	42245	FGW	42327	EMT
42045	FGW	42115	FGW	42182	ICE	42247	FGW	42328	EMT
42046	FGW	42116	ICE	42183	FGW	42250	FGW	42329	EMT
42047	FGW	42117	ICE	42184	FGW	42251	FGW	42330	ICE
42048	FGW	42118	FGW	42185	FGW	42252	FGW	42331	EMT
42049	FGW	42119	EMT	42186	ICE	42253	FGW	42332	FGW
42050	FGW	42120	EMT	42188	ICE	42255	FGW	42333	FGW
42051	AXC	42121	EMT	42189	ICE	42256	FGW	42335	ICE
42052	AXC	42123	ICE	42190	ICE	42257	FGW	42337	EMT
42053	AXC	42124	EMT	42191	ICE	42258	FGW	42339	EMT
42054	FGW	42125	ICE	42192	ICE	42259	ICE	42340	ICE
42055	FGW	42126	FGW	42193	ICE	42260	FGW	42341	EMT
42056	FGW	42127	ICE	42194	EMT	42261	FGW	42342	AXC
42057	ICE	42128	ICE	42195	FGW	42263	FGW	42343	FGW
42058	ICE	42129	FGW	42196	FGW	42264	FGW	42344	FGW
42059	ICE	42130	ICE	42197	FGW	42265	FGW	42345	FGW
42060	FGW	42131	EMT	42198	ICE	42266	FGW	42346	FGW

Data Tables

No.	Code
42347	FGW
42348	FGW
42349	FGW
42350	FGW
42351	FGW
42352	ICE
42353	ICE
42354	ICE
42355	ICE
42356	FGW
42357	ICE
42360	FGW
42361	FGW
42362	FGW
42363	ICE
42364	FGW
42365	FGW
42366	AXC
42367	AXC
42368	AXC
42369	AXC
42370	AXC
42371	AXC
42372	AXC
42373	AXC
42374	AXC
42375	AXC
42376	AXC
42377	AXC
42378	AXC
42379	AXC
42380	AXC
42381	FGW
42382	FGW
42383	FGW
42384	EMT
42385	FGW
42401	GTL
42402	GTL
42403	GTL
42404	GTL
42405	GTL
42406	GTL
42407	GTL
42408	GTL
42409	GTL
42501	FGW
42502	FGW
42503	FGW
42504	FGW
42505	FGW
42506	FGW
42507	FGW
42508	FGW
42509	FGW
42510	FGW
42511	FGW
42512	FGW
42513	FGW
42514	FGW
42515	FGW

No.	Code
44000	FGW
44001	FGW
44002	FGW
44003	FGW
44004	FGW
44005	FGW
44007	FGW
44008	FGW
44009	FGW
44010	FGW
44011	FGW
44012	AXC
44013	FGW
44014	FGW
44015	FGW
44016	FGW
44017	AXC
44018	FGW
44019	ICE
44020	FGW
44021	AXC
44022	FGW
44023	FGW
44024	FGW
44025	FGW
44026	FGW
44027	EMT
44028	FGW
44029	FGW
44030	FGW
44031	ICE
44032	FGW
44033	FGW
44034	FGW
44035	FGW
44036	FGW
44037	FGW
44038	FGW
44039	FGW
44040	FGW
44041	EMT
44042	FGW
44043	FGW
44044	EMT
44045	ICE
44046	EMT
44047	EMT
44048	EMT
44049	FGW
44050	ICE
44051	EMT
44052	AXC
44054	EMT
44055	FGW
44056	ICE
44057	ICE
44058	ICE
44059	FGW
44060	FGW
44061	ICE
44063	ICE
44064	FGW
44065	GTL

No.	Code
44066	FGW
44067	FGW
44068	FGW
44069	FGW
44070	EMT
44071	EMT
44072	AXC
44073	ICE
44074	FGW
44075	ICE
44076	FGW
44077	ICE
44078	FGW
44079	FGW
44080	ICE
44081	FGW
44083	FGW
44085	EMT
44086	FGW
44088	GTL
44089	GTL
44090	FGW
44091	FGW
44093	FGW
44094	ICE
44097	FGW
44098	ICE
44100	FGW
44101	FGW
45001	AXC
45002	AXC
45003	AXC
45004	AXC
45005	AXC
45018	WCR
45026	WCR
45029	DBS
80041	RIV
80042	RIV
99035	SUP
99040	SUP
99041	SUP
99080	SUP
99108	VTN
99120	SUP
99121	WCR
99125	WCR
99127	WCR
99128	WCR
99132	WCR
99193	WCR
99194	WCR
99195	WCR
99241	SUP
99304	WCR
99311	WCR
99312	SUP
99316	WCR
99317	WCR
99318	WCR

No.	Code
99319	WCR
99326	WCR
99327	WCR
99328	WCR
99329	WCR
99348	WCR
99349	VTN
99350	WCR
99353	VTN
99354	WCR
99361	VTN
99371	WCR
99402	WCR
99405	SUP
99530	VSO
99531	VSO
99532	VSO
99534	VSO
99535	VSO
99536	VSO
99537	VSO
99539	VSO
99541	VSO
99543	VSO
99545	VSO
99546	VSO
99678	WCR
99679	WCR
99670	WCR
99671	WCR
99672	WCR
99673	WCR
99674	WCR
99675	WCR
99676	WCR
99677	WCR
99680	WCR
99706	WCR
99710	WCR
99712	WCR
99713	WCR
99717	WCR
99718	WCR
99721	WCR
99722	WCR
99723	WCR
99782	SUP
99792	SUP
99884	WCR
99953	SUP
99966	WCR
99968	VSO
99969	VSO
99991	SUP
99995	SUP

NPCCS Stock

No.	Code
6260	NRL
6261	NRL
6262	NRL
6263	NRL
6264	NRL

No.	Code
6321	SIE
6322	SIE
6323	SIE
6324	SIE
6325	SIE
6330	FGW
6336	FGW
6338	FGW
6340	ICE
6344	ICE
6346	ICE
6348	FGW
6352	ICE
6353	ICE
6354	ICE
6355	ICE
6358	ICE
6359	ICE
6376	GBR
6377	GBR
6378	GBR
6379	GBR
6392	EMT
6395	EMT
6397	EMT
6398	EMT
6399	EMT
9393	ICE
9394	ICE
9701	NRL
9702	NRL
9703	NRL
9708	NRL
9714	NRL
72612	NRL
72616	NRL
72630	NRL
72631	NRL
72639	NRL
80204	SUP
80217	SUP
80220	SUP
82101	VWC
82102	AEA
82103	AEA
82104	DBR
82105	AEA
82106	DBR
82107	AEA
82109	OLS
82110	DBR
82111	NRL
82112	AEA
82113	DBR
82114	AEA
82115	NRL
82116	DBR
82118	AEA
82120	DBR

Data Tables

82121	AEA	92114	NRL	94411	DBS	94548	DBS	977994	NRL
82122	DBR	92159	OLS	94412	DBS	95300	DBS	977995	NRL
82124	NRL			94413	DBS	95301	DBS	977996	PRE
82125	OLS	92901	OLS	94416	DBS	95400	DBS	977997	NRL
82126	VWC	92904	VSO	94420	DBS	95410	DBS		
82127	AEA	92931	OLS	94422	DBS	95727	DBS	999508	NRL
82129	NRL	92939	NRL	94423	DBS	95754	DBS	999550	NRL
82132	AEA	94103	DBS	94427	DBS	95761	DBS	999602	NRL
82133	AEA	94104	DBS	94428	DBS	95763	DBS	999605	NRL
82136	AEA	94106	DBS	94429	DBS	96100	OLS	999606	NRL
82137	DBR	94116	DBS	94431	DBS	96139	OLS		
82138	DBR	94121	DBS	94432	DBS	96175	WCR		
82139	AEA	94137	DBS	94433	DBS	96181	OLS		
82140	OLS	94147	DBS	94434	DBS	96371	DBS		
82141	DBR	94153	DBS	94435	DBS	96372	DBS		
82143	AEA	94160	DBS	94438	DBS	96373	DBS		
82145	NRL	94166	DBS	94440	DBS	96374	WAB		
82146	DBS	94170	DBS	94445	DBS	96375	DBS		
82148	DBR	94176	DBS	94451	DBS	96602	COL		
82149	OLS	94177	DBS	94458	DBS	96603	COL		
82150	DBR	94192	DBS	94462	DBS	96604	COL		
82152	AEA	94195	DBS	94463	DBS	96605	COL		
		94197	DBS	94470	DBS	96606	COL		
82200	ICE	94207	DBS	94479	DBS	96607	COL		
82201	ICE	94208	DBS	94481	DBS	96608	COL		
82202	ICE	94209	DBS	94482	DBS	96609	COL		
82203	ICE	94213	DBS	94488	DBS				
82204	ICE	94214	DBS	94490	DBS	99666	NRL		
82205	ICE	94217	DBS	94492	DBS				
82206	ICE	94221	DBS	94495	DBS	**Service Stock**			
82207	ICE	94222	DBS	94497	DBS	930010	EMT		
82208	ICE	94225	DBS	94498	DBS	950001	NRL		
82209	ICE	94227	DBS	94499	DBS	960010	CRW		
82210	ICE	94229	DBS	94501	DBS	960014	CRW		
82211	ICE	94302	DBS	94504	DBS	960015	CRW		
82212	ICE	94303	DBS	94512	DBS	960201	NRL		
82213	ICE	94304	DBS	94514	DBS	960202	NRL		
82214	ICE	94306	DBS	94515	DBS	960301	CRW		
82215	ICE	94307	DBS	94518	DBS				
82216	ICE	94308	DBS	94519	DBS	971001	NRL		
82217	ICE	94310	DBS	94520	DBS	971002	NRL		
82218	ICE	94311	DBS	94521	DBS	971003	NRL		
82219	ICE	94313	DBS	94522	DBS	971004	NRL		
82220	ICE	94316	DBS	94525	DBS				
82222	ICE	94317	DBS	94526	DBS	975025	NRL		
82223	ICE	94318	DBS	94527	DBS	975081	NRL		
82224	ICE	94322	DBS	94528	DBS	975091	NRL		
82225	ICE	94323	DBS	94529	DBS	975280	NRL		
82226	ICE	94326	DBS	94530	DBS	975464	NRL		
82227	ICE	94331	DBS	94531	DBS	975486	NRL		
82228	ICE	94332	DBS	94532	DBS	975814	NRL		
82229	ICE	94333	DBS	94534	DBS	975984	NRL		
82230	ICE	94334	DBS	94536	DBS				
82231	ICE	94335	DBS	94538	RIV	977337	NRL		
		94336	DBS	94539	DBS	977868	NRL		
82301	DBR	94338	DBS	94540	DBS	977869	NRL		
82302	DBR	94340	DBS	94541	DBS	977969	NRL		
82303	DBR	94343	DBS	94542	DBS	977974	NRL		
82304	DBR	94344	DBS	94543	DBS	977983	NRL		
82305	DBR	94400	DBS	94544	DBS	977984	NRL		
82306	ATW	94406	DBS	94545	DBS	977985	NRL		
82307	ATW	94408	DBS	94546	DBS	977986	NRL		
82308	ATW	94410	DBS	94547	DBS	977993	NRL		

Data Tables